THE OFFICIAL
AMERICA ONLINE
FOR WINDOWS 3.1 TOUR GUIDE

THIRD EDITION

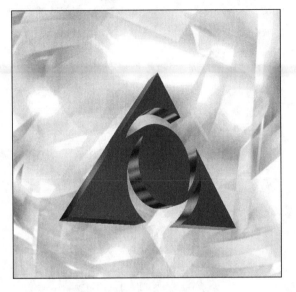

COVERS VERSION THREE

THE OFFICIAL
AMERICA ONLINE
FOR WINDOWS 3.1 TOUR GUIDE

THIRD EDITION

COVERS VERSION THREE

Everything You Need to Begin Enjoying the Nation's Most Exciting Online Service

Tom Lichty

VENTANA

The Official America Online for Windows 3.1 Tour Guide, Third Edition

Library of Congress Cataloging-in Publication Data
Lichty, Tom.
   The official America Online for Windows 3.1 tour guide: everything you need to begin enjoying the nation's most exciting Online service / Tom Lichty. — 3rd ed.
      p. cm.
   Rev. ed. of: Official America Online for Windows tour guide. 2nd ed. ©1994.
   Includes index.
   ISBN 1-56604-374-3
   1. America Online (Online service) 2. Microsoft Windows (Computer file) I. Lichty, Tom. official America Online for Windows tour guide. II. Title
   QA76.57.A43L523 1996
   004.69—dc20   96-12644
                                                       CIP

Third Edition 9 8 7 6 5 4
Printed in the United States of America

Limits of Liability and Disclaimer of Warranty
The author and publisher of this book have used their best efforts in preparing the book and the programs contained in it. These efforts include the development, research, and testing of the theories and programs to determine their effectiveness. The author and publisher make no warranty of any kind, expressed or implied, with regard to these programs or the documentation contained in this book.

   The author and publisher shall not be liable in the event of incidental or consequential damages in connection with, or arising out of, the furnishing, performance or use of the programs, associated instructions and/or claims of productivity gains.

Trademarks
Trademarked names appear throughout this book. Rather than list the names and entities that own the trademarks or insert a trademark symbol with each mention of the trademarked name, the publisher states that it is using the names only for editorial purposes and to the benefit of the trademark owner with no intention of infringing upon that trademark.

President/CEO

Josef Woodman

**Vice President of
Content Development**

Karen A. Bluestein

Production Manager

John Cotterman

**Technology Operations
Manager**

Kerry L. B. Foster

**Product Marketing
Manager**

Scott S. Johnson

**America Online Marketing
Account Manager**

Marisa A. Paley

Art Director

Marcia Webb

Acquisitions Editor

Neweleen A. Trebnik

Project Editor

Jessica A. Ryan

Copy Editor

Marion Laird

Cover Design

Image Communications
of Vienna, VA

Desktop Publisher

Patrick Berry

Technical Reviewers

Brian Little, Imagination
Workshop

David O'Donnell,
America Online

Proofreader

William R. Stott

Indexer

Dick Evans

About the Author

Tom Lichty writes computer and design books from his home in Damascus, Oregon, where he's accompanied by two dogs and five computers in a tiny studio overlooking Mount Hood. He has been trying to retire for four years now, but never quite finds the time to get around to it.

Acknowledgments

A book like this could never be the work of a single person. Hundreds of AOL in-house and remote staff have contributed to its genesis. Marisa, Matt, Thea, Lisa, Jill, Jay, Jeff, Bill, Ellen, Serge, Katherine, Randy, Julia, Clarisse, Tim, Maura, David, Dave, Chris, Walt, Daye, Jon, Sarah, Tom, Charlie, Teach, Mary, and (of course) Steve: I thank you all for your benevolence.

Even the writing process is a group effort. Jennifer, Jim, Michael: I thank you for your wordsmithery.

Somehow holding it all together, the people at Ventana Communications serve as my bedrock. Elizabeth, Joe, Patty, Neweleen, Pam, Marion, Karen, Amy, Jessica, John, and Brian: bless you for your patience.

Kudos to Matt, Bill, and Maureen at Waterside Productions for the arbitration for which you're renowned.

Namaste to Leonard, for providing continuity in MajorTom's patchwork life.

Most of all, I thank you, the readers of *The Official America Online Tour Guide*. I have received thousands of suggestions for improvements to this book and many of them are reflected in this edition.

Throughout this book I refer to AOL as a community. As you can see, the *Tour Guide* is, perhaps, the consummate community effort.

Tom Lichty
June 1996

Contents

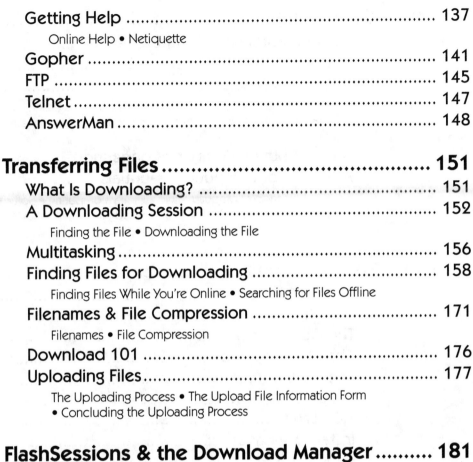

Foreword

I first got interested in online services in the early 1980s. I didn't know much about them then, but I knew enough to realize that they had a lot of potential. So when I bought my first personal computer in 1982, I decided to buy a modem and get online. This proved to be a very frustrating experience. It took me several months before I had all the equipment properly configured and was able to connect for the first time. Once I got connected, I found the services themselves hard to use and expensive. Nevertheless, despite all the hassles and shortcomings, I thought it was amazing that such a wealth of information and services were out there, waiting to be tapped into.

That was more than a decade ago. When we founded America Online, Inc., our objective was simple: to make online services more accessible, more affordable, more useful and more fun for people like you and me. America Online now serves more than a million customers and is the nation's fastest-growing online service.

Our success has been driven by a constant focus on making the power of online services accessible to everyone. In designing America Online, we worked hard to make it very easy to use. We didn't want people to have to read a book in order to get connected, so we made the software easy to install and easy to use. As a result, people are usually up and running with America Online in less than 15 minutes.

Although we've done a good job of making the process of connecting to America Online hassle-free, we still have a problem: once you're connected, what do you do? America Online has grown so quickly, and now contains so many different services, finding the services that best meet your specific needs can be a bit of a challenge.

That's where this book comes in. Think of it as your personal tour guide, helping you get the most out of America Online. It highlights a wide range of useful and fun services, so you can begin enjoying America Online immediately. After you're comfortable with the basics, it will take you to the next step by explaining some of the more advanced capabilities that are built into the service.

When Ventana Press first contacted us about publishing an America Online book, we thought it was a great idea. Our members had been asking for a book for some time, so we knew there was interest. And we felt that by working with an independent publisher, we'd end up with a better book than if we tried to write it ourselves.

Ventana's choice of Tom Lichty as the author was inspired. Tom had written a number of popular computer books, so he knew how to communicate information in an interesting and humorous manner. (A lot of computer books are deathly dull; Tom's are funny and engaging.) And since Tom was a novice user of online services, we felt his insightful observations as a novice would help others get the most out of America Online.

When the first edition of this Tour Guide was published in 1992, it got raves from readers, so this new, expanded version—highlighting our broader array of services (including Internet access), and introducing you to our new Main Menu and multimedia look—is certain to be even more popular.

As you'll soon discover, America Online is more than easy-to-use software and a collection of useful and fun services. It's a living, breathing "electronic community" that comes alive because thousands of people all across the country don't just passively read the information that scrolls by on their screens, they get involved and participate, exchanging ideas on hundreds of topics. We provide the basic framework; beyond, that, America Online is shaped by the collective imagination of its participants.

A new interactive communications medium is emerging, and it will change the way we inform, educate, work and play. America Online is at the forefront of this exciting revolution. Come join us, as we work together to shape this new medium.

Steve Case, President, America Online, Inc.
AOL E-Mail Address: SteveCase

CHAPTER 1

Introduction: Starting the Tour

We stood just inside the doorway, the auditorium walls dramatically curving away from us on either side. A soft susurration filled the air: a chorus of muffin fans, droning in the deserted expanse, melancholic, as only the sounds in an empty auditorium can be.

It was October 30. All day, I had seen America Online staffers roaming the halls, dressed in various degrees of whimsy. Even Steve Case was in costume. Now they had all gathered upstairs on the third floor for an after-hours Halloween fest, leaving us alone in a room built to accommodate hundreds—just Matt Korn and me . . .

. . . and 75,000 others, invisible and silent, ethereal as shadows.

Korn extended his hand to a switch on the wall and suddenly the room was a moonless night, black as a Halloween cat, aswirl in the breeze from the fans.

"Hold still a moment," he said. "Let your eyes adjust."

Slowly, flickering lights began to appear in the darkness. As my eyes adjusted, thousands of them became visible, winking randomly across the expanse of the auditorium. It was as if we were descending from a night flight, emerging from a cloud cover above a midnight city.

In time, the random flickers resolved into a pattern, revealing clusters of lights arranged in columns, miniature office buildings twinkling in the dark. I was later to learn that we were watching hundreds of *session controllers*: machines about the size of a VCR, each catering to the commands and caprices of AOL members.

The ability to accommodate capricious chaos is one of America Online's founding virtues. Members often leave multiple windows open on their screens—chat windows, Internet windows, library windows—and switch among those windows at will. Linearity isn't mandated by the software: there's no need to return to some kind of main menu before following another path. If a destination is visible on the screen, clicking its window takes you there. AOL's visionaries refer to this as their *modeless strategy*. For many of us who use AOL, following our impulses is as natural as respiration, and like respiration, we're unaware of the underlying "system" that makes it possible—unless, for some reason, it's withheld from us.

The electronic session controllers sense the members' clicks, determine where they want to go, and route them to the AOL computer that's appropriate for that task. Each session controller routes the commands of up to 64 members; cabinets the size of refrigerators each hold four to seven session controllers. That evening, there were perhaps 300 cabinets in operation: around 75,000 people were logged on.

The lights were busy: it was Friday night; the members were playing. The lights wouldn't have been as active that afternoon when most people were working. Play is capricious; work tends to be more linear. On Friday night, most of those signed on were playing.

"That's New York," said Matt, pointing to a vertical array of lights. "That's Columbus, and Dallas, and Philadelphia. Los Angeles is over there; Seattle, Miami, Nashville . . . ."

An auditorium of lights reflected people clicking mice all over the country. I felt like a voyeur. And I was mesmerized by what I saw.

Matt Korn

Matt Korn joined the firm in the early 1990s. He is a senior member of AOL's technical staff (Vice President of Operations, to be specific). Matt represents the median employee demographic: young, a participant in the employee stock-option plan, well educated, intelligent, and monomaniacally dedicated to his job: he had arrived at work around 8:00 this morning; it was now 7:30 in the evening and he still had a couple of hours of work ahead before going home. He seemed to be just getting his second wind. I wondered if he was married.

Soon after he arrived at AOL, Matt Korn became coordinator of the project that converted the auditorium into AOL's second computer room. A defense contractor had occupied the lower floor of the building before AOL purchased it; the auditorium served as the theater for extravagant presentations to the military—millions of public dollars riding on 10-minute productions! Though high technology still permeates the building, the fact that it's private telecommunications rather than public defense provides a microcosmic reflection of contemporary societal priorities.

What Is America Online?

I hope I haven't given you the wrong impression with this introduction. AOL is many things other than an auditorium-size room filled with machines and wires.

A term like "America Online" doesn't give many clues as to its composition. We can safely deduce its country of origin (it's in America, all right: Vienna, Virginia, to be exact—just outside Washington, DC). But what's this "online" business? You won't even find the word in your dictionary if it's an older edition.

A definition is in order, and I am going to pursue that definition not only in terms of features and functions but also in relation to the "community" we join when we become AOL members. Over the next few pages, we'll allow America Online's technological capabilities to dazzle us, but by the end of this chapter you'll see that the true rewards are found in the *people* who await us on AOL.

It's One Big Thunder Lizard Computer

One way of defining AOL is by describing its hardware. Coordinating thousands of simultaneous phone calls and storing tens of thousands of files requires one Thunder Lizard of a computer complex. No little Stegosaurus will do. We're talking Brontosaurus here, a beastie who relocates continents whenever he gets the urge to sneeze. Forget prefixes like *kilo* and *mega*. Think *giga* and *tera*. When they turn on the power to this thing, lights dim along the entire Eastern seaboard.

Open Architecture

I hate to disappoint you, but America Online isn't a single Brontosaurus-sized mainframe; it is, in fact, a number of refrigerator-size computers, each having more in common with the adaptable Velociraptor than a leviathan as benign as the Brontosaurus.

Figure 1-1:
A few of the many systems that are the heartbeat of America Online. A number of manufacturers are represented here, each product selected on the basis of suitability to a specific task. The homogenization factor is open architecture, which allows all of these diverse systems to work in concert.

Perhaps the best way to tackle this technologically complex subject is to return to that darkened room where we were standing a few pages back.

Our eyes fully adjusted now, Matt Korn and I walk among the session controllers as he continues his litany of cities: "Boston, Portland, Atlanta . . . ." Each cabinet is labeled, though Korn has them memorized.

One thing strikes me as peculiar about these cabinets: the equipment mounted in them carries a variety of brand names. This isn't a place where a single manufacturer's equipment monotonously dominates the scene. I expected everything to say IBM or DEC on it, with matching colors and shapes like a model kitchen. Instead, what's inside of Korn's cabinets is a mélange of electronic diversity, more akin to a customized home entertainment system. AOL's cabinets hold equipment from a variety of manufacturers. IBM is there all right, but so are Hewlett-Packard, Cisco, Tandem, Silicon Graphics, Stratus, and a few others.

Using equipment from a single manufacturer, and connecting it with proprietary cables and communications protocols—so-called *closed systems*—used to be commonplace in mainframe computer installations. Today, however, closed systems are no more tolerated there than they are in home music systems. In my living room I have a Pioneer receiver, a TEAC tape deck, and a Sony CD player. Each had the features I wanted when I bought it, and the price was right. I was able to plug them all together using standardized cables with never a worry that they might not work together properly.

In the computer business, this is called *open architecture*, and it's almost a mantra at AOL. Because of the common standard (TCP/IP, or *Transmission-Control Protocol/Internet Protocol,* for those of you who care about those things), Korn can now buy mainframe components much as we buy components for our stereo systems: the best one for each job, at the best price.

All of which is to say that from a mechanical perspective, AOL is a diversity of computer systems interconnected with TCP/IP open architecture—most of which resides in that cavernous auditorium in Vienna, Virginia, about 14 miles from downtown Washington, DC.

Hosts & Clients

Let's define a couple of terms up front. You'll encounter them often, and without clarification they'll seem like that much more technobabble—and we all know how irritating that can be.

AOL's computer complex in Virginia is often referred to as the *host*. There are millions of us and only one AOL; we all "visit" AOL when we sign on; AOL's machines attend to our needs: these are the kinds of hostlike things that provoke the term.

Our computers—and the AOL software running on them—are the *clients*. Clients are served by the host; clients are numerable; and in this case, clients are patrons.

Client/host terminology is common in the networking industry, and when you think about it, AOL *is* a network. The meanings behind the terms aren't complex. Don't let the dweebs intimidate you.

Common Carriers

There's more to the technology of AOL than computers, however. There's also the nagging little problem of delivering the signal from your location to Vienna. Again, an analogy is in order.

If you wanted to get a package to a friend who lives across the country, you could probably hop in your car and drive it there yourself. But compared to the alternatives, driving across the country would be impractical, to say the least.

More likely, you'd hire a *common carrier*—a service such as United Parcel Service or FedEx—to deliver the package for you. For a fraction of what it would cost you to do the job yourself, common carriers can do it more reliably, less expensively, and much more conveniently.

AOLnet

In the early 1990s, when AOL was experiencing almost meteoric growth, even the largest common carriers couldn't keep up. It was as if you and I and everyone we know were to call FedEx for a pickup every 15 minutes. The common carriers clogged up, connections with AOL were difficult to establish during peak usage periods, and when connections were made, they were often sluggish.

Taking matters in its own hands, AOL established its own private network, *AOLnet*. AOLnet is your best choice of all the carriers because all of AOLnet's access numbers are high-speed, and AOLnet's backbones—the transcontinental lines that run from city to city—are state-of-the-art. For more information about AOLnet, sign on, press Ctrl+K (for "keyword," AOL's navigational shortcut system), enter the keyword: **AOLnet**, and read the information you find there.

Figure 1-2:
High-speed tele-
communications
equipment in use
at America Online
headquarters.

For much the same reason, AOL hires common carriers to deliver goods to its members. And, typical of AOL, it hires multiple common carriers to ensure reliability. There's SprintNet, a service of US Sprint, and there's DataPac, a subsidiary of Bell Canada, for Canadian members. There are others as well. These common carriers offer *nodes*—local telephone numbers—in most cities in North America. They charge AOL for phone calls (placed or received) just as FedEx would charge you to deliver a package.

AOL is quickly installing AOLnet nodes in as many cities as possible, but for those cities that AOLnet doesn't serve, SprintNet or DataPac are used. No matter which carrier you use, the important thing to understand is that the carrier is as much a part of the AOL network as are the machines in Vienna.

It's a Telecommunications Service

Now *there's* a polysyllabic mouthful: *telecommunications*. As the term is used here, the word telecommunications refers to two-way communications via telephone lines. A phone call, in other words, is a form of telecommunicating. Telephone lines are good for things other than phone calls. Fax machines use telephone lines to transfer documents; video phones use them to transmit pictures; and modems use them to transfer computer data (the term *modem*—and many other terms—is defined in the Glossary at the back of this book). I'm not talking about expensive dedicated telephone lines here—I'm talking about the very same telephone lines that are already in our homes and offices.

Now we're getting somewhere. If you have a computer and I have a computer and we each have a modem, we can use our existing telephone lines to connect our computers to one another. Once connected this way, our computers can exchange data: text, graphics, sounds, animation—even programs.

Of course, you have to be at your computer and I have to be at mine—at the same time—and we have to know how to make our computers talk to one another, and we have to check for errors encountered in the transmission, and I'm just me and you're just you, and there's only so much computer data two people can exchange with one another before the whole thing gets to be pretty dull.

What we need is a *service* that will store our data so that we don't have to be at our computers at the same time. Instead of calling your computer, I have my computer call the service and store my data and messages there. When you're ready for that data, you can instruct your computer to call the service and retrieve the data at your convenience.

As long as we're imagining a service, we might imagine it to automate all the electronic technicalities as well. If we imagine it right, the service can mediate communications between the two computers, check for errors (and fix them when they're encountered), and even dial the telephone.

And who's to say that you and I should have the service all to ourselves? We can let everyone else with a computer in on it as well, regardless of the type of computer they own. Carried to its extreme, this scenario might result in hundreds of thousands—millions, actually—of people using the service, exchanging and storing thousands of computer files. Most of this data can be public rather than private, so the exchange becomes multilateral.

Which is precisely what telecommunications services—and AOL—are: a vast network of "members," each of whom uses a computer, a modem, and a telephone line to connect with a common destination—to "go online." Members can exchange public and private files; they can send and receive e-mail; and members who are online at the same time can "chat" in real time. They can even play online games with one another.

And what does this service cost? The economies of scale allow expenses to be distributed among the members. Moreover, even though AOL is near Washington, DC, very few members pay for long-distance calls. America Online has local telephone numbers in nearly every city in the contiguous United States. Even if you live in "the sticks," chances are you'll find a local number you can call—or one that's a "short" long-distance call away. If that's too expensive, there's always AOL's 800 number. (To find out more about access to AOL via the toll-free 800 number, sign on and use the keyword: **Access**.)

It's Software Installed in Your Computer

Conceptualizing AOL as nodes and mainframe computers isn't very comforting. For many of us, America Online is much more parochial than that: AOL is software in our computers—software on a disk bundled with the computer, ordered from a magazine ad, or provided in the *Official America Online Membership Kit*.

Figure 1-3:
America Online's
logo appears
whenever you run
the software in-
stalled on your
computer.

That's more like it. The software you use on your computer to sign on to AOL more accurately represents the personality of the service than anything we've discussed so far. It makes friendly noises (if your computer is equipped with sound), it's resplendent with windows and icons, and it automates tasks and procedures that only a few years ago used to exclude most semi-normal people from using telecommunications systems.

Here's what I mean. Nearly every telecommunications program assumes you know how to set certain arcane but necessary attributes and protocols, such as data bits, stop bits, parity, and flow. Frankly, though I've used telecommunications software for years and have adjusted my data bits and parity, I have no idea what they are, and I have always been kind of nervous about shooting in the dark like that. America Online, on the other hand, uses its own custom software at both ends of the line. After you install the software on your computer (a simple process I describe in Appendix A, "Making the Connection"), all the technicalities are coordinated by the host computer and your machine. They simply talk things over and make adjustments as required. This is as it should be.

We're getting closer to the mark. The phrase "user-friendly" is properly used to describe this service. America Online's new Windows software is familiar, predictable, and comfortable for the Windows user. The File menu says Open, Save, Close, and Exit. Its windows have title bars and minimize buttons.

Another unique aspect of the AOL software is its interface and communication strategy. The software is highly graphical, and trans-ferring graphics online takes time—much more time than transferring text, for instance—which could make the service as sluggish as a hound in July. However, this should not cause problems because most of AOL's graphical components are transferred to your machine only once, then they're stored on your hard disk. After that, text is the primary information that flows between you and AOL, and text travels very quickly.

Software Updates at Signoff

Occasionally, you'll encounter a message just after you issue the Sign Off command (the Sign Off command is under the Go To menu). The message will indicate that a change needs to be made to your application—the AOL client software running on your computer—and that an update needs to take place (see Figure 1-4).

Figure 1-4: The signoff update routine assures that your AOL software is always up to date.

INFORMATION

A download of the updated versions of the required tools is going to start before logout. Do you want to continue the downloading now?

Yes   No

File Transfer - 12%

Now Downloading AOLBLANK.BUT

12%

About 1 minute remaining

America Online

The application will now be restarted to put the software update into place. This will take a few moments. Please press OK to continue.

OK

Updates such as this usually amount to nothing more than the download of a few graphical elements—a button is being downloaded in Figure 1-4—that keep your software up to date. The download can amount to much more: AOL can add major features to your software this way.

Regardless of the complexity of the download, if you click the Yes button in the Information window pictured in Figure 1-4, AOL will stop your online clock—you won't be billed for the time other than any long-distance telephone charges you're incurring—and conduct its update without requiring your attention. You can walk away from the computer, or you can minimize AOL and move on to some other computer activity. When AOL completes its update, it signs you off and restarts the software, if required, all automatically.

AOL's multimedia interface is constantly changing, to add more enhancements. That's part of what makes AOL so exciting. The concession, however, is that if you want the bells and whistles, they'll have to be transferred at some time or other. The best time for this is sign-off. Do it then.

Here's the point: AOL is an advanced and progressive telecommunications service that grows daily and contains the features necessary to accommodate that growth. The software features I describe here reflect a progressive attitude, and that attitude is a better way of defining AOL.

It's a Resource

News, sports, weather—sure you can get them on radio and television, but not necessarily when you need or want them. You can get them in a newspaper, too; but it's going to cost the environment a tree or two, the pictures are fuzzy, and about all you can do with a newspaper you've read is throw it away (consult the Environmental Forum at keyword: **Environment** for recycling information). America Online offers the news, sports, and weather as well—available at your convenience and without sacrificing any trees. It's in electronic form, so you can file it, search it, and include it in documents of your own.

On an average day, I begin by reading the latest news and weather (discussed in Chapter 10, "Staying Informed"); then I check up on the investments in my modest portfolio (discussed in Chapter 12, "Personal Finance"), and read my mail (discussed in Chapter 3, "Electronic Mail & the Personal Filing Cabinet"). Not long ago I researched the purchase of a new hard disk for my computer (see Chapter 15, "Buying & Selling"), and I often make my travel plans using AOL's airline reservation system. I constantly search the online video reviews before I rent a tape (the airline reservation system and video reviews are discussed in Chapter 11, "Divertissements"). Past issues of *Windows Magazine, WIRED, National Geographic,* and *Smithsonian* are online for my review, as is *Compton's Encyclopedia,* the *Merriam-Webster Dictionary,* and "the Gray Lady": the *New York Times* (see Chapter 14, "Reference"). As a professional member of the desktop publishing community, I constantly collect graphics, fonts, and utilities (AOL has tens of thousands of files online—described in Chapter 5, "Transferring Files").

In other words, I could describe AOL as a resource of almost infinite potential. You don't have to drive anywhere to use it; it's continuously maintained and updated; and it's all electronic—available for any use you can imagine. Many members find the resource potential alone ample justification for signing on to AOL, but to limit your participation this way would be a disservice to AOL and to yourself. Above all, AOL is people: friends, associates, consultants—even lovers. It's a resource all right, but it's also a community. And therein lies its greatest value.

It's a Community

I've taken the easy way out. Yes, AOL is a telecommunications service. Yes, it's the host computer. Yes, it's client software in your computer. And yes, it's a resource. But that's like saying that Christmas is just another day of the year. There's much more to it than that. Christmas is reverence and good things; but for many of us, Christmas means people: family, friends, and community. AOL, too, is best defined by its people. America Online is a *community*. My dictionary defines community as "a social group sharing common characteristics or interests," and that is the best definition I can imagine for AOL.

As members, we have common interests, we all have computers, and we love to share. *That's* what AOL is all about. After a few weeks, the novelty of interconnection and graphical images wears off. After a few weeks, we stop wondering about the host computer and data bits. After a few weeks, we all discover the true soul of AOL, and that soul is its people.

Futuring

This is certainly a medium for futuring—for envisaging, musing, and aspiring. I future with nearly everyone I meet at AOL: they're the people who are shaping the future of telecommunications, and they're always a couple of years ahead of the rest of us. Fascinating discourse.

Steve Case is President of America Online. He is paid to future, and he loves his job. On this spectacular fall afternoon, sitting in his office with Virginia's autumnal splendor outside the window, Steve talks of what lies ahead for telecommunications.

Not even 9 percent of American homes were online in the fall of 1995 when we talked. Steve compares this to television in the late 1940s: "No one remembers television then. It was in less than 10 percent of America homes. It was an emerging technology, a curiosity, and the things television did in the '40s are all but forgotten."

He goes on to cite television's emergent moment, which he feels was the 1960 Presidential election. We couldn't help but take notice of television after that: the debates, after all, could very well have swayed the election.

Steve Case futures about the online medium in ten years, when it has reached the same point along its developmental curve. Will the candidates appear in an online Rotunda of some sort, debating issues and answering questions from members? Will they offer an e-mail address and respond to all queries? Steve suspects that the online industry might very well influence the viability of a third political party in this country. What medium is better prepared to develop a party of the people? The online medium is the embodiment of the elusive flat playing field, where everyone is equally empowered and there is little cause for class, race, gender, or age discrimination. In an era where political candidates are perceived as media stars—inaccessible, almost chimerical—we're primed for a candidate who seems to be one of us, and the online medium is where such a creature might best be nurtured.

I never asked Steve Case if he thought he might ever be President. I doubt that he would take the job. He's having too much fun being Steve Case.

When I first agreed to write this book, community was the last thing on my mind. I have been a telecommunicator for years. I thought I'd seen it all. Now, however, I spend as much of my online time corresponding with friends—new friends in every part of the country—as I do conducting research. In Chapter 3, I admit to getting despondent if I don't hear the familiar mail notification when the Welcome screen comes up. Throughout this book, I'll offer little tips on how to make friends online. Follow these tips, and you'll become as much a part of this community as I am.

You really couldn't do much better.

Tom Lichty

Allow me to introduce myself. My name is Tom Lichty (say *lick'-tee*). I'm a full-time writer, living on a small farm in rural Oregon where the air is clear and the politics are liberal. I often ply the waters of the Pacific Northwest and Alaska aboard Pick Pocket, my Spartan little aquatic cruiser. If you ever happen to be in Desolation Sound on a peaceful July evening and notice a small boat with a fellow bent over the keyboard of his laptop computer, it's probably me.

➡

I'd be flattered if you'd check out my home page on the World Wide Web (the Web is discussed in Chapter 4, "Using the Internet"). Sign on to AOL, press Ctrl+K and type **http://members.aol.com/majortom/private/index.html**. Be sure to type it exactly as shown, then click the Go button.

The people at America Online have an uncommonly altruistic attitude toward the documentation for their service. *The Official America Online Tour Guide* is a book, not a manual. I'm an independent author, not a staff technical writer. And AOL chose a traditional publisher—Ventana Communications—to produce and distribute this book. It's not an AOL production. I therefore have the autonomy and elbow room to explore the subject with you independently, thoroughly, and candidly. The people at AOL are to be commended for their courage in choosing this path. It could be perilous. Confidence in their product, however, emboldens them, and rightfully so.

How to Use This Book

I suppose this book is the documentation—the "user's manual"—for America Online. You no doubt already know that documentation can be dull. Few people take a software manual to the hammock for a lazy afternoon of reading. As you might guess from the title, this is not your typical prosaic how-to instruction manual; you will find no inscrutable "technobabble." I hope you'll find it more of an odyssey—a pleasant journey of discovery—to the interesting places and people in America Online's virtual universe. Nonetheless, as your guide to all the diverse experiences AOL has to offer, I've included organizational and reference tools that will help you find your way around.

Finding Answers

I want you to be able to turn to *The Official America Online Tour Guide* whenever you have a question about AOL. I want you to be able to find the answer to your question with a minimum of effort, no matter how many different places the subject may appear in the book. Pursuant to that, a number of tools are at your disposal:

- The *table of contents* lists titles, section heads, and subheads for every chapter. When you need information on a specific subject, turn first to the table of contents. Nine times out of ten, it will be all you need.

▲ A thorough *index* appears at the end of the book, with references to subjects, procedures, and departments. If the subject you're after doesn't appear in the table of contents, turn to the index.

▲ Secondary tables of contents appear at the beginning of each chapter. Use these listings not only to preview the contents of a chapter before you read it, but to help you find specifics when you're using this book for reference.

▲ A *listing of keywords* appears in Appendix B. Keywords are the interstate highway system at AOL. If you want to get somewhere in a hurry, use a keyword. As you discover places that appeal to you, add them to your list of favorite places in your Personal Filing Cabinet (described in Chapter 3, "Electronic Mail & the Personal Filing Cabinet").

▲ A *glossary* of terms used in the book follows the appendices. The glossary is especially thorough in its inclusion of telecommunications terminology that is unique to AOL. People often talk in shorthand when they're online—typing is so *slow*—and the glossary offers the necessary translations.

Activity Listings

With the exception of the first and last chapters, I've organized this book according to the way people use AOL. Chapters 2 through 15 each describe a typical online activity and how that activity is best pursued.

▲ Chapter 2, "The Abecedarium," comes up next. AOL is a big place. Lots of things are going on here, and when you first sign on it's like your first day on a new job: everyone seems to know what to do except you. Chapter 2 is like a neighborly coworker—showing you an *orderly, effective* approach for getting to know AOL and spending your time there productively. This chapter also defines the word *abecedarium*.

▲ Chapter 3, "Electronic Mail & the Personal Filing Cabinet," describes AOL's most popular feature: e-mail. You can communicate with people all over the world—not just fellow AOL members but anyone with e-mail access to the Internet—using AOL's mail filing system, which is second to none.

- Chapter 4, "Using the Internet," briefly introduces the Internet and AOL's tools for using it. I say "briefly" because the Internet is subject enough for an entire second book—something which I've written. See the bibliography at the end of this book.

- Chapter 5, "Transferring Files," focuses on tricks and techniques for receiving (downloading) and sending (uploading) files from and to AOL.

- Chapter 6, "FlashSessions & the Download Manager," shows you how to read and write your mail offline, when you're not paying AOL for the time. You can also instruct your computer to perform your downloads automatically and unattended, in the middle of the night if you want, when the load on the system is minimal.

- Chapter 7, "Computing," explores AOL's computing resources: programs, drivers, and utilities, and offers commiseration and advice.

- Chapter 8, "The Community," introduces you to chat rooms and Instant Messages, where conversations occur in real time and strangers rarely remain strangers for long. This chapter also discusses the people who comprise that community: kids, seniors, and everyone in between.

- Chapter 9, "Boards & Forums," opens the doors to AOL's clubhouses, where people of similar interests gather to exchange wisdom and develop communities.

- Chapter 10, "Staying Informed," describes AOL's profound informational resources, including news, sports, and weather.

- Chapter 11, "Divertissements," makes an effort to acquaint you with the spectrum of interesting things you can do online. Though it's by no means comprehensive, this chapter includes online games; book, film, and television reviews; ABC, MTV, and *Entertainment Weekly*; the comics; and travel, including EASY SAABRE, the Travel Forum, Travelers' Corner, and Preview Vacations.

- Chapter 12, "Personal Finance," offers a mini-primer on the subject of online finance. Not only can you buy and sell publicly traded issues with AOL, but you can also maintain a detailed portfolio, chart its performance and consult the wisdom of experts when transactions must be made.

- Chapter 13, "Learning," explores learning opportunities for the student and teacher, Berkeley Online, the Nature Conservancy, the Library of Congress, the Smithsonian, and the incomparable Odyssey Project.

- Chapter 14, "Reference," spotlights one of the online medium's most unique benefits: information retrieval. Encyclopedias, cookbooks, dictionaries—they're all electronically searchable, continually updated, and eminently quotable.

- Chapter 15, "Buying & Selling," runs the gamut from the classifieds to real estate. The online medium has become fertile ground for commerce—you can't beat it for convenience, after all—and AOL offers scores of ways to participate.

- Chapter 16, "Ten Best," offers my ten-best lists—the ten best tips for using AOL, the ten questions most frequently asked of the AOL customer support team, the ten best files for downloading—that kind of thing. No fair reading this one first!

Moving On

Our lights-out experience in the auditorium concluded, Matt Korn sits in his office. The sounds of nocturnal revelry downstairs still sift through the building, but Matt has better things to do. He talks of an online future that incites the imagination. Virtual realities, video chat, personal agents—things that require new vocabularies to comprehend. I feel honored to be among his *beau monde*.

I'm honored, too, to share this extraordinary resource with you. Matt may be enamored with AOL's future—that's his job, after all—but I'm dazzled enough with its present. You will be too. Turn the page—a remarkable journey is about to begin.

The Abecedarium

CHAPTER 2

- New Member Info
- Road Trips
- Getting Help
- Guides
- My AOL
- Parental Controls
- Terms of Service (TOS)

Isn't that a *great* word? "Abecedarium." Pronounce the first three syllables as you would pronounce the first three letters in the alphabet: A-B-C, then add "darium" (it rhymes with "aquarium"). Indeed, the letters "ABC" are the root of the word, for in the original Medieval Latin, *abecedarium* meant "alphabet." Later the term was used to describe books for people who are learning the alphabet, and later still—as it is today—abecedarium was used to describe a primer on any subject. That's what we're doing with this chapter: presenting a primer for those of you who are new to this abecedary we call online telecommunications.

The Newbies, the Ditzels, and the Dummies

In the fall of 1995, a long-term discussion broke out on the staff message boards at AOL: What term do we use to describe people who are new to online telecommunicating? "Dummy" is popular, but it's not a very flattering term. Its success as a book title, I suspect, relates more to a person's self perception, not to the person's status among others. "Ditzel" is perhaps too colloquial a term, and even less flattering than "dummy."

The consensus among the staff was that "newbie" would have to do, though it wasn't a unanimous sentiment. The term is often used derisively, in spite of its original intent.

> I like "abecedarian." No word with that many syllables can be derisive. No word that appears to be so confoundedly unpronounceable can possibly be colloquial. And its meaning is understood by so few that it will never be used unflatteringly—it's hardly used at all.
>
> Perfect. We'll call ourselves abecedarians and perplex them all with our pedantic pedagogy. They're all a bunch of dweebs anyway. ;-)

New Member Info

Somewhere, the Godiva people must have a chocolate warehouse. I'll bet it's huge. Imagine standing just inside of the door, confronted by shelves of chocolates, stacked to the ceiling in a warehouse that's measured in acres. Your host just told you to "Eat whatever you want." *Holy confections*! Where to begin?

Once the stupefaction wears off, most AOL abecedarians wander around aimlessly for their first few weeks, biting their nails and cultivating futility. This is no more productive a method of exploring AOL than it is of exploring Godiva's warehouse. We need some direction here: something or someone to show us where the best stuff is so we can get down to the business of prodigal consumption.

I don't know about Godiva, but AOL offers such a place, and it's right on the menu. To get there, choose New Member Help from the Help menu, or use the keyword: **Orientation**. This is where all of AOL's new member help is consolidated, and there's a wealth of it.

> ### Keywords
>
> I mentioned *keywords* in the previous chapter and I just mentioned them again, but more emphasis is appropriate. Keywords are shortcuts to specific destinations within AOL. Without keywords, accessing Family PC Online, for example, via menus and windows requires that I click the Computing button on the Main Menu, click the ZD Net button, click the Explore icon, and finally click the Family PC button. *Whew*! That's a lot of button-pushing, and I had to know which buttons to push. There's gotta be a better way.
>
> ➡

And there is: keywords. The keyword(s) for Family PC Online are **Family PC**. Once I know the keyword or keywords, all I have to do is choose Keyword from the Go To menu (or click the keyword button on the toolbar, or press Ctrl+K) and enter **Family PC** into the area provided. Instantly, AOL takes me directly to Family PC Online, bypassing all the steps in between.

A list of keywords is available in Appendix B of this book. Keywords are also available within the Directory of Services (discussed later), which you can search right in the Keyword window. Just enter your criterion where the keyword would normally go and click the Search button.

A final note: Keywords are not case sensitive. **FAMILY PC** works just the same as **family pc**. You can leave out spaces too: **Family PC** works no better than **FamilyPC**.

Without getting specific, perhaps the best way for you to explore the New Member Help area is exactly the way you should *not* explore AOL: by wandering around aimlessly. You won't cultivate futility here: every corner you turn will reveal a new aspect of AOL, without having to explore the plenitude of the entire service.

Road Trips

AOL's Road Trips are guided tours of the service. Virtually speaking, you climb aboard a bus (usually with 20 or so others) and take off on a magical adventure conducted by tour "Guides"—people who know where they're going and identify features along the way (see Figure 2-1).

Figure 2-1:
Road Trips are
probably the best
way to get to know
AOL. Take the hand
of an expert and
participate in a
methodical, reveal-
ing tour of America
Online—and have
fun along the way.
Road Trips are
available at the
keywords: **Road
Trip**.

Are You Current?

As is the case with many other areas in this book, the Road Trips discussion assumes you have the latest version of AOL's software. Do you? Here's how to find out:

- Sign on and use the keyword: **Upgrade.**

- Find the latest copy of AOL's software available for download in the upgrade area, then read its description to discover its version number.

- Choose "About America Online" from the Help menu and note the number of the version you're now using.

- If the versions don't match, you need to download the upgrade. Begin by printing the file's description that appears on your screen. *Don't neglect this step.*

- Download the upgrade, then sign off.

- Exit from the AOL software, then follow the directions in the description you have printed.

Road Trips aren't passive. At each stop, your Guide will let you "off the bus" to explore the area for a while on your own. You can wander around in the Florida Wildflower Web page, for example (see Figure 2-2), and your tour guide will be at your side, ready to answer questions and point out features.

Figure 2-2:
The Florida Wild-
flower Web page
invites my explora-
tion in the top half
of the Road Trip
window. In the
lower half, my
Guide is identifying
features of the site.
The very bottom of
the window offers
a text box where I
can submit my
questions and
comments. The
Guide or anyone
else on the bus can
reply.

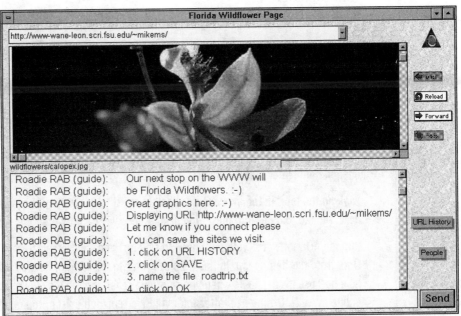

Road Trips aren't the exclusive purview of AOL's staff, by the way. Anyone can be a guide—even you. It's a great way to introduce friends to AOL, even if they're in another part of the country. It's really quite easy to prepare your own personal tour: press the Help button at keywords: **Road Trip** for more information.

Getting Help

Speaking of help, I'll never forget my first online experience. It was many years ago—long before America Online. But, like AOL, the service I subscribed to was a commercial service, and the clock was running whenever I dialed their number. Anxiety had no finer ally.

In other words, I empathize with those of you whose fingers turn to cucumbers whenever you sign on—and so does America Online. Things have changed. Today there is help—plenty of help. Not only does AOL offer an abundance of help, it's most often free. I'd be five years younger today if the early days of the online industry had been that considerate.

Getting Help: A Methodical Approach

If you have a question about AOL and require help, *don't write to me!* I'm just one person, with one person's knowledge of the system. AOL offers an army of experts, each of them is thoroughly acquainted with the system, and each is trained in member assistance. To make effective use of them, I suggest you use the methods described below, in the order in which they appear. Most of the topics mentioned are explained in detail later in this chapter.

1. Look up the topic in the index of this book to see if your question is answered here. I'd like to think that most of your questions will be answered this way.

2. Run the AOL software (you don't need to sign on) and choose Search for Help On... from the Help menu. In this chapter I refer to this kind of help as *offline* help because it's available when you're offline (even though it's available online as well). Offline help offers an extensive searchable list of topics and will often answer your question, especially if it has to do with the most commonly asked AOL questions.

3. Sign on and click the question mark button on the toolbar (the toolbar is that bar of icons just under the menu bar). Click the Yes button in response to the "Are you sure..." message. This will take you to AOL's Member Services, a particularly comprehensive (and free) resource. There's a Member Services button on each channel's screen as well.

4. Sign on and use the keyword: **Questions**. This will take you to the One Stop InfoShop, where you can review a slew of FAQs (Frequently Asked Questions) covering a wide variety of topics. From this keyword, you can also jump to a search of the Member Services answer database. This is an amazingly comprehensive collection of answers to almost any AOL or Internet-related question you might have, and it's keyword-searchable.

➡

5. Sign on and use the keyword: **MHM**. This will take you to AOL's Members Helping Members message board. Post your question in the appropriate folder there. Within a day or so you will have a response to your question from another member. Peer help is often the best help you can find.

6. Sign on and use the keywords: **PC Help**. This will take you to the PC Help Forum. They have a searchable *New Member Guide*, a file folder of hints and tips, and a textual map of AOL. The PC Help Forum has message boards as well, and they guarantee a reply within 48 hours.

7. Sign on and use the keywords: **Tech Live**. This will take you to the Member Services department. Click the button for Tech Support Live, where you can consult AOL's Technical Support staff. This feature is free and available from 8:00 a.m. to 3:45 a.m., seven days a week except when the AOL system is down for maintenance.

8. Send e-mail to Customer Relations. Sign on and use the keyword: **Questions**. You might encounter some intervening windows (AOL is always trying more effective methods for providing help) but eventually you'll end up at the One Stop Infoshop window (see Figure 2-5). All of the categories of help listed in that window offer a "Write to Our Staff" option.

9. Call Customer Relations at 1-800-827-6364. They're open from 6:00 a.m. to 4:00 a.m. Eastern time, seven days a week. It's a toll-free call in the continental United States, and there's never any charge for support from AOL.

Altruistically, AOL offers both online and offline help. One set of help files resides on your hard disk and is available at any time regardless of whether you're online. I call this version AOL's *offline* help. The other version—*online* help—is always available online, without charge. We'll discuss both in this chapter.

Offline Help

Let's talk about offline help first. America Online's offline help is especially configured to answer the kind of questions you'll encounter when you're disconnected from the service. How do I connect when I'm away from my usual location? What's the Customer Relations telephone number and when are they on duty? How do I sign up my friends?

A Familiar Face

With Windows 3.0, Microsoft inaugurated a policy that was new to the industry at the time: a Help application common to all programs. In the Windows environment, Help is a separate program that's called by other programs when the user wants help. When you choose an item from AOL's Help menu, AOL starts the Help application. When you ask for help from Microsoft Word, the same thing happens. The Help files themselves are different; the Help application is the same (see Figure 2-3).

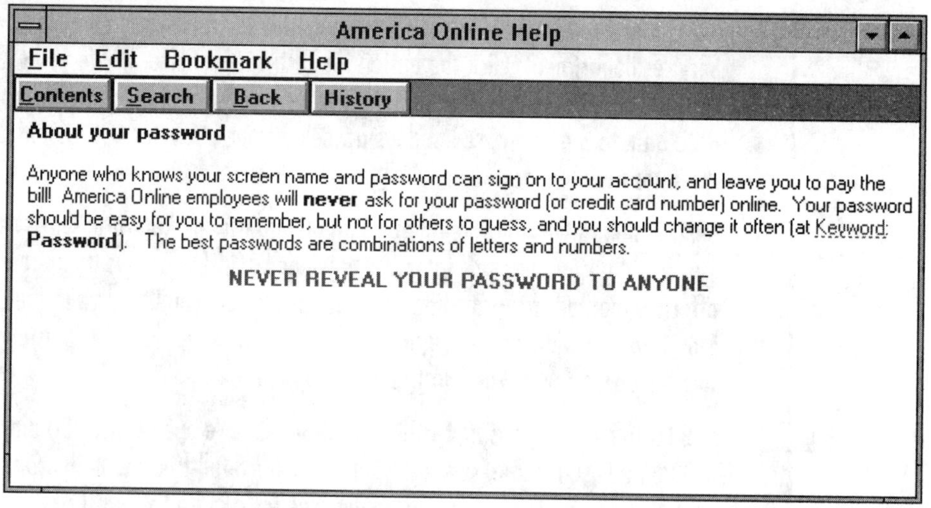

Figure 2-3:
A familiar face:
AOL's Help utility
looks and acts just
like the Help utility
in any other Win-
dows program.

This means there's no need to learn how to use the Help feature over again for each application. Help is the same for all Windows applications.

America Online utilizes the Windows Help application to its fullest. The AOL Help file is very large, and there are plenty of links to cross-reference Help topics with one another. Any Help topic can be searched and printed; bookmarks can be placed to lead you back to topics of particular interest; and an extensive list of tips and tricks is available.

As is always the case with items that aren't grayed out on Windows menus, Help can be chosen at any time, whether you're online or off. These Help topics are stored in a file on your hard disk and so don't require that you go online to access them; you just need to launch the AOL program and pull down the Help menu.

Downloading the Help File

AOL's offline Help file is an encyclopedic piece of work. It's so large, in fact, that it won't fit on the program disk that AOL distributes. For most member installations, AOL downloads the Help file to you at the conclusion of (or during) your first online session. You'll see a message to that effect—probably just before you sign off— and the option to accept the download or ignore it. Unless you're calling AOL via a toll line (that is, unless you've had to dial a "1" before AOL's number), there won't be a charge.

In other words, when you're offered the download, take it. If you don't, you'll miss one of AOL's better Help mechanisms.

How to Use Help

One of the topics on the Help menu is How to Use Help. If you've never used the Windows Help feature before, this is the place to start. Get to know Help inside and out; become comfortable with it. Once you've gained that kind of confidence, you won't hesitate to use Help the next time it's needed.

Figure 2-4:
Searching America Online's Help files for "local access," I discover plenty of resources. This information is available whether I'm online or off.

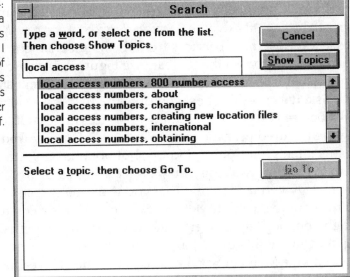

```
┌─────────────────────────────────────────────────────┐
│ ─ │              Search                               │
├───────────────────────────────────────────────────── │
│ Type a word, or select one from the list.   ┌─────────┐│
│ Then choose Show Topics.                     │ Cancel  ││
│                                              └─────────┘│
│ ┌──────────────────────────────────────┐    ┌─────────┐│
│ │ local access                         │    │Show Topics││
│ └──────────────────────────────────────┘    └─────────┘│
│ ┌──────────────────────────────────────────┐ ↑        │
│ │ local access numbers, 800 number access  │ █        │
│ │ local access numbers, about              │ █        │
│ │ local access numbers, changing           │          │
│ │ local access numbers, creating new location files│   │
│ │ local access numbers, international      │          │
│ │ local access numbers, obtaining          │ ↓        │
│ └──────────────────────────────────────────┘          │
│                                                       │
│ Select a topic, then choose Go To.         ┌─────────┐│
│                                            │  Go To  ││
│                                            └─────────┘│
│ ┌─────────────────────────────────────────────────┐ │
│ │                                                 │ │
│ │                                                 │ │
│ │                                                 │ │
│ │                                                 │ │
│ └─────────────────────────────────────────────────┘ │
└─────────────────────────────────────────────────────┘
```

Victoria, my wife, is a medical student. She learned a long time ago that it's impossible to memorize all of the things she has to know to become a successful practitioner. The sheer magnitude of the task was dragging her down until she realized that all she really had to know was where to look for information. She has a well-organized library and knows which books discuss which topics. When she needs assistance, she goes to her library and gets help.

You should do the same. Don't worry about memorizing all the petty details—for any computer program. Instead, learn how to use Help. It will take 20 minutes and it will be the most productive 20 minutes you'll ever spend with your computer.

Online Help

America Online's online Help is especially comprehensive. Moreover, because the online Help files are stored on the host computer (and not on your hard disk), they can be updated quickly, whenever an update is required. In addition to the help you get using the online files, AOL staff and members stand ready to help you as well. This is world-class help, and its breadth is unique to AOL.

Member Services

AOL doesn't call their online Help area "Online Help." In the true spirit of altruism, they call it *Member Services*. To access Member Services, choose Member Services from the Members menu, click the question mark icon on the toolbar (see Figure 2-5) or use the keyword: **Help**. You must be signed on for this: online Help isn't stored on your hard disk. It's on AOL's host computer.

Just before you enter the Member Services area, AOL flashes the message pictured near the top of Figure 2-5. Unprovoked dialog boxes like this often spell trouble, I know, but not this one. America Online is trying to say that you're about to pass through the "free curtain" (to use the AOL vernacular) and that you won't be charged for the time you're about to spend in Member Services. That's a comforting thought: online Help is free. You can spend all day perusing online Help and AOL will never charge you a dime.

Once in the Member Services area, click the "Have Questions?" folder, then on the "One Stop Infoshop" icon to enter the One Stop Infoshop pictured in Figure 2-5. The Infoshop is a great place to poke around, getting to know the service.

Random Acts of Help

The next time you sign on to AOL, click the toolbar's question mark icon and venture into the One Stop Infoshop. Once you're there, relax (the clock's not running) and explore this area casually. Poke around as you would at a flea market. Don't try to memorize anything. Get the feel of the place. Get to know what's there and where it's found. Consider this an exploratory mission without any particular agenda. After 20 minutes or so, move on to something else.

You will be amazed at what this kind of unstructured behavior can do for you. You will acquire a familiarity with the layout of the place, and you will gain confidence in the use of online Help. Most important, the next time you need help, you won't hesitate to use the keyword. And that, in the long run, is perhaps the most productive attitude you can adopt toward the use of AOL.

Figure 2-5:
Online Help is available whenever you're online by clicking the question mark icon on the toolbar. The best part: it's absolutely free.

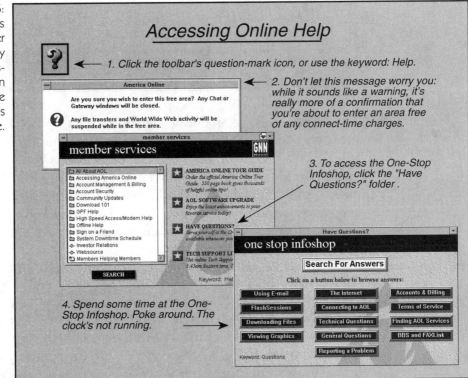

The subjects pictured in the One Stop Infoshop window offer immediate answers for nearly anything you encounter while online. Each of these Help topics can be saved, printed, or both. The list of topics is extensive, and the detail offered within each topic is bountiful (see Figure 2-6).

Figure 2-6:
A few of the e-mail
Help topics available in the One
Stop InfoShop.

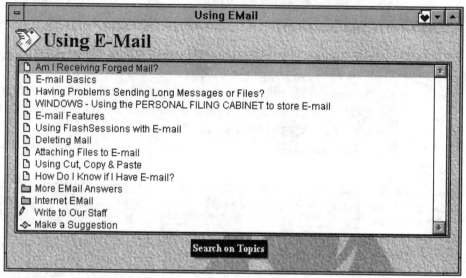

Saving Help   To save an online Help topic that's on your screen, simply choose Save (or Save As—they're the same command in this context) from the File menu. America Online asks you what you want to name the file and where you want to save it. Provide the information it needs, and that Help topic will be stored on your disk, ready for any purpose you might have in mind. You can open the file containing the information you saved with a word processor or your AOL software: just choose Open from the File menu.

Printing Help   More likely, you'll want to print a Help topic for ready reference. As you might expect, all you have to do is choose Print from the File menu, or click the Print icon in the toolbar. Printing from AOL works about like printing from any other Windows application. You'll receive the print dialog box associated with the printer you've selected via the Print Setup command under the File menu. Configure this dialog as you please, and print. By the way, you can print just about

any text file you read online, not just the online Help files. If you run across a file description or news article you want to print, just choose Print from the File menu—AOL will print whatever text is in the frontmost (active) window.

The Directory of Services

Try the keyword: **Services**, which will take you to AOL's Directory of Services, a searchable database of information on all the services available online. Information for each service includes the following:

- The service's name.

- Any keywords associated with that service.

- A menu path for access to that service.

- A description of that service.

- A button to take you there.

Searching the Directory of Services   The Directory of Services is AOL's answer to the question: "I wonder if they have anything that addresses my interest in..." Are you interested in model airplanes? Search the Directory of Services. How about music, poetry, or fine food? Use the Directory of Services.

I was having trouble with Microsoft Word the other day. Couldn't get it to do things I knew it was capable of doing. What to do? Call five friends on the phone and get their voice mail? Call Microsoft long distance and wait as they play unendurable Microsoft deejayed music while I'm on hold?

None of the above. I simply signed on and consulted the Microsoft Knowledge Base. The Knowledge Base is the summation of nearly everything Microsoft knows about its products, including answers from their technical support staff. It's updated periodically and re-leased on CD-ROM. You can subscribe if you wish (if you have a CD-ROM player)—it's only $295 a year.

Or you can use AOL. America Online offers a link to Microsoft's Knowledge Base Web page, complete with a search mechanism to find what you're after. If you forget Microsoft's keyword, use the Directory of Services to find it for you. That's just what I did the other day, and my question was answered within a few minutes (see Figure 2-7).

Figure 2-7:
The Directory of
Services found the
Microsoft Knowl-
edge Base for me,
and the Knowledge
Base had my
answer.

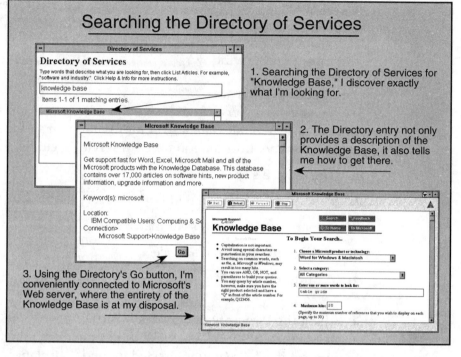

Note that the middle window in Figure 2-7 offers the keyword(s) for the Knowledge Base, its location (the menu path that gets you there) and its description. If it isn't what I need, the description saves me the trouble of going there. If it is what I need, not only do the keyword and location tell me how to get there quickly, a Go button is provided at the bottom of the window. Clicking on it will take me there in a flash.

Locating the Directory of Services   There are at least three ways to get to the Directory of Services. You can use the Find area (click the Find button on the toolbar), or the keyword: **Services**, but you'll access the Directory of Services most often via the Keyword window. Type **Ctrl+K**, enter your criterion, and click on the Search button.

Tech Support Live

Let's talk about rooms for a moment. At AOL, a *room* (you might hear it referred to as a *chat room*) is a place where a number of people gather to talk about a subject of common interest. There are classrooms, for instance, where you'll find a teacher and students (the Online Campus is discussed in Chapter 14, "Reference"). There's People Connection (the two-heads button on the toolbar), where people go to mingle and meet other people. In fact, AOL offers scores of rooms, and we will explore a number of them in Chapter 8, "The Community."

Look again at Figure 2-5. There you'll see an icon for Tech Support Live in the Member Services window. If you click that icon (or better yet, use the keywords: **Tech Live**), you'll eventually find yourself in a room with at least one Customer Service representative and probably a number of other members, all with questions about the service. Conversations in the room are real-time: you don't have to wait for replies. This isn't mail, and it's not a message board. It's a room, and as in real rooms in real buildings, people there can hold real-time conversations. Tech Support Live is available from 8:00 a.m. to 3:45 a.m., seven days a week, excepting those periods when the AOL system is down for maintenance. If you need an immediate response, this is the place to find it (see Figure 2-8).

Figure 2-8: A glimpse of the Tech Support Live service. To get there, use the keywords: **Tech Live**.

Tech Live	

Rooms	People	Interact	Chat Rows

People on Stage:

Tech Live

Tech Live
Tech Live1

TECHLIVEDB:	(2) Welcome to Tech Live! How may I help you?
Tech Live:	To ask a question, type in the TEXT BOX, then select SEND, or
Tech Live:	CHAT IN ROW. Do not use the INTERACT button.
Tech Live:	In order to help our customers more quickly, we ask that you
Tech Live:	leave Tech Live when your questions have been answered. Thank you. :)
Member1:	(2) How do I paste an ad in the classifieds from one section to another?
Member2:	(2) Got a question... actually a few...
Member1:	(2) Tried and failed.
Member2:	(2) I ordered a mug from AOL... I received it in less useful condition... (busted)
TECHLiveDB:	(2) Member1 - highlight the desired text - from the menu select Edit/Copy
TECHLiveDB:	(2) Go to the desired location, Select Edit/Paste
Member1:	(2) Ok, Thanks.

Send

Take the Time

Tech Support Live, as you can imagine, is a popular place. At any one time, hundreds of members might be there, each asking questions to which they want answers *right now!*

Rather than toss everyone in the same "room" where they're forced to clamor for attention like reporters at a press conference, AOL arranges the Tech Support Live room in a series of "rows," each with its own tech representative, and each with a limited number of members. Of necessity, it's an elaborate structure with strict protocols—a structure that takes a bit of understanding in order to use it.

As you pass into the Tech Support Live area, AOL offers a number of windows explaining the protocol and offering general help. When you make your first visit to Tech Support Live, take the time to read that information, or search for a reply to a specific question. Once you get into the room and receive a prompt reply to an urgent question, you'll be glad you did.

The Help Rooms

Tech Support Live is widely promoted and always free, and that often leads to a crowd. An alternative is the Help Room (more properly, the Help *Rooms*—there are usually more than one). The Help Room is a chat room in People Connection, and though it's not free, it's staffed by a Guide, and it's open every day from 3:00 p.m. until 3:00 a.m. Eastern. Read Chapter 8, "The Community," to learn about People Connection and chat rooms.

Members Helping Members

On my IRS 1040 form, right there next to the word *Occupation*, it says "educator." Though I've retired from the classroom, I still write books and do some consulting. As an educator, I attend a number of conferences. Most of these conferences are academic, each featuring a number of speakers and seminar leaders.

Reflecting back on those conferences, I must admit that the greatest benefit I receive from them is not from the speakers or the seminars, it's from the other people attending the conference. I get my education in the hallways and at lounge tables. People talking to people, peer to peer—that's where I find the Good Stuff.

America Online is no different. Some of the best help online is that received from other members. America Online knows that; that's why it provides Members Helping Members—a formalized version of peer support (Figure 2-9).

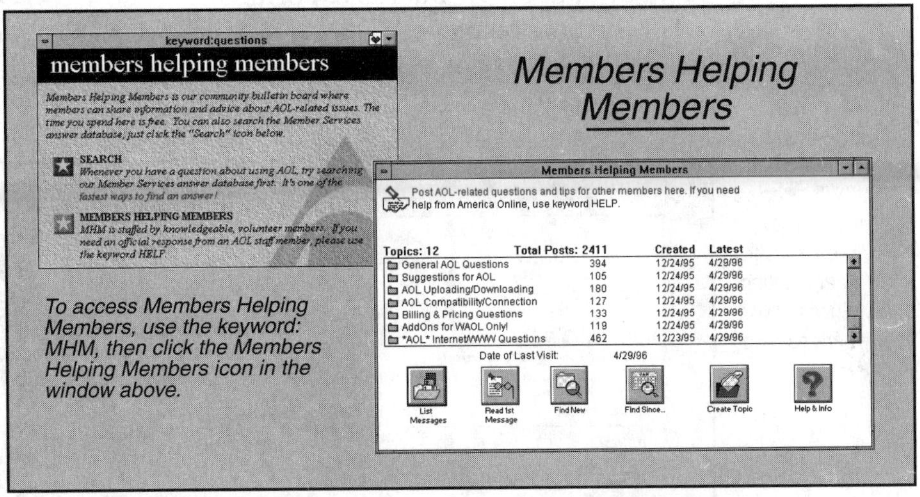

Figure 2-9:
To access
Members Helping
Members, use the
keyword: **MHM**.

Members Helping Members is a free feature at AOL. There's no cause to feel rushed while you're there.

Message Boards   Members Helping Members is a *message board*. Though we'll discuss message boards in Chapter 9, "Boards & Forums," the subject is worth a brief mention here as well.

Throughout AOL you'll see little pushpin icons. This is AOL's way of identifying message boards. A message board is analogous to the bulletin boards you see hanging in the halls of offices and academic institutions. People post things there for other people to see: postcards, lost mittens, announcements, and messages. America Online's message boards are exactly the same (though you might not see lost mittens on AOL's boards).

Look again at Figure 2-9. Note how AOL's boards are organized by using folders. The bulletin board analogy weakens a bit here, but AOL's boards get a lot of messages (the Members Helping Members board pictured in Figure 2-9 has 2,411). Unless they're organized in some fashion, 2,411 messages posted on a single board would be chaotic and overwhelming. The solution is folders.

You can read all the messages in a folder, browse through them (viewing only their subjects, rather than the messages themselves), or specify only those messages that have been posted since a specific date. This is a very convenient message-reading system and is described in detail in Chapter 9, "Boards & Forums."

For the time being, let's select a folder and read its messages. I picked the AOL Hints & Tips folder and found the series of messages pictured in Figure 2-10.

Figure 2-10: N7WS needed help on saving messages for later printing. JenuineOne was there to help.

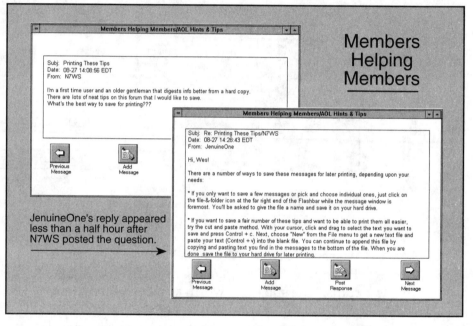

JenuineOne's reply appeared less than a half hour after N7WS posted the question.

The Value of Member Help   Look at the last message pictured in Figure 2-10. Not only does JenuineOne suggest three ideas for N7WS, she explains why and when each idea would work best. This is superb help, and it came from another member. The full text of the message from JenuineOne appears in Figure 2-11.

Figure 2-11:
JenuineOne offers
not one, but three
solutions to a
question.

JenuineOne's Message

```
Subj:  Re: Printing These Tips/N7WS
Date:  08-27  14:28:43 EDT
From:  JenuineOne

Hi, Wes!

There are a number of ways to save these messages for later
printing, depending upon your needs:

* If you only want to save a few messages or pick and choose
individual ones, just click on the file-&-folder icon at the far
right end of the Flashbar while the message window is foremost.
You'll be asked to give the file a name and save it on your hard
drive.

* If you want to save a fair number of these tips and want to be
able to print them all easier, try the cut and paste method. With
your cursor, click and drag to select the text you want to save and
press Control + c. Next, choose "New" from the File menu to get a
new text file and paste your text (Control + v) into the blank file.
You can continue to append this file by copying and pasting text you
find in the messages to the bottom of the file. When you are done,
save the file to your hard drive for later printing.

* If you want to save *all* the messages, use a log to capture
everything. To open a log, select "Logging..." from the "File"
menu and open a Session Log. Now all text you come across will be
captured and saved in the log, whether you read it all or not! When
you are done, go back to Logging and close the log. You can read and
print it right in AOL (if it isn't too big) or in a word processor.

I hope these ideas are helpful!

JenuineOne  O;>
```

Note another small detail: JenuineOne must have looked up N7WS's profile, as she addresses her message to "Wes." That's a nice touch. JenuineOne didn't have to do that, but it makes her message all the more personable. How, you may wonder, do I know that JenuineOne is a she? *I* looked up *her* profile! Profiles are discussed later in this chapter.

I'm reminded of community again. Visiting a big city a few months ago, I was struck by the isolation that seemed to surround everyone I passed on the street. Perhaps it's a defense mechanism for dealing with high population density, but it seemed that everyone was in a cocoon, oblivious of everyone else. No one smiled. No one ever looked anywhere but straight ahead. Thousands of people jostled together, yet no one was talking. An incredibly lonely place.

On the other hand, in Damascus—the little Oregon town closest to my home—there are no strangers. People stop on the street and say hello, swap some gossip, and perhaps offer advice.

America Online is more like Damascus. I spent years on other services and never felt like I belonged. I never got mail, I never contributed to a message board, and I never knew where to find help. It was like a big city to me, and I was always anxious to leave. At AOL I'm walking the street in a small town on a sunny day, and everyone is smiling. The first day I arrived at AOL, I got a letter from Steve Case. People like JenuineOne go out of their way to offer assistance. This is my kind of place. I'm at home here.

The New Member Lounge

The New Member Lounge is exactly what it promises to be. This is a place where new members can get to know one another, get to know the "feel" of the service, and become familiar with chat rooms.

Chat rooms—and the New Member Lounge—are discussed in Chapter 8, "The Community," and I don't want to scoop that chapter here. At the moment, I just want you to be aware of the New Member Lounge. If you're feeling impatient; if you absolutely *must* participate in a chat session before you get to Chapter 8, click the two-heads button on the toolbar and visit the New Member Lounge. Figure 2-12 offers a sample of what you'll find when you get there.

Figure 2-12:
There's never a
stranger in the New
Member Lounge.

The New Member Lounge

```
OnlineHost:
OnlineHost: *** You are in "New Member Lounge". ***          This is an ongoing
OnlineHost:                                                  conversation I walked
MajorTom: Hi all!                                            in on.
PianoPlayr: me either.  ◄─────────────────────────────
Member1: i might go as the denorex chick. is that a good idea?
PianoPlayr: Hello Major
Member2: Might Morphine Power Rangers!
PianoPlayr: HA, great
Member2: Hi Major.
PianoPlayr: : - ))  ◄─────────────────────────          Big smile—perhaps
Hunchbacks: good-bye all                                 a double chin?
MajorTom: Hi Playr. Hi Member2.
MajorTom: Nice place you have here
Mamber3: It's not mine
Member2: Where you from Major.
PianoPlayr: SO  how are you doing Major
MajorTom: Oregon. Doing fine. Sunny here today
PianoPlayr: Do you go to school there?
Member2: Sunny here too
Grrrilla: hi all .Hows things?  ◄──────────────          Another new arrival.
MajorTom: Well, no. Not exactly. Used to teach it, tho!
PianoPlayr: Hello Grr
PianoPlayr: So Major, you were a teacher then.
MajorTom: At the University of Oregon, yes.
PianoPlayr: What did you teach?
Member3: lady, I thought it was ya'll
MajorTom: And you, Playr. You a piano player?
PianoPlayr: Yes.
MajorTom: Any particular style?
PianoPlayr: Classical!  But also like to listen to the other styles.
MajorTom: Ah yes: Rachmaninoff, Chopin?
PianoPlayr: Yes, my favorite!
MajorTom: A romantic no doubt. Etudes & such
PianoPlayr: You sound like that you are very into classical music yourself.
MajorTom: Yes. I hosted a classical music program on public radio for years
MajorTom: Don't play, though. Wish I did
PianoPlayr: Wow!
PianoPlayr: It is ok, as long as you enjoy listening to it.
MajorTom: It's been fun, but I gotta run. Seeya!
```

Guides

I recall an art gallery I visited once in Amsterdam. There were a number of Rembrandts there, hanging on the wall just like any other pictures. No glass cases or protective Lexan—just those radiant Rembrandts, emancipated and free. A gentleman in uniform stood near. He wasn't a guard; the uniform wasn't that severe. He was a guide. He was a volunteer. He got to spend his days in a room full of the Rembrandts he loved and at the same time share his interest with other people. He explained the Rembrandts to us in a fatherly way, exhibiting a proprietorial regard for his fellow countryman's legacy.

Which is precisely what AOL's *Guides* are. They're members just like the rest of us—experienced members, with particularly helpful online personalities, but members all the same. They remain politely in the background, leaving us to our own explorations, silent unless spoken to. If we need help, however, Guides are always nearby, ready with friendly advice and information. If you have a question—any question at all—about AOL, its services or its policies, ask a Guide.

Like the guide in Amsterdam, you can identify Guides by their appearance: their screen names have the word "Guide" in them. If Figure 2-11's JenuineOne was to be a Guide (she should be), she would probably be "Guide JEN," or something like that.

Figure 2-13:
A stop by the
Lobby for some
help from
Guide MO.

A Night in the Lobby

```
MajorTom    : Hi all!
Guide MO    : Hey MajorTom :)              ←
Lthrneck    : :::::getting out ostrich feather:::::
Guide MO    : Nonononononono!!!
Lthrneck    : :::::TICKLE, TICKLE:::::
Guide MO    : ::giggling::
Guide MO    : Hey Cantoni!! :)
Cantoni     : Hi MO!
Guide MO    : Hiya NyteMaire :)
NyteMaire   : Hiya MO :)
CountStixx  : Maire!!!!   {}{}{}{}{}{}       ←
NyteMaire   : {{{{{{Count}}}}}}}} **
LovlyVix    : Nyte {}{}{}{}{}{}{}{}{}{}{}{}{}
NyteMaire   : {{{Vix}}}}
LovlyVix    : How are you Nyte?
NyteMaire   : Getting crazy, and you? ;)
LovlyVix    : Pretty good Nyte :)
MajorTom    : Anybody know of a utility to convert JPEG to TIFF?
Guide MO    : Let me check the libraries for you, T :) I always use Photoshop :)
PC Kate     : <--trying to type while holding ice pack on face. :)
Lthrneck    : ACK Kate, what happened?
Guide MO    : Kate :( Dentist??
AFC Borg    : Is the ice pack inside or outside the paper bag?
PC Kate     : Lthr, had 3 hours of oral and sinus surgery yesterday.
              They say I should be able to eat again next Friday.
GWRepSteve  : Alchemy would probably be the converter to use, MajorTom...
Lthrneck    : Ouch!  Kate!! {}{}{}{}{}{}{}{}
Lee123      : awww Kate.    * to make it better.....    ←
LovlyVix    : <--needs to go to dentist for Kates new diet :)
PC Kate     : Vix, works real well... lost just under five pounds  in 2 days. :)
LovlyVix    : Perfect ...that would put me just where I want to be, Kate :)
Guide MO    : MajorTom - I 'm sorry - I don't see what you need offhand,
              though I know we must have it here :/    ←
Guide MO    : I'll check later and email you, if that's any help.
MajorTom    : Thanks Guide. Appreciate it. I have a Plus. Can't run PhotoShop.
Guide MO    : Ok - I just wrote a note to myself -
              I'll check for you when I get off shift at 9 and email you :)
MajorTom    : Great! Thanks for the help. G'Night all!
Guide MO    : Night MajorTom :)
```

To help you follow what's going on, my part of the conversation appears in bold.

These are hugs for a new arrival in the Lobby.

The asterisk is a kiss.

Chagrin.

I got an answer the next day.

Figure 2-13 is a little hard to follow if you're not used to AOL's so-called chat rooms. Though chat rooms are discussed in Chapter 8, "The Community," a little explanation seems in order here as well. Twenty-one people were in the room when I visited. Many were just watching ("lurkers"), but others seemed to be old friends. The room was full of "smileys" (turn your head counterclockwise 90 degrees and :-) becomes a smile) and hugs. The entire illustration is a "chat log" (see your File menu for the Log Manager command).

Chat rooms can be intimidating to the first-time visitor. Don't be shy. Jump right in with a Hello, look for the Guide's name and ask your question. More important, note that I received one immediate answer to my question (from GWRepSteve, a member) and another the next day from Guide MO. I got just what I needed (Alchemy worked perfectly, though now the AOL software handles a conversion like this for me), and it only took 10 minutes.

The Guidepager

Sometimes you'll need a Guide in a hurry. Someone could be harassing you, or hassling people in a room. This kind of behavior, lamentable as it is, is intrinsic to an online community that's larger than most cities in the country today.

Though I'll discuss this subject in Chapter 8, "The Community," it's worth noting here that you don't have to wander the lobbies looking for a Guide when you need one in a hurry. Just use the keyword: **Guidepager** and select one of the categories there (see Figure 2-14).

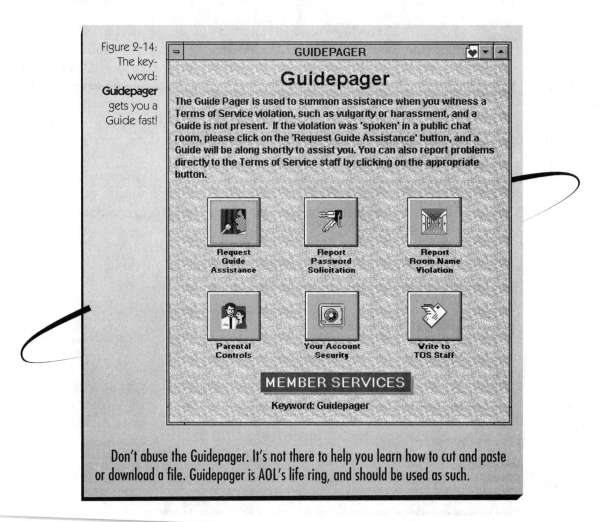

Figure 2-14:
The key-
word:
Guidepager
gets you a
Guide fast!

Don't abuse the Guidepager. It's not there to help you learn how to cut and paste
or download a file. Guidepager is AOL's life ring, and should be used as such.

Guides are on duty 24 hours a day, seven days a week, 365 days a
year. To find a Guide, click on the two-heads button on the toolbar, or
select the People Connection option from the Channels screen. Find the
name of a room you like (Lobbies are good) and look for a Guide there.
They're easy to spot: they all have the word "Guide" in their screen
names.

My AOL

We're all guilty of a nesting instinct, some of us more than others. Faced with a new living space, many of us immediately turn to wallpaper samples and paint chips. A new office might sprout posters, bulletin boards, and a favorite lamp—all within minutes of taking possession. Or how about the people who put wobbly-head critters on the parcel shelf of a newly acquired automobile before they drive it off the lot? Regular robins in the spring, we are.

If you're a nester, you'll love the degree of personalization AOL offers. You can not only control AOL's environment, you can even control the way you're presented within that environment. AOL is a nester's Shangri-la.

All of these nesting controls are found at one location, appropriately called *My AOL*. To get there, click the My AOL icon on the toolbar.

Figure 2-15:
The My AOL button on the toolbar allows you to configure your online environment exactly as you wish.

Changing Your Password

As you are in the My AOL area, you will often be reminded that AOL staff members will never ask for your password, and that you should change your password often.

That's good advice, but how, exactly, *do* you change your password? None of the admonishments explain the process.

It's easy: just use the keyword: **Password**, then follow the directions.

A number of the MY AOL controls are so extensive that I've dedicated exclusive sections of the book to them. Others are best presented in contexts other than this one. Though I'll discuss many of the My AOL controls here, others are addressed elsewhere in the book:

- *Preferences* deserve an entire appendix, look for them in Appendix E of this book.

- *FlashSessions* are discussed in Chapter 6, "FlashSessions & the Download Manager."

- The *Personal Filing Cabinet* is discussed in Chapter 3, "Electronic Mail & the Personal Filing Cabinet."

- *Favorite Places* are discussed in Chapter 4, "Using the Internet."

- *Buddy Lists* are discussed in Chapter 8, "The Community."

There are a number of others features in the My AOL area, however, and we'll discuss them next.

Member Profiles

America Online offers you the opportunity to post a voluntary *member profile*. Profiles are the way AOL members describe themselves: hobbies, home towns, age, gender—that kind of stuff. It's all very enticing, but the operative term here is "voluntary." America Online values the individual's privacy, and if you wish to remain secluded in the online community, you may do so.

On the other hand, your profile is your opportunity to be anyone you want to be: if you've always wanted to be Jell-O Man, be Jell-O Man; if you have a fascination with wobbly-head critters, mention it in your profile and you'll probably meet some other wobbly heads online.

The Masquerade

The text mentions your profile, but be aware that you are by no means limited to a single one. Your AOL account provides for up to five account names, and each of those account names can have its own profile. Businesses might use these account names for individual employees, and families might use them for individual family members, but most people use them as *nom de plumes*. At AOL, you never know whether you're talking to a real person or someone behind a mask. It's a regular masquerade here, for better or worse.

➡

> And that's my point: if you want to avoid the potential of meeting a misdirected personality concealed behind a mask, withhold any confidentialities until you're on reliably firm ground. Anonymity breeds impudence in some people, as does any mask; and like a mask, one's visage is not necessarily one's self. Contrary to Mother's adage, feel free to talk to strangers here. Just don't get in the car with them until you know who's driving and where the journey might go.
>
> This masquerade is all part of the AOL community, which is discussed in Chapter 8.

As I mentioned a moment ago, member profiles are voluntary. If you elect not to complete a profile, however, you cut yourself out of a number of opportunities to become involved in the online community. If you elect to post a profile (or if you've already posted a profile and want to edit it), use the keyword: **Profile**. When you do, the Create or Modify Your Member Profile window pictured in Figure 2-16 will appear.

Figure 2-16: Be who you want to be: fill in as much or as little of this form as you wish.

Edit Your Online Profile

To edit your profile, modify the category you would like to change and select "Update." To continue without making any changes to your profile, select "Cancel."

Your Name:

City, State, Country:

Birthday:

Sex: ⦿ Male ◯ Female ◯ No Response

Marital Status: ⦿ Single ◯ Married ◯ Divorced/Separated ◯ No Response

Hobbies:

Computers Used:

Occupation:

Personal Quote:

[Update] [Cancel] [Help]

Figure 2-16's caption reveals a secret that many of AOL's members don't know: you can complete as much or as little of the profile window as you wish. If you don't want people to know your name, put your screen name there, or your first name only. Many people include only their birth day and month, preferring to keep the year of their birth to themselves.

In fact, here are a few profile secrets:

- If you include your birth day and month, people can send you birthday wishes via e-mail.

- If you include your first and last names *and* your city and state, people can use directory assistance to reach you by phone. Is that what you want them to do?

- You must be online to make any changes in your profile.

- Definitely do fill out a profile. You can't really participate in AOL's online community until you do.

- The Hobbies, Computers Used, and Occupation fields are often used by people looking for others with similar interests. If you enjoy quilting and you include quilting among your hobbies, there's a good chance you'll meet up with other quilters online.

- You're not committed to the information you include in your profile: you can add, modify, or delete it whenever you want—just use the keyword: **Profile**.

The Member Directory

There are two primary reasons for filling out a profile. Most often, someone will see your screen name online—in a chat room (chat rooms are discussed in Chapter 8, "The Community"), or in some e-mail—and they will want to know more about you. They'll choose Get a Member's Profile from the Members menu, enter your screen name, and your profile will be displayed.

The other use for profiles is the *Member Directory.* The Directory is AOL's database of everyone's profiles, and it's searchable. You can search for a member by real name, screen name, or by anything in their profile. You might see a screen name online and wonder who is behind it: search the directory. You might wonder if a friend is signed up with AOL: search the directory. You might wonder if a friend or relative is signed up with AOL: search the directory and you'll know in seconds. One of the more interesting things you can do with the directory is to search for people with interests similar to yours. Once you've found them, you can send them mail and, perhaps, strike up a friendship. It's all part of the electronic community.

I, for instance, enjoy cruising the waters of the Pacific Northwest. Thinking I might find someone to share my interest, I search the Member Directory for members with similar interests by specifying "cruising" and "boat*" as my criteria (Figure 2-17).

Figure 2-17: Much to my delight, there are lots of other cruisers on America Online.

Member Directory

Type words that describe what you are looking for, then click Search. For example, "biking and swimming" or "Hollywood, CA." Click Help & Info for more instructions.

cruising AND boat*

Items 1 - 20 of 189 matching entries.

USDMan	PETER W. CLARKE
Deck watch	STEVE
MisterStew	STEVE
H20pilgrim	GLENN BURCH
RichAJr	RICH A
RoberteD	ROBERT E. DIDIO - "BOB"
CHNTICLR	Toms River Yacht Club
CFTA	CHRIS TAURIELLO
Ldysailing	Ladysailing

Search   More   Help & Info

Note that one of my criteria was "boat*" and that I use the Boolean function AND. The asterisk is a wildcard, and most Boolean functions are supported. Do terms like *wildcard* and *Boolean* make sense to you? Don't worry if they're mysteries, but if you plan to make much use of the Member Directory, you *will* want to learn about them: just click the Help & Info button pictured in Figure 2-17.

The Gallery

If you want to know even more about a person, check out the Gallery (keyword: **Gallery**). Members can send their photographs to a scanning service and the electronic result is posted in the Gallery; or they can post scans of their own. There's a search button, so you don't have to look through long listings. Steve Case is there; so am I. Printed gallery photos make great trading cards: "I'll trade you one Steve Case for two MajorToms."

Personal Publisher & My Place

The Member Directory is searchable—quite a feat when you realize that AOL has well over five million members and each of them has five potential screen names—but that's its finest quality. It's textual, after all, and its fields are small. Most people can talk forever about themselves, and would love to post pictures of themselves, their dogs and cats, their cars, and their families. They might even want to post the *sound* of their cat, or a short movie of their family. They might want to post this information in such a way that it's open to everyone—not just AOL's membership but anyone with access to an online service or the Internet. You can't do that with the Member Directory. For that you need AOL's *Personal Publisher* or *My Home Page*.

Personal Publisher

Personal Publisher is an area within AOL where you can create your own World Wide Web home page and post it online for others to see. (In fact, as I write this, AOL is beginning to call this area *My Home Page*, reflective of its purpose.) Though the World Wide Web is discussed in Chapter 4, "Using the Internet," you should know that a Web *page* is essentially a screenful of text and (optionally) graphics, sound, and video. A *home page* is typically a Web page describing a person or company. AOL has a home page: press Ctrl+K, enter **http://www.aol.com/** in the space provided (type carefully!), then click the Go button (see Figure 2-18).

Figure 2-18:
America Online's
home page. You
can make one of
your own by using
the keywords:
**Personal
Publisher**.

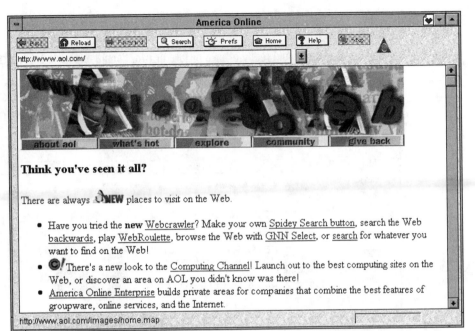

This is not the chapter, nor is it even the book, to detail the operation of AOL's Personal Publisher. Fortunately, there's no need to. The Personal Publisher window (see Figure 2-19) offers plenty of help on the subject, and the process itself is a sequential procedure, with explanatory messages almost every step of the way.

Figure 2-19:
Personal Publisher
offers a Frequently
Asked Questions
file, a message
board for help, and
even a tutorial.

Scanners Optional

Your home page should really offer a picture or two. People expect to see a picture of you at least, and probably another one of your dog Spam.

Home page pictures, however, imply scanners, and a good color scanner is simply too expensive for most of us. What we need is a nice, friendly place where we can take our pictures and have them scanned for us.

Figure 2-20:
Send them
your pic-
tures, they
send you
files, at
keyword:
PicturePlace.

That place exists, it's remarkably inexpensive and fast: you send them your pictures (via the U.S. Mail), they scan them and post the resulting files online for you to download. They're called PicturePlace (see Figure 2-20) and they're waiting to tell you their story at keyword: **PicturePlace**.

How does Personal Publisher compare with the Member Directory? Pictures are the big difference: you can run rampant with graphics (within the 2MB limit), whether they're photographs or graphics from AOL's own clip-art collection (look again at Figure 2-19: see the Home Page Graphics button?). You can search the Personal Publisher pages as well, to see if your favorite AOL member has a page of their own.

My Place

Personal Publisher isn't perfect, however. The generation of Personal Publisher pages is highly automated and somewhat restricted by that

automation. Multiple Web pages, for example, aren't possible via Personal Publisher. If you want more versatility (and you know how to use the HTML scripting language), you need My Place (see Figure 2-21).

Figure 2-21: My Place isn't very thrilling to look at, but it offers a place for your home page, no matter how complex it may be.

members.aol.com:/majortom

Connected to members.aol.com

Uploaded:	Filename:	Byte Size:
11/11/95	private	-

Open	Download Now	Utilities	Upload	Create Directory	Help	More

We're way out of this book's league now. Companies hire consultants to design and construct home pages—some have paid over $100,000 for the privilege. You should be familiar with hyperlinks, FTP, and UNIX directory structures before you mess around in My Place. But if you want a home page that's available to the entirety of the Internet, My Place offers the facility—*if* you know what to do with it.

The Web Diner

Constructing and posting a personal home page is a complex task. You can spend a great deal of time trying to figure everything out and have nothing to show for your efforts. Errors in design, in function, in content—especially errors for all of the Internet to see—can be embarrassing or even devastating.

Unless you know all there is to know about the World Wide Web and home pages, become familiar with the Web Diner (see Figure 2-22). The Web Diner is where AOL has assembled all of its Web expertise and support services for its members. It's comprehensive, germane, and all at the keywords: **Web Diner**.

Figure 2-22:
Tips, tours, tutori-
als, and more: the
Web Diner is where
to learn it all, at
keywords: **Web
Diner**.

Yes, MajorTom has a home page. You'll find it at **http://members.aol.com/majortom/private/index.html.** Sign on, press Ctrl+K and type that address into the space provided. Click the Go button and come by to say hello.

Parental Controls

In Chapter 1, I described AOL as a community. On a political level, communities range from socialism to anarchism. But in this country we think of something in between. There *is* a government, after all, but it's not authoritarian; people do pretty much as they please, within certain bounds.

Our politics are reflected in our families: we seek a balance between despotic authority and profligate anarchy. Parents struggle with this balance: equanimity is elusive. Nowhere is this more evident than in matters of censure.

Every parent adopts a personal level of censorship: that's as it should be. Recently, however, the media have offered their assistance: all motion pictures are rated, many television cable companies offer selective channel blocking, a rating system is emerging for video games, and AOL offers a feature called *Parental Controls* (see Figure 2-23).

Figure 2-23: Parental Controls allow the master account holder to determine how many or how few of AOL's services are available to the screen names associated with the account.

Parental Controls can only be used by the master account. The master account is the permanent screen name that was created during your first sign-on to AOL. Parental Controls enable the master account holder to restrict—for other names on that account—access to certain areas and features available online. It can be set for one or all screen names on the account; and once it is set for a particular screen name, it is active each time that screen name signs on. Changes can be made only at the master account level, and therefore only by the person who knows the master account's password.

Figure 2-24:
Using my master
account I am able
to control access
to certain areas
within the service
for all my other
accounts.

Refer to Figure 2-24: the master account holder can set any or all of the following four Parental Control features:

- *Block instant messages* turns off all Instant Messages to and from the screen name. (I'll discuss Instant Messages in Chapter 8, "The Community.")

- *Block all rooms* blocks access to People Connection (which is also discussed in Chapter 8).

- *Block member rooms* only blocks access to the member-created rooms within People Connection.

- *Block conference rooms* blocks access to the special-interest rooms found throughout AOL, such as the classrooms in Education, the technical forums in Computing, and the Neverwinter Nights role-playing game in Entertainment.

The Parental Controls feature is an elective, not an imperative. Use it if you want; ignore it if you wish. That's a level of intervention that accommodates any parental attitude, and that's the way most of us prefer to have it.

Terms of Service (TOS)

You're probably not aware of it, but you have a contract with AOL, and even though it's not a signed contract, you waived the need for your signature when you first signed on. The contract defines exactly what you can and cannot do online, and it defines exactly what AOL can do if it determines that you have violated the terms of contract.

The contract is called *Terms of Service*, or *TOS* for short. It's always available for review or downloading at keyword: **TOS** (see Figure 2-25). Time spent there is free of AOL's normal connect-time charges.

Figure 2-25:
The contract that exists between all members and AOL is available at keyword: **TOS**.

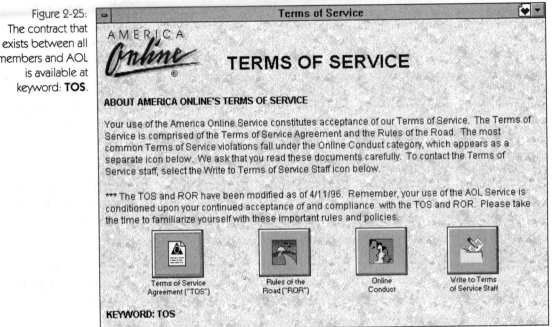

Unless you have joined AOL with the specific intention of disrupting the service (snerts, phishers, and trolls are discussed in Chapter 8, "The Community"), TOS exists to protect you. Specifically, TOS describes violations such as offensive e-mail, impersonation of AOL staff, and online harassment. It also describes what you can do if you witness these violations. Among other things, AOL's TOS team is the online "police," and they can take quick and effective action when provoked. I've seen it happen: it's not an experience soon forgotten.

TOS, like your local 911 service, exists to make the community a better and safer place to live. Like a 911 service, however, TOS can be abused—even by those with good intentions—through ignorance. If you think you might ever require TOS enforcement, read this information.

Here are some interesting TOS conditions:

- You agree that you are an individual, not a corporation.

- You agree that you are at least 18 years of age.

- You agree to notify AOL within 30 days if your billing information changes (e.g., your credit card is stolen).

- You are liable for all expenses incurred on your account—even if someone steals your password—until you notify AOL by telephone.

- AOL does not intentionally monitor or disclose any private electronic communications (such as e-mail or private chat rooms) unless required to do so by law.

- AOL *does* monitor public communication (public chat rooms, message board postings), though AOL "... has neither the practical capability, nor does it intend, to act in the role of 'Big Brother' by screening public communication in advance." (Quoted from "Rules of the Road.")

- Unless you tell AOL otherwise (see Appendix E, "Preferences"), AOL has the right to distribute your name and address to third parties (for example, mailing lists). This right does not extend to your billing information, however.

- Both the Terms of Service agreement *and* the Rules of the Road (review Figure 2-25) constitute your contract with AOL. You should read them both.

I mention all of this not to infuse you with an Orwellian fear of AOL but rather to offer a wake-up call: TOS has some very specific and significant conditions in it, conditions to which you have legally agreed. You should know your rights and know how to recognize others' wrongs. Read this agreement.

AOL's Voice

The male voice you hear when you sign on is that of Elwood Edwards, a professional announcer who, last I heard, works for Channel 50 in Washington, DC.

El's story is one of online romance made good. He was a member like the rest of us when, in the late 1980s, he met a female member online and began to chat with her. It turned out that the lady worked for AOL, where they were in the process of adding a voice to AOL's software. When she discovered El's profession, she asked him if he would like to record the voice tracks.

El and his newfound acquaintance met face-to-face for the recording session, discovered lots of things they had in common, and were married soon thereafter.

The voice tracks were recorded on a cassette recorder in 1989, and their quality isn't state of the art. El rerecorded his material digitally in late 1995 (including a fix for the grammatically incorrect "You've got mail"). To get the new tracks, use the keywords: **File Search**, then search with the criteria: **Edwards AND voice**. If the file is still around, you'll see it as AOL_NEW.ZIP, available for downloading. Downloading is discussed in Chapter 5, "Transferring Files." The procedure for installing the new voice is discussed in the file's description.

Moving On

All of this talk about TOS notwithstanding, I hope this chapter has made you feel more comfortable and welcome at AOL. America Online offers more help—and more kinds of help—than any software I've known. It's online, it's offline, it's Tech Support Live, it's Members Helping Members, and it's Guides. Everyone at AOL—members included—helps someone else sooner or later. That's comforting. Not only is AOL a community, it's a *considerate* community, where no one remains a stranger for long.

Without a doubt, the mechanism that members most often use to communicate among themselves is electronic mail, or e-mail for short. AOL places notable emphasis on its e-mail features, and it shows. To see what I mean, turn the page. . . .

CHAPTER 3

Electronic Mail & the Personal Filing Cabinet

- What Exactly Is Electronic Mail?
- A Circular Exercise
- The Mail Menu
- Attaching Files to Messages
- Receiving Attached Files
- Internet Mail
- The Address Book
- The Personal Filing Cabinet
- E-mail Alternatives

Cicero sent mail to his brother a hundred years before Christ was born. Pliny the Younger sent mail from Rome in the first century. Thoreau wrote from Walden, Louisa May Alcott wrote from the battlefield, and Emily Dickinson wrote from seclusion. As late as the 1950s, Anne Spencer Morrow Lindbergh used the mail to express her views on women's issues, but as a letter writer, she was by then in the dwindling minority. People used to spend hours every week composing lavish prose to one another, but by the middle of this century, letter writing was almost a forgotten art. The U.S. Postal Service had become a vehicle not for rhapsodic prose but for junk mail, magazines, and nasty little envelopes with glassine windows. When it came to correspondence, most of us let our fingers do the walking.

A lamentable condition, that correspondence thing. People took time to search their souls when they corresponded via the mails—they reflected and introspected. They were exacting in choosing their words, reviewed what they wrote, and eagerly anticipated replies. It was a very considerate, unselfish, compassionate thing to do. And though it was common a century ago, by the 1950s it was as scarce as a 3-cent postage stamp is today.

There's cause for optimism, however. People are writing to each other again. There's a renaissance of correspondence, a revival of colloquy. Personal communication is no longer a phone call that interrupts dinner, it's a thoughtful process. And again the writer awaits a reply, expectant and hopeful as a bride.

The salvation, of course, is electronic mail. Electronic mail brings the convenience and immediacy of the telephone to written communication, yet it reflects contemplation, and retains—even encourages—the eloquence of the written word. It's a vehicle not only for communication but expression as well. And, significantly, not only the content but the costs of communication have rolled back to yesteryear.

What Exactly Is Electronic Mail?

Electronic mail (*e-mail* for short) is simply mail prepared on a computer and sent to another computer. There are lots of private e-mail networks—computers wired together and configured to send and receive mail. America Online is one of these. Many of these networks (including AOL) are connected to the Internet (discussed in Chapter 4, "Using the Internet"; Internet mail is discussed later in this chapter), and you can send mail to (and receive mail from) the people who are connected across these networks.

Most e-mail systems share common characteristics:

- Messages are composed of pure ASCII text. ASCII is an acronym (see the glossary), and even though the "AS" part stands for "American Standard," the standard is used around the world, on virtually every computer.

- Messages can thus be sent between dissimilar computers—PCs, Macintoshes, Amigas, mainframes—even terminals.

- The addressee must be known to the respective mail system.

Some of the features below are offered by some e-mail systems; AOL offers them all:

- Messages can be replied to by anyone or forwarded to anyone, including people connected to networks outside of AOL. This includes commercial services, such as Prodigy and CompuServe.

- Files—graphics, sounds, programs, spreadsheets—can be attached to messages, including those sent to Internet addresses outside of the AOL network.

- Messages can be addressed to multiple recipients. "Carbon copies" can be sent to people other than the addressee, and "blind" carbon copies (copies sent without the other addressees' knowledge) can be specified as well.

- Messages—both incoming and outgoing—can be filed in a hierarchical filing system similar to an office filing cabinet. Not surprisingly, AOL calls this feature your *Personal Filing Cabinet*. It's discussed later in this chapter.

- Messages need not be composed while you're online. Likewise, received messages need not be read while you're online. Any incoming message can be filed for later retrieval and read offline at your convenience. If you choose to reply, you can compose your reply offline as well. You need to sign on only to send and receive mail, a process that rarely consumes more than a couple of minutes online, and the process can even be automated—something we'll discuss in Chapter 6, "FlashSessions & the Download Manager."

A Circular Exercise

Before we get to the details, here's a little exercise just to show you how e-mail works. This exercise is somewhat futile: sending mail to yourself is a bit pretentious and rarely productive. Nevertheless, do it just this once. Nobody's looking.

The Mini Toolbar

The mini toolbar immediately above the message field in Figure 3-1 allows you to change the font size, style, color, and alignment of selected text in the mail window. Fiddle with these buttons during this exercise. Select some text, then click a button. See what happens.

Note also that if you leave the cursor atop one of the buttons for a moment, a tool tip pops up, explaining the button's purpose.

1. With America Online up and running, sign on. Leave the Welcome screen showing, and choose Compose Mail from the Mail menu (or click on the pen-and-paper button on the toolbar). A Compose Mail form will appear (see Figure 3-1).

Figure 3-1: This window appears whenever you're about to compose some mail. AOL has already identified you as the sender; it's now waiting for you to identify the recipient.

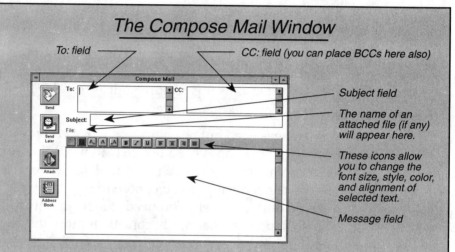

2. The insertion point is now flashing in the To: field, where you are required to enter the screen name of the recipient. Type in your own screen name. This is the futile part of the exercise—sending mail to yourself—but the rewards are immediate, and there will be no guessing as to whether the mail ever made it to the addressee.

3. In the Subject: field, enter the word **Test**.

4. Type something into the message text box. Don't overdo it. People will talk.

5. Click the Send button.

If your PC is equipped with sound, a voice instantly announces, "You've got mail!" Even if you don't hear anything, the mail flag will pop up in the mail button at the far left of the toolbar. There's a particular comfort in that. Mail moves around the AOL circuit quite literally at the speed of light. You'll never wonder again if your mail will get to its destination by next Thursday. It gets there the instant you send it.

Note also that two things have happened: (1) the little flag in the mailbox icon on the toolbar comes up; and (2) the You Have Mail icon on the Welcome Screen is now active (Figure 3-2).

Figure 3-2:
You have mail! You get two doses of visual indication and one aural announcement every time mail is waiting for you at America Online.

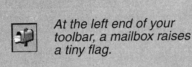
At the left end of your toolbar, a mailbox raises a tiny flag.

And in the Welcome window, another mailbox appears, stuffed with your mail.

4. By now, the Compose Mail window has closed and you're back at the Welcome screen. Click the You Have Mail button.

5. The New Mail window appears (see Figure 3-3). This window is a little redundant when you only have one piece of mail waiting, but soon you'll be a popular person, and dozens of entries will appear here every time you sign on.

6. Double-click the entry, which represents the mail you sent a moment ago.

7. The message window appears, with your "Test" message therein (see Figure 3-4).

It's probably best for you to toss this mail now, before anyone sees what you've been up to. To throw it away, double-click its close button, or press Ctrl+F4. I just wanted you to see how simple, fast, and easy the process really is. That's the whole idea—above all, e-mail should be convenient, global, and inexpensive, and AOL certainly makes it so.

A Case for Exactitude

America Online is, perhaps, excessively lenient when it comes to e-mail addresses. At AOL, screen names are not case-sensitive. MajorTom works no better than majortom. Even spaces are ignored: mail addressed to Major Tom is always delivered to MajorTom.

On the Internet, however, the user name occasionally *is* case-sensitive, and spaces simply aren't tolerated.

Even if you don't know what the Internet is (you will if you read this chapter and the next), and even if you think you'll never exchange mail on the Internet, it's wise to develop the habit of entering e-mail addresses *exactly* as you encounter them. If your friend tells you that she's **JulAnnF**, send mail to **JulAnnF**. If she tells you that she's **julannf@umich.edu** (an Internet address—you can tell by the "@" sign), send mail to **julannf@umich.edu**. Many matters in life require adherence to rules. Like traffic lights, this is one of them.

The Mail Menu

Nearly all day-to-day mail activities are performed using the Mail menu (see Figure 3-5).

Figure 3-5:
The Mail menu
handles most of
your daily e-mail
activities.

Mail
The Mail Center
<u>C</u>ompose Mail   Ctrl+M
Read <u>N</u>ew Mail   Ctrl+R
Check Mail You've <u>R</u>ead
Check Mail You've <u>S</u>ent
<u>F</u>ax/Paper Mail
Edit <u>A</u>ddress Book...
Setup FlashSession...
Activate FlashSession Now
Read <u>I</u>ncoming FlashMail
Read <u>O</u>utgoing FlashMail

Choosing the first option on the Mail menu takes you to the Mail Center, where AOL has gathered an arsenal of material to support you in your e-mail endeavors, no matter what they might be. If you ever have any questions about e-mail, visit the Mail Center first.

Composing Your Mail

The second option on the Mail menu is Compose Mail, which you choose whenever you want to send mail to someone. This option is available whether you're online or off; you can compose mail offline and send it later—a feature I'll discuss in Chapter 6, "FlashSessions & the Download Manager."

When the Compose Mail command is issued, America Online responds with a blank piece of mail titled "Compose Mail" (review Figure 3-1). Note the position of the insertion point in Figure 3-1. It's located within the To: field of the window. America Online, in other words, is waiting for you to provide the recipient's screen name. Type it in. (If you don't remember the screen name, use your Address Book, which I'll describe later in this chapter.)

You can type multiple addresses in the To: field if you wish, *separating them with a comma and a space.* If you want to send mail to Steve Case and Tom Lichty, type **Steve Case, MajorTom** in this box. Note that the field is actually a scroll box. You can type as many addresses as you want, up to 14,000 characters.

Press the Tab key and the cursor jumps to the CC: (carbon copy) field. Here you can place the addresses of those people who are to receive "carbon copies" of your mail. Carbon copies (actually, they're called "courtesy copies" now—carbon paper isn't around much anymore) are really no different than originals. Whether a member receives an original or a copy is more a matter of protocol than anything else. Capacity limitations for this field are the same as those for the To: field.

Blind Carbon Copies

As is the case with the traditional CC: (or cc:) at the bottom of a business letter, the addressee is made aware of any others who will receive an electronic carbon copy of the letter—a traditional courtesy.

On the other hand, you might want to send a copy of a message to someone without letting the addressee(s) know you have done so. This is known as a "blind" carbon copy, and at AOL it works whether you're mailing to another AOL member, an Internet address (I'll discuss Internet mail later in this chapter), or a combination of both. To address a blind carbon copy, place the address (or addresses) of the blind carbon copy recipient(s), *enclosed in parentheses*, in the To: or the CC: field. The parentheses are the trick. No one but the recipient of the blind carbon copy will know what you've done. (The ethics of this feature are yours to ponder.)

Press the Tab key to move the insertion point to the Subject: field, and enter a descriptive word or two. The Subject: field can contain no more than 80 characters. **Note:** The Subject: field *must* be filled in—AOL won't take the message without it.

Press the Tab key again. The insertion point moves to the message field. Type your message there (see Figure 3-6). **Note:** This field also must contain something: you can't leave it blank.

Figure 3-6:
The completed
message is ready to
send. Click the
Send button (if
you're online) or
the Send Later
button (if you're
not online).

Compose Mail

To: MajorTom   CC:

Subject: Frogs in Heaven

File:

Hi Tom --

   I'm pleased that you have found my essay "Frogs in Heaven" to be of interest. Few people consider the potential of the subject: frog heaven, after all, is an emormous place, significantly larger than most other heavens I know, and of particular interest to the entire amphibious community. Frogs, after all, go to the same heaven as lizards and Gila monsters -- a very crowded place indeed. Overcrowding is rampant, and the residents are becoming restless.

It's subtle, but note that the Send button in Figure 3-6 is dimmed: this message is being prepared offline (see the "Preparing Mail Offline" sidebar).

Preparing Mail Offline

Consider preparing mail when you're offline and the meter isn't running. You can linger over it that way, perfecting every word. When you complete a message, click the Send Later button. The next time you sign on, send the mail by choosing Read Outgoing FlashMail from the Mail menu, then clicking the Send All button (see Figure 3-7).

Figure 3-7:
Three mes-
sages in the
Outgoing
FlashMail
window await
sending. All I
have to do is
click the Send
All button.

Outgoing FlashMail

10/21	BillyJoMc	Toads or frogs?
10/21	fig@path.n	Re: Good to hear from you
10/21	MMjyc95674	Thanks for the mail

Edit   Delete   Send All

For more information on preparing and reading mail offline, see Chapter 6, "FlashSessions & the Download Manager."

Alternative Mail Sources

Occasionally you might want to send a text file via e-mail. Perhaps it's a file you have created with AOL's New command (File menu) or a text file you captured online. Regardless of the source, you can send a text file as mail (rather than as a file) by copying and pasting it into a Compose Mail window.

This feature is especially useful for those who prefer to use a word processor to compose messages. Word processors feature spelling checkers and productivity tools that AOL's Compose Mail utility doesn't offer. If you prefer to use your word processor (and it's a Windows word processor—few DOS word processors are appropriate for this), here's how to do it:

- Prepare your message using your word processor. Don't bother with formatting details: see the "Fancy Text" sidebar.

- Select the portion of the message you wish to send, then copy it by choosing Copy from the word processor's Edit menu. This places a copy of the selected text on the Windows clipboard, ready for transfer to any application.

- Assuming your AOL software is running, switch to it now. You can use Alt+Tab to toggle between programs quickly.

- Choose Compose Mail from AOL's Mail menu, click within the message field of the Compose Mail form, then choose Paste from AOL's Edit menu.

- Supply the recipient's e-mail address in the To: field and a subject in the Subject: field. Sign on and send your mail on its way.

Fancy Text

If the recipient is an AOL member and uses AOL for Windows, you can embellish your mail with changes in font, size, color, style, alignment—even the background color. Prepare your mail normally, select the text you want to embellish, then click the *right* mouse button. A pop-up menu will appear, offering all of the choices mentioned here and more.

In fact, this feature will be correctly interpreted by any e-mail program that recognizes *HTML code*—the markup language that's common on the World Wide Web (the World Wide Web is discussed in Chapter 4, "Using the Internet"). Few e-mail programs are capable of interpreting HTML code at the moment, but their number is increasing every day. In other words, if the recipient is not an AOL member—that is, they receive their mail via the Internet—they might be able to see your fancy text. If you want to send formatted text to someone on the Internet, send them a test message: experimentation won't hurt.

Checking Mail You've Sent

Occasionally you may want to review mail you've sent to others: "What exactly did I say to Billy Joe that caused him to visit the Tallahatchee Bridge last night?"

Even if you don't file your mail, AOL retains (for a few days) everything you send, and stores it on their hard disks in Vienna. You can review any sent mail by choosing Check Mail You've Sent from the Mail menu. AOL responds by displaying a listing of all the mail you've sent recently (see Figure 3-8). Choose the mail you want to know about from that list, then click the Read button to review what you've written.

Figure 3-8:
You can reread any
mail you've sent by
using the Check
Mail You've Sent
menu option.

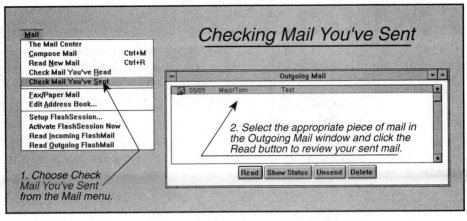

Figure 3-8:
You can reread any mail you've sent by using the Check Mail You've Sent menu option.

As you're reading your sent mail, you can select and copy it, then paste it into other documents. This works especially well for reminder notices, clarifications, and nagging. It may save you some typing as well: you may need to send a message that's a near-duplicate of one you sent four days ago. Rather than retyping text from the old message, just reopen it using Check Mail You've Sent under the Mail menu, copy the sections you need, and paste them into a new message window. Alternatively, you can forward the entire message (including its headers and any comments) by using the Forward button.

Buttons in the Outgoing Mail Window

Don't let the title of this window confuse you. You might interpret "Outgoing Mail" as meaning mail that is scheduled to be sent, as if it's queued in some sort of "out box." In this case, outgoing mail is mail you have *already* sent.

A number of buttons appear across the bottom of the Outgoing Mail window pictured in Figure 3-8; each serves a specific purpose.

The Read Button

Select a piece of mail from the list, then click the Read button to read that message. Double-clicking a particular piece of mail in the Outgoing Mail window does the same thing.

The Show Status Button

The Show Status button tells you when the mail was read by the recipient (or recipients, if the mail was sent to more than one address). Though we'll talk about Internet mail later in this chapter, note that the time displayed will be accurate for mail sent to other AOL members— it doesn't apply to Internet mail. AOL forwards Internet mail to the Internet within a few seconds after you press the Send button, but when is it actually "sent"? When it's posted? When it's routed to the recipient's country or mailbox? There are no answers to these questions. Thus, when you select a piece of Internet mail and click the Show Status button, AOL will display the message "Not Applicable."

The Unsend Button

The Unsend button allows you to retrieve mail you have sent from the mailboxes of all recipients, as well as from your Mail You've Sent list. To unsend a piece of mail, highlight the mail you wish to unsend and click the Unsend button. This feature, however, will be disabled in the following circumstances:

- Any addressee was an Internet mail address.

- Any recipient has read that piece of mail (including you, if you were on the addressee list).

- Any recipient was a fax or U.S. Mail address (more about fax and U.S. Mail later in this chapter).

If you Unsend a piece of mail, it will be permanently deleted from the AOL archives. It won't show up on your Outgoing Mail list when you check it again. AOL will remind you of this when you click the Unsend button. If you want to modify or save an unsent message, open it while it still appears in the Outgoing Mail list, then either modify it (and resend it if you wish), or copy and paste it into some other document. Then you can Unsend it without fear of losing the original.

The Delete Button

This button simply removes the selected piece of mail from your Outgoing Mail list—from the list only, remember: this isn't a list of mail that's about to be sent, this is a list of mail that has been sent. It does not affect the message's destiny: AOL will still deliver it (and probably already has, by the time you find your way to this button). It's really a feature for people who get lots of mail and prefer to keep their Outgoing Mail lists short.

Reading New Mail

The third option on the Mail menu—Read New Mail—refers to mail you've just received. I don't use this menu item. To me, mail is like Christmas morning: I can't wait to get to it. Immediately after hearing that I have mail, I click the You Have Mail button (see Figure 3-2) and start unwrapping my presents.

Night Mail

My passion for new mail is shared by plenty of others. In *Night Mail,* the poet W. H. Auden once wrote:

And none will hear the postman's knock
Without a quickening of the heart.
For who can bear to feel himself forgotten?

Perhaps that's e-mail's greatest virtue: it makes us feel appreciated. That little mailbox full of envelopes in the Welcome window says "Somebody's thinking of you," and there are few of us whose hearts don't quicken a bit when we see it.

Nonetheless, there are those who don't share my enthusiasm. That, I suppose, is why AOL provides this menu option. When it's chosen, America Online presents the New Mail window (Figure 3-9).

Figure 3-9:
To read new mail,
click the You Have
Mail button in the
Welcome window,
press Ctrl+R, click
the leftmost icon
on the toolbar,
or choose Read
New Mail from the
Mail menu.

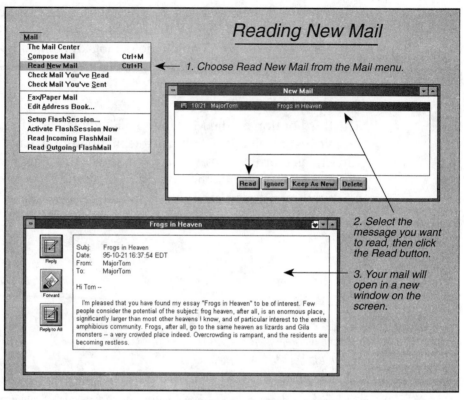

Figure 3-9:
To read new mail, click the You Have Mail button in the Welcome window, press Ctrl+R, click the leftmost icon on the toolbar, or choose Read New Mail from the Mail menu.

Though Figure 3-9 shows only one unread piece of mail, a number of pieces may appear here. If more than one shows up, they'll appear in the order in which they were received at America Online. The oldest mail will be at the top, the most recent at the bottom. In other words, to read your mail in chronological order from oldest to most recent, read your messages from top to bottom.

Buttons in the New Mail Window

A number of buttons appear across the bottom of the New Mail window pictured in Figure 3-9. They can be confusing at first:

The Read Button

This button displays the selected piece of mail on the screen for reading. It's the default button: double-clicking an entry on the list does the same thing.

The Ignore Button

This option will mark a selected piece of mail as read without your actually having to read it—in effect "ignoring" it. If the sender is an AOL member and issues a status check, he or she will see the word "Ignored" beside your screen name. Be sure that's what you want the addressee to see if you use this command.

The Keep As New Button

Clicking this button will return the selected piece of mail to your New Mail list, marking it as unread even though you have already read it. The mail is, however, still considered read as far as other members' status checks are concerned. In other words, if someone checks the status of a piece of mail that you read and then kept as new, they will see the time you read the mail, regardless of whether you kept it as new or not.

The Delete Button

This feature allows you to remove a piece of mail permanently from your new mail mailbox. It will not appear on the Mail You Have Read list either (I'll discuss the Check Mail You've Read command below), nor will it appear in the Outgoing Mail window pictured in Figure 3-8. Status checks performed by other members on deleted mail say "Deleted." Compare this button with the Ignore button mentioned earlier.

Checking Mail You've Read

We all forget things now and again: "What did I promise to get my mother for Valentine's Day?" That's why AOL provides the Check Mail You've Read option under the Mail menu. When you choose this command, AOL responds with the Old Mail window (see Figure 3-10).

Figure 3-10:
The Old Mail win-
dow lists the mail
you have read, just
in case you forget.

10/21	MajorTom	Fwd: Frogs in Heaven
10/21	MajorTom	Frogs in Heaven
10/21	MajorTom	Test

Old Mail

[Read] [Show Status] [Unsend] [Delete]

There are no surprises here. Double-click any message in the window to reread it. Mail that's been reread in this fashion can be forwarded and replied to just like any other mail.

Online Only
The Check Mail You've Read and the Check Mail You've Sent commands are only available when you're online. This mail is stored on AOL's machines, not yours; you have to be online to access data stored there.

As mentioned earlier, the Check Mail You've Read command brings up a list of the mail you've read that's available on AOL's machines in Vienna. AOL only holds mail for a few days (the exact period varies), and you have to be online to access this list. A superior method of checking mail you've read is to store and retrieve it from the Personal Filing Cabinet, which is filed on your hard disk and remains there until you remove it. The Personal Filing Cabinet is discussed later in this chapter.

Printing & Saving Mail

You can print or save any piece of mail that occupies the frontmost (active) window by choosing the appropriate command from the File menu or clicking the appropriate icon on the toolbar. If you choose Print, AOL displays the standard Windows dialog box identifying your default printer (as selected through the Windows Control Panel). Click the OK button to print, or change to another installed printer through the Setup button.

If you choose Save or Save As (in this context they're the same command), AOL responds with the traditional Windows Save As dialog box. Give your mail a name (use the .TXT extension for maximum compatibility with other programs) and put it wherever you please. It will be saved as a standard text file and you will be able to open it not only with AOL's software but with any word processor (or text editor such as Windows Notepad).

Alternatively, you can select and copy any text—mail included—appearing on your screen. Once it's copied, you can open any text file on your disk (or start a new one via the New command under the File menu) and paste your mail into that file. You can also paste copied AOL text into other Windows applications' files if you wish. You might want to do that to obtain more control over the appearance of the printed output. Like most e-mail programs, AOL's print command offers few options regarding the appearance of text.

Replying to Mail

You'll probably reply to mail more often than you forward it. Actually, all the Reply button does is call up a compose mail window with the To: and Subject: fields already filled in with the appropriate information (see Figure 3-11). Aside from these two features, a reply is no different from any other message. You can modify the To: and CC: fields, if you wish, and discuss any subject that interests you in the message text. You can even change the Subject: field or remove the original recipient's screen name from the To: field, though this somewhat defeats the purpose.

Figure 3-11:
The reply window.
The Subject:
and To: fields
are already com-
pleted for you.

Re: Frogs in Heaven

To: MajorTom   CC:

Subject: Re: Frogs in Heaven

File:

Thanks, Tom. I'll look it over.

Katie

Send

Send Later

Attach

Address Book

Hyperlinks in E-mail

Cruising the Net, you come across the "Travelsickness Bag as Art" Web page. Thinking of your friend Harry, who—how shall I say it?—can't keep it to himself when it comes to air travel, you compose some mail to tell him about it.

Telling him about it, however, could be a chore. You will have to tell him how to use the Web, and then identify the specific Web address for the page—a lengthy thing, filled with nonsense words and exacting punctuation.

There's an alternative. If you've already added the page to your list of Favorite Places (Favorite Places and the World Wide Web are discussed in Chapter 4), all you have to do is click the heart icon on the toolbar (to open the Favorite Places window), then drag the Travelsickness entry from the Favorite Places window to the message field of the compose mail form. When you do, the Travelsickness entry will appear in the compose mail form, underlined and in a different color than the rest of the message, if you have a color monitor.

When Harry receives the mail, all he has to do is click the underlined text. AOL will launch the Web browser and connect with the page, all automatically. It's a great way to exchange the names of interesting places with friends.

Any entry on your Favorite Places list will work. It doesn't have to be a Web address. In fact, the entry doesn't even have to be on your list of Favorite Places: just highlight some text in the message field of a compose mail form and right-click on it. AOL will produce a dialog box where you can supply a location's address—a *hyperlink*—manually.

The fine print: Harry will have to be using Version 3.0 of the AOL client or later. So will you.

By the way, there really *is* a "Travelsickness Bag as Art" Web page. Pages of this ilk are fleeting and it might be gone by the time you read this, but it's worth a try; I found it at http://www.pvv.unit.no/~bct/spypose/

Replying to All

Look once again at the lower window in Figure 3-9. Note that there are two reply buttons, including one marked Reply to All. Reply to All allows you to reply to everyone who was sent a message, including any CC: addressees. In other words, you have your choice of replying only to the original sender (the Reply button) or to everyone who receives a message (the Reply to All button).

Like the Reply command, the Reply to All command really only completes a few fields of a New Mail form. You can add or delete recipients and change the Subject: field if you want. This command is a convenience, not an imperative.

Replying to Blind Carbon Copies

The Reply to All button does not necessarily reply to blind CC: addressees. The rule here is: Reply to All replies to all the addresses visible in the Mail window. If you don't see an address (which would be the case if someone received a blind carbon copy), that person will not receive your reply.

Quoting

Some people get mountains of mail and don't remember everything they've said. You might be responding to something someone e-mailed to you a week ago, and even though their message is right in front of you at the moment, it might be hundreds of messages in their past. If you respond with something like, "Yes. Next Thursday at 2:00 would be good," they might have to search laboriously through their mail filing system (assuming they have one) to discover what provoked your response.

To avoid such a situation, it's a common courtesy to quote the significant part(s) of the message to which you're replying. A typical quote might look like this: "In a message dated 5-12, you said <<Would you like to have lunch soon and discuss the contract?>>" Following that, your message, "Yes. Next Thursday at 2:00 would be good," makes a great deal more sense.

Those "chevron" brackets in the paragraph above (<< >>) indicate that you are *quoting*. Quoting can be tedious, but AOL's software makes it easy. Just select the portion of the message that you want to quote *before* you click the Reply button. There's no need to copy the selection. When you click the Reply button, AOL will automatically quote the selection in either the AOL style (which I'm using here as an example) or the Internet style (there's a preference command for this—see Appendix E in the back of this book). It works with forwarded mail, too.

Forwarding Mail

Once you have read your mail, you can forward it, reply to it, or throw it out. Each of these options is accomplished with a click of the mouse. To forward a piece of mail, click the Forward button pictured in the lower window of Figure 3-9. America Online will respond with the slightly modified compose mail window that appears at the center of Figure 3-12.

Figure 3-12:
Forwarding mail is
as easy as clicking
an icon, identifying
the recipient,
and typing your
comments.

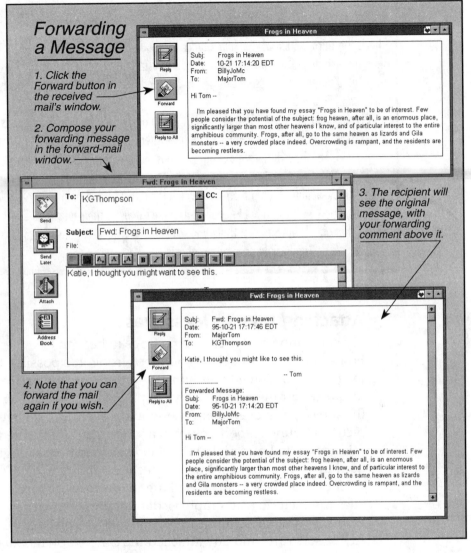

The center window pictured in Figure 3-12 is where you enter your forwarding comment and the address of the person who is to receive the forwarded mail. The new recipient then receives the mail with your comment preceding it. America Online clearly labels the mail as forwarded and identifies the person who forwarded it (see the bottom window in Figure 3-12).

There Are No Frogs in Heaven

This is the Third Edition of the *Tour Guide*. This book has been in circulation for more than three years; lots of people have read it. During that time, I've received an uncounted number of messages asking me to send "the 'Frogs in Heaven' essay" pictured in Figure 3-12.

Perhaps there *are* frogs in heaven, but to the best of my knowledge there is no essay about them. Frogs in heaven? I've never heard a celestial croak—only choirs, harps, and the wispy fluttering of angels' wings. Surely frogs don't grow wings. (In reviewing this manuscript, my technical editor commented that if Frogs *did* have wings, "they wouldn't bump their butts when they hop." Good point and typically well put, Brian.) It's improbable enough that they *un*grow their tails. And everyone knows that angels have necks. Have you ever seen a frog with a neck? Frogs in Heaven: it's as implausible as metamorphosis.

Attaching Files to Messages

My contention that there are no frogs in heaven (see the "There Are No Frogs in Heaven" sidebar) could be wrong. It's possible that there *are* long-necked, winged amphibians up there, playing harps and singing in chorus. Stranger things have happened. If I *were* to write an essay on the subject, however, mere text would never do. I'd have to include pictures, sounds—perhaps even a video. And if I wanted to exchange this nontextual material with other esteemed herpetologists, I would need more than e-mail. I would need the ability to *attach files* to e-mail.

Understand that I'm not talking in the abstract here: files are files. Files can include text, graphics, data, sound, animation, even programs. Any of these files can be attached to a piece of e-mail using AOL's software, and any attached file can be downloaded in its native format (the format used by the creator of the file), ready for viewing, hearing, or (in the case of program files) running.

File transmission requires elaborate protocols and error checking. Not a single bit, nibble, or byte can be displaced. Most other telecommunications services require you to decide upon one of many protocols with cryptic names like XModem and Kermit. You also have to determine the number of data bits and stop bits, and the parity setting your system needs. All told, of the 50 or so potential configurations for file transfer, usually only one of them will work in a given situation.

Forget all of that. You need not become involved. America Online handles it all invisibly, efficiently, and reliably. If you want to send a file, all you have to do is click the Attach button (review Figure 3-1) and AOL takes care of it from there.

Cheap Insurance

If your work involves travel and you take your laptop with you on the road, send e-mail to yourself, attaching important files you've constructed while away from the office. America Online will hold them for you. If something untoward should happen to your data while you're on the road, you can download your files when you return. It's cheap insurance.

Figure 3-13 follows a telecommunicated file from beginning to end. The journey spans half a continent—from Oregon to Mississippi—but only costs pennies.

Figure 3-13:
Sending an MG
across the country
is as easy as click-
ing a mouse.
(Illustration by
Rich Wald.)

Sending a File

1. To send the graphic at right, click this button and select the file. The file name appears here.

Compose Mail

Send

To: KatieG6732   **CC:**

Subject: MG Pix

Send Later

File: C:\MG.TIF

Attach

Hi Katie --

Remembering your love of MGs, I found this graphic online and thought I'd send it your way,

Tom

Address Book

File Transfer - 36%

Now Uploading MG.TIF

36%

Less than a minute remaining

☐ Sign Off After Transfer

Finish Later   Cancel

2. A thermometer monitors the progress at the file uploads.

New Mail

📧 10/21   MajorTom   MG Pix

Re

3. Later, Katie sees this notice of received mail (note the disk-and-mail icon at the far left).

MG Pix

Reply

Subj:　MG Pix
Date:　95-10-21 19:27:20 EDT
From:　MajorTom
To:　KatieG6732

Forward

File:　MG.TIF (16854 bytes)
DL Time (14000 bps): < 1 minute

Hi Katie --

Reply to All

Remembering your love of MGs, I found this graphic online tonight and thought I'd send it your way.

Download File   Download Later

4. AOL has inserted this note into my message.

File Transfer - 38%

Now Downloading MG.TIF

38%

Less than a minute remaining

☐ Sign Off After Transfer

Finish Later   Cancel

5. Katie clicks this button, sees this thermometer, and receives the file. →

Note: The button marked "Detach" in the upper window of Figure 3-13 will be labeled "Attach" until you actually declare an attached file. When you do, the label for the button will change to "Detach," as shown in the illustration.

Use Attached Files Appropriately

Before the recipient can do anything with an attached file, it has to be downloaded, saved, and (usually) viewed with some kind of program other than AOL itself. This is something of a nuisance for the recipient. In other words, don't send attached files when a simple e-mail message will do.

You might be tempted, for instance, to send a word processing file instead of a conventional message to another member. Perhaps the message is long, or you just prefer your word processor over AOL's text editor. Resist the urge. No one expects fancy formatting when it comes to e-mail (if they do, AOL's HTML formatting should suffice—see the "Fancy Text" sidebar earlier in this chapter), and you can always send unformatted word processing files by copying them and pasting them into a Compose Mail window. Attached files should never be sent when simple messages will do.

Attaching a File

You can attach a file to any e-mail message by clicking the Attach button in the message's window. America Online will respond with the sequence of windows pictured in Figure 3-14.

Figure 3-14:
Attaching a file
amounts to little
more than clicking
a button and
locating the file on
your disk.

Attaching a File

1. Click the Attach button in the Compose Mail window. The window below will appear.

2. Select the file from the Attach File dialog box.

Compose Mail

To: KatieG6732   CC:

Subject: MG Pix

File:

Hi Katie --

Remembering your love of MGs, I found this graphic online and thought I'd send it your way,

Send

Send Later

Attach

Attach File

File Name:
mg.tif

mg.tif

Directories:
d:\aol\download

🗁 d:\
🗁 aol
🗁 download

OK

Cancel

Compose Mail

To: KatieG6732   CC:

Subject: MG Pix

File: D:\AOL\DOWNLOAD\MG.TIF

Hi Katie --

Remembering your love of MGs, I found this graphic online and thought I'd send it your way,

Tom

Send

Send Later

Detach

Address Book

3. When you click the OK button above, the file name will appear within the mail window, ready for sending.

When you click the Send button pictured in the bottom window of Figure 3-14, you trigger the sequence of events pictured in Figure 3-13. America Online will hold the mail and the file until the addressee is ready to read the mail and download the file. If you address the mail to multiple recipients—even if they're receiving carbon copies or blind carbon copies—each will be afforded the opportunity of downloading the file.

And downloading files attached to received mail *is* optional. Though the MG Pix window pictured in step 4 of Figure 3-13 offers both Download File and Download Later buttons, the recipient might elect to ignore them both. (Keep that in mind if you ever receive mail with attached files you don't want.)

Attaching Multiple Files

You can attach more than a single file to an e-mail message if you wish, in the form of a *zip archive*. Though the subject is discussed in Chapter 7, "Computing," you should know that a zip archive is often a collection of several files rolled into one. Typically, a zip archive is compressed as it's compiled, streamlining the file-transfer process even further.

Two commonly used shareware packages are used to create (or *zip*) archives such as this—PKZip and WinZip, but you don't need either one to receive zipped attachments: your AOL software unzips (decompresses) most archives automatically. It will often make a new directory on your disk and place the individual (unzipped) attached files within that directory, leaving both the zipped archive *and* the directory of individual files on your disk.

Perhaps the best way to learn more about zipped archives (aside from reading Chapter 6 of this book) is to download an evaluation copy of WinZip and read the program's help files. They're well written and extensive. There's even a tutorial. To download WinZip, go online and use the keywords: **File Search**, then search for WinZip.

Receiving Attached Files

When you receive mail with an attached file, whether it's from another AOL member or from someone on the Internet, two buttons will appear at the bottom of the message, marked "Download File" and "Download Later." (See Figure 3-15.)

Figure 3-15:
Receiving attached
files. Pay particular
attention to the file-
saving dialog box
in the center win-
dow. Knowledge
of where you
saved the file and
what you called it
is required when
you need to find
it later.

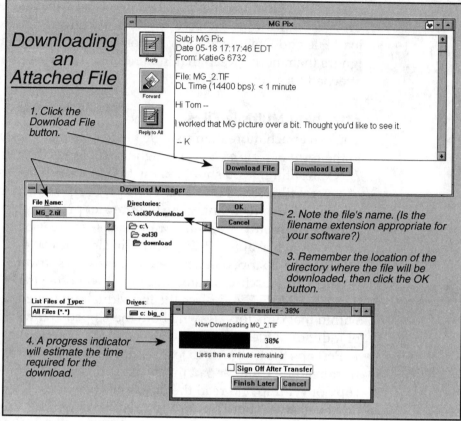

The Download Later button is actually a function of the Download Manager, which is discussed in Chapter 6, "FlashSessions & the Download Manager."

The Download File button will produce the standard Windows file-saving dialog box, allowing you to give the file a name and declare its destination. *Pay attention to this dialog box!* It determines where the file will be when you've signed off and are trying to remember where you put it. The file-saving dialog box also allows you to declare the file's extension, which can determine the software that opens it.

When you click the file-saving dialog box's OK button, AOL will download the file and save it where instructed. A progress indicator will keep you abreast of the process.

Internet Mail

As much as Steve Case and his fellow shareholders would prefer it, not everyone is a member of AOL. Some receive their mail via the Internet (which we'll discuss in Chapter 4, "Using the Internet"); others prefer AOL's competitors (which, as you might suppose, this book doesn't discuss).

We haven't yet made it to Chapter 4, so discussing Internet mail is somewhat premature. But this is the e-mail chapter, after all, and e-mail is a big part of the Internet, so an Internet e-mail discussion follows.

For the time being, understand that the Internet is a worldwide interconnected network of networks, each of which is similar to AOL. Something like 50 million people use Internet mail, and you can send mail to (or receive mail from) any one of them via AOL, a privilege for which you pay nothing extra.

Internet Addresses

To identify an Internet addressee, the following format is used:

paul_williams@oregon.uoregon.edu

Everything to the left of the at sign (@) in an Internet address is the user's name (**paul_williams**, in the example). Unlike AOL screen names, Internet user names aren't subject to a 10-character limit, so they can become quite elaborate. Everything to the right of the @ sign is the addressee's *domain*—the name of the network the addressee is using (**oregon.uoregon.edu,** in the example—a computer network at the University of Oregon). Our domain is AOL, which is known as **aol.com** on the Internet. My Internet address, then, is the combination of my screen name, an @ sign, and AOL's domain name: **majortom@aol.com**. Note AOL members' Internet addresses appear in all-lowercase letters: that's not always the case for other people's addresses on the Net. As I mentioned earlier, always use Internet addresses exactly as they're provided to you. Some are a mixture of upper- and lowercase letters. Some have underscores in place of spaces, others just run everything together. The Internet is a stern master; there's no margin for error.

The Directory of Internet Users

Users come and go on the Internet like nighttime talk-show hosts. There are 50 million of us, after all, and thousands log in and out every day. Keeping a directory of them would be nearly impossible.

"So what?" you say. "There are well over 50 million telephone users in this country, and they're all listed in directories." Your point is well taken, but the telephone system is composed of a number of coordinated authorities, each charged with the responsibility, among others, of maintaining a directory of its users. Not so with the Internet. No one's charged with the responsibility of maintaining Internet member directories. A few lists are produced voluntarily, but these volunteers all have lives beyond their spare-time member directories. Moreover, many Internet users would consider any such directory a violation of their right to privacy.

In other words, there's no accurate, up-to-the-minute, all-inclusive Internet membership directory. You must have the exact mailing address for someone you intend to send mail to via the Internet. You'll have to obtain those addresses from a source other than AOL or the Internet: there's no Internet membership directory to consult.

Here's a tip: Keep a written record of your important Internet addresses. Don't just put them in your AOL address book (you might need an address when you're away from your machine, and AOL's software stores your address book on your hard disk), and don't trust them to memory (few people remember the alphabet soup of Internet addresses accurately). If you carry an old-fashioned (hard-copy) address book with you, that's the best place to keep your Internet addresses.

Sending Internet Mail

Internet e-mail is composed and sent conventionally. To address an Internet user, simply place the recipient's Internet address in the To: field of the compose mail form (see Figure 3-16).

Figure 3-16: Sending mail via the Internet requires entries in the To, Subject, and message fields. You can't leave any of them blank.

Compose Mail

Send

Send Later

Attach

Address Book

To: paul_williams@oregon.uoregon.edu   CC:

Subject: NCCE

File:

Hi Paul --

I'm speaking at NCCE this year and was wondering if you might be there. If so, perhaps we can sip a brandy together?

Tom

Once you click the Send button (or once you run a FlashSession containing outgoing Internet mail), your outgoing mail is immediately posted on the Internet. There's no waiting.

Undeliverable Internet Mail

Because Internet addresses are complex, you might occasionally misaddress a piece of Internet mail. Fortunately, your fallibility has been anticipated in the form of Internet "postmasters." Should you include a nonexistent domain or user name, the receiving site's postmaster will intercede and send the mail back to you. It's no problem, really, as the postmaster sends back the body of the message as well (shown in Figure 3-17). All you have to do is select and copy the message text, paste it into a new mail window, enter the proper address, and resend the mail. Your mail won't end up in some kind of Internet dead letter box: the Internet always delivers.

Figure 3-17:
At top, a
misaddressed
Internet mail mes-
sage looks as good
as any other, but a
few minutes later I
receive the "User
unknown" message
pictured in the
center window.

Undeliverable Internet Mail

Subj: NCCE
Date: 10-21 19:13:37 EST
From: MajorTom
To: pd_williams@oregon.uoregon.edu

Hi Paul --

I'm speaking at NCCE
might be there. If so, p

Tom

*Though the message
at left looks acceptable,
the user name is
incorrect. The mail
is undeliverable.*

Subj: Returned mail: User unknown
Date: 10-21 21:06:45 EST
From: MAILER-DAEMON@mailgate.prod.aol.net
To: MajorTom

----- Transcript of session follows -----

While connected to oregon.uoregon.edu [128.223.32.6]
(tcp):
>>> RCPT To:<pd_williams@oregon.uoregon.edu>
<<< 553 unknown or illegal user:
pd_williams@OREGON.UOREGON.EDU
550 pd_williams@oregon.uoregon.edu... User unknown

----- Unsent message follows -----

Hi Paul --

I'm speaking at NCCE this year and was wondering if you
might be there. If so, perhaps we can sip a brandy
together?

Tom

*A few hours later,
the mail is returned
from the Internet
postmaster. Note
that the body of the
undelivered message
is included in the
postmaster's
message.*

*Noting the "user
unknown" message,
I recheck Paul's
address, find the
error, and re-send
the mail to the
proper address.*

In Figure 3-17, note the inclusion of my message's text in the postmaster's message in the bottom window. When I later copy and paste the mail into a new mail window (and correct the address), the mail will be delivered satisfactorily.

Daemons

Look at the sender's address in Figure 3-17. Isn't that a vicious-sounding word: *daemon*? My dictionary defines the word as a "subordinate deity." In this context, however, a daemon (pronounced day'-mon) is an innocuous little Unix program—one that's usually transparent to the user—which is anything but a deity, subordinate or not. PCs have daemons, too (though we don't call them that). Perhaps the most familiar example is the PrintMonitor—the background program that spools the print output from your applications to your printer.

Sending Mail to Other Commercial Services

I'm going to fudge a bit here and refer you to an online resource. Addressing e-mail to CompuServe and some of the other commercial online services can be tricky. Moreover, the number and names of commercial online services is changing—it seems like every day.

Fortunately, AOL maintains a ready (and current) reference for Internet e-mail addressing techniques, including the instructions on how to address mail to the other online services. Use the keywords: **Mail Gateway** to access it.

Be aware of one thing: not all of the commercial online services are as lenient as AOL. Many of them charge their members for Internet mail. Before you send mail to a friend on another commercial online service, be sure they want to receive it.

Receiving Internet Mail

Internet mail is received like any other AOL mail: it's announced when you sign on, and you can read it by clicking the You Have Mail button on the Welcome screen. The only way you'll know it's Internet mail is by looking at the sender's address, which will contain an @ sign and a domain name. You'll also see the Internet "header" at the end of the message. Reading Internet headers is a little like reading the Bible in its original Hebrew: enlightening perhaps, but not requisite to effective use of the medium.

Internet Mail Conundrum

A perplexing mail question, frequently received at AOL, has to do with blind carbon copies and Internet mail. It's possible that you might receive a piece of Internet mail, yet your name will not appear in the header as a recipient. "Was the mail misdirected?" you'll ask.

Probably not. More than likely, you were sent a blind carbon copy (a "BCC"). When you are a recipient of BCC Internet mail, your name will not appear among the recipients in the header, yet you *will* receive the mail. If you think about it, it makes sense: if your name appeared in the header—or anywhere else for that matter—the BCC effort would be thwarted. It's confusing, I know, but comforting to know that your anonymity is assured.

A few notes regarding received Internet mail:

- If you want to give your Internet address to someone else (it's very impressive printed on your business cards), remove any spaces, change everything to lowercase, and follow it with @aol.com. As I mentioned earlier, my Internet address is **majortom@aol.com**. Steve Case's Internet address is **stevecase@aol.com**.

- America Online offers plenty of help with Internet e-mail, including a message board and an avenue for communication with the AOL Internet staff. Use the keywords: **Mail Gateway** to explore this feature.

Internet Mail Trivia

Actually, this isn't trivia at all. I was trying to attract your attention with a sidebar. If you're an Internet mail user, this is Really Important Stuff:

▲ Though AOL places no prohibitions on the length of e-mail messages, some other e-mail systems do. If you must send a message longer than about 20 pages (30K) via the Internet, cut your mail into smaller pieces, and mail the pieces independently. Identify your strategy in the Subject field: "Letter to Mom 1/2," and "Letter to Mom 2/2." This is common shorthand for split mail on the Internet.

▲ If you use a word processor to prepare outgoing Internet mail (and you copy and paste it into a new mail form as mentioned earlier in this chapter), all character and paragraph formatting will be removed from your message when you paste it.

▲ Don't use any special characters (such as copyright symbols or the "smart quotes" offered by some word processors) in Internet mail. The ASCII standard doesn't recognize them, therefore it's unlikely they'll make it to the destination. They might survive after you've pasted them into the Compose Mail window, but they'll never make it to the destination.

▲ America Online doesn't charge you anything extra for Internet mail, sent or received. If you're counting your blessings, add that to the list.

Attaching Files to Internet Messages

Because there's no universal standard for attaching files to e-mail on the Internet, you can't directly send files (or receive them) via Internet mail. Internet mail, like all e-mail, is pure ASCII text, and most files take the form of binary data, not ASCII text. Don't worry if you can't define the term *binary data*; just understand that it's not ASCII text and therefore not native to e-mail.

With that said, it will seem contradictory when I tell you that you *can* attach a file to Internet mail, but it's true. A few comments follow:

▲ If you attach a file to Internet mail, AOL will convert it to text before it's sent. This may seem anachronistic: how can you send a picture of a frog (or the sound of a frog), for example, as text? Simple: use a program that converts binary data into ASCII text. AOL does this for you, via a technique called *MIME* (Multipurpose Internet Mail Extensions) *base64 encoding.*

- The recipient's e-mail program must understand MIME base64 encoding and be able to decode it. If that's not possible, the recipient will have to decode it manually. There are a number of programs that can do this, most notably a little shareware application called MIME64. It's available in AOL's libraries. Downloading files from AOL's libraries is discussed in Chapter 5, "Transferring Files."

- There are other binary-to-text-and-back techniques for transferring files on the Internet—one called *uuencoding* comes to mind, and Macintosh users are fond of *BinHex*—and if someone sends an attached file to you, it might be encoded using one of these other techniques. If that happens, your AOL software will not be able to automatically decode the message and offer to download the file to your machine. You'll have to do this manually. A description of that process—a process that can take many forms depending on the encoding method used—is beyond the scope of this book; but again, you can find answers (and ask questions) by visiting the keywords: **Mail Gateway**.

- It should be apparent that file attachments to Internet mail are not universally supported, just barely standardized and fraught with the potential for error. Both you and the intended recipient should be prepared for a period of experimentation and adjustment. The system doesn't always work the first time it's tried.

With all of the disclaimers out of the way, and though the convert-to-text-and-back process sounds a little bit like a sow's ear, it is in fact a technique that's been used for years on the Net. It works flawlessly when it works, and thousands of people do it every day. My friend Jim and I often exchange architectural drawings (in CorelDRAW! format) this way.

The Address Book

America Online provides an address book just like the address book next to your telephone. In effect, AOL's book is a cross-reference, listing people's real names and their corresponding e-mail addresses. My recommendation is that you use the Address Book, even if you only have a name or two to put there now. E-mail addresses (especially Internet addresses) are tricky; you're not going to want to type them very often. Typing them is too much work, and it's too easy to make mistakes.

Adding a Name to the Address Book

No one memorizes Internet addresses. Internet addresses are eccentric composites of alphabet, punctuation, and symbol characters—for example, **speterman@lemming.uvm.edu**. Addresses like this are eminently forgettable. AOL's addresses are less complex but, like most addresses, they too are forgettable. That's why America Online provides an Address Book.

Of course, before you can use the Address Book you have to put some addresses there. It's easy. Online or off, choose Edit Address Book from the Mail menu and America Online will provide the Address Book editing window pictured in Figure 3-18.

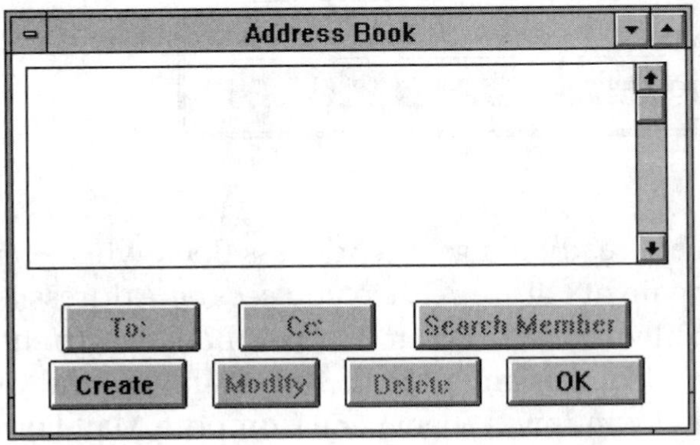

Figure 3-18:
The Address Book Editor window allows you to create, modify, and delete members' names and screen names, or to search for a specific member.

Address Book

To: Cc: Search Member
Create   Modify   Delete   OK

To add an entry to your Address Book, click the Create button. AOL provides the editing form pictured in Figure 3-19.

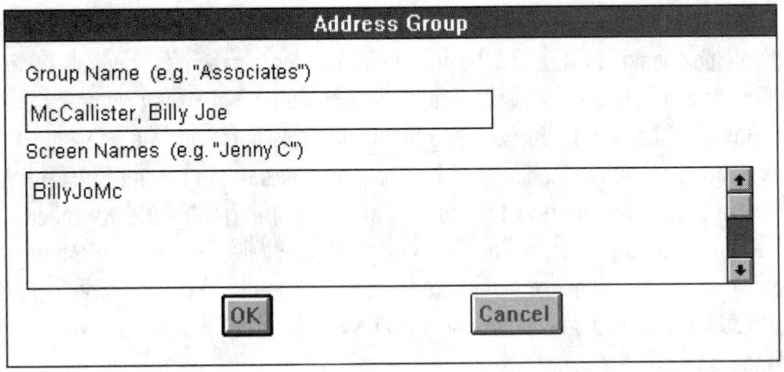

Figure 3-19:
The Address Group editing form.

Address Group

Group Name (e.g. "Associates")

McCallister, Billy Joe

Screen Names (e.g. "Jenny C")

BillyJoMc

OK   Cancel

Place the person's full real name, or a nickname you know them by, in the Group Name field, then place their e-mail address in the Screen Names field. The next time you choose Address Book from the Mail window, the new name will appear there (see Figure 3-20).

Figure 3-20:
The Address Book
now contains the
new entry.

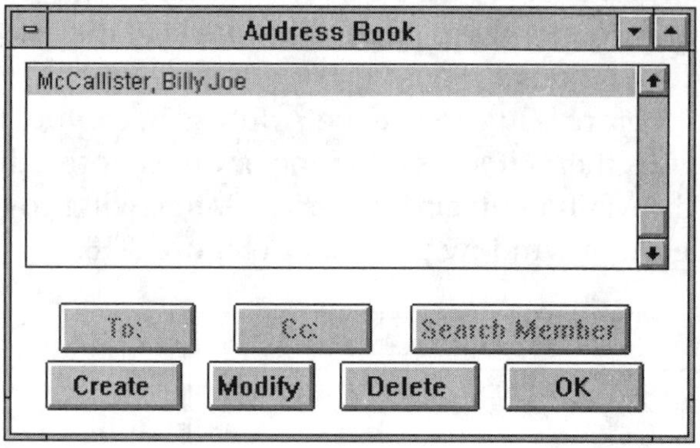

Now you are ready to use the Address Book whenever you prepare mail. Look again at Figure 3-1. Do you see the Address Book icon in the Compose Mail window? If your Address Book is current, you can use it to look up addresses and plug them into the To: and CC: fields of the Compose Mail window. Whenever a Compose Mail Form is displayed on your screen, all you have to do is click that icon. From then on, it's only a matter of clicking the mouse.

Multiple Accounts

If you look again at Figure 3-19, you'll notice that there's room for multiple addresses in the Screen Names field. Notice that it's Screen *Names*, not Screen *Name*.

Imagine that you're participating in an online discourse on frog heaven with three other esteemed theologians. Nearly every piece of mail on the subject has to be sent to all three. In this situation, you might want to create an entry called "Froggers" in your Address Book, and list all three addresses—with a comma and a space between each address—in the Screen Names field. Once you have done so, all you have to do is select the Froggers entry from your Address Book to send mail to them all.

The Personal Filing Cabinet

I have a number of friends who live far away, and I use e-mail to keep in touch with them. Jim, for example, lives on Whidbey Island in Washington state. I also do almost all my business via e-mail. When e-mail becomes something other than a casual dalliance, a system for filing it becomes strategic. Fortunately, such a system is included in your AOL software, and it's called the *Personal Filing Cabinet*.

Mail Preferences

Though preferences are discussed in detail in Appendix E at the back of this book, two mail preferences deserve mention here. Note the "Retain all mail" preferences pictured in Figure 3-21. These preferences are available by choosing Set Preferences from the Members menu, then clicking the Mail button.

When they're selected, the two "Retain all mail..." preferences, shown in Figure 3-21, cause your local AOL software to save every piece of mail you send or read. This is a new feature, and it's truly a blessing.

Figure 3-21: When they're turned on, the two "Retain all mail..." preferences, shown here in the "on" condition ("off" is the default), cause all of your mail to be saved automatically in the Personal Filing Cabinet on your hard disk.

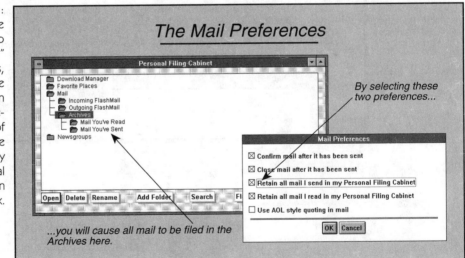

When they're turned on, the Retain all mail... preferences route all your mail—sent and read—to the Archives folder pictured in Figure 3-21. Once the preferences are on, copies of all of your mail are retained locally for your review.

After an online session has concluded, when you're offline and the clock isn't running, you can choose Personal Filing Cabinet from the Mail menu and sort through your mail leisurely, reading, replying, filing, and deleting. This is real mail, too; it's not just text. When you open a message, it appears in a mail window, complete with Forward and Reply buttons (see Figure 3-22). If you use mail as much as I do, this is one of the best features AOL has to offer—and lots of people aren't even aware of it!

Figure 3-22:
Mail stored in your
Personal Filing
Cabinet isn't simply
text, it's AOL mail.
When it's opened,
it appears in a mail
window, complete
with Forward and
Reply buttons.

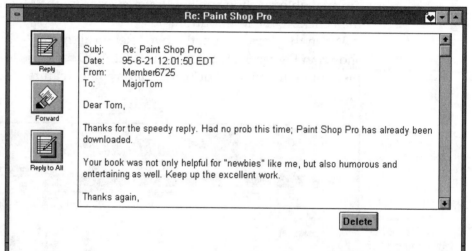

Keyword: Suggestions

The Retain All Mail feature described in the text is not only one of the best features AOL has to offer for avid e-mail users; it also represents an idea that came from a member. That member used the keyword: **Suggestions**, then proposed the feature. Not long after that, the feature appeared in the AOL client.

In other words, AOL listens. If you have a great idea that AOL could use, tell them about it. Like any community, this one functions better when people give back to the community whenever they can, and the keyword: **Suggestions** makes it easy.

Managing Your Mail

Leaving mail in your Mail You've Read and Mail You've Sent folders is not a good idea. Though it will accumulate there in chronological order, there will be no other organization whatsoever. Once a few dozen entries pile up, you will realize that you need some kind of filing system.

Filing Schemes

Filing schemes are very personal things. As you observe the illustrations in this section of the book, you'll note that I file my mail using folders with people's names on them. You may prefer to file by date, by project, or by geographical location. There are no limits. Filing schemes can be multilayered: you might have two primary folders— "Friends" and "Business," for example, in which items are filed by date. My friend Leonard gets so much mail that he has alphabetical sections—"A-F," "G-P," and "Q-Z"—and folders with people's names on them within each of those sections. Some people argue the merits of their particular system the way the boys down at the pub compare Fords and Chevys. It really doesn't make much difference how you set up your system; just pick one and do it. You can always reorganize later if you have to.

Back It Up!

Many of us configure our backup programs to back up only a portion of our hard disk—the portion that contains data. The portion that contains programs might not get backed up as often, or at all. This makes sense: why back up program files, which normally don't change and are stored already on floppies or CD-ROMs?

Although the theory is sound, the data we're discussing in this section—your Personal Filing Cabinet data—are stored in your ORGANIZE subdirectory, and that's inside your AOL30 directory, which is a *program* directory.

If you value the contents of your Personal Filing Cabinet, be sure to back it up. Ideally, back up your entire AOL30 directory and all the subdirectories within it, and perform that backup regularly.

Making New Folders

No matter what kind of filing scheme you elect to use, it will be done with folders. Think of a real filing cabinet: to organize your stuff, you visit the stationery store and buy a box of tabbed folders. You label them according to your filing scheme, put them in the filing cabinet, and store papers inside them. You might even store folders inside of folders. That's the metaphor used in your Personal Filing Cabinet.

Making a new folder is better done if you select the folder (the "parent" folder) in which you want the new folder to appear before you click the New Folder button. In Figure 3-23, for example, note that I selected the Mail folder before I made the Jim folder. Doing so causes my new folder to appear automatically within the Mail folder. I don't have to drag it around once it has been created.

Figure 3-23:
Select the in-
tended parent
folder before you
click the New
Folder button.

Personal Filing Cabinet

Favorite Places
Mail
    Incoming FlashMail
    Outgoing FlashMail
    AOL
    Archives
    Articles
    Broker
    Cruising
    Damascus
    Internet Book
    Jennifer
    Leonard
    Marion
    Matt
    Misc.
    Orientation Express
    Permissions
    Rooster
    Sue
    Ventana
    Walt
    Wadsworth
Newsgroups

Open | Delete | Rename | Add Folder | Search | Compact PFC | FlashSessions | Help

*Adding
a Folder*

*1. Select the folder in
which you want your
new folder to appear.*

*2. Click the Add
Folder button.*

*3. Enter the new
folder's name.*

*4. The new folder will
appear at the bottom
of the list.*

New Folder

Folder Name: Jim   OK

    Sue
    Ventana
    Walt
    Wadsworth
    Jim
Newsgroups

Open | Delete | Rename | Add Folder | Search | Compact PFC | FlashSessions | Help

You can name a folder anything you choose. Folder names can
include spaces and punctuation, and the limit of 69 characters is more
than you'll ever need.

Your ORGANIZE Folder

If there's a "flaw" in the Personal Filing Cabinet, it's that you're going to use it, and
use it extensively. You'll save everything. Doing so, of course, implies storage
considerations: if you store too much, your Filing Cabinet can become unwieldy.

This is significant. The contents of your Personal Filing Cabinet are stored on your
hard disk, not on AOL's machines, in a file with your screen name on it. You'll find it
in the ORGANIZE folder in your AOL30 directory. You might find as many as five
files there, one for each of your account names. Check them often, and if matters
get out of hand, start cleaning house.

Drag & Drop

To organize mail within folders, simply drag and drop it. Figure 3-24, for example, illustrates the process of dragging a selected piece of mail from my Mail You've Read folder to my Leonard folder. You can drag and drop mail up, down, or across your hierarchy using this method. You can drag and drop folders as well.

Figure 3-24:
To move mail from
one folder to
another, drag and
drop it.

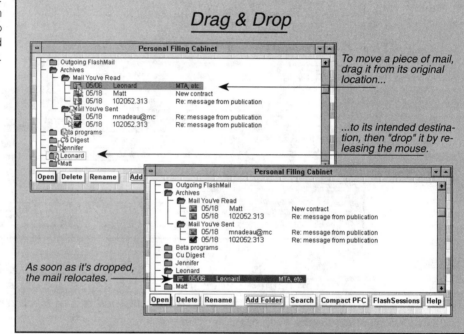

You can reorganize your mail within a folder using the same drag-and-drop method. If you have three entries named "Baker," "Charlie," and "Able" in a folder, and you want to alphabetize them, just drag "Able" up to "Baker" and release the mouse. **Note:** This applies to reorganizing mail only, it does not apply to reorganizing folders. Read the "Sorting Folders" sidebar for more.

Sorting Folders

While rearranging mail within a folder is a simple matter of drag and drop, re-arranging folders is not. If you try to move a folder within its parent—trying to alphabetize folders is a good example—you'll drop the folder you're dragging into another folder more often than not. Folders appear in chronological order, with the newest at the bottom (note how the Jim folder in Figure 3-23 appeared at the bottom). If you want to rearrange their order, you'll have to employ a little chicanery.

The method I use is to shuffle them via their parent folder. To insert the Jim folder between the Jennifer folder and the Leonard folder, for example, I drag all of the folders that are to appear after the Jim folder to the parent (Mail) folder, and drop them there. This causes the folders I've dragged to be "added to" the list, thus they appear after the Jim folder. This is much more difficult to describe than it is to accomplish. AOL is no doubt working on a more elegant solution, but until it's offered, this works for me.

Deleting Mail

Earlier I mentioned the need for housecleaning. No matter how well it's organized, your Personal Filing Cabinet can become unwieldy if you don't clean it out now and then. I copy my Filing Cabinet to a floppy disk on the first day of each month, then go through it methodically and delete all mail that's more than a month old. On May 1, for example, I copy my Filing Cabinet to a floppy, then delete all the mail from March. This keeps the volume of mail in my Filing Cabinet at manageable levels. It also provides a comprehensive monthly backup, and if I have to refer to outdated mail, I can always restore my Filing Cabinet file from the floppy.

Compacting the Personal Filing Cabinet

Deleting pieces of mail from your Personal Filing Cabinet doesn't really delete them from your hard disk, they just disappear from the Cabinet's display. They're still on your hard disk, and they still take up some room.

There's a reason for this: the physical process of deleting mail could take a lot of time. It's much faster for your software to simply mark a piece of mail as deleted—leaving it otherwise undisturbed—than it is to actually remove it.

Think of one of those sliding-tile games you might have played years ago. To fill a vacated space, many tiles have to be shuffled, a process that takes time. Physically deleting mail from your Personal Filing Cabinet would leave little "holes" on your hard disk, and utilizing that space vacated by deleted mail would require a process not unlike sliding game tiles.

Rather than shuffling hundreds of pieces of mail around on your hard disk every time you delete mail from your Personal Filing Cabinet, your AOL software offers a specific, automated routine for that process. That routine is available whenever the Personal Filing Cabinet window is open: just click the button marked "Compact PFC" (review Figure 3-23). Do this when you're offline and only when you have some time: the process can be lengthy.

There are a number of preferences to control the behavior of the Compactor feature. Refer to Appendix E for details.

You can delete mail from your Personal Filing Cabinet either by opening it and pressing the Delete button pictured in Figure 3-22, or by selecting it and pressing the Delete button pictured in Figure 3-25. The three Routing Request messages selected in Figure 3-25, for example, will be deleted when I click the Delete button. The Delete key on your keyboard will do the same thing.

Figure 3-25:
Delete mail by first
selecting it, then
pressing the Delete
button in the Per-
sonal Filing Cabinet
window.

Personal Filing Cabinet
Cu Digest
Jennifer
Jim
Leonard
Matt
Netsurfer Digest
Ventana
☑ 05/17 VentanaPam new address
☑ 05/18 lynnj@vmedia.com Re: Routing request
☑ 05/18 lynnj@vmed Re: Routing request
☑ 05/18 lynnj@vmed Re: Routing request
05/18 lynnj@vmed Outline is OK
Queries/replies
Sue
Walt
Open	Delete	Rename	Add Folder	Search	Compact PFC	FlashSessions	Help

Multiple Selections

You can select multiple messages or folders—or a combination of both—in the Personal Filing Cabinet by using the modifier keys used by many Windows applications today. The three contiguous files pictured in Figure 3-25 were selected by clicking on the top message, holding down the Shift key, then clicking on the bottom message. This selected all the messages in between.

If I had preferred to select messages in *discontinuous* order, I would have held down the Ctrl key as I selected them. The Shift and Ctrl keys also work for folder selection.

Once selected, multiple folders or messages can be moved or deleted as if they were one.

Searching Your Files

With all of the functionality described so far, the Personal Filing Cabinet offers even more, in the form of two elegant searching commands. Let's say I was engaged in a discourse with an associate on the subject of the Communications Decency Act, the so-called "Cyberspace Bill" that rocked the online community in the spring of 1995. I remember reading something about that bill in the "Computer Underground Digest," a mailing list I subscribe to.

But where did I see it? I save my back issues of the Digest for reference, but the "Digest" is a lengthy publication, and searching manually through 10 or 20 issues looking for a specific item can be tedious.

The solution is the Search button pictured in Figure 3-26. That button invokes the Search dialog box that's also pictured in Figure 3-26. All I need to do is fill it in and tell it to search for me.

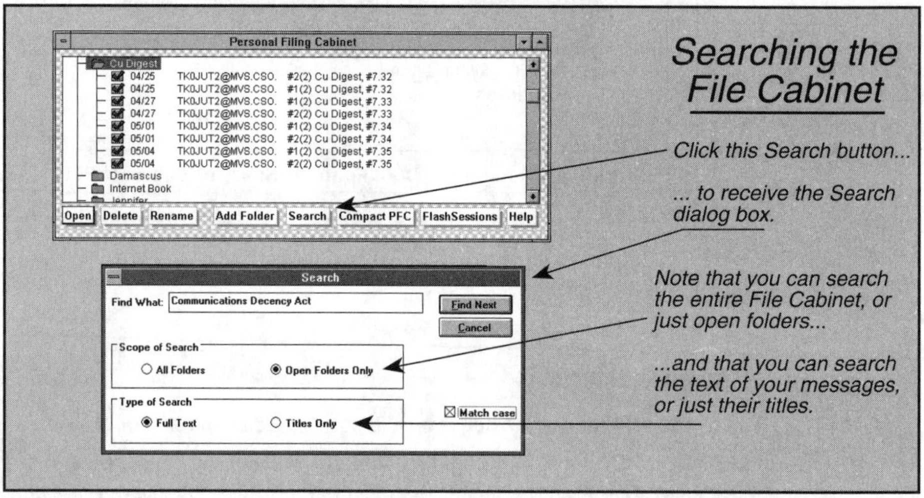

Figure 3-26:
The Search button allows you to search your entire Personal Filing Cabinet, or portions of it, for either a specific message title or a string of characters in the message body.

Searching the File Cabinet

Click this Search button...

... to receive the Search dialog box.

Note that you can search the entire File Cabinet, or just open folders...

...and that you can search the text of your messages, or just their titles.

Searching through your messages in this way is remarkably fast, and when AOL finds a match, it highlights the message containing the found text (see the top window in Figure 3-27). The Find Next button (Figure 3-26) will direct the software to find the next message containing the search text, if there is one. And so on.

Finding the message containing the text is only half the task, however. The other half is finding the text itself. This is accomplished with the Find in Top Window command that's pictured in Figure 3-27. Once the Search command has found a message, open it and choose Find in Top Window from the Edit menu. You'll see the Search window pictured in Figure 3-27, and once it's completed, the matching text will be found in no time.

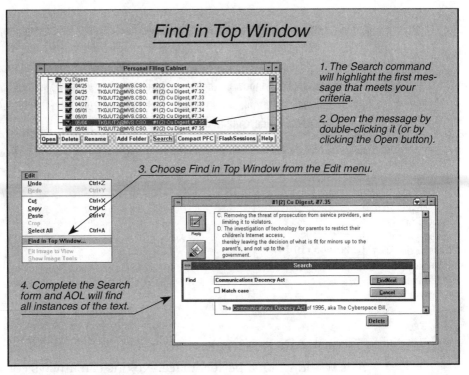

The Find in Top Window command applies to any window, by the way, not just to those windows containing mail in your Personal Filing Cabinet. You can use it to find text in articles, newsgroup postings—any text file you can open with AOL's Open command.

The Alternate Mouse Button

It won't take long: shuffling files like a Vegas gambler, you suddenly discover that no matter how you manipulate your Filing Cabinet display, you can't fit both the window containing the source file and its intended destination on the screen at the same time.

What you really need is another window—one showing the destination, for example—that can share the screen with the source.

And you can have it. All you have to do is point to the folder (the destination folder, in this example) and click on the alternate mouse button. The menu pictured in Figure 3-28 will appear, allowing you to create a new window for the selected folder. With the second window on the screen, arrange your windows so that both the source and the destination are displayed, then drag and drop the message. This is much more difficult to describe than it is to do. Give it a try!

Figure 3-28: This pop-up menu appears when you click on a Filing Cabinet folder with the alternate mouse button.

```
Rename
Delete
New Window
```

E-mail Alternatives

The world is not a perfect place. No one can always correctly predict the weather, computers don't always address envelopes reliably, and *some* people still aren't online. What if you want to communicate with these heathens? You could write them a letter, but that requires paper, an envelope, a stamp, and a trip to the mailbox. You could phone them, but an answering machine will probably take the call (and your money as well, if it's long distance). You could try telepathy or ask Scotty to beam you there, but these are emerging technologies and you know how reliable they are (remember "The Fly"?).

U.S. Mail

Instead, use AOL to send 'em a letter. All you have to do is prepare normal e-mail and include a special address (see Figure 3-29). A few days later, a real paper letter in a real paper envelope will arrive at your specified destination, looking for all the world like you typed it yourself. There is an additional charge for this, but it's not much: somewhere between the cost of a first-class stamp and a long-distance phone call; and it's no more difficult than sending e-mail. This brings such a convenience to communicating that it almost eliminates procrastination.

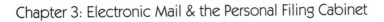

Speaking of procrastination, when was the last time you wrote your mother?

Figure 3-29: Sending a message via U.S. Mail involves completing return address and mailing address forms before confirmation.

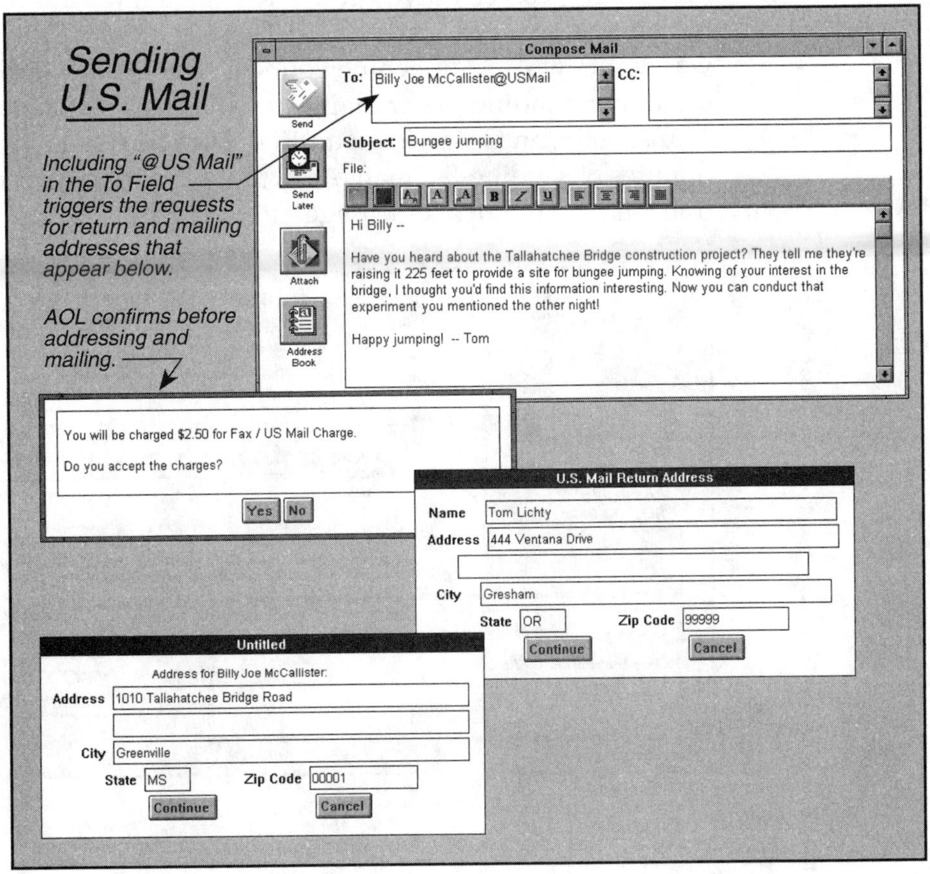

Note that the only difference between sending regular e-mail and sending U.S. Mail is the address. If AOL sees **@usmail** in an e-mail address, it automatically triggers the address request dialogs you see pictured in Figure 3-29.

Note: ZIP Codes are required, and AOL verifies that they match the cities in both the return and mailing addresses. If they don't, you will receive an "invalid US Mail address" error and be sent back to the offending entry.

Sending a Fax

Perhaps your mother owns a fax machine or fax/modem (doesn't everyone?). You can save a few cents and a few days over paper mail by sending her a fax instead. Again, AOL stands ready to serve, even if you don't own a fax machine yourself. The process is no more complicated than sending paper mail—or e-mail, for that matter (see Figure 3-30). Again, an @ sign in an address triggers the dialog. Within a few minutes of sending fax mail, AOL sends e-mail to you confirming the transmission of the fax message.

Figure 3-30: Fax mail differs little from normal e-mail.

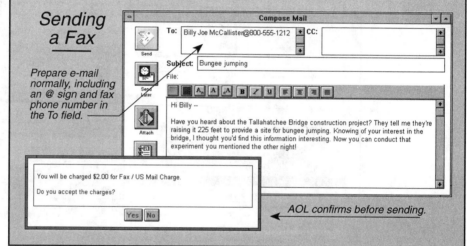

Sending a Fax

Prepare e-mail normally, including an @ sign and fax phone number in the To field.

AOL confirms before sending.

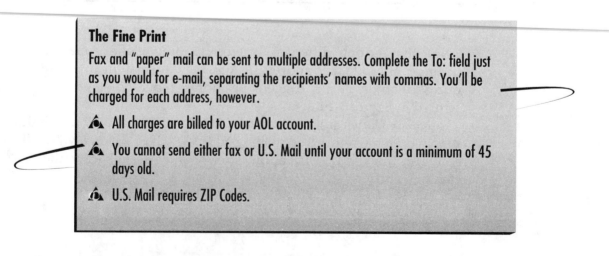

The Fine Print

Fax and "paper" mail can be sent to multiple addresses. Complete the To: field just as you would for e-mail, separating the recipients' names with commas. You'll be charged for each address, however.

⚠ All charges are billed to your AOL account.

⚠ You cannot send either fax or U.S. Mail until your account is a minimum of 45 days old.

⚠ U.S. Mail requires ZIP Codes.

- Fax addressee names cannot exceed 20 characters, including spaces and punctuation. U.S. Mail addressee names are limited to 33 characters.

- You can't attach files to fax or U.S. Mail messages. Both services are plain-text only.

- Both fax and U.S. Mail messages wrap to 70 characters on a line. Fax pages contain a maximum of 60 lines. U.S. Mail messages contain 40 lines on the first page (to make room for the address) and 53 lines on all others.

- Forced page breaks may be declared: Type >>> **PAGE BREAK** <<< on a line by itself. This works for both fax and U.S. Mail.

- U.S. Mail is limited to four pages. Fax mail is limited to 24K.

- Include your real name (not your screen name) in the text of both fax and U.S. Mail.

In either case, you'll receive a confirmation identifying all charges before AOL sends your mail (refer again to Figures 3-29 and 3-30). If, after reviewing the charges, you decide you don't want to send the mail or the fax, you can cancel at that point. You will also receive a confirmation (via e-mail from AOL) that your fax has been transmitted a few minutes after you click the Send button.

Moving On

As you can see, AOL's e-mail facility is effective and easy to use. It holds your mail for you, even after you've read it, and even if you don't file it yourself. It allows you to reply to and forward mail at the click of a button. It offers a filing system that's the best in the business. Perhaps best of all, it rarely costs you any more than your monthly AOL membership fee.

Very impressive indeed.

E-mail, however, is not a local thing. Just like U.S. Mail, you aren't limited to sending and receiving mail within your community (AOL) itself when you use AOL's mail feature. You can send e-mail to anyone who can receive it and vice-versa, regardless of the community—or even country—they live in. The tool for that is the Internet. I've mentioned the Net a number of times in this chapter; now's the time to get to know it better. Read on.

Using the Internet

CHAPTER 4

Most students of mathematics can recall that humbling moment when, with algebra mastered, and buoyed by an embryonic self-confidence, they opened a door marked *Calculus*—and stepped into an abyss. At that moment, pride of accomplishment turned to humility, confidence to catatonia. Everything learned prior to that event was reduced to insignificance in the shadow of this megalith, this inscrutable, unfathomable vastness.

And no small comfort came from the discovery soon after that this phoenix of fancy was developed in the 17th century, by people *in their twenties!!*

Welcome to the "calculus" of communications, the Internet. Like algebra, America Online is but a subset of an infinitely larger universe—a single star in a galaxy of telecommunications grandeur. And the galaxy, of course, is the Internet. While AOL counts members in the millions, the Internet counts them in the *tens* of millions—and like calculus, many of these people are in their youth, Newtons of the Net, Mozarts of the metaverse, Rembrandts of the right-of-way.

Figure 4-1: "NET01," by Jeff Stewart, is the artist's conception of how the Internet might appear in virtual reality. Jeff has a number of images posted online. Use the keywords: **File Search**, then search for OBJECT1.

Jeff Stewart
Object01@aol.com
(C) 1995

Imagine connecting your computer not just to AOL, not just to computers outside of AOL, but to thousands of other computer *networks*, many with forums, e-mail, and thousands of files to download. It's not unlike the wonder you might feel while gazing at stars in a summer sky—each star itself a sun, many with planets—except that these stars are attainable. The Internet takes you there.

Three Years in Search of 75 Cents

Speaking of the stratosphere, meet Cliff Stoll, who is an astronomer. Since astronomers do a lot of computer modeling, Cliff is fairly adept at using computers. That's a good thing, because there *isn't* much work for astronomers, and there *is* for computer operators, especially at Cliff's level.

Which is how Cliff Stoll came to be involved with the Internet and Milnet, an Internet branch that ties together thousands of unclassified computers in the Army, Navy, and Air Force. When I asked Cliff to contribute to this book, he wrote:

➡

"Hmmm... military computers on a network? A group of German programmers, adept at breaking into computers, decided to make money from their skills. For a year, they snuck into dozens of systems across the Milnet, copied data from them, and sold this information to the Soviet KGB. They were high-tech spies. With keyboards and modems, they exploited security holes in distant computers. Once on a system, they scanned for sensitive material, passwords or pathways to other computers. For a year, they went undetected. Then they bumped into me.

"In August 1986, while managing an astronomy computer in Berkeley, California, I noticed a 75-cent accounting error. Someone had used a few minutes of computer time without a valid billing address. Curious... just nickels and dimes, but worth checking into. Zooks, but what I found! Using a printer and several PCs, I watched someone sneak through my system, onto the Milnet, and then steal information from military systems a thousand miles away.

"Instead of locking him out of my system, I let him prowl through it, quietly tracking him back to his roost. The trace took a year; but in the end, we proved that five guys were spying over the computer networks. They were convicted of espionage in 1990."

For the whole story, read Cliff's book, *The Cuckoo's Egg*. It's the true story of tracking a spy through the maze of computer espionage, and it ought to be required reading for any Internet user.

Cliff also has a new book called *Silicon Snake Oil*. Buy a copy of his books, read them, then send Cliff some e-mail telling him you heard about it here. His screen name: CliffStoll.

A Superset of AOL

The Internet, then, is a superset of AOL. It's everything AOL is—forums, mail, files to download, chats—only bigger. Much bigger. At the moment, AOL is more than five million people in only five countries; the Internet is as many as 50 million people in more than 100 countries. No one owns it; it has no central facility; there are no Guides or Terms of Service. And there's no Steve Case. An advisory committee is at the helm; its concerns are primarily technical; and its members are all volunteers.

Now that I read the previous paragraph, I hasten to add that there's no "it," either. The Internet isn't a singular entity. It comprises scores of independent networks—some military, some academic, some commercial—all interconnected. Indeed, these *inter*connected *net*works are the very basis of the Internet name.

Nouns & Adjectives

If you're going to live in the neighborhood, you're going to have to speak the language. Used as a noun, the Internet is referred to as "the Internet." One would never say, "Send me a message on Internet"; it would be, "Send me a message on *the* Internet."

Used as an adjective, the article is dropped. It's "Internet mail," not "the Internet mail."

If you really want to speak in the vernacular, just call it "the Net," and refer to yourself as a "netter." That'll keep 'em guessing.

Military Preparedness

The best way to define the Internet is to examine what it was: like democracy, the Internet is best understood by observing its past.

Most important, the Internet began as a military contrivance. Most Net users know this, but many have never grasped its significance. The Internet's early military credentials have more to do with what it is today than any other factor.

The Internet is a collection of an uncounted number of independent computers distributed worldwide. Most are networked (wired) together locally and connected to a hub of some sort—a server. These servers—and, in some cases, other independent computers—belong to a *domain*: a network that's connected to the Internet and listed in the Domain Name System (a name registry).

Using leased high-speed digital lines (not modems), each domain is wired to at least one other domain on the Net (often more). The slowest of these lines operates at 56 kbps—more than five times faster than a

9600 baud modem. Many of these domains maintain a constant connection to the Net. They don't sign on and off as we do with AOL, they're online all the time.

A simplified map of this arrangement might look like that pictured in Figure 4-2.

Figure 4-2: The Internet extends around the globe as a web of independent domains interconnected continuously, around the clock, by high-speed dedicated connections.

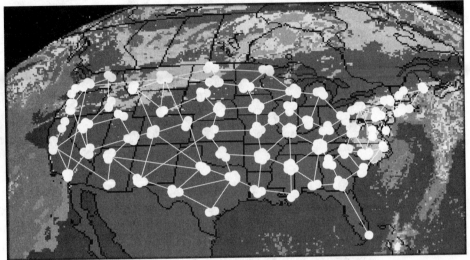

Don't interpret either Figure 4-2 or 4-3 literally. I drew the white lines, and they're not intended to represent actual Internet or AOL nodes (especially because all I've included is the U.S. mainland—a politicocentric decision if there ever was one). It would take a map the size of a picture window to display all these nodes. While there might be such maps somewhere, this isn't the place to present them. The image of the continent is from the GEOS satellite. Use the keyword: **Weather**, then investigate the weather maps there.

Compare the Internet's strategy with that of AOL. America Online consists of a host computer system (in Virginia) and thousands of client computers (our PCs). While the Internet strategy looks like a web, the AOL strategy looks more like a star (see Figure 4-3).

Figure 4-3: America Online's starlike network consists of a host computer and thousands of intermittently connected clients.

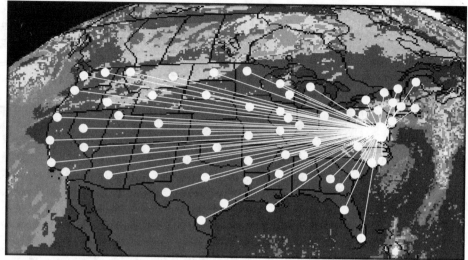

Now the military part: look again at Figure 4-3. If Ace Excavation were to dig up a fiber-optic cable in Vienna, Virginia, most of us would be without AOL—an unpleasant prospect indeed. On the other hand, if a backhoe unplugged a domain in the Internet, communications would simply be routed around it. Indeed, a large percentage of the Net's domains could be eliminated and the Net would still function.

Forever prepared, the Defense Department commissioned the Advanced Research Projects Agency (ARPA) to configure a computer network that would accommodate just such a possibility. This plan was implemented in the late 1960s; the network was called the ARPANET.

Academic Anarchy

By the early 1980s, educators discovered the value of sharing research information and computing resources through interconnected computers—especially supercomputers, which are as precious as gold (literally—an older Cray-1 supercomputer has thousands of dollars worth of gold connectors in it). The educators weren't interested (primarily) in security; their interest was access. Their computers held vast amounts of data and, true to form, they wanted to share that information objectively, without bias, with anyone in the community who wanted access.

ARPANET was a possible answer, but there were—how shall I put it?—fundamental differences in the military and academic attitudes. The academic community elected instead to develop its own network which it called NSFNET (named for the National Science Foundation, the academics' primary source of funding). Significantly, NSFNET used the same networking strategy ARPANET used: interconnected domains randomly distributed around the United States. The result could have been dysfunctional anarchy, but by definition a computer network implies some form of universal protocol—electronic standards that everyone agrees to observe. The result is best described as *consensual anarchy*, whereby everyone marches to his or her own drummer but all agree on a common route for the parade.

And that's how the Internet is today: an agglomeration of independent domains drawn from both ARPANET and NSFNET, each owned by organizations that are independent of one another, interconnected by high-speed data lines, and not subject to any form of central control. There's no central data storage, either. Data are scattered about the Net like dyed eggs on Easter Sunday, hidden in faraway places, awaiting discovery. It amazes me that the thing even exists—it's one of the few working models of functional anarchy today, and it works extremely well.

WIRED Magazine

WIRED is the "magazine of the digital generation"—covering interactive media, the networking community, and the toys of technology. Started in early 1993, *WIRED* has quickly advanced to the vanguard of the literary aristocracy. Its design is precocious, its content acerbic, its language always provocative (and often offensive to some). The information age has few perspectives that can match *WIRED*'s insight, candor, or irreverence, and none can match them all.

Best of all, *WIRED* is available online at AOL. Only past issues of *WIRED* are available—you'll have to visit your newsstand for the latest edition—but its focus isn't so myopic that its content becomes obsolete in a month or two. If this chapter interests you and you're not yet a *WIRED* devotee, read this magazine. Use the keyword: **WIRED**.

Until recently, military and academic users dominated the Internet community. It might have been an anarchistic community, but it was also very exclusive. Things have changed. Commercial accounts were allowed access in the early 1990s, opening the door to businesses as well as millions of everyday computer users like you and me. Now all of us with AOL accounts are offered Internet access. And there's no extra charge.

Internet Addresses

Before we go any further, we need to discuss Internet addresses. I touched on them briefly in Chapter 3, but they deserve more than that. They're really not much different from the addresses the U.S. Postal Service uses, though rather than being sent to you at your home, Internet mail is sent to your *domain*. Domain or domicile, they're the same thing: they're the places where you receive mail.

International Top-Level Domains

When my friend Kyoko writes to me from Japan, the address she places on the envelope goes from the specific to the general: she starts with my name and ends with "U.S.A.," in the *name/address/city/state/usa* format.

International Internet addresses are exactly the same. At the far right you'll find the name of the country. This is called the *top-level* domain. Well, *almost* always. The Net's an anarchy, after all. Figure 4-4 identifies the abbreviations for some common international top-level domains.

Figure 4-4: Country abbreviations are the top-level domain of international Internet addresses.

Abbreviation	Country
au	Australia
at	Austria
ca	Canada
dk	Denmark
fi	Finland
fr	France
de	Germany
it	Italy
jp	Japan
no	Norway
uk	United Kingdom
us	United States

Perhaps the best-known example of an international top-level domain is

username@well.sf.ca.us.

indicating a user on the Whole Earth 'Lectronic Link (the WELL) in San Francisco (sf), California (ca), U.S.A. (us).

Note that the segments of Internet addresses are separated by periods. It's always that way. (Well, here again, *almost* always. You occasionally will see other address formats. They're rare, however, and assuredly the exception to the rule.)

U.S. Top-Level Domains

At the risk of sounding politicocentric again, most domains are within the United States, and the *us* top-level domain is typically omitted from American domain names, just as it is on paper mail that's to stay within our borders. Instead, top domains for U.S. users typically identify the type of system they're using. Figure 4-5 identifies the common U.S. top-level domains.

Figure 4-5: U.S. top-
level domains
identify the nature
of the user's
affiliation.

Abbreviation	Affiliation
com	business and commercial
edu	educational institutions
gov	government institutions
mil	military installations
net	network resources
org	other (typically nonprofit)

My Internet address, as mentioned in Chapter 3, is **majortom@aol.com**. Anyone looking at my top-level domain can determine that I'm affiliated with a commercial organization—in this case, America Online.

Domain Names & Computer Names

Immediately to the left of the top-level domain is the location of the network that's actually connected to the Internet. Thus, a domain name such as **uoregon.edu** implies that there's a network named "uoregon" somewhere, and it has a direct line to the Internet.

Many institutions—especially educational ones—have more than one local area network (LAN). Most of my academic associates work at the University of Oregon, but the U of O has at least seven satellite networks connected to the university's central mainframe, which is connected to the Net. One of those networks is located within a building called Oregon Hall, and the users on that network add **oregon.uoregon.edu** to the string, which identifies the Oregon Hall (oregon) LAN, which is connected to the University of Oregon domain (uoregon), which is an educational institution (edu).

User Names

Most Internet activity takes the form of e-mail, and e-mail is sent to individuals. To identify an individual, the format **username@oregon. uoregon.edu** is used. Everything to the left of the at sign (@) in an Internet address is the user's name. Internet user names aren't subject to AOL's 10-character limit, so they can become quite elaborate.

Many people on the Net use their first initial and last name as their Internet name. This format is unique (at least to the domain), and it's not gender-specific (an issue which many Net users prefer to avoid). Spaces aren't allowed (so you'll often see underscores in their place: **fred_morgan@mit.edu**), and Internet addresses are usually not case-sensitive. None of this should make a whit of difference to you: your screen name (minus any spaces) automatically becomes your Internet user name. Your domain (sounds regal, doesn't it?) is **aol.com**.

The World Wide Web

Cultivated in UNIX and nurtured by computer professionals, the Internet became a patchwork of disjointed fragments: USENET, FTP, Telnet, and e-mail. The Internet almost seemed to take pride in its incoherence. Now that the Net has evolved from its experimental stage, coherence, convenience—even hospitality—are not only appropriate but essential.

Apparently, the scientists at CERN—the European Particle Physics Laboratory in Geneva, Switzerland—agree: in 1989 they set out to take the Internet another step up the evolutionary ladder. The result—introduced in 1990—is the *World Wide Web*, which has become some-what like a department store: a gathering of FTP, Gopher, WAIS gateways, e-mail, and newsgroups. The Web puts all these things under one roof, in familiar and convenient surroundings. If you can use a mouse, you can use the Web. Indeed, the Web is so obliging, it might become your only means of using the Internet (other than e-mail) from now on.

Hypermedia

The Web's cosmos consists of *hypermedia*. In my experience, the use of polysyllabic buzzwords usually indicates that the words' true meanings are obtuse and opaque. The word "hypermedia" is no exception, but it's the heart of the Web, and you must understand one to understand the other. Perhaps Figure 4-6 will help.

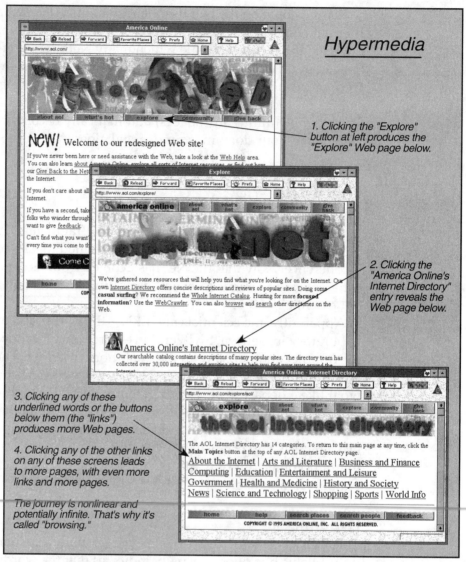

Each Web *page* consists of text and graphics (and more—such as sound and video—if it's a really ambitious page), usually marked with *links* (*hyperlinks*, actually) or areas on the page that when clicked lead to something else. Links can lead you to more Web pages, graphics, sounds, or videos: there are no limits other than the capability of your hardware and the link designer's imagination. The path shown in Figure 4-6 is only one of an infinite number of paths we could have explored. A click on the Community or What's Hot buttons on AOL's Welcome to the Web page would send you down other paths, just as fertile and just as infinite as the one in the illustration. Indeed, the Web is a vast cosmos of resources, linked to related resources all over the world. This, perhaps, is why it's called the World Wide Web.

Nomenclature

So far, we've defined the *World Wide Web, page,* and *link,* but there are a few other terms that require interpretation before we continue.

A *Web browser* is software designed to access the World Wide Web—the Internet's graphical interface. Web access requires a hefty piece of software; you'll see Web browsers for sale at software stores and in mail order catalogs, and they're not cheap. You needn't fret: your AOL software contains a superb Web browser; you don't need anything else to browse the Web.

The *URL* is the Uniform Resource Locator, or the address for each article of text, and each graphic, sound, or video on the Web. There are millions of URLs, thus their addresses are lengthy and specific. They can be typed directly into the text field just below the toolbar in AOL's Web Browser window. They can be pasted there, too, which is probably a better idea.

HTTP stands for HyperText Transfer Protocol. Appearing at the left end of a URL, HTTP tells the browser to expect a hypertext Web document.

HTML is HyperText Markup Language, the scripting language that's used to create Web pages.

Favorite Places

As you explore the Web, you'll discover pages you'll want to return to. And when you return, you won't want or need to type URLs again from the keyboard. That's what the *Favorite Places* feature is for.

I've enlarged a section of the AOL screen in Figure 4-7 to identify the two icons you need to use when accessing Favorite Places. Most Web pages have a little heart-shaped icon on the right of the title bar. This icon serves as a bookmark: if you want to "mark" a page by adding it to your list of Favorite Places, simply click its little heart icon or drag it to the Favorite Places icon on the toolbar (see Figure 4-7).

Figure 4-7: Adding
Favorite Places is
as simple as click
or drag.

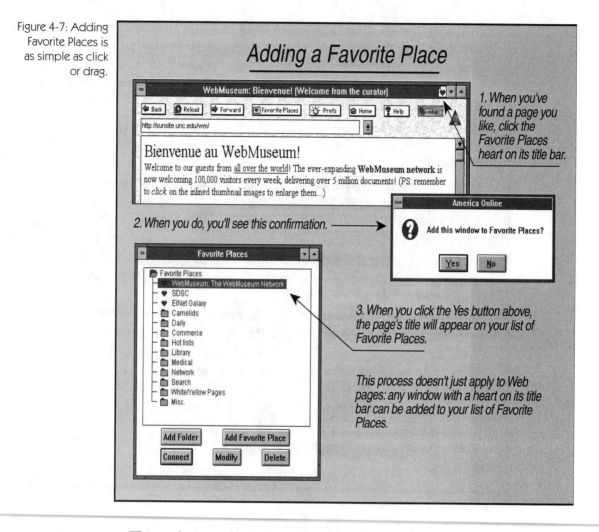

This technique doesn't apply only to Web page windows: many
areas within AOL offer a heart icon on their title bars; whenever you
see one you can use it to add your current location to your list of
personal Favorite Places.

To open the Favorite Places window, click the Favorite Places icon on the toolbar at any time, whether you're online or off. To go to one of your favorite places, just double-click it in the Favorite Places window.

Finding Stuff on the Web

There are a number of Web pages that allow you to search the Web for a subject of interest. One of the more popular sites is *Webcrawler*, a technology now owned by AOL. I use it more than any other because it's so convenient: just use the keyword: **Webcrawler**. When you do, AOL will launch its Web browser and call up the Webcrawler page, automatically. All you have to do is specify what you're looking for and click the Search button.

Browsing

This is not a place to become mired in procedural details. As the AOL software presents it, the Web really requires no instructions. It's a place for leisurely browsing, like an art gallery (try the WebMuseum at **http://sunsite.unc.edu/wm/**) or the shelves of books in a public library (try the World Wide Web Virtual Library at **http://www.w3.org/hypertext/DataSources/bySubject/Overview.html**). Be prepared to wander and wonder at all the remarkable rewards the Web has to offer. Drag and drop bookmarks when you find places you want to return to, and surf the sea of the Internet the way the people at CERN intended. (The people at AOL hope you'll make extensive use of the Web too: look at Figure 4-8.) This is the Internet at its best; it will bring you back time after time.

Figure 4-8:
The World Wide
Web is integrated
throughout
America Online.
Look for "world"
buttons or "WEB"
selections.

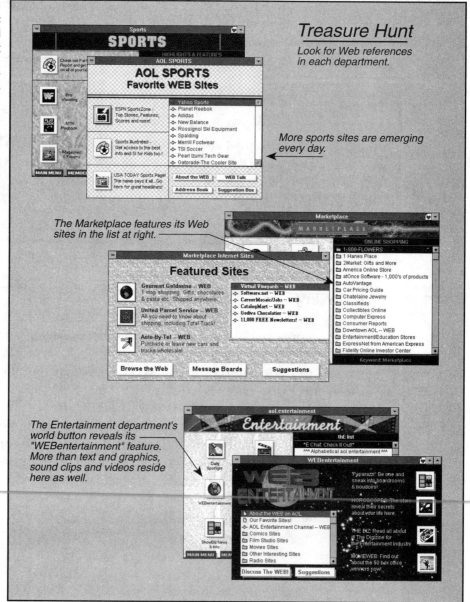

Mailing Lists

Internet mailing lists are something of a cross between Ed McMahon and Rush Limbaugh (a vivid, if not particularly adept, analogy if there ever was one).

Mailing lists are like Ed McMahon in that they arrive in your mail-box frequently and seemingly unbidden. They're like Rush Limbaugh in that they accept material from listeners (subscribers in this case) and broadcast those contributions to everyone else on the list.

Shameless Plug

This chapter's description of mailing lists and the Web is necessarily abbreviated. Other Internet features covered in this book will be abbreviated as well. This is a tour of AOL, after all, not the Internet. If you want to become better acquainted with the Net and AOL's gateway to it, read my *America Online's Internet*, also published by Ventana Communications. Use the keywords: **AOL Store**, or look for it at your local bookstore.

Think of AOL's message boards. Mailing lists, like boards, are where people discuss issues of common interest. There are thousands of lists, and the issues range from ablation to zymurgy.

Lists are sometimes called *reflectors*: mail you send to a list is broad-cast (reflected) to everyone else who subscribes to the list. Conversely, you will automatically receive—as Internet mail—any message sent to the list by any other subscriber.

In that way, mailing lists are similar to the AOL Address Book feature. Using the Address Book, you can associate a number of screen names with a single address book entry; when you select that entry, multiple screen names are plugged into the To: (or CC:) field of an outgoing mail form. An Internet mailing list is much the same: mail sent to it is normally received by every subscriber to the list. One name represents many.

America Online offers a direct line to its Internet mailing list feature; just use the keywords: **Mailing Lists** (see Figure 4-9).

Figure 4-9: The
keywords: **Mailing
Lists** provide
access to Internet
mailing list informa-
tion, including a
searchable data-
base of lists cur-
rently available.

Subscribing to a good mailing list can be entertaining, stimulating, enlightening—and overwhelming. You should subscribe to one just for the experience. Before you do, however, understand a few mailing list basics:

- It's not unusual for a list to generate a prodigious volume of mail. For this reason, it is important that you check on your mail box often to avoid losing your mail. Your AOL mailbox—the one in Virginia, where your unread mail is held—is limited to 550 pieces of mail, including both read and unread mail. Unread mail disappears five weeks after the date it was sent. Mail you've read disappears one week after the date it was sent—even sooner when the mail load at AOL is heavy. If your total mailbox mail count (both read and unread) exceeds 550 pieces, the AOL system will start to delete excess mail, starting with read mail and then unread mail.

- Find out whether any mailing list you wish to join has a "digest" mode, which compiles all of the day's (or week's—it depends on volume) messages into a single mailing. You can usually spot a digest version of any particular mailing list by looking for the word *digest* in the list's name. If a digest is offered, subscribe to it.

- ◭ Don't subscribe to a mailing list unless you plan to read it.

- ◭ When reading a list's description, be sure to take note of how to "unsubscribe," in case you change your mind about receiving it. (Often, once you subscribe to a list, you'll be a sent a confirming message that also explains how to unsubscribe—put this message in a safe place in case you need that information.)

- ◭ If you subscribe to any mailing lists, sign on regularly to read your mail and clear your mailbox.

- ◭ Some lists are "moderated"; some are not. Moderated lists are comparable to AOL's hosted chat rooms in that their content never strays too far off the subject and rarely becomes offensive. Lists that are not moderated embody the anarchistic nature of the Internet and can become quite idiosyncratic and immoderate.

America Online offers a searchable directory of lists (review Figure 4-9). Again, the keywords: **Mailing Lists** will take you there. Don't be surprised if the subject you have in mind isn't listed. Do spend some time exploring the directory: it searches the list descriptions by content rather than by keyword. A search using the criterion *flying*, for example, produces all the lists with the word *flying* in their descriptions, including high-flying and flying by the seat of your pants. While searches like this can drift off the subject quickly, you never know what gems you'll unearth.

Note: Because the Mailing List Directory is intended to be a resource for Internet users worldwide as well as AOL's members, it is being migrated to a series of World Wide Web pages and may already have been converted by the time you read this. The keywords: **Mailing Lists** will always bring you to the proper location, no matter what format the Directory is in. You can also obtain the Directory via FTP; instructions are at keywords: **Mailing Lists**.

Newsgroups

Newsgroups are similar to mailing lists in that they provide forums for the free exchange of ideas, opinions, and comments, usually confined to a specific field of interest. You visit a newsgroup, read the messages you find there, reply to those that inspire a response, post new messages when you have a new topic to propose, and come back another day to see what responses you've provoked.

Unlike mailing lists, no mail is involved with newsgroups, and you needn't subscribe—all newsgroups are open to everyone. Most activity occurs while you're online, including reading and responding to postings. Thus, some will say that newsgroups are more immediate, more interactive, and more conversational than mailing lists. Newsgroups or mailing lists? For most it's a matter of preference. You probably will want to dabble in both for a while.

Figure 4-10: The America Online Newsgroups screen. To reach it, use the keyword: **Newsgroups**.

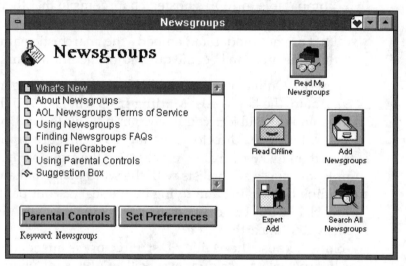

At the moment, more than 17,000 newsgroups flood the Internet. This figure is more than four times the 4,000 mentioned in Adam Engst's *Internet Starter Kit* (copyright 1993), which is in turn more than double the 1,500 mentioned in Ed Krol's *The Whole Internet* (first edition, copyright 1992). If the number of newsgroups keeps doubling and tripling every year, we'll have more than half a million of them by the turn of the century.

Bizarre Talk

The Internet is a diverse place. Scientists exchange formulae for the creation of life. Programmers exchange code for the creation of daemons. And others exchange palaver in the newsgroup talk.bizarre. To wit, the following:

```
Subject:    The Solbergs Do The Zoo
From:       andsol@cml.rice.edu (Andrew Solberg)
Date:       17 Jul 1994 22:53:59 -0500
Message-ID: <9407180354.AA01851@cml.rice.edu>
```

```
Andy: Ah, the heady aroma of the zoo.
Dema: Buy me a Slushee.
                    - * -
Andy: Dema, are the moats around these critters
      meant to keep them in or little kids out?
Dema: I think they're actually meant to trap little kids.
      They fall down the steep walls and die there, kind of
      like pitcher plants.
Andy: I get it! The kids die and their bodies decompose into
      a thick, nutrient-rich mulch........
Dema: .....which plants grow in, which the elephants eat....
Andy: Oo! Oo! Let me say it!
Dema: Okay.
Andy: "....And Thus Is The Cycle Of Nature Renewed."
Dema: People are staring.
                    - * -
Dema: They don't have a meerkat!
Andy: A what?
Dema: A meerkat!  Like in The Lion King!
Andy: Are you sure that's a real creature?
Dema: Of *course* it is!  Disney wouldn't *dare* invent it!
Andy: I don't buy it.
Dema: Then buy me another Slushee.
```

Special thanks to Professor Andrew J. Solberg from the University of Oslo, Norway, for his wit and permission to display a bit of it here.

One thing's for sure: few newsgroups have anything to do with the news. Newsgroups aren't groups assembled to discuss *Washington Week in Review*. This is an anarchy: there are no restrictions whatsoever on newsgroup topics. That's why there are 17,000 of them.

The Internet doesn't have a monopoly on newsgroups. America Online has hundreds of them, though AOL prefers to call them message boards. CompuServe has "forums"; GEnie has "bulletin boards"; and Delphi has "round tables." They're all the same thing, and they all exist to satisfy our passion for discourse. Accordingly, newsgroups are arguably the most popular resource on the Internet.

And they *are* an Internet resource, meaning they're outside of AOL's sphere of influence. No one polices the Internet. Newsgroup subject matter and use of language are appropriate to the Internet anarchy. In a way, AOL is performing a service similar to that of the telephone company when it comes to newsgroups: AOL is just the medium, not the message.

Because newsgroups are an Internet resource, AOL's own internal Terms of Service (TOS) don't apply. There are guidelines, however, and AOL's USENET Newsgroups TOS is a codification of these guidelines. The USENET TOS is always available in the list box at the keyword: **Newsgroups**, where it's called "AOL Newsgroups Terms of Service." Be sure to read it—it might save you considerable newsgroup face.

The Ringmaster Pub

The Ringmaster Pub and Deli is just up the street from AOL—an easy walk, even in the rain. It's inside the building that houses the offices of Ringling Brothers and Barnum & Bailey's Greatest Show on Earth. If you enter the wrong door on your way to the pub, you land in Barnum & Bailey's foyer surrounded by the stuffed remains of Gargantua the Gorilla and a magnificent wall mural, measuring perhaps 20 by 35 feet. It's an elaborate painting—exquisitely detailed—of a three-ring circus with clowns, tigers, and trapeze artists, all caught in mid-air.

AOLers don't frequent the Ringmaster Pub, preferring to walk another couple of yards uptown—figuratively and literally—to the American Cafe. I'm more of a pub guy and I try to visit the Ringmaster every time I travel to AOL. Gargantua and I are old friends.

It's appropriate that AOL and the circus occupy neighboring office buildings. Both services make a living by juggling balls in the air. Both services have their tigers and their clowns, and both services have amassed their fortunes a couple dollars at a time. AOL could place that three-ring mural in its foyer and nothing would seem out of place.

Getting Help

As I mentioned earlier, space limitations preclude a full description of operational details for AOL's Internet features here. I have written another book exclusively for that. Fortunately, however, help is never far away when you're using AOL's Internet features. A number of methods are available for accessing help, from AOL, from other members, or from the Internet community at large.

Online Help

Nearly every Internet window on AOL offers a potential for online help. Figure 4-11 offers a sampling.

Figure 4-11: Help topics abound at the Internet Connection.

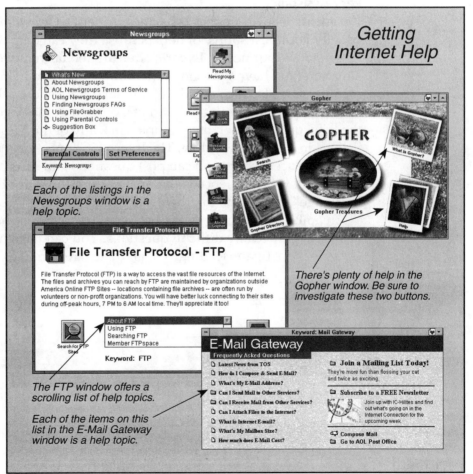

The good news is that because the newsgroup help files are stored at AOL (and not on your hard disk), they can be changed whenever the Internet staff wants to change them. These help files, in other words, always reflect changes made in response to suggestions from users as well as changes in the Net itself.

The bad news is that you have to be online to access them, and for that you pay.

Here's a tip: print 'em. Whenever a help window is open, all you have to do is choose Print from the File menu, and you'll have a hardcopy of the online help file that's currently open. You can print them all in this manner if you like.

Peer Assistance

I'm a firm believer in peer assistance. America Online members are usually your best source of help because they can empathize; they understand your needs. Experts often are too far removed from your situation (and have too many other things to do) to help the way other members can. In other words, if you have a question, ask around.

You might start with the Internet Connection message boards. Use the keyword: **Internet**, then double-click any of the Message Board listings in the main window. The Internet Connection's message boards provide places where you can post questions and receive replies from others who've experienced similar situations. Look for the "Internet Exchange" item in the Internet Connection window's list box.

An ambitious team of "CyberJockeys" patrols these boards as well, answering especially difficult questions. You can recognize CyberJockeys by the leading "CJ" in their screen names.

Figure 4-12: The Internet Exchange offers a comprehensive help compilation at keywords: **Net Exchange**.

The Internet Exchange

Internet Exchange

What's Your Favorite World Wide Web site?

Swap URLs with other AOL members in the WWW message board

▣ Message Board

Internet experts, here's

'Newsgroups About the 'Net

▢ alt.best.of.internet
▢ alt.life.internet
▢ alt.culture.internet
▢ alt.internet.media-coverage
▢ alt.online-service
▢ alt.online-service.america-online
▢ comp.infosystems

Mailing Lists About the 'Net

▯ BESTWEB
▯ McLuhan-List

The Internet Exchange offers quick access to two local message boards, seven newsgroups and two mailing lists—all available for problem solving.

Subj: Off AOL but on Internet
Date: 05-20 09:27:42 EDT
From: ME

In attempting to print from WWW, succeeded in some then got error message: Cannot read TEMP file created by Print Manager. May be corrupted. Try again...

Was bumped off AOL, but when I signed on again, found myself still at the Web page I had been printing.
a) Cause for error message?
b) Was I being charged for
computer was at Windows P
c) AOL software problem or

Thanks, ME

ME needs help, posts a request for information, and receives a Cyber-Jockey reply two hours later. ⟶

Subj: Re:Off AOL but on Internet
Date: 05-20 11:43:26 EDT
From: CJ Jon

Hmmm .. that *is* strange ...

First .. if you were already signed on .. and tried to sign on again, AOL wouldn't let you, so either A) you were signed off, or B) you never actually signed off ..

Did you re-dial the number and everything?

Well .. in any event it would be interesting to know if you could re-create the situation!

.oO
jon

aol.newsgroups.help

Finally, be sure to subscribe to the **aol.newsgroups.help** newsgroup (it is part of the default newsgroup subscription list—you're probably already subscribed). This is the most active location for newsgroup assistance, and it's not broadcast throughout the Internet—your questions are only seen by fellow AOL members, and your responses will come from fellow AOL members.

Netiquette

Nowhere is the etiquette of online conduct more critical (or more abused) than in newsgroups. Most *faux pas* are committed by newbies—people like you and me. The Internet is a community, after all: one with a particularly stalwart camaraderie and an intense adherence to a set of unwritten guidelines for interactions with others. Most specialized social organizations are that way, and to become a member of one without first becoming familiar with its catechism invites disgrace. A minicourse in Netiquette, then, might help:

- Having stung myself a number of times, I've taken to writing my missives and *waiting* for at least a couple hours before posting them. I save them and recall them the next time I sign on. For some reason, this obliges me to read them again before I click the Post button—and it has often saved me considerable newsgroup face.

- There are real people on the other end of the line: people with emotions and feelings. Honor them.

- Honor yourself as well. You are known on the Net by what you write. Project the image you want others to see.

- Brevity is admirable; verbosity is disfavored (among other things, because it wastes time, disk space, and network bandwidth). Say what you have to say succinctly; your words will carry greater authority and impact.

- Read before writing. Add something to the conversation; don't simply repeat what's already been said. Subscribe to the **news.answers** newsgroup and read the Frequently Asked Questions file (FAQ) for your newsgroup before posting. By reading before you write you'll have a better sense of the tenor and conventions of the newsgroup to which you are posting.

- Quote the messages to which you're responding. Edit the quoted material for brevity (and indicate when you've done so), use the quoting fashion you see in other messages and always acknowledge the person you're quoting. (Quoting is also discussed in Chapter 3, "Electronic Mail & the Personal Filing Cabinet.")

- Contribute something. Some people speak simply to be heard; these same people post mainly to see their material online. Don't contribute to the tedium: look for a new perspective, ask a probing question, make an insightful comment. If none come to mind, wait for another opportunity. There are plenty of opportunities on the Net; we all have something worthwhile to contribute eventually.

- Use Help. If the Help files described in this chapter don't answer your question, post a message in **aol.newsgroups.help**. Lots of people are willing to help you if you ask.

Emily Postnews

Brad Templeton originally created Emily Postnews a number of years ago; Steve Summit keeps her alive today. Emily is a satirical document, providing witty examples of what *not* to do when using newsgroups. Here's an example:

Q: What sort of tone should I take in my article?

A: Be as outrageous as possible. If you don't say outlandish things, and fill your article with libelous insults of net people, you may not stick out enough in the flood of articles to get a response. The more insane your posting looks, the more likely it is that you'll get lots of followups. The net is here, after all, so that you can get lots of attention. If your article is polite, reasoned and to the point, you may only get mailed replies. Yuck!"

Emily Postnews is posted every couple of months in the **news.answers** newsgroup. She might be satirical but she's effective at conveying the spirit of the newsgroup community without being condescending. Be sure to read her.

Gopher

Growth on the Internet is a stupendous thing. Most everyone agrees that it exceeds 100 percent a year; some contend that it's as high as 20 percent *per month*. Regardless of the figure, navigating the Net has become about as convenient as navigating the Atlantic Ocean: relatively easy if you have the right tools, but impractical—some might say perilous—if you don't.

One such tool is *Gopher*. Originating in 1991 at the University of Minnesota (where the school mascot is the Golden Gopher), Gopher is a system of sites containing amazing numbers of files (mostly text), all listed in hierarchical menus. All you have to do is keep choosing menu items until you find what you're after, then Gopher "goes for" (it's kind of a double pun: mascot and "gofer") your material on the Net.

People new to the Net tend to think of e-mail, USENET, and the Web as the only resources available on the Internet. Those who do are doing themselves a lamentable disservice. The Gopher system has been around for over seven years now—nearly a third of the Internet's lifetime—and the amount of data that's stored there is extensive and for many Internet users, undiscovered (see Figure 4-13). And Gopher has a measurable advantage over many Web resources: it's fast. Most Gopher pages are textual, and a textual Gopher page transfers much more quickly than a Web page filled with graphics and links.

Figure 4-13: The keyword: **Gopher** takes you to AOL's redesigned Gopher service where vast—and often overlooked— Internet resources await your exploration.

The Gopher system is actually composed of a number of *Gopher servers* located around the world. Each server is like a good librarian: it organizes content for your convenience. (Librarians organize libraries with card files; Gophers organize the Internet's content with menus.) When you find what you're looking for, the Gopher retrieves the information for you. Better yet, Gophers reference other Gophers:

AOL's Gopher, for example, offers access to hundreds of other Gophers. It's as if you were given access to a librarian's convention, and the librarians, every one, brought their card files with them.

Though there are a number of Gopher servers, you're rarely aware of them individually: AOL simply groups them all into one massive menu tree that you're free to peruse as you wish. In a way, that's too bad, because you're usually unaware of the vast distances you're traveling when you access the various Gopher servers on AOL's menus. You might be in Switzerland one moment and Germany the next. That's the nature of the Net: distance has no meaning in cyberspace.

That's about all there is to lament, however. AOL wraps up Gopher in a fine cloak of colors, offering its Gopher menus in the Web browser window, where everything is familiar and comfortable. If you're used to browsing the Web, you won't have any trouble using Gopher. In fact, some folks are beginning to rediscover Gopher, thanks to some enterprising individuals who are making Gopher content available via the Web.

The Comics Come to the Net

The original Gopher server at the University of Minnesota was established to bring convenience to the Net. Since copies of all the Internet sites' directories were stored on the server, searching was local. No time was spent connecting to and disconnecting from the individual sites during the data searches.

In time, more Gopher servers came along. There are scores of them now, and searching the *servers* has become a task.

Enter *Veronica*, a tool that is a database of the Gophers' directories.

Prior to Veronica, some wag of a programmer created a utility to search FTP sites, and called it Archie. Not to be outdone, another programmer created a Gopherspace search tool and named it Veronica (for the *Archie* comic book character). She was followed shortly by Jughead, another Gopher searcher. Searching for a name for your latest creation? Pick up the nearest literature—Betty and Moose can't be far behind.

To access Veronica, click the Search button in the main Gopher window—the one with a gopher wearing a hard hat. Be warned: Veronica is *not* fast, and AOL has no control over that. It's just that way.

If you know how to use the Web, you already know how to use AOL's Gopher interface. About all I can add is an explanation of the icons. Take a moment to look at Figure 4-14. Note the variety of icons pictured to the left of the menu topics.

Figure 4-14: Each icon on America Online's Gopher menus has a specific meaning.

> gopher://isumvs.iastate.edu/1%7edb.VIDEO
>
> Back | Reload | Forward | Search | Prefs | Home | Help | Stop
>
> gopher://isumvs.iastate.edu/1%7edb.VIDEO
>
> Select one of:
>
> - Video and Movie Review database information
> - Quick Pix from Movies/Video recently released
> - This month's video reviews!
> - Last month's video reviews!
> - This year's video reviews!
> - Last year's video reviews!
> - Search for a specific video title (Enter one word)
> - Link to full Video Search capabilities
> - Complete alphabetical list of all video review titles
> - Critic's Honor Roll of Superior Video Reviews
> - Add a new video review [11:19:10]
> - The Video DMZ (WWW Version of Video db)
> - USENET Movie Review Archive

The Gopher Icons

Note the Uniform Resource Locator (URL) address for this page: it's clearly a Gopher resource.

Tiny text pages are textual articles.

Little menus lead to more Gopher menus.

Binoculars reveal a searchable Gopher index.

Typical of AOL, the *page* icon represents an *article*: a textual document suitable for reading onscreen, or for saving or printing.

The *menu* icon represents another Gopher menu. Double-click a menu icon, and you get another set of choices. This is the nesting structure that's the standard in Gopher-based information.

A *blank* icon (not pictured) leads to a Gopher resource that AOL isn't able to resolve. Often, these references are outdated.

The *binocular* icon is a searchable Gopher database. When you double-click it, you will see a criteria entry form. You'll then be able to enter search criteria and conduct the search itself.

Like the World Wide Web, the Gopher system invites exploration. It's easy to use, it's one of the Internet's most rewarding resources, and it's always available at keyword: **Gopher**.

FTP

Gopher, newsgroups, and the Web are nifty tools, but what if you want more direct access? What if you want to log on to another machine on the Net, see a directory of its files, and download a few of them? We're talking now about the "engine room" of the Internet, where you access other machines' files as if they were on your own hard drive. FTP, or *File Transfer Protocol*, provides that kind of access; it's how you download files (including programs, sound, sound video, and graphics) from other machines.

Figure 4-15: Using FTP to download a Windows program that helps manage information.

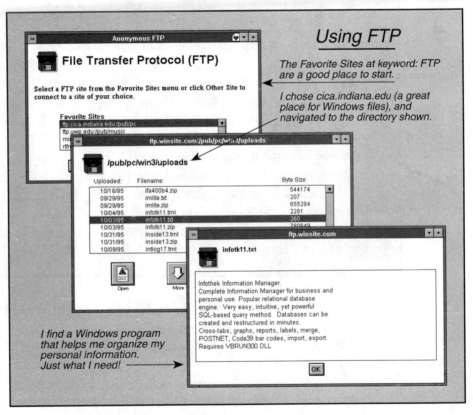

FTP is two things, actually. First, it's a protocol, allowing machines on the Net to exchange data (files) without concern for the type of machine that originated the file, the file's original format, or even the operating systems of the machines involved. FTP is also a *program* that enables FTP. Just as the word *telephone* denotes both a device you hold in your hand and a system for international communications, FTP is both the message and the medium.

The term also is used as both noun ("It's available via FTP") and verb ("FTP to **ftp.aol.com** and look in the pub directory"). It's hard to misuse the term, in other words. Just don't spell out the words— always use the initials.

Anonymous FTP

Originally, most FTP sessions occurred between a site and a person at a remote location who had an account at that site. The person would log on by supplying an account name and a password, then conduct the appropriate file activities.

The need soon became apparent, however, for less restrictive access. What if a site wanted to post a file for *anyone* to download? A number of publicly funded agencies required such an arrangement. NASA's space images, as an example, are funded by public money; therefore, it was decided that the public should have access to them.

The solution they came up with was *anonymous FTP*. During an anonymous FTP session, the user logs on to the remote site using the account name "anonymous" (AOL does this for you unless you supply a specific user name). The password for anonymous login, typically, is the user's Internet address—a common courtesy so the people at the remote site can determine, if they wish, who is using their system. Again, AOL does this for you unless you supply a specific password.

Operating FTP successfully and acquiring a library of fertile FTP locations (and knowing when to access them) is a skill worthy of development, but it *does* require time to develop. Begin by reading the Help files available at the keyword: **FTP** (and pictured in Figure 4-11), and practice for a while using AOL's "Favorite Sites" pictured in Figure 4-15. If you feel you need more help, post questions on the Internet Connection message boards. AOL's community is always ready to help you learn.

Telnet

Yet one more tool remains for us to discover: Telnet. A number of Internet users require operating-system access to machines on the Net, not for the purpose of transferring files (which is FTP's job) but to run programs on those remote machines. Often these programs are games, but chat applications are common as well.

People who require Telnet access to the Internet have specific needs, and most of these people have favorite programs—Telnet clients—that they prefer to use for the task. This isn't a situation where AOL can provide a client for you, Telnet is too idiomatic for that.

Instead, AOL provides a "socket" into which you plug your Telnet client. The AOL client—your AOL software—recedes to the background under these circumstances, and the Telnet client assumes command. At AOL's end, signals from your computer are routed directly to the remote computer you're accessing. AOL's host computers remain transparent until your Telnet session concludes.

Figure 4-16: Telnet allows you to connect the client of your choosing directly to the Internet.

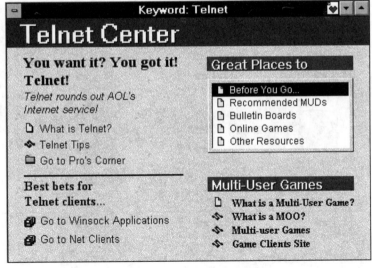

If you require Telnet access to the Net, use the keyword: **Telnet**. You'll find a number of clients available there, as well as the sockets I've mentioned. Take the time to review the informational resources pictured in Figure 4-16 if you're not already familiar with this technology.

AnswerMan

Speaking of a community that's eager to help you learn, if you want to learn more about the Internet, use the keyword: **AnswerMan**, and investigate the AnswerMan area (see Figure 4-17). It's intended for newcomers to the Internet who might be feeling a bit overwhelmed by it all. AnswerMan doesn't have all of the answers, but he does have a message board to which he replies (click the Ask AnswerMan icon). His live appearances are frequent and informative (click the Talk with AnswerMan icon for a schedule). The AnswerMan Resources area offers a compilation of some of the best stuff the Internet has to offer. Be sure to check it out.

Figure 4-17: Find answers to your Internet questions at keyword: **AnswerMan**.

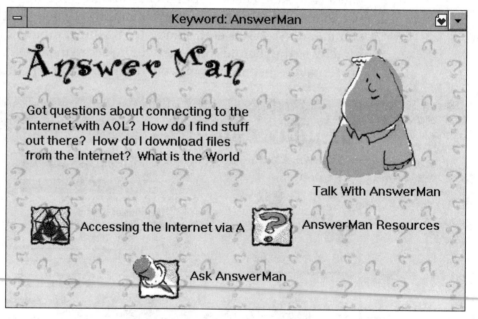

Moving On

Each Internet resource described on these pages is an existing AOL feature. Others will no doubt come along. That's part of the fun of telecommunications: this is just the beginning, and there's always more to come. Becoming a member of AOL (and exploring the Internet) is a little like planting a fruit tree: there are many rewards (blossoms, bees, fruit, firewood), and each year there's a more bountiful harvest than there was the year before.

It's positively organic. ;-)

In this chapter, we might have temporarily lost our focus. This is a book about America Online, not the Internet, and AOL offers a motherlode of resources for the intrepid electronic explorer. Many of these appear in the form of files: programs, graphics, fonts, sounds, and video ready for transfer to your computer at the click of a mouse. It's remarkably easy to do, and we will discuss all of these file types in the next chapter.

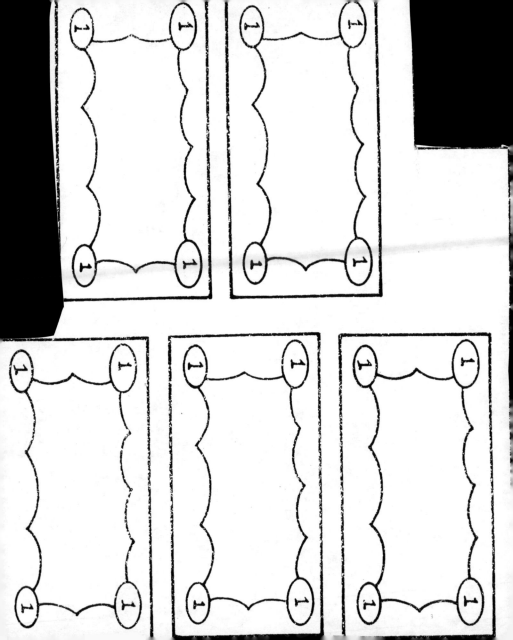

$$13 + 15 = 28$$
$$28 + 14 = 42$$
$$42 + 11 = 53$$
$$53 + 5 = 58$$
$$58 + 25 = 83$$
$$83 + 19 = 9?$$

22

30

unicorn

Transferring Files

A staff member wrote to me the other day. "If I had a nickel for every time I was asked how to download or what a download is," she said, "I would be a rich woman."

Exaggeration, perhaps—it takes 20,000,000 nickels to make a millionaire—but her message is clear: people want to know what this "downloading" business is all about. And, well they should: downloading is one of the top five activities people do online, and more than 100,000 files are available for downloading on AOL, spread across the service like flowers in a meadow. Members graze this meadow, smiling, downloading bouquets of files. People must be on to something here, and those who aren't want to be. A chapter on the subject seems warranted. Here it is.

What Is Downloading?

Simply put, *downloading* is the process of transferring files—for example, transferring a file from AOL's computers to a disk in your computer. Files can be programs, utilities, drivers, fonts, graphics (many of the graphics in this book have been downloaded), sound, animation, and, of course, text. On AOL, downloads don't cost extra money: your normal AOL access charges are in effect whenever you download; you pay nothing additional for this privilege.

And that's it. You may have heard horror stories about downloading, but they probably had something to do with computer viruses or complex downloading protocols. Fortunately, those are things of the past. All of the appropriate files on AOL are checked for viruses before they're made available for downloading, and AOL's software handles the protocols automatically.

Note: This chapter discusses the process of downloading files stored in AOL's libraries. Another form of downloading—FTP, or File Transfer Protocol—has to do with downloading files stored on the Internet, via AOL. There's a considerable difference. File Transfer Protocol is discussed in Chapter 4, "Using the Internet."

A Downloading Session

Perhaps the best way to explain downloading is to download a file for you and explain the process as it's happening. If your computer is nearby, you might want to sign on and follow along.

Finding the File

Before you can download a file, you have to find it. There are lots of ways to find files, but for the purposes of this exercise, we'll go directly to a known location. Later, we'll discuss methods of finding a file when its location is *not* known, or when the name of the file isn't at hand.

Begin by signing on and using the keywords: **Windows Forum**. Though we'll discuss forums in Chapter 9, "Boards & Forums," it's enough for the moment for you to know that most forums offer libraries, as does this one. Simply stated, a *library* is an online reservoir of files. Some of these files are placed online by the forum's staff; others are uploaded by AOL members (I'll discuss uploading later in this chapter). There's usually a forum staff member who maintains the library, checking files for viruses, clarifying file descriptions, and removing outdated entries.

By now you should see a Software Libraries button in the Windows Forum window. Click it (see Figure 5-1).

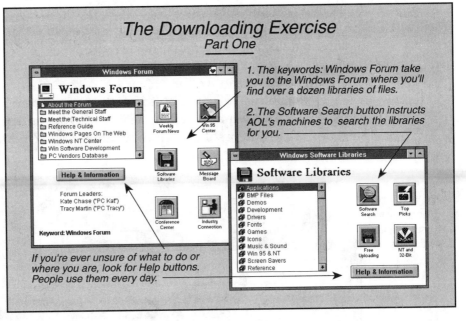

Figure 5-1:
The Windows
Forum is an espe-
cially rewarding
place to find files
for downloading.

As a computing forum, the Windows Forum offers not just one library but more than a dozen of them. Each of the entries in the scroll box shown in the lower window of Figure 5-1 is a library, and each library offers hundreds of files for downloading. This is the motherlode of Windows stuff.

Writing on Water

This exercise is a litany of specifics, and when it comes to the telecommunications industry, describing specifics is like writing on water. By the time you read this, the Windows Forum's appearance may change, the forum's libraries might be restructured, and WinZip 6.0 could be superseded by a new version.

Assuming this *fait accompli*, I suggest adaptability. The Windows Forum will always exist, and so will its file libraries. WinZip will probably be with us for a long time, though you might find a later version online when you conduct your search. Tolerate change, and your online life—not to mention your experience with this book—will come a lot easier.

Wandering aimlessly, looking for one particular nugget in a motherlode isn't a very effective thing for you to do. There are machines that do this much more quickly and reliably. AOL's machine is called *File Search.* We'll discuss File Search in detail later, but we'll make quick use of it now.

Click the Software Search button pictured in Figure 5-1. The Windows File Search window will appear, with your cursor flashing in the text box at the bottom of the window. Enter "WinZip Mak" as shown in Figure 5-2.

Figure 5-2:
With the proper criteria, file searching is specific and fast.

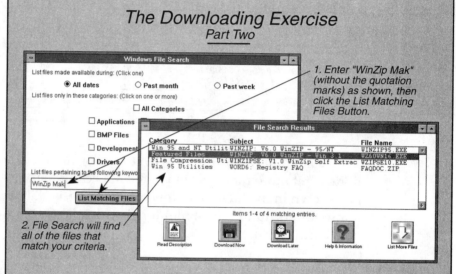

WinZip

You can't survive long in the downloading environment without some form of compression/decompression software. Compression and decompression are as common to downloading files as stink is to skunks. Though I'll discuss file compression later in this chapter, you're going to need file compression software eventually, and now's a good time to get some. WinZip is an excellent choice, and since this exercise requires that you download something, we might as well make it something useful.

The search phrase "WinZip Mak" tells File Search to search for files with both *WinZip* and *Mak* as criteria. WinZip is the name of the file, but lots of files have been compressed with WinZip and still others require WinZip or something like it to be extracted (decompressed). Those files might match our criterion if we simply specified "WinZip," so we include "Mak"—the name of the file's publisher, Nico Mak—to state our objective specifically.

When you click the List Matching Files button in the File Search Window, AOL should find at least a few files that match the criteria, as shown in the lower window in Figure 5-2. The Windows 3.1 version of WinZip is selected in the illustration. It's appropriate to my needs, so I click the Download Now button and the transfer begins (see Figure 5-3).

Figure 5-3:
Determine where you want the file to go on your hard disk, then click OK. The remainder of the transfer is automatic.

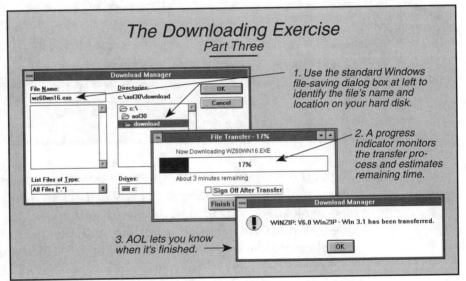

Downloading the File

The standard Windows file-saving window appears next. Choose a place for WinZip on your hard disk, then click the OK button. The progress indicator shown in Figure 5-3 appears, estimating the amount of time required to download the file and providing visual indication of the file's progress. When the transfer is finished, the announcement you see at the bottom of Figure 5-3 appears and the process concludes. It's as easy as that.

Filenames & Destinations

Look again at Figure 5-3 and note the proposed filename. If you want to use a filename other than the one proposed, all you have to do is select the name (if it isn't selected already) and start typing. I don't recommend this, unless the proposed filename conflicts with one already on your disk. The file's documentation, for example, might refer to the file by the original name; if you change the name, the reference might be unclear. Also, forum discussions might refer to the file's original name. If you search for an update to the file, you'll need to use its original name. So stick to the original name unless you have a good reason not to.

The \aol30\download directory pictured in Figure 5-3 is the default destination for downloaded files. Some would say that this directory isn't the best place to use: there will no doubt be an update to Version 3.0 some day, and when it comes along you will probably make a new directory for it—something like c:\aol35. When the installation of the update is complete, you might be tempted to delete the old \aol30 directory, forgetting that you have a number of valuable downloads in a subdirectory there. By the time you remember, it might be too late. The file-saving dialog box in Figure 5-3 allows you to declare any directory on any disk as a destination. Don't hesitate to change the destination.

Sign off now if you've nothing else to do online (the Sign Off command is under the Go To menu). Navigate back to the folder where you downloaded WinZip, and double-click the .exe file you downloaded. WinZip's installation is routine, with plenty of Help buttons available along the way. When installation is finished, execute WinZip and choose Brief Tutorial from its Help menu. That's the best way to get to know the program, and since this is a book about AOL—not WinZip—I'll move on to a different subject now. The important thing to mention is that you have downloaded a file from AOL—a particularly useful file—and all you had to do was click a few buttons.

Multitasking

America Online offers three ways to download files: (1) You can simply click the Download Now button and sit in front of your machine like a fossil, watching all the excitement the progress indicator provides; (2) You can queue files for downloading and wait until the end of your online session (or for another part of the day) and download then. (This is a function of the Download Manager, which we'll discuss in Chapter 6); or (3) You can do something else with your PC while the download concludes in the background, like write that letter you owe your mother or pay the bills.

Doing more than one thing at a time with your computer is known as *multitasking*, and it might come as a surprise to you (even many veteran AOL members are ignorant of this feature) to discover that your AOL software offers true multitasking capabilities: start a download, then do something else with your PC.

Here's how it's done:

- Sign on, locate the file you want to download, and start the downloading process by clicking the Download Now button pictured in Figure 5-2.

- Once the progress indicator appears (pictured in Figure 5-3), you can do whatever you please with the programs on your computer, including the AOL program itself. If you want to read mail or visit a forum, do it. If you want to run another program on your computer, minimize AOL and run the other program. AOL will continue downloading in the background in either case.

When the download concludes, AOL will announce that it has completed the task. If you were working in another application, AOL will become the active application then make its announcement.

With all that said, a few caveats are in order:

- You will notice some degradation in your computer's performance. It's doing double duty after all, and each task gets its little slice of your computer's power.

- Some software doesn't tolerate multitasking very well, especially software that relies heavily on disk activity or your computer's central processing unit. Games are notoriously unsuited to the multitasking environment.

- If you've got them, watch the lights on your modem. If the Receive Data (RD) light goes out or flickers badly while you're multitasking, you're asking too much of your system. Let AOL have your system to itself while you stretch a bit or go for a walk. If that won't do, find another task to perform with your computer that isn't quite so demanding.

Multitasking seems a bit magical to me, and at first I didn't trust it. But it works. In three years I've never had a download go bad or a file become corrupted because of a multitasking problem. In fact, I'm writing this sentence as a download is underway. It's a great way to magnify your potential.

Finding Files for Downloading

Now that you've seen how easy it is to download a file, you probably have come to realize that it isn't downloading that requires your understanding, but *finding the files* for downloading. There are over 100,000 of them, after all, and like prospecting for gold, the search is 99 percent of the expedition.

Searching through 100,000 files would be a horrendous task were it not for AOL's searchable database of online files. This database contains all of the files stored in the computing forums, and it's constantly maintained. Every file in the computing forums' libraries appears in this database within a few hours after it's posted. As you might expect, access to the database requires only a click of your mouse.

Finding Files While You're Online

There are two ways you can find files while you're online: you can search for them or you can browse among them. Searching implies that you know what you're looking for; browsing is a more leisurely activity. Each requires its own strategy.

File Search

You've already seen the most common method of finding files: File Search. Though I took you into the Computing Forum to conduct your search earlier, you can search at any time, from any place online. All you have to do is click the FIND button on the toolbar (see Figure 5-4).

Figure 5-4:
The FIND button on
the toolbar or the
keywords: **File
Search** take you
directly to a data-
base of files stored
on AOL. There you
can enter specific
criteria to help you
find exactly the file
you want.

Using File Search

Keyword

To quickly access an area, type its keyword below and click Go. To access a
page on the World Wide Web, type the Web address below and click Go. To
locate areas that match your topic of interest, type words that describe what you
are looking for and click Search.

Enter word(s): file search

Go

*The keyword: FileSearch
take you directly to AOL's
searchable database of
online files.*

*Better yet, use FIND
button on the toolbar.*

FIND

Software Search

List files released since: (Click one)

⦿ All dates   ○ Past month   ○ Past week

List files in the following categories: (Click one or more)

☐ All Categories

☐ Applications   ☐ Games   ☐ OS/2

☐ Development   ☐ Graphics & Animation   ☐ Telecommunications

☐ DOS   ☐ Hardware   ☐ Windows

☐ Education   ☐ Music & Sound

List files pertaining to the following keywords: (Optional)

winzip mak

List Matching Files   **Get Help & Info**

Look again at the Software Search dialog box pictured in Figure 5-4. Two sets of check boxes are provided: you can specify only those files that have been uploaded recently (the Past week option is great for finding only new files), or only those files that fit certain criteria.

More important, there's also a text box within the File Search dialog. Here you can specify your own criteria. Words entered here are matched against keywords appearing in the following areas:

▲ The person who uploaded the file.

▲ The file's name.

▲ The subject line.

▲ Keywords assigned to the file.

There are three special words you can use in a match phrase: AND, OR, and NOT. I might receive dozens of matches to the search phrase "Versailles," most of which would be references to the suburb of Paris or the palace, not to my objective—the Versailles font. The search phrase "Versailles AND font," on the other hand, narrows the search. (The AND modifier is the default, by the way. Whenever more than one word appears in a search phrase, AOL assumes there's an AND between them. Thus the phrase "Versailles AND font" is the same as the phrase "Versailles font.")

Perhaps you want the Utopia font as well as the Versailles font. Here is where the OR modifier comes in. The phrase "Versailles OR Utopia" finds either one.

The NOT modifier narrows the search by excluding material matching the criterion that follows it. The phrase "Versailles NOT France" would provide a listing of all references to Versailles that aren't associated with France.

Combining modifiers can be unclear. The phrase "Versailles OR Utopia AND font" is ambiguous. Do we mean "Versailles, or Utopia and font," or do we mean "Versailles or Utopia, and font"? To clarify, use parentheses. The phrase "(Versailles OR Utopia) AND font" says "look for Versailles or Utopia, excluding everything but fonts from either category." It pays to be specific.

File Descriptions

In my haste to download WinZip, I neglected an important step in the file searching process: the file description. Look again at the lower window in Figure 5-2. During the exercise at the beginning of this chapter, I simply asked you to click the Download Now button. Normally, you wouldn't click that button until you had read the file's description. To read the file descriptions shown in Figure 5-2, you would select the file in the File Search Results window's list box, then click the Read Description button. (Double-clicking the file's entry in the list box would do the same thing.) Figure 5-5 pictures WinZip's file description.

Figure 5-5:
Read file descriptions before you download.

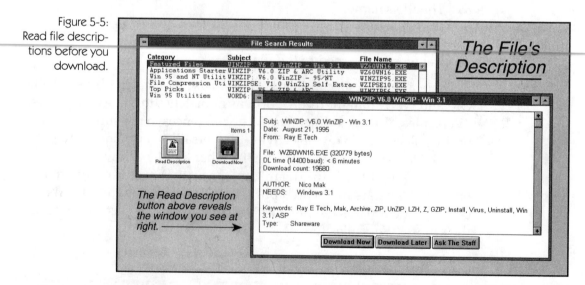

When I click Figure 5-5's Read Description button, AOL provides a complete description of the file. This intermediate step is critical. There are lots of things I need to know about this file before I can decide whether to download it.

Let's look at WinZip's file description in its entirety (see Figure 5-6).

Figure 5-6:
A wealth of information is found in file descriptions.

```
Subj:  WINZIP: V6.0 WinZIP - Win 3.1
Date:  August 21, 1995                        WinZip's
From:  Ray E Tech                           File Description

File:  WZ60WN16.EXE (320779 bytes)
DL time (14400 baud): < 6 minutes
Download count: 19768

AUTHOR:   Nico Mak
NEEDS:    Windows 3.1

Keywords: Ray E Tech, Mak, Archive, ZIP, UnZIP, LZH, Z, GZIP, Install, Virus, Uninstall, Win
3.1, ASP
Type:     Shareware

Version:  Official Release


New with this version:
* The File Manager Extension is now implemented under Windows 95, Windows NT and Win32s.

* WinZip now allows you to view multiple files in an archive without first closing the first
file (earlier versions of WinZip restricted you to closing the first file before viewing the
second file).

* The WinZip installation procedure now includes "Express Setup" and "Custom Setup" options.
Custom Setup results in the "old" WinZip 5.6 behavior.  Express Setup, the default, skips the
Program Locations dialog box, the File Manager Configuration dialog box, and "Create Program
Group" prompt.

* With more and more people using the Internet, virus scanning is more important.  As a
result, WinZip's support for virus scanners has been improved.

* The number one new support problem in WinZip 5.6 was caused by the "TAR File LF to CR/LF
Conversion".  This option, intended for text files only, caused problems for binary files.
The option has been replaced by the "TAR File Smart CR/LF Conversion" option.

WinZip brings the convenience of Windows to the use of ZIP files. Includes PKZIP-compatible
built-in zip and unzip, so PKZIP is not needed for basic archive operations.

Also included is the ability to install, try, and UNINSTALL software distributed in ZIP
files.  This feature runs the install program in a ZIP, gives you a chance to try the
program, and OPTIONALLY deletes any new files, icons, program groups, and restores any
altered INI files.

WinZip includes a powerful yet intuitive point-and-click drag-and-drop interface for viewing,
running, extracting, adding, deleting, and testing files in ZIP, LZH, and ARC files,
including self extracting archives. Optional virus scanning support is included.

Note: This is a Self-extracting, Self-installing file. To install, RUN the program
WZ60WN16.EXE

Documentation: README.TXT, WHATSNEW.TXT, WINZIP.TXT plus Online Help

Downloads for previous version: 94,939
```

The *Subject, From,* and *File* lines are all searchable criteria. Don't confuse the From line with the Author line. The From line contains the name of the person who uploaded the file. That person is often a Forum Assistant or another member, not the author. Note that the File line tells you both the file's name and its size.

What Is Shareware?

You might note that WinZip is *shareware*. There are two major channels for the distribution of computer programs and data. The traditional commercial channel involves the publisher, the distributor, and the retailer—each of whom, in order to make a living, must add a bit to the cost of the product. There's a considerable distance between the creator of the software and the people who purchase and use it.

A software product distributed by the alternative method is called *shareware*. With shareware, there's usually a direct connection between the user and the creator. Shareware programs and data are posted on telecommunications services like AOL, where they can be downloaded whenever we, the users, please. Individuals or user groups also can distribute shareware among themselves without fear of recrimination. As a rule, shareware authors welcome this kind of distribution.

If you download a shareware program, you normally get the complete program—not a "crippled" version. It usually comes with documentation as well. You can try it out for a few weeks before you decide to buy. If you decide to keep it, in most cases the author expects you to send money. Since the money goes directly to the author—no publishers, distributors, or retailers are involved—shareware theoretically can cost much less than commercially distributed software. The author's share is all you pay for shareware, and the author's share is a very small portion of the total cost of the software distributed through commercial channels.

With shareware, there's also a direct channel for communication between user and author. If you have a complaint or a suggestion for improvement, send e-mail to the author. Chances are you'll get a reply. This is a significant feature: to whom do you send mail if you think your car or your refrigerator can be improved? And do you really think anyone will ever reply?

While most shareware authors request financial remuneration, a few simply give their material away (freeware). Others request a postcard from your city or town (postcardware), or a donation to a favored charity.

The shareware system only works if users pay, and payment is voluntary. Sadly, only about 10 percent of the people who use shareware programs actually pay for them. This is undoubtedly the biggest fault in the shareware concept. Shareware can be a boon to us users, but only if we obey the honor code that's implicit in the system. In other words, if you use shareware, pay for it—and encourage others to do the same.

File indicates the actual name of the file as it will download to your machine. This is what you'll see in the File Manager after you've downloaded the file.

The *date* is used when you specify "Past month" or "Past week" in the File Search dialog box.

The *download time (or DL time)* is AOL's best guess as to how long it will take to download the file. The time is estimated based on the baud rate at which you're connected. If you're connected at 14,400 bps, the estimate is based on that baud rate. This number is only an estimate. If you signed on during a peak-use period (for example, around 9 p.m. Eastern time), this number might be slightly optimistic. If you're signed on at 4 a.m., this number will be pessimistic. I downloaded WinZip—which AOL estimated to be a six-minute download—in less than five minutes during a mid-morning session at 14,400 bps.

The *Download Count* is a rough indication of the file's popularity. If you're looking for a graphic of a cat, for example, and 40 files match your search criteria, you might let the number of downloads direct you. Often, however, the number of downloads says more about the catchiness of a file's name or description than it does about the nature or quality of its content. Sometimes you have to balance the download count and date to gauge the quality of a file. If something has been online for a year, and only has 20 downloads, you can normally assume that it's of limited usefulness. WinZip 6.0, on the other hand, was uploaded November 13, 1995, and by May of 1996 had already racked up over 32,000 downloads. It's a pretty safe bet that this is a good program. You'll get a feel for this sort of thing as you peruse and sample the various files available.

The *Equipment* line, if present, indicates any hardware and/or software beyond a basic PC and 400K of memory you'll need to run the file. Sometimes, though, this line is used to indicate what hardware or software the author used to create the file.

The *Needs* line is critical: if your PC isn't up to the task, or if you need special software, it's nice to know before you download the file. For example, you'll need Windows 3.1 to run WinZip 6.0.

Keywords are those that provide matches when you enter your own search criteria. Read these. They offer valuable insight into how best to word your search phrases. That's how I knew to specify "WinZip Mak" when I originally declared my search phrase. Keywords are assigned by the AOL staff to each file.

Note: In this context, a keyword is a word assigned to a shareware file that is used to help categorize and describe it for easy search and retrieval. These keywords are separate from and can't be used by AOL's navigational keyword function (accessed by typing Ctrl+K or by clicking the keyword button on the toolbar).

The *description* itself is provided by the person who uploaded the file. WinZip's description, for example, indicates that a help file is available with the program—an important consideration for a program like this.

File descriptions can be saved for later reference. Choose Save from the File menu before you close the description window. America Online will ask where you want to store the description, which it saves in ASCII text format. All the text you read on your PC's screen is formatted this way, and it can be read offline (after you've saved it to a separate file) with any word processor or the AOL software (just choose Open from AOL's File menu).

Browsing for Files

File Search is not the only way to locate files while you're online. What if you're simply looking for a nice graphic? You don't necessarily know *which* graphic you're looking for, just a graphic.

Here's a real-life situation: the other day I needed a provocative graphic for use as Figure 4-1 in the previous chapter. I had no idea which graphic that would be, so File Search was out—"provocative" isn't a very precise search criterion. An abyssal reservoir of graphics resides in the Graphic Arts Forum. Whenever I'm in the mood for something pretty to brighten up my screen, or something intriguing to pique my visual curiosity, this is where I go to browse. (The Graphic Arts and Windows Forums are discussed in Chapter 9, "Boards & Forums.")

I used the keyword: **Graphics**, clicked the Software Libraries button, and began to browse (see Figure 5-7).

Figure 5-7:
The Graphic Arts
Forum at keyword:
Graphics is a great
place to browse
for images.

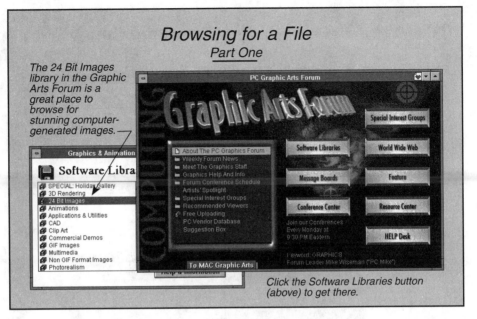

I know from experience that the 24 Bit Images library contains hundreds of particularly sublime images—the kind that make my books look better—so I chose it. I've seen a number of ray-traced images, and every one has been something of a heady experience, so I chose the 24BIT: Renderings & Ray Tracings folder pictured in Figure 5-8. Among those images, I selected 24BIT: Renderings & Ray Traces, and then the 24BIT: Rendered Abstract & Conceptual library. These decisions are illustrated in Figure 5-8, along with the library listing for The Internet 1, Jeff Stewart's evocative image of the Internet, which I eventually chose, to use as Figure 4-1.

Figure 5-8:
24-bit rendered ray
tracings are among
the most captivat-
ing images avail-
able online. That's
one in the back-
ground: "AOL
Spheres" by Mike
Wiseman.

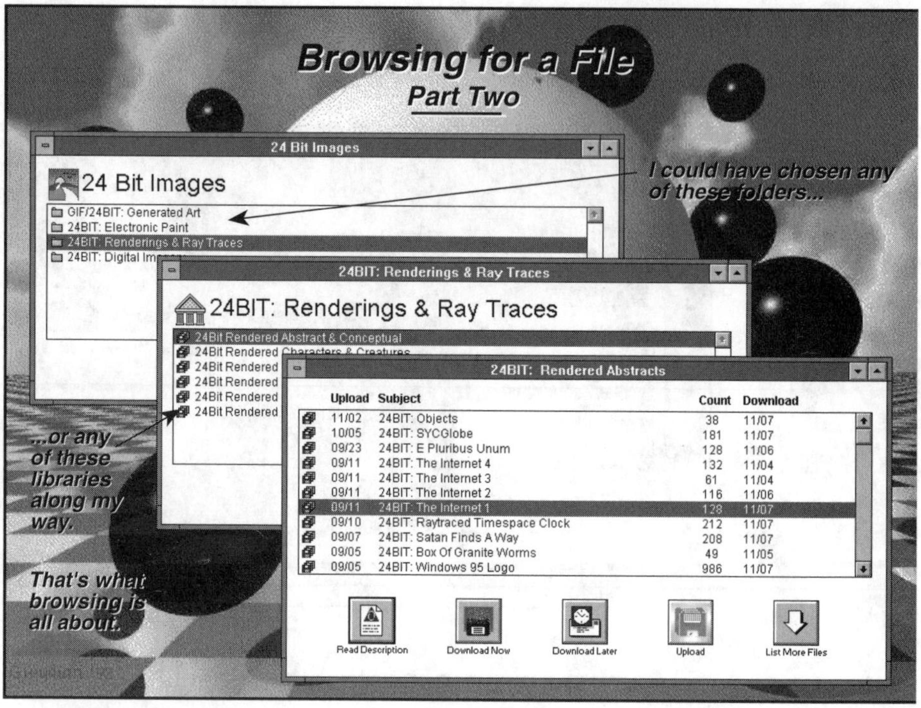

Note that I could have chosen any other library or folder along the way. I could have browsed the Graphics Forum for hours, peeking at thumbnails (see the "Thumbnails" sidebar) and downloading images that caught my eye. Browsing for files is a leisurely pursuit—most browsing is—with plenty of opportunity for detours and new discoveries. Finding files on AOL is like shopping: if you know what you're after, you can go directly to your destination and nab the merchandise; or you can meander, grazing in meadows of opportunity. The choice is yours.

Thumbnails

A feature recently added to the AOL software allows you to view *thumbnails* of graphics files before they're downloaded. This is a boon to members: thumbnails allow us to see a graphic before we spend time downloading it. Thumbnails appear in the top left corner of a graphics file's description window (see Figure 5-9). You can't miss them.

Figure 5-9:
Most graphics
offer thumbnail
views so you
can preview
the graphic
before you
make the deci-
sion to down-
load it. The
thumbnail in
this illustration
is in the upper
left corner.

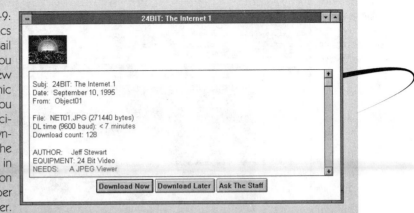

**Not all graphics offer thumbnails. Older graphics, for example, do not. Thumb-
nails are created when graphics are uploaded, thus graphics uploaded with older
AOL software don't display them.**

The Graphics Viewer

Your AOL software offers a graphics viewer which allows you to see
graphics as they're downloaded. The viewer is especially valuable
when there's no thumbnail (see the "Thumbnails" sidebar) available
and you're downloading in the dark, so to speak.

Assuming the graphic you're downloading is either in the PCX,
BMP, JPG, or GIF format (more about formats later in this chapter), and
assuming it has either a .pcx, .bmp, .jpg, or .gif filename extension,
AOL will display the graphic on your screen as soon as enough of it is
received for you to see. (There's a preference available to turn the
viewer off, though its default setting is On. Preferences are discussed in
Appendix E.)

You don't need to do anything to invoke the viewer: it just appears
when it's supposed to. Figure 5-10 shows the viewer in action as Jeff
Stewart's graphic is being received.

Figure 5-10:
The graphics
viewer allows you
to see graphics as
they're received.

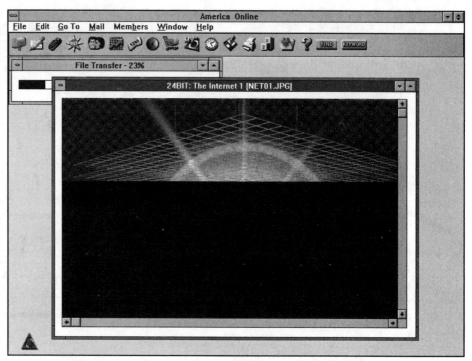

Let's face it: not all graphics are of archival quality. You'll occasionally encounter one that in spite of an acceptable thumbnail isn't worth the time it takes to download it. File descriptions and thumbnails go a long way toward avoiding that potential, but sometimes you just have to see an image full size to pass judgment. That's what the graphics viewer is for. By the time a third of a graphic is received, you'll probably know whether you want it or not. Just keep your eyes on the screen and be ready to click that Cancel button (it's mostly hidden behind the viewer in Figure 5-10) if you don't like what you see.

Graphics Viewer Trivia

Many regular users aren't aware of it, but AOL's graphics viewer can be used to open existing graphics stored on your hard disk—whether you're online or off—and store them in either the BMP, GIF, or JPG format. In other words, you can not only use your AOL software to download graphics, you can use it to open them whenever you want—online or off—and change their formats if you need to.

To change a graphics format, choose Save As from AOL's File menu whenever a graphics window is open, then select the format you desire from the List Files of Type list box in the file-saving window. AOL will change the filename extension automatically.

There's more: ten image-modification tools are available whenever you have a graphics image open. You can adjust the graphic's brightness and contrast, flip or mirror the image, convert it to grayscale, or even make a negative out of it. To see the image toolbox, choose Show Image Tools from AOL's Edit menu whenever a graphics window is active.

Aimless Roving

The graphics example I've been using assumes your browsing is focused: I was looking for a graphic when I found that picture—a graphic that was to serve a specific purpose.

Often, browsing is less deliberate. Sometimes you go to a bookstore for a novel; sometimes you go to a bookstore for a book. There's a big difference. Browsing for files is much the same.

If you're browsing for browsing's sake, investigate AOL's Software Center at keywords: **Software Center** (see Figure 5-11). The Software Center is a bookstore of files. As you would expect, it supports browsing of the specific variety, but it also offers a splendid opportunity to browse aimlessly.

Figure 5-11:
The Software Cen-
ter is the place to
find AOL's best
downloading fare.

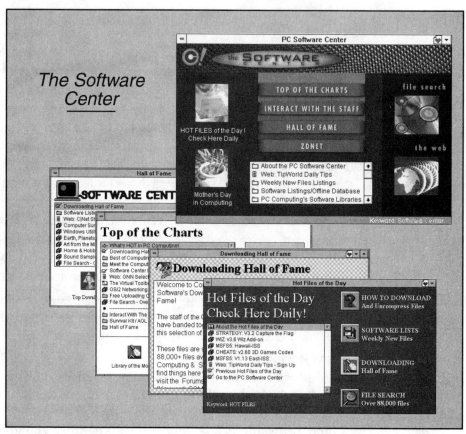

Look at those categories in Figure 5-11: The Downloading Hall of Fame, Top of the Charts, Hot Files of the Day—the list goes on, as you can see.

The libraries in the Software Center are updated every week; make it one of the places you visit on a regular basis.

Searching for Files Offline

If you're a dedicated downloading zealot, you should know about the Software Center's downloadable database of files. All you need to do is download the database each week and search it offline, on your own time. The database is in dBase format: if you have dBase or a dBase-compatible program, you can use it to do the searching. If you don't have such a program, AOL provides a public domain database program for the purpose (see Figure 5-12). It sure beats poking around while the clock's running.

Figure 5-12:
The AOLDBF pro-
gram, running
inside of a DOS
window. OK, it's
not Windows and
it's not very pretty,
but it allows you to
search AOL's librar-
ies offline, and
that's a moneysaver.

```
┌─────────────────────────────────────────────────────────────────┐
│ ─                          MS-DOS Prompt                    ▼ ▲▼ │
│ Record # 20/61                        File: GR2      Last Update: 10/16/95 │
│                       America Online, Inc.                        │
│                    PC Software Center Database                    │
│                  Computing and Software Libraries                 │
│                  Public Domain Software by Joe Nuvolini           │
│                                                    ╔══ Version 2.0 ═╗│
│  Filename:  ACROBAT.JPG              Filesize (K):  135           │
│                                                                   │
│  Subject:   24BIT: Stunt Plane                                    │
│                                                                   │
│  Uploader:  Holvenstot                                           │
│                                                                   │
│  Forum:     Graphics               Library:     24Bit Transprt/Mil│
│                                                                   │
│  Keywords:  Holvenstot, Airplane, Flight, Vehicle, 24 Bit, DF, JD │
│                                                                   │
│  Forums:   Applications    Games             OS/2                 │
│            DeskMate        Graphics          Telecom              │
│            Development     Hardware          Windows              │
│            DOS             Music and Sound   Software Center      │
│                                                                   │
│  Next Prev Top Bottom Search Libr Edit Add Del View Report Clean Join File Quit │
└─────────────────────────────────────────────────────────────────┘
```

To download the database, visit the Software Center at keyword:
Software, or use the keywords: **File Search** and the criterion: AOLDBF.
You'll find both the program and the database listings. Download the
program once. Download the listings each week as they're updated.

Filenames & File Compression

The number of potential file formats for downloaded files is staggering.
Fortunately, some standards and conventions help to organize the
confusion.

Filenames

All downloadable files for Windows follow DOS naming conventions.
DOS filenames allow a maximum of eight characters, followed by a
period, followed by a three-character filename extension:
wz60wn16.zip, for example. The three-character extension is particularly useful. All you have to do is look at an extension to see what kind
of file it is. Filenames ending in .xls are Excel worksheets, for example.
Those ending in .txt are text files and are readable by most word
processors and text editors, including the AOL software itself. Those
ending in .zip are files compressed using a file-compression utility
(more about these later in this chapter). And those ending in .jpg are
graphics files.

The chart pictured in Figure 5-13 identifies some of the common filename extensions and their meanings. Your AOL software is compatible with a surprisingly large number of these formats. It really can open sound and video files, and play them too—assuming you have the hardware for it.

Figure 5-13:
Filename extensions for some of the most common file formats you'll find online. Those marked with an asterisk can be opened with your AOL software.

Filename Extensions

Textual formats

*TXT	Unformatted ASCII text
RTF	Rich Text Format
DOC	Microsoft Word, WordPerfect

Graphic formats

*BMP	Windows bitmaps
TIF	Tagged-image file format
*GIF	Graphic interchange format
*JPG	Joint Photographic Experts Group
*PCX	PC Paintbrush, Windows Paintbrush
WMF	Windows Metafile
EPS	Encapsulated PostScript

Compressed formats

ZIP	PKZip (AOL unzips automatically)
EXE	Executable self-extracting archive
SIT	StuffIt (Macintosh)
ARC	Archives (AOL decompresses automatically)

Other formats

*WAV	Windows audio
*MID	Musical Instrument Digital Interface
*AU	Sun workstation audio
*AVI	Video for Windows
MPG	Motion Picture Experts Group

File Compression

Look again at Figure 5-13. Four *compressed* formats are identified there, and they require further explanation.

Why compress files? There are three good reasons: (1) compressed files are much smaller than files that haven't been compressed and thus take significantly less time to download; (2) compressed files require less storage space; and (3) compressed files are often stored in an archive (several files compressed into a single file). Archives are a convenient way of grouping multiple files for storage and downloading.

Amazingly, compressed files can be reduced to as little as 20 percent of the original size; yet when they're decompressed, absolutely no data are lost. I don't know how they do it. Smoke and mirrors, I suppose.

Figure 5-14: The original image on the left measures 21,394 bytes. The image on the right was compressed to 9,111 bytes (43 percent of the original), then decompressed for printing. No data were lost; both pictures are identical. (Scanning and retouching by David Palermo.)

What's wrong with compressed files? They're useless until they're *de*compressed. The compressed image in Figure 5-14 couldn't be included in the illustration until it was decompressed. In other words, you must have decompression software before you can use compressed images. That's the bad news. The good news is that you already have decompression software: it's part of the AOL software package installed in your PC.

PKZip

A shareware program called *PKZip* is responsible for a great deal of the file compression encountered in the PC environment. PKZip can compress (or *zip*, as it's called) a single file or a multitude of files into a single file—an archive. PKZip archives are identified by the .zip filename extension.

Like all archives, PKZip archives must be decompressed (unzipped) before use, and, incredibly, it happens automatically when you use AOL. (A caveat: Only versions 2.5 and later of the AOL software decompress all forms of zipped files automatically. Be sure you're using the latest version by choosing About America Online from the Help menu. The version will be clearly identified there. If you need to upgrade, use the keyword: **Upgrade**.) If compression is done with smoke and mirrors, automatic decompression must be done with smoke and mirrors and an eye of newt. Whatever the technique, it works—and we're the beneficiaries.

When your AOL software downloads a file with .zip in its filename, it makes a note to itself to unzip the file immediately after you sign off. (You must have this option in effect. It's a preference, and preferences are discussed in Appendix E of this book.) An unzipped copy of the file appears on your disk after decompression, ready for use. Your AOL software also automatically decompresses any files with the .arc (for "archive") filename extension.

America Online only gives you the unzipping part of PKZip, and it only unzips (decompresses) archives downloaded using the AOL software. If you want to zip your own files, you'll need your own copy of PKZip. Fortunately, PKZip is available online: use the keywords: **File Search**, then search for PKZip. You'll find a number of files meeting the criterion; be sure you get the latest. PKZip is shareware. If you like the program, pay the shareware fee and you can use it indefinitely with a clear conscience.

WinZip

As great as PKZip is, it's not Windows software. In fact, PKZip steadfastly clings to the archaic DOS interface of command lines and obtuse, exacting syntax. Though a number of shell programs came along—programs that wrapped up PKZip in a pretty Windows interface—they were usually slow and they all required PKZip. The double shareware fees—one for PKZip and one for the shell—were an insult; until *WinZip* came along.

WinZip is available in a Windows 3.1 version that's fully self-contained and does its work effectively, without the need for PKZip. It's fully compatible with PKZip, it's almost as fast—quite a compliment—and it's easy to use. Perhaps best of all, WinZip offers an extensive help file for those few occasions when you need it.

The downloading exercise at the beginning of this chapter describes how to locate and download WinZip.

Self-Extracting Archives

You now know all about compressed files, but there is another type of archive you'll find online: the *self-extracting archive*. Just as the name implies, these are archives that decompress themselves when you run them. Self-extracting archives look like DOS programs because they usually end with the .exe filename extension. But so do many decompressed files, so check the download's description. (Refer again to Figure 5-3: WinZip is shipped as a self-extracting archive.)

For example, let's say you find a file online called dummit.exe, and you see this line in the file description:

This file is self-extracting, requiring 112,500 bytes.

That tells you dummit.exe is a self-extracting archive, and it gives you an idea of how many bytes it will take up on your disk when you extract it. You would download it just as you would any other file; but because it's self-extracting, AOL's automatic decompression feature won't work here. That's not a worry. All you need to do is specify dummit.exe after choosing Run from the File Manager's File menu. The files contained within dummit.exe will decompress themselves, if there are more than one (it might be a single file), and you're ready to run the program according to the instructions contained in the online file description.

StuffIt

While PKZip is the file compression standard for Windows, a program called *StuffIt* is the standard for the Macintosh platform. Instead of being zipped and unzipped, StuffIt files (followed by the .sit extension) are "stuffed" and "unstuffed." A number of files suitable for use on either platform—graphics, mostly—were originally constructed on Macintoshes and are stuffed rather than zipped. (This is beginning to sound like a recipe for baked turkey: First stuff, then zip the carcass, then bake at 350 degrees for four hours.)

Stuffed files won't decompress automatically on a PC, nor are they self-extracting archives. To use them, you have to acquire unstuffing software. My favorite is a program called UNSTUFF. I forgive its DOS command-line interface because it's written by the people who wrote StuffIt, which means compatibility is ensured. UNSTUFF is available as freeware on AOL. Use the keywords: **File Search**, then search for UNSTUFF.

Download 101

Even with AOL's automation and downloading conveniences, downloading can be confusing. And though I've tried to explain it thoroughly here, some people are better served by another voice. I'm not offended if you're one of them.

If you have any downloading questions, try using the keywords: **Download 101**. Download 101 is AOL's center for downloading questions and answers, and it's rich in downloading tips and techniques. There's also a downloading simulation there that walks you through the process, explaining each step along the way.

Figure 5-15: Download 101 is the place to get hands-on downloading experience, free of charge.

Best of all, Download 101 is free. Spend as much time there as you need to become familiar and comfortable with the downloading process. All it costs is your time.

Uploading Files

With all this talk about downloading, it's easy to forget that before a file can be *down*loaded, it first must be *up*loaded. True to its community spirit, AOL depends on its members for most of its files—members like you and me. Uploading isn't the exclusive realm of AOL employees and forum staff, nor is it the realm of the weenies and the dweebs. Most of the files you can download from AOL—I'd guess more than 90 percent—have been uploaded by members, using PCs just like yours.

Earlier I defined downloading as "the process of transferring a file from AOL's computers to a disk on your computer." Uploading is just the reverse: the process of transferring a file from a disk on your computer to a disk on AOL's computers. Once received, it's checked for viruses and the quality of its content, then it's posted. The process rarely takes more than a day. Upload a file on Monday, and you'll probably see it available for downloading Tuesday morning.

The Uploading Process

Begin the uploading process by visiting the forum where your file seems to fit (forums are discussed in Chapter 9, "Boards & Forums"). If it's a graphic, post it in the Graphic Arts Forum. If it's poetry, post it in the Writers Club. Once you're in the forum, select the library that's the most appropriate place for your file (if there's more than one library in the forum) and click the Upload File button. (Some forums have a button marked Submit a File; use this button if it's available.) Also note that some forums have very specific libraries marked Free Uploading and New Files—send your uploaded files there. Be sure, too, to read any files marked "Read This Before Uploading," or the like. They usually contain information specific to uploading material to that forum.

Recently I uploaded a magazine article to the Writers Club. When I clicked on the Upload button, I received the Upload File Information form pictured in Figure 5-16. You'll encounter this form every time you upload a file to AOL.

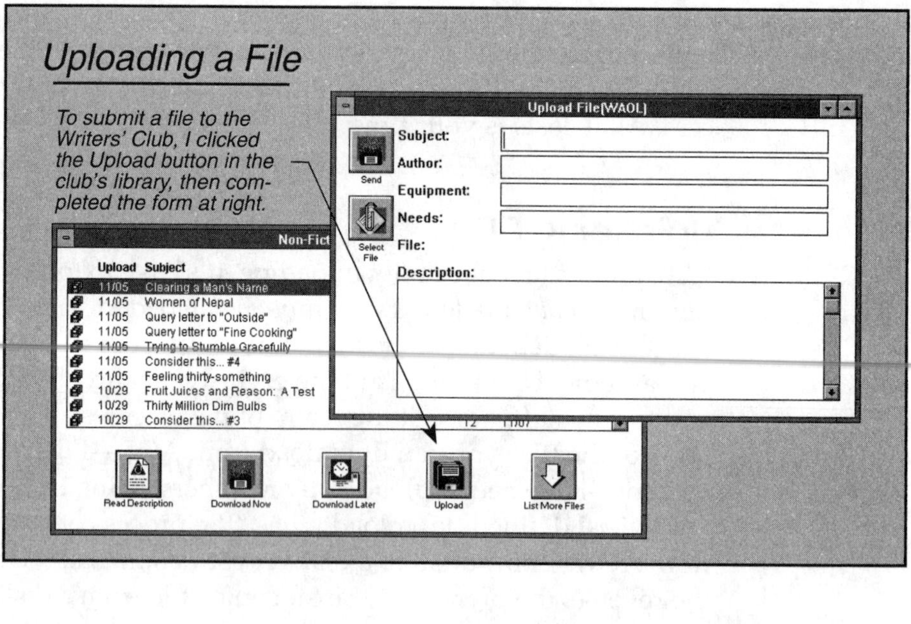

Figure 5-16:
You'll be asked to fill out the Upload File information form for every file you upload to America Online.

Uploading a File

To submit a file to the Writers' Club, I clicked the Upload button in the club's library, then completed the form at right.

The Upload File Information Form

All too often, uploaders fail to complete the Upload File information form adequately. This form "sells" your file to other members, and what you have to say about it determines whether a member will take the time to download it. Here are some hints for creating accurate, useful, and compelling descriptions of files you upload.

- The *Subject* field should be descriptive and catchy, in that order. Look at Figure 5-16. Do you see how the subjects are listed there? The subject line is your headline. If you want members to read your story, hook 'em with a really great subject line.

- The *Equipment* line should identify any special equipment required to access the file. A 24-bit graphic requires a 24-bit color card; VGA won't do. As mentioned earlier, some people use this line to list what they used to create the file, although this is generally not proper protocol.

- The *Needs* line is where you specify the particular software application or program required to access your file. An Excel worksheet, for example, requires the Excel spreadsheet program.

- The *Description* field is where you get specific. Here you differentiate your file from others that might be similar. If you're submitting a program, you should include the version number. Be specific and persuasive: you're selling your file here. Think about what you would want to read if you were considering downloading the file. Make it sound irresistible.

If you're submitting a number of related files, or if your file is larger than about 50K, compress it (or them) using PKZip or something equivalent. This saves downloading time, and it's the polite way to offer your material. There are many different versions of PKZip. Before you upload, ask your Forum Leader which version is preferable.

Concluding the Uploading Process

America Online's by-now-familiar progress indicator will keep you entertained while the upload is under way, followed by a dialog box announcing your success. The time spent uploading your file will be credited back to you. Though you might not see the credit before you sign off, it will appear soon thereafter.

To check your billing information, use the keyword: **Billing**. A day or so after your upload is completed, you should see a note crediting your account with any time you have spent uploading files. The billing area is free, so you won't be charged for whatever time you spend online checking your account's billing information.

Moving On

It's time for you to get your second wind. Though we've covered a parking lot full of technicalities, there's more.

Much more, in fact. Your AOL software is not only capable of downloading, it's not only capable of downloading multiple files in one session, it's also capable of downloading multiple files in only one *unattended* session—in the middle of the night, if that's when you choose to do your downloading (and you might: system activity is minimal in the middle of the night; files transfer faster). Your AOL software is also capable of conducting all of your mail activities at the same time, so your new mail is already retrieved and waiting for you first thing in the morning. These are the features of FlashSessions and the Download Manager. We discuss them next.

FlashSessions & the Download Manager

The greatest volume of mail I receive from my *Tour Guide* readers comes in response to this chapter. These people are thrilled. They've discovered AOL's two automation features—FlashSessions and the Download Manager—and they are dancing rapturously on the virtual sidewalks of the electronic community. If AOL has to deliver your mail with a forklift and you've been reading and responding to it online, you're going to love what this chapter has to say.

There's more: if you're a downloading zealot—if you collect shareware, utilities, fonts, and graphics the way Woody Allen collects troubles, you too will want to read this chapter. Your AOL software can sign on in the middle of the night—to take advantage of minimum online traffic and maximum transfer speeds—and download a queue of files you've scheduled for downloading. It can even resurrect partially downloaded files—files that were interrupted in mid-download when you lost the connection or the cat chewed the phone line in half.

AOL offers solutions to all of these problems: FlashSessions and the Download Manager.

What Are FlashSessions?

A *FlashSession* is an automated online session. At its highest level of automation, a FlashSession signs on at a predetermined time, downloads all of your incoming e-mail, downloads any files you identified earlier for transfer, and uploads any e-mail you've prepared but not sent. When all of that is completed, the FlashSession signs off, leaving a note on your screen telling you what happened and when, along with notification of any errors encountered.

Many people use FlashSessions in a spontaneous fashion, invoking them manually as they work (I just invoked one a moment ago, to check my mail while I write this paragraph), or at the conclusion of an online session—sort-of an "I'm ready to sign off now: clean everything up for me and sign off" command.

Others—people who conduct business via e-mail and need to check their mailboxes frequently during the day—schedule their Flash-Sessions to run automatically every hour or half-hour, maintaining an almost continuous connection with AOL and, therefore, with their e-mail community.

There are even a few people who schedule their FlashSessions to occur in the wee hours of the morning, preferring to conduct the majority of their online events when network traffic is light and connect times are minimal. These are people who delight in seeing their e-mail waiting for them when they awaken, sort of like breakfast in bed.

Futility Revisited

In Chapter 3, you sent yourself a letter. Yes, it was an exercise in futility, but you saw e-mail in action. We're about to repeat the exercise, but this time we'll have the computer do it for us. We'll experience not just futility; we'll experience *automated* futility. This is *not* what computing is supposed to be, but it might prove to be enlightening.

Do not sign on. Rather, run your AOL software and choose Compose Mail from the Mail menu. As you did in Chapter 3, prepare a short message to yourself. Your Compose Mail window should look something like the one pictured in Figure 6-1. (Be sure to put your screen name, *not mine*, in the To: box. You'd be amazed at the amount of mail I receive with "This is a test of FlashSessions" in the message field.)

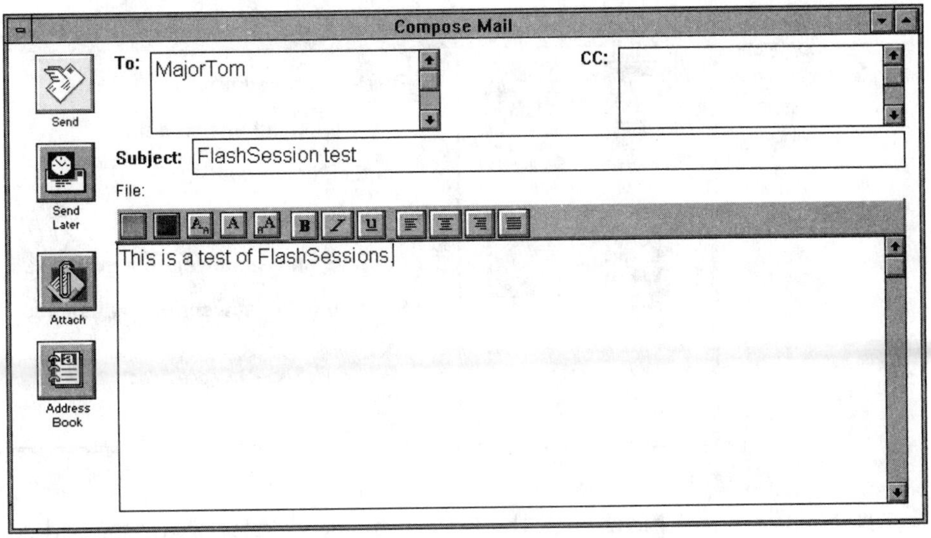

Figure 6-1:
Compose a
message to your-
self, using *your*
screen name in the
To: field.

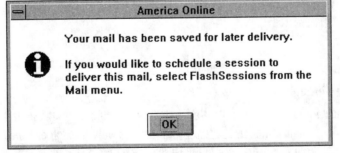

> Note that the Send button is dimmed. Since you're not online, this command is not available. Instead, click the Send Later button. Unless you've changed your preferences from the default (preferences are discussed in Appendix E, "Preferences"), AOL will reply with the message pictured in Figure 6-2.

Figure 6-2:
America Online
confirms your
request to Send
Later.

> Note that the dialog box shown in Figure 6-2 suggests that you "...select FlashSessions from the Mail menu." Do that now by choosing Setup FlashSession from the Mail menu.

> A FlashSession window will appear (see Figure 6-3), including all the check boxes.

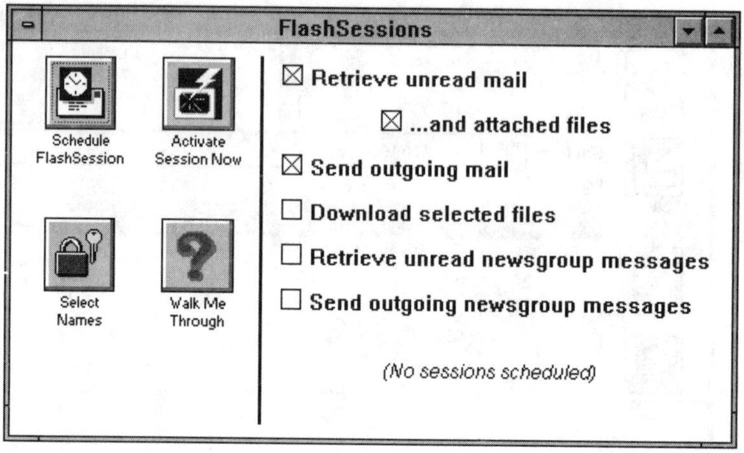

Figure 6-3:
Configure
FlashSessions in the
FlashSessions
window.

FlashSessions

Schedule
FlashSession

Activate
Session Now

Select
Names

Walk Me
Through

☒ Retrieve unread mail

    ☒ ...and attached files

☒ Send outgoing mail

☐ Download selected files

☐ Retrieve unread newsgroup messages

☐ Send outgoing newsgroup messages

(No sessions scheduled)

🔺 Now click the button marked Select Names, and complete the resulting form as pictured in Figure 6-4. Select the screen name you want to use (if you have more than one) and enter the password you use (for that screen name) when you sign on to AOL. Your screen name will appear in place of mine, and the number of characters in your password will probably differ as well. (Notice that your password isn't displayed as you type: asterisks representing each letter in your password appear instead. That's as it should be. You never know who's looking over your shoulder.) When you have completed the Select Screen Names form, click the OK button.

Walk Me Through

If you're new to FlashSessions, AOL offers a step-by-step tutorial on the subject (see the Walk Me Through button in Figure 6-3). In fact, the walk-through executes automatically during your first visit to the FlashSession area, walking you through the FlashSession setup process with extensive verbal instructions along the way. It might even escort you through this exercise.

    The walk-through only executes automatically once. After that, you can always click the Walk Me Through button to invoke it again. If you're an infrequent FlashSession user and prone to absentmindedness, this feature always stands ready to serve.

Figure 6-4:
Complete the
Select Screen
Names form.

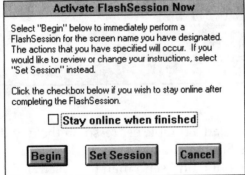

 Back at the Sign-On window, choose Activate Session Now from
the Mail menu. America Online will respond with the form pictured in Figure 6-5.

Figure 6-5:
If this is your first
FlashSession, read
these instructions
carefully and
review your
FlashSession
actions if you want.

 The "Stay online when finished" feature allows you to run a
FlashSession—sending and receiving mail and newsgroup postings,
uploading and downloading files—then stay online for more events
after the FlashSession concludes. That's not our intention at the
moment. For the purposes of this exercise, be sure the Stay online
when finished option is cleared, as shown in Figure 6-5.

 Click the button marked Begin. America Online takes over
(Figure 6-6).

Figure 6-6:
The FlashSession
signs on, "flashes"
your mail to AOL
Headquarters in
Virginia, and signs
off—all in seconds.

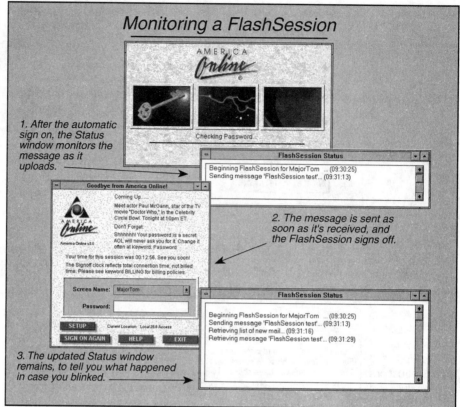

AOL must have had a double espresso on the day that I produced Figure 6-6: this FlashSession has resulted in both an upload and a download. Not only did I send mail to myself, I also received it— all during the same FlashSession. This isn't always the case. Sometimes the e-mail system is too busy to turn a piece of mail around and send it back before the FlashSession signs off. Don't be surprised if you have to run your FlashSession a second time in order to receive the sent mail.

Regardless of whether you've had to run a second FlashSession or not, you've got mail, and you need to read it. But you're not online. How do you read mail when you're offline?

♠ Pull down the Mail menu. Choose the Read Incoming FlashMail command, which should now be available (see the top portion of Figure 6-7).

Figure 6-7:
You can read mail offline when it's convenient for you and the clock's not running.

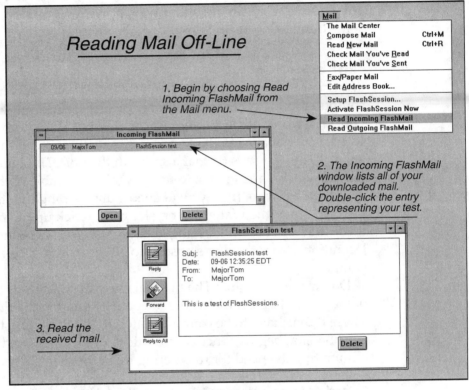

♠ The Incoming FlashMail window will appear (see the middle portion of Figure 6-7). Double-click the entry representing your test.

♠ A second window will open (Figure 6-7, bottom), containing the text of your test. After you've read it, delete it by clicking the Delete button in the lower right corner.

I'm reminded of a big Mercedes sedan I read about the other day. In an irrational effort to remain the technological leader among automobiles, Mercedes equipped the car with *motorized headrests*! Now *that's* technology. Our exercise was a little like that. We threw technology at a task that was no doubt best left undone. At least we're in good company.

Scheduling FlashSessions

You can invoke a FlashSession at any time, whether you're online or off. Alternatively, you can schedule FlashSessions to occur at predetermined intervals: every day, every hour—whenever you please. Before any FlashSession can get under way, however, you have to tell AOL some things it needs to know.

FlashSession Setup

I can hear it now: it's 4:00 a.m. and the AOL voice calls from my computer in the other room. "Tom," it says, "come out here and type in your password!" Bleary-eyed, I stumble to my PC and type my password. I crawl back into bed and start to drift off when the voice calls again. "Tom," it says (is that a smirk in the voice?), "come out here and tell me which screen name to use!" Again, I stumble to the PC, tripping over the dog, who, rudely awakened, runs yelping into the hall table, knocking over the Waterford crystal vase. I pick up the pieces, hiding those that don't seem to fit together any longer, and Band-Aid the laceration across the dog's nose. I do all this smiling, of course. Always smiling.

Do I make my point? The manual entry of passwords and screen names would defeat the whole purpose of unattended FlashSessions. These things have to be communicated to the PC before the first FlashSession begins. Once communicated, they're stored on disk, eliminating the need for re-entering them for each subsequent session.

Selecting Screen Names & Entering Stored Passwords

Many AOL members use more than one screen name. Perhaps more than one member of your family uses the service. Maybe you have an alter ego. Perhaps you're shy, or famous, or reclusive, and you don't want anyone to see your real name on the screen. Whatever the reason, if you use more than one screen name, you have to tell your PC which of these names to use for FlashSessions, and if you want them to run unattended, you'll have to enter a password for each screen name.

Selecting names and entering passwords is easy, and once it's done you won't need to do it again unless you want to reconfigure your FlashSessions. I won't linger here, as we've already selected a name and entered a password during the exercise that led off this chapter. Figure 6-8 shows you how to do it.

Figure 6-8:
The Setup
FlashSessions
command under
the Mail menu takes
you to the entry
form for selecting
names and storing
passwords.

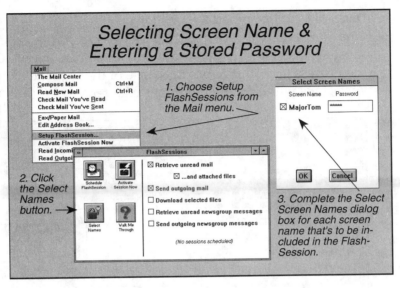

Though Figure 6-8 illustrates the selection of a single screen name (and entry of a password for that screen name), the Select Screen Names form will include all of the screen names you are using for your account, up to the maximum of five. Activate only the check boxes for the screen names you want included in your FlashSessions, and include the password for each (only if you intend to have your FlashSessions occur while you're away).

Caution!

There's a minor potential for unauthorized use of your account whenever you store your passwords, even if you store them only for the use of FlashSessions. I'm getting ahead of myself, but peek ahead at Figure 6-10 and note the check box labeled "Stay online when finished." This check box allows anyone with access to your computer to invoke what's called an *offline* FlashSession, which normally signs on in response to the operator's command, does all of its FlashSession activities, then signs off. That last step, however, is omitted if the Stay online when finished box is checked. In effect, this allows anyone with a little AOL savvy to run a FlashSession on your account, then stay online to do as he or she pleases, for as long as he or she wishes—all without needing to know your password. If there's a potential for this kind of abuse around your machine (and there always is with laptops, which are frequently stolen), don't store passwords.

Declaring the Download Destination

One more setup task remains before you can start a FlashSession: you must declare a destination for downloaded files. Figure 6-9 illustrates the process and offers a brief glimpse of the Download Manager, a subject we will discuss later in this chapter.

Figure 6-9:
The Download
Manager lets you
specify where you
want to save
downloaded files.
The DOWNLOAD
subdirectory in
your AOL30 direc-
tory is the default.

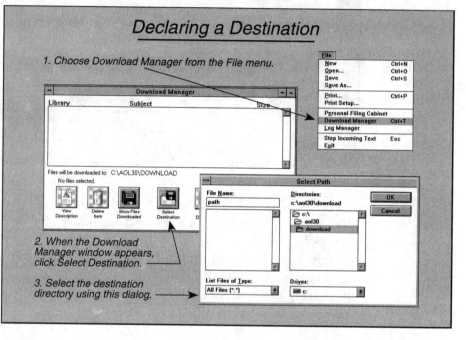

Attended FlashSessions

Now that you've stored your screen names, passwords, and destinations, you're ready to run a FlashSession. The exercise that began this chapter describes an *attended FlashSession*—one that occurs when you issue a FlashSession command. Let's examine attended FlashSessions first.

Many FlashSessions occur when you're about to wrap up an online session. There's something organic about the flow of an online session: after a couple of months online, you'll glide from one task to another with all the fluidity of warm honey. About the last thing you'll want to do is interrupt your progress with a download or the transmission of a piece of mail. Instead, you can schedule a FlashSession to take care of these things when your session has concluded. More about this in a moment.

Another kind of attended FlashSession occurs when you're offline and want your PC to sign on, transfer mail and files, and sign off. As you saw during the earlier exercise, the advantage here is speed. FlashSessions "know" exactly what they're doing; they waste no time, they waste no money, and you don't have to stick around while they're under way.

Offline Attended FlashSessions

This is exactly what we did during the earlier exercise in this chapter. You begin an offline FlashSession not by signing on but rather by choosing Activate FlashSession Now from the Mail menu (shown at the top of Figure 6-10). When the Activate Session Now form appears (see the bottom of Figure 6-10), click the Begin button.

Normally, this is all you need to do to run an offline attended FlashSession. When you click the Begin button, your PC signs on, does everything it's been told to do, then signs off. It repeats the process for each of the screen names you've indicated. When the dust settles, a FlashSession Status window remains on your screen to inform you of what happened (Figure 6-11). This is more a necessity than a convenience. Without the FlashSession Status window, you might have to perform some major sleuthing to find out what happened during a FlashSession, especially one that occurred in your absence.

Figure 6-10:
Once your screen
name and pass-
word are stored, a
menu selection and
a mouse click are
all it takes to run an
offline attended
FlashSession.

Running an Off-Line FlashSession

Mail

The Mail Center	
Compose Mail	Ctrl+M
Read New Mail	Ctrl+R
Check Mail You've Read	
Check Mail You've Sent	
Fax/Paper Mail	
Edit Address Book...	
Setup FlashSession...	
Activate FlashSession Now	
Read Incoming FlashMail	
Read Outgoing FlashMail	

1. Choose Activate FlashSession Now from the Mail menu.

Activate FlashSession Now

Select "Begin" below to immediately perform a FlashSession for the screen name you have designated. The actions that you have specified will occur. If you would like to review or change your instructions, select "Set Session" instead.

Click the checkbox below if you wish to stay online after completing the FlashSession.

☐ **Stay online when finished**

| Begin | Set Session | Cancel |

2. When you click the Begin button, AOL will use the screen names you identified earlier.

Do You Know Who You Are?

There's a bit of a trap waiting for you if you follow the two steps illustrated in Figure 6-10 and aren't paying attention. It's not apparent what screen names AOL will use during the upcoming FlashSession. Review the Select Screen Names window in Figure 6-8, if necessary. Note that AOL will run a FlashSession for each name that's selected in the Select Screen Names window, not just the screen name that's currently showing in the Welcome (sign-on) window. Be sure you know which names are selected in the Select Screen Names window before you allow your FlashSessions to run.

Figure 6-11:
The FlashSession
Status window lets
you know what
happened during a
FlashSession, just in
case you weren't
watching.

FlashSession Status

```
Beginning FlashSession for MajorTom   ... (12:38:38)
Retrieving list of new mail... (12:39:21)
Retrieving message 'testamonial'... (12:39:25)
Retrieving message 'Chicago Book'... (12:39:26)
Retrieving message 'The Comedy Club'... (12:39:28)
Retrieving message 'Heavenly frogs'... (12:39:29)
Retrieving message 'Parise for the Tour Guide'... (12:39:30)
Downloading files attached to mail... (12:39:30)
Downloading file AMONLINE.TXT (12:39:30)
testamonial has been transferred. (12:39:35)
P4PS: V2.01 Postscript Print Util has been transferred. (12:41:30)
Batch file transfer ended (12:41:30)
FlashSession is complete. (12:41:31)
member P4PS.EXE successfully extracted. (12:41:32)
```

Look again at Figure 6-11. I received five pieces of new mail (one with an attached file) and downloaded a file I'd scheduled for download earlier. The America Online software even extracted (decompressed) my downloaded file for me.

It isn't uncommon for only two entries to appear there, representing the start and finish of a FlashSession, with nothing in between. This isn't as meaningless as it might seem. If there was no activity during a session I had scheduled for the middle of the night, I would be aware of that the next morning, and I wouldn't waste time looking for mail or files that weren't there. Of additional benefit is notification of errors. If I incorrectly addressed some mail or if the session was interrupted for some reason, I'd read about it here.

Online Attended FlashSessions

Another form of attended FlashSession is the one that occurs at sign-off. During a typical online session, you might visit a forum or two, mark some files for downloading, reply to some mail, and perhaps compose some new mail. Downloads in particular can disrupt the flow of an online session. Sitting at your PC watching a progress indicator is not the best use of your time. That's why AOL provides sign-off FlashSessions.

When you've done everything you want to do online, choose Activate FlashSession Now from the Mail menu (rather than selecting Sign Off from the Go To menu—see the top of Figure 6-12), click the Sign off when finished option, then click the Begin button (see the bottom of Figure 6-12). This is one alternative to the Sign Off command; the other is the Download Manager, which I'll discuss later in this chapter. Either one will work if activity remains that doesn't require your involvement.

Note that you can choose either to stay online after the FlashSession concludes (which is the default, as shown in Figure 6-12), or to have the software automatically sign off after your FlashSession activities have ended (see Figure 6-13). You will have to specifically activate the Sign off when finished option if it's your preference.

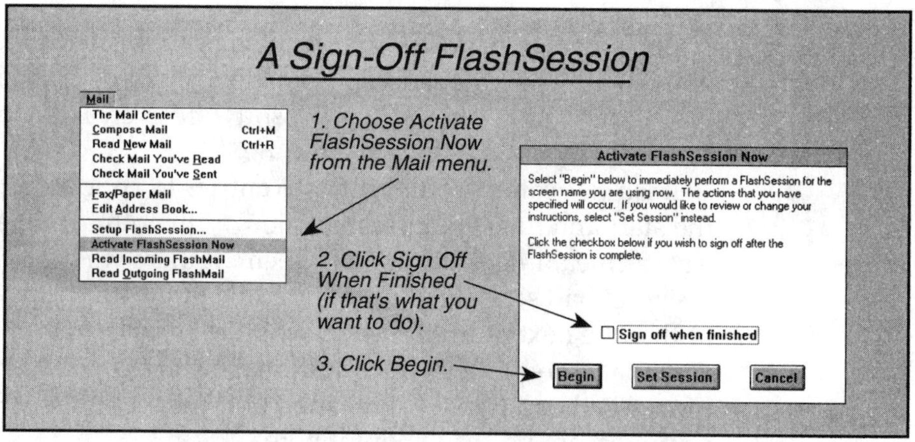

Figure 6-12:
Rather than choose Sign Off from the Go To menu, choose Activate FlashSession Now from the Mail menu. All your queued downloads and mail routines will become a part of the sign-off routine.

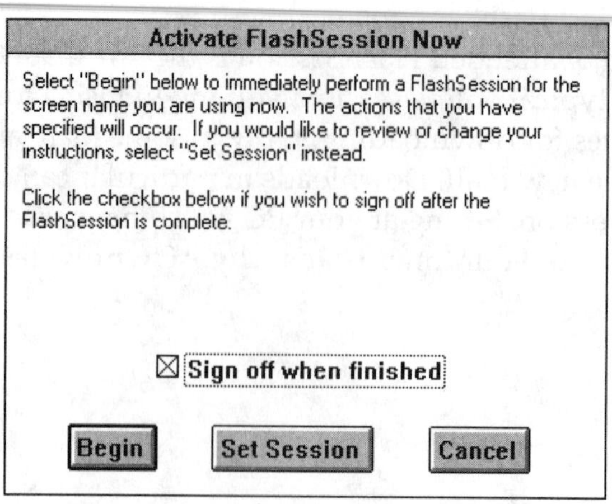

A Sign-Off FlashSession

Mail
The Mail Center
Compose Mail   Ctrl+M
Read New Mail   Ctrl+R
Check Mail You've Read
Check Mail You've Sent
Fax/Paper Mail
Edit Address Book...
Setup FlashSession...
Activate FlashSession Now
Read Incoming FlashMail
Read Outgoing FlashMail

1. Choose Activate FlashSession Now from the Mail menu.

Activate FlashSession Now

Select "Begin" below to immediately perform a FlashSession for the screen name you are using now. The actions that you have specified will occur. If you would like to review or change your instructions, select "Set Session" instead.

Click the checkbox below if you wish to sign off after the FlashSession is complete.

2. Click Sign Off When Finished (if that's what you want to do).

3. Click Begin.

☐ Sign off when finished

Begin   Set Session   Cancel

Figure 6-13:
Turn on the Sign off when finished option to sign off automatically when a FlashSession concludes.

Activate FlashSession Now

Select "Begin" below to immediately perform a FlashSession for the screen name you are using now. The actions that you have specified will occur. If you would like to review or change your instructions, select "Set Session" instead.

Click the checkbox below if you wish to sign off after the FlashSession is complete.

☒ Sign off when finished

Begin   Set Session   Cancel

Where'd That File Go?

FlashSessions not only receive any mail that AOL is holding for you, they also download any files that are attached to that mail. Unfortunately, the destination of those downloads is often obscure and you're forced to scour your hard disk after the FlashSession, looking for the e-mail attachments it has downloaded.

Like all computer programs, AOL only does what it's told. In the case of files attached to e-mail, it defaults to the directory identified by the Download Manager. Though I'll discuss the Download Manager later in this chapter, all you have to do to find your files is choose Download Manager from the File menu. The path to the downloading directory will be plainly identified in the resulting window.

Unattended FlashSessions

My agent uses e-mail. My publisher uses e-mail. My editor uses e-mail. Indeed, most authors and many others in the book-publishing business work at home, and most manuscripts and related communications are exchanged electronically. There are days when communication sparks across the continent like migrating locusts. Contracts are negotiated, manuscripts are edited, illustrations tweaked—sometimes five or six times a day.

The literary profession isn't unique in its reliance on e-mail. For lawyers, salespeople, brokers, and others who need to send messages— across town, across the country, or around the world—*unattended FlashSessions* are beyond mere conveniences, they're necessities.

On locust days like these, I instruct my FlashSessions to check for mail every half-hour. This they do, in the background, as reliably as clockwork, regardless of what I'm doing with my computer. There's no need to interrupt my train of thought: the FlashSession simply signs on, sends queued mail, receives new mail, and signs off. I don't even have to be in the building. That's why they're called "unattended FlashSessions."

You're not limited to a half-hourly schedule either: you can run unattended FlashSessions as frequently or as infrequently as you desire. Some people even run them in the predawn hours to take advantage of off-peak hours when traffic is light.

Predawn FlashSession Tips

Lots of people run FlashSessions in the middle of the night. Many of these people are downloading zealots: their download sessions often last for hours. Under these conditions, downloading when system activity is minimal—around 4:00 a.m. eastern time—makes significant economic sense.

If a 4:00 a.m. FlashSession appeals to you, be sure to leave your computer on with the AOL software running. Don't forget to leave the modem on too (if it's the external variety), but turn off the monitor if you can: monitors (color, especially) consume a lot of power.

Scheduling Unattended FlashSessions

In addition to choosing screen names and entering stored passwords, one significant task remains: scheduling the time of day and the days of the week that you want AOL to conduct its FlashSessions. Figure 6-14 illustrates the procedure.

Figure 6-14: The Schedule FlashSessions window lets you declare the days and times you want unattended FlashSessions to run. Be sure to check the Enable Scheduler box (it's easy to neglect) or the FlashSession won't run.

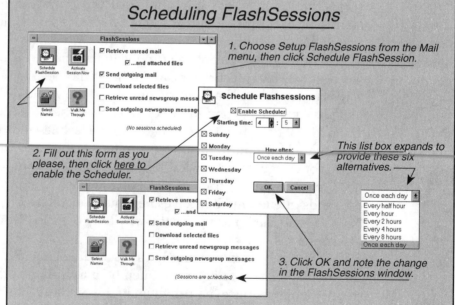

I've assumed here that you've used the FlashSessions window (pictured at the top of Figure 6-14) to check all the activities you want AOL to carry out during a FlashSession. Usually you'll want to select all the activities shown in the illustration.

I've also assumed that you have declared the appropriate screen names (and stored passwords) for which you want the FlashSession to apply. Review Figure 6-4 if you're unsure.

Look again at Figure 6-14. Note that my FlashSessions are scheduled for 5 minutes after the hour. In fact, I only have two choices: 5 or 35 minutes after the hour. America Online arbitrarily assigned these times when I joined. Yours will differ from mine, and so will those of everyone else. America Online staggers FlashSession times to distribute the load on AOL's host machines. If given our druthers, most of us would probably choose to run our FlashSessions on the hour or the half-hour—that's human nature. But AOL's machines would bog down, answering thousands of simultaneous phone calls. Offering limited random times is AOL's way of avoiding FlashSession overload.

Excepting Incoming Files

Just last week, I attempted to send some e-mail to a friend. Attached to the message was a 270K file. Unfortunately, I misspelled his screen name in the To: box of the Compose Mail form. Even more unfortunately, the misspelling meant the mail went to another legitimate AOL screen name—along with the 270K file. Though I re-sent the mail to the proper person later, the person who was on the receiving end of the misdirected mail was no doubt quite displeased with me if his FlashSession downloaded my file. My error might have cost him 10 minutes or more of connect time.

In other words, to protect yourself from encountering a mistake like the one I inadvertently inflicted on that unsuspecting AOL member, you might want to deactivate the "...and attached files" option in the FlashSessions window (see the top window in Figure 6-14). "On" is the default; you might want to change that. After all, you can always sign back on to download files, but you can't undo the cost of a lengthy unwanted download once it's done.

Reading FlashMail

It only makes sense that AOL lets you read incoming FlashMail. What's interesting is that you can read *outgoing* FlashMail as well. This is especially comforting for those of us who suffer from occasional bouts of irresolution. Until it's actually sent, outgoing FlashMail is ours to edit, append, or "wad up and throw away." (Now that I think about it, you can edit, append, or wad up and throw away mail even after it's sent—as long as it's not Internet mail and as long as no one has read it. Refer to Chapter 3, "Electronic Mail & the Personal Filing Cabinet," if you're not familiar with this feature.)

Reading Incoming Mail

Incoming FlashMail is stored in the Incoming FlashMail folder in your Personal Filing Cabinet. (The Personal Filing Cabinet is discussed in Chapter 3, "Electronic Mail & the Personal Filing Cabinet.") To read incoming FlashMail, use the Read Incoming Mail command under the Mail menu (or choose Personal Filing Cabinet from the Mail menu), open the Mail folder, then open the Incoming FlashMail folder. Most folks use the Read Incoming Mail command under the Mail menu. To read incoming mail using this command, follow the steps illustrated in Figure 6-15.

Figure 6-15:
Reading incoming mail is easy. Because incoming FlashMail is stored on your machine, not AOL's, you can read it when you're offline.

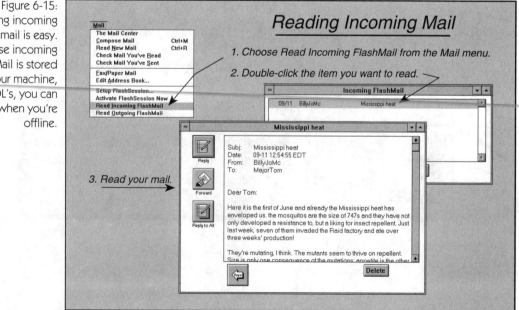

Don't confuse the Read Incoming Mail command with the Check Mail You've Read command, which also appears under the Mail menu. Check Mail You've Read is an online command that allows you to review mail you've already read. The Read Incoming Mail command discussed here is usually issued offline, after a FlashSession has concluded. (Again, review Chapter 3 for a thorough explanation of e-mail commands.)

Watch Those Screen Names!

It's important to note that the only mail appearing in the Read Incoming Mail window is that addressed to the screen name currently appearing in the window that is onscreen when you issued the Read Incoming Mail command. If you've used a FlashSession to download mail for more than one screen name, you must change the screen name in the welcome window (or the goodbye window, if you've signed on and signed off earlier) to identify incoming mail for each of your screen names. Only then will you find all the mail that came in during the session.

Avoid Clutter

As I mentioned earlier, incoming FlashMail is stored in the Incoming FlashMail folder in your Personal Filing Cabinet. All incoming FlashMail messages are stored there until they're deleted or moved, even after they have been read. This is no place to file your mail. Mail left in this folder continues to appear in the Incoming FlashMail window, with the oldest at the top. Discovering new FlashMail under these circumstances can be awkward, and you might even miss a piece or two.

Either file incoming FlashMail in your personal mail folders, or delete it after you've read it. Remember also that if you've set your mail preferences to retain copies, all incoming FlashMail will appear in *two* places in your Personal Filing Cabinet: in the Incoming FlashMail folder and in the Mail You Have Read folder in the Archives folder. Be sure to delete both copies if you delete mail, or file one and delete the other.

The Personal Filing Cabinet is discussed in Chapter 3, "Electronic Mail & the Personal Filing Cabinet." Mail preferences are discussed in Appendix E, "Preferences."

Reading Outgoing Mail

The Read Outgoing Mail command allows you to read outgoing FlashMail before you send it. This command can be invoked either online or off, as long as you've prepared FlashMail for sending but haven't sent it yet.

Again, don't confuse this command with the Check Mail You've Sent command. Check Mail You've Sent is an online command letting you review mail you've sent during the past five days. The Read Outgoing Mail command pertains only to mail you've scheduled for delivery but haven't sent yet.

Figure 6-16:
The Read Outgoing
Mail command is
available only
when mail has
been scheduled
for delivery but
hasn't been sent.

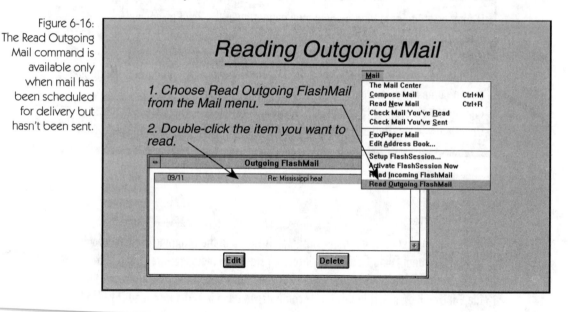

The Download Manager

Downloads probably offer more potential than any other AOL feature. There are tens of thousands of files on AOL's hard disks, and every one of them can be downloaded to your computer. There are millions more on the Internet, and many of those are available to you as well. Using the Download Manager, you can establish a queue of files while you're online, reading descriptions and estimating time. When your session is almost over, you then instruct the Download Manager to download the files and sign off—or schedule a FlashSession to download your files for you later, when system activity is less intrusive. Either way, once the process has begun, you can walk away.

Let's watch a typical Download Manager session to see what the screens look like. We'll schedule two files for downloading; then we'll instruct the Download Manager to handle the downloading process and sign off automatically.

Selecting Files for Downloading

Figure 6-17 illustrates the process of selecting a graphic from the VH1 area (at keyword: **VH1**). This is a particularly rewarding area if you're looking for something to download. It's full of graphics, sound, and—of course—video.

Figure 6-17:
The last step in selecting a VH1 graphic for delayed downloading is to click the Download Later button, which calls up the dialog box at the bottom of the illustration.

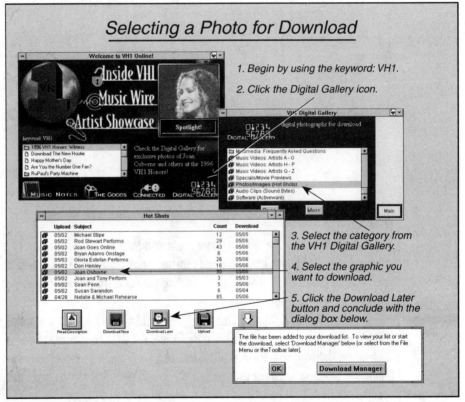

We might as well give the Download Manager more than one thing to do, so let's select another file to add to the download queue. A Mike Keefe political cartoon seems appropriate (see Figure 6-18).

Figure 6-18:
Selecting a Mike
Keefe cartoon for
delayed down-
loading.

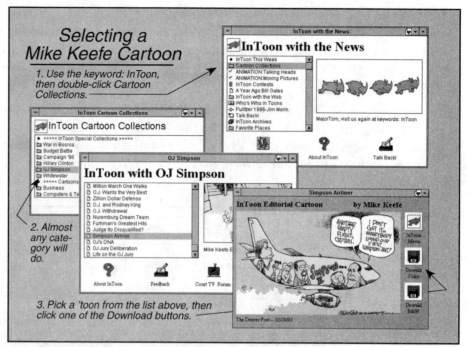

The Control Room

After a couple of hours in the hardware room with Matt Korn (see Chapter 1), my comprehension of things electronic had reached overload. I felt like a tourist inside of a nuclear power plant. You might be feeling the same way, immersed as you are here in AOL's lofty automation features.

Sensing my fatigue, Matt led me to a steel door that opened into a room of contradictory calm and quiet. As I stepped inside, the steel door whooshed shut behind me, latching with the metallic *thunk* of a bank vault. Scores of 21-inch computer monitors lined the room, stacked two and sometimes three high. Seven people scurried about on wheeled chairs, answering incessantly ringing telephones in hushed tones, responding to Instant Messages, and conversing with AOL's online staff working the chat rooms.

This is AOL's control room. Some of its monitors displayed graphical images of AOL's host computer system: webs of interconnections radiating from scores of system processors. Other monitors watched the communications system that connects AOL to the world, displaying, quite graphically, the network of communications links described in Chapter 1. A few text-only monitors tallied the total number of users on the system and the number of logins per minute. The operators watched these seemingly insignificant displays like a driver watches a fuel gauge.

I was reminded of the control room in the movie *The China Syndrome*. The place was alive with drama. I expected the clatter of a klaxon to pierce the air at any minute, and Jack Lemmon to emerge from behind a glass wall, proprietary and custodial. I fantasized myself as Michael Douglas, clandestinely taking pictures from beneath a coat folded over my arm. Where's Jane Fonda when I need her?

Running the Download Manager

Eventually, the time will come to reap the harvest. Rather than sign off, choose Download Manager from the File menu. This is a second alternative to the Sign Off command (the first being Activate FlashSession Now—under the Mail menu—described earlier in this chapter). The Activate FlashSession Now command accommodates both delayed mail and downloading activities, but it doesn't offer the control that the Download Manager does. The Download Manager— under the File menu—doesn't send or receive queued mail or newsgroup postings, but it offers access to all the options pictured in Figure 6-19. If you have mail to send and files to download when you sign off, choose Activate FlashSession Now (and configure the Download Manager ahead of time). If you have only files to download, choose the Download Manager.

Figure 6-19:
The Download
Manager window
lists all files sched-
uled for download,
including sizes,
destinations, and
the estimated
amount of time
required to down-
load the entire
queue.

Download Manager		
Library	**Subject**	**Size**
Chart Library (Daily	Dow Jones Averages	20K
Mike Keefe Editorial	Cuban Migration (bk&wt)	8K

Files will be downloaded to: C:\AOL30\DOWNLOAD

Selected file size: 29K. About 1 minute to download.

View Description	Delete Item	Show Files Downloaded	Select Destination	Start Download	Download Preferences	Help

Note the buttons across the bottom of Figure 6-19. This is an impressive array of commands. America Online wants you to have complete
control over the downloading process, especially now that it's about to
begin.

🔺 *View Description* is the same as the View Description button you
encounter when you're browsing a file library. It's handy to have
this command here. Though you probably read the file's description a half-hour ago, chances are you remember nothing about it
now that you've reached the Download Manager window. Lots of
things could have happened in the interim. This button saves a
long trip back to the file's original location to review its description.

🔺 *Delete Item* allows you to remove a file (or two, or three) from the
list. Sometimes enthusiasm exceeds resources.

🔺 *Show Files Downloaded* lets you review your past downloads. The
number of downloads available for review is set with the Download Preferences button (which we'll discuss in a moment). There's
no value in downloading the same file twice. Though AOL will
warn you if you try to download a file you've already downloaded, you can save yourself the trouble by checking this list first.

- *Select Destination* allows you to declare a destination folder other than the AOL30\DOWNLOAD folder, which is the default. **Note:** All the files in the queue must download to the same folder.

- *Start Download* begins the downloading process. We'll use it in a moment.

- *Download Preferences* allows you to determine whether images are displayed during an attended download. (See Chapter 5, "Transferring Files," for a discussion of the online graphics viewer.) A number of decompression options are presented here (again, see Chapter 5), as is the number of downloads available for review when you click the Show Files Downloaded button. Refer to Appendix E, "Preferences," for a comprehensive discussion of all the AOL preference options.

- The *Help* button produces the Download Manager help screens. These are offline help screens—they reference the help files that are stored locally on your hard disk—thus they're available whether you're online or off.

Pick Up Where You Left Off

Occasionally, the downloading process is interrupted. Lightning strikes. A power cord gets tripped over. The phone line develops a stutter. These kinds of things don't happen often, but when they do they always seem to occur when you're 80 percent of the way through a 47-minute download. *Poof!* There goes 35 minutes of connect time.

Don't worry about it. If a file was interrupted during a download, your AOL software makes a note of it and will resume the download queue where you left off the next time you return to the Download Manager.

The downloading process commences when you click the Start Download button (see Figure 6-20).

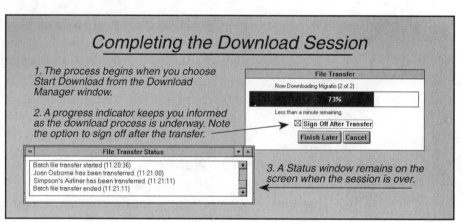

Completing the Download Session

1. The process begins when you choose Start Download from the Download Manager window.

2. A progress indicator keeps you informed as the download process is underway. Note the option to sign off after the transfer.

File Transfer
Now Downloading Migratio (2 of 2)
73%
Less than a minute remaining.
☒ Sign Off After Transfer
Finish Later   Cancel

File Transfer Status
Batch file transfer started (11:20:36)
Joan Osborne has been transferred. (11:21:00)
Simpson's Airliner has been transferred. (11:21:11)
Batch file transfer ended (11:21:11)

3. A Status window remains on the screen when the session is over.

Look again at Figure 6-20. When the Sign Off After Transfer option is selected, you can walk away from the computer while all this is going on, secure in the knowledge that the Download Manager will sign off when everything has been downloaded satisfactorily.

Figure 6-21:
Tack a couple of
downloaded
printouts to your
wall each day;
people will think
you're clever,
erudite, and
urbane.

Suitable for Framing

Moving On

All this time spent talking about FlashSessions and the Download Manager might make you feel like a real yahoo if you don't use them. Don't worry about it: not all AOL members get enough mail or download enough files to make FlashSessions and the Download Manager worthwhile. In other words, you've got plenty of company: the yahoos are the majority.

There's a political statement there, I'm sure; but to explore it would hardly be the way to conclude a chapter. Instead, reward yourself for reading this far by turning the page. The "Computing" chapter follows. That's one subject we all have in common, and AOL offers plenty of information on computers. Read on.

Computing

CHAPTER 7

- The Computers & Software Channel
- Live Events
- Computing Media
- The Computing Company Connection
- A Medley of Computing Essentials

I have a boat—a little cruiser that I can live on for a few weeks at a time, and I do that a lot, here on the splendid waters of the Pacific Northwest. Parts of this book—some would say the better parts—were written afloat.

I won't bore you with boat talk, but I got to thinking that it would be nirvana if I could sign on to AOL and find any- and everything to feed my aquatic habit, at no charge other than my normal connect fee. Just think of it: boat stuff, boat advice—even boats themselves—all available online! Elysian waters, indeed.

Boating

If you are also a boating enthusiast, AOL won't disappoint you. Try the keyword: **Boating**. You'll find *Boating* magazine there, the Sailing Forum, and a place called The Exchange, with ongoing discussions about navigation, tow vehicles, cruising, personal watercraft—the gamut. There are plenty of boating newsgroups too. Use the keyword: **Newsgroups**, then search using the Search All Newsgroups button. The World Wide Web has recently added a variety of boating sites. Use the keyword: **Web**, then use Webcrawler to search for boating subjects (newsgroups and the Web are discussed in Chapter 4, "Using the Internet").

Now if only I could figure out a way to download a nice, 32-foot trawler....

OK, it ain't gonna happen. But my other habit—computing—is amply served in exactly the way I've described. I can get computer programs, drivers, fonts, graphics, sounds, movies, accessories—even the computers themselves—here on AOL. And, with the exception of the hardware, it's all available at nothing more than the cost of my normal connect time and an occasional shareware fee. AOL's computing resources are the consummate carnival—an opiate, a tabernacle, a jubilation for Windows weirdos.

In fact, even if you're not a Windows weirdo, you'll spend a lot of time with AOL's computing resources. There are thousands of files available—fonts and graphics in particular—that will appeal to even the casual Windows user. And if you need help with either your PC or the software you run on it, AOL is ready to oblige. There are stimulating forums here, ranging from the fundamental to the existential. This place is as rife with opportunity as a sunny Saturday in August, and you can enjoy it any day of the year.

The Computers & Software Channel

Almost everything we'll discuss in this chapter falls under the custody of the Computers and Software Channel (see Figure 7-1). You'll find the Computers and Software Channel listed on the listing of channels, or you can use the keywords: **Computers & Software** to get there.

Figure 7-1: The
Computers &
Software Channel
serves as the head-
waters for almost
everything dis-
cussed in this
chapter.

The resources offered by this channel are so vast that I've had to divide them up and present them in various chapters of this book. You'll find a discussion of the Computers & Software Channel forums, for example, in Chapter 9, "Boards & Forums." Many of the Computers & Software Channel's Help resources are discussed in Chapter 2, "The Abecedarium."

Remember that you have two ways to reach any destination available on AOL. You can use either menus (in this case, the Computers & Software Channel would be your "top" menu), or keywords. Menus are effective when you're on a discovery mission; keywords get you where you want to go when you know where that place is and want to get there in a hurry.

Although I'll be offering keywords throughout this chapter, remember that you can also get to most of these places via the Computers & Software Channel's main window, pictured in Figure 7-1. You can take the expressway (keywords) and get to a place quickly, or you can use the Computers & Software Channel to explore an alternate route. The best rewards are often found when you travel the back roads.

Live Events

A unique benefit offered by the online community is real-time conferencing. Although this subject is discussed in Chapter 8, "The Community," it warrants special mention here. Perhaps you've noticed already: people who use computers are never shy when the topic of discussion turns to computing. We have more opinions about computers than Andy Rooney has about politics.

Live computing events occur each week. Many feature celebrities, others feature a computer company representative, and others bring a noted columnist or writer to the stage. Don't confuse these events with one-way media like television or magazines: these are bilateral discussions, and you the member are as much a part of them as the guest. Where else could you sit down and chat with Bill Gates or Steve Wozniak?

Keeping up with the schedule of these appearances, however, is like keeping up with a television schedule. We need some kind of "channel listing" of upcoming live events, and it's available in the Computers & Software Channel's Rotunda window (click the Rotunda icon), where it's called "Upcoming Rotunda Events" (see Figure 7-2).

Figure 7-2:
Tonight in The
Upcoming Rotunda
Events is your
guide to upcoming
live computing
events on AOL.

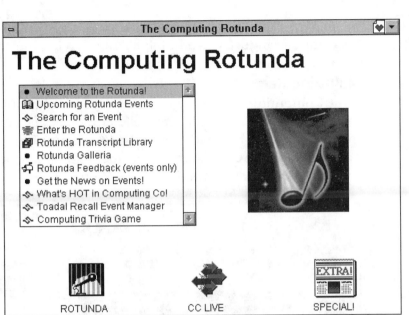

At Your Doorstep

Just like subscribing to *TV Guide*, you can receive notifications of upcoming live events via e-mail. The people at AOL will send you a notice every week listing all of the events scheduled for the following week, including their start times and key-words.

Unlike *TV Guide*, the service is free. Just send e-mail to the screen name: MailEvents. Ask to be placed on the list of upcoming Computing Rotunda events. They'll take care of the rest.

Computing Media

You simply cannot find a computer magazine that doesn't participate in the online medium in some way. In fact, almost every magazine offers an e-mail address. With magazines, an online presence is a conditioned reflex. Magazines aren't the only computing medium that has discovered the online community—television, radio, newspapers, books: they all offer a presence in some way or other, many on AOL. Many are computer industry publications, a few of which I'll describe in the paragraphs that follow. For a discussion of online media beyond the computer industry, read Chapter 10, "Staying Informed."

Magazine Rack

If the Computing Forum is a clearinghouse for everything online that relates to computing, the Magazine Rack area is a clearinghouse for all media online that relate to computing (see Figure 7-3). Here's where you'll find all of AOL's online magazines and radio features, plus links to the most popular computing-media Web sites.

Figure 7-3: Use the keywords: **Magazine Rack** to access all of the computing media resources from one central location.

PC World Online

There's so much great media stuff here, it's hard to know where to begin. One thing I know we all have in common is our PCs, so PC World Online (see Figure 7-4) is probably a good starting point.

Figure 7-4:
Everything but the
ads: nearly every-
thing in the current
issue of *PC World* is
online, plus past
issues and software
libraries. Use the
keywords: **PC
World** to get here.

I visit PC World Online once a month without fail, and whenever I'm contemplating a purchase—hardware or software—I consult the reviews. Last year I researched high-speed CD-ROM drives. After briefly searching past issues, I discovered that the price of the drive I needed—and eventually purchased—was about to drop. I recently heard that 6X CD-ROM drives are available, so once again I consulted the *PC World* archives (see Figure 7-5).

Figure 7-5:
Searching past
issues of *PC World*,
America Online
found an article
describing the
first available 6X
CD-ROM drive.

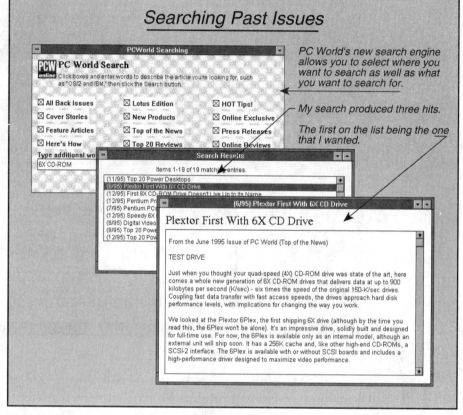

While past issues are a primary feature of PC World Online, hundreds of news stories, reviews, and files also are available—all searchable, and all in a form you can use in documents of your own. In addition, a special section called Message Exchange features message boards that put you in touch with *PC World*'s editorial staff. And a library of files offers indices to past issues, macros, and programs (see Figure 7-6).

Figure 7-6:
A software library,
feature stories, a
question-and-
answer message
board, and an
exclusive area full
of online informa-
tion round out PC
World Online.

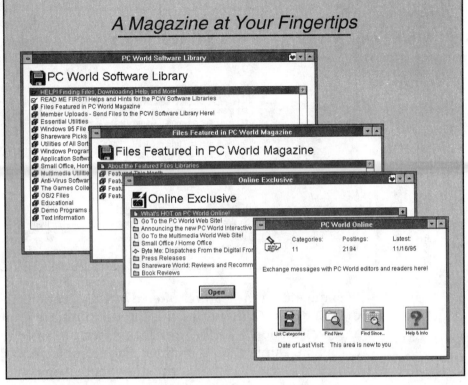

Windows Magazine Online

I subscribe to both *Windows* and *PC World* magazines. Over the past few years I've thought about allowing one of the subscriptions to lapse. But in the end, I realized that I depend on both equally, and simply didn't want to let go of either one.

Imagine my delight when *Windows Magazine* appeared online. This magazine's presence is substantial: everything in the printed version is online, and an extensive library of files for Windows users—including games, drivers, utilities, sounds, and music—complements the textual material.

Figure 7-7:
Windows Maga-
zine online focuses
on information and
resources for the
Windows user.

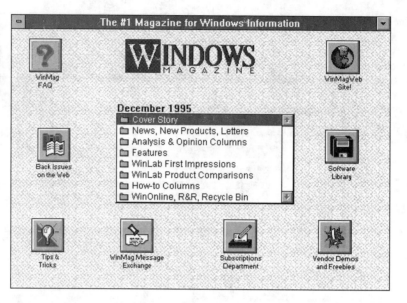

Enumerating the features offered by this forum would be redundant: the Windows Magazine and PC World forums are similar in design and presentation. Like the print magazines, however, the forums differ in content. Duplication is minimal. Each complements the other. Just as I chose to continue my subscriptions to both magazines, so it is with the forums: you gotta have both.

The Windows Magazine forum offers a unique and significant feature: a library of programs written by the magazine's staff. There are scores of programs here, including the industry standard WinTune, a performance-measuring utility with a wealth of reporting features (see Figure 7-8).

Figure 7-8:
WinTune can mea-
sure the perfor-
mance of your PC
and find possible
problems with
your hardware or
setup. A review of
the program's
exhaustive Help file
will offer some
solutions.

A real-world example best illustrates the value of online support for the computer user. My new machine was acting erratically—one of those nagging problems that left no signature and defied positive identification. I used WinTune to isolate the problem; with the results, I traveled to the Gateway forum (keyword: **Moo**) to see if anyone there had a solution.

Sure enough, many others had experienced the same problem. The solution turned out to be an improved driver for my Western Digital hard drive, something that Gateway conveniently posted on AOL. I downloaded the driver, installed it, and improved my hard disk's performance *by a factor of 20* in just a few minutes. This I did at night on a holiday weekend, when no other resources were available (or neces-sary, as it turned out). I have Windows Magazine Online (and Gate-way) to thank for my redemption.

Business Week Online's Computer Room

You know about *Business Week* magazine. It's online, at keyword: **BW**, and there are few that can compare with its immediacy and depth in reporting on current issues. If you're an incorrigible digit-head, you also know that *Business Week* is the first general-interest magazine to break out a separate department to provide weekly bulletins from the world's technology fronts. That was 15 years ago, and now it's all available online. There's no keyword for this area—yet (there might be one by the time you read this). But it's available in the Magazine Rack window, at keywords: **Magazine Rack**.

The Cyberscooter

One of the more eccentric stories available in the Business Week Online Computer Room is about the Cyberscooter: a Neimann-Marcus offering in their 1995 Christmas catalog (see Figure 7-9).

Figure 7-9: The Cyber-scooter.

It seems that Motorola Cellular Service has teamed up with underwear maker Joe Boxer to create the Cyberscooter—just the thing for fashion-conscious and technology-minded road warriors. The polka-dotted Vespa is equipped with a cellular phone and a digital communicator, allowing simultaneous I-way and byway cruising for the terminally bored. Also included in the deal are a bright yellow "happy face" helmet and antenna flag, 30 pairs of boxer shorts, and your very own page on Joe Boxer's World Wide Web site, all for a trivial $10,000. And you thought this computer stuff was just for dweebs.

An Embarrassment of Riches

The three online computer magazines I've described are only a few of AOL's online publications. Be sure to investigate Home Office Computing, CONNECT Magazine Online, Multimedia World Online, Computer Life Online, FamilyPC Online, WIRED Magazine, and PC Today Magazine Online. Each is available by using the italicized portion of its title above as the keyword.

Keyword Tricks

If you take the time to thumb through Appendix B, you'll see that AOL's list of keywords is epic, and more are being added every day. In fact, almost every keyword has a synonym or two—or three—and those synonyms are typically common-sense words.

Let's say you want to go to the *New York Times* online area. Actually its online name is "@times," but you've forgotten that. Don't fret: try the keywords: **New York**, or **Times**, or **NYC**, or **NYTimes**—they'll all get you there.

This tip doesn't just apply to *The Times*, nor does it just apply to the computer-related online magazines mentioned in the text: it applies to almost every area online. Forget the keyword? Press Ctrl+K, then type in almost anything that describes where you want to go. What's to lose? The worst that can happen is that you'll get an "Invalid Keyword" error, and no one has failed to recover from that.

Thanks to Sean Stallings (who uses a HAL 9000 for his online travels) for this tip.

The Computing Company Connection

Computer users often need help with hardware or software, which leads us directly into a discussion of the Computing Company Connection. There are a number of ways to solve problems with your computer:

- Worry at the problem, trying solutions as they come to mind. This might take a week.

- Look up the solution in the manual (if you can remember where you put it). This usually takes half a day.

Call the publisher or manufacturer—which can involve 20 minutes on hold (listening to a bad radio station playing commercials for stores in a city 3,000 miles away) then several days waiting for someone to return your call.

 Or you can sign on to AOL, type in the software publisher's key-word, and post your question. Within 24 hours you will receive not only a response from the vendor you're trying to reach but also helpful advice from fellow users who have experienced the same problem (see Figure 7-10).

Figure 7-10: No waiting on hold: post your question online and read a response at your convenience a few hours later.

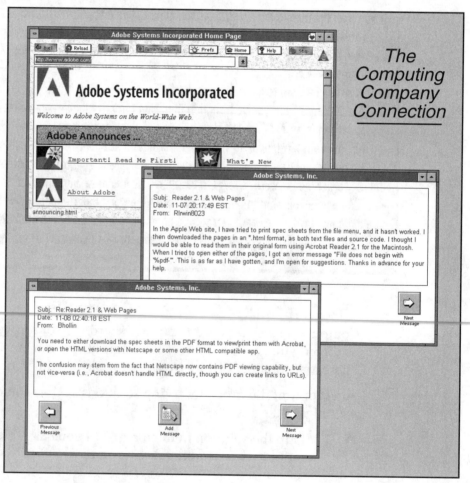

The Adobe Systems Incorporated Web page window, visible at the top of Figure 7-10, is a good example of how World Wide Web pages are integrated into forums on America Online (the Web is discussed in Chapter 4, "Using the Internet"). Adobe, a software provider to the international market, has chosen the World Wide Web as home for its information area. Rather than try to duplicate that resource, AOL includes Adobe's Web page in their area. It's an interesting blend of local and worldwide resources—and certainly worth investigating at keyword: **Adobe**.

No Place for Vilification

Look again at Rlrwin8023's question in Figure 7-10. He identifies the complexity of his problem, including methods he's using to work around it. He resisted the temptation to take out his frustration on the manufacturer. Instead, he is concise, specific, and nonantagonistic.

If we all communicated our problems this courteously—no matter how frustrating and agonizing the problems might be—we'd be more likely to receive prompt, courteous responses like Bhollin's. Requesting support—whether it's from the industry or from a peer—is not the proper time to show off our expertise or shower abuse on those who are trying to help us.

Prepare your question in advance, before you sign on. Include the hardware brand name, software version number, system configuration, additional boards—those kinds of things. Spend a few moments checking your message for clarity, brevity, and courtesy. Sign on and post your message only after it has passed this kind of scrutiny. You can prepare a message offline, away from a message board, by choosing New from the File menu (or pressing Ctrl+N). After you have prepared the message, select it all and copy it. Now sign on and find the message board you want, then paste your message into the form used for posting messages on the board. The Select All, Copy, and Paste commands are all under the Edit menu.

The service that provides this help is AOL's *Company Connection* shown in Figure 7-11 (use the keyword: **CC**). Hundreds of vendors currently maintain message boards on AOL, and each vendor checks its board at least once a day. Not only is excellent vendor support found here, but also peer support, libraries of accessories and updates, announcements from the industry, and tips from other users.

Figure 7-11: The Computing Company Connection is your direct route to hundreds of software and hardware manufacturers.

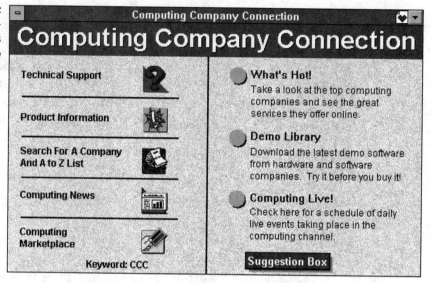

Figure 7-11: The Computing Company Connection is your direct route to hundreds of software and hardware manufacturers.

Software libraries usually round out the company support area online. These libraries boast a variety of programs for downloading, including patches, demo versions, diagnostic tools, and hardware and software drivers—programs that would otherwise only be available directly from software manufacturers.

A Medley of Computing Essentials

I've been a regular visitor to AOL's computing areas for over four years now, and I still haven't seen it all. This place is as vast as Bill Gates's ambition. Though I'm going to describe a number of computing areas on the upcoming pages, the list is by no means comprehensive. Don't confine yourself to those mentioned in this book. Use the keyword: **Computing**, and explore. When it comes to doing things online, a healthy curiosity is as rewarding as a fast modem.

Kim Komando's Komputer Klinic

You might have heard of Kim Komando. You might have seen her on Fox TV or read her columns in *FamilyPC* magazine. She has a couple of books on the shelves and a regular talk radio show too.

Most of all, Kim Komando knows how to answer questions about computers. She does that in plain English, without affectation or embroidery. Moreover, she's accessible: she's willing to help members

regardless of how simple their questions might seem. Computerdom needs more Kim Komandos, but at least we have *one* (see Figure 7-12, and use the keyword: **Komando**).

Figure 7-12: Kim Komando's Komputer Klinic is one of the best places online for straight talk about hardware and software. That's Kim in the lower-right corner—proof positive that she is *not* Mr. Science, in spite of rumors to the contrary.

You'll find answers to common questions about buying and upgrading a computer, DOS, downloading and uploading, CD-ROMs, scanners, sound and video, memory, networking and the Internet (be sure to check out her Internet Hot Spots). Naturally, you can submit questions of your own and receive a reply within a couple of days.

You'll also find the highly respected American Computer Exchange—AmCoEx—listing of used computer systems and related equipment pricing. Take a look and you'll know exactly the high, low, and average price paid on just about any piece of computer hardware.

Kim Komando is also one of only two people who actually know the identity of radio's Mr. Science, and apparently she has an in with him, as her area is one of the few places in *any* medium that offers a direct connection to the man who phones in his radio interviews from a telephone booth outside a WalMart store in Medina, Arkansas.

Komando (pronounce it "commando") really is Kim's last name, she doesn't wear a pocket protector and she admits to being a blonde.

Family Computing

I'm going to let you in on one of AOL's little secrets: the Family Computing Forum is one of AOL's most popular areas—in fact, it's among the Computers & Software Channel's top five performers. And when it comes to popularity among members, few areas can compare to the Computers & Software Channel.

Figure 7-13: The Family Computing Forum is one of AOL's worst-kept secrets.

Why is this area so popular? There are a number of theories, but 10 minutes in the forum tells all: people are made to feel welcome here. You'll learn about your computer, in a refreshingly shirtsleeve atmosphere—one where you can take the family and learn about computers together. You'll find pictures of members and their families in the Family Photo Album, and the "Refrigerator Door," where young artists hang their computer graphic originals. There's a chat room where you can take your grandmother, if you want, without fear of snerts or trolls or phishers offending her (snerts, phishers, and trolls are discussed in Chapter 8, "The Community"). There's a rec room for family game-playing and a Hot Tips area where family members can go to learn new things about using AOL (probably the best tips area on the service!).

Excellence, it seems, is often discovered in the most unlikely places. The Family Computing Forum is one of them.

Software/Hardtalk with John Dvorak

You probably know who John Dvorak is. You might listen to his *Software/Hardtalk* on public radio stations and Armed Forces Radio, or read his monthly column in *PC Magazine*.

Dvorak's Software/Hardtalk area on AOL publishes all of his radio interviews and provides a discussion area for the subjects and issues covered on the program. You'll see some commentary that hasn't appeared in other media, and there's a library of his favorite shareware. Get all the skinny at keyword: **Dvorak**.

Figure 7-14: John Dvorak's Software/Hardtalk offers a reprise of his radio broadcasts, commentary, discussions, and frequent live events.

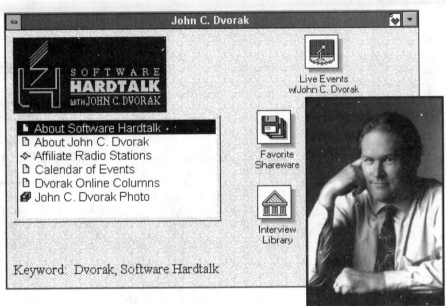

Fonts

Fonts are the chocolate of computing: you can never have enough. To many of AOL's members, fonts are the most tempting downloads AOL offers. They're relatively small (most download in less than a minute at 14.4 kbps) and inexpensive. Most of these fonts are shareware or freeware; the shareware fees rarely exceed $15. Best of all, they enhance your documents with personality and individuality, like icing on a cake. Chocolate icing, of course. Yum.

Windows fonts come in two flavors: TrueType and PostScript (the Applications Forum—where you'll find vast libraries of fonts—calls these "ATM" fonts). Most general Windows users seem to prefer

TrueType, though desktop publishers prefer PostScript. Neither group could ask for much more than these extensive Application Forum offerings. Researching this chapter, I found more than 190 PostScript Windows fonts online. I didn't bother to count the TrueType ones, but there were just as many, or more. In addition, a number of Macintosh-to-Windows font converters were available, which means the entire Macintosh desktop-publishing font library (keyword: **MacDTP**) is accessible as well. We're talking about thousands of fonts here. If fonts are chocolate, AOL is the passkey to the Godiva kitchens (Figure 7-15).

Figure 7-15: The Applications Forum's "Font Petting Zoo" allows you to see fonts before they're downloaded.

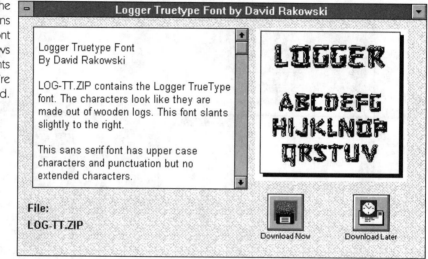

Redgate/New Products Showcase

The Redgate/New Products Showcase area at keyword: **Redgate** offers information and services you're unlikely to find anywhere else—events, trends, and innovations in the high technology industry, including multimedia and interactivity. Unlike most other information, the information you receive via the New Product Showcase comes to you directly from the source: from the high-tech manufacturer or service company—in their language, unedited, and unfiltered.

Figure 7-16:
Events, trends, and
innovations at
keyword: **Redgate**.

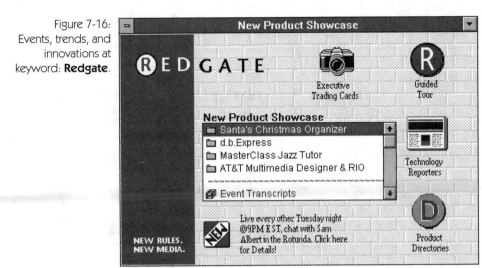

You'll find photos, press kits and demos, transcripts of live press announcements and comprehensive product directories here—brought to you by Redgate, a technology marketing consulting firm and creators of *En Passant*, the world's first home shopping CD-ROM.

Electronic Frontier Foundation

Out here in the west, it wasn't long ago that we called ourselves a frontier. There were no population centers, no organized form of government. Things ran pretty much according to chance. It was survival of the fittest.

When you stop to think about it, computer-based communication media are becoming the basis of a new form of community. This community—without a single, fixed geographical location—comprises the first settlement in an electronic frontier, not unlike that of the west a couple of hundred years ago.

According to the Electronic Frontier Foundation's charter, "The Electronic Frontier Foundation has been established to help civilize the electronic frontier; to make it truly useful and beneficial not just to a technical elite, but to everyone; and to do this in a way which is in keeping with our society's highest traditions of the free and open flow of information and communication."

Figure 7-17: The
Electronic Frontier
Foundation serves
as our advocate in
the frontier we call
cyberspace.

> **Electronic Frontier Foundation**
>
> ⬅ Back   🔄 Reload   ➡ Forward   ⏹ Stop
>
> **The Electronic Frontier Foundation**
>
> A non-profit civil liberties organization working in the public interest to protect privacy, free expression, and access to online resources and information.
>
> EFF Info
> **Alerts**
> Current Newsletter
> Archives
> Sponsors
> For-Sale/Wanted
>
> Click This Button to Change the World:
>
> EFF Services, Forums & Publications
>
> The EFF Mission
>
> Discuss the Issues with EFF
>
> File Libraries
>
> Keyword: EFF

The Electronic Frontier Foundation (at keyword: **Netorgs**) promotes educational activities, lobbies policy makers, advocates civil liberties, and develops new tools to afford telecommunications access for non-technical users. If you're at all interested in the future of our industry as a society, you should be a regular visitor here. Like the wagons on the Oregon Trail, the EFF is blazing new ground every day, and those of us who feel a responsibility for this medium find the EFF to be an effective delegate and a capable paladin.

All the Rest

There's much more for the computer enthusiast online. The Desktop Publishing Resource Center and the Electronic Publishing Resource Center serve print and electronic journalists, respectively. Craig Crossman's Computer America offers a radio simulcast and the Programmer University serves up a savory plate of support for computer programmers. CyberLex reports legal developments affecting the computer industry.

There are more, and new computer-related areas are arriving every day. Search the Directory of Services (look under your Go To menu) with the criterion: Computer, for a comprehensive list, and be sure to use the keyword: **New** every couple of days to catch new ones as they arrive.

Moving On

This has been a long chapter steeped in technicalities. Computers are inherently technical, and almost everything discussed in this chapter has been technical as well.

But America Online is much more than technicalities. Many members use it for the community alone: e-mail, chat, kids, and seniors. In fact, community is the heart of AOL. There are millions of wonderful people here. Turn the page. I want you to meet a few.

CHAPTER 8

The Community

- People Connection
- The Guidepager
- Chat Room Sounds
- The Auditoriums
- AOL Live!
- Instant Messages
- Buddy Lists
- Kids & Parents
- Seniors
- Women's Issues
- Guttersnipe

For many AOL members, the online community is what it's all about: chat, Instant Messages, games, auditoriums—telecommunicating in real time with real people all around the world. This is a two-way medium; it's a level playing field; it's egalitarian, attainable, and less expensive than cable TV. On the other hand, these very qualities are its greatest weaknesses: parity of access and freedom of expression don't necessarily promote honor and virtue. Thieves and scoundrels find this medium to be just as inviting as do scholars and prophets. Along with brotherhood and beneficence, there be dragons here. It's a community as diverse as America itself, and like America, America Online warrants scrutiny under strong light. Thus, this chapter.

People Connection

I discussed e-mail in Chapter 3, newsgroups and mailing lists in Chapter 4, and I'll discuss message boards in Chapter 9. All of these tools foster dialog between people, but none of the dialogs occur in real time. *People Connection* is the real-time, member-to-member communications headquarters of AOL. I was about to compare People Connection dialogs with telephone conversations, but at People Connection any number of people can be involved, there's rarely a long-distance toll to pay, and many of the people you talk to are strangers—but never for long.

People Connection is the heart of the AOL community. Here is where you make the enduring friendships that keep you coming back, day after day. Here, in a "diner," you can order a short stack and a cup of coffee, and talk over the weekend ahead. You can also sip a brew in a "pub" after a long day on the job. There are "events" here as well, where you can interview eminent guests and hobnob with luminaries.

Doesn't that sound like a community to you? This isn't couch-potato entertainment; this is interactive telecommunication—where imagination and participation are contagious, and the concept of community reaches its most eloquent expression.

It sure beats reruns.

A Haven for Shy People

America Online is a haven for shy people. Shy people usually like other people and they're likable themselves; they just don't do well with strangers. Most shy people want to make friends—and all friends were once strangers—but they aren't very adept at doing it.

This is why shy people like AOL. Nobody can see them online; nobody seems to notice if they don't talk much; and if they're uncomfortable, they can always escape when they wish by signing off. Perhaps best of all, if you're a shy person, you can use a *nom de plume* and no one will even know who you are. We're back at the masquerade ball I mentioned in Chapter 2: you can wear the mask of a different screen name and be whatever or whomever you want to be. There's something comforting yet exciting about those possibilities.

Shy people can begin the AOL journey in a "safe" place like a forum (forums are discussed in Chapter 9, "Boards & Forums"), where no one's the wiser when they read a few forum messages or download a file or two. The next step would be to make an online friend and exchange some mail. Regardless of the path taken, it takes some time to work up the courage to venture into People Connection. It invariably means ending up in a room full of strangers, and this is not where shy people feel most comfortable.

The irony is that shy folks love People Connection once they become acquainted with it. It's the perfect outlet for years of pent-up longing for sociability. I'm a shy person. It took me months to work up to People Connection. Yet now it's one of my greatest online rewards. I go there whenever I have time. You will too, once you get the hang of it.

The Lobby

Unlike other areas within AOL, a visit to People Connection requires first passing through the "Lobby." The Lobby is one of AOL's so-called *chat rooms*, where real people communicate in real time. No messages are left here. There are no files to download. America Online's Lobby is similar to the lobby of a hotel: it's an area people pass through, often on their way to some other destination. Every so often, people bump into an acquaintance. Or they just sit there a moment to rest.

If you've never visited People Connection, come along with me and we'll give it a whirl. Click the two-heads icon on the toolbar, choose People Connection from the Main Menu window, or use the keyword: **Lobby**. No matter which method you use, you will soon find yourself in the Lobby (see Figure 8-1).

Figure 8-1: The Lobby screen seems empty just after I enter.

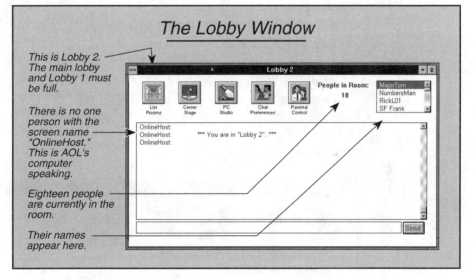

Note that the message in the chat room window pictured in Figure 8-1 says "You are in Lobby 2." When I entered the Lobby, AOL routed me to Lobby 2. This happens whenever traffic on the system is heavy. When the main Lobby reaches capacity (rooms are considered filled when they contain 23 members), AOL places people in the secondary lobby—Lobby 1. It, too, must have filled by the time I arrived, so I got placed in Lobby 2. Note that it was also approaching capacity, so new arrivals were about to be routed into yet another lobby. This isn't un–common. There are often dozens of lobbies in operation at any one time.

> **Have Faith**
>
> If you really are following along with me, you've been in a lobby for a couple of minutes now. Your screen is full of chat, some of it indecipherable, some of it scurrilous, and some of it from people just as confounded as you are. Some people find lobby chat to be provocative; other people think it's insipid; still others would say it's simply vulgar. If your first experience in a lobby doesn't pique your interest in AOL's chat rooms, don't give up. Finish this chapter: there are rooms where the conversation is enlightening, urbane, and predictably polite. Read on and I'll tell you how to find them.

Also note that of the 18 people in Lobby 2 at the time, a few of their names appear in the scroll box in the upper right corner of Figure 8-1's window. My preferences are set to arrange these names alphabetically (preferences are discussed in Appendix E, "Preferences"). Your scroll box may list the members in the order they appear.

Finally, note that there is no text in the main (conversation) portion of the window other than the announcement telling me where I am. The only true conversation appearing here occurs after my arrival, and I have just walked in the door. That situation changes the moment I speak (see Figure 8-2).

Figure 8-2: No matter how shy you're feeling, say hello when you enter a room.

| | | | | | People in Room: | MajorTom |
| List Rooms | Center Stage | PC Studio | Chat Preferences | Parental Control | 20 | NumbersMan RickL01 SF Frank |

```
OnlineHost:
OnlineHost:      *** You are in "Lobby 2". ***
OnlineHost:
MajorTom:        Hi all!
```

Lobby 2

Send

Look again at Figure 8-2. This lobby is active today. People are rushing through it with hardly a pause. By the time I've said hello—a matter of seconds—two more people have arrived. America Online's lobbies are something like a hotel lobby just after a large meeting has let out: people are scurrying everywhere. (This is particularly true during periods of heavy usage. The session pictured occurred on a Sunday morning. America Online is almost always busy on the weekends.)

Password Surfing

You've no doubt seen messages to this effect already, but if you're new to People Connection it's worth repeating here: *no one from AOL's staff will ever, EVER ask you for your password.* I don't mean to imply that other people won't ask you for your password: password thieves are always a problem. I'll discuss the problem of password thieves later in this chapter, but just in case a message pops up on your screen while you're "lobbying" with me asking for your password, simply close its window and forget about it—at least for the time being. You probably won't hear from that person again.

Seconds later, a conversation has begun (see Figure 8-3).

Figure 8-3: Catchy screen names come in handy when you first enter a room.

Lobby 2

People in Room: 22

MajorTom
NumbersMan
RickL01
SF Frank

List Rooms | Center Stage | PC Studio | Chat Preferences | Parental Control

```
OnlineHost:
OnlineHost:      *** You are in "Lobby 2". ***
OnlineHost:
MajorTom:        Hi all!
RickL01:         Hey Tom!
NumbersMan:      Hi, MajorTom!
HarpoonU:        ground control to............
MajorTom:        I'm the one, Harpoon.
```

Send

Though I immediately became involved in a conversation, don't feel obligated to do so yourself. It's perfectly all right to say hello, then just watch for a while. In fact, I recommend it: it gives you a chance to adapt to the pace of the conversation—to get to know who is in the room and what they're like. Lobbies are good for this. They're lobbies, after all. It's perfectly natural for people to sit in a lobby and watch other people.

Lurkers

It's not a very flattering term: *lurker*. It always makes me think of dark alleys and trench coats. In the online context, however, a lurker is one who visits a chat room and chooses not to participate in the conversation. There's nothing wrong with online lurking. I always lurk for a few minutes after I enter a room and say hello, to see who's in the room and to get a feel for the tenor of the conversation. You can lurk online for as long as you want to, but leave the trench coat in the closet.

As is the case with hotel lobbies, however, you won't want to stay in AOL's lobbies indefinitely. Awaiting you are lots of other rooms where conversations are more focused and residents less transitory. These rooms can be great fun; all you have to do is find the one that suits you best.

Kinds of Rooms

People who are new to AOL often have trouble understanding all of the kinds of rooms AOL has to offer. Each type of room serves a different purpose. Entering one without understanding what's inside is a bit like opening meeting room doors in a large hotel: some might welcome you enthusiastically, others might make you feel unwelcome, and still others might be engaged in conversations that are of no interest to you whatsoever.

Public Rooms

If you're still in a lobby, you'll soon discover the List Rooms button at the top left of the lobby's window (review Figure 8-2). This leads to the Public Rooms window pictured in Figure 8-4. Here, you can scan lists of all the public rooms available at the moment, and choose the one that suits you best.

Figure 8-4: This Public Rooms list appears whenever you click the List Rooms button in a chat window.

Public Rooms

Members   Double-click Room

19	Lobby
16	Chat About the Web
20	Best Lil Chathouse
4	Game Parlor
8	Game Parlor Chat
22	Game Parlor Teen
5	Game Parlor Too
20	Gay and Lesbian
19	Hollywood Tonight

Member Rooms
Private Room
Help
Feedback

Go   Who's Here?   More

Moving Target

As I write this, AOL has announced plans to change the room-selection interface—the screen pictured in Figure 8-4. The problem is a growing membership and consequently too many public rooms: listing them all in a single scroll box has become too cumbersome. Eventually, the public rooms list will be categorized, a change that should make matters much easier for those who use the rooms list to visit public rooms. The new interface is in the planning stage; I'm including a screen shot of how it might look (see Figure 8-5), but it's anything but finalized.

Figure 8-5: A preview of the new room-selection interface, captured in its early stages of development.

Public Rooms

Double-click to
Select a Category

Town Square
Arts and Entertainment
Lifetime
News, Sports, and Finance
Places
Romance
Special Interests

Select a Room
Members   Room Name

Member Rooms   Feedback   Go   Who's Here?
Private Room   More   Help

There's even a chance that AOL will do away with the mandatory lobby visit mentioned earlier in this chapter and send you directly to the dialog box pictured above when you first enter People Connection. The online industry is a moving target for those of us who try to paint a picture of it in print. It's sometimes frustrating, but that's what makes reporting on this business so much fun.

The rooms appearing in the list box in Figure 8-4 all represent so-called *public* rooms at America Online. Public rooms share a number of common characteristics:

- As you might expect, they're open to the public. Anyone can enter (unless the room is full) and leave whenever they wish.

- Most public rooms are limited to 23 people (there are exceptions, but they're few). I don't know where that number came from, but it's appropriate: conversations in rooms with more than 23 people would be hard to follow, especially if those people were all in a garrulous mood.

- Public rooms are named by AOL employees. Most of them are *self-replicating*: when Lobby 2 fills, for example, Lobby 3 is automatically created.

The Best Seat in the House

The best way to find a "seat" in a self-replicating room is to attempt to enter one that's already full: if you want to enter a lobby, for example, try Lobby 1—even if it's full. AOL will display a message telling you that room is full and ask you if you want to enter another one that's like it. Answer yes. Chances are, someone just walked out of one of the full lobbies and AOL will put you in that person's seat. AOL always tries to find you the best seat in the house if you use this technique.

- Guides visit public rooms occasionally, either to offer assistance or to generally police the place. (Guides were discussed in Chapter 2, "The Abecedarium.") Aside from the occasional Guide, however, most public rooms are occupied by members only: there are no staff members present.

- The names of all public rooms are "published" via the windows pictured in Figure 8-4.

To enter a public room, scroll the list box in Figure 8-5 until you find the room you want, then double-click its name. (Be sure to read the "Best Seat in the House" sidebar to find a good seat.) As soon as you arrive (the chat window on your screen will tell you—review Figure 8-2), be sure to say hello.

To find out more about the people in the room, refer to the scroll box in the upper right corner of the room's window. The screen names of all of the people in the room are listed there. To see a "roommate's" profile, double-click his or her screen name, and click the Get Info button (see Figure 8-6). Not only will you be able to call up a profile of that person (profiles were discussed in Chapter 2, "The Abecedarium"), but you can send them an Instant Message as well (we'll discuss Instant Messages later in this chapter).

Figure 8-6:
Double-click any name on a people list to find out more about that individual.

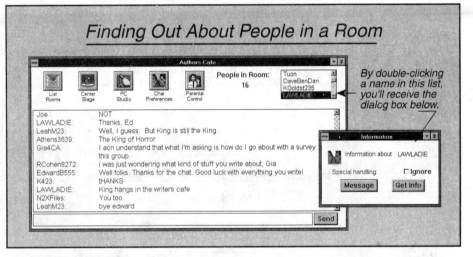

Special Handling

The person named "Joe" in Figure 8-6 was harassing the room, posting nonsense like the "NOT" pictured at the top of the Authors Cafe window. (I've changed his name and cleaned up his language—"Joe" was a vile little muck.) Though there are a number of ways of dealing with his type, I simply double-clicked his name in the list box, then clicked the Ignore option illustrated in Figure 8-6. From that moment on, Joe went out of my life. It appears that the other room residents did the same thing, for everyone is ignoring him. Don't you wish real life could be this convenient?

Conference Rooms

While the Authors Cafe illustrated in Figure 8-6 is a public room, the *Writers* Cafe is a *conference room*. Conference rooms are usually associated with forums (I'll discus forums in Chapter 9), and are typically accessed through those forums. You can't get to them via the Lobby, and they're not listed when you click the List Rooms button shown in Figure 8-2. Other than that, conference rooms aren't much different than public rooms, but since they require a bit more savvy to find, they're less privy to the kind of harassment I alluded to in the "Special Handling" sidebar.

Refer to Figure 8-7: the Writers Cafe is only available via the Writers Club. You can't get there with Ctrl+L or the two-heads icon on the toolbar; you've got to venture through the Writers Club first—and encounter a friendly prequel about the room—before you get to the Writers Cafe.

Figure 8-7: You have to travel through a forum to reach most conference rooms.

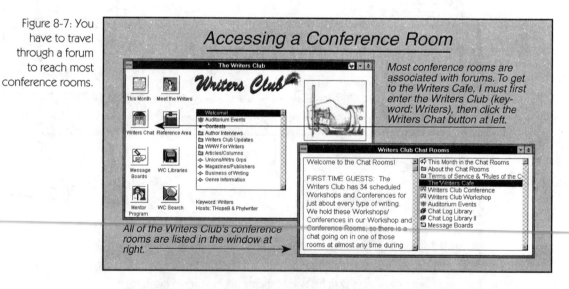

Because they're associated with forums (the Writers Club is a forum; we'll discuss forums in Chapter 9, "Boards & Forums"), and because they're slightly less accessible than public rooms, conference rooms exhibit some characteristics not common in public rooms:

- Most conference rooms can hold more than a public room's maximum of 23 people. Thirty or forty people aren't uncommon. In spite of the crowd, conversations are rarely difficult to follow, due

to the use of *protocol* in most conference rooms. (See the "Protocol Rooms" sidebar.)

▲ You're more likely to find staff members in conference rooms. They're forum staff—not Guides—and sometimes you can't determine they're staff without checking their profiles, but their presence usually makes a room more orderly and focused.

▲ Conference rooms are often scheduled: forums hold regularly scheduled meetings in their conference rooms during which a staff member is usually present and the subject matter is carefully regulated. (Review Figure 8-7: do you see the mention of "34 scheduled Workshops" there?) Become familiar with a conference room's schedule before you enter it: you don't want to walk in on a scheduled conference unaware of what you're doing.

▲ Even during unscheduled times, conference room topics are more focused. I wouldn't expect to find people discussing model airplanes in the Writers Cafe (unless they were writing *books* about model airplanes), and hobbyists wouldn't expect to find me talking about agents and deadlines in their conference rooms either.

▲ The people in conference rooms are less transitory. People often graze among public rooms, looking for The Perfect Chat like a remote-wielding couch potato seeking The Perfect Channel. Such is not the case with conference rooms. People often stay in conference rooms for hours.

I'm trying to make a subtle point here: if you're attracted by chat but repelled by public rooms, seek out a forum that aligns with an interest of yours and see if it has a conference room. If it does, pop in. You might find yourself coming back again and again.

Protocol Rooms

At times, some conference rooms operate with *protocol*, usually when there is a guest speaker or a specific topic under discussion.

You can usually tell when you've entered a protocol room because you'll be greeted by a message informing you of the protocol. Protocol rooms invariably have a moderator as well, and the moderator's influence on the conversation will be readily apparent. One way or another, it doesn't take long to tell you're in a protocol room: just watch the conversation. Here are some of the conventions you'll see:

- Type a question mark **(?)** if you have a question and wait until the moderator calls on you.

- Type an exclamation point **(!)** if you have a comment and, again, wait.

- Type **GA** (for Go Ahead) or **/end** when you're done with your question or comment. It's also wise to have your material typed and ready to go before you're called on.

A final comment about conference rooms before we move on: many people use them as a "back door" to public rooms. To get to a public room you usually have to travel through a Lobby. If that's not to your liking, find a little-used conference room in a forum somewhere and memorize the keyword that got you there. The next time you want to access a public room, go to the conference room you've memorized—be sure there's no conference going on there at the time—then click the List Rooms button in the conference room's window. All of the public rooms will be displayed and you can enter any one that's available. It works just as if you were in the Lobby.

Parlor Games

A particular type of protocol room (see the "Protocol Rooms" sidebar) that's dedicated to games is the *Game Parlor*, where mental challenges mingle with casual socializing (use the keyword: **Parlor**, and see Figure 8-8).

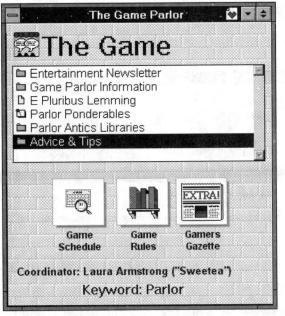

Each game has an official host and scorekeeper and most have a greeter. The greeter will provide you with the host's and scorekeeper's names, and some of the rules. The action is usually fast and erudite but don't let that intimidate you: everyone has a first time and new visitors are always made to feel comfortable.

Parlor game schedules are always changing; you can see the latest at keyword: **Parlor**.

Member Rooms

Member rooms are named and created by members. The subject is entirely up to the member who creates the room and is usually identified by the room's name (see Figure 8-9).

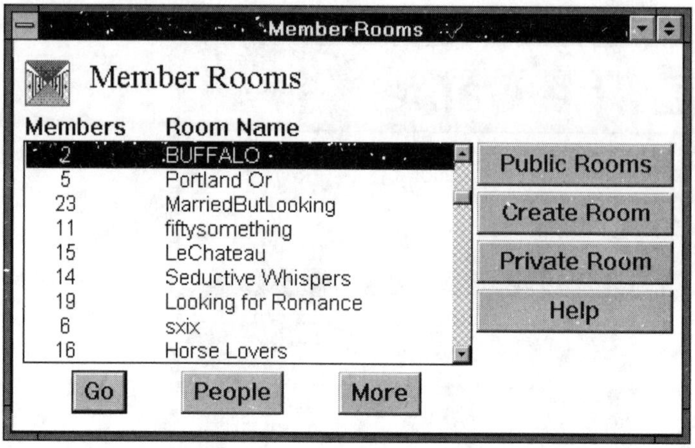

Figure 8-9: Member
room topics vary
from the innocuous
to the scurrilous.

Member Rooms

Members	Room Name
2	BUFFALO
5	Portland Or
23	MarriedButLooking
11	fiftysomething
15	LeChateau
14	Seductive Whispers
19	Looking for Romance
6	sxix
16	Horse Lovers

Public Rooms
Create Room
Private Room
Help

Go   People   More

Figure 8-9 identifies the three types of member rooms that you'll encounter most often:

🔺 The first two rooms are representative of regional topics. If you live near a large city, you're likely to find a room for your locale if you're visiting on a busy night.

🔺 The "Horse Lovers" room is interest-oriented. These rooms usually adhere to their subject. Most interest-oriented rooms are conference rooms and are accessed via forums, but if there's no particular forum for that, members will often take it upon themselves to establish an appropriate room.

🔺 The remaining rooms no doubt contain members who are engaged in online flirting of one kind or another.

Member rooms share a number of common characteristics:

🔺 Member rooms are open to the public unless they're full.

🔺 Member rooms have a maximum capacity of 23 people and are not self-replicating.

A list of member rooms is available by clicking the Member Rooms button pictured in Figure 8-10.

Figure 8-10: The
Member Rooms
window lists rooms
that members
have created.

Member Rooms	

Members Double-click Room Name

16	jacksonville
18	nyc
21	trucker
21	La Chateau Dungeon
21	TV Chat
21	crazy times
22	Hopelessly Romantic
21	new hampshire
21	fiftysomething
21	millionaires lounge
21	MIAMI
16	Arizona
19	LadyRedhead

Create Member Room
Public Rooms
Private Room
Help
Feedback

Go   Who's Here?   More

⚫ Member rooms are created and named by members (I'll tell you how in a moment). Member room names must abide by AOL's TOS (Terms of Service—TOS is discussed in Chapter 2, "The Abecedarium"); those with names found to be in violation of TOS are closed by People Connection staff.

⚫ Member rooms are never hosted by staff members, though they *are* often hosted. The hosts in these circumstances are often host "wannabe's." I'm not using that term derogatorily: many conference room hosts get started by hosting a member room.

⚫ Member rooms are rarely patrolled by Guides. Guides only enter member rooms when summoned via the Guidepager (see the Guidepager section of this chapter for more).

Anyone can create a member room: just follow the sequence described in Figure 8-11.

Figure 8-11:
Creating a member
room of your own
amounts to little
more than clicking
a button.

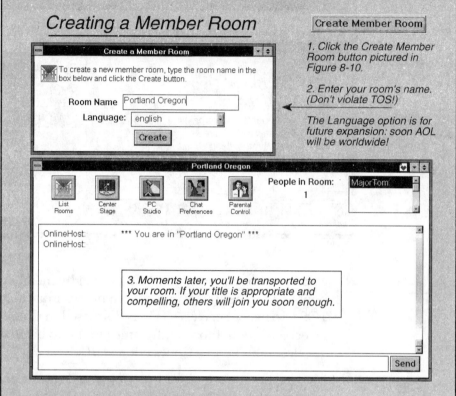

I hope the picture is coming into focus by now: the content, quality, and integrity of member rooms differ considerably from room to room. Some of the best rooms on the service are found here; so are the worst. I often visit the Portland, Oregon, room: one of our local TV meteorologists hangs out there, and weather is a subject about which Oregonians *always* have an opinion. However, there are other member rooms that are like the dark under the stairs to me: their names usually tell all.

Private Rooms

Like member rooms, private rooms are created by members and can hold 23 people. That, however, is where the similarity ends. Here are the specifics:

- Private rooms are not available to the public. There's no way to see a list of private rooms.

🔺 Since you can't see a list of private rooms, you must know the
exact name of a private room in order to enter it. You'll never
know about a private room unless you create one of your own or
someone invites you into theirs by providing you with its name.

🔺 Private rooms are never patrolled—AOL's Terms of Service, in fact,
specifically prohibits AOL staff from monitoring private-room
conversations (TOS is discussed in Chapter 2, "The Abecedarium").

🔺 You can leave a private room whenever you want to: just click its
close box.

Refer to Figure 8-12. The Private Room button pictured there allows
you to create or visit a private room. When you click this button, AOL
asks you for a room name. If you enter a name and the room already
exists, AOL takes you into that room. If it doesn't exist, AOL creates it
and takes you there. If you create a room, the only people who can
enter it are those who know its name.

Figure 8-12:
Private rooms are
created in exactly
the same fashion as
member rooms.

Creating a Private Room

Private Room

Enter a Private Room

To create or enter a private room, type the room name in the
box below and click on the Go button.

Room Name: MajorRoom

Language: english

Go

1. Click the Private Room button
pictured in Figure 8-4.

2. If the room already exists,
AOL will take you to that room.
Otherwise, you'll see the win-
dow at left. Fill it in as you wish.

MajorRoom

List
Rooms

Center
Stage

PC
Studio

Chat
Preferences

Parental
Control

People in Room:
1

MajorTom

OnlineHost:
OnlineHost: *** You are in "MajorRoom". ***
OnlineHost:

3. Other people will have to know your room's name
in order to visit: it will not be listed anywhere.

Send

Online Conference Calls

Consider the private room as an alternative to the conference call. We don't tend to think of them that way, but private rooms are essentially mechanisms whereby people from around the country can hold real-time conferences. America Online's private rooms are much less expensive than the phone company's conference calls, and participants can keep a log of the conversation for review once the conference has concluded (for a discussion of logs see Chapter 10, "Staying Informed"). Conferences are often more productive when participants have to write what they say (makes 'em think before they speak) and vocal inflections don't cloud the issue.

To hold a private-room conference call (or to simply meet some friends for a chat in a private room), tell the participants the name of the room and the time you want to meet beforehand, then arrive a few minutes early and create the room. Instruct the participants to enter the Lobby (the two-heads icon on the toolbar gets you there in a hurry) when they sign on, click the List Rooms button, click the Private Room button, then type in the name of your room (try to keep the name simple). Try it: it's in many ways superior to a conference call—and cheaper to boot.

Using Favorite Places to Get to a Room

I discussed *Favorite Places* in Chapter 4, but only in the context of Web pages. In fact, any AOL window with a little heart icon in its upper right corner can be added to your list of Favorite Places. Once a location is added to the list, you can return to it quickly and easily by choosing Favorite Places from the Go To menu or clicking the folder-and-heart button on the toolbar.

With that said, you might notice that most of the rooms we have discussed so far offer Favorite Places hearts on their title bars. The implication, then, is that you can add any room to your Favorite Places list and return to it later with a few clicks of the mouse. Are you fond of the Star Trek Club's "The Bridge" conference room? Add it to your Favorite Places list. The next time you want to go there, call up the list and double-click the entry for The Bridge. You'll bypass the Lobby and the List Rooms windows and be teleported (an appropriate Star Trek term) directly to your destination. It's as if Scotty were handling the controls.

Remember too that Favorite Places are available even when you're offline. If you're offline and want to sign on and visit The Bridge, just call up your Favorite Places list and double-click the entry for The Bridge. AOL will sign on (and ask you for your password if you haven't stored one—see Chapter 6 for a discussion of stored pass-words) and burrow directly to The Bridge. You'll hardly have time to dust off your communicator pin.

Chat Room Tips & Etiquette

It's appropriate that we wrap up the People Connection part of this chapter with a few comments about chat room etiquette and technique:

- Review America Online's Terms of Service (discussed in Chapter 2 and available free at keyword: **TOS**), and get to know terms like *scrolling, impersonation, disruption, polling, chain letters,* and *pyramid schemes* as they pertain to the online environment.

- Don't give your password to anyone, no matter how convincing their argument to the contrary might be. Read about trolls, phishers, and snerts in the "Guttersnipe" section of this chapter for more on this subject.

- Say hello when you arrive in a room. Say goodbye before you leave.

- When you first enter a room (and after saying hello), watch the conversation for a few minutes to see which way the wind is blowing. Only then should you enter into the conversation.

- Don't type in uppercase. That's shouting.

- Speak when spoken to, even if you say nothing more than "I don't know."

- A catchy screen name works wonders. When I enter a room using my business screen name—which isn't catchy at all—I encounter far fewer rejoinders from its inhabitants than I do when I enter using my MajorTom screen name.

- Your screen name should contain a convenient "handle"—ideally your first name. Talking to TLic6865 is like talking to a license plate. "MajorTom" allows people to call me "Major," or "Tom," or "MT."

The New Members Lounge (a public room) is a great place to begin.

 Keep a log of your first few chat room visits (logs are discussed in Chapter 10, "Staying Informed"). Review the log offline when the session has concluded. You'll learn a lot about chats this way.

 Get to know *smileys* and *emoticons*. These are the shorthand symbols you'll encounter online such as ROTFL (Rolling On The Floor Laughing), BTW (By The Way), ;-) (a wink: turn your head 90 degrees counterclockwise) and hundreds of others. There are a number of files available for downloading that list them all. Use the keywords: **File Search**, then search with the criterion: Emoticons. I'm fond of the *Unofficial Emoticons Dictionary* by L.L. Drummond.

 You might want to see who's in a room before you enter it. A screen name often tells a lot about a person. You can see who's in a room by clicking *once* on any name in the Public Rooms window (review Figure 8-4) or the Member Rooms windows (review Figure 8-10), then clicking the Who's Here? button.

 Learn what to do if you witness a TOS violation.

That last item points us directly toward the subject of the Guidepager: AOL's equivalent of an online 911. Read on.

The Guidepager

Freedom within the online community is threatened by a number of things—legislation, access, resources—but the most insidious and menacing threat to online freedom is abuse of the medium. And abuse, most frequently, appears in chat rooms.

Often the abusers are simply ignorant of the society. Sometimes they're brats on a lark, and a few are vandals, plain and simple. In all cases, the best way to deal with them is to report them, quickly and resolutely. This isn't tattling or hiding behind Mommy's apron; it's an imperative that we should all observe if we want to keep this community a healthy place. Those who would inflict online abuse represent a "social virus" to the online community: the scourge spreads like typhoid if left unchecked.

AOL's Guides are much more than the charitable souls they might seem to be. Think of them as you would think of the police: while they prefer to travel about benevolently assisting people in need, they are also vested with considerable authority. Guides can remove a member from a room, sever a member's access to People Connection for a period, or even terminate an account.

The *Guidepager* is a device used to summon a Guide for help, especially in the event of a TOS violation. The Guidepager is *not* a method of getting general help on AOL: read Chapter 2 for information on that. The Guidepager is available at any time, 24 hours a day, 7 days a week, at the keyword: **Guidepager** (it's pictured in Figure 8-13).

Figure 8-13: Use the Guidepager whenever you witness a violation of AOL's Terms of Service.

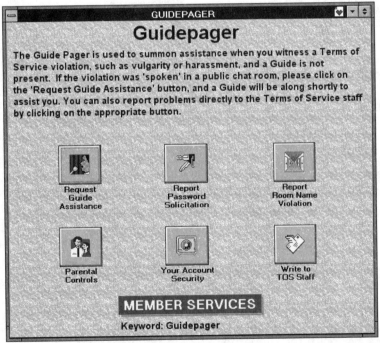

Before you use the Guidepager, be sure to note the room you are in, the screen name of the member causing the problem, and a brief description of the problem. Within five minutes, the Terms of Service Advisor or an on-duty Guide will come to your assistance. Don't abuse this service: sending false or frivolous pages can result in the termination of your account.

Chat Room Sounds

Interestingly, the online medium offers potential for much more than the textual exchange of dialog. In a few years you will probably command an *avatar*—an online visual presence of yourself—just as you "wear" a screen name now; and when your avatar enters a chat room you will see other members' avatars in the room. Members in the room will likewise see your avatar when you enter, just as they see your screen name when you enter a room now.

It's all very radical, I suppose (and aptly described in the novel *Snow Crash*), but not inconceivable. In fact, part of this scenario is here now, in the form of *chat room sounds*.

You can broadcast chat room sounds to a room just as you send text; people in the room will hear the sound just as they would read the text. There are a couple of caveats, however:

- Your PC needs a sound card and speakers. If you don't hear "Welcome" when you sign on, you won't hear sounds in chat rooms. Almost any sound card and speaker combination will work, but buy the good stuff if you can afford it. This is destined to become a multimedia medium; elaborate multimedia content is on the way, and it will make extensive use of sound.

- Likewise, the only people who will hear sounds you send are those with similarly equipped computers.

- The person sending the sound and all those who want to hear it must have the sound already installed on their hard disks. America Online doesn't transmit the actual sound file when you send a sound (sending the actual sound itself would take too long using a modem); rather, it sends a *notification* to play the sound. Members' machines will play the sound only if they have the sound on file.

- The only sound files that work in chat rooms are those that end with the filename extension .wav. You already have a number of them: take a look at your \windows and \waol directories.

- To broadcast a sound in a chat room, type a line matching the format below, then click the chat window's Send button.

  ```
  {S WELCOME.WAV}
  ```

Notice that the command above is enclosed in braces {} and that it begins with a capital *S* (a lowercase *s* won't do). There's a space after the *S*, then the name of the sound. The .wav filename extension is optional in the command.

Finding & Installing Sounds

Hundreds of sounds are available online, where they're referred to as *waves* because of their .wav filename extension. For a listing of some of them, use the keywords: **PC Music**, then browse the wav Sounds library. A similar library of sounds is available in the Macintosh Music and Sound Forum (keyword: **MMS**). To convert Macintosh sounds to .wav format, use one of the many utilities available from the PC Music and Sound Forum. I use "Makin' Waves," from Geoff Faulkner (file search using the criterion: Faulkner), but there are lots of others available.

Once you have downloaded (or converted) a .wav file, move or copy it to your \waol directory. From then on, you can use it in chat situations by following the directions above.

Sound files are great fun, especially in those chat rooms where they're used extensively. LaPub (keyword: **LaPub**) is a good example. More than a room, LaPub is a microcosmic community, complete with its own library of sounds. With a sound card, speakers, and LaPub's library of sounds on your hard disk, a visit to the Pub is reminiscent of the TV series "Cheers," replete with the clinking of glasses and the occasional splat of a pie hitting a face.

Earmuffs

Under some circumstances, chat room sounds can be disruptive. There are both technical and societal reasons for this, but the important thing is that chat room sounds can be turned off if you don't want to hear them. Read Appendix E, "Preferences," for more information.

The Auditoriums

So far, all we've discussed are rooms with a relatively small capacity: 23 persons, for the most part. But what if President Clinton were to make an online appearance? (He has.) How about Billy Joel, Oprah Winfrey, Anthony Edwards, or David Bowie? (They all have.)

Such a vehicle exists. In fact, a number of them do. Collectively they're known as AOL's auditoriums, and each one has a name: Cyber-Plex, Odeon, Globe, Bowl, Coliseum—there are twelve of them in total.

Collectively, AOL's auditoriums can hold up to 60,000 people at a time (see the "Media Melding" sidebar). When you enter, you're assigned a "row" in the auditorium. Each row holds 13 people, and the 13 of you can talk among yourselves all you want: no one else can hear your conversation.

Participating in an Auditorium Event

AOL's auditoriums are significantly different from other chat rooms. They have to be: thousands of people populate the auditoriums—many, many more than a normal chat room's maximum of 23. Here's how it works:

- When you're ready to interact with the people on stage, click the Interact button pictured in Figure 8-14. Your question or comment will be placed in a queue for the moderator's consideration. With audiences numbering in the thousands, not all questions are answered, but the dialog is always engaging, whether you participate or not.

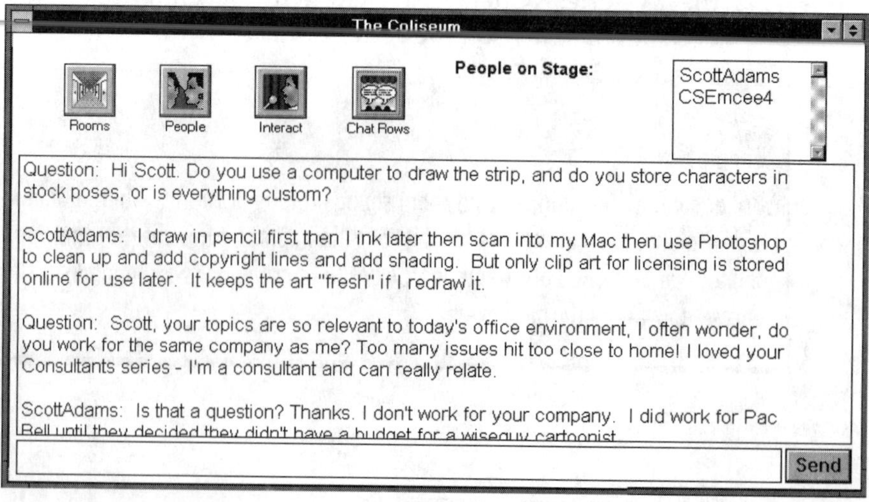

Figure 8-14: In the auditoriums with Scott Adams, creator of the "Dilbert" comic strip.

The Coliseum

People on Stage:
ScottAdams
CSEmcee4

Rooms　People　Interact　Chat Rows

Question: Hi Scott. Do you use a computer to draw the strip, and do you store characters in stock poses, or is everything custom?

ScottAdams: I draw in pencil first then I ink later then scan into my Mac then use Photoshop to clean up and add copyright lines and add shading. But only clip art for licensing is stored online for use later. It keeps the art "fresh" if I redraw it.

Question: Scott, your topics are so relevant to today's office environment, I often wonder, do you work for the same company as me? Too many issues hit too close to home! I loved your Consultants series - I'm a consultant and can really relate.

ScottAdams: Is that a question? Thanks. I don't work for your company. I did work for Pac Bell until they decided they didn't have a budget for a wiseguy cartoonist.

Send

🔺 If you simply type a comment into the lower text box pictured in Figure 8-14 and click the Send button, your comment will appear in the main text box, *but only on the screens of the people in your row*. Comments such as this are easy to recognize: they're preceded by your row number, which appears in parentheses.

🔺 Figure 8-14's People button will display a listing of the other people in your row. You can send them Instant Messages or view their profiles as if you were in a normal chat room (review Figure 8-6).

🔺 The Chat Rows button in Figure 8-14 will produce a listing of all of the rows in use within the auditorium, and the number of people in each one. You can use this button to jump from one row to another, or to find out about people in the auditorium who aren't in your row.

Media Melding

It was a media first: Michael Jackson appearing in a simulcast with America Online and MTV. It also set a record for Auditorium attendance at AOL. In fact, over 16,000 people were "in" the auditorium with Michael Jackson that night, sitting in virtual seats, reading the conversation on their computer monitors while they watched The Man on their television screens. It wasn't the first, nor will it be the last multiple-medium online event: President Clinton's appearance was simulcast on the "Larry King Live" program on CNN, and the cast and crew of "Wings" appeared online while an episode was being taped!

Out of context, 16,000 is a meaningless number. Let's put it in perspective: the previous record for Auditorium attendance was 2,035, set a few months earlier by actress Sandra Bullock. President Clinton drew 1,364 and Anthony Edwards (from NBC's "ER") drew 1,846.

Michael Jackson's auditorium event was, in other words, a Big Deal—probably the biggest online event in the history of the medium. You owe it to yourself to witness at least one of these events. Use the keyword: **Live!** to see the schedule of celebrity appearances. On the appointed evening, use the keyword indicated on the schedule to join the fun.

AOL has twelve auditoriums: Odeon, Globe, Rotunda, Bowl, Coliseum, AOL Live, AOL Sports Dome, News Room, Hollywood Live, Main Stage, CyberRap, and CyberPlex. Each can hold up to 5,000 people. There really isn't any difference between them besides their names—they all have the same capacity and they all work the same way. There are twelve of them so that AOL can accommodate simultaneous online events. AOL's auditoriums are similar to the auditoriums in a multi-screen theater: some want to watch the "Rocky Horror Picture Show"; some want to watch "On Golden Pond." To each his own.

The Game Parlor

Celebrity appearances aren't the only things that happen in AOL's auditoriums. Games are big events as well. Every Saturday night is game night, and gamers turn out by the thousands.

By way of example, I'll pick something familiar. *Wheel Watchers* is a popular offering, based on the syndicated "Wheel of Fortune" TV game show. Three players are selected at random for each of the two preliminary rounds of play, each consisting of two puzzles. Once in play, a puzzle is displayed with asterisks representing the missing letters of the puzzle.

The "spins" of the wheel provide the value for the letters that players guess. If a "7" is spun, its value is 700 points for each time the letter appears in the puzzle. Players with at least 250 points can buy vowels. If you're familiar with the TV game, you're familiar with Wheel Watchers.

There are scores of other games: *Lucky 7, Stump the Standup, Roll 'Em, Scrambled Eggs, Hands Up!, 3-in-a-Row, Mixups*—there are more. And this isn't Hollywood: not only does everyone get a good seat in the audience, in most games, everyone gets to play!

With all of these luminaries and games appearing online—sometimes over a dozen a day—how do you tell who's appearing, and when, and where? And how can you get there? Read on...

Auditorium Help

People, hosts, guests, etiquette, protocol—they can overwhelm the first-time visitor, I know. Any large gathering is that way.

Fortunately, there's help, and it's available right from the AOL Live! Main Screen. Use the keyword: **Live**, then click the Help button.

AOL Live!

Auditoriums, the Game Parlor, conference rooms—at any moment (especially in the evenings) scores of them are active. Keeping track of them all would be an unrealistic undertaking, were it not for *AOL Live!*

Simply put, AOL Live! is your *TV Guide* for online events. Want to know what's playing? Use the keyword: **Live** and look over the schedule of Coming Attractions (see Figure 8-15). You can check the schedule according to time of day, or search for a specific guest, room, or time.

Figure 8-15: Use the keyword: **Live** to see what's happening in AOL's auditoriums and conference rooms.

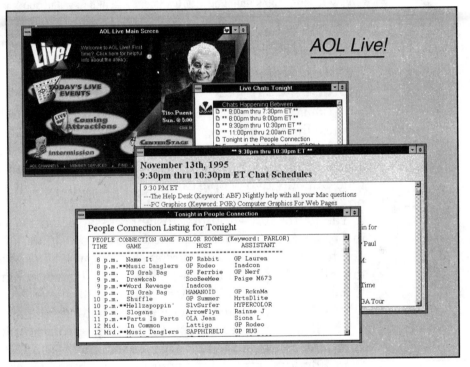

So how do you get to all of these nifty auditorium events? Here's a tip: you can get to any auditorium, at any time, by using the keyword: **Intermission**, then clicking the Auditorium Entrances button. When auditorium events are advertised (especially on the Welcome screen), you're usually given a keyword that will take you to the forum or sponsor for the event. That's fine—especially if you want to know more about the sponsoring organization—but if you simply want to get there fast, use the **Intermission** keyword.

Express Delivery

Often, online promotions for auditorium events—you'll see them on the Welcome screen all the time—mention the name of the auditorium in which the event is occurring.

When you know an auditorium's name and want to get there as if Scotty beamed you, use the auditorium's name as a keyword, *preceded by an @ sign*. If something is happening in the Odeon at 7:30, for example, wait till 7:30, then use the keyword: **@Odeon**. You'll materialize in the Odeon just like Kirk and Spock on a distant planet, ready for action.

Instant Messages

An *Instant Message* is a message sent to someone else online. Don't confuse Instant Messages with e-mail or chat rooms. Unlike e-mail, Instant Messages work only if both the sender and the recipient are online at the same time. Like chat rooms, Instant Messages occur in real time, but only two people can participate in an Instant Message: there's no "room" for others.

You'll probably encounter Instant Messages most often when you're in a room. It's then, after all, that the greatest number of people know you're online. Under those circumstances, an Instant Message is something like whispering in class, though you'll never get in trouble for it. Instant Messages aren't limited to chat rooms, however: they work whenever you're online, wherever you might be.

You'll also often receive Instant Messages from people who have your screen name on their Buddy List. Receiving an Instant Message from a Buddy—especially if your PC is equipped for sound—is always a welcome intermission.

Earlier in this chapter I suggested a private room as an alternative to conference calls. You might also consider Instant Messages as alternatives to long-distance phone calls. Pam Richardson (formerly my primary contact at Ventana Press) and I needed to have a number of discussions nearly every day. Unfortunately, Pam, located in North Carolina, was about as far away from Oregon as one can be without being in a different country. Instead of making long-distance telephone calls across the country and four different time zones, we agreed on mutual times to

go online, allowing us to "talk" without worrying about the cost. The cost amounted to nothing more than the normal connect-time charge. A conversation we had recently appears in Figure 8-16.

Figure 8-16: The "Instant Message From VentanaPam" window contains a running log of our conversation in the upper text box, along with the response I'm composing in the lower one.

Send Instant Message

To: VentanaPam

Hi Pam. I have some answers for you!

Send   Available?

Instant Message from VentanaPam

VentanaPam: Great--please send the message along now. I'll be online for awhile.
MajorTom: Those characters slipped in during the PageMaker-to-text conversion process. They're the things like open and close quotes -- that stuff.
MajorTom: Just search and replace them out with inch-marks (") and foot marks (').
VentanaPam: OK--Thanks for your help on this. I hope it works out.

Let me know if it doesn't work. I'll fix it here if you can't fix it there.

Send   Cancel

To send an Instant Message, choose Send an Instant Message from the Members menu, or type Ctrl+I. Enter the recipient's screen name and your message, as shown in the upper window of Figure 8-16, and click Send. After that, a running log of the conversation is maintained in the Instant Message window, as pictured in the lower window of Figure 8-16.

Before you send an Instant Message, use the Available? button in the Instant Message window pictured at the top of Figure 8-16, or the Locate a Member Online command under the Members menu. If the recipient isn't online when you send an Instant Message, AOL tells you, and you'll have to wait for another opportunity. (If a member is not available online, consider sending e-mail instead. Electronic mail is discussed in Chapter 3.)

Available or Locate?

The Available? button in the Send Instant Message window does the same thing as the Locate a Member Online command under the Members menu. I prefer the button. Most of the time, if a member is online you're going to want to say hello, right? If you discover the member online via the Locate command and want to say hello, you have to call up the Send Instant Message dialog box anyway; but in the time it takes to produce that box, you might lose your opportunity.

OK, it's a small matter, and locating members online isn't like locating pike: they aren't liable to disappear in a matter of seconds. Nonetheless, it's one less command to learn, and every time you don't use the Available? button, you'll wish you did.

- Figure 8-16's lower window has been enlarged from the default. Like all of AOL's windows, the Instant Message window can be resized. If you want to change the size of a window permanently, choose Remember Window Size Only from the Windows menu after you have sized the window to your satisfaction.

- You cannot send Instant Messages while in a free area, though you can compose them while you're there. America Online closes any open Instant Message windows when you enter a free area, and exits a free area as soon as you attempt to send an Instant Message.

- Use the Available? button in the Send Instant Message window to determine where the intended recipient is before sending an Instant Message. This feature tells you if the recipient is online and, if so, whether he or she can receive Instant Messages. It also tells you if a member is in a chat room, in which case you might want to go to that room rather than send an Instant Message.

- Instant Messages are accompanied by a "tinkerbell" sound (assuming your machine is equipped to play sounds), and the Instant Message window will appear on your screen. See the "Ongoing Instant Messages" sidebar for more.

Ongoing Instant Messages

Occasionally, you'll find yourself engaged in an ongoing Instant Message conversation. You might want to do something else online while it's under way—read the postings on a board, for example, or check the weather.

Doing something else online, however, pushes the IM window to the back, and if your PC can't play sounds, you'll need another method of determining when your correspondent has replied. How can you tell with the IM window in the background?

Easy: before you pursue another task, position the IM window on your screen (it's a window like any other and you can move it by dragging its title bar) so that its title bar will show, even if it's in the background and other windows have come to the front. While you're working on another task, keep your eye on the IM window's title bar. When your friend sends a reply, the > symbol will appear in the IM window's title bar, even if it's in the background. Then it's a simple matter of bringing the IM window to the front and composing your reply.

- You can log Instant Messages (handy for telephone-style Instant Messages such as those I exchanged with Pam) by choosing Log Manager from the File menu. Use the "Chat Log" option: it logs Instant Messages as well as chat discussions.
- If you don't want to be disturbed by Instant Messages, you can turn them off at any time by sending an Instant Message to "$im_off" (without the quotation marks, with the dollar sign, and always in lowercase). Include a character or two as text for the message; otherwise AOL will respond with a "cannot send empty Instant Message" error. A single character will do. To turn Instant Messages back on, send an Instant Message to "$im_on."

Buddy Lists

Supply and demand: classical economics expounds on the balance between equilibrium and chaos, citing theories and pointing to business graphics that look like the Grand Tetons and apple pies—all very arcane and inscrutable.

It's not that complex at America Online. At AOL, the supply-and-demand theory is simple: if we the members demand it, AOL will supply it. Such is the case with *Buddy Lists*. By mid-1995, the demand from members for Buddy Lists warranted AOL's examination of the matter. Six months later, the feature was available.

What's a Buddy List? The flaw in the Instant Message scenario that we've been discussing is that you have to know if the recipient is online before you can send an Instant Message. The Locate a Member Online command under the Members menu serves the need after a fashion, but what if the person you're trying to locate signs on four seconds after you've tried to locate him or her? What if that person is online when you sign on? Wouldn't it be nice to know that as soon as the "Welcome" greeting is finished?

Buddy Lists are the solution. Once defined, your Buddy List patrols AOL's front gates like a faithful doorman, checking all members' screen names as they sign on. If there's a match—if a member signing on is on your Buddy List—you're immediately notified. And if a buddy of yours is already online when you sign on, you'll be notified similarly (see Figure 8-17).

Figure 8-17: Once a Buddy List is active, you'll receive automatic notification of a buddy's arrival whenever the buddy signs on.

Your Buddy Has Arrived!

1. When a buddy arrives online, AOL will signal you by bringing the window at right to the front of your screen.

2. The name of your recently-arrived buddy will be selected: click the IM button to make contact.

Buddy Lists

Buddies Online
Buddies1 (1/5)
BillyJoMc

Keyword: BuddyView

You're not limited to a single Buddy List. You can have as many of them as you like—for each of your screen names. As MajorTom, I might have a group of buddies on my "Readers" Buddy List, and another group of buddies on my "Business" Buddy List. If I was online doing work, I'd activate my Business list. If I was there to be social, I'd use the Readers list.

You can create Buddy Lists; and you can add, edit, or delete buddies on those lists using the windows pictured in Figure 8-18 (at keyword: **Buddy**). You can also specify those members whose Buddy Lists you want your name to appear on (and those you don't) by using the Buddy List preferences discussed in Appendix E.

Figure 8-18: Create, Add, Edit, and Delete buddies and Buddy Lists using these routines.

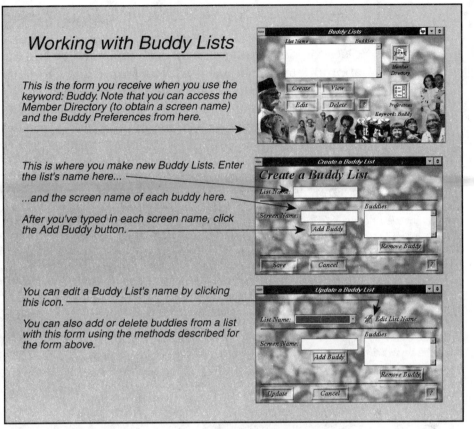

Kids & Parents

In its early years, the online industry was almost exclusively composed of adult males. The online services of the early 1980s concentrated almost exclusively on computer topics and issues. (AOL was no exception: it was called *PC Link* in those days, and was devoted exclusively to users of the Commodore computer—remember the Commodore Pet?) The Internet was up and running then, but military and academic users dominated its use—hardly a forum for kids, or seniors, or even women.

Things have changed. Kids, women, and seniors are the fastest-growing segments of the online community. Probably no other segment of our society adapts as well to computers as our kids do, and kids have no qualms about striking up a new online friendship, uploading original art, or speaking their minds on a board topic.

Kids Only

Kids Only (keyword: **Kids**) is a full-fledged channel on AOL. It's AOL's place for kids to interact with each other and to find information appropriate to their age level. Not surprisingly, parents (and other adults) are asked to refrain from posting on the kids' boards or chatting in the rooms, though browsing the channel is a delight for people of all ages (just look at Figure 8-19 for an indication of the wealth of offerings in this area).

Figure 8-19: The visual abundance of Kids Only is apparent even in black and white. What you can't see or hear are the animations or sounds that accompany each of these areas. For that, you'll have to use the keyword: **Kids**, and explore the channel for yourself.

Take Five for Online Safety

I'm lifting these five rules directly from the Kids Only Channel. It's important for kids to realize that people online aren't always who they say they are. These five rules will help kids—of all ages—manage in our community to their greatest benefit:

- Don't give your AOL password to anyone, even your best friend.

- Never tell someone your home address, telephone number, or school name without asking a parent.

- Never say you'll meet someone in person without asking a parent.

- Always tell a parent about any threatening or bad language you see online.

- If someone says something that makes you feel unsafe or funny, don't just sit there—take charge! Call a Guide (keywords: **KO Help**). If you're in a chat room, leave the room. Or just sign off.

Nickelodeon Online

As you would expect from an organization with a rich visual heritage like TV's *Nickelodeon*, Nickelodeon Online is a hit with kids. Oh sure, there are the *de rigueur* plugs for Nickelodeon shows—popular and colorful events in themselves—but there are also scads of events, message boards, and chat rooms.

Figure 8-20: Nickelodeon Online is home to much more than a cable TV channel.

The *Blabbatorium* is a huge chat room where Nickelodeon viewers from all over the world discuss TV. *Smorgasboards* is the home of the Game Domain, an area devoted to the fine art of game playing online—and while we're on the topic of fine art, kids can upload their own drawings in the *Nick Art Room*. And there's *The Dump*, where kids download Nickelodeon sights, sounds, and videos. (I hesitate to mention this, but Nickelodeon Online also offers a free how-to downloading manual titled *How To Take a Dump*. Whatever you might think of the title, it's a great downloading primer, and it will save parents hours of frustrating—and perhaps futile—tutelage.)

What makes Nickelodeon Online a premier area? The attitude and talent of the people who put it together. This is online programming for kids at its best.

KidzBiz Invention Connection

There are few things more encouraging than a kid with an idea. Unfortunately, parents are often ill-equipped to deal with such a potential, and out of ignorance, or lack of time, end up quashing it.

In fact, ambition is best shared with peers, and that's what KidzBiz is all about. KidzBiz is where kids can share inventions, ideas, job and money issues—even fads (see Figure 8-21).

Figure 8-21: KidzBiz is where creativity and ambition meet: peer support for tomorrow's business and technology leaders. It's all at keyword: **KidzBiz**.

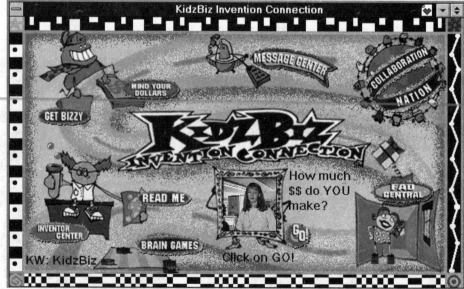

Fad Central

I remember trying to keep up with my daughter's fads when she was a kid. They changed every week, it seems. If only I wudda had KidzBiz Fad Central. Just the other day I found out what a Pog is (and I also found out that they're on their way out—passed me right by!), and the message in Figure 8-22 clarified something I always suspected: expansion team jerseys are poison!

Figure 8-22: A one-day program for success. If only I'd known about football jerseys when I was in school...

```
┌─────────────────────────────────────────────────────────────┐
│ ─  ·          KidzBiz Invention Connection             ▼ ▲  │
├─────────────────────────────────────────────────────────────┤
│  ┌────────────────────────────────────────────────────────┐ │
│  │ Subj: JERSEYS                                          │ │
│  │ Date: 11-10 16:13:20 EST                               │ │
│  │ From: Kid844                                           │ │
│  │                                                        │ │
│  │ EVER TRY WEARING A FOOTBALL JERSEY. POPULARITY GOES UP │ │
│  │     1 DAY!!!!!!!!!!! NEVER EXPANSION TEAMS             │ │
│  │                                                        │ │
│  └────────────────────────────────────────────────────────┘ │
│                                                             │
│  Previous   Read 1st    List       Add       Post    Next   │
│  Message    Response   Responses  Message   Response Message│
└─────────────────────────────────────────────────────────────┘
```

Blackberry Creek

There's no better use of this medium than the exchange of kids' artistic creations, and Blackberry Creek exists for that single purpose (see Figure 8-23). Kids love to create, and they love to share their work. At Blackberry Creek, they reach an audience potential of millions.

Figure 8-23:
Blackberry Creek is
where kids can
post their creations
for all to enjoy.

Blackberry Creek isn't just graphics: *Party People* is a trove of party ideas—by kids, for kids (scout leader alert!), *Story Tellers* is a collection of stories by kids, and *The Players* offers scripts for the stage and screen.

Kids Chat

If there's one thing kids like to do even more than exchange their creations, it's exchange their opinions. All kids have an opinion about something, and most of them have opinions about everything. And there's no medium better suited for that purpose than America Online.

There are chat rooms all over the Kids Only Channel. Nickelodeon has the Blabbatorium, Warner Brothers has the Chat Shack—there are lots of others. These rooms serve a distinct audience; they're not the same as conference rooms or the rooms in People Connection. A few suggestions and specifics on features, restrictions, and unacceptable behavior:

- Some kids rooms (all of those in Kids Only, for example) are for kids of a specific age. Determine a room's age restrictions before you enter.

- The age restrictions are for participants, not observers. Parents should visit these rooms—observe the conversations—before their children become participants.

- Most kids rooms are staffed at peak times; some are staffed round the clock. It's not uncommon to find three or four "nicks" (Nickelodeon staff) in the Blabbatorium, for example, on any weekday afternoon.

- Profanity is not allowed anywhere on America Online. Use of such language in chat rooms and message boards will result in a TOS violation. Using symbols to disguise these words is also a violation.

- Rudeness to a guest, verbally or by behavior, will be considered a room disruption and is subject to TOS review.

- Harassing a staff member or another member in a chat room is not allowed. If someone harasses *you*, do not respond in the same manner. If the harassment appears in the form of an IM, use the Ignore feature (discussed earlier in this chapter) and report the violation to TOS. Don't let one person's rudeness make you behave in the same way.

- Talk of illegal activity is forbidden on America Online.

- *Scrolling* (when a user repeatedly hits the return key so that previous chat room messages move too fast for the users to see) is forbidden. Scrolling is specifically defined as a TOS violation.

- *Polling* (asking a question and requiring all present to post a specific letter, number, or word in response, such as "Type '3' if you love David Bowie.") isn't specifically a TOS violation, but it's a little moronic and always disruptive.

- Before coming to a Kids Chat room, check the calendar. If there is a scheduled event, the room is reserved. You're welcome to join the event in progress, of course, but if you're looking for a social chat, wait until the scheduled event is finished.

- Do not post age/sex checks (requests for room occupants' age and gender) during scheduled events. This disrupts a discussion, is rude to a guest, and makes it difficult to play a game. Ask in Instant Messages if you really can't wait till the event is finished.

There's Much More

I'm only describing a portion of the kids areas available online in this chapter. An exceptional offering of educational resources for students of all ages is described in Chapter 13, "Learning."

Parental Considerations

Though it occurs throughout the service, harassment and exploitation are particularly obstructive in any kids area. To be effective, AOL must be a place where kids are made to feel welcome: it's their online home, and a home—above all—must always be comfortable.

TOS & Kids

America Online's Terms of Service (TOS is discussed in Chapter 2) clearly define the rules of acceptable online behavior—for all members, including kids. Parents should understand these rules and make sure their children understand them before signing on. In the perspective of TOS and kids it's important to remember that the person who is the master account holder is responsible for all of the users whose screen names are on the account.

An extra measure of security

Here's a nifty little tip from remote Forum Leader Tom Quindry: use the Edit Stored Passwords command under the Members Menu to store your kids' passwords. The kids won't need a password to sign on—which might be convenient—but more important, they won't be able to see the passwords on the screen, even if they choose the Edit Stored Passwords command. (Note in Figure 8-24 that stored passwords are displayed as asterisks)

Figure 8-24: Passwords entered via the Edit Stored Passwords command don't show up on the screen.

Edit Stored Passwords

Screen Name	Password
Master Account	
MajorTom	
Kid 1	********
Kid 2	******

OK   Cancel

If your kids don't need a password to sign on, if they can't see their stored password on screen, and if you don't tell them what it is, they can't possibly reveal it to friends or password surfers, no matter how persuasive the come-on. An interesting proposition. Give it some thought.

KO Help

When your child witnesses a TOS violation, he or she should be encouraged to use the keywords: **KO Help** and ask a Guide to enter the room where the violation is occurring (see Figure 8-25). KO Help is sort of a Guidepager for kids. It's a bit more kid-friendly, but it carries the same degree of authority as any other Guide online. Not only will the offender be made to understand the significance of TOS enforcement (that's as politely as I can put it), but your child will see what happens when these rules are broken. A witness to a "TOS event" rarely forgets the experience.

Figure 8-25: Making AOL a better place for all kids: KO Help is only a keyword away.

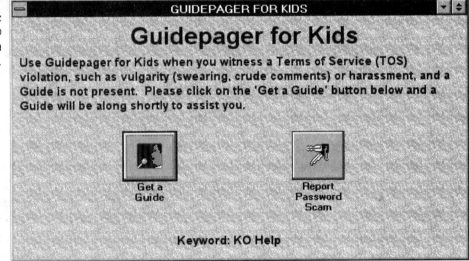

Instant Messages & Kids

Instant Messages often arrive unbidden, and when kids are involved these messages are occasionally unwelcome as well. Your child should know how to turn Instant Messages off, a procedure described in the "Instant Messages" section of this chapter.

Online Time

A friend of mine once recounted her horror when she discovered that her daughter had fallen asleep for two hours while making a call to a 900 number. While 900 numbers usually charge by the minute and AOL charges by the hour, AOL's charges can add up quickly when a child—who can hardly be expected to understand the significance of a month of six-hour Saturdays in the KOOL Tree House—is left unattended online. The Kids Only staff suggests you teach your children how to use FlashSessions for collecting and posting mail (FlashSessions are discussed in Chapter 6, "FlashSessions & the Download Manager"). Set limits on the amount of time they are allowed online, in much the same way you limit their television viewing. KOOL should be a fun electronic clubhouse but not a financial burden. America Online cannot be held responsible for charges you might deem excessive.

The Internet & Kids

As I mentioned in Chapter 4, the Internet is a vast superset of AOL, extending around the world. It is, therefore, an environment over which AOL has no control. There is no Internet TOS, and even if there was one, there would be little authority for its enforcement: the Internet is still an anarchy in many ways.

On the other hand, an increasing number of schools are going online via the Internet, and the array of services available there is constantly growing. This is not an appropriate resource for parents to prohibit, though it *is* one to restrain and monitor (we'll discuss that later in this chapter, when we get to "Parental Controls").

By all means, encourage your children to explore the Internet, but do so only after you've explored this section of the book and visited the keywords: **Parental Controls**. Should you become aware of the transmission, use, or viewing of child pornography while on the Net, immediately report it to the National Center for Missing and Exploited Children by calling 1-800-843-5678. The Center has an excellent brochure on this subject titled *Child Safety on the Information Highway* (see Figure 8-26). The brochure was written by Lawrence J. Magid, a syndicated columnist for the *Los Angeles Times* and author of a number of books on the subjects of computers and the Internet.

Figure 8-26: Parents who intend to allow their children to explore the Internet should order this brochure from the National Center for Missing and Exploited Children. Call 1-800-843-5678 to order.

Parent Soup

We discussed Parental Controls in Chapter 2, "The Abecedarium", but have you heard of *Parent Soup?* Being a parent myself, I know all about parent soup: parents never have enough time for the job of parenting; and all parents can use information, advice, and empathy on the subject. Unfortunately, the online community hasn't made the job any easier.

Or has it? Parent Soup is available from the comfort of your own home, at whatever time of day or night you've got a moment. You can drop by to ask a question, talk to other concerned and involved parents, go to a talk by a leading expert, even get some comic relief. You may be in pajamas or in bagged-out sweats, you might even be dressed for a meeting, but wherever you are, whatever you're doing, the real advantage of Parent Soup is that whenever you're ready, someone there is ready to take your question, hear your sigh, boost you up, or just listen—no small thing when you're a parent.

Note that I said "someone there is ready." The implication is that Parent Soup is a live resource. Many parenting issues require answers *now*, not tomorrow or the next day. Parent Soup offers a profusion of resources, but wherever you travel in Parent Soup, you'll see a Help button. When in doubt, just press it and someone there will come running.

Parent Soup is an antidote for parental paranoia—especially the kind that's provoked by the online community. If you're a parent, take the time to get to know what's available. It's at the keywords: **Parent Soup**, of course.

Seniors

I've remarked on the value of online community. The kids are certainly aware of it, and so too are the members of another demographic sector: seniors. Sometimes isolated, occasionally sedentary, but often gregarious—seniors are perfect candidates for the convenience and camaraderie the online medium offers. True to form, two of the most active areas on the service are in the seniors' domain.

The Communities Center

Kids, seniors, women—they're all discussed in this chapter. But how about Hispanics, Native Americans, African Americans, Twentysomethings, Lions, Eagles, Toastmasters & Jaycees?

There are message boards for each of these communities, and many more. To reach them all, use the keyword: **Communities**.

AARP Online

The American Association of Retired Persons (AARP) is the nation's oldest and largest organization of older Americans, with a membership of more than 33 million. Membership is open to anyone age 50 or older, both working and retired. Over one-third of the Association's membership is in the work force. Whether you're a member of the AARP or not (information about joining is available online), you'll find AARP Online (keyword: **AARP**) a supportive network of people concerned with issues such as caring for parents, grandparenting in the '90s, planning for a sound retirement, re-entering the work force, and consumer fraud (see Figure 8-27).

Figure 8-27: AARP Online offers a wealth of research and information.

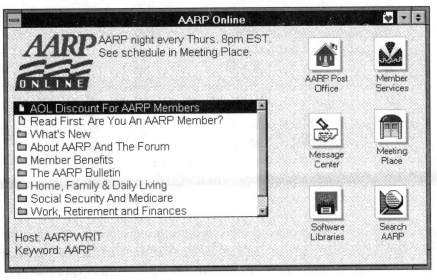

Of particular interest is the forum's searchable database of senior issues. Through its research center and its magazine, the AARP has developed a wellhead of senior-oriented information over the years. The database puts it all online, and it's available to AARP members and nonmembers alike (see Figure 8-28).

Figure 8-28: The AARP's database of senior issues is a pertinent and extensive resource.

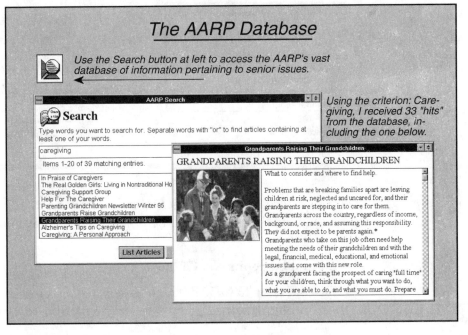

AARP Online also offers a Reporters' Resource Center and a message board, where visitors discuss generational issues, consumer affairs, transitions, finances, and many more topics germane to the senior lifestyle. And I've saved the best for last: AARP members receive a discount on their AOL monthly charge. If you're an AARP member, be sure to take advantage of this offer.

SeniorNet Online

The AARP isn't the only nationwide resource established to serve America's senior population. There's a second one—SeniorNet—that's more focused but every bit as lavish in content as AARP. And fortunately for AOL's senior membership, they're both available online. SeniorNet, the parent organization of SeniorNet Online, grew out of a research project begun in 1986 at the University of San Francisco to determine if computers and telecommunicating could enhance the lives of older adults—in this case, those who are 55 or older.

Figure 8-29:
SeniorNet Online is home to thousands of SeniorNet members. Just use the keyword:
seniornet.

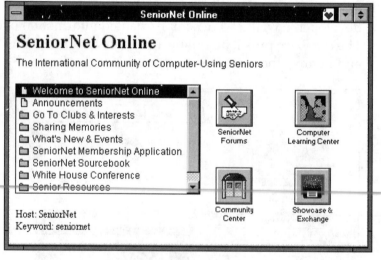

Though access to SeniorNet Online is afforded to any AOL member, those who qualify for and join SeniorNet receive a number of other benefits:

- Unlimited SeniorNet Online access.

- Discounts of 25 to 50 percent on selected magazines and books (including this one).

- Significant discounts on computer hardware and software.

- *Newsline*, SeniorNet's quarterly newsletter, which includes step-by-step computer workshops, computer product reviews, computer tips, and other articles of interest to computer-using seniors.

- Discounted admission to the national SeniorNet conference. The 1993 conference was held in Hawaii.

SeniorNet Online's boards are especially well designed and appropriate for the membership. Topics range from wellness to writing, and hundreds of postings appear every day. When I last visited, more than 20,000 messages were available. This is one of the most active forums on AOL.

The History of the World

Peeking at the SeniorNet libraries the other day, I happened across this gem from history teacher Richard Lederer. Richard has pasted together the following "history" of the world from certifiably genuine student bloopers collected by teachers throughout the United States. Read carefully: you might learn something!

"The inhabitants of ancient Egypt were called mummies. They lived in the Sarah Dessert and traveled by Camelot. The climate of the Sarah is such that the inhabitants have to live elsewhere, so certain areas of the dessert are cultivated by irritation. The Egyptians build the Pyramids in the shape of a huge triangular cube. The Pyramids are a range of mountains between France and Spain.

"Without the Greeks, we wouldn't have history. The Greeks invented three kinds of columns—Corinthian, Doric and Ironic. They also had myths. A myth is a female moth. One myth says that the mother of Achilles dipped him into the River Stynx until it become intolerable.

"Achilles appears in the Iliad, by Homer. Homer also wrote The Oddity, in which Penelope was the last hardship that Ulysses endured on his journey. Actually Homer was not written by Homer but by another man of that name.

"Socrates was a famous Greek teacher who went about giving people advice. They killed him....

"In midevil times, most of the people were aliterate. The greatest writer of the time was Chaucer, who wrote many poems and verses and also wrote literature. Another tale tells of William Tell who shot an arrow through an apple while standing on his son's head.

"The Renaissance was an age in which more individuals felt the value of their human being. Martin Luther was nailed to the church door at Wittenberg for selling papal indulgences. He died a horrible death, being excommunicated by a bull....

"It was an age of great inventions and discoveries. Gutenberg invented the Bible. Sir Walter Raleigh invented cigarettes. Sir Francis Drake circumcised the world with a 100-foot clipper....

"Delegates from the original thirteen states formed the Contented Congress. Thomas Jefferson, a Virgin, and Benjamin Franklin were two singers of the Declaration of Independence. Franklin had gone to Boston carrying all his clothes in his pocket and a loaf of bread under each arm. He invented electricity by rubbing cats backwards and declared, 'A horse divided against itself cannot stand.' Franklin died in 1790 and is still dead."

Surely you know more now than you did a few minutes ago, even though I've cut more than half the article in the interest of brevity. If you want it all, snoop around in the SeniorNet libraries (snoop hard: it's there, under the title "The History of the World"). There's great reading to be found there.

SeniorNet Online also offers the SeniorNet "headquarters," where they've put all the information you want to know about SeniorNet (the club), such as Member Benefits, Member Discounts, and a list of SeniorNet Learning Centers. Naturally, if you're not already a member you can sign up online to join SeniorNet. It's that easy.

Women's Issues

Sitting at your computer, probably in private, it's difficult to imagine the sheer magnitude of the AOL community. There are over five million people here: more people "live" in the AOL community than in the metro areas of San Francisco, Madrid, or Sydney. Every community this size has its share of societal rewards—and problems. AOL is no exception.

Perhaps no segment of AOL's society benefits more from these rewards—and suffers more of the problems—than women. A section on Women's Issues, then, is not only appropriate for this book; it's integral to the understanding of the community. This is a responsibility I don't take lightly.

I'm not a woman however, nor am I so arrogant as to assume that I can speak on women's behalf. For that purpose I have drafted the perspectives of five women of online significance and vision. They're all active participants in the online community, and they've all been here long enough to have things in proper perspective. Short biographies appear as sidebars; I'm using the women's screen names to identify them.

Future Tense

My interviews with Jennifer, Gwen, Eva, Sue, and Sooze occurred in mid-November of 1995, more than three months before the official launch of the Women's Channel. Buddy Lists weren't available at that time either. For this reason, you won't see much mention of either of these pertinent women's features in their comments. This should in no way be interpreted as dilution of their message or their lack of awareness.

Screen Names

Any woman who has ventured into People Connection with a gender-specific screen name probably has a shocking tale to tell. Instant Messages overlap on your screen like paper emerging from a hyperactive photocopier. Most of the senders are men, and most are shy and relatively innocent. Some are not.

What's a woman to do? Take a gender-neutral screen name? Avoid People Connection? Cancel her account? All of the women on our panel use gender-specific screen names. Here's why.

Jennifer: "I've always used a primary gender-specific screen name simply because, quite simply, *I'm* gender-specific. <grin> After I'd been on AOL for a few weeks, I considered the idea of having a gender-neutral name, but it seems like "hiding" or sacrificing my identity in some way. So I didn't, and I'm glad I made that choice. I've met many women who refuse to use a gender-specific screen name because they feel that they will be harassed and/or discriminated against. I've only been harassed while in the People Connection chats (and that is no big deal to me), and rarely (if ever) discriminated against. So I use a gender-specific screen name because I like my name (most names have been a variation on Jennifer) and because I am female. It is just who I am."

Jennifer

Jennifer became an America Online member many years ago—with few expectations; but she found an extraordinary world filled with promise and discovery. In an effort to give something back to the online community, she became a volunteer and consultant. Among her many hats, she is the remote staff coordinator for OMNI Magazine Online, Saturday Review Online, and Longevity Online, as well as the keyword list compiler and author of several AOL-related articles and guides. She also assists and trains other online community leaders.

EvaS: "I've always used my own name. The only time I didn't was in order to see how different my experience might be were I to sign on and go to a chat room using a man's name. It was interesting. I was ignored. :(. . . I'm a woman and like being one. I like my own name. I've learned how to deal with harassment. I ignore it completely. . . ."

SueBD: "In contrast to some of the rest of you, I do get sick of harassment in chat rooms. Most of the time I deal with it by either not going in there to begin with, or by going in under a gender-neutral name. I have noticed, however, as Eva has, that I get less attention that way.

"Entirely naively, I may have gotten myself into a worse situation than those who 'merely' have female screennames. SueBD was really just my initials when I joined AOL in 1993, but I have discovered since then (to my chagrin) that B & D also stands, in some circles, for bondage and discipline, and suggests all *kinds* of kinky things to some folks. Since doing kinky things is the *last* place I want to be online, I finally resorted to making a pretty blatant statement in my profile. As someone else suggested, it works most of the time. I've toyed with the idea of changing my screenname, but I'm on a billion mailing lists, and everyone online knows me by this name, and it just seems like a big undertaking at this point. Furthermore, SueBD is the top name on my account, and if I delete the whole account to get rid of it I lose my mailing list names, too."

SueBD

SueBD works in the medical profession and is a graduate student, preparing to practice in women's issues therapy. She also runs a medical profession mailing list (mailing lists are discussed in Chapter 4) with over 200 members in 10 countries.

GwenSmith: "Both [my business screen name] and my "civvie" one. . . are gender-specific. Why? Because I like to feel that I am showing 'me' online, that I am not hiding myself from others. When I started on AOL, I did have a more 'obscure' name, which allowed me to wander around without anyone knowing who I was—in fact (as it's my original log-on) I still have it and use it, now and again. However. . . people can see a gender-specific name and, well, hormones get the best of 'em, I guess. But I am not going to hide myself because they can't control themselves."

Sooze50: "I closed my account and restarted twice, out of paranoia, to get new screen names. If I were giving advice, I'd say, stow your main screen name, never use it, create one suitable changeable alter ego screen name, and use that for actual online activities. That way, you can dump the alternate screen name without going through the bother of canceling the account. My local police suggested I should never use my real name or give my real address. That proved impractical, since I wanted to exchange books and manuscripts with writers I met online. There is something of depth, an opportunity for mind to mind communication, a surprisingly high level of intimacy of thought, that is worth the risk. E-mail cuts across all the boundaries—age, gender, race, religion, location, time of day. It sounds corny, but, since the picture of the earth that was taken from the moon, I think that the biggest opportunity for world peace is going to be world wide communication by e-mail and the Internet. In worrying about the problems, I say, let's not lose sight of the Big Picture."

Self Defense

Using a gender-specific name, however, eventually provokes an unwanted advance or two. Here's how the members of our panel deal with them:

Jennifer: "I got a lot of these my first year here, and I almost never get them now. I think the biggest reasons are that I don't frequent the same places (People Connection chat rooms), I don't attract that kind of attention anymore, and I know what to do with those who do bother me. There are definitely places online that will bring more unwelcome advances than others, but that shouldn't be a reason to stay away if you want to visit them. Women just need to know that they don't have to respond to all the IMs they get (it *is* OK to close that IM window if you don't want to reply!), how to turn off IMs if necessary, and how to report problems. These days I just ignore the IMs, but if I'm in a particularly talkative mood, I may try to explain to them that asking a woman what she looks like isn't necessary when you are online, and that they have the opportunity to get to know someone from the inside out here. . . .

"Another more 'controversial' way to avoid unwelcome advances is to not call attention to yourself. That means skipping the 'cute' screen names, sticking to basics in your profile, and not giggling and blushing a lot in a chat room. It is similar to walking with confidence down a street when you are worried about muggers. If you act in a strong, self-confident manner online, you will be overlooked more often in favor of those who don't. This doesn't mean you have to act tough at all. Just that you won't take any nonsense."

GwenSmith: "I find if I'm entering a room I haven't been in before, I tend to lurk and get the feel of the area. This often 'comes off' as 'avoiding being cute'—and saves me a lot of trouble! Another thing is to be wary about how much personal information you give out—like addresses and phone numbers, stuff like that. I never list my actual city in my profile (I'll use geographic locales instead), and will usually tell others who ask where I am that I'm 'Near (name a nearby city), CA'. . . ."

GwenSmith

GwenSmith has been an America Online member since spring of 1993, and has seen the system—and herself—grow and change during that time. Gwen is a graphic designer by trade and spends much of her time online with a very close circle of friends in the Gazebo chat room.

EvaS: "[The] first line of defense is to ignore unwelcome IMs. If they're salacious, lewd, report them to TOS. In other words, there I am—or, actually, was—hosting The Womens Room in People Connection. And an IM comes in: "Wanna go private?' I don't answer. I just click the IM box off. . . . Same is true of unwanted e-mail.

"Before I was a host, though, I tried this technique. It would go something like this:

"IM to EvaS: 'Wanna go private?'. . .

"EvaS's reply: 'Hey, I'm old enough to be your grandmother!'

"IM to Eva: 'How old are you?'

"Reply: '52' (which is what I was five years ago;))

"::long pause::

"IM to Eva: 'I like older women!'

"So, with that kind of reply, I decided they weren't going to be put off by my age, that this approach was useless, that most of them are lonely guys of various ages. . . and that every woman who's willing to engage in cybersex looks the same. ;) From then on—and it did take me a couple of months to learn that my response was not working—I simply ignored them."

EvaS

EvaS is the Online Coordinator for the new Women's Channel on AOL. She is also the Forum Leader of the Women's Issues Conferences. In addition, in September of '91, she started The Womens Room, now Womens POV, in People Connection. "I'm really excited by the fact that more and more women are signing on to AOL," Eva says. "What I'd like to see is a true representation of women reflecting the population. Fifty percent women is my goal. And I do think we'll get there someday!"

Sooze50: "I was expecting to meet Stephen Hawking online and argue chaos theory. Virgin me, I knew nothing about 'hot chat.' I ventured innocently into the chat rooms with a feminine screen name. . . and, via IM, immediately met 'Lefty' of Florida who claimed to make 'XXXX videos.' There was also 70 year old Frank from Maryland who was interested in writing 'personal erotica.' I teach testosterone, and consider myself a 'woman of the world,' and I am familiar with the male libido. But I was surprised to find the Electronic

Bonejumpers online, so quickly!, so eager to peek up my Cyberskirts, and with so little foreplay! Initially I was frightened by the horny porny guys. I found, however, that simply saying I 'was not interested in that sort of thing' put an end to it. My advice on the handling of this problem is a combination of a sense of humor, caution, and faithful logging. You can always 'forward' to TOS." (**Note:** logging is discussed in Chapter 10, "Staying Informed." TOS is discussed in Chapter 2, "The Abecedarium.")

Sooze50

Sooze50 is Professor of Biology at Temple University. She has taught courses and written textbooks on biological clocks, the pineal gland, and endocrinology. She is 51, and planning an active future with her retired husband in the Rocky Mountains.

GwenSmith: "Undesired IMs are promptly ignored. If the conversation isn't going to go past 'What are you wearing?,' then what's the point. Of course, if it's vulgar, off it goes to the TOS staff. A couple tips I have passed on to folks include:

"1. Don't bother to IM with a person who won't enter the chat room [you're in]. If they won't enter the room and talk, but want to carry on a conversation with you, then there is probably good reason to be suspicious of their intentions. Usually, I will "invite" the person to come in and talk, just to see what their response is.

"2. Add something into your profile. Just putting a quick 'No Cybersex' or such in a profile can really help keep people away. A lot of the 'cruisers' check those profiles, and if they see 'No'—well, some of them will actually listen."

The Value of Online Friends

Most of us who have used this medium over time can attest to its greatest reward—finding and making friends online. Of my very few "best friends," I've met two online. Over the years we've shared death, marriage, retirement and, of course, philosophy. Intellectual and emotional exchange with these people tends to be more intimate and intense than it is with my other good friends. The medium does that.

I have an unfair advantage, however. Scores of readers write to me every day, so I don't have to look very far for opportunities to make online friends. People tend to write to me using their primary account names rather than their alter egos. And I'm a man: few who write to me have ulterior motives. These are advantages few other people have, and for women, soliciting friendships online is an exceptional vulnerability.

Sooze50: "In the beginning, I thought, what the heck can I do with this? As an author, I had talked only to editors and readers. Wouldn't it be fun to be friends with some authors? So, I thought, I'll try to find some. I found them, and some surprises, by searching the AOL Membership Directory. For example, searching Melville produced everybody interested in Herman Melville—and also everyone who lived in the town of Melville. I found Edward (name changed) while searching for the ghost of Moby Dick. He wrote, 'please write anytime' and launched into a discourse on Skylab blowing up. Edward was as scary as Stephen King with the black humor of John Irving. Edward and I wrote over 600,000 (!) Strictly Platonic biting witty words to one another in the course of a year before he got [angry with me] the second, and Final time. . . . Therein lies the pleasure, and the danger. Because, when Edward disappeared, both the first and the second time, my feelings were hurt. . . we wrote for a long time, and I still miss him."

EvaS: "I have Chronic Fatigue and Immune Dysfunction Syndrome. Being online saved my life. I started a CFS support group, The Womens Room in PC, and so on. To put it yet another way, I found support through finding others with this rotten illness. And I found friends in the support group, people who didn't think I was a malingerer, who knew the illness was/is real. . . . One of the things I've learned about a lot people of online is that they find out new things about themselves. They can try out being more assertive, are less shy. They can speak up more. And all these experiments they try finally do leak over into their offline life. They actually try their wings here, unseen, unheard, and learn to speak out—not only here, but at work and at home."

GwenSmith: "All of my closest (other than my spouse and some long time friends from high school) are from friendships gathered online. . . . Back in [the] halcyon days of '93, I met friends who are *still* here, friends that I have since met offline and who mean a lot to me. We all, I think, have had to make the first step in gaining friends, whether it was from opening up rooms, or from seeing someone else online who seemed like a nice person, and opening up a dialogue. I know that I usually get folks contacting me over hobbies, etc., in my profile, and think the [idea of an] 'extended profile' is a great idea!" (**Note:** No sooner said than done. Read the "Personal Publisher" section in Chapter 2.)

Sooze50: "Here's my best story: My husband joined CompuServe. Which was better? I said, 'Let's try both.' He is sitting in His Home Office, I am sitting in My Home Office. We are separated by a bedroom, bathroom, and laundry room, a long hallway, and an electronic highway. I've been married to this man thirteen years, and my eyeballs popped when his hot poetry burned my screen. . . . I didn't even know the man could rhyme. He's turned out to be a regular e e cummings."

Making Online More Female Friendly

I don't have figures for this, but I'll bet that the fastest-growing segment of the online community is women. If it isn't, I'm sure it will be someday soon. This might be a medium of snakes in the grass, but the grass itself is a verdant meadow of grace and regard.

Like any crop, however, this one benefits from fertilizing. Below, the panel's comments.

Sooze50: "America Online already took the first big step. Free diskettes, easy to use, lots of help. The Best Little Tour Guide in America. :) It may be the 80% of the membership that don't read the Tour Guide that have the most problems, because the Tour Guide tells about Parental Chat Control, etc."

Thank you, Sooze, for the plug. Readers of these pages, however, are poor candidates for Tour Guide sales. :-(Her implied advice, however, is sound: if you haven't read Chapter 2, "The Abecedarium," or the other sections of this chapter, be sure to do so.

EvaS: (speaking somewhat as staff) "We can tell them how we handle snerts. We can teach them how we handle snerts. Part of this is what AOL—meaning, the new Women's Channel—will try to do. [We] have been working on a course to teach women how to help themselves deal with the mean streets here. ;)

"Just because you're sitting at home at your very own computer doesn't mean that you won't have to deal [with sexual problems online]. Second thing to get across is that there are ways to deal. . . we've covered a lot of these already. The main one being that we don't

have to answer someone who talks to us, either in a chat room, via IM or e-mail. Click off the IM. Put the jerk on Ignore. Don't answer the e-mail.

"The problem is that most women are taught to speak when spoken to. Men are not as bound by that stricture as women. The other problem is that we're taught, as women, that what happens to us *vis a vis* men is our doing, our fault. So, if a man whistles at us on the street, we wonder if we're wearing clothing that is too provocative, whether we gave some kind of come on, whether we're emitting pheromones of sexual invitation. So, there we are at home, and a man IMs us, asking what we're wearing. . . . We *must* have asked for this in some way. Maybe he's a mind reader, and we've had our sexual desires, needs, thoughts, read. This a blame-the-victim mentality which is very much alive and well. :(

"It's compounded in another way by the new things that are finally happening—successful sexual harassment suits, empowerment of women, and so on. So, she sits there, thinking: 'Why should I have to take this kind of thing?? I didn't ask for it. Who the hell does he think he is?? I'm paying for this damned service and look what happens!! This is s**t and I'm going to tell him a thing or two!'

"Wrong thing to do, of course. And if women can be taught that this is really a large city, that if you're on 42nd St. in NYC, you have to watch it, that you don't have to respond to the guy who's whistling at you, or the equivalent, just because you're female, that you have to ignore the come-ons, etc. And, most important of all, you didn't ask for this.

"We have to direct women to areas online that are safer, more women-friendly already. And there will be a new women's area soon, a big one, that will be that way. Not that women will be protected from snerts, but that it will be women in the majority."

Jennifer: "Female-friendly means many things to me. It means educating our friends, family, colleagues, and passers-by on general online etiquette and matters of consideration. Not just educating women, and not just educating them about women's issues online.

"Being female-friendly also means getting more women online to level out the playing field. AOL is still predominately male, and it can be intimidating to be in the minority. We should encourage the women in our life to use the computer, get online, and discover the opportunities.

"Another aspect of being female friendly is to help women realize that this medium is as much theirs as anyone else's. Personally, I won't pander to self-depreciating jokes some women make about how they don't know how to use AOL or their computers. Too many women are still afraid of the computer, or expect their husband or boyfriend to do all the 'techie' stuff for them. Woman need to understand that it isn't 'unfeminine' to use a computer and to *like* it—it is simply a tool that helps us accomplish things and realize dreams.

"Other things are:

"—Don't assume the owner of a non-gender-specific screen name is male. (It happens a *lot*.)

"—Don't act different around those who you know are female. Take advantage of one of the great benefits of being online and treat everyone equally.

"—Report problems you see happening online. If you don't, no one may.

"—Talk about this subject with others. Not only does it increase awareness, but you may learn more!"

GwenSmith (in summation): "I feel it is up to those of us who are on staff to provide 'female-friendly' content and environments online, and it is up to those of us who are members (all of us) to make sure people know we are here."

Community awareness comes slowly. We tend to explore first, exchange some mail, and maybe visit a room or two. Later, we might develop a few friendships and find a few favorite haunts. Most of us, however, take a year or two before we become of the AOL community as a whole. It's a revelation when we do: AOL is vibrant and diverse, and like any vital community, it requires teamwork to prosper and grow. Gwen, Sue, Jennifer, Eva, and Sooze all endeavor to put back into the community more than they take from it. We should all aspire to their benevolence.

Interesting Places for Women Online

As I write this chapter, a whole new women's area of America Online is under construction. It will probably become a full-fledged Women's Channel, offering expanded women's resources and a place for women to go. Though not exclusively so, this will be a women's space—a "private space," as writer Deborah Tannen calls it—where women's communication will prosper.

The Women's Channel & Women's Issues Conferences

Unlike the Women's Channel, the Women's Issues Conferences exist now. It's the online equivalent of Tannen's private space and will no doubt remain so even after the Women's Channel is launched. There's a terrific Women-to-Women area, ". . . a place for all of us to communicate about what concerns us, to share our experiences, thoughts and feelings. Only through seriously listening to and reading others' ideas and sharing our own can we widen our views, challenge our assumptions, and find common ground." (Quoting the Conference description.) Look also in the Reading Room, the Gallery, and the Library; and visit the Conference Room every Tuesday from 9-10:30 p.m. The schedule is always available under the Schedule of Events.

Figure 8-30: The Women's Issues Conferences offer women a place to find common ground online. They're available at keyword: **Women**.

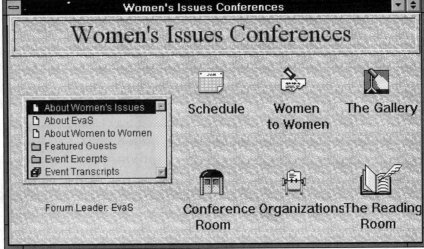

NetGirl

Irreverant, perhaps. Outspoken, without a doubt. The *Berkeley Barb* of online, maybe. One thing is for sure: NetGirl doesn't paint with pastels. This is women's online programming with an attitude, and if you're a woman, the attitude is decidedly positive (use the keyword: **NetGirl**, and see Figure 8-31).

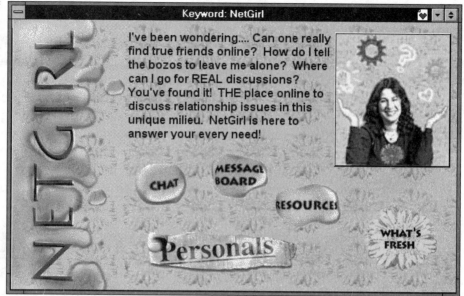

The World Wide Web (discussed in Chapter 4) is rapidly becoming a primary medium for women's exchange, and true to her name, NetGirl lists hundreds of women's Web resources, and the list is getting longer every day. Click the Resources button.

Unique to the commercial online medium, however, are NetGirl's Personals. These are the alternative-newspaper personals you've seen: people seeking partners, parent to parent, friends seeking friends. That last one is one you might want to investigate: it's organized by region, and it's one of AOL's best methods of finding people—people nearby—for online friendships.

Lifetime TV

Lifetime Television—"Television for Women"—was created by the merger of Daytime and Cable Health Networks in 1984. Since then, Lifetime's original programming has received over 200 awards and Emmys. Lifetime Online is a Web page, and the number of links is not only enormous, it's significant as well: the links represent a compendium of the best women's resources on the Internet.

Figure 8-32: Lifetime Television offers in-depth programming information and lots of Web links at keyword: **Lifetime**.

ELLE Online

As a leading women's fashion magazine, *ELLE* continues to break new ground as the first magazine in its category to be featured online. In addition to its fashion and beauty areas, ELLE Online offers an extensive Fitness and Health focus. Look for Susan Blumenthal's comments in ELLE's Health Newsletter—Dr. Blumenthal is the Assistant Surgeon General and U.S. Deputy Assistant Secretary for Women's Health.

Figure 8-33: ELLE
Online offers fea-
tures on fashion,
beauty, fitness,
and health at
keyword: **Elle**.

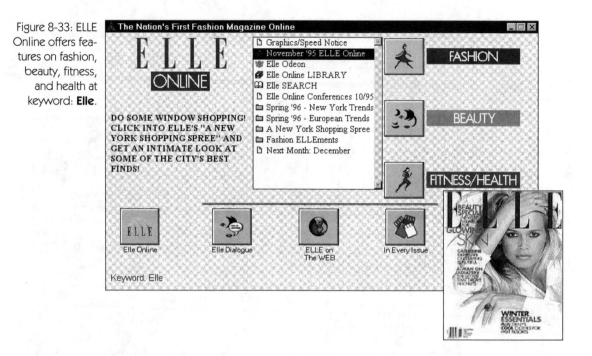

Woman's Day Online

With my wife Victoria in medical school and our daughter Sybil long
ago on her own, I have become, of necessity and convenience, a home-
maker. And in this capacity, I admit to visiting the Woman's Day
Online area for homemaking tips and recipes. There's much more,
including a superb resource center and message board for breast cancer
issues. If you visit and see me there, be sure to say hello.

Figure 8-34: For a discussion of practical issues for both sexes, use the keywords: **Woman's Day**.

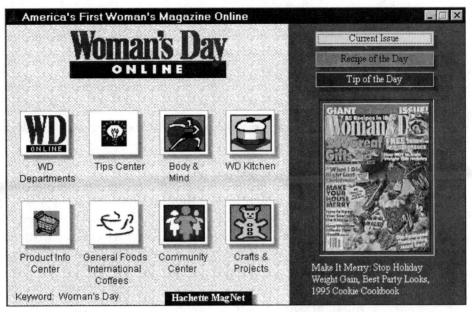

Guttersnipe

In a community of five million, it should come as no surprise to learn that there are a number of interlopers online. And typical of an industry that embraces acronyms and sobriquets, AOL members fastidiously categorize these gremlins according to the severity of their pestilence.

Trolls

Least sinister are the *trolls*. Trolls dawdle along the information highway, impeding traffic and undermining good will. Trolls enter chat rooms with palaver like "Is anyone horny?" or "Press 3 if you like Spam." They're a bit more loquacious on message boards, but their posts usually disappear when the staff makes its first sweep of the day. Trolls send me e-mail all the time that says "Did you know your name is in the Tour Guide?" Recondite discourse, that.

Trolls are easy to manage: just ignore them. They're seeking attention, after all, and if it's granted, they have their reward. Trolls are the first category of urchin to Ignore in a chat room (the Ignore button was discussed earlier in this chapter). If a troll sends you e-mail or IMs you, copy his screen name and close his window. He probably won't be back. Use the copied screen name to block yourself from his Buddy List (blocking Buddy Lists is a preference and is discussed in Appendix E) and forget about it. You just passed a ragamuffin on the street; don't break your stride and he won't break his.

Phishers

We're moving up the scavenger's food chain now. *Phishers* are trolls who have graduated from misdemeanors to larceny. Phishers snack on passwords, and they feast on credit card numbers.

The common phisher appears in the form of an unsolicited IM on your screen. The message therein identifies the phisher as a member of AOL's staff. There will be a comment about damaged files at AOL and a request for your password "so that we can reconstruct our database."

More sophisticated phishers will send you an IM or e-mail claiming to be a member of AOL's staff, offering an irresistible discount on an article of merchandise. Who can resist a 28.8 modem for $24.95? The hitch, of course, is that they're not AOL staff, they have no modems, and the conversation will eventually get around to a request for your credit card number.

Other phishers, also masquerading as AOL staff, will ask you to send specific files on your hard disk to them. Though the files might seem benign and the request might seem sanctioned, this is phishing nonetheless. The requested file probably contains your encrypted password—for use by unattended FlashSessions, for example—and some phishers are sophisticated enough to decipher them.

If you ever receive a message—e-mail or IM—asking for your password, a file, or your credit card number, you can be sure it's a phisher. It is *not* a member of AOL's staff, no matter how eloquent or convincing the request.

FOOLED YOU!

Many phishers use the old "0 and L" trick. The word "GUIDE" will be rejected if it appears anywhere within a proposed screen name, but the word "GUlDE" will not (the third character is a lowercase *L*, not an *I*). Thus, you might receive a message from "GUlDE Tom" and think he's an official of some sort. Beware of zeros as well: "A0L Tom" is not a staff member. Though AOL is a blocked sequence for screen names, A-*zero*-L is not.

Phishers should always be reported. Don't close that IM window! Instead, click somewhere within the message, choose Select All from the Edit menu, then choose Copy from the same menu. Write down the phisher's screen name, then use the keyword: **Guidepager**. You'll find your way from there.

The term *phisher* probably originated with the phone freaks of the 1970s and early 1980s—they called themselves "phreaks." They were the first (phirst?) of the breed, and unfortunately this breed is especially prolific. They can be *very* sophisticated: don't be phooled.

Snerts

Trolls troll for attention. Phishers phish for passwords. *Snerts*, however, are virtual voyeurs. Their primary goal is an indiscriminate assault on privacy. They live under tenement stairs where there is no light and an abundance of virulence. There they concoct schemes specifically designed to wreak havoc online, and harassment is their preferred bounty. When they discover a technique that seems especially repulsive, they broadcast it to other snerts (usually via the Internet) and come knocking on AOL's electronic doors.

A small army of AOL technicians vigilantly patrols for snerts (read the "The Control Room" sidebar in this chapter), but the battle is often an impasse.

Recidivistic Trolls

The word *snert* is an acronym: Sexually Nerdishly Expressive Recidivistic Trolls. Hardcore snerts, however, eschewed sex in the traditional sense of the word a long time ago—if they ever knew about it in the first place. They prefer the online medium for their carnal romps now; they don't have time for the triviality of substantive matters. Perhaps we should be thankful for that: their arrogance surpresses procreation. Snerts may be a vanishing species.

Unfortunately, snerts are as hard to catch as an arsonist, and every bit as destructive. When you encounter one, use the keyword: **Guidepager** immediately and report them.

Moving On

There's another form of community: the community of association. You might live in one community, but you might also travel to meet with people with similar interests. My trailerboating community has no specific body of water: I take my boat to waterways all over the northwest, and I meet with other boaters when I do.

Thus, we move from the general to the specific; from the online community to the forums, each a microcommunity of its own—an association of members sharing similar tastes and attitudes. If you have a hobby, a vocation, or a belief, AOL probably has a forum of folks with similar interests. Turn the page to find out.

Boards & Forums

CHAPTER 9

- Message Boards
- Computers & Software Forums
- Community Forums
- Gaming Forums

'm having a semantics problem: in the second edition of this book, I called the subjects of this chapter "clubs," but the word *club* implies exclusivity, and that isn't quite right. AOL's attitude toward exclusivity is similar to that of Groucho Marx: in a letter to Hollywood's Friar's Club, Groucho wrote "Please accept my resignation. I don't care to belong to any club that will have me as a member." Kinda puts exclusivity in its place, don't you think?

I suppose the proper term is *forum*. It has a certain Roman quality to it: Roman forums were public meeting places for sharing ideas and interests. That's close to where we're headed with this chapter. On the other hand, whole Roman cities were laid out with forums as their focus. That's a bit pretentious in this context, but it will have to do.

AOL's forums are where people with a common interest gather to exchange opinions, solicit advice, and hobnob with celebrities. Forums are the *vox populi* of AOL's living room referendum; they're as diverse as Pacific Northwest weather and as abundant as its rain; and if you can't find a forum to your liking, there are always the Internet newsgroups, there are more than 17,000 of those, and AOL carries nearly every one.

How to Find a Forum

AOL offers hundreds of forums. How can you tell if one exists that addresses your interest in, say, celestial navigation? Here's a methodical approach:

Search the Directory of Services. Use the keywords: **Directory of Services**, then specify your interest. Try a variety of search phrases: if the phrase **celestial navigation** doesn't work, try "navigation." If that doesn't work, try some general or related topics such as "boating" or "flying."

Try using your specific interest as a keyword. Press Ctrl+K, then enter **celestial navigation**. If that doesn't work, use keyword search. Press Ctrl+K, enter a few words describing your interests, then click the Search button. Again, don't hesitate to experiment.

Perhaps there's a newsgroup on the Internet that matches your interest. Use the keyword: **Newsgroups**, then click the Search All Newsgroups button. This is especially effective if your interest is regional. Be sure to read Chapter 4, "Using the Internet," before you participate.

AOL's forums usually consist of a conference room, where meetings are held and guest appearances are scheduled; a library, where members submit software they find useful, or files of their work—text, graphics, music, video—for others to enjoy; and message boards, where members converse without the boundaries of time or place.

We discussed libraries in Chapter 5, and conference rooms in Chapter 8. Message boards, however, provide a more direct, more personal, and sometimes more interesting route to the sources than rooms and libraries put together. This chapter, therefore, begins with a discussion of boards and their operation. After that, we'll examine some of the forums themselves.

Message Boards

America Online's message boards are the electronic analog of the familiar cork board and pushpins. Message boards (call them "boards") are especially appropriate to online forums. One of the unique advantages boards offer is convenience: you can drop in any time of the day or night, read the messages, and post your replies.

Most of us visit our favorite boards every time we sign on and anxiously read all the messages posted since the last time we visited. The feeling is remarkably immediate, and withdrawal sets in after about three days' absence. In other words, boards are addictive—but that's part of the fun.

Reading Messages

One of my favorite forums is the Cooking Club (keywords: **Cooking Club**). These folks like their food, and their libraries of recipes range from elegant appetizers to tantalizing desserts. The Cupboard offers articles and reviews of cookbooks and cooking software, and The Kitchen (a chat room, a topic we discussed in Chapter 8) opens each Sunday at 8:00 p.m. Eastern time for a cooking class, new recipes, and lively camaraderie. (This is an especially nonthreatening chat room by the way. If you're new to chat rooms you might try this one first: there's very little aggression among people who spend their Sundays sipping sherry and discussing soufflés.)

Editing the Go To Menu

Once you've found a forum to your liking, you might want to visit it every time you sign on. Rather than navigating a stack of menus or typing a keyword, give the forum a place on your Go To menu. Items at the bottom of the Go To menu are under your control; you can add or delete any one you please. The only requirement is that the item must have a keyword.

Once a place is added, you can go there via its keystroke shortcut: Ctrl+1, Ctrl+2, and so on. This is even easier than using the Favorite Places feature described in Chapter 4. Only ten places can be added to your Go To menu, however, so save these entries for your most frequently visited places.

Let's say you've become an active participant in the Cooking Club. To add it to your Go To menu, follow the procedure illustrated in Figure 9-1.

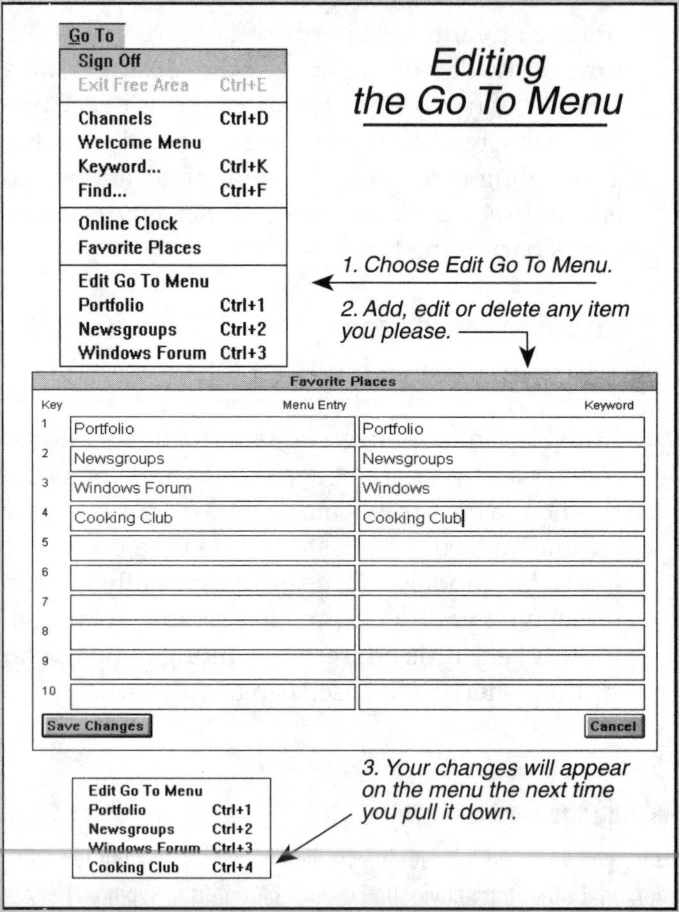

Figure 9-1: Adding menu items is accommodated via the Edit Go To Menu command.

Editing the Go To Menu

Go To	
Sign Off	
Exit Free Area	Ctrl+E
Channels	**Ctrl+D**
Welcome Menu	
Keyword...	**Ctrl+K**
Find...	**Ctrl+F**
Online Clock	
Favorite Places	
Edit Go To Menu	
Portfolio	**Ctrl+1**
Newsgroups	**Ctrl+2**
Windows Forum	**Ctrl+3**

1. Choose Edit Go To Menu.

2. Add, edit or delete any item you please.

Favorite Places

Key	Menu Entry	Keyword
1	Portfolio	Portfolio
2	Newsgroups	Newsgroups
3	Windows Forum	Windows
4	Cooking Club	Cooking Club
5		
6		
7		
8		
9		
10		

[Save Changes]   [Cancel]

3. Your changes will appear on the menu the next time you pull it down.

Edit Go To Menu	
Portfolio	**Ctrl+1**
Newsgroups	**Ctrl+2**
Windows Forum	**Ctrl+3**
Cooking Club	**Ctrl+4**

Note that there are ten positions for you to customize on the Go To menu and that mine only has five positions active. You don't have to have all ten filled if you don't want to, nor do you have to use those that AOL initially provides. You can change any item (select it and type over), or delete items (select the item, then use the backspace key on your keyboard). Changes to the Go To menu are in effect only on the computer used in making them, by the way, and not to any particular screen name. They won't appear when you're using another machine, but they *will* appear when you're using another screen name on the original computer.

Once you have added a forum, all you have to do to get there is choose that forum from the Go To menu or use the Control key equivalent. My Go To menu contains the names of the places I like to check every time I'm online. By choosing each one in order, I never neglect to visit places I'm likely to forget.

But I'm getting ahead of myself. I've chosen this forum because it's an excellent example of message boards. In fact, it has eight of them. Everyone eats food, after all, and most of us who eat it aren't shy when it comes to talking about it. For this discussion, we'll examine the Cooking Club's recipe-exchange boards in The AOL Cookbook (see Figure 9-2).

Figure 9-2: Type the keywords: **Cooking Club** to open the Cooking Club's main window, then click The Cookbook icon to visit the boards.

Look at Figure 9-3. Six buttons appear across the bottom of The Desserts window: List Categories, Read First Message, Find New, Find Since, Create Topic, and Help & Info. We'll examine each of these, beginning with the one marked List Categories (see Figure 9-3). Because this is a complex board—it's a cookbook after all, and cookbooks are typically large and organizationally complex—a click on Figure 9-2's List Categories button produces a list of categories (the bottom window in Figure 9-3). Each category is followed by a list of *topics*. The Desserts & Sweet Treats category, for example, is further subdivided into more specific topics (Angel Food Cakes, Bundt & Tube Pan Cakes, and so on). Note that these topics are the members' creations: almost every folder was a member's idea. While this is a little anarchistic, it's also democratic; and that's the way message boards should be. If you feel like making a comment that's off the subject, use the Create Topic button to make a new folder for it.

The Creation Issue

No, I'm not going to debate Darwinism. This is a computer book and we're discussing cooking. That's off-subject enough. The Cooking Club offers examples of a board that allows members to create folders. The Create Topic button pictured in Figure 9-3's center window allows you to create a folder on the board, in which you or any other interested member can post a message.

You'll find other boards where there's no Create Topic button. The topics are established by the board's staff; members can't change them.

To allow creation or not to allow creation: the decision is up to the forum's staff. I mention it because I don't want you to expect a Create Topic button on every board you visit.

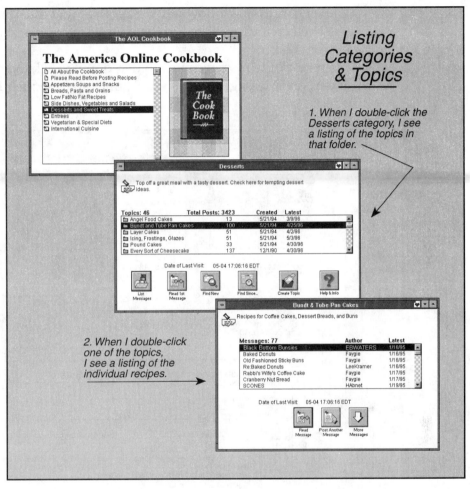

Figure 9-3:
The eight catego-
ries posted on The
Cookbook's recipe
board are followed
by 46 member
topics. Each topic
folder contains a
number of indi-
vidual recipes.

The bulletin board metaphor is distorted a bit here. Individual messages aren't normally posted on boards; *folders* are posted on boards (the messages themselves are inside the folders). Look again at the center window in Figure 9-3: this board is currently holding more than 3,000 messages. If all 3,000 were posted independently, the board would be a mess. You would never find a thing. The board's nested folders are merely organizational tools intended to help you locate topics of interest to you.

To read the messages placed in a folder, double-click the folder. By double-clicking the Bundt & Tube Pan Cakes topic folder shown in Figure 9-3's center window, we reveal the 77 recipes listed in the Bundt

& Tube Pan Cakes window at the bottom of that illustration. Although only seven recipes are listed in the window, you can scroll down to view the rest.

To read all the messages in a folder, double-click the first one, then use the Next Message button (see Figure 9-4) to sequentially display the rest.

Figure 9-4:
Once you have read the first message in a folder, click the Next Message button to read the remaining messages in the order of their posting.

Reading Every Message in a Folder

Desserts

Subj: Black Bottom Bunsies
Date: 06-01 14:57:42 EST
From: EBWATERS

Black Bottom Bunsies

1 1/2 C all purpose flour
1 tsp. baking soda
1/2 tsp. salt
1 C sugar

Next
Message

Subj: Black Bottom Bunsies   06-01 14:57:42 EST
From: EBWATERS

Black Bottom Bunsies

1 1/2 C all purpose flour
1 ts
1/2   Subj: Chocolate Sauce   07-24 18:13:44 EST
1 C   From: EBWATERS
1/4
1 C   Chocolate Sauce
1/3
1 tb   1 C
1 tb   1/2   Subj: BUCKEYES (SORT OF)   10-25 12:28:33 EST
1 8   1/4 (From: IreneN2130
1 eg   1 tbs
1/2   2 sq   2 cups peanut butter
1/8   1 tsp   1 stick melted butter
1 6   pinc   2 cups powdered sugar
                4 cup
Cor   Diss   Coati   Subj: Carmel Apples   10-30 10:08:24 EST
Cor   Boil   4 tbls   From: Brian 1305
Spo   pinc   Melt
Cor   Roll i   I am trying to make carmel apples because I can't eat chocolate. If anyone
cho   boile   has any suggestions for those or any other tasty non chocolate desserts,
cho   choc   please send some to Brian 1305.   Thanks

Sprinkle top

Makes 5 dozen   Subj: Caramel Apples   10-30 21:36:03 EST
                   From: Bev In CA

                   Caramel Apples

                   5 medium apples
                   1 cup granulated sugar
                   3/4 cup dark corn syrup
                   1 cup cream
                   2 Tablespoons butter
                   1 teaspoon vanilla
                   coarsely chopped nuts (optional)

                   Wash apples, remove stems, and stick skewers into stem ends of apples.
                   Cook sugar, syrup, cream, butter, and vanilla to firm-ball stage, 245F. Do not
                   stir. Remove from heat. Dip apples into syrup; spoon syrup over apples to
                   cover completely. Remove apples; hold skewer between palms of hands
                   and spin for a moment to cool caramel. If desired, roll in coarsely chopped
                   nuts. Place apples upright on waxed paper.

The Next Message button is the key to reading all messages. Every message will offer one except the last.

Brian's morning plea for help was answered that evening.

Log Those Messages

Reading messages is one of the most time-consuming activities AOL offers. Rather than read messages online, save a log of them (we'll discuss logs in Chapter 10, "Staying Informed") as they download to your computer. Let them scroll off your screen as fast as they can; don't try to read them while you're online. When you have finished the session, sign off, open the log (choose Open from AOL's File menu, or open it with a word processor if it was a lengthy session) and read it at your leisure. You can always add messages to boards by signing back on again.

Browsing, Finding & Reading Messages

I need to take a side trip here. The verbs *browse, find,* and *read* have particular, unequivocal meanings when it comes to message boards; it's important that you understand how to use them. Think of a public library: you might go to the library simply to pass the time. You walk in and browse, picking up a book here and there as different titles strike your fancy. On another day, you might visit the library with a specific title already in mind, in which case you go straight to the card or electronic files and find that particular book. Regardless of how you come across a book, you eventually want to sit down and read it, page by page.

America Online attaches the same meanings to these verbs. Look again at the Desserts window at the center of Figure 9-3. Six buttons parade across the bottom of the window, representing variations on the three verbs we're discussing.

The List Messages button displays the folder's message subjects, authors, and dates, not the messages themselves (see the Bundt & Tube Pan Cakes window at the bottom of Figure 9-3). Using the List Messages feature is like browsing through the books in a library: the concept is the same for both. The leftmost button (List Messages, in this case) is the default: if you double-click a folder, you'll see the list that appears in the lower window of Figure 9-3.

Clicking the Read 1st Message button produces a window displaying the first message in the folder (see the top window in Figure 9-4).

The Subject Line

As you read through this section, note the role played by a message's subject line. A subject line like "Comment" doesn't illuminate its contents very well. Alternatively, a subject line like "Savory Béarnaise Sauce Recipe" clearly summarizes the content of the message and intrigues the reader. Spend a moment thinking about subject lines when you post your own messages; they're significant.

This might be a board you read often. You might visit it every time you sign on. If you do, you can go right to the Find New button, which displays only those messages posted since you last visited (see Figure 9-5).

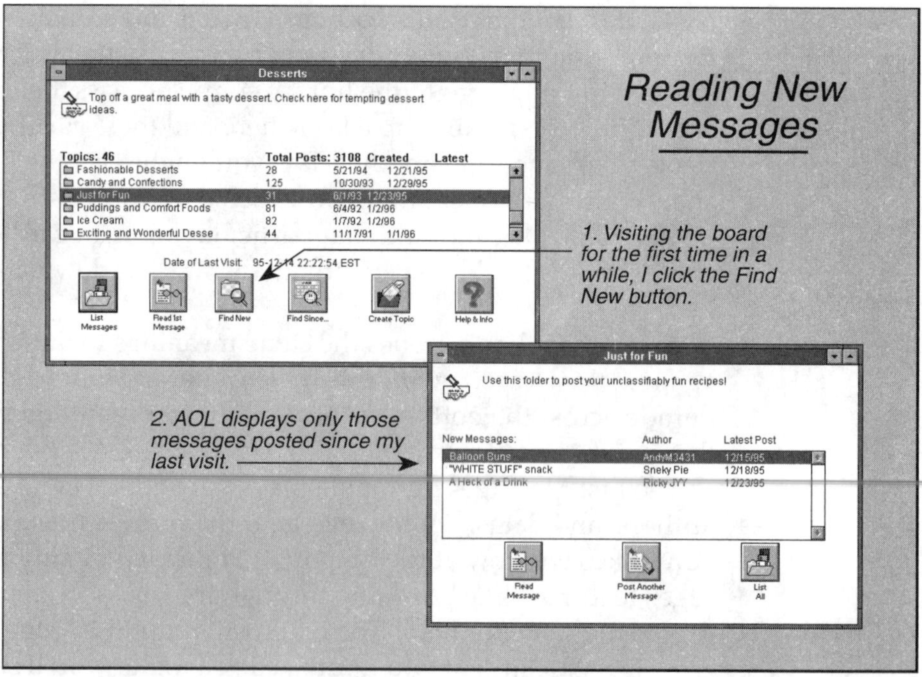

Figure 9-5: Only new messages appear when you click the Find New button. You can read them, add to them, or list all the messages in the folder.

Reading New Messages

1. Visiting the board for the first time in a while, I click the Find New button.

2. AOL displays only those messages posted since my last visit.

Note the Post Another Message button at the bottom of Figure 9-5. This is how you add messages to the folder. All you need to do is click the button, enter the subject and text of your message, then click Post to submit your effort. Your message will be added to the folder immediately. I'll discuss this further in a moment.

Your Personal Date

Your personal "date of last visit" is marked the instant you visit a board. This implies two things: (1) No matter how many (or how few) messages you read while visiting a board, none of the messages posted prior to that visit are displayed when you next click the Find New button; and (2) If anyone (including you) posts a message on a board while you're reading, that message will appear when you next click the Find New button.

Note that I'm talking about *boards* here, not folders. If a board contains 600 messages in 24 folders and you read one message in one folder, none of the remaining messages will show up the next time you click the Find New button. In other words, your date of last visit applies to *every* folder on a board, whether or not you actually read every folder during your last visit. It's a significant subtlety, so don't let it trip you up.

Your Date of Last Visit is associated with your screen name, and it's recorded on AOL's hard disks, not yours. Thus your Date of Last Visit reflects the date you last read messages on the board, regardless of the machine you used.

Most boards contain hundreds of messages. No matter how interested in the subject you might be, it's doubtful you'll want to read every message the first time you visit a board. Or maybe you've been away from the board for a few months and don't want to be deluged with all the messages posted since your last visit. These are two of the reasons why AOL provides the Find Since button (see Figure 9-6).

Figure 9-6:
The Find Since
button allows you
to specify the
extent of a mes-
sage list.

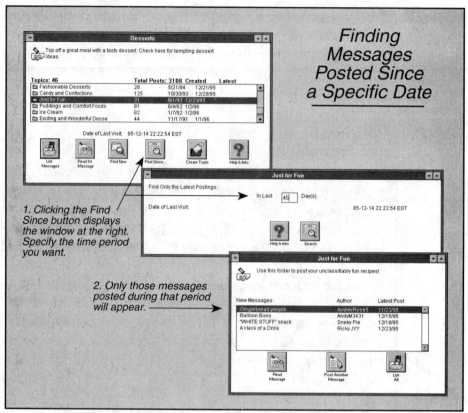

It took me months to figure out just how the List Messages, Find, and Read buttons work. I hope this little discussion saves you the trouble. Regardless, find a board that interests you and start reading its messages. Start with just one or two folders, read the last week's worth of messages, and become familiar with the subject and the people. When you feel confident, post your own messages. It is at that mo-ment—when you have joined the fray—that message boards start to get really interesting. This is part of the fun; don't deny yourself the opportunity.

Posting Messages

A moment ago, I suggested you post your own messages. It might help if we review that process. There is not much to it: take a look at Figure 9-7.

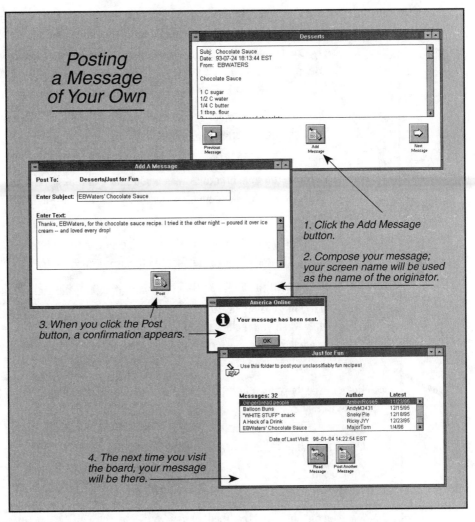

Figure 9-7: Posting your own message is as simple as clicking a button.

Online Etiquette

If you want to be heard, if you want replies to your messages, and if you want to be a responsible online citizen, you should comply with a few rules of telecommunications etiquette. Because Emily Post and Miss Manners haven't yet spoken on the subject, we'd best discuss it here.

- Post messages only when you have something to say, phrase the subject header effectively, and be succinct. The best messages have provocative headers and pithy prose. If your message fills more than a screen of text—if it requires a trip to the scroll bar to read—edit it.

- Stick to the subject. If the folder you're participating in is entitled "Weasels in Wyoming," don't discuss armadillos in Arizona.

- If your message wanders, summarize before responding. You might quote a previous posting (do so in brackets: "When you said <<I really prefer Macintosh>> were you talking about apples or Apples?"). This will help others stick to the topic.

- Don't post chain letters, advertisements, or business offers unless the board was created for it. And never send junk mail to unsuspecting recipients.

- HEY YOU! CAN YOU HEAR ME??!! (Did I get your attention? Did you like the way I did it?) All-caps are distracting, hard to read, and, worse, arrogant. Use all-caps only when you really want to shout (and those occasions should be rare). For emphasis, place asterisks around your text: "I *told* you he was a geek!"

- Do not issue personal attacks, use profanity, or betray a confidence. If criticism is specifically invited, remember that there is no vocal inflection or body language to soften the impact and remove the potential for misinterpretation. E-mail is a better forum for criticism than boards are.

- For the same reason, subtleties, double entendres, and sarcasm are rarely effective.

- Avoid emotional responses. Think before you write. Once you've posted a message, you can't take it back.

- Remember your options. Some replies are better sent as mail than as messages. If you're feeling particularly vitriolic, send mail to the perpetrator. This saves face for both of you.

Posting effective messages is something of an art. Messages like "Me too," or "I don't think so" don't really contribute to a board. Before you post a message, be sure you have something to say, take the time to phrase it effectively, and give it a proper subject header.

Threaded Boards

Some boards offer *message threading*: messages arranged so that you can elect to read responses to a specific message. Compare this with the Read 1st Message command pictured in Figure 9-6. Reading the first message displays the first message on a board with the option to read all the remaining messages on the board as well.

Threaded message boards allow you to choose to read only the replies to a specific message. This is especially appropriate where the subject of a particular folder is likely to be broad, and its messages are numerous and varied. To examine a threaded board, let's visit the Pet Care Forum (use the keyword: **Pets**). A number of veterinarians from universities and private practices visit this board regularly, some of whom are on the board's staff. If you have pets—dogs, cats, reptiles, birds, even farm animals—this is a forum you will want to visit often (see Figure 9-8) For now, let's look for information about cats. Click the Cats button at the lower left of the screen, then select the Cat Message Board.

Figure 9-8:
The Pet Care Forum offers boards for not only dogs and cats but farm animals, fish—even reptiles.

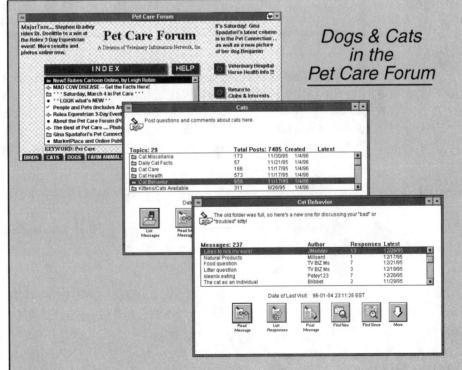

Until now, threaded boards look just like unthreaded boards. But look what happens when I double-click the folder labeled "Cat Behavior" (see Figure 9-9).

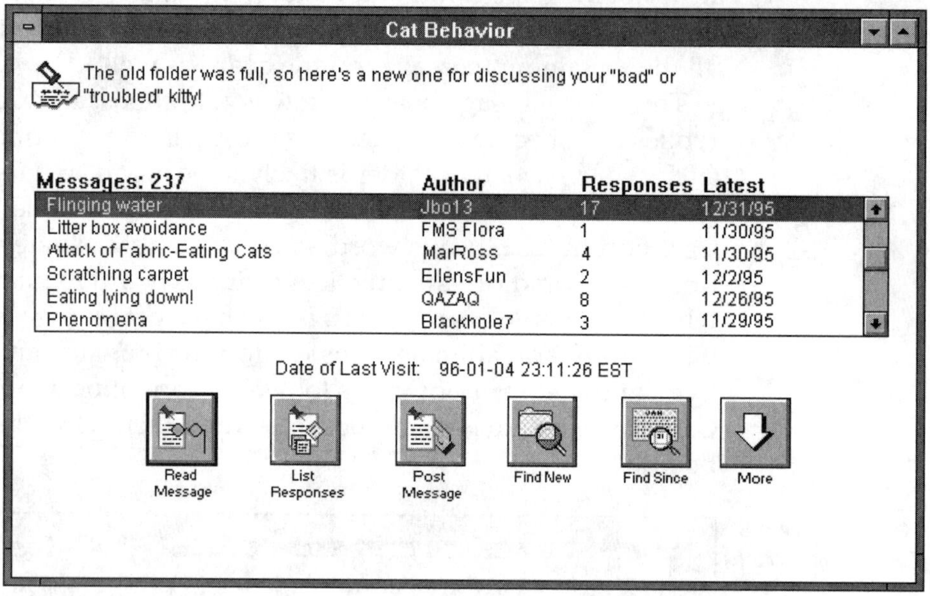

Figure 9-9:
Threaded boards
offer a Responses
column and a List
Responses button
at the bottom of
the window.

Look carefully at Figure 9-9: a Responses column appears, identifying the number of responses that have been posted to any particular message. A new List Responses button appears at the bottom of the window as well.

Now watch what happens when I double-click the "Flinging water" posting (see Figure 9-10).

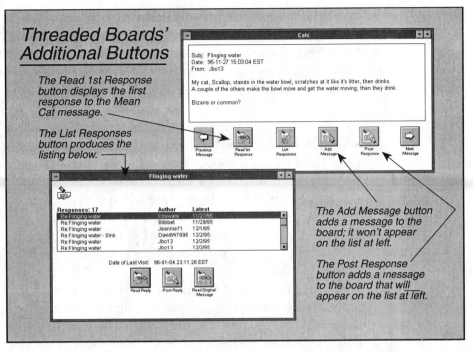

Figure 9-10:
Note how the list
of responses to the
"Flinging water"
message allows me
to post a reply or
reread the original
message in case
I've forgotten a
detail.

The Read 1st Response and List Responses buttons are new to the message window, as is the Post Response button. When I click the List Responses button I see a listing of only the responses to the "Flinging water" message. This allows me to stick to the "Flinging water" subject, rather than wander all over the board.

Proper Replies

Be sure you post replies to messages properly. Look again at the upper window in Figure 9-10: two reply buttons appear there—Add Message and Post Response. The Add Message button simply adds a message to the board; the added message is posted independently and not identified as a response to any other message. A message posted via the Post Response button will appear as a response in a list of responses, similar to those pictured in the lower window of Figure 9-10. It's not just a matter of semantics; it's an organizational imperative. Give consideration to your replies on threaded boards: post them where they're most appropriate.

Not all boards are threaded. Some lend themselves to threading, some don't. Some of my favorites aren't threaded, and I'm glad: threading discourages the kind of browsing that favored boards merit. Don't look upon an unthreaded board as old-fashioned or anarchistic. Welcome them and celebrate their diversity.

Computers & Software Forums

Enough of this talk about boards. Before you can participate on a board, you need to visit a forum. There are no membership requirements: you don't need to register when you first enter a forum; you don't have to prove your expertise or anything more than a passing interest. You never know whether you'll like a place until you visit, and visiting AOL's forums requires nothing more than knowledge of how to get there.

Perhaps the busiest forums on AOL are found in the Computers & Software Channel. The computer industry is a moving target, and those who try to keep it in their sights seek information with eagerness that borders on the fanatical. The Computers & Software Channel offers forums for every level of computer enthusiast, from beginners to developers, and these forums are all extremely popular.

The PC Help Forum

Perhaps there's no better example of a forum for us to discuss than the PC Help Forum (keywords: **PC Help**). We all have an interest in AOL, and this is a traditional AOL forum, with a conference room (open every night from 9 to 11 p.m. Eastern time to provide you with immediate AOL help), a library of files (a New Member Kit, keyword lists, a text map of AOL, and even the New Member Guide in downloadable form), and a message board (official responses are guaranteed within 48 hours—guaranteed responses are very rare—and they even send you a copy of the response via e-mail).

Figure 9-11:
Among all of the
things mentioned
in the text, note
that the PC Help
Forum also offers a
New Member
Guide. It's an in-
valuable tool for
anyone just starting
out on AOL—just
click the question
mark button.

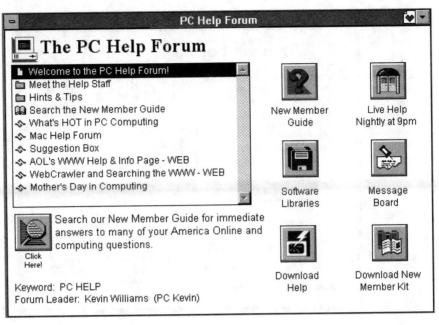

The Windows Forum

Another topic in which we all have an interest is Windows. Probably
the most fertile field for those of us who use Windows is the Windows
Forum itself. You can either choose the forum from the main Computers & Software Channel window at keyword: **Computing**, or use the
keywords: **Windows Forum**.

Figure 9-12:
The Windows
Forum offers pro-
grams, fonts,
games, graphics,
demos, utilities—
even sounds. A
bounty among the
bountiful.

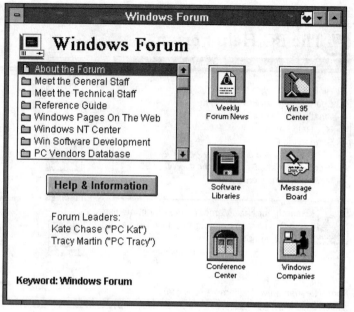

The Family Computing Forum

This forum (at keyword: **FC**) is exactly what its title promises it to be, with one significant exception, the "Novice Member Playground." The Playground offers a place for you to practice participating on a board and downloading from a library—without connect charges! Look for it in the Life's Workshop area (at keyword: **Workshop**).

Figure 9-13:
The Family Computing Forum offers a virtual family room for computer users and a free area where you can practice participating in a board and downloading graphics.

December 28

Throughout this book, I have suggested that you try to time your online events to align with slack time on the network—before 6:00 p.m. Eastern time. I say "the network" because the stress is placed more on the communications system between you and AOL than on AOL's host computer system itself. The telecommunications system that knits us all together is vast and difficult to modify. Growth in such a system takes time.

There's another time when the system is stressed: a few days after Christmas. Lots of people receive a computer for Christmas, and most of those computers now include a modem and a free sign-on kit for AOL or one of its competitors. When the relatives have departed and the wrapping paper is disposed of, people set up their new computers and go about the process of signing on for the first time. This is not an insignificant number of people. In fact, AOL's busiest day of the year is invariably December 28th.

Invite the relatives to stay another few days. Go for a sleigh ride. Haul some wood for the fire, but find another day for your AOL journeys. In cyberspace, December 28th is the busiest day of the year.

The PC Hardware Forum

You just bought a new machine and want to know the best way to use it. Maybe you're interested in upgrading and aren't sure what to buy. Or you have a new printer and want the latest driver for it. The PC Hardware Forum (keywords: **PC Hardware**) offers all of this and more. The message boards are great for peer support (some would say this is the best support available), and the file libraries offer a treasure trove of utilities and drivers. There's also a hardware reference guide, a computing newsletters collection, and an expanded conference schedule.

Figure 9-14:
The PC Hardware Forum is a great place online for hardware help and support.

The PC Applications Forum

If there's a PC Hardware Forum, you would expect a PC Software Forum. There is one, but it's called the PC Applications Forum (keywords: **PC Applications**). A few sentences back I indicated that peer support is probably the best available, a claim that's easily substantiated by exploring this forum's extensive message boards. All popular name brands of software are supported here; hardly a question goes unanswered.

Figure 9-15:
The PC Applica-
tions Forum's mes-
sage boards are a
reliable source of
software support.

Don't conclude your visit to this forum without investigating the "Starter Kit" of applications in the software libraries. Everything you need for productive use of your PC is here: compression, word processing, spreadsheet, database, and desktop publishing shareware—a complete shareware suite!

The PC Multimedia Forum

With the advent of the World Wide Web, multimedia has taken on all the importance of oil in Texas. Suddenly, everyone is anxious to hear sounds, watch movies, and publish electronically with their PC. With the Web as its medium, multimedia is the computing industry's darling of the '90s.

Fortunately, The PC Multimedia Forum is prepared to help us get on board. A Desktop & Web Publishing Resource Center, an extensive multimedia library, Multimedia World Online, and many others are all standing by, ready to serve you (see Figure 9-16).

Figure 9-16:
The Multimedia
Forum offers
support and moti-
vation for Web
authors, game
players, and elec-
tronic publishers.

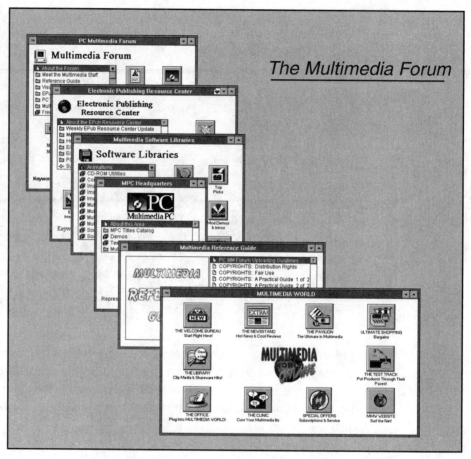

The Multimedia Reference Guide pictured in Figure 9-16 is particularly valuable for anyone who is considering online publishing. Accurate information on copyrights for electronic materials can be an elusive objective. If you're interested in copyright, be sure to read the
Reference Guide's series on the subject.

Finding Leadership Online

If you've ever wondered who's in charge of running the forums, you've probably
run into the answer if you spend much time online: the *Forum Leader*. Forum
Leaders are responsible for the day-to-day management of the forums in their

charge. But forum life online is so busy that each Forum Leader maintains a staff of forum assistants and consultants, usually selected from the general membership for their expertise in a given area. The Forum Leader, consultants, and assistants work as a team to provide technical support, answer member inquiries, process file uploads, and help direct forum conferences. You can identify forum personnel quickly by looking for one of these three prefixes on a screen name: PC (Forum Leader), PCA (Forum Assistant), or PCC (Forum Consultant). (AFL prefixes denote Forum Leaders for the Mac and Apple II forums.) Look for these folks when you have a question: they're among the best.

The PC Graphic Arts Forum

Imagine having access to tens of thousands of graphics files, with more becoming available every day. Imagine a database of these files, searchable by keywords, author names, and filenames. Imagine reviews of graphics software, tips from graphics experts, and a comprehensive manual describing the ins and outs of online graphics. This, of course, is the PC Graphic Arts Forum (keyword: **Graphics**).

Figure 9-17:
The Graphic Arts
Forum offers 12
categories of
graphics files and
utilities, ranging
from simple line
art to complex
ray-traced
photorealistic
images. In addition,
there is usually a
"special" library
listed pertaining to
some impending
holiday or special
occasion.

No Place for Chauvinism

Only half the graphics available online reside in the PC Graphic Arts Forum. An equal number await the adventurous in the—dare we say it?—Macintosh Graphics Forum (keywords: **Mac Graphics**, or click the button pictured at the bottom of Figure 9-17). This sister forum is just as plentiful as the PC forum, and many of the graphics there are in GIF or JPEG format, meaning they can be viewed and used on almost any PC with your AOL software. So go ahead, slip into the Mac Graphics Forum. They're up to some pretty interesting stuff over there.

The PC Development Forum

Computer programmers range from hobbyists to professionals, and they're both served well by the PC Development Forum (keywords: **PC Development**). Message boards play a leading role here, as programmers assist programmers with sticky problems and eternal bugs.

Figure 9-18:
The PC Development Forum offers utilities, examples, and advice for computer programmers—both amateur and professional.

Development Forum

- About the Forum
- Meet the Development Staff
- Reference Guide
- Game Designers Area
- Microsoft Knowledge Base
- PDA Development
- Programmer U
- Free Uploading

Weekly Forum News
Visual Basic Programming

Help & Information

Development Forum Leader:
Bob Dover ("PC BobD")

Conferences:
Saturdays at 10:30 pm

Keyword: PC Development

Software Libraries
Message Board
Conference Center
Development Companies

Community Forums

The computing forums represent the category of forums dedicated to the support of a specific subject. There are many, many more, however, ranging from the Adoption Forum to the Writers Club. This forum category, in which the primary subject is *community*, offers resources, debate, and fraternity—the elements that define and support all vital communities, virtual or otherwise.

The Gay & Lesbian Community Forum

If ever there was a community that stood to benefit from the peer support and organized resources that forums provide, it's the Gay & Lesbian Community Forum. And if ever there was a sympathetic medium for those activities, it's AOL. We go back to the late 1980s for this one, when the gay and lesbian community operated under the name of GLUE (Gays & Lesbians United Electronically). GLUE quietly operated behind the scenes, making its voice heard to the AOL management team. The effort did not fall upon deaf ears, and the result is the Gay & Lesbian Community Forum as we know it today: comprehensive, compassionate, and supportive not only to the gay and lesbian community but to the transgender and AIDS communities as well. This is one of AOL's most proactive forums, with a membership of staggering proportions and a staff that's as large as AOL itself was back in the days when GLUE was getting underway. With its elegant redesign in the winter of 1995, this forum warrants your investigation regardless of your sexual orientation (see Figure 9-19).

Figure 9-19:
The Gay & Lesbian
Community Forum
is one of AOL's
largest and most
active forums.
The benefits are
generous and the
compassion is
sincere—for par-
ticipants of all
predilections.

There is no hostility or insularity here: it's a forum of support and sympathy. As forum member GLCF Wendy puts it:

"Anyone who feels they have no place. . .

"Anyone who feels alone. . .

"Anyone who is scared. . .

"And anyone who feels that no one cares. . .

". . . is welcome here."

Let's look at each of the Forum's features:

🔺 *News & Politics* is where the forum's staff monitors the print, music, and electronic media for developments pertinent to the community. You'll also find the forum's *Pride Press*—a twice-monthly newsletter of exceptional quality and awareness. (Keywords: **GLCF News**)

🔺 *Events & Conferencing* gathers all of the forum's chat and conference rooms (chat rooms are discussed in Chapter 8) in one place, for easy access. You'll find the forum's chat schedule here as well. (Keywords: **GLCF Chat**)

- Text, graphics, and even sounds are available in the *Resource Library*. Look for the Lambda Rising Bookstore here too, with books, music, videos, apparel, and accessories (even refrigerator magnets!) available for purchase. (Keywords: **GLCF Library**)

- *Organizations* offers the Organizations Database, a space for members to contact and receive information about various local and national organizations within the lesbian/gay/bisexual/transgender community. The database is searchable and exceptionally comprehensive. (Keywords: **GLCF Orgs**)

- *Travel* offers a listing of tour operators and cruise companies, and an exclusive connection to the International Gay Travel Association—a network of travel industry professionals dedicated to encouraging and assisting in the promotion of gay and lesbian travel. (Keywords: **GLCF Travel**)

- *Message Boards* gathers the forum's myriad message boards together in one place for easy access. (Keywords: **GLCF Boards**)

There's more to the Gay & Lesbian Community Forum. Read on.

Gaymeland

::dancedancelaughdance:: So begins your introduction to Gaymeland, the GLCF's "Island Oasis of Constant Fun." The heart of Gaymeland is *The Romping Room*, with live interactive "gaymes" every night of the week. In *The Zilla Scrolls* you'll find fake astrology, brainteasers, interactive stories, wisecracks, challenges—anything and everything "Gaymezilla" can come up with for inclusion on a message board. The *National GaymEnquirer* is "more than just your father's newsletter," and the *Library Lagoon* offers a library of sounds used in the Gaymeland conference and chat rooms. There's a healthy irreverence here, served up with disarming wit and charm. Use the keyword: **Gaymeland** and *::dancedancedance::* the night away!

The Positive Living Forum

The Positive Living Forum is a place for people to find information and support about HIV and AIDS. It's appropriate for people infected with the virus, people interested in learning how to avoid the virus, caregivers, and family (see Figure 9-20).

Figure 9-20:
The Positive Living Forum offers support and resources for people who need or seek help with HIV and AIDS.

The forum offers a comprehensive resource of AIDS/HIV information, whether it be online articles, file libraries, or folders in message boards. Like the GLCF, the Positive Living Forum's emphasis is on compassion and caring, and its large complement of health care professionals, researchers, and social service workers underscores its benevolent charter.

The Transgender Community Forum

The Transgender Community Forum offers support and provides education and outreach about transgender issues. The forum welcomes the transgendered, transsexuals, transvestites, crossdressers, significant others, family, supportive friends, medical and legal professionals—without regard to race, sexual preference, or lifestyle.

The forum is also a resource for all America Online members. Everyone is welcome to contribute and participate; all viewpoints are welcome. You'll find them at keyword: **TCF**.

Better Health & Medical Network

Not so many years ago, the common approach to health care was one of repairing the human machine. The primary character was the friendly family doctor, the focus was on symptoms, and the medical profession was a staid and reliable community fixture.

Paralleling technology's move toward integration, today's health care has shifted toward a broader concept of health that includes information, lifestyle, mental health, making informed decisions, the family unit, gender-specific health, alternative medical approaches, health problems of the workplace, stress, learning disorders, and issues focused on specific age groups.

Best of all, health care now recognizes the vital importance of the patient in his or her own health care decision-making and healing. Healing no longer means repair of a part but a comprehensive approach to the whole person, a perspective America Online shares and addresses in its Better Health and Medical Network (see Figure 9-21). To get there, just use the keywords: **Better Health**.

Figure 9-21: The Better Health & Medical Network is your connection to personal health care information, advice, and support groups of people who share your problems or concerns.

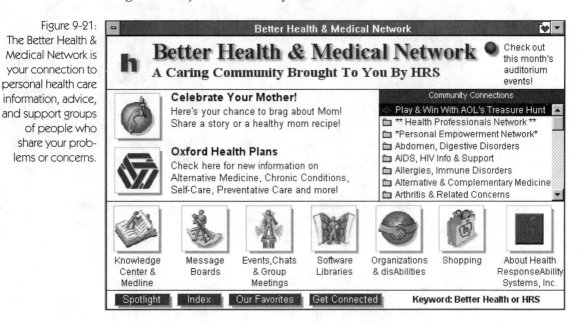

The Religion & Beliefs Forum

Here's a singular combination: the newest of all human creations—electronic communication—in concert with perhaps the oldest of all human traditions—religion. (See Figure 9-22.) Actually, the focus of this forum is not entirely old, for the forum is shared equally by long established religious traditions, relatively young traditions, and modern discussions in ethics and philosophy.

You'll find file libraries and lively message boards on Buddhism, Hinduism, Christianity, pagan beliefs, New Age thought, philosophy, Humanism, Islam, and Quakerism, to name just a few. Be sure to check out the religious art exhibits and message boards where religious and ethical dialogs regarding current events and issues take place. You'll find it all at keyword: **Religion**.

Figure 9-22: The Religion & Beliefs Forum is a place to discuss and learn about the ultimate human question.

The Garden Spot

The Garden Spot is America Online's gardening message and information center (see Figure 9-23). If your fuchsias are faltering, or you want to know exactly how to prune your pear tree, here's where you can find out. The Gardening Message Boards can put you in touch with experts in every area of gardening, from aquatic plant life to weed control.

Of particular value are the regional gardening boards—message centers dedicated to plant health solutions for specific geographic areas of the country. If you need horticultural information fast, the Garden Spot (keyword: **Garden**) is a great place to start.

Figure 9-23: The Garden Spot is your connection to horticultural experts and master gardeners in your own geographical area.

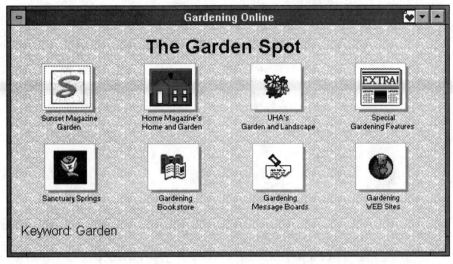

The Genealogy Forum

Genealogical research has taken three great steps forward with the arrival of personal computers: new software has made family tree organization simpler; connection via modem to major genealogical archives has broadened and accelerated information searches; and e-mail facilitates personal communication among family members all over the world.

America Online's Genealogy Forum (see Figure 9-24) represents another step forward for genealogy hobbyists and researchers by combining message centers, file and software archives, live genealogy conferences, and genealogical research guides into one easy-to-find location. The Genealogy Forum is one of AOL's most popular areas, and no wonder: whether you'd like to do a simple surname search or initiate the creation of an extensive family tree, you'll find all the tools and pointers you'll need by typing the keyword: **Roots**.

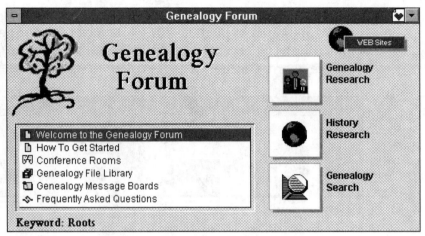

The Writers Club

Writers, often by choice as much as necessity, swim alone and only
occasionally come up for air. And when they do, their first breaths fuel
the need to find and converse with their peers. America Online, which
constantly relies on hundreds of writers, understands this full well and
has created a place and structure for writers of all genres and persua-
sions (see Figure 9-25).

You'll find genre-specific message boards and chats, of course,
serving the creative gamut from technical writing to poetry. You'll also
find workshops and conferences—34 scheduled when I looked—for
just about every type of writing. And for those whose schedules are
staunchly idiorhythmic, the Writer's Cafe is open for conversation 24
hours a day.

Three areas of the Writers Club deserve special mention. The New
Writers Market News, found under the main menu's Articles and
Columns listing, provides tips and information for those developing
their writing craft. Job announcements may be found via the Writers >
Messages > Writer's Market Message Center trail. And, thanks to AOL,
you can establish a personal relationship with a published author via
the Mentor program. You'll find all of this and much more at keyword:
Writers.

Figure 9-25:
Whether you're a
beginning writer or
a seasoned pro,
the Writers Club
offers tips, ideas,
information, and
contacts.

Figure 9-25:
Whether you're a
beginning writer or
a seasoned pro,
the Writers Club
offers tips, ideas,
information, and
contacts.

Gaming Forums

It's not difficult to become obsessed with a game: chess, Nintendo, flight simulation—they often consume inordinate amounts of time and cerebral energy. There's rarely any harm in that, of course—in fact, friends are often made in the pursuit. That's where the gaming forums come in: this is where gamers meet gamers, where strategies are discreetly disclosed, and where obsessions feed obsessions. It's all good fun, and it often leads to improved scores. If this sounds like your trump suit, read on.

Flight Simulation Resource Center

Flight simulation is, indeed, a virtual world unto itself, and AOL has provided flight simulation aficionados with a place to meet and exchange hangar talk. The Flight Simulation Resource Center (see Figure 9-26) is where newcomers can find advice on flight simulation software, and experienced virtual pilots can download the latest utilities, sound, scenery, program add-ons, and images.

Are you captivated by the Golden Age of Flight, or is hyperspace your arena? You'll find people here who share your passion in software-specific flight simulation clubs with themes ranging from the early days of flight to space flight of the distant future. You can even join (or create and operate) your own virtual airline. Just use the keyword: **Flight**.

Figure 9-26:
If your joystick
hand convulses
after ten hours
away from the
computer; if you
practice Immelman
at your nonvirtual
desktop while
you're supposed to
be earning a living;
if you race out the
front door when
the sound of a Pratt
& Whitney radial
fills the sky, the
Flight Simulation
Resource Center
had better be
among your favorite places.

> **Flight Simulations**
>
> **Flight Simulation
> Resource Center**
>
> - About this Area
> - News & Information
> - Product Information
> - Message Board
> - Add-Ons
> - Microsoft Flight Sim 4.0
> - Microsoft Flight Sim 5.0
> - Utilities & Misc.
> - FSRC Club Files
>
> Virtual Airlines
>
> Conference Room

Star Trek Club

The signature phrase of the "Star Trek" television program, "where no one has gone before" is an apt description of the online medium. What better place than AOL, then, for fellow Trekkers to meet and converse.

The Star Trek Club (keyword: **Trek**) features information and meeting areas dedicated to the original TV show, the Star Trek movies, "Star Trek: The Next Generation," "Deep Space 9," and "Voyager." You can join the Star Trek writer's group on The Bridge to help create the continuing saga, or officially enlist in the Star Fleet Academy (keyword: **Starfleet**) to begin your quest for promotion and power in the Starfleet ranks.

Figure 9-27:
The Star Trek Club
feeds the Trekkie
fancy, while
Starfleet Online
offers online simu-
lations of Trek
adventures—and
you're invited to
participate. They're
all at keyword:
Trek.

Strategy & WarGames Forum

The very fact that you're reading this book indicates you are a person
who enjoys mental activity, the acquisition of information, and problem solving. And that's what the Strategy and WarGames Forum is all
about—conversation about games of all types which use strategy and
tactics to solve problems (see Figure 9-28). (**Note:** The games themselves are discussed in Chapter 11, "Divertissements.")

Figure 9-28:
Use the keyword:
Strategy to share
your game-playing
skills or to start up
an e-mail game of
your own.

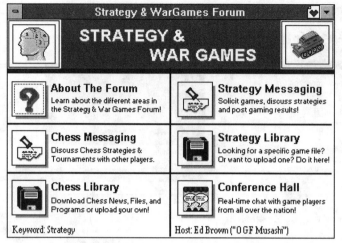

Not surprisingly, this forum is also the home of America Online's Chess Forum, where you can converse with other players, study chess strategies, research game collections from national and international tournaments, review chess books and software, access news reports from the world of professional chess, and read commentary and answers to members' questions from AOL's resident Grand Master Gabriel Sanchez.

All these features clearly make the Chess Forum a valuable resource for chess fans, but there's more. Here you can always find someone to play by posting a message in the Looking for a Game folder. And when you think you're ready to move up to a new level, you'll find tournaments and USCF rated game opportunities to test your knowledge and provoke your creativity. Curious? Just use the keyword: **Strategy**.

Nintendo Power Source

History is filled with dates signifying the beginning of important trends. Some future historian will no doubt note the "then unrecognized" importance of the industrious Mario Brothers. Lest we err by disregarding those energetic little workmen, now familiar to an entire generation, we should remember the ultimate success of a certain singing mouse some fifty-odd years before.

The Nintendo Power Source (see Figure 9-29) is the home of the Nintendo Forum, and while the forum is undeniably an information, message, and chat center for the avid fans of the Marios and other Nintendo home video games, it is also a picture window into the emerging world of recreational virtual reality, a world that is evolving no less rapidly than that of home computers. Whether you're looking for help with your latest game, or looking through the game into the future, you'll find there's much to be learned at keyword: **Nintendo**.

Figure 9-29: You'll find the Nintendo Forum under the Play It Loud button on Nintendo's main screen.

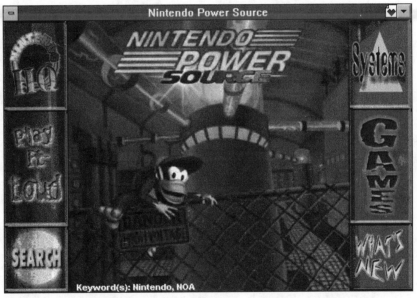

Moving On

As good as AOL is at helping you pursue an interest—a hobby or an avocation—it's even better at keeping you informed. The online medium, after all, doesn't have to wait for "film at 11" or the morning edition. If there's news worth breaking, it's online immediately. Some of AOL's weather maps are never more than 15 minutes old. This could very well be information's ideal medium. Turn the page to see what I mean.

Staying Informed

In the beginning of the information age, people got their news from newspapers. At best, newspapers offered the news once a day—a small inconvenience considering the limited expectations of the public in those days. Radio emerged 70 years ago, offering immediate "on-the-scene" coverage. But there were no pictures, and if you weren't listening when the news was broadcast, you missed it. Forty years ago, television brought pictures, but even today you're at the mercy of TV scheduling if you want the latest.

What if you had access to the most up-to-date news and information all the time—exactly when and how you wanted it? What if you could see the pictures and hear the sounds while you're seated in front of your computer? That's the way America Online thinks news should be. And as you can tell from the abundance of opportunity pictured in Figure 10-1, the potential supply is inexhaustible.

Figure 10-1: The
keyword: **News**,
the keyword:
Sports, and the
keyword: **Weather**
connect you with
an arsenal of infor-
mation resources,
continually
updated and
maintained.

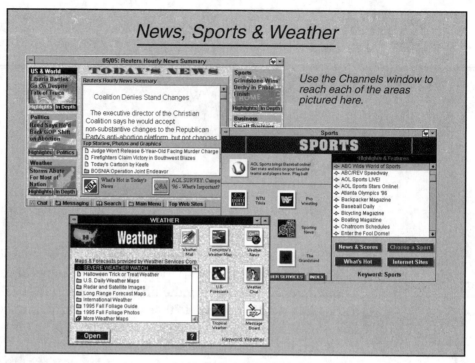

The News

AOL's Today's News window, pictured in Figure 10-1, is where most of your informational journeys will begin. The contents of this window are changing continuously, as are the stories to which they lead.

The Top Stories

Look again at the Today's News window in Figure 10-1. The list you see at the left side of this window is always current; it changes as events change. These are the stories that lead the news; the online "front page." By simply double-clicking a headline, Today's News calls up the complete text of the story.

Some headlines are complex and contain several related story lines. Note the small "folder" icon beside the Bosnia listing in Figure 10-1. Double-clicking a line with a folder icon displays a window containing story menus, and often a headline banner and lead story (see Figure 10-2).

Figure 10-2: Folder icons identify items that include collections of related stories.

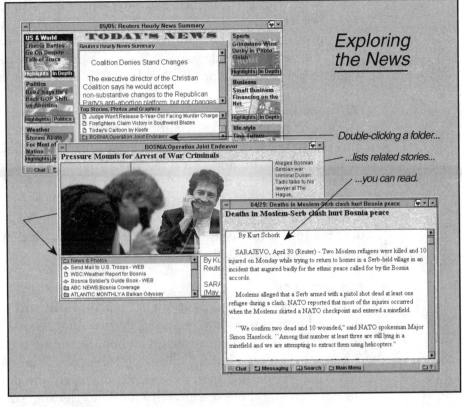

Double-clicking a folder...

...lists related stories...

...you can read.

Informational Preparedness

Before we go much further, we need to discuss some of the tools available to you as you browse the information resources available on AOL. You'll want to save some of the material you see, or print it, or specify the scope of your wanderings. Here's how it's done.

Saving Articles

Whenever an article appears on your screen in the frontmost window, it's available to be saved on your hard drive or a floppy disk. To save an article (news or otherwise—I'm talking about *any* article, at any time), just choose Save from the File menu. You'll see a standard Windows Save As dialog box, where you can assign the article a name and file location.

Saved articles are pure text and can be opened with any word processor. (**Hint:** use the .txt filename extension so the material you save offers the most compatibility with any software you might use.) You can open any articles saved this way with AOL's software—whether you're online or off—by choosing Open from the File menu.

Printing Articles

You can print any article that appears in AOL's frontmost window. This is best done offline, when the clock's not running. Using the File menu, choose Print and you'll see your PC's standard print dialog box. Make any necessary changes to the print configuration and click OK. America Online will print the article to your PC's currently selected printer. When you print directly like this, you won't have much control over the formatting of the printed page; if you want that kind of control, open the article using your word processor.

Keeping a Log

While articles like those pictured in Figure 10-2 are informative, invaluable, and often fascinating, reading them online is not. I prefer to absorb information like that at my leisure, when the online clock isn't running.

The solution is found in AOL's *Log Manager*. When a log is turned on, all text appearing on your screen is recorded on your disk. You can zip through an online session without delay, letting articles flash across your screen at the tempo of an MTV video. Then, when you've accessed what you need, sign off and review the log. Any word processor will open a log file, as will your AOL software. Just choose Open from the File menu.

Now that I've read the paragraph above, I feel compelled to make a disclaimer: some things offer their own saving routines (World Wide Web pages—discussed in Chapter 4, "Using the Internet"—are a good example); others may have to be copied and pasted into a new document for saving. Generally, the logging feature is used for articles—AOL text files—so that they can be saved for later review.

To start a log: while you're online, choose Log Manager from the File menu. In the Logging window, open a Session Log by clicking the Open Log button in the lower part of the window. America Online will display a standard file-open dialog box complete with a suggested filename and location (see Figure 10-3). Make any filename/location changes you want, then click Save. From then on, all the text you see onscreen will be saved on your disk.

Figure 10-3: Log files capture and save onscreen activity to disk for later review.

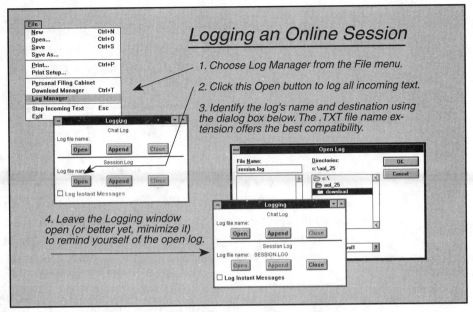

Logging an Online Session

1. Choose Log Manager from the File menu.

2. Click this Open button to log all incoming text.

3. Identify the log's name and destination using the dialog box below. The .TXT file name extension offers the best compatibility.

4. Leave the Logging window open (or better yet, minimize it) to remind yourself of the open log.

A Few Notes About Logs

- To capture the complete article in your log you must double-click (open) the article's headline while you're online and allow AOL to finish the transmission of the article to your PC (be sure it's complete: if the More button is active, then there's more to follow). When the hourglass cursor changes back to the arrow cursor, transmission is complete. You don't have to read it online—you don't even have to scroll to the end of it—you just have to receive it in its entirety.

- Log files can be as large as you want them to be, but they can grow quickly if you don't pay attention. Monitor your activity online while a log file is open as you would monitor your fuel gauge while traveling through Death Valley.

- You can always close the log or append an existing one with the buttons in the Logging window (refer again to Figure 10-3). This is handy when you want to turn your log on and off: you can use the Close and Append buttons as you would the pause button on a tape recorder, capturing the material you want and excluding what you don't want. The Logging window works while you're offline as well, so you can start a log even before you sign on. You'll never miss a thing that way.

> ⚠ If you look carefully at the bottom window in Figure 10-3, you will note two types of logs. The Session log is the one that captures articles like those discussed in this chapter; it doesn't capture chats and instant messages (I discussed those in Chapter 8, "The Community").

Searching the News

Look again at the Today's News window pictured at the top of Figure 10-1. In the lower center of the window you'll see a button labeled "Search News." This is an extremely powerful tool. It's powerful because it searches not only world news but also news about business, entertainment, sports, and even weather. If you know of a subject that's in the news and you want to know more, click this icon.

Figure 10-4: Using the criterion: *Virus*, I receive 82 "hits" in an America Online news search. By specifying *Computer Virus*, I narrow my search to only 15 hits, including four articles that are exactly what I'm looking for.

Searching the News

```
News Search
Type words that describe what you are looking for, then click List Articles. For example,
"Clinton or Congress." Click Help & Info for more instructions.
VIRUS
Items 1-20 of 82 matching entries.

BSW:  TouchStone announces PC-cillin  95, new anti-virus utility protects again
KRT:  The Sacramento Bee, Calif., Technology Talk Column
RTR:  Australia faces deadly animal viruses, exotic fly
RTR:  FEATURE-Australia faces deadly animal viruses, exotic fly
RTR:  Montagnier says HIV drug mix could prolong life
RTR:  Possible new Ebola virus threat looms in Zaire
RTR:  HIV can be infectious despite antibodies -- study
BSW:  Cytel acquires full ownership of Sequel Therapeutics, Inc.
PRN:  NEW STUDY FINDS BLOOD SUPPLIES CAN BE RENDERED

         List Articles   More   Help & Info
```

A single word often has several meanings, and single word searches may include articles you don't want.

```
News Search
Type words that describe what you are looking for, then click List Articles. For example,
"Clinton or Congress." Click Help & Info for more instructions.
COMPUTER VIRUS
Items 1-15 of 15 matching entries.

KRT:  The Sacramento Bee, Calif., Technology Talk Column
BSW:  TouchStone announces PC-cillin  95, new anti-virus utility protects again
BSW:  DATAWATCH announces software distribution  agreement with Apple Computer;
PRN:  SYMANTEC ANNOUNCES 61% NET INCOME GROWTH FOR THE SEPTEMBER 1995
BSW:  Critical Data Service Company Finds Unusual  Niche In Japan
BSW:  VASCO Data Security celebrates first anniversary  of Access Key II; ships
BSW:  AST outlines direction for Intel Pentium Pro on Business Desktops and Per
BSW:  New Media Centers Adds Kaleida Labs;  Corporate Participation Growing in
BSW:  NetPro Computing announces Admin ToolBox 3.0  for Windows

         List Articles   More   Help & Info
```

To find exactly what you're looking for, focus the search by adding one or more words to the primary search word, then run the search again.

Searching for the word *Virus*, AOL found 82 stories in the news, with topics ranging from Australian animal viruses to antibody research. Along the way, AOL even found a story about African National Soccer. Because my true interest was in new computer antivirus programs, I focused my search by using the criterion: Computer Virus. This time AOL's narrowed search produced 15 "hits" (pictured in the lower window of Figure 10-4).

Specifying effective search criteria for AOL's database searches takes a bit of practice and a working knowledge of the so-called Boolean operators—the modifying terms (AND, OR, and NOT) used to clarify a search. If necessary, review the discussion of these modifiers in the File Search section of Chapter 5, starting on page 158.

> **No Criteria**
>
> Here's a little trick you might find revealing: conduct a news search using no criteria whatsoever. Press the spacebar to place nothing more than a space in the criteria field (where the words *Virus* and *Computer Virus* appear in Figure 10-4), then click the List Articles button.
>
> This tells AOL to search for *anything*, and it will find every article in Today's News. Typically, you'll see several thousand of them, which gives you an idea of just how large the Today's News area really is. America Online subscribes to scores of news services. Few news sources are this extensive.

News Sources

We've arrived at your "16th birthday." You know how to operate the machine—how to search for news; how to log, save, and print your selections—and now you're ready to venture forth onto the information highway. What you need now is a road map: something to identify the roadside attractions that America Online has to offer. Let's consider that road map.

U.S. & World News

America Online's top story menus and News Search provide access to every news article on file in the Today's News area—19,900 of them on the day I researched for this chapter. If you prefer a more structured approach to your daily news, use the buttons arrayed throughout the Today's News window (review Figure 10-1).

Looking under the "U.S. & World," section, you can see an "In Depth" button (several of the sections have one), which leads you to an organized presentation of the day's U.S and World News (see Figure 10-5). Use the keywords: **US News** if you want to access this feature directly.

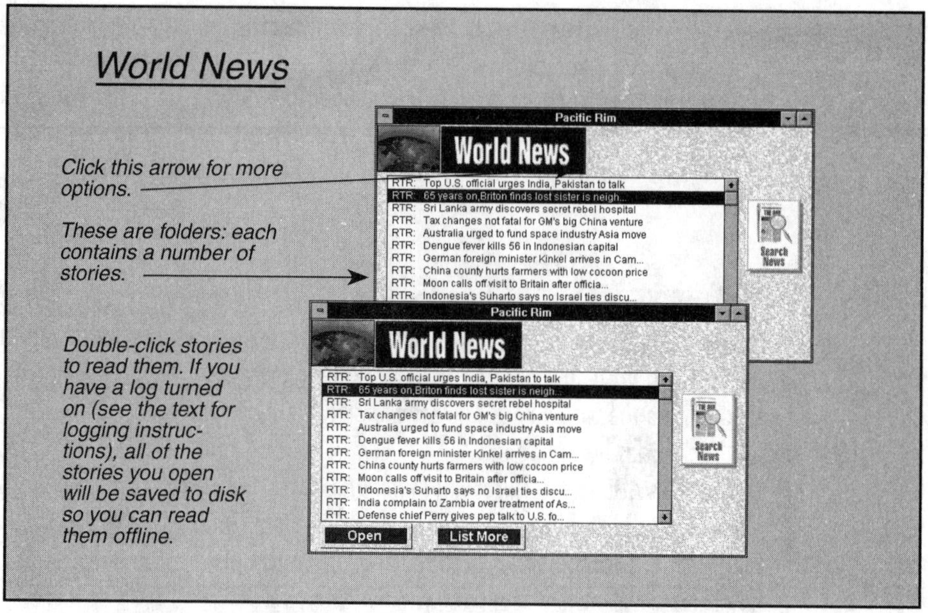

Figure 10-5: AOL categorizes World News by region. By first selecting the "World" entry in the U.S. & World News category drop-down window, and then the "Pacific Rim" entry from the World menu, I'm pre-sented with a menu of associated regional news stories.

World News

Click this arrow for more options.

These are folders: each contains a number of stories.

Double-click stories to read them. If you have a log turned on (see the text for logging instruc-tions), all of the stories you open will be saved to disk so you can read them offline.

The six mini headline windows along the sides of the Today's News window (again, refer to Figure 10-1) are analogous to the sections of your daily newspaper. They're especially useful if you're just browsing the news, with no particular subject in mind. Each also allows you to skim the day's highlights, or pursue the area in greater detail, depend-ing on which button you click.

Business News
Don't confuse Today's Business News with the Personal Finance Channel I'll describe in Chapter 12, "Personal Finance." Like all the other items found in Today's News, the business news offered there is just what its title implies: today's most recent business news from around the world. Other business information, such as investing advice, stock market timing charts, and mutual fund analysis is cov-ered in Chapter 12.

Like the U.S. & World News area, the Business News area brings a coherent structure to an array of news articles. The main Business News window presents the "lead stories"—not only of the day but of the *moment*. You can peruse the Top Business news stories listed in the opening window by double-clicking a story line, or you can click the down arrow button to the right of the Top Business category box to explore articles found in other business categories (see Figure 10-6).

Figure 10-6: The Business News section offers multiple categories of news, each containing selected items from the day's key business news stories.

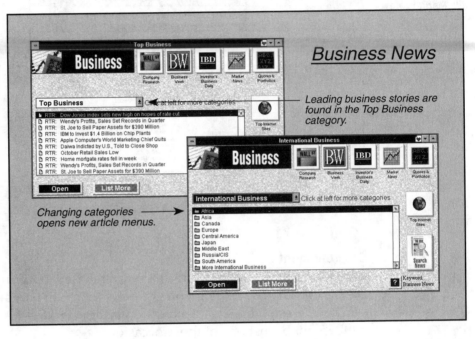

Market News

Look again at Figure 10-6. Do you see the button labeled "Market News"? This is another stock market resource offered by AOL (see Figure 10-7); many others are discussed in Chapter 12, "Personal Finance." All the information you expect to see in your newspaper is here, with one significant difference: AOL's stock market information is updated continually during periods of stock market activity.

Figure 10-7:
America Online's
Market News rarely
trails the NYSE
ticker by more than
20 minutes during
trading. To get
there in a hurry, use
the keywords:
Markets News.

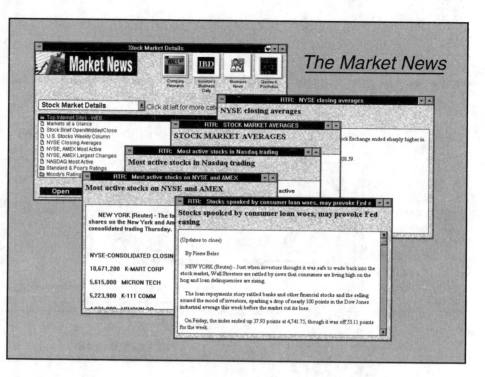

Entertainment

Can you recall an occasion when you purchased a product and were pleasantly surprised when you got more than you bargained for? If you're interested in news from the entertainment field, signing on to AOL might be just one of those occasions.

I say this because the Entertainment News section of Today's News offers articles from *Variety*, the preeminent industry magazine that profoundly influences people in the entertainment capitals of our nation.

It's posted each day on AOL. All you have to do to reach the Entertainment News area is click the In Depth button under the life.style window at the bottom left of the Today's News main window (see Figure 10-8). In addition to individual stories, AOL carries *Variety*'s front page in a single file.

Figure 10-8: The Entertainment section of Today's News features news of the entertainment industry, most of which is drawn from *Variety* magazine.

This is one of AOL's best-kept secrets. *Variety* magazine is the entertainment industry's "Bible," and now you know where to find it.

The Newsstand

If the immediacy of Today's News is the online analog to television, the Newsstand compares with the magazine section at the library, the main difference being that it offers a distinctly different, but profoundly significant, journalistic advantage: capacity.

Most magazine readers value the printed medium; but if you're like me, you've given up on filing past issues. After a few months, I just recycle most of my magazines. And, all too often, after I dispose of them I decide to review something I saw in an issue that's now gone.

I have good news, periodical patrons: the Newsstand is AOL's answer to the problem of that stack of magazines in the garage, a place where you can read current issues, save articles, download files, and even talk to the editors online. Perhaps best of all, the Newsstand is not only horizontally comprehensive (lots of publications), it's vertically comprehensive as well (most back issues are searchable). Chances are, if you search for a subject of interest, it's there. That's what I mean by the benefits of capacity. To get there, click the Newsstand button in the Channels window, or use the keyword: **Newsstand**.

There's so much great stuff in the Newsstand, it's hard to know where to begin. One thing I know we all have in common—our PCs. So we'll begin our exploration by double-clicking Computer Publications, the second listing from the top in the Newsstand's opening menu (see Figure 10-9).

Figure 10-9: The Newsstand gathers all of AOL's online magazines into one central location— use the keyword: **Newsstand** to get there.

Though we discussed a few of AOL's computer-oriented magazines in Chapter 7, "Computing," other entries in the Newsstand's Computer Publications menu include *Home PC, Home Office Computing, FamilyPC,* and *Game Pro*—four publications focusing on subjects of interest to home computer users (see Figure 10-10). However you use your computer at home, you'll find these publications have lots to offer.

Figure 10-10:
Games, resources,
contests, trouble-
shooting, message
boards, hardware
and software re-
views—diverse
features chosen to
address the diverse
interests of home
computer users.

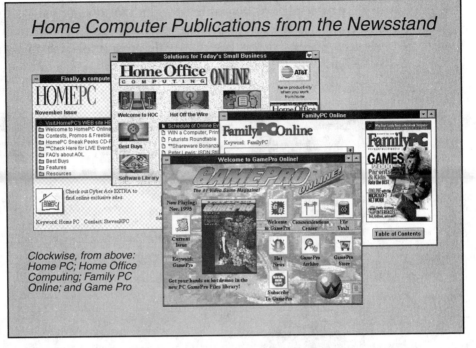

Clockwise, from above: Home PC; Home Office Computing; Family PC Online; and Game Pro

By now you may be wondering if any of your old print media favorites have made the leap to online publication. They probably have: most major magazines are already publishing online, and more are joining the list every week. We'll discuss two of them below.

Business Week

September 7, 1929: Volume 1, Number 1 of *Business Week* magazine appeared on the shelves, just in time to forewarn its readers of "dangerous overheating" in the stock market. On October 29th—only a few weeks later—*Business Week*'s prophecy became an infamous entry in the history books, and the Great Depression began.

An auspicious beginning for the world's largest business magazine, which has been pointing the way for business and financial leaders ever since. *Business Week* is available online—not only the domestic edition but international editions as well. And not only the current issue but back issues as well—dating to January 1994.

Figure 10-11: Each Thursday night, Business Week Online uploads all of its domestic and international editions, hours before the magazine hits newsstands on Friday. It's all available at keyword: **BW**.

Naturally, the text and some selected illustrations from the magazine are available online, but you can also attend live conferences with *Business Week* editors and newsmakers; learn all about the Best Business Schools (including how to apply, in some cases electronically); browse Business Books Online and order books through the Bookstore; search the Business Week Online Corporate Directory (which lists the names and addresses of *Business Week* 1000 companies and is only available online); and, as you might expect, search the magazine's archives for the electronic text of stories you want to review or might have missed.

How Sweet It Is

In the cover story for the January 8, 1996, issue of *Business Week*, Steve Jobs, cofounder of Apple Computer, was mentioned as an entrepreneur of the year. Anyone who follows Steve's journeys might wonder what qualified him for such a prestigious honor: he has been trying to come up with a second hit (after he left Apple) for a decade, after all. If you've followed Steve's career *very* carefully (or if you read *Business Week*), however, you're aware that in late November of 1995, Steve's company, Pixar Animation Studios, makers of the smash hit movie *Toy Story* (see Figure 10-12), went public with a bang. The stock, priced at 22, zoomed to 49, and Jobs's 80 percent stake was briefly worth $1.1 billion—yes, that's a "b". What's next? His other company, NeXT, is making software for the World Wide Web, and Jobs may have profited from his third public offering by the time you read this.

Figure 10-12: For a brief period in late 1995, Pixar's *Toy Story* put Steve Jobs on the billionaire list. (I found this graphic in Business Week Online's file libraries.)

Business Week Online is a trove of multimedia treasures—indeed, the variety of material offered here is unique in the online medium (and most certainly not available via the printed version of the magazine). Not only will you find audio and video clips but also HTML scripts (for viewing World Wide Web pages associated with *Business Week* stories) and Adobe Acrobat documents, featuring searchable and printable magazine-like presentations, complete with photos and charts. To look them over, use the keyword: **BW**, then click the button labeled Search & Downloads. Look in the Downloads window that appears for file libraries with names like HTML Files and Audio & Video Files.

@times

Business Week isn't the only place for contemporary multimedia, however. @times—the *New York Times* online area—is just as splendid, especially since its redesign in late 1995. If you're like me, and Sunday morning simply isn't Sunday morning to you unless you have a copy of the Sunday *Times*, you're going to gravitate toward @times.

One of the great strengths of the *Times* is its cultural coverage and criticism. For decades, readers have relied on the *Times's* critics for guidance in choosing everything from books to videos. Now, with @times, thousands of *Times* reviews—movies, videos, books—are available in one place (see Figure 10-13).

Figure 10-13: @times offers, among other things, the crème de la crème of the *New York Times*: its entertainment and arts features. To get there in a hurry, use the keyword: **@times**.

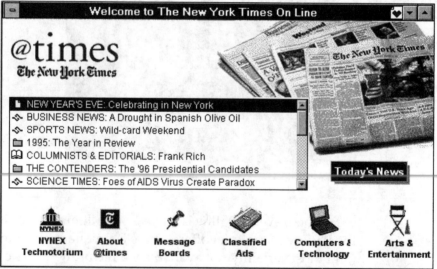

Look for the *New York Times* Best Seller List here, along with the *Times* weekday book, video, and movie reviews. @times also features the top international and domestic news, business, and sports stories. These stories appear before they're printed in the paper: articles from the next day's newspaper begin appearing after 11 p.m. Sunday through Friday, and after 9 p.m. Saturday.

The New Republic

I'll describe one more venerable publishing giant, but there are many more, especially the special-interest magazines. Be sure to investigate them all at keyword: **Newsstand**.

At the 1994 National Magazines Awards—where *The New Republic* magazine was presented with the General Excellence award—the judges said: ". . . every issue is informed by a muscular intelligence that makes you keep reading no matter how tough or familiar the subject. In a period of intense concern with the direction of American politics and policy . . . *The New Republic* offers lucid analysis, sophisticated reporting, and the zest of a good argument. . . ."

These accolades refer primarily to *The New Republic*'s in-house staff. There are plenty of other contributors to the magazine, including Vice President Gore, Norman Mailer, John Updike, Gail Sheehy, and Naomi Wolf.

Figure 10-14: Some of the most sagacious insights into our culture are available when you use the keywords: **New Republic**.

Who reads the *The New Republic*? The list is a Who's Who of America: Bill and Hillary Clinton, Les Aspin, Bob Dole, David Geffen, Mitch Kapor, Yo-Yo Ma, Richard Dreyfuss, Ted Koppel, Diane Sawyer, and Rush Limbaugh, among others. You should be reading it too, and you can—not only the current issue but past issues as well—by using the keywords: **New Republic**.

Other Sources

There are scores of online versions of print publications in the Newsstand. Some—such as Bicycling Magazine, Car & Driver, Cycle World, Flying Magazine, and Stereo Review—cater to specific interests. Others—such as American Woodworker, DC Comics Online, Nintendo Power Source and Popular Photography—cater to the hobbyist. Others serve more general needs. Among the general interest publications you'll find online are OMNI, Smithsonian, WIRED (mentioned in Chapter 4, "Using the Internet"), Saturday Review, Worth, and many others that might appeal to you. This place is a quarry of priceless literary nuggets, and you pay nothing extra for access to it.

Digital Cities

Times have changed. Though paper grows on trees, as a society we've discovered that trees don't necessarily grow at the rate at which we use paper. Every form of paper-based media from catalogs to postcards has felt the pinch, and the pressure is unrelenting. Just a few months ago, *OMNI* magazine was forced to cease publication due to rises in the cost of paper. Others are following.

(All hope is not lost, however. *OMNI* still maintains a significant online presence—at keyword: **OMNI**—and is, indeed, fortifying its online staff.)

The medium that has most painfully felt the increasing cost of paper, however, is the newspaper. Once the parapet of timely information, newspapers are suffering not only from escalating costs but from the superior immediacy of electronic media as well.

On the other hand, newspapers are local. In most markets, their coverage can't be beat. To many communities, losing its newspaper is like losing the community itself.

A savior has emerged, in the form of the online medium. The almost insignificant cost of the medium itself is a boon to financially strapped local news operations, and access is rapidly becoming commonplace. The medium offers a rich blend of not only print and graphics but sound and video as well. And, if you please, it can be printed. Reader's choice. It's no wonder that in the past year, over a dozen newspapers in major markets around the country have gone online. In fact, the potential is so rich that AOL has created a new channel for them: Digital Cities. In this section I'll discuss just one, but you should investigate them all. Click the Digital Cities icon in the Channel window to find the Digital City nearest you.

Chicago Online

When I first visited AOL's headquarters, the staff was particularly optimistic about a newly launched service called Chicago Online. At that time, Chicago Online represented two significant innovations that made the inauguration of the Newsstand auspicious and that today offer a glimpse into the future of online journalism.

First, Chicago Online is a stand-alone municipal communications service—a parochial service, optimized for the people of Chicago, by the people of Chicago. It has its own message boards, chat rooms, news, sports, and weather (plenty of the latter, actually). In a way, Chicago Online is like a local newspaper. The nation has *USA Today* and the *Wall Street Journal*, and Chicago has the *Chicago Tribune*. The nation has AOL and Chicago has Chicago Online. Neither precludes the other. Nearly every community in the country has its own newspaper; we might someday all have our own little online areas as well. After all, local communications channels are as much a part of the community as national ones. America Online knows that, and that's why it tested the waters with Chicago Online (see Figure 10-15).

The test was a success. For additional evidence of the potential of this alliance, visit the Mercury Center, an online publication of the *San Jose Mercury-News*. Use the keyword: **Mercury** to get there. Also check out AZ Central and *The Arizona News/Phoenix Gazette/Arizona Business Gazette* at keyword: **Arizona**.

Figure 10-15:
Chicago Online
offers a tantalizing
glimpse of future
telecommunica-
tions, as well as a
banquet of suste-
nance for the
online appetite.

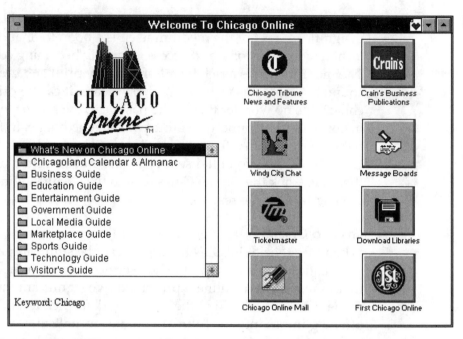

Chicago Online also is a *strategic alliance*. The service is the product of an alliance between the *Chicago Tribune* and AOL. The *Tribune* gains a communications channel that's significantly more bilateral (and less costly) than a daily newspaper, and AOL gets a test bed for another avenue in the electronic community. Perhaps best of all, we all get to observe the formative moments of a new communications medium. Ecologically speaking, the "electronic newspaper" (or something like it) will become increasingly appropriate, and through this alliance, two of the most progressive representatives of the electronic and print media are exploring its potential. There's lots of hope here, for all of us.

But enough existentialism. The *Chicago Tribune* is no lightweight when it comes to information, after all. There's a wealth of practical information for us outlanders. Check out Gene Siskel's Flick Picks (as well as reviews by Dave Kehr, Roy Leonard, and Sherman Kaplan).

Take a look at Ed Curran's Technogadgets and the Chicago Tribune Cookbook Online. Chicago Online isn't a half-hearted experiment in alternative media; it's a mature, expansive, and resourceful communications medium. Give it a half-hour of your time. It will reward you eloquently.

Sports

Back in the old days, football was played in the mud by men in leather helmets, boxing was gloveless and bloody, and families went to baseball games on Sunday afternoons.

Those, of course, were the days before TV and the couch potato. Until recently, sports had become a solitary activity, practiced by supine sluggards in dark living rooms brandishing TV remotes and dissipative bowls of Cheetos.

I'm happy to report that sports have again become interactive, team-oriented activities. Oh, there's still the glow of a cathode-ray tube in the living room on Sunday afternoons, but it's probably displaying AOL now, and the gamester at the controls is enlightened, participatory, and fraternal.

Once again, the nation can be proud of its pastime.

Sports News

The sports fan who clicks the Sports In Depth icon at the top right of the Today's News main menu (see Figure 10-1, or use the keyword: **SportsNews**) enters a sports news area that has few peers (see Figure 10-16). The default category, Top Sports, displays the current headlines of the sports world. And near the top of this list is Sports Roundup, a collection of the top sports stories of the hour.

Figure 10-16:
Sports News offers
not only the top
stories but routes
to the sports dis-
cussion boards,
sports score-
boards, and
various topical
sports news areas
as well.

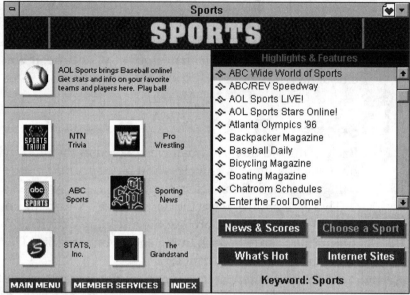

It's not surprising that America Online's Sports News is organized like AOL's other news areas; AOL's method is the fastest way for you, the user, to find what you want. And once you've learned how to look for news in one news channel, you'll find the same information structure in any other channel, whether it be Politics, Business, Sports, life.style, or Weather.

You can browse headlines in the Sports News window, click the category box arrow to display stories in other categories, double-click storylines to read stories, and use the News Search button at the right on the Sports News main window to explore stories further. It's really pretty simple.

The Sports Channel

There's a lot more to sports than news, however. Look again at Figure 10-16. The button near the top center is labeled "Sports Channel." This is your pathway to the AOL Sports Channel's main window (see Figure 10-17), where you'll find a broad array of sports information, services, products, message boards, and interest groups. You can also go directly to the Sports Channel from anywhere in AOL by using the keyword: **Sports**.

Once you've arrived at the Sports Channel, AOL makes it just as easy for you to return to the Sports News window.

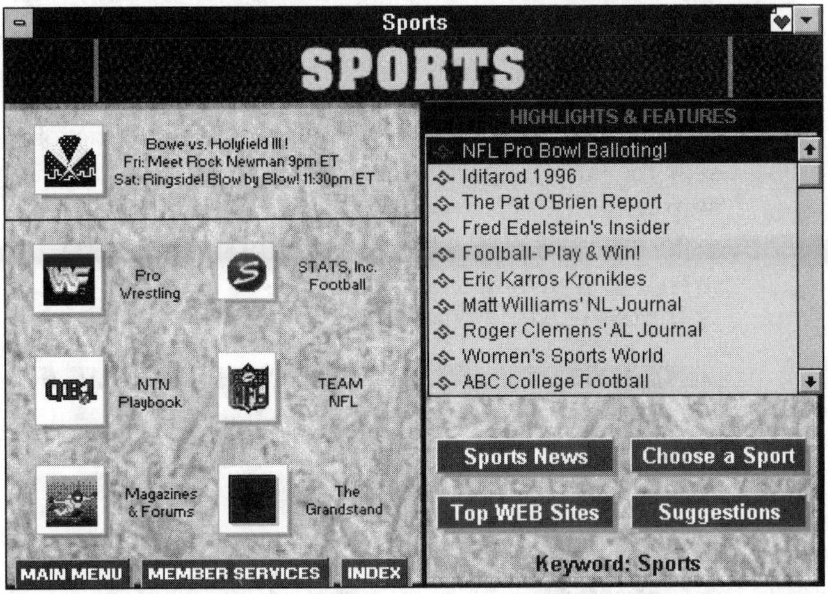

Figure 10-17: Use the keyword: **Sports** to access the top level of AOL's Sports Channel.

If you've come to the Sports Channel windows to browse a specific sport, save yourself a mouse click or two and select the "Choose a Sport" item from the main Sports window, then go directly to the sport of your choice. On the other hand, if you're not in the mood for browsing and you'd like to explore a specific Sports News story, the best strategy is to use the News Search button in the Sports News window. It's just a mouse click away.

So far in this chapter, I've written only about News. The introduction of the Sports Channel has broadened our discussion, and some clarification is in order. To better understand how Sport News is related to the Sports Channel, think of Sports News as a fast flowing river of information; then think of the Sports Channel as a great lake into which the river pours. But read on. As you'll see, AOL's sports arena is very large indeed.

ABC Sports

If you were AOL and you wanted a sports channel that honored the medium and the members, you probably wouldn't start from scratch. Starting from scratch would necessitate crews of photographers and reporters at all of the key games; libraries of knowledge, images, and videos; and armies of staff members and consultants.

No, if you were AOL and you wanted to do the job properly, you'd seek the largest sports organization in the country and form a partnership with them. You would do what you do best—offer a medium and expertise in its use—and allow your partner to do what it does best: event coverage and analysis. AOL has such a partner, and the partner, of course, is ABC Sports (see Figure 10-18).

Figure 10-18:
ABC Sports is the nation's venerable sports authority, and its partnership with America Online spells nothing but enrichment for the membership.

Depending on the season, ABC Sports offers major league baseball, the National Hockey League, Monday Night Football—even thoroughbred racing! Figure 10-18's Monday Night Football button, for example, leads to comprehensive background information for the upcoming game, videos of last week's game, graphics of key players, biographies, statistics—enough data to make any couch potato a savant among supplicants.

Behind the Scenes

For the broadcast of the 1995 Kentucky Derby, ABC used no fewer than 26 cameras, including its unmanned "cablecam" at trackside (the one that races down the backstretch alongside the horses), miniature cameras on the starting gates, and its trademark airborne camera aboard a hovering blimp.

Figure 10-19: One of ABC's 26 cameras at the 1995 Kentucky Derby.

Details such as this are rife in the ABC Sports area (which is where I found the camera information): just look for "Behind the Scenes" buttons.

The Grandstand

If you enjoy sports, you'll love the Grandstand (use the keyword: **Grandstand**; it's the most effective way of getting there). America Online's homage to the sports enthusiast is current, relevant, and vast (see Figure 10-20). In the interest of sports widows everywhere, however, I suggest moderation. The walls of prehistoric caves the world over are covered with pictographs of smashed keyboards and fractured computer screens. It's not a pretty sight.

Figure 10-20: The Grandstand offers something for every sports enthusiast.

THE GRANDSTAND℠

- About the Grandstand
- Grandstand Publications
- Grandstand Contest Area
- Grandstand Feedback Area
- Sports News
- Play ProPicks Here!
- Grandstand Flash Football!
- Sideline Views (Geoff Nathanson)
- Dugout (Baseball)

Sports Flash

Sports Rooms

Fantasy Leagues

Sports Boards

Sports Libraries

Keyword: Grandstand

E-Mail Contact: SportsFan

While investigating the Grandstand the other day, I found scores of graphics uploaded to AOL by members and organizations (four are pictured in Figure 10-21). I even discovered an online club dedicated entirely to baseball cards. It provides news, price polls, and conferences for card collectors throughout the nation.

Figure 10-21: A quick browse through the Grandstand turns up a picture of a Ferrari 412 T1 uploaded by Nigel Mans, a screen capture from an about-to-be released golf game from Accolade, an NFL Playoffs forecast uploaded by Jeeperjo, and the Grandstand Toolbox window, a treasure of downloadable sound and video programs to let you access all that the Sports Channel has to offer.

Chapter 10: Staying Informed

Sports fans like to talk about their interests with other sports fans. Sports talk is especially rewarding when it's with people who are outside your usual circle of acquaintances—who live, in fact, all over the country. If this sounds appealing, consider visiting the message boards. Just click on the Sports Boards icon on the right side of the Grandstand window, or open the folder of the sport that interests you (see Figure 10-22).

Figure 10-22: Browse your favorite sport's message board or take in all the boards. Either way, you'll find a wealth of information.

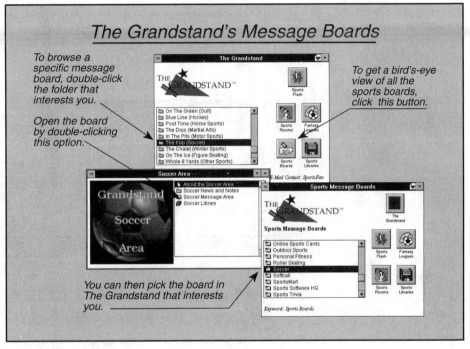

Messages on the sports boards are diverse and occasionally unexpected. Consider the thread of messages I found on the Hockey board (pictured in Figure 10-23). It's great to see unbridled appreciation.

Figure 10-23:
A slice of online
camaraderie.

On the Message Boards

From The Point [Pro Hockey]

Subj: Mike Lange
Date: 94-01-30 10:28:00 EST
From: Pen Quinn

HEEEEE SHOOTS AND SCORES!!! Too bad not every team has an announcer like Lange.
Wouldn't you have loved to here Lange do the All-Star game? Imagine what he would have
sounded like with 17 goals being scored?

Previous
Message

From The Point [Pro Hockey]

Subj: Re:Mike Lange
Date: 94-01-30 13:10:25 EST
From: JTomko

You could not be more correct. Mike is one of the best announcers in the league. I have moved
from Pitts and miss his work greatly.

Previous
Message

From The Point [Pro Hockey]

Subj: Mike Lange
Date: 94-02-21 01:38:31 EST
From: BenCa

Yes even out in Ca mike is well known, and loved.
Even my 4 year old can say " michael michael motor-cycle!"

Next
Message

From The Point [Pro Hockey]

Subj: Re:Mike Lange
Date: 94-02-03 00:55:14 EST
From: Mordaxacis

Anyone that followed the KBL broadcaster negotiations this past summer/fall knows how
much Mike means to Pittsburgh. I mean, the guy gets worked over in Toronto and still calls
the game. Reminds me of Tocchet's performance against the Blackhawks the season before
last. You have to have heard Mike to really appreciate him.

Mordaxacis

Previous
Message

Add
Message

Next
Message

Message boards are wonderful things, but it takes some learning to use them effectively. You can find more about using them in Chapter 9, "Boards & Forums."

Perhaps the most interesting aspect of the Grandstand is its assortment of fantasy teams assembled by members—make-believe teams made up of real players in the sport. The Grandstand Fantasy Baseball League (GFBL), for example, is modeled after "Rotisserie League Baseball," as described in the book of the same name by Glen Waggoner (Bantam Books). Team owners (that's us—the members of AOL) draft 23 players from the available talent in the American or National Leagues. The players' actual big-league performances are used in computing the standings of the GFBL team. Standings, stats, newsletters, and other league information items are found in the message and library sections of the GFBL (see Figure 10-24), and members follow them fanatically. Double-click any of the folders in the scroll box of the Grandstand's main window to access the leagues.

Figure 10-24:
The GFBL window,
and the 1995 GFBL
Champions.

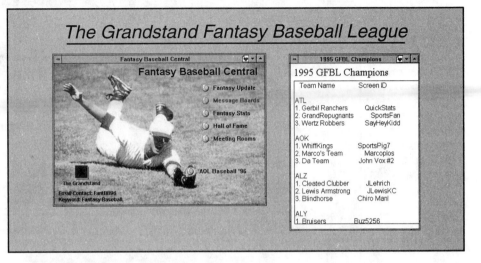

Special Coverage

Without the restrictions imposed by commercial broadcast, America Online is free to devote as many resources as necessary to the appropriate coverage of not only the major, but the not-so-major sporting events as well. AOL goes beyond the "who and what" to provide in-depth answers to the "why and how" of the U.S. Olympic Festival, U.S. Open Tennis, and Wimbledon, to name a few. You'll find extensive background information from a variety of sources, graphics and sounds, Web pages and message boards, for a free exchange of knowledge and opinions with other members (see Figure 10-25).

Figure 10-25:
Preparations for the
1995 Iditarod
dogsled race were
underway as I
prepared this
chapter; I discov-
ered (clockwise,
from the upper
left) the Iditarod
Race window, an
Iditarod history
article, the Pat
O'Brien Report,
Women's Sports
World, and Surflink,
the surfer's online
hangout.

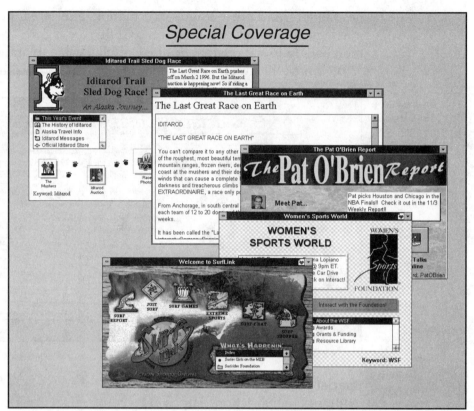

The Online Pace of Change

The Sports Channel, as well as many other areas on AOL, has under-
gone significant change during the last few months, so if it's been a
while since you visited here, give it a try and see all that's been added.
(And don't be surprised if something on your screen looks a little
different than it appears in this book—AOL can change quickly. That
is, after all, the beauty of this medium.)

Weather

Naturally, AOL is brimming with weather information. This is where the online medium really excels. America Online's weather is not only always up to the minute, it's also graphic and colorful.

The primary Weather window (see Figure 10-26) not only offers access to the day's weather news (check here before traveling or when the weather is particularly interesting or threatening), forecasts (updated continuously and organized by state), and boards (lots of experts hang out here; post questions freely), it also offers a route to the color weather maps. And that's where the fun begins.

Figure 10-26: America Online's primary Weather window offers a wealth of current weather information, including maps.

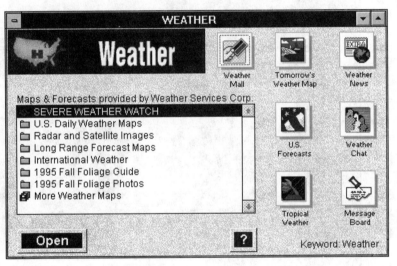

The maps are from Weather Services Corporation, which provides forecasting and consultation services for *USA Today*, among others. Those colorful weather maps on the back page of *USA Today* are derived from the same data that's available on AOL when you use the keyword: **Weather**.

The precipitation, jet stream, and tropical outlook maps are released between 10 a.m. and 11 a.m. Eastern time each day; the temperature bands for the next day will be available between 6 p.m. and 7 p.m. (see Figure 10-27).

Figure 10-27:
You'll have to
imagine it here, but
each of these maps
is displayed in 16
colors and down-
loads in less than a
minute. To get to
them quickly, use
the keyword:
Weather and
double-click on the
U.S. Daily Weather
Maps folder (or
one of the several
other Weather
Maps folders
available).

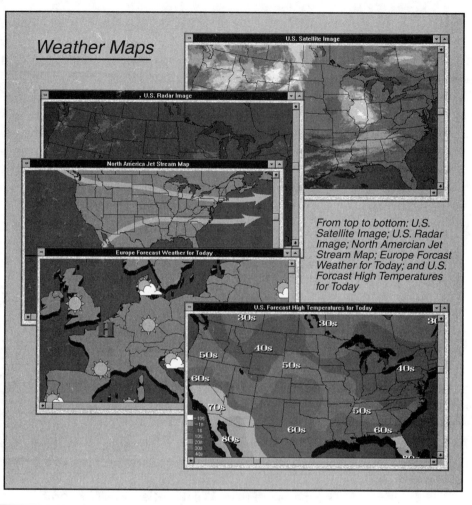

*From top to bottom: U.S.
Satellite Image; U.S. Radar
Image; North Amercian Jet
Stream Map; Europe Forcast
Weather for Today; and U.S.
Forcast High Temperatures
for Today*

You don't need special software to view these maps: simply double-
click any listing, read the description if you wish, then click the Download Now button. If you're using Version 1.5 (or a later version) of the
AOL software, the maps will be displayed onscreen as they're downloaded. None of them takes more than a minute to download at 9600
baud; they'll display satisfactorily even if you don't have a color monitor (or printer); and the files are always available for viewing after
you've downloaded them (even after you sign off) by choosing Open
from the File menu.

Moving On

As I come to the end of this chapter, I see that I've barely scratched the surface of AOL's abundant online resources. After all, we've only explored news, sports, and weather. There is so much more to discover—online games, resources for self-reliance in the health arena, travel information, critics—AOL seems as vast as the Pacific ocean sometimes.

What we need to do is a bit of "channel surfing," much as one might do with a TV remote. I'll bet it won't take much surfing to come upon something that really appeals to you. Turn the page.

CHAPTER 11

Divertissements

- Games
- Entertainment Media
- Travel
- MusicSpace

The outline for this book is posted on the bulletin board here in my office. Having it at my side helps me keep perspective—something that's easy to lose in the midst of a 700-page book project.

This morning, that outline reminds me that so far we've discussed things like the AOL community, the Internet, staying informed, and transferring files. That's all necessary information, but what if we want to have some fun? We're here partly for the fun of it, after all. What's in it for us?

The answer is "plenty." As evidence, I offer this chapter of divertissements: diversions, amusements—places where fun is foremost and duty is disenfranchised. Loosen your tie. Kick off your shoes. Admit intemperance into your life. The night's young.

Games

There's a world of game lovers who find the game-playing arena online to be their hermitage, the place where games are paramount and challenges abound. It's here that knights slay dragons, space voyagers conquer aliens, and residents of the late 20th century scratch their heads in bewilderment. You owe it to yourself to try an online game if you never have: the challenge of playing with remote competitors— unseen and unknown—is unmatched by any other. And if you get hooked, the gaming resources at AOL stand ready to nourish your obsession.

Neverwinter Nights

Neverwinter Nights is an online Advanced Dungeons & Dragons (AD&D) fantasy role-playing game. There's no other online experience quite like it; and there's no better way to play AD&D than with real people in real time, in a medium that combines color, sound, graphics, and unbounded intellectual stimulation.

Neverwinter Nights uses its own software, which you must download and install on your hard drive (a process I'll describe in a moment). Once that's done, you sign on, enter the Neverwinter Nights Forum (keyword: **Neverwinter**), then start the Neverwinter Nights software on your hard drive (see Figure 11-1). Windows and AOL disappear, and Lord Nasher, Neverwinter's brave leader, assumes control. There's great treasure here. And if you and Nasher succeed in returning peace to the land, bounty can be yours.

Figure 11-1:
AD&D greets you
with flashy colors
and sound effects.
It's here that the
adventure begins.

The Neverwinter Nights software offers spectacular sound and 3D graphics. Anyone who has played the game can tell you that there's nothing lightweight about Advanced Dungeons & Dragons. America Online is aware of this and graciously provides a number of AD&D experts to give help whenever you need it. At the top of the list are the official Neverwinter Nights AD&D staff members—easily recognizable by the "NW" or "NWA" in front of their names.

> **Neverwinter Nights Software**
> To play Neverwinter Nights, you will need special software, which you can download for free. For those who just want to take a peek inside Neverwinter Nights, use the keyword: **Neverwinter** and click on AOL Games Download Center. Once there, select Download AOL Online Games, and then retrieve the Neverwinter Nights software. The download is free (you will pass through the free curtain on your way to the download area), and you'll find complete instructions detailing how to download and install the software.

When I tried out the game, I was a little overwhelmed by its immensity until I happened upon NW Snowie (AD&D Online NWN Coordinator) and Trollsbane (a fellow member). They kindly showed me some of the ropes (there are a lot of them). They let me follow them around; helped me acquire gold, treasures, and weapons; cast spells upon my character to make it stronger and less vulnerable to the terrible beasts it met along the way; and saved my character's life on more than one occasion. This isn't special treatment: anyone who needs help has only to ask. People are incredibly helpful and congenial here. There's a Neverwinter Message Center and Lord Nasher's Lounge where you can relax and get to know other players. Either one is fertile ground for members new to the game who need help.

Neverwinter Nights offers a degree of interactivity and realism that entices the new member and challenges the veteran player. Many people join AOL solely to play this game—it's that good. While you may not be quite so fervently committed, you should at least explore the game. It's a remarkable realization of the telecommunications medium.

Strike-A-Match

Julann Griffin created the television show *Jeopardy!* years ago, and you know how successful that endeavor has been. Now, Julann is back. This time the game is Strike-A-Match and the medium is online, and as you might assume, the game plays like a TV game—players buzz in and solve puzzles—only there's a big difference: you get to play, not just watch. You'll find it at the keywords: **Strike a Match** (see Figure 11-2.)

Figure 11-2: Quickly: can you find the two words that match in this puzzle? If you can, you should be playing Strike-A-Match. (Wally and Beaver were brothers on the *Leave It to Beaver* TV series.)

Like Neverwinter Nights, Strike-A-Match requires additional software to run, but the software is free and so is the download. The game is a feature of Boxer*Jam (see Figure 11-3); keep your eye on these people: more is in the works.

Figure 11-3: Boxer*Jam is host to Strike-A-Match (use the keyword: **Boxer*Jam**). If you like online game shows, keep your eye on this keyword. There is more to come.

Murder Mysteries Online

"Hello. My name is Inspector Forsooth, and I'd like to welcome you to my office, otherwise known as Murder Mysteries Online . . . ." Just reading this message is a bit of a mystery, as you must first learn your way around Forsooth's "office," which you'll enter when you use the keywords: **Cyber Sleuth** (see Figure 11-4).

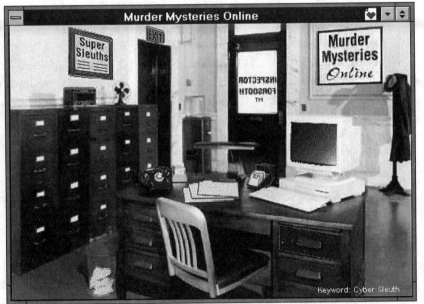

Figure 11-4: Everything but the ash tray: politically correct Inspector Forsooth's office is loaded with buttons, but you have to find them in order to make Murder Mysteries Online come to life.

Two forms of mystery confront you at Murder Mysteries Online. The first type is the daily mini-mysteries (see the "A Lion in Sheep's Clothing" sidebar), which are proposed and solved via message boards (message boards are discussed in Chapter 9, "Boards & Forums").

Also, every Sunday night, the sleuths gather, live, in the area's conference room to attempt to solve a murder mystery. The first sleuth to solve the case wins free connect time on AOL. It's all great fun, but I warn you: it's addictive too!

WeaK RaP in Cincinnati

Here's an example of a daily mini-mystery, direct from Inspector Forsooth's files:

"Scott Gable is a wanted man in Ohio. Just last year he had set up an illegal betting operation there; the authorities uncovered the operation and dismantled it, but not before Gable fled the area. He began to live life as a fugitive.

"His gambling passion eventually persuaded him to tempt fate, though. He decided to board a plane for Cincinnati. He had some financial matters to attend to in nearby Covington, then he planned to head straight to the race track. Upon landing at the Cincinnati airport, though, something happened that might surprise you. What happened was that Gable walked right by several state policemen, but they did nothing whatsoever to stop him!

"In fact, Gable proceeded to carry out his business and arrived at the race track without the authorities laying a hand on him. To cap it all off, he made thousands of dollars when the horse he bet on came through! What I ask of my cybersleuths is to figure out how in the world Mr. Gable got off scot-free. Good luck!"

Think about this while you read. Forsooth and I will tempt you with a clue now and then. You'll find the solution at the end of the chapter.

E-mail Games

There's a genre of online games that doesn't require you to be quick or even be present while the game is taking place—an important consideration for those who must keep a regular working schedule and can only sign on when they get home in the evening. Even then, there might only be enough time to fetch mail and sign off.

No problem. These are *e-mail games,* where everything takes place via e-mail. They're brought to you by Yoyodyne Entertainment (keyword: **Yoyo**), they're lots of fun, and the prizes are spectacular (see Figure 11-5).

Figure 11-5:
The e-mail games
at keyword: **Yoyo**
are designed for
your convenience
and are surprisingly
rewarding.

Figure 11-5:
The e-mail games
at keyword: **Yoyo**
are designed for
your convenience
and are surprisingly
rewarding.

Here are a couple of examples. In the game of Writer's Block, you get to use your creativity and wit to respond to a humorous premise. There's a deadline, but you'll have plenty of time if you check your mail daily. After twelve rounds each winner gets to compete in the final round. And the grand prize? An autographed, first-edition book of poems by Robert Frost! The winner of Down for the Count—a sports trivia game—wins a real bag of gold, worth more than $500! The prizes are subject to change, but they're always of similar value, and prizes like this make the competition even more interesting.

Cincinnati Clue #1
No, the police weren't paid to look the other way. There was no payoff or bribing of any sort.

Federation
There's another category of online games that we haven't discussed: those that involve more than one player at once. This is where things get interesting, as the dynamic of the situation is as unpredictable as a lottery.

Federation is an adult space fantasy multiplayer game, set within a future scenario of interstellar trade, exploration, and intrigue. You can buy drinks for space princesses, swap tips with hardened traders, and gossip with aliens.

These characters are, of course, other players. That's the first thing you do before you enter the game: devise a character. You can be any sex, race, type, or even any species you want.

Though science fiction in nature, Federation is about commerce, politics, intrigue, power, and money—real-life stuff. There's little reward for violence, thus it's rarely encountered. It's called an "adult" fantasy game (not an "adult fantasy" game) because its emphasis is on pragmatic themes rather than violence and subterfuge. But that doesn't stop it from being fun. Give it a try at keyword: **Federation** (see Figure 11-6).

Figure 11-6: Federation features real-time, multiple-player role playing. You never know who you'll encounter there, or what will be on their minds.

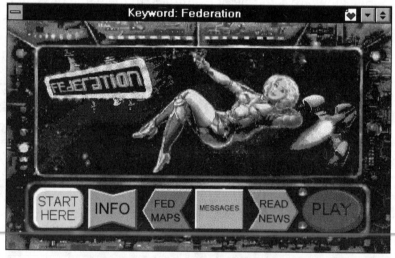

Get Caught!

In less than two years, the World Wide Web has become a focus of online game players. Where else can you meet up with players from all over the world, and explore enticing titles like Mr. Edible Starchy Tuberhead, Gigabox, and Hairball? There are more traditional games as well, like Virtual Vegas and Bridge—plus 9 electronic gaming magazines and 24 video game companies (numbers that are bound to change by the time you read this).

All of these goodies are found at keywords: **Game Sites**, where the people at the Games Channel not only provide the connections but also prowl the Web constantly on your behalf, searching for the best games and monitoring new additions.

Chess

As I write this chapter, AOL is working on an ambitious project: constructing an area dedicated to the game of chess. Chess lovers with enlightened Internet connections have long been able to participate in the Internet Chess Club, but participation in the Club required a Telnet connection, and save for the chess board itself, the interface was primarily textual.

The Internet Chess Club, however, is home to tournament players, Masters, International Masters, and even some International Grandmasters. Without these people, a chess area—even a chess area in a community as large as AOL—wouldn't be worthy of an avid chess player's pawn.

As you might expect, AOL has entered into an agreement with the Internet Chess Club and is building a graphical interface for the area that will provide complete access to the Club, including tournament play and chat. To see the results of their labor, use the keyword: **Chess**.

Figure 11-8:
A fanciful rendition of a chess board displaying a game between Bobby Fischer and Josef Kupper in 1959. The POV-Ray image was created by David Shrock and is available in full color by using the keywords: **File Search**, then searching with the criterion: Shrock.

Cincinnati Clue #2

Gable ended up driving almost 100 miles before he reached his ultimate destination.

Entertainment Media

I've made a number of online friends over the years, and I've developed ongoing philosophical discussions with a few of them. It's my brain food, and I enjoy it.

The other day a friend and I were discussing some of the significant changes in the American lifestyle over the past 100 years. Our conclusion: three major developments have changed that lifestyle forever: (1) the automobile, (2) the computer, and (3) the media.

That last development is the one that brings us to the subject at hand: Entertainment. Imagine entertainment when there were no movies, no videos, no television, no magazines, and very few books! What did those people do with their time? They certainly couldn't hang around AOL's Entertainment Channel.

That opportunity, it would appear, is uniquely ours. And it's one you're not going to want to miss. This place is rife with the spangles of technoglitter.

Critics' Choice

Critics' Choice (see Figure 11-9) is actually a multimedia syndicate, specializing in entertainment reviews. You'll find their reviews not only on AOL but in newspapers as well. Their mission is to serve as a provident guide to entertainment—a mission they fulfill admirably. Use the keyword: **Critics**.

Figure 11-9:
Though there are lots of places to find reviews of books, television, videos, and movies online, I prefer Critics' Choice.

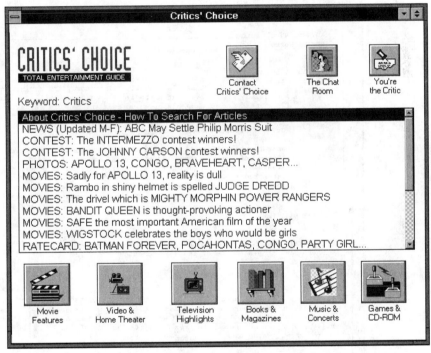

A Review of Online Reviews

While Critics' Choice is AOL's sovereign source of media reviews, you'll find a number of others. Hollywood Online (discussed later in this chapter) is one; @times/The New York Times, Mercury Center (keyword: **Mercury**), and Chicago Online (discussed in Chapter 10, "Staying Informed") are a couple of others.

The Afterwards Coffeehouse (keyword: **Arts**) discusses art; The Atlantic Monthly (keyword: **Atlantic**) and The Saturday Review (keyword: **Saturday**) review a wide variety of media; and SPINonline (keyword: **SPIN**) reviews music. Try each of these services: it's the only way to find the reviewers whose preferences match yours.

Figure 11-10:
A sampling of the reviews (and reviewers) available online.

Critics'
Choice
Reviews

```
Hardcover Bestsellers List - Fiction

The 37th Mandala

Critic: Teressa L. Elliott

AUTHOR: Marc Laidlaw
GENRE: Horror
PUBLISHER: St

The novel beg
Khmer Rouge m
mandalas.

The mandalas
are f
for a
free-

Back
too t
Manda
merel
reape
```

```
Critic: Chris Gardner

For a series that started off with the infamous words "You are
standing in an open field west of a white house, with a boarded
front door. There is a small mailbox here," "Zork" has come a
long way, baby. What started off as a "type-'till-you-bleed"
text-parser game has grown up over the past 19 years (and 6
```

```
Critic: Brandon Judell

What Franco Zeffirelli accomplished for Shakespeare with 1968's
"Romeo and Juliet," Frederic Mitterand, nephew of France's late
President, has realized for Puccini with this lush, superbly
cast "Madame Butterfly": a film that will transform youthful
opera illiterati into devoted buffs. From the opening strains
here to the final death pulsation, no matter what your opera
```

```
Critic: Bill Mann

ABC's "The Drew Carey Show" looks like one of the new season's
winners--and it's also one of the best comedies of the new
rookie crop.

In this new sitcom, Carey, the necktie-adjusting, crewcutted
stand-up who used to break up audiences on the "Tonight Show,"
plays an assistant personnel director in Cleveland who hangs
out a lot with his buddies. One of them is funny stand-up Ryan
Stiles, whom you may recognize from Comedy Central's British
improv show, "Whose Line Is It, Anyway?"

Carey's deliciously mean-spirited material delivered with his
trademark grin is irresistible, and the one-liners seldom stop
on the premiere show. This new sitcom is basically an
extension of Carey's irreverent stand-up act, which is fine by
me. This show has a great time spot--it's "hammocked" between
ABC hits "Ellen" and "Grace Under Fire," shows also hosted by
comedians (neither of whom is half as funny as Carey).

I'm hoping Carey's refreshing new show will knock off CBS'
pedestrian "Dave's World" on Wednesday nights. It certainly
deserves to.
```

Cincinnati Clue #3
Had he landed at Columbus instead of Cincinnati, chances are he'd be in jail.

The remainder of Critics' Choice offers consummate, relevant reviews of all of today's media (see Figure 11-11). While you're there, note the Coming Soon feature in the movies section and the Laserdisc Report in the video section. The television section describes this week's episodes of nearly all shows; the magazine section describes the feature stories of dozens of popular magazines; the music section offers a gift guide; and the games section offers strategies and tips.

Figure 11-11: The contents of Critics' Choice. Nearly every current attraction is reviewed, and all reviews are searchable.

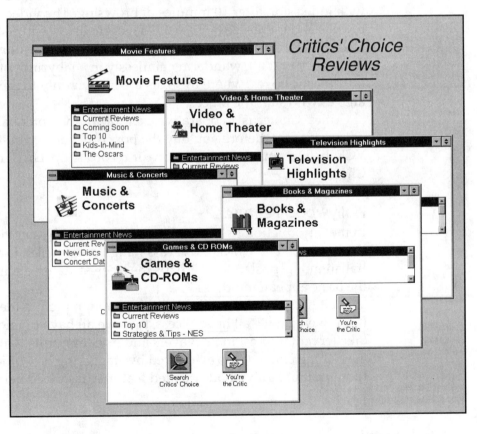

Search Tips

All the reviews in Critics' Choice are searchable—just click any of the search icons pictured in Figure 11-11. Want to see a really great movie? Search for "4STAR." Want to take the kids to a matinee? Search for "MPAAG." Want a review of a Scott Turow novel? Search for "thriller and legal." Search methods are described in "About Critics' Choice—How to Search for Articles," available from the area's main screen.

Don't forget the Critics' Choice video reviews. If you're like me, you can spend hours in a video store and leave with nothing to show for it. Unless I know what I want before I walk in the door, I'm tormented with indecision after 10 minutes of browsing. The video store in my town is about the size of Texas. It's hard to browse in a store the size of Texas. Either you know what you want or you're swallowed by the immensity of it all, wandering aimlessly in a labyrinth of racks and little plastic boxes, where the exits are known only to the pubescent knaves who staff the place.

Critics' Choice is an operative example of the potential of today's online services. Before you buy the popcorn, before you fire up the VCR, before you visit a bookstore or record shop, check out Critics' Choice.

Hollywood Features

In the introduction to her book *Kiss Kiss Bang Bang*, movie critic Pauline Kael wrote, "The words 'Kiss Kiss Bang Bang,' which I saw on an Italian movie poster, are perhaps the briefest statement imaginable of the basic appeal of movies."

A bit harsh, I suppose, but true: the motion picture medium is the art form to which we all have access, thus we all have opinions and we all take fervent interest in its players and its community. Our passion for everything cinematic is evidenced by staggering box-office receipts and the surfeit of Hollywood-oriented features described below.

Hollywood Online

Hollywood Online offers all the things you'd expect from its title: pictures of your favorite stars from the Pictures and Sounds library, cast and production notes in Movie Notes, and discussion on the Movie Talk message board (see Figure 11-12).

Figure 11-12: Hollywood Online (keyword: **Holly-wood**) is AOL's window on everything cinematic.

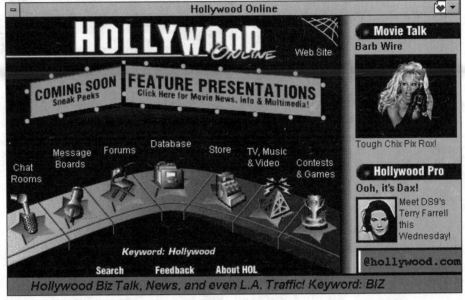

Two other things, however, are worthy of your investigation at Hollywood Online: (1) you can download sneak previews of selected motion pictures before they're released, and (2) multimedia figures heavily in Hollywood Online's contents. Film clips come complete with color, sound, and animation; and interactive "kits" give you a chance to browse a film's contents, allowing you to replay scenes that interest you and skip those that don't.

Figure 11-13:
The Hollywood
Online Database
boasts not just
reviews and com-
ment, but graphics,
sound, and even
video.

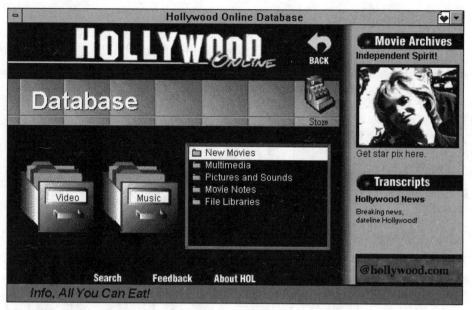

Follywood

The problem with critics is that their opinions don't always align with ours. The problem with box-office success is that it's the result of all kinds of marketing efforts that have little to do with the movie itself.

Yet the critics and the box office are the two most influential factors in our movie decision-making process. Samuel Goldwyn once said, "Why should people go out and pay good money to see bad films when they can stay at home and see bad television for nothing?" That's the trouble: decisions based on flawed filters can be expensive.

The solution is Follywood's "Fool Factor," an amalgam of four factors: critical appraisal, box-office success, popular opinion (yours and others on AOL), and "foolishness" (staff opinions). Each week, Follywood rates each current film by its Fool Factor and publishes the results. I consult the Fool Factor every Saturday afternoon before I head for the silver screen. You should too.

Figure 11-14:
Follywood's "Fool
Factor" is available
every week at
keyword:
Follywood.

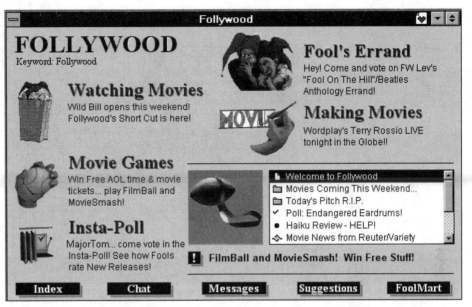

Books

Two features in the Books area are of particular interest. The first is the bestseller lists (see Figure 11-15), compiled via a recurring survey of national distributors and booksellers and presented in the Book Nook. These lists are an alternative to those that appear in the *New York Times* (discussed in Chapter 10, "Staying Informed"). Compare them: the differences are occasionally enlightening.

Figure 11-15:
The bestseller lists
and reviews found
in the Book Nook.
Use the keywords:
Book Nook to get
there quickly.

Bestseller
Lists

```
Hardcover Bestsellers List - Fiction

HARDCOVER BESTSELLERS

*  COMPILED BY THE WALL STREET JOURNAL  *
* COPYRIGHT 1994 BY DOW JONES & COMPANY INC. *
* REPRINTED WITH PERMISSION *

FICTION -
```

```
        Hardcover Bestseller List - Nonfiction

        HARDCOVER BESTSELLERS
        *  COMPILED BY THE WALL STREET JOURNAL  *
        * COPYRIGHT 1994 BY DOW JONES & COMPANY INC. *
1.   "The Gi * REPRINTED WITH PERMISSION *

2.   "The Ch  NONFICTION -
```

```
                                              LAST    WSJ
                                              WEEK    SALES
                                                      INDEX
Kirkus Book Reviews - Fiction

BOOK REPORT

CAPSULE REVI
COMPILED BY
                 Kirkus Book Reviews - Nonfiction
FICTION -
                 BOOK REPORT
1.   Joseph
     needed     CAPSULE REVIEWS OF NEW BOOKS OF UNCOMMON MERIT OR POPULAR APPEAL
                COMPILED BY KIRKUS REVIEWS, NEW YORK, NY
2.   Insomni
                NON-FICTION -
3.   Haunting
     collect    1.   Not P.C.: Richard Bernstein unmasks the Dictatorship Of
                     Virtue.  Release September 7.
4.   Cees No
     in The     2.   Doris Kearns Goodwin illuminates the complex Roosevelt
                     marriage in No Ordinary Time.  Release September 23.
CLOSING TIME
                3.   David Halberstam looks at a pivotal moment: the World Series
   The long-         of October 1964.  Release August ?

  In 1961 He    NO ORDINARY TIME:Franklin and Eleanor Roosevelt: The Homefront in
about a group   World War II
brutal assau
the ruthless       A superb dual portrait of the 32nd President and his First
Catch- 22, He   Lady, whose extraordinary partnership steered the nation through
sequel. Yoss    the perilous WW II years.
68 and in Ma
Tappman again       In the period covered by this biography, 1940 through
consultant f    Franklin's death in 1949, FDR was elected to unprecedented third
company. The    and fourth terms and nudged the country away from isolationism
learn that h    into war. It is by now a given that Eleanor was not only an
                indispensable adviser to this ebullient, masterful statesman, but
                a political force in her own right. More than most recent
                historians, however, Goodwin (The Fitzgeralds and the Kennedys,
                1987) is uncommonly sensitive to their complex relationship's
                shifting undercurrents, which ranged from deep mutual respect to
```

The second feature is the reviews available in Rogue Print. These are independent reviewers, so the reviews often are more diverse than those appearing in the *Times*. Again, compare for yourself and—if you are truly of the literati—give thanks that AOL offers such alternatives.

Don't forget the Book Bestseller boards (in the Reading Room). This is the place for your review—often the most incisive of all.

Cartoons

Let's take a little survey. What's the first section you read when you pick up the Sunday paper? If you're like me, you read "the funnies" before anything else. Often they're the *only* thing I read, depending on how dreary the world has been that week.

America Online is particularly rich in cartoons, and you don't have to wait until Sunday morning to enjoy them. A number of nationally acclaimed cartoonists contribute to AOL each week. They include the following:

- Scott Adams's comic strip "Dilbert," reaching more than 30 million newspaper readers in nine countries. "Dilbert" was the first syndicated comic strip to appear online, where fans have initiated more than 30,000 comic downloads monthly and generated over 50,000 e-mail messages. "Dilbert" is at keyword: **Dilbert**.

- The Comic Strip Centennial, where you can learn about the history of one of the very few art forms "born in the U.S.A." This area is presented in cooperation with the Newspaper Features Council in honor of the 100th anniversary of the birth of the comics, and it includes exhibits from the Library of Congress and the U.S. Postal Service (see Figure 11-16).

- The Cartoon Network, with its own forum of 'toons and comments.

- AOL Out of Line from ABC, where you supply the caption and win prizes.

Figure 11-16: Cartoons abound at keyword: **Funnies**. The main screen appears at upper right; then the logo from The Comic Strip Centennial; two postage stamps from the U.S. Postal Service; America Out of Line's Caption the Cartoon contest; and "Bungee Boss," a Dilbert strip from Scott Adams.

Visit the Cartoon Forum at keyword: **Cartoon**, for even more 'toons and comment. New cartoons are posted there every week, including those from the AOL membership. This is your chance to get your 'toons published online!

Columnists & Features Online

Columnists & Features Online is the best way to read provocative newspaper columnists and communicate with them online (see Figure 11-17).

Figure 11-17:
Columnists & Features Online offers current material as well as an extensive searchable library. Use the keyword:
Columnists.

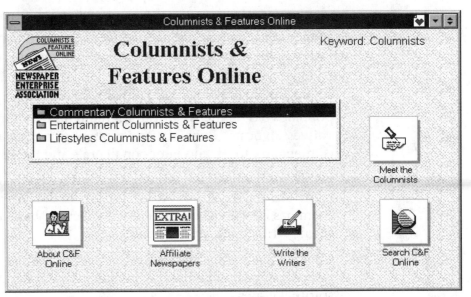

The Newspaper Enterprise Association (NEA) syndicates distinguished writers and political columnists to newspapers nationwide, including the 29 (a number that's sure to grow) featured on AOL (see Figure 11-18).

Figure 11-18:
A sample of the columnists assembled for bilateral discourse via Columnists & Features Online.

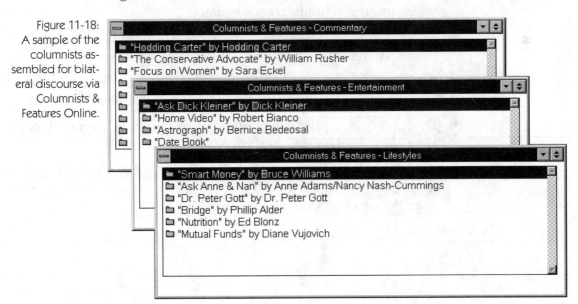

The text of each column appears the same day it is released to the newspapers and remains online for a week. After that, past columns are posted in the library. Use standard AOL criteria to search them. Some of the columnists include the following:

- William Rusher, the former publisher of the *National Review* and a popular voice of the American Right. In his column "The Conservative Advocate" Rusher uses a mixture of humor and political commentary to jab and lampoon liberals and the American Left.

- Nat Hentoff, one of the foremost authorities on the First Amendment. Hentoff's column, which appears in the *Washington Post*, examines how legislative decisions affect our basic freedoms to speak, write, think, and assemble.

- George Plagenz, an ordained minister and news veteran who writes "Saints and Sinners," a personal look at family values and spiritual issues.

- Ian Shoales, a popular humor columnist from National Public Radio and the *San Francisco Examiner*, known for his amusing social commentary.

- Joseph Spear, an advocate for the average American, who offers witty, insightful political commentary.

- Robert Bianco, a *Pittsburgh Post-Gazette* journalist who writes "Home Video," up-to-the-minute reviews of home video releases.

- Radio personality Bruce Williams, whose column "Smart Money" gives incisive answers to personal finance questions.

- Dr. Peter Gott, a practicing physician and patients' rights advocate who offers readers free medical advice.

- Astrologer Bernice Bedeosal, the author of "Astrograph." What's in the stars for you? You'll find it in "Astrograph," one of the most popular astrology columns in America.

Horoscopes

Mention of Bernice Bedeosal's "Astrograph" column reminds me that horoscopes play a transcendental role in the Entertainment Channel. Daily horoscopes for each of the astrological signs are posted each week; you're welcome to consult them before you do anything rash. Use the keyword: **Horoscope** to access this area quickly. And if you'd like something a little more specific, stop by the Crystal Ball Forum (keywords: **Crystal Ball**) to see what the tarot cards have to say about the future.

Figure 11-19:
That's my horo-
scope you're read-
ing there. Let's see
. . . it seems today
would be a good
day to call my
broker (a Leo) and
buy 431 shares of
AOL stock. . . . Or
maybe I should
consult the cards
to be sure.

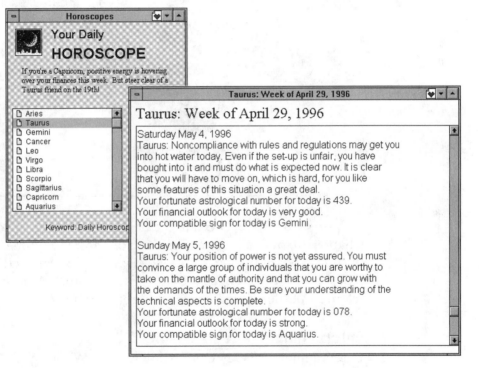

ABC Online

ABC Online is one of the most dazzling areas available at AOL. A vast reservoir of images, sounds, and videos is available in the libraries, along with pertinent talk and commentary on today's media (see Figure 11-20).

Figure 11-20:
ABC Online is one
of AOL's showcase
expositions.

Sports fans will appreciate the depth ABC Sports (discussed in Chapter 10) delivers online, and aficionados of daytime TV will wallow in suds at SoapLine Daily (keywords: **ABC Soaps**). And don't neglect ABC beta (keywords: **ABC Beta**), especially the "America Out of Line" feature. A little irreverence is good for all of us.

Entertainment Weekly Online

Entertainment Weekly Online (keyword: **EW**) brings AOL subscribers the full text of *Entertainment Weekly* magazine each week: feature stories and reviews of movies, TV, music, books, videos, and multimedia.

That's the official line, but if you're an *Entertainment Weekly* reader, you know there's much more to the magazine than that. Just this week I dropped in and caught Mary Makarushka's encore piece about Jim Croce. *Rolling Stone* noted that the critics were content to consign him to the status of a likable nonentity, yet Makarushka reminds us of some of his most poignant lyrics—"Time in a Bottle" is still one of my favorite lyrics of all time, and Makarushka agrees. There's insightful, contemporary journalism here.

Figure 11-21: Entertainment Weekly Online offers not only the full text of the magazine each week, but you can chat with staffers and participate in guest events.

Be sure to check out the notable programs for the week in the TV section every Monday, and parents should avail themselves of their weekly Parents' Guide.

Cincinnati Clue #4

The horse he bet on was named Thunder Gulch. Does that name sound at all familiar?

Travel

Who hasn't indulged in an "If I had a million dollars. . ." fantasy? My favorite is travel: South America, the British Isles, a blue-water cruise, the Orient Express. . . . Heck, I'd be happy if someone just gave me a ticket to Tucumcari.

Of course, fantasies require money. That's why they're fantasies. If you want money-optional indulgences, try AOL's Travel Channel (keyword: **Travel**). Not only can you indulge your fantasies here, you can actually fulfill them as well. You can find exceptional travel bargains; book airline, car, and hotel reservations; consult with other travelers before you depart. They say there are only two types of people in the world: those who are on vacation, and those who wish they were. The Travel Channel serves both types.

One World Travel

Perhaps one of the most specific advantages offered online is the ability to shop for your own airline reservations. For years, travel agents have peered at computer screens and applied their expertise to interpret cryptic displays for tyro travelers. Now, however, the computer screen is your own; the display is graphical and precise; you can examine the alternatives yourself and make your own decisions; you can even book the tickets from your keyboard.

Changes Ahead

It's frustrating to describe an area that's under construction, especially when it's as integral—both to this book and to AOL—as the airline reservation feature. What am I to do? I can't leave it out.

My best strategy is to be frank and tell you that as I write this, the One World Travel feature is in an early phase of development. Consequently, I must omit the system's preliminary screens where you provide your traveler's profile, billing information, and seating, class, meals, airline, home airport, and frequent flyer information. I must also omit the fare information and itinerary verification dialogs. Thus, interpret this section of the book as a glimpse of a far greater whole. If you look carefully at Figures 11-22, 11-23, and 11-24 you'll note that all of the One World Travel screens offer Help buttons. The information under these buttons will be comprehensive and germane. Use them, liberally, when you have questions.

Itinerary Planning

One of my favorite jaunts is a trip to North Carolina in the summer. They have some delectable cuisine there (to say nothing of the mint juleps); it's a pleasant and friendly place; and the natives talk with a lilt that could melt even Jack Palance's heart. (Did I mention that my publisher is there, too? And that my publisher usually pays for the trip? It's amazing how a travel allowance can make a place seem even more endearing.) Let's use One World Travel to see if there's a flight that will get me there.

I begin by entering my departure and destination cities, and my preferred time and date of departure (see Figure 11-22).

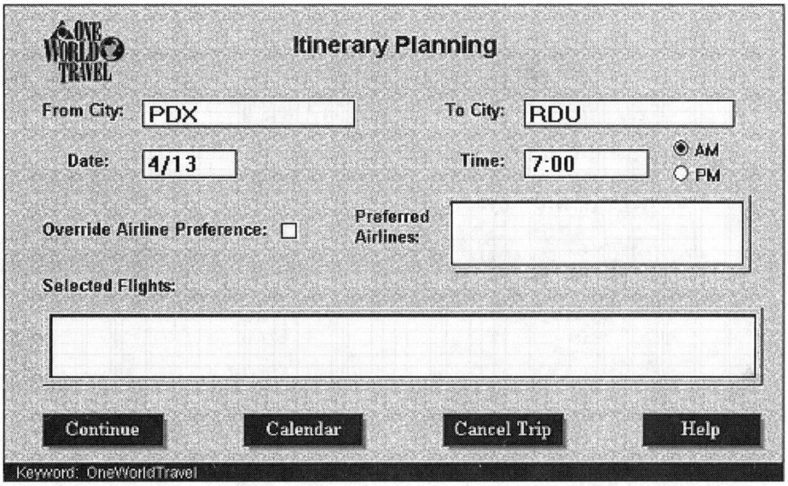

Figure 11-22:
I begin by identifying where and when I want to travel.

> **One World Travel**
> **Itinerary Planning**
>
> From City: `PDX` To City: `RDU`
>
> Date: `4/13` Time: `7:00` ● AM ○ PM
>
> Override Airline Preference: ☐ Preferred Airlines: [   ]
>
> Selected Flights: [   ]
>
> [Continue] [Calendar] [Cancel Trip] [Help]
>
> Keyword: OneWorldTravel

There are three points I should make about Figure 11-22: (1) I didn't have to use the departure and destination codes (PDX, RDU) that you see in the illustration. I could have answered the questions in plain English and One World Travel would have determined my need or asked me to clarify my meaning. (2) The Preferred Airlines box would contain the airlines that I defined earlier, when I indicated my preferences. (3) The Selected Flights list box would contain earlier flights in this itinerary: a departure flight, for example, if I was booking my return.

Once I've entered the information, pictured in Figure 11-22, I click the Continue button.

Flight Selection

The Flight Selection window appears next, displaying the flights One World Travel has discovered that meet my travel criteria. To select a flight, all I need to do is click on it, then click the Select Flight button.

Figure 11-23:
To select a flight,
click the Select
Flight button.

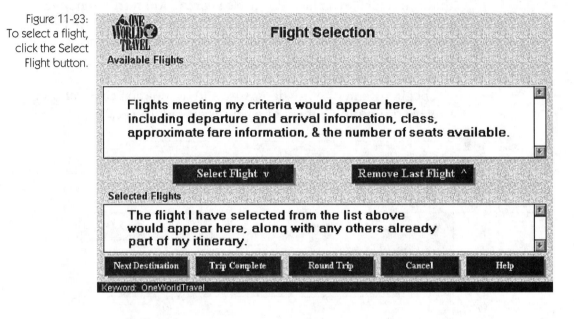

As Figure 11-23 indicates, approximate fare information would appear in the upper list box along with the flights meeting my criteria. Using this information, I could select a flight for inclusion in the itinerary I'm building below.

The Fare Display

When you've decided upon your departure and return flights—and any others in between—you'll click Figure 11-23's Trip Complete button. This will provoke the Fare Display window appearing in Figure 11-24.

Figure 11-24:
You can review
your trip plan,
change it, select a
lower fare, or
accept via this
window.

Fare Display

Your Trip:

Rules

All of the flights on your itinerary would appear here.

Total Base Fare: ⬚   Total Tax: ⬚   Total Fare: ⬚

Lowest Trip:

Rules

If the system found less expensive alternatives, they would appear here.

Total Base Fare: ⬚   Total Tax: ⬚   Total Fare: ⬚

| Keep Your Trip | Select Lowest Trip | Change or Cancel Trip | Help |

Keyword: OneWorldTravel

Note that One World Travel looks for less-expensive seats on the flights chosen, and reports them in Figure 11-24's lower list box; a convenient Select Lower Trip button appears at the bottom of the window should you wish to take advantage of the lowest fares.

The itinerary process concludes after you complete passenger and billing information. Your ticket is sent by 2nd-day air. It won't be long before you'll be able to reserve a rental car and a hotel room this way too, with confirmations arriving just as quickly.

You don't have to complete the online reservation process. You can always click a Cancel button. No one will tattle if you indulge in a little fantasy travel. It's a great cure for the summertime or wintertime blues; and who knows, maybe you, too, will visit the beautiful Raleigh-Durham-Chapel Hill Triangle area of North Carolina. Sip a mint julep while you're there: there are none better in the South.

The Travel Forum

As long as we're in a traveling mood, let's check out the Travel Forum. Articles, message boards, and a library offer a wealth of information and tips for the domestic or world traveler (see Figure 11-25).

Are you looking for a romantic hideaway for your getaway weekend? Check the cruise message board. If you're looking for the best itinerary for your train trip through Europe, check the World Traveler message board. If you're traveling overseas, check out the U.S. State Department Travel Advisories and the Forum's special events with travel experts. In-depth articles cover topics such as "How to find hotel discounts" and "Should I buy trip cancellation insurance?"

Travel plans, perhaps above all else, benefit from peer support. The Travel Forum is where you can solicit the advice of peers and pros alike. No travel plans are complete until you talk to those who have been there. For this purpose, check the Travel Forum's message boards. Lots of people travel, and most who do like to talk about it. Their comments are candid and relevant, and because it's a message board, everything is current.

Figure 11-25:
The Travel Forum offers packing tips, a Bargain Box, great programs like Geoclock that show the current time in terms of daylight around the world, and much more.

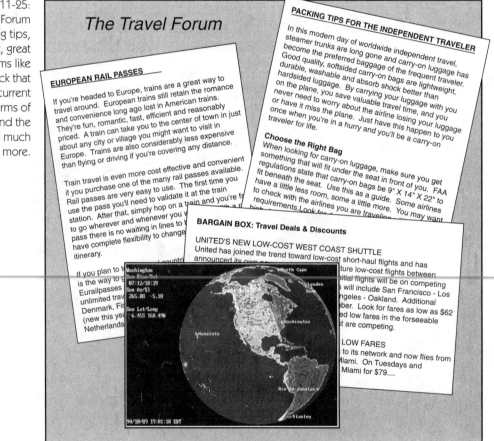

The Travel Forum

PACKING TIPS FOR THE INDEPENDENT TRAVELER
In this modern day of worldwide independent travel, steamer trunks are long gone and carry-on luggage has become the preferred baggage of the frequent traveler. Good quality, softsided carry-on bags are lightweight, durable, washable and absorb shock better than hardsided luggage. By carrying your luggage with you on the plane, you save valuable travel time, and you never need to worry about the airline losing your luggage or have it miss the plane. Just have this happen to you once when you're in a hurry and you'll be a carry-on traveler for life.

Choose the Right Bag
When looking for carry-on luggage, make sure you get something that will fit under the seat in front of you. FAA regulations state that carry-on bags be 9" X 14" X 22" to fit beneath the seat. Use this as a guide. Some airlines have a little less room, some a little more. You may want to check with the airlines you are traveling... requirements. Look for...

EUROPEAN RAIL PASSES
If you're headed to Europe, trains are a great way to travel around. European trains still retain the romance and convenience long ago lost in American trains. They're fun, romantic, fast, efficient and reasonably priced. A train can take you to the center of town in just about any city or village you might want to visit in Europe. Trains are also considerably less expensive than flying or driving if you're covering any distance.

Train travel is even more cost effective and convenient if you purchase one of the many rail passes available. Rail passes are very easy to use. The first time you use the pass you'll need to validate it at the train station. After that, simply hop on a train and you're fr... to go wherever and whenever you... pass there is no waiting in lines to... have complete flexibility to change... itinerary.

If you plan to t... is the way to g... Eurailpasses... unlimited trav... Denmark, Fir... (new this yea... Netherlands...

BARGAIN BOX: Travel Deals & Discounts

UNITED'S NEW LOW-COST WEST COAST SHUTTLE
United has joined the trend toward low-cost short-haul flights and has announced its own... ...ture low-cost flights between ...itial flights will be on competing ...s will include San Francisco - Los ...ngeles - Oakland. Additional ...ber. Look for fares as low as $62 ...ed low fares in the forseeable ...t are competing.

...LOW FARES
...to its network and now flies from ...Miami. On Tuesdays and ...Miami for $79....

Cincinnati Clue #5
If you knew the full name of the Cincinnati airport, the mini-mystery would be easily solved!

Travelers Corner

Don't confuse the Travel Forum with Travelers Corner. Though the two serve similar purposes, there's a subtle but significant difference in their focus.

Arnie Weissmann began planning for an around-the-world journey in the early 1980s. To his dismay, he couldn't find information about his destinations. He knew how he was traveling, he knew what his costs were going to be, he knew what to pack and how to dress. But what he needed were friends, chaperones familiar with his destinations who could tell him where to go and what to do when he arrived—how to behave, how to find the good stuff and avoid the bad. He needed what the Travelers Corner calls "destination profiles" (see Figure 11-26). The Travel Forum, in other words, concentrates on planning, transportation, and reservations. The Travelers Corner focuses on what to do once you get there. You should become familiar with both.

Figure 11-26: The Travelers Corner offers destination information for thousands of locations around the world.

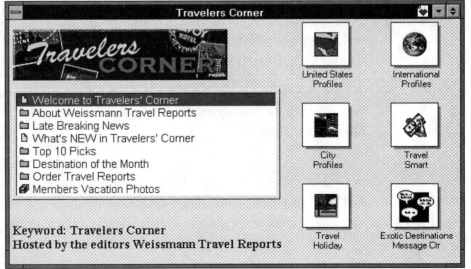

Preview Vacations Online

With their television and online productions, Preview Media is preparing the travel agency of the future. They have the world's largest collection of vacation videos and images, agents on duty seven days a week, and weekly opportunities to win a free vacation. At AOL, they're known as Preview Vacations Online. To find them, use the keyword: **Vacations**. (See Figure 11-27).

Figure 11-27: Preview Vacations Online offers dozens of competitively priced vacation packages. You can examine the accommodations and fares online—from the world's largest vacation image library—then make the booking, without ever having to leave your keyboard.

Preview Vacations Online is a full-service travel agency. They not only offer a kaleidoscope of travel images, they not only leverage their extensive media exposure to gather great package deals, but they also make bookings—including transportation, hotels, and rental cars where appropriate—online. The human touch isn't ignored either: you can always talk to an agent via their toll-free line when you have specific questions.

Be sure to fill out your vacation profile so that Preview Vacations can contact you when an irresistible deal pops up that fits you perfectly. And don't neglect to enter the drawing for a free vacation: you can't beat that price!

Your Wallet Is Safe at AOL

All this talk about travel agencies, renting cars, and booking airline tickets may make you a little squeamish: "Does my AOL membership obligate me for anything beyond the standard monthly fee and connect charges?" No, not at all. All the additional-expense items I've discussed in this chapter are voluntary—not at all requisite to membership in AOL. This is the Travel Channel, after all, and most travel is discretionary—and an additional expense.

ExpressNet

ExpressNet from American Express offers a comprehensive online resource for American Express cardholders. Using a password, you can query the status of your American Express account, including all billed and unbilled charges. You can download billing details to your computer for use with Quicken, Managing Your Money for Windows, and Kiplinger's Simply Money software. By providing American Express with your checking-account information, you can even pay your American Express bill online!

Figure 11-28: ExpressNet offers an extensive array of services for American Express cardholders.

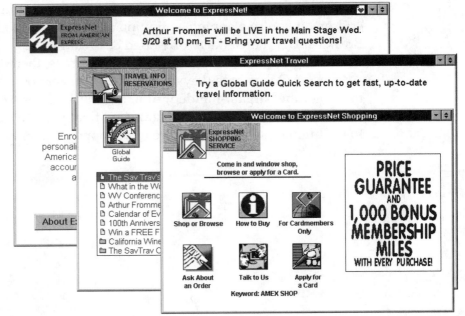

ExpressNet members (there's no charge, though you must have an American Express card) also have access to the following:

- The American Express Travel Service for airline, hotel, and car rental reservations.

- The ExpressNet Shopping Service, where every purchase builds bonus miles in the American Express Membership Miles feature.

- A database of the special discounts and value-added offers exclusively available to American Express Cardmembers.

There's more, but you have to have an American Express card to access all of the features ExpressNet has to offer. Naturally, you can apply for a card online—just use the keyword: **ExpressNet**.

Other Travel Services Online

Space limitations simply don't permit me to explore the entirety of the Travel Channel. Still, I'd be remiss if I didn't mention at least some of the other major travel areas offered by AOL. If you've ever thought about taking an ocean cruise, discover Cruise Critic (keywords: **Cruise Critic**), an online cruise guide with in-depth, candid reviews of cruise ships and cruises. You'll find the latest cruise bargains, cruise tips, reviews of more than 100 ships—plus the advice of your fellow AOL cruisers. If you're planning a vacation at a bed & breakfast, the Bed & Breakfast U.S.A area (keywords: **Bed & Breakfast**) is where you'll find everything you need. If you're the outdoors type, then the Outdoor Adventure Online area (keyword: **OAO**) will get you where you want to go. For the bargain-minded, AOL has the Traveler's Advantage area (keywords: **Traveler's Advantage**). And finally, there's complete access to the Internet, where even more travel opportunities and interests await.

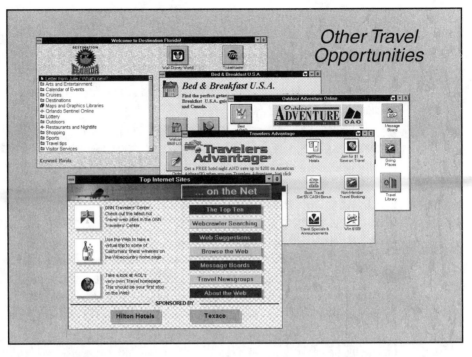

Figure 11-29:
Just a few of the
many other travel
areas offered by
AOL.

MusicSpace

We tend to think of the online medium as one that's primarily textual, with a few graphics for window dressing. That perception isn't far off the mark, but the mark is a moving target. The online medium of today bears little resemblance to what we'll be using tomorrow. We are the pioneers. Future generations will remember us as we remember the pony express riders back in the days when mail was carried on horseback.

Perhaps the most profound change will occur in the music business (see the "Thea McCue" sidebar). Music recording technology is already almost exclusively digital; even some musical *instruments* are digital. Digital is the language of computers. It's only a matter of time before digital music and your computer are wedded via the online medium.

Thea McCue

Thea McCue is an Account Coordinator for AOL. Her purview is MusicSpace (described later in this chapter). Like many of AOL's creative staff, her job is not only to manage the day-to-day operation of her area, but to stay an appropriate distance ahead of it as well.

In perhaps five years, when "the bandwidth" opens up and we're all able to connect to AOL at, say, 256 kbps—a megabyte every ten seconds—Thea sees a MusicSpace that's considerably different from the one that exists today. "Music producers today are at the mercy of the broadcast media: if radio stations don't play it; if MTV or VH1 doesn't run the video, the music dies." The consumer, in other words, sees and hears new music only after it has passed through the broadcast media's filters—hardly an unbiased selection.

In five years you might be listening to music—perhaps even watching videos—that you've downloaded from Thea's libraries. These libraries will offer all of the new music that's available, not a subset passed through a filter. You'll listen to it when you want and it will be digital quality—the same as CDs today. AOL will keep track of the downloads—just as they do today—and those selections with large download numbers will become hits. Feedback from listener to artist will be direct via message boards and download numbers. You might even furnish your credit card number and have AOL download the entire album to your writeable CD-ROM. Consumer and producer will share a distribution channel that's equitable and immediate.

Music is a personal thing. This scenario will not only complement that intimacy, it will promote it. There are changes ahead, and many of them will be for the better.

In 1969 I camped across from the launch site of Apollo 11, the first rocket to land a man on the moon. The night before launch, the anticipation among the people gathered there was electric. Something big was about to happen and we were all there to see it. AOL's MusicSpace (see Figure 11-30) is like that. It is home to some of the most creative people in mass communications—people drawn to both music and the online medium. They're camped out here, waiting for Something Big. If you want to be there when it happens, visit MusicSpace often.

Figure 11-30: MusicSpace is the conductor's podium for all things musical on AOL. If you enjoy music—be it classical, hip-hop, or anything in between—use the keyword: **MusicSpace** every time you sign on.

MTV

Writing in the San Francisco *Examiner*, Robert Rossney recently referred to AOL as "bringing American commercial culture to the online world as fast as it can." His description of AOL made it sound about as exciting as flat beer by citing areas of the service where you can obtain instructions for making masks from paper plates and throwing block parties.

Obviously, Rossney never visited MTV Online (keyword: **MTV**). This place is about as indicative of American commercial culture as Las Vegas on Halloween. The people at MTV—with screen names like MTVomit, MTVixen, and MTVacuum—love to get "in your face," and the online medium hardly cramps their style (see Figure 11-31).

Figure 11-31:
MTV Online is
about as reverent
as a fraternity house
on a Saturday night
in June.

Here's a hint: get the map. The list box in the main MTV screen offers an online diagram of the MTV areas and describes what's in each one. How else would you know that you can find a historically signifi-cant video every month in the *Buzz Been* section of MTV Past Out, or that Beavis and Butthead hang out at the Head Shop?

With your map in hand, be sure to check out MTV Yack!, the Wave-length, and the Stream Of Consciousnews areas.

Even if you can't make sense of what they're saying, the place flaunts the best Eye Candy that's available online. Be sure your color is turned on!

The Corner Tavern

Anyone who has attended the showing of a good film in a full theater knows that most people prefer their entertainment in the company of other people. We go to the movies not just to see the film, but to see the film in the company of others. We laugh more at sitcoms when we're not alone. We travel to the corner tavern for Monday Night Football so that we can comment to one another while the game is in progress.

➡

It comes as no surprise to the people at AOL, then, to learn that there's a significant coincidence between message board usage and broadcast television. Visit MTV Yak someday while your TV is tuned to the MTV channel, on a weekday, after school has let out. Chances are, the discussion will coincide with the events onscreen. The same can be said of the Melrose Place board—though peak activity might occur just after an episode ends—or, indeed, Monday Night Football. It's a peculiar but quantifiable phenomenon. Someone should write a thesis.

VH1

Shall we mellow the demographic somewhat? On cable, VH1's appeal is to a slightly older market than MTV's, with artists such as Emmylou Harris, Billy Joel, k.d. lang, and Mariah Carey. The same can be said of VH1's online offering (see Figure 11-32).

Figure 11-32: VH1 online spotlights music, of course, and much of it is downloadable. VH1 is a compelling multimedia resource that's available now, at keyword: **VH1**.

VH1 offers all of the chat rooms, message boards, and artist features you would expect from a resource such as this, but two features warrant special mention:

- The *Digital Gallery* offers a spectacular library of video clips and sound samples. Some of the latter are available in digital stereo and sound every bit as good as a CD played on the proper equipment. This is a great way to sample material from a new release to see if it's something you want to buy.

- The *Goods* offers a direct connection to Blockbuster Music, so you can buy the music you've read about—perhaps even sampled—without leaving your keyboard!

Music Message Center

The Music Message Center is the Big Daddy of all of the message boards on AOL. It's one of the busiest places you'll find anywhere online—it requires a staff of almost 20 people—and because of its size, there's bound to be a music category that suits your needs (see Figure 11-33).

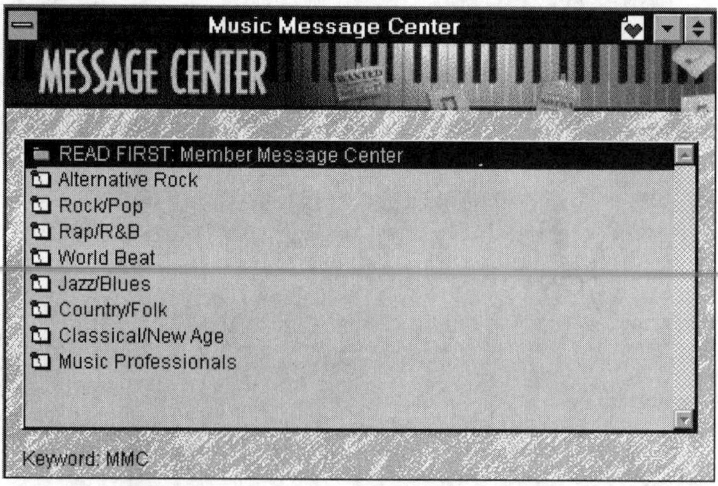

Figure 11-33:
The Music Message Center is the place for you to exchange views and queries about music of all forms.

Figure 11-33 hardly does the Music Message Center justice. Each of the broad categories appearing in the illustration contains scores—sometimes hundreds—of individual folders. The Rock/Pop category, for example, offers over 280 boards, discussing topics from ABBA to Frank Zappa.

The Message Center's success is, most likely, attributable to its attitude. The Center's focus is fans, not the media, and the participants appreciate the lack of industry intrusion. If you like music and you want to talk with others who like music, use the keyword: **MMC**, and become involved with the Music Message Center.

SPINonline

As you would expect from the people who produce *SPIN* magazine, SPINonline offers creative irreverence and verbal spaghetti. It's all in fun, and every corner of the online medium is exposed along the way. These guys push the envelope (see Figure 11-34).

Figure 11-34: The Digital Mosh Pit, The Wasteland, Suspicious Minds, and the SPINonline Garage—they're all waiting to be explored at key-word: **SPIN**.

If you're in a band—even if you're solo—try uploading a sound clip to the SPINonline Garage. The mechanics there review everything received and post the best for everyone else to hear. There's also the SPIN College Radio Network Online. Each week *SPIN* Magazine produces a program that airs on more than 300 college radio stations from coast to coast, and SPINonline is where you'll find out about upcoming shows, and meet new artists and your neighborhood college radio programmers.

> **Cincinnati Clue #6**
> This truly was a borderline case. Unless you live in Cincinnati, a map might come in real handy!

House of Blues

The House of Blues is the jazz industry's answer to rock's Hard Rock Cafe. Nestled in the French Quarter of New Orleans, the House of Blues plays host to Al Green, Little Feat, Ray Charles, Koko Taylor, and scores of others.

In the spring of 1995, the House of Blues hosted an online area for the live coverage of the New Orleans Jazz & Heritage Festival (see Figure 11-35). Not only was the festival a success, so was the online area. Such a success, in fact, that the House of Blues is now a permanent feature on AOL, a becoming home to blues and jazz lovers nationwide.

Figure 11-35: The House of Blues is headquarters for blues and jazz lovers nationwide.

WEB TopStops

AOL's MusicWeb site is a *tour de force* in Web page design. In addition to its changing list of top ten music sites, AOL also has a number of innovative sites of its own. Look for the "Music Mood Ring," with blue (the blues), red (party music), yellow (mellow, acoustic, profound), pink (bubbly), green (underground), and black (heavy metal). Each of these colors takes you to a Web page that's festooned with links to Web sites from all over the world, with audio and video clips galore. The Music Mood Ring isn't all: AOL has also cooked up the "Browse-O-Matic," where a new recipe for Web sites appears each week, and each of the ingredients is a hyperlink to even more Web sites. The World Wide Web (discussed in Chapter 4) is almost overburdened with music resources, but the Web TopStops brings organization and fun to what could be an overwhelming mire of excess.

Figure 11-36: AOL's WEB TopStops brings order to the chaos of music Web sites at keyword: **MusicWeb**.

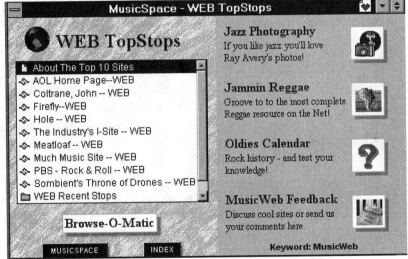

SOLUTION: WeaK RaP in Cincinnati

Earlier in this chapter, while we were discussing Murder Mysteries Online, Inspector Forsooth proposed a mystery (see page 378). Did you solve it? Here's the Inspector's solution:

"Although Gable flew in to the Cincinnati airport, that airport is actually the Greater Cincinnati/Northern Kentucky International airport, and is located in the state of Kentucky. That's why the state police paid no attention to him—he was a wanted man in Ohio, not Kentucky. (Covington, the other locale mentioned in the text, is quite close to Cincinnati but is just across the Kentucky border.)

"The time was May 1995, and Scott Gable was on his way to Churchill Downs, in Louisville, Kentucky, for the annual running of the Kentucky Derby. Obviously the trip worked out well for him. He bet on Thunder Gulch, who proceeded to win the Derby and give Mr. Gable a handsome return. (You did notice that 'Mr. Gable' is an anagram of 'gambler,' didn't you?)"

Warner/Reprise Online

I saved this one 'til last because it always invokes the image of Porky Pig's head emerging from the old Warner Brothers logo, saying "Th-Th-Th-That's all, folks!" Thus, it seems to fit at the end of our entertainment media section well.

As you would expect, Warner/Reprise online exists to keep fans informed about artists on the Warner/Reprise family of labels, which includes Warner Bros., Reprise, Sire, American Recordings, Giant, Slash, 4AD, Qwest, Luaka Bop, Kinetic Records, the Medicine Label, and Maverick (see Figure 11-37). You'll find music industry news here too, and a kaleidoscope of multimedia files, including an extensive library of videos.

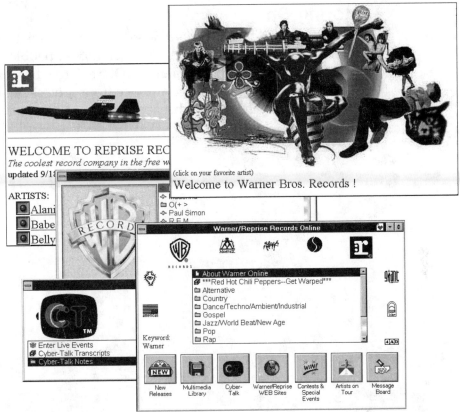

I find Warner's CYBER-TALK, however, to be the area's spectacle among spectacles. CYBER-TALK is an interactive talk show, occurring every Monday evening at 9:30 (Eastern time). The list of guests is impressive: k.d. Lang, Vince Neil, Christine McVie, Fleetwood Mac, Carlene Carter, Chris Isaak, Elvis Costello, Peter, Paul, and Mary, Bob and Hillary James, Joni Mitchell, Van Halen, Jeff Foxworthy—these are just a few of the artists who appeared in the fall of 1995. Check the CYBER-TALK area at keyword: **Warner** for the current schedule. See you Monday nights!

And that—as Porky used to say—is all, folks!

Moving On

From the trivial to the profound—we now make the transition to the world of the Personal Finance Channel. Lots of people subscribe to AOL for financial purposes alone. AOL rewards them with relevant (and current) information, and advice from professionals and fellow investors alike. Grab your checkbook and turn the page.

Personal Finance

Have you ever seen those little radios that pick up weather reports? I use one every day. It's tuned to the local National Oceanic and Atmospheric Administration (NOAA) station, which broadcasts nothing but the weather, 24 hours a day. These gadgets are the ideal information machine: always current, always available, and nearly free. Now if I could only find a similar source for financial information.

Aha! What about AOL? If ever there was a "machine" for instant financial news, America Online is it. Unlike television or radio, AOL's market information is available whenever you want it: there's no waiting for the 6 o'clock news or suffering through three stories (and four commercials) that you don't want to hear. Unlike newspapers, AOL's financial news is always current. It's not this morning's news; it's this *minute's* news. It's current, it's always available, and it's almost free.

I wonder if Ted Turner knows about this?

Your Personal Stock Portfolio

Let's begin this chapter with a financial exercise. This one is risk-free but nonetheless quite real. A portfolio of investments is a fascinating thing to follow and nourish, even if it's only make-believe. And if you want to add some real punch to it, AOL offers a brokerage service. You can invest real money in real issues and realize real gains (or real losses).

Whether you intend to invest real cash or just funny money, join me as we create a personal portfolio of stocks and securities.

Quotes & Portfolio

Begin the journey by clicking the Personal Finance button on the Channels Menu, or by typing Ctrl+K and entering the keyword: **Finance**. America Online responds by transporting you to the Personal Finance department (see Figure 12-1).

Figure 12-1: America Online might be the perfect financial information machine: it's always current and it's available 24 hours a day.

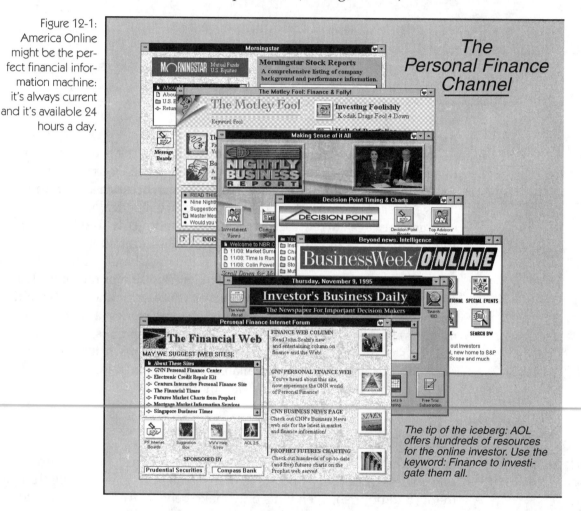

A wealth (pun intended) of financial information awaits you here, as does opportunity. You not only can seek counsel on your investments, you also can actually buy them here—and maintain a portfolio as well. And the portfolio, for the moment, is our focus. Click the icon labeled Quotes & Portfolios, and let's invest our surplus cash (see Figure 12-2).

Figure 12-2:
The Quotes &
Portfolios window
allows you to
access market
news, look up an
issue, build a
portfolio, and
actually buy and
sell issues. It's
available from the
main window of
the Personal
Finance window,
through the jagged-
arrow button on
the toolbar or the
keyword: **Quotes**.

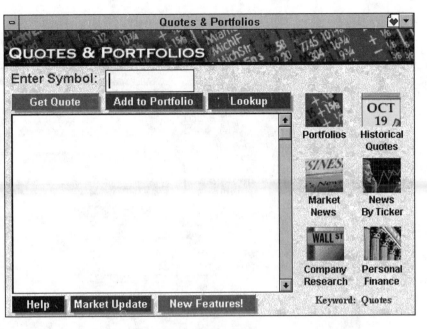

The Quotes & Portfolio section of the Personal Finance Channel is a comprehensive financial information service equaled by few others in the telecommunications industry, and available on AOL without surcharge. The only thing you pay when you're visiting here is your normal connect-time charges. America Online is connected to the financial centers of the world via high-speed data lines, providing financial information that is updated continuously during market hours—usually about 15 minutes behind the action.

Finding a Stock Symbol

America Online is waiting for us to enter a stock symbol. Stock symbols are those abbreviations you see traveling across the Big Board in a stockbroker's office. What shall we buy? Because it's something that we all have in common, let's look up AOL. America Online is a publicly traded issue, after all, so we should offer a reference to it here.

But what's AOL's symbol? Hmmm . . . Let's try the Lookup button in the Quotes and Portfolios window, shown in Figure 12-2. When you click that icon and follow the path pictured in Figure 12-3, you discover that AMER is the symbol for America Online.

Finding a Stock Quote

Click the symbol above
in the Personal Finance
main window.

Then, in the Quotes and
Portfolios window, click
the Lookup button.

Enter the first few letters
of the company name. →

AOL finds the issue and
its symbol...

...which you can double-
click for a current
update.

QUOTES & PORTFOLIOS

Enter Symbol:

Get Quote   Add to Portfolio   Lookup

OCT
19

Portfolios   Historical
Quotes

Market   News
News   By Ticker

Search Symbols

Enter the first few characters of the
company name or symbol you want to scan
for: america

Search By Company   Search

Help   Market Update

Symbol

AMFD   AMERICA NATIONAL FOO
AMER   AMERICA ONLINE INC
ASGR   AMERICA SERVICE GROU
ATCO   AMERICA TECHNOLOGY
AWA   AMERICA WEST AIRLINE
AWAWS   AMERICA WEST AIRLINE
AADBX   AMERICAN AADVANTAGE
AADEX   AMERICAN AADVANTAGE
AAGAX   AMERICAN AADVANTAGE

Get Quote

Quote Detail

Symbol: AMER

AMER - AMERICA ONLINE INC
Last Price: 58 3/8 at 10:55
Change: Up 3/4 (+1.30%)
High: 60 at 9:35
Low: 58 1/8 at 10:49
Open: 59 at 9:30
Previous Close: 57 5/8 on 5/9
Volume: 2,375,800
Shares Outstanding: 82,280,000
52-Week High: 68 1/8
52-Week Low: 16 3/4
Yield: 0.00%
P/E Ratio: 5,837.5

Prices delayed at least 15 minutes.

Add to Portfolio

Once you have the symbol, enter it into the box as shown in Figure
12-3 and click on the Get Quote button (or simply double-click the
symbol's line). The results are pictured in Figure 12-3's scroll box.

Building the Portfolio

Note the current price, then click the Add to Portfolio button. America
Online responds with the dialog box shown in Figure 12-4.

Figure 12-4:
Enter the current
price and the
number of shares
you want, then
click OK. The "in-
vestment" will be
added to your
portfolio.

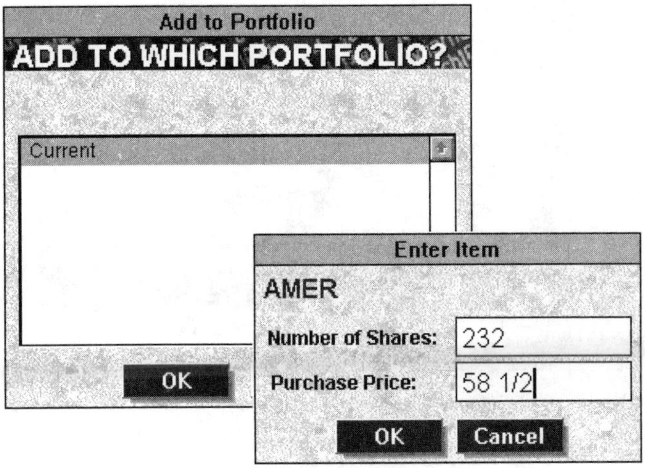

Add to Portfolio

ADD TO WHICH PORTFOLIO?

Current

OK

Enter Item

AMER

Number of Shares: 232

Purchase Price: 58 1/2

OK   Cancel

Figure 12-4:
Enter the current price and the number of shares you want, then click OK. The "investment" will be added to your portfolio.

Note that you can have more than one portfolio—up to 20, in fact, with as many as 100 issues in each one. You might have to create a portfolio before you can add your "investment" to it; but eventually you'll encounter the windows in Figure 12-4.

Because this is only make-believe, buy as many shares as you like. Don't worry: AOL doesn't share your portfolio with anyone, and you won't be charged any special fees for this exercise; it's a private matter between you and your computer.

To view your portfolio, click the Portfolios button in the Quotes & Portfolios window shown at the top of Figure 12-3, or use the keyword: **Portfolio**. AOL will provide the Portfolio Summary window in Figure 12-5: double-click the portfolio you want to view.

Figure 12-5:
Your portfolio is
always available at
keyword: **Portfolio.**
To make it even
easier to access,
add it to your list of
Favorite Places.
(Favorite Places are
discussed in
Chapter 4.)

Viewing Your Portfolio

Use the keyword: Portfolio, then
double-click the name of the portfolio you want to view.

Portfolio Summary

Current

Create Portfolio
Delete Portfolio
Rename Portfolio
Display Portfolio
Add Item

Keyword: Portfolios

Portfolio Detail: Current

QUOTES & PORTFOLIOS

Current Value: $13,630.00

Symbol	Shares	Last/NAV	Change	%Growth	Gain/Loss	Value
AMER	232.00	58 3/4	+1 1/8	+38.24%	+3,770.00	13,630.00

Note the variety
of porfolio man-
ipulation tools
available
here...

...and the issue
manipulation
tools available
here.

| Help | Details | Add | Edit | Remove | Print | Refresh | Click here for multiple portfolios! |

Printing & Saving Your Portfolio

The Print button at the bottom of Figure 12-5 prints the data displayed in the Quotes & Portfolios window, as you would expect.

Few people are aware, however, that by clicking the Print button, you can also *save* your portfolio, for advanced analysis by spreadsheet and database programs.

The File > Save command is disabled when the primary Quotes & Portfolios window is displayed, but when you click its Print button, the contents of the window are reformatted (in Courier, for printing) and the Save command is enabled. Your portfolio data will be saved as a text file which many programs—word processing and spreadsheet in particular—can interpret. Microsoft's Excel spreadsheet can even resolve the mixed fractions and decimals in the Last/NAV column.

This is a godsend for those of us who used the portfolio-saving command that was available in earlier versions of the software.

Company Research

You can conduct a significant amount of company research on any one particular issue right from the Quotes & Portfolios window: just select the issue you want to know more about, then click the Details button. AOL will respond with the Stock Quote window illustrated in Figure 12-6.

Figure 12-6:
You can obtain extensive current and historical information about any issue in your portfolio by clicking the Details button.

Getting the Details

Portfolio Detail: Current

QUOTES & PORTFOLIOS

Current Value: $13,630.00

Symbol	Shares	Last/NAV	Change	%Growth	Gain/Loss	Value
AMER	232.00	58 3/4	+1 1/8	+38.24%	+3,770.00	13,630.00

1. Select the issue for which you want details.

Help Details Add Edit Remove Print Refr

2. Click the Details button above to see the window at right.

Stock Quote - AMER - AMERICA ONLINE INC DEL

AMER

AMER - AMERICA ONLINE INC DEL	
Last Price:	58 7/8 at 12:37
Change:	Up 1 1/4 (+2.17%)
High:	59 1/2 at 9:35
Low:	58 1/8 at 10:49
Open:	59 at 9:30
Previous Close:	57 5/8 on 5/9
Volume:	3,081,800
Shares Outstanding:	82,280,000
52-Week High:	71
52-Week Low:	16 3/4
Yield:	0.00%

Market News Historical News By Ticker

Two buttons at the bottom of the Stock Quote window shown in Figure 12-6 deserve special mention. Refer to Figure 12-7 as you read on.

🔺 The News by Ticker button leads to a variety of financial news stories regarding that particular issue. The stories that appear are drawn from Reuters, Knight-Ridder, and the PR Newswire over the past couple of weeks. Read them all and there won't have many unanswered questions about your investment.

🔺 The Graph button calls upon AOL's built-in graphing routines to graph the high-low-open-close performance of your investment over time. Be sure to investigate the mini-toolbar in the Graph window: just leave the mouse pointer over any one of them for a moment to see a pop-up tool tip.

The amount of company research that's available directly from the Quotes & Portfolios window is impressive. If you take investing seriously, be sure to investigate what's available—and that includes the Help buttons!

The PC Financial Network

Though you can pretend all you want, eventually you're going to want to make some real investments, and that's what the PC Financial Network is for. To get there, use the keyword: **PCFN**. There's a considerable—but free—art download if you've never been here before, and it's worth the wait: this is one of the most handsome areas on the service (see Figure 12-7).

Figure 12-7: The PC Financial Network. It's here that you can buy and sell investments online.

PC Financial Network (PCFN) is a service of the Pershing Division of Donaldson, Lufkin & Jenrette Securities Corporation, an independent operating subsidiary of the Equitable Life Assurance Society of the United States. Pershing has been a leading provider of brokerage services for more than 50 years and currently handles about 10 percent of the daily volume of the New York Stock Exchange and 8 percent of all listed options trades. With total capital of more than $1 billion and total assets of about $40 billion, Pershing is America's largest online discount brokerage service.

Online investing offers a number of advantages over broker-assisted transactions, and opening an account takes only a few minutes.

- You can buy or sell 24 hours a day via AOL.

- You receive fast, accurate executions. Orders are sent directly to PCFN's computer and then to the markets—all electronically.

- Commissions are significantly lower than you'll find elsewhere. In most cases, the PCFN commissions are even lower than "discount" brokerages. To verify that claim (and set your mind at ease), PCFN offers a "commission calculator," which allows you to see what the commission will be for any particular investment, and then compare that cost to those of other brokerages.

- You can call PCFN day or night to place a trade or ask a question.

- You receive 100 real-time quotes per trade. You also receive 100 real-time quotes when you open an account.

- More than 500 mutual funds are available for trade online.

- You pay no extra monthly or usage fees—only your regular AOL connect-time charges, plus PCFN's low discount commissions.

Trading online is easy and can be fun. To see for yourself, try PCFN's free online demo account. You can "buy and sell" without spending a dime. Furthermore, PCFN's "MegaHelp" is available on every screen: all you have to do is click your mouse. If the thought of online trading has ever appealed to you, this is the most comprehensive and convenient way to give it a try.

Company Research

Let's see: we talked about managing your portfolio, then we talked about making the investment. Seems a bit out of order, I suppose. Oh well: as long as I'm presenting things from the end to the beginning, let's talk next about the Personal Finance Channel's Company Research area (keywords: **Company Research**, and see Figure 12-8).

Figure 12-8:
The Company
Research area is a
harbinger of future
online investing.

Easter Egg

"Easter eggs" are tiny secrets hidden within computer programs where they remain hidden for only a few to discover. AOL doesn't have many, but there are a few, and the Company Research screen pictured in Figure 12-8 contains one of them.

Move the tip of your arrow cursor until it points to the top of the triangle inside of the "A" in the "Wall St" sign on the main Company Research screen, then click the mouse button. If it doesn't work the first time, move the mouse a bit and click again—the "hot spot" is small. I won't tell you what happens when you hit it, but you'll know when it does.

Research: it's not a provocative title for a subject, I know, but in fact, this is where the delight is to be found in the Personal Finance Channel. There's no pressure here—no sweaty brow—not if you don't want it. And AOL dedicates an arcade of multimedia catalysts to the purpose. There's no reason why financial research shouldn't be enjoyable as well as informative, and a well-informed investor is more likely to be a successful investor. Successful investors are what Company Research is all about.

The Motley Fool Online

Take financial advice, for example. The image of a stern patriarch comes to mind, humorless and intransigent. But these are the 90s: today's investor was reared on a diet of situation comedies and rock & roll. Musty tweed is as well suited (forgive the pun) to the task as a one-pronged pitchfork. An alternative is requisite, and that alternative is the Motley Fool (keyword: **Fool**).

Perhaps the best way to introduce the Motley Fool is to let the Fools themselves (brothers David and Thomas Gardner) do the talking:

"Once upon a time there was the *Motley Fool*. It was a print publication founded in July of 1993 whose subscription cost $48 a year. The *Motley Fool* had three aims: to inform, to amuse, and to make the reader good money at the same time. It was a literary-cum-investment rag with its own real-money portfolio designed so that any reader could learn from and duplicate it. It was highly Foolish, and there was nothing else quite like it.

"Then one day, the Editors discovered America Online. They started a message board, called 'The Motley Fool.' They answered any question that came their way about anything, and slowly developed a faithful Foolish following. In fact, the Editors soon found themselves spending more time answering questions and talking stocks online than they did in putting their publication together!

"This was perplexing and deeply troubling, and something had to be done about it.

"Just as the Editors prepared to check themselves into a Decyberspacification Center, a nice person who was NOT wearing a white coat came along and offered to start up a new area online, called The Motley Fool Online. The Editors, who were just a couple of kids with the corny old dream of one day making it out of their dusty old town, agreed. Recognizing instantly that their print publication would be rendered obsolete by the advantages of real-time cyberspace, they shut up shop, and sent out tardy refund checks to all of their subscribers.

"The Editors had gotten to know cyberspace quite well by this time, having both racked up budget-busting online bills AND written extensively on the subject. They believed they had come to understand the strengths and weaknesses of the medium, how it could be used well, and how others might abuse it. . . ."

Figure 12-9:
Come to the
Motley Fool for
a provocative
personal investing
perspective.

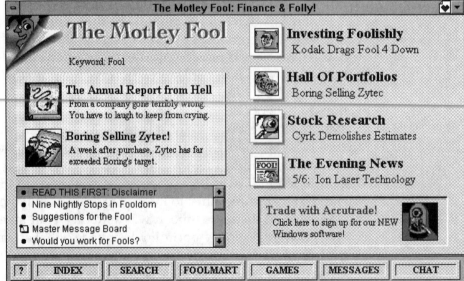

The Motley Fool is one of AOL's true success stories, and you should wonder why. In addition to their astute observations and advice on the state of the market, the Fools offer the following:

- *An area for learning.* More and more people today are seeking to understand investing, to do it themselves and in so doing gain a new measure of control over their finances. For no more than the cost of connect charges, the Fool's School offers fun, Foolish, and informative articles on many different aspects of investing. It gets novices up and running, investing for themselves in no time. And for those who want to test their new knowledge, there's always the Monthly Novice Quiz.

- *A fully managed, real-money online portfolio.* The Fool Portfolio is a real-money portfolio, not pie-in-the-sky or make-believe. In the Fool Portfolio, all related costs—including commissions and spreads—are accounted for. There's no hype and nothing ambiguous. If you prefer to learn by watching, here's your classroom.

- *Message boards.* The Motley Fool offers a dynamic exchange on hundreds of message boards; it's dedicated to broader investment approaches in general and scads of individual stocks in particular. The Fools claim that these boards are the best organized and most informative anywhere in cyberspace, and they're probably right.

- *Foolish games.* Fools love games, and the Motley Fool Online offers a few Foolish Games that challenge your mind and offer free online time to the winners. Check out Today's Pitch and Port Folly, via their buttons on the Fool Games screen.

Every online investor should visit the Motley Fool Online regularly. Learning is best accomplished in a supportive, peer-intensive, and *entertaining* environment, and that's exactly what the Fool has to offer.

Morningstar Mutual Funds

I began investing a couple of years ago. I located a broker—Dave is his name—with whom I found mutual trust, and in whom I found a kindred soul. Trading through him has never been stressful.

As I would expect, Dave is extremely knowledgeable about the market—especially mutual funds and bonds, which is where I've done most of my investing. I asked him one day where he got his information. "Morningstar," he said, adding obliquely, "It's an interdictory association." That evening I looked up the meaning of the word "interdictory" and felt that I was right privileged to walk among the ranks of the plutocracy.

Then I browsed around AOL and found Morningstar online, complete with User's Guide and Guided Tour (see Figure 12-10). The plutocracy had come to the proletariat, and the plutocrats didn't even know. Now I read Morningstar just as Dave does. I'm sure I'm a better investor (and a better client) because I do.

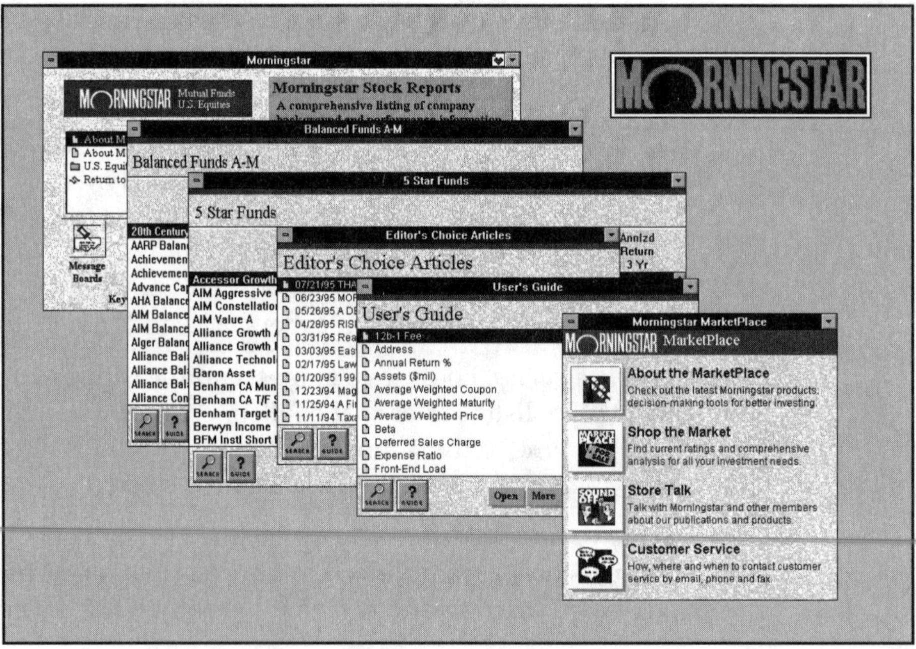

Figure 12-10:
Morningstar offers data, publications, and software for analyzing more than 6,000 mutual funds, closed-end funds, variable annuities, variable life, variable universal life, Japanese equities, and American Depository Receipts. Use the keyword: **Morningstar**.

Hoover's Business Resources

Morningstar isn't the only investor's reference available on AOL. If your investing interests exceed the scope of mutual funds and bonds, investigate Hoover's Business Resources (keyword: **Hoovers**). Hoover's collection of searchable databases includes profiles of more than 1,100 of the largest, most influential, and fastest-growing public and private companies in the world. In addition, there are monthly updates on these and 6,200 other major companies. They've even got business rankings from a number of perspectives and industry profiles. The voice is lively and interesting; the data are pertinent to every investor; and the price—free of surcharges to AOL members—is as affordable as old clothes used to be.

The Decision Point Forum

Now we're getting serious. The Decision Point Forum provides a platform and materials to help you learn, refine, and profitably use technical analysis skills and market timing information. You're encouraged to assimilate information and opinions, then arrive at your own conclusions. There are no magic systems here, only aids that help you make your own decisions. And there are plenty of them:

- *The buy/sell signals* generated by the forum's timing models are summarized in the Decision Point Alert, updated every Saturday morning.

- Each market day the forum posts *chart tables* of the 150 stocks and 160 mutual funds being followed. Featured are four proprietary timing models that can help you identify stocks that might be starting a new trend. The forum also offers two-year charts for the stocks and funds in this portfolio.

- There are *message boards*, where you can post questions and exchange ideas with other members about the technical condition of the market and the stocks you own or follow.

- There is a vast collection of *chart libraries* (see Figure 12-11) with files of stock, mutual fund, and market indicator charts. These libraries are updated each week.

Figure 12-11:
The Decision Point
Forum is the home
of America
Online's stock
market charts.
There are hundreds
of them here, and
they're all available
for downloading
and viewing with
your America
Online software.

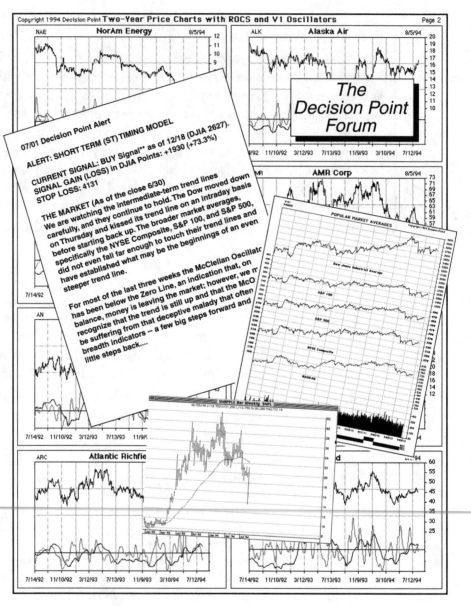

Free of Extra Charges

Most commercial online services offer news and finance features similar to those found on AOL. None offers them all, however, and none offers them at the price AOL charges: nothing beyond the normal connect-time charges. This is unique to AOL. In this industry the word "premium" usually translates to "extra charge." Aside from sending the occasional fax or piece of mail via the U.S. Postal Service (which is discussed in Chapter 3, "Electronic Mail & the Personal Filing Cabinet"), you rarely will find an extra charge for any of the services AOL offers. With all the money you save, perhaps you can invest in the stock market or buy a small business. If you do, AOL stands ready to help—at no extra charge, of course.

- A collection of *historical data files* of market indicators and indexes is available for download in the database libraries, allowing you to construct your own charts. These data, too, are updated weekly.

- A collection of *essays and articles* covering various subjects is available in the reading libraries under Instructions & Definitions. Of particular importance is the "Timing Model Documentation"—a thorough explanation of how to use the timing models found elsewhere in the forum.

- The *Top Advisors' Corner* features comments by prominent stock market advisors.

- The *Investor's Resource Center* lists sources of investing information, products, and services.

If you're a serious investor—or if you've considering investments in the stock or mutual funds markets, the Decision Point Forum should be a frequent stop in your AOL journey.

Worth magazine

No serious investor should conclude an AOL journey without exploring the articles of Worth Online, the electronic version of *Worth* magazine, the magazine of financial intelligence. Here you can download current and past articles written by such Wall Street experts as Peter Lynch, Graef Crystal, Gretchen Morgenson, Bob Clark, Jim Jubak, and John Rothchild. It's available in the main Personal Finance window, or by using the keyword: **Worth**.

Chart-O-Matic

The financial market is a moving target. Trying to take aim at it by observing a static chart is like trying to shoot skeet with a cannon: impressive to behold, but hardly nimble enough for the job.

That's why AOL's Chart-O-Matic provides "live" charts for your observation of stock-market activity. Choose Live Charts from the list box pictured in Figure 12-8, then pick the issue or the index you want to track. When the chart appears, leave it on your screen: it'll be automatically updated every few minutes (see Figure 12-12).

Figure 12-12: AOL's Chart-O-Matic live charting feature provides an animated look at stock market activity as it happens, all day long.

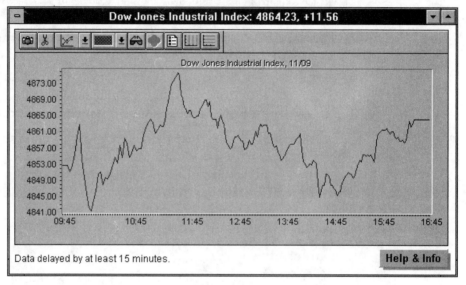

There are a number of controls on the live chart screen—a sort of mini-toolbar—that might at first seem baffling. Don't let them intimidate you. There's a Help & Info button in the lower right corner that leads to plenty of assistance. And each of the buttons on the mini-toolbar offers an explanatory info balloon when you click it with your right mouse button.

Your Business

Is "entrepreneurial community" an oxymoron? Your Business (keywords: **Your Business**) doesn't think so. In fact, Your Business exists specifically to promote the entrepreneurial community—an independent and often remote anarchy of unconventionalists in search of community whether they're aware of it or not (see Figure 12-13).

Figure 12-13: Your Business brings community to a broad range of individuals involved in independent business ventures.

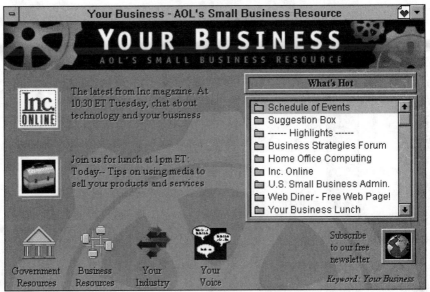

Your Business's service and content are significant (more about that later), but what makes it all work is the diversity of business experience that AOL's members bring to the forum. Your Business welcomes all forms of entrepreneurs: dreamers, consultants, small business owners, and those who work at home. Whether your plans are small or large, a peer group is not only beneficial, it's almost mandatory, and Your Business is where your community makes its home.

The Business Strategies Forum Message Boards

Perhaps nowhere is the spirit of community more active than on the Business Strategies Forum message boards (at keyword: **Strategies**). People all over the country find others working in the same field here, and their discussions enlighten casual readers as effectively as the participants themselves (see Figure 12-14).

Figure 12-14:
The Business
Strategies Forum
message boards
offer peer-to-peer
comments and
suggestions.

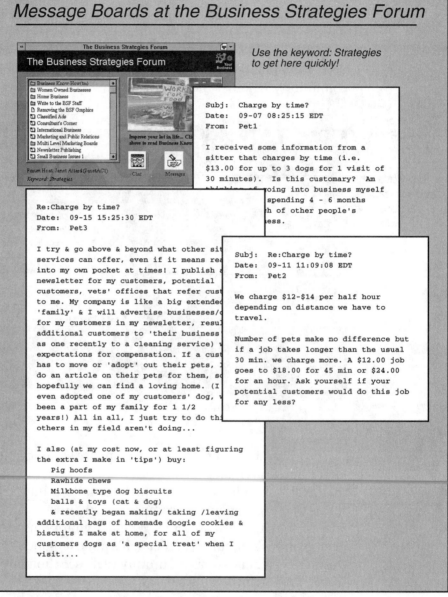

Inc. Online

YB's bedrock, perhaps, is Inc. Online (keyword: **Inc**). *Inc.* magazine has been serving entrepreneurs for years with timely information, relevant and vital to entrepreneurs nationwide. It stands to reason, then, that *Inc.*

should have an online presence offering research potential, analysis, entrepreneurial resources, comment, and guests. Inc. Online offers all of that and more; Figure 12-15 offers a snapshot of what it's all about.

Figure 12-15:
Inc. Online offers
a fountain of
entrepreneurial
resources at
keyword: **Inc**.

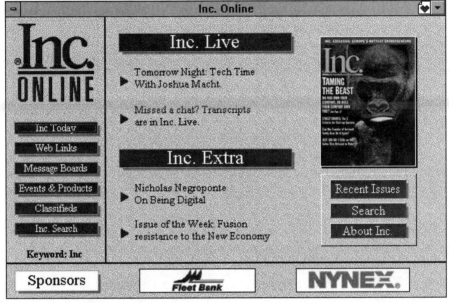

If you're an entrepreneur—or thinking of becoming one—be sure to visit Your Business regularly. This is a field where even minor advantages pay off—directly—and Your Business is an advantage indeed.

Moving On

It's a disservice to the Personal Finance Channel to end this chapter here. There's much more than I've described, and I don't want you to misinterpret my emphasis. I've tried to present the diversity of features offered, not a listing of its best stuff.

Too much time in the Personal Finance Channel, however, can lead to monetary overload. There are plenty of nonmonetary features available on AOL, and we should spend some time examining those. Turn the page and we'll do just that.

Learning

CHAPTER 13

- The Online Campus
- The Nature Conservancy Online
- The Library of Congress Online
- Smithsonian Online
- Scientific American Online
- Saturday Review Online
- The Odyssey Project
- Princeton Review
- The Career Center
- The Academic Assistance Center
- College Board Online
- Education for the Teacher
- The Broadcast Media

My dictionary defines the word *inquisitive* as "inclined to investigate; eager for knowledge." While the online medium's chat, e-mail, and files for downloading receive the lion's share of media attention, and while they might be the enticements that lured many of us here in the first place, we soon discover that the true value of the medium is personal enrichment via the pursuit of knowledge. Nothing can compare to the online medium's seemingly limitless variety, hair-trigger immediacy, and extensive multimedia capabilities. If you're "eager for knowledge," the Learning & Culture Channel is your citadel (see Figure 13-1). Use the keyword: **Learning**, or click on the channel's button on the Main Menu.

Figure 13-1: Alvin Toffler, author of *Future Shock*, once said that ". . . knowledge is the most democratic source of power," referring, perhaps, to its accessibility. The Learning & Culture Channel brings directly to your PC an infinite resource that can increase your knowledge and, thus, your power. Use the keyword: **Learning** to investigate.

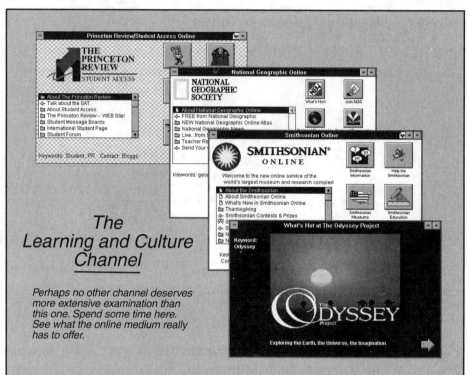

The Online Campus

I used the word "enrichment" earlier. It's a great word. There's a wholesome ring to it. Bread is enriched with vitamins; nitrogen enriches soil; learning enriches us all.

The online campus (keyword: **Campus**) offers a "community enrichment" curriculum, including academic, professional, and special-interest courses. Scores of courses are offered every term—all you have to do is sign up, pay your tuition, and attend.

Accreditation

The Online Campus isn't limited to learning exclusively for the purpose of personal enrichment, no matter how honorable an intention that may be. By the time you read this, courses will be available for college credit as well, from no less honorable an institution than the University of California, one of the nation's most prestigious communications research centers. Details aren't available as I write this—negotiations are still under way—but you can obtain them all at the keyword: **UCX**.

An example of Online Campus offerings is in order. "Writing the Novel" is an eight-week course covering what you need to know to write a good, publishable novel. A twenty-chapter textbook prepared by the instructor is included (exclusively available to students of this course), as well as access to live question-and-answer conferences, scores of files (including proposals, timelines, character biographies, and recommended books and agents), and a private message board. And for those who wish to pursue their literary potential even further, an eight-week follow-up course is available.

The class meets (virtually, but in real time) once a week for an hour, and is taught by Lary Crews, author of three published mystery novels, 405 published magazine articles, twenty published poems, two recorded songs, one published short story, two produced plays, and twenty-five radio news documentaries—including one that won an Associated Press award in 1976. He is a four-time winner in the Writer's Digest National Writing Competition and is currently writing a new book, a suspense novel. See Figure 13-2.

Figure 13-2: Lary Crews shares his novel-writing experience weekly at the Online Campus.

"Writing the Novel" is but one of many courses offered every term at the Online Campus. Classes are available in the arts, business & professional studies, English & writing, hobbies, the humanities, languages, mathematics, religion and spirituality, and science and nature. The Online Campus also offers the Afterwards Cafe, a hot spot for lively discussions of the arts; the Bull Moose Tavern, where the conversation spins around social and political issues; the Lab, a hang-out devoted to discussions of the realms of science and nature; the International Cafe, where you can brush up on your language skills;

the Reading Room, where you can join fellow book lovers in discussions of authors, publishers, and favorite works; the Scholars' Hall, where lecture series and graduation ceremonies find a home; and the Teachers' Lounge, where you can hobnob with your instructors after class. Few places offer as much potential for fostering the online community, a community not only of colleagues and companions, but one of knowledge as well.

The Nature Conservancy Online

The Nature Conservancy purchased its first parcel of ecologically significant land—60 acres in New York state—in 1951. Since then, acreage under the Conservancy's protection in the United States has increased to 7.9 million, with another 42 million acres in foreign countries. Nearly three-quarters of a million people contribute to the Conservancy's stewardship, and now they have a common resource at the Nature Conservancy Online (use the keyword: **Nature**, and see Figure 13-3).

Figure 13-3: The Nature Conservancy uses a science-based, nonconfrontational approach to conservation of the earth's biodiversity.

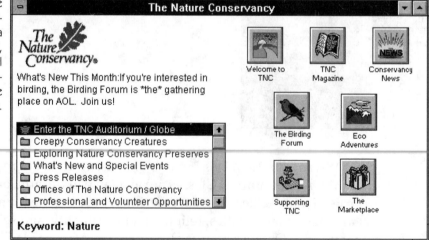

The Library of Congress Online

The Online Russian Archives are a temporary "exhibit" in the Learning & Culture Channel, not unlike the exhibit on which they are based in the Library of Congress (keyword: **Library**). In the museum business, temporary (or traveling) exhibits don't stay in any one museum permanently; after an appropriate length of time, they move on to other museums where others will have a chance to see them. Indeed, the Library of Congress returned the Russian Archives exhibit to Moscow in July 1992.

I include the Online Russian Archives as an example of the topical material endemic to this channel, and to impress you with the quality and opulence of its "traveling" exhibits. The appearance of the Russian Archives on America Online represents the world's first online version of a major national exhibit.

The Online Russian Archives (more properly, *The Secret Soviet Archives*) is a collection of documents culled from several declassified secret files of the former Soviet Union. The full exhibit of some 300 Soviet documents, photographs, and films—which were on display in the Library of Congress in the spring of 1992—was the first such exhibition in the West. It shed new light on some of the major events of the 20th century, from the Russian Revolution to recent times. Included in the exhibit are materials relating to such topics as Stalin's reign of terror, the Gulag system, censorship, the workings of the secret police, substandard construction practices at the Chernobyl nuclear plant, and the 1962 Cuban Missile Crisis.

The online exhibit consists of excerpts from 25 of the 250 documents in the museum exhibit. Scans of the original documents are posted in .GIF format (.GIF is a graphics format, discussed in Chapter 5, "Transferring Files").

Each scanned original is accompanied by an English translation (which you can read online or save to your hard drive for further study) and a piece providing the appropriate historical background. Reading these documents is an experience you'll never forget—a John Le Carré novel come to life, illuminated by the Russian originals, downloaded and displayed on your screen, in heirloom color and Cyrillic mystery (see Figure 13-4).

The Russian Archives have been placed on exhibit on America Online "indefinitely." They make up a unique and most rewarding area on the service. Don't pass this one by!

Figure 13-4: The Chernobyl report exceeded 1,000 words and filled nearly six pages. The page shown here, which documents early construction flaws, was written in early 1979. The plant exploded at 1:21 a.m. on April 26, 1986—a little more than seven years later.

Revelations from the Russian Archives

CHERNOBYL
Central Committee of the CPSU
USSR COMMITTEE OF STATE SECURITY [KGB]
February 21, 1979   No. 346
Moscow

Construction Flaws at the Chernobyl Nuclear Power Plant [AES]

According to data in the possession of the KGB of the USSR, design deviations and violations of construction and assembly technology are occurring at various places in the construction of the second generating unit of the Chernobyl AES, and these could lead to mishaps and accidents.

The structural pillars of the generator room were erected with a deviation of up to 100 mm from the reference axes, and horizontal connections between the pillars are absent in places. Wall panels have been installed with a deviation of up to 150 mm from the axes. The placement of roof plates does not conform to the designer's specifications. Crane tracks and stopways have vertical drops of up to 100 mm and in places a slope of up to 8.

Deputy head of the Construction Directorate, Comrade V. T. Gora, gave instructions for backfilling the foundation in many places where vertical waterproofing was damaged. Similar violations were permitted in other sections with the knowledge of Comrade V. T. Gora and the head of the construction group, Comrade IU. L. Matveev. Damage to the waterproofing can lead to ground water seepage into the station and radioactive contamination of the environment.

The leadership of the Directorate is not devoting proper attention to the foundation, on which the quality of the construction largely depends. The cement plant operates erratically, and its output is of poor quality.Interruptions were permitted during the pouring of especially heavy concrete causing gaps and layering in the foundation. Access roads to the Chernobyl AES are in urgent need of repair.

Construction of the third high-voltage transmission line is behind schedule, which could limit the capacity utilization of the second unit.
As a result of inadequate monitoring of the condition of safety equipment, in the first three quarters of 1978, 170 individuals suffered work-related injuries, with the loss of work time totalling 3,366 worker-days.

The KGB of Ukraine has informed the CPSU Central Committee of these violations. This is for your information.

Chairman of the Committee [KGB]
[signed] IU. Andropov..Secret

As I write this, the Library of Congress features five additional online exhibits, including the Treasures of the Vatican, the Columbus Quincentenary, the Scrolls from the Dead Sea, the Comic Strip Centennial, and the African-American Mosaic. The Mosaic exhibit marks the publication of *The African-American Mosaic: A Library of Congress Resource Guide for the Study of Black History and Culture*. A noteworthy and singular publication, the Mosaic is the first Librarywide resource guide to the institution's African-American collections. The Library of Congress Online is not only fascinating and educational, it's a capital example of the benefits online access has to offer.

Smithsonian Online

The Smithsonian Institution in Washington, DC, is probably America's most popular museum. Occupying a significant percentage of the District of Columbia, the Smithsonian is really a collection of 17 museums and galleries, including a zoo. You'll find Smithsonian Online in the main Learning & Culture menu, or simply use the keyword: **Smithsonian** (see Figure 13-5).

Figure 13-5: Smithsonian Online offers round-the-clock electronic access to one of America's most comprehensive resources.

In addition to descriptions, articles, and photos from many of its museums, Smithsonian Online also provides a comprehensive guide for anyone intending to visit the institution—just click the Smithsonian Information button. Making a visit to the Smithsonian is not a casual event; planning is not only recommended, it's essential. And you can do all your pretrip planning using America Online. (See Figure 13-6.)

Figure 13-6: Final flight: the SR-71 Blackbird spy plane touches down on the runway at Dulles International Airport near Washington, DC, having just set a new cross-country speed record on its way to its permanent home at the Smithsonian Institution. The photo is available online and appears here courtesy of the Smithsonian.

The thousands of Smithsonian Photos images are scrupulously indexed; the Smithsonian Education area offers ideas, outlines, and publications for teachers; and the Education Resource Guide catalogs educational materials available from the Smithsonian and several affiliated organizations. This is one of the richest environments available on the service, and it warrants your exploration.

Constant Change

Perhaps you've noticed: telecommunications is not a conservative, tranquil industry. Its waters are about as placid as an Atlantic storm. For this reason, America Online is constantly in a state of change.

Case in point: as I write this, Smithsonian Online has just announced its plans to establish a distinguished-speaker series, including interviews and classes. I can't provide the details yet because they're not available, but don't let omissions like this annoy you. Seek them out and rejoice in their significance: AOL is always improving, and we—AOL's members—are the reason. To stay abreast of the changes, use the keyword: **New**.

Scientific American Online

Quickly now: name every mass communications medium you can think of that's 150 years old. Remember, there was no radio or television 150 years ago, no telephones or C-SPAN, and certainly no Internet or AOL. Newspapers and magazines were *it*, and only one magazine from 150 years ago still survives: *Scientific American* (see Figure 13-7).

Figure 13-7: Scientific American Online offers the current issue of the magazine online (before it goes on sale at newsstands) and a searchable database of back issues.

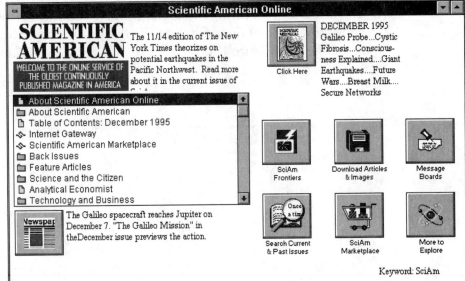

Scientific American Online offers the latest from the current issue of *Scientific American* magazine—before it hits the newsstands—and more than a year's worth of back issues; access to the magazine's journalists and fellow readers via the message board; an archive of articles, selected images, and even video clips; the bulletin contents of *Scientific American Medicine* and *Scientific American Surgery*; and abstracts of all *Scientific American* articles published from May 1948 through December 1994. That's quite a résumé of features, and it's all available at keyword: **SciAm**.

Saturday Review Online

Archibald MacLeish, George Bernard Shaw, W. Somerset Maugham, Oscar Wilde—they all appeared in *Saturday Review* during its 50-year run. A premiere journal of culture, literature, and the arts, politics and the sciences, leisure and business, and even brain-teasers, *Saturday Review* was the periodical medium at its best for many of us.

You might be happy to know that *Saturday Review* is back and available online. Under Norman Cousins's leadership, *Saturday Review* dealt with the greatest works of art and the most crucial issues of its time. Yet it was never a rarefied, highbrow, elitist publication. Cousins believed that art and culture belonged to everyone, and Saturday Review Online continues that tradition. If you mourn the passing of the magazine, lament no more. Just use the keywords: **Saturday Review** to get there (see Figure 13-8).

Figure 13-8:
Saturday Review
Online offers a
treasury of opinion,
arts, and culture at
keywords: **Satur-
day Review**.

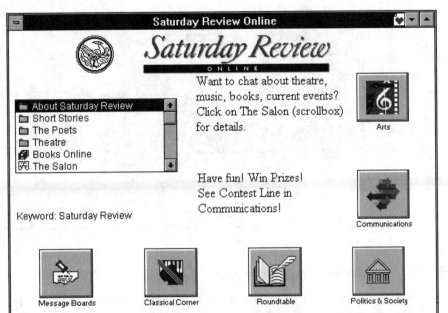

The Odyssey Project

Pictures in magazines and newspapers are usually entertaining, especially the really good ones, but the Odyssey Project (keyword: **Odyssey**) puts you right beside the photographer. Not only are the project's
pictures majestic and sometimes awe-inspiring—as well they should
be, considering the world-class photographers who take them—but
you get to listen and watch as these professional adventurers share the
"rest of the story" in first-hand sessions. The Odyssey Project (see
Figure 13-91) is a window on the pleasures of intensely focused travel,
a collection of perspectives on people, cultures, and animals—and a
way to scratch the travel itch. It's an experiment with new forms of
visual publishing and a community of organizations that encourage us
to get out and taste the world for ourselves.

Figure 13-9:
The Odyssey
Project attracts
world-class photo-
graphic talent, then
sits you down with
the photographers
for a personalized
look at their
portfolios.

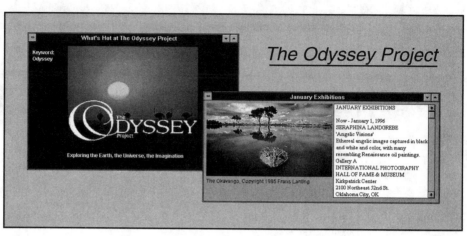

Princeton Review

A number of resources are available to help students get more out of
college, expand their graduate school and career options, and network
with other students nationwide. The Princeton Review, the nation's
most effective test-prep organization, has brought them together as an
AOL service called Princeton Review Online (see Figure 13-10).

Figure 13-10:
Princeton Review
Online offers a
number of educa-
tional, financial,
and career
services.

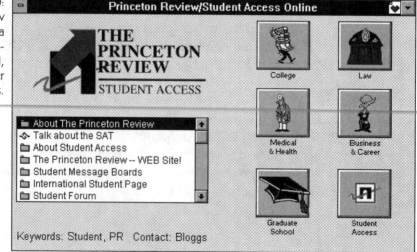

Membership in Princeton Review Online gives the student access to
a variety of exclusive educational, financial, and career services, including the following:

- Financial planning

- Internship opportunities

- Admissions counseling

- Job-placement services

- Group buying power (hundreds of products and services at discounted rates)

- The service's greatest asset—the Student Access members themselves. Student Access forums and trips connect thousands of college students nationwide.

Princeton Review Online almost gives students an unfair advantage, yet it's open to anyone. And at this writing, this wealth of opportunity is FREE to AOL members! All you have to do is complete the enrollment form.

Kaplan Online

In introducing the Princeton Review area, I indicated that a number of resources are available to help students get more out of college. That's true, but there's a resource that's specifically intended to help students get into college as well, and its name is Kaplan Online.

Kaplan offers courses for over 30 standardized tests including college admissions exams, such as the SAT and ACT; graduate and professional school entrance exams, such as the GMAT, GRE, LSAT, and MCAT; professional licensing exams for medicine, nursing, dentistry, and accounting; and specialized exams for foreign students and professionals. The organization has been doing this for 55 years, since young Stanley H. Kaplan first created the test preparation industry in his Brooklyn basement.

Kaplan Online offers sample test questions, examples of how to prepare for the test, a countdown to the test day—even what to do after the test. Best of all, there's no charge. It's all available at keyword: **Kaplan**.

Kaplan Online is not limited to test preparation, however, and its recently redesigned windows reflect the rapid changes occurring throughout the education arena. Allow Kaplan to expand your educational perspectives by checking out the Career and International Centers. If you're about to enter college, graduate school, business, law, medicine, or nursing, get to know Kaplan Online.

The Career Center

Let's see, now: we've helped you select a college and even helped you prepare for entry, and now that you've graduated it's time to find a job. We can help with that too, in the form of the Career Center (see Figure 13-11).

Figure 13-11: The Career Center is the first electronic career and employment guidance agency in America.

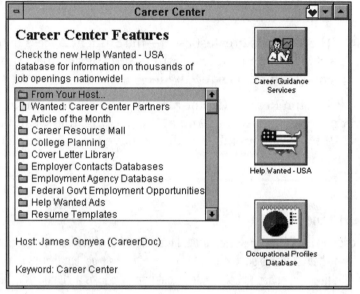

The Career Center offers career counseling, articles on hiring trends, libraries of résumé and employment letter templates, profiles of those elusive home computing business opportunities, and a database of employer contacts. There's information on over 200 occupations—job descriptions, entrance qualifications, salaries, future prospects, and working conditions—in the occupational profiles database, and help-wanted and employment agency databases as well. You can even list your professional skills in the Career Center's talent database. If you're looking for work, this place is a gold mine of opportunity. Use the keywords: **Career Center**.

The Academic Assistance Center

Perhaps I got ahead of myself. You might not be in the job market yet. Lots of AOL members are still students. For students, the Academic Assistance Center (keyword: **AAC**) offers tutoring, help with homework, or assistance in polishing skills that have become rusty. In particular, this is the place to find teachers—teachers who are online and dedicated to the pursuit of academic goals (see Figure 13-12).

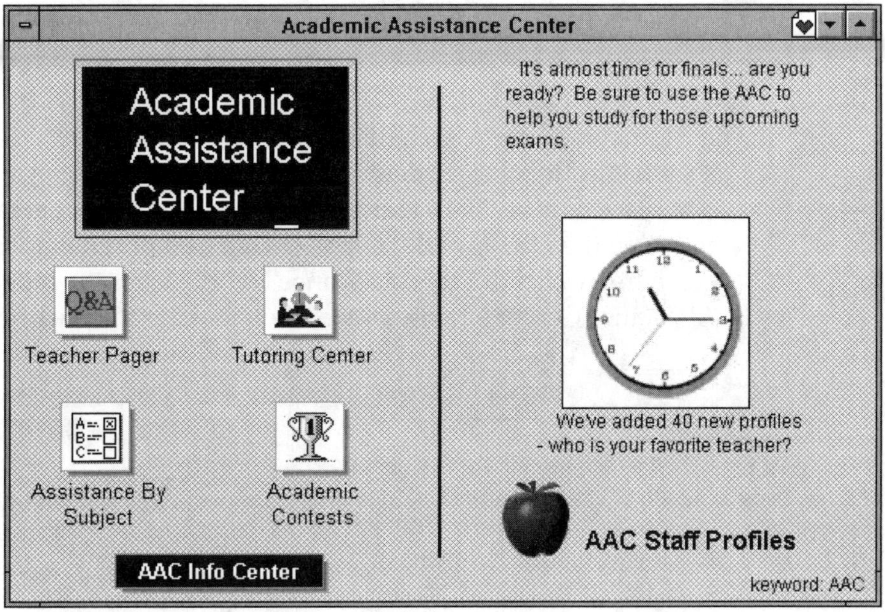

Figure 13-12: The Academic Assistance Center is where students can find teachers and other professionals who will help them with their school work.

The Academic Assistance Center is dedicated to helping the student—online, without surcharge. And it's guaranteed: all the message boards mentioned below are closely monitored; if a student posts a message on any of them and doesn't receive a response within 48 hours, AOL credits the student with an hour of free time.

🔺 In the Academic Assistance help area, students can find live, real-time help with a general or specific subject area. They can post questions, attend one of many regularly scheduled sessions on a variety of subjects, or sign up for an individual session with one of AOL's instructors.

The Teacher Pager

During the evening, the Teacher Pager is ready to connect a student—any AOL member, actually; people of all ages use this feature—with a teacher, online and live. All you need to do is use the keyword: **TeacherPager**. You'll receive an online form to fill out—in which you identify your question and talk a bit about yourself—and within five minutes, a teacher will reply. More than 500 teachers and professionals are on the Teacher Pager staff. You can't remain in the dark for long with a service such as this.

Homework is one area that's often foremost on a student's mind, and it's what leads most students to the Academic Assistance Center in the first place. Figure 13-13 identifies a few of the subject areas that were active on the Homework Help Message Center when I visited. You can get there by clicking the Assistance by Subject buttons on the Academic Assistance Center's main screen, then looking for pushpin icons.

Figure 13-13: At the beginning of the academic year, thousands of messages fill the Homework Q & A message board.

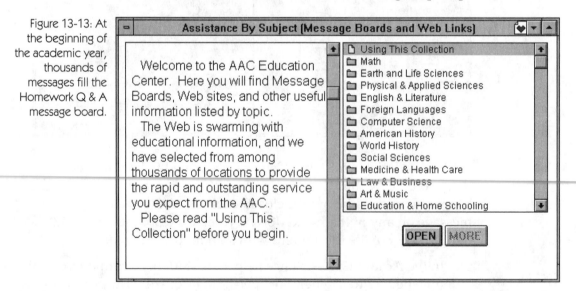

College Board Online

Founded in 1900, the College Board is a national, nonprofit association of more than 2,500 institutions and schools, systems, organizations, and agencies serving both higher and secondary education. The College Board assists students moving from high school to college with services that include guidance, admissions, placement, credit by examination, and financial aid. In addition, the board is chartered to sponsor research, provide a forum to discuss common problems of secondary and higher education, and address questions of educational standards.

Which is a mouthful. What it means is that the College Board Online (keywords: **College Board**) is an invaluable service to the student faced with all the college-related questions: Where should I go? How much will it cost? What are the admission requirements? What are my chances of being accepted? (See Figure 13-14.)

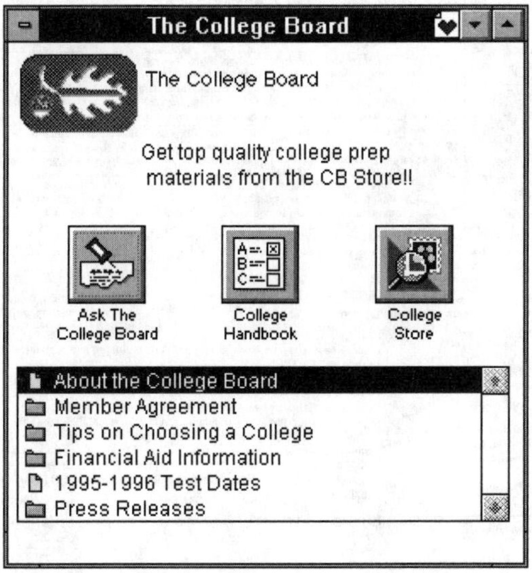

Figure 13-14: The College Board Online is invaluable for the student contemplating a college education.

Perhaps the best way to introduce the College Board is to play the part of a prospective student and query the College Board Handbook. The handbook contains descriptions of more than 3,100 colleges and universities. Information about each school includes majors offered, academic programs, freshman admissions, student life, and athletics. You can search the Handbook either by topic or by college name.

Let's say I'm interested in journalism and black history, and I've decided to pursue the combination of the two as a career. For this, I need an education. Perhaps the College Board Handbook has the answer (see Figure 13-15).

Figure 13-15: A query of the College Handbook identifies the University of Virginia at Charlottesville, Virginia, as a possible destination for someone interested in studying journalism and black studies.

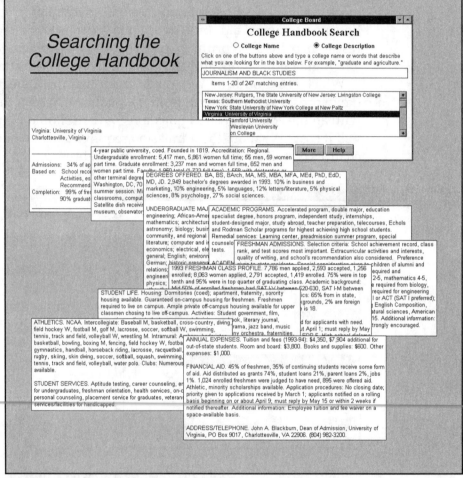

My search criteria for Figure 13-15 were "journalism" and "black studies." The College Handbook found 247 colleges that matched my criteria, one of which is the University of Virginia at Charlottesville. By selecting the University of Virginia listing, I received all the text that's pictured in Figure 13-15. This is a profusion of information, and it's available for each of the other 246 candidates as well.

One thing I notice as I read the UVA admission requirements is that this is one tough school to get into. My credentials will have to be sterling. For this I need help, and for help I turn to the College Board Store (see Figure 13-16).

Figure 13-16: Shopping the College Board Store, I discover the perfect book/video combination to help me submit a winning application.

Shopping the College Board Store

College Store

- About the Store
- Choosing A College
- Applying To College
- Test Preparation Materials
- Academic Preparation Materials
- Guides for Parents
- How to Order
- Order Here

Document

WRITING YOUR COLLEGE APPLICATION ESSAY

by Sarah Myers McGinty

This College Board "classic" has helped tens of thousands distinctive college application essays.

It provides up-to-date information on application essay polici institutions, types of essay questions most frequently asked questions. Students will find this informative and reassuring

* timely examples of the prewriting process
* a detailed review of the basics of writing a well-constructed
* simple procedures for making essays truly personal
* analyses of 6 essays to help students pinpoint strengths a

Document

YOUR COLLEGE APPLICATION (Video)

Based on the book, YOUR COLLEGE APPLICATION, this video takes students through the various stages of the application process. Interviews with college admissions officers as well as high school and college students provide important first-hand information, suggestions, and strategies for approaching the three basic sections of the college application--the academic section, personal section, and supporting documents.

Item number 003276, 1988, VHS videotape, 32 minutes, $29.95

Transmitted: 93-10-18 11:44:33 EDT

Education for the Teacher

Education is not an isolated activity. Education involves the transfer of knowledge, and the transfer of knowledge typically begins with a teacher. The people at America Online know that; that's why the Learning & Culture Channel features a number of areas specifically intended for teachers. Four service areas deserve specific mention:

- ⚫ The Teachers' Information Network (keyword: **TIN**) not only provides information on education, it's also a gathering place where teachers can exchange information, ideas, and experiences.

- ⚫ CNN Newsroom Online is one of America Online's most popular offerings for teachers. CNN (Cable News Network) is the largest news-gathering organization in the world, and CNN Newsroom Online brings the power of CNN to the classroom, complete with ready-to-use outlines and materials for the teacher. You'll find it at keyword: **CNN**.

- The National Education Association (keywords: **NEA Public**) is a teachers' union providing benefits, support, networking, and—through related associations—accreditation for teachers and institutions. NEA Online is an ideal communications vehicle for the association: most teachers have access to a computer, and communication of this sort is best handled quickly, efficiently, and bilaterally.

- The American Federation of Teachers (keyword: **AFT**) offers an electronic hub for AFT news, resources, and activities—a place where AFT members can stop by for timely updates on what's happening, current information on major issues, and an exchange of views and ideas.

The Broadcast Media

Although I've already mentioned CNN, there are two other broadcast services that should be of interest to you: National Public Radio Outreach and C-SPAN. An article I once read (from *WIRED* Magazine—see Chapter 4, "Using the Internet") discussed the future of broadcast media and suggested that the era of passive, one-way broadcast communication is rapidly drawing to a close. I agree. Our curiosity seeks an astounding diversity of information, and AOL's broadcast (and magazine) forums are burgeoning answers to that need.

National Public Radio Outreach Online

This is NPR's avenue of communication with educators and listeners alike. Educators will find a wealth of teachers' guides, newsletters, and brochures (found under Ed. Guides and Newsletters) that tie in with NPR programs—not unlike the strategy employed by CNN. The rest of us will find press releases, biographies (and photos) of on-air personalities, programming schedules, and member-station listings (see Figure 13-17).

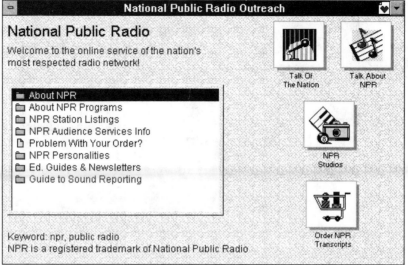

Two items are of particular interest: (1) "Talk About NPR" provides direct access to NPR's listener-feedback loop. You're not only assured that your comment will be read, but you may receive a reply as well. (2) The Audience Services Info area provides information on books, music, and films reviewed on NPR's *All Things Considered, Morning Edition,* and *Talk of the Nation.* Typically, contact information is included for individuals and organizations discussed in program features. The keyword? **NPR**, of course!

C-SPAN Online

Former U.S. House of Representatives Speaker Jim Wright once called C-SPAN (Cable-Satellite Public Affairs Network) "America's Town Hall." Indeed, since 1977, C-SPAN has been providing live, unedited, balanced views of government forums that are unmatched in the broadcast industry. Now C-SPAN Online brings C-SPAN's viewers even closer to cable television's public affairs network (see Figure 13-18).

Perhaps the most significant parts of the online service are its program descriptions and long-range scheduling information: finally, we can tell what's coming up next!

Figure 13-18:
C-SPAN Online
offers schedules,
feedback, educa-
tional services and
a searchable
database for its
viewers.

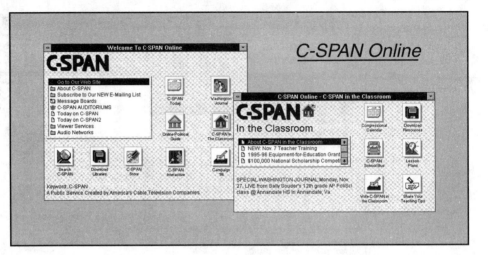

Educators who are interested in using C-SPAN as a teaching resource can join the network's free membership support service: C-SPAN in the Classroom. This service offers teaching guides, access to C-SPAN's archives, a toll-free educators' hotline, and special issues of the *C-SPAN Digest*. Together with CNN and NPR, C-SPAN in the Classroom offers a gold mine of current affairs study material that's professionally produced, contemporary, and—not to be forgotten—almost free. I wish my teachers had had access to this material when I was in school.

Moving On

The Learning & Culture Channel is a vast collection of resources: a joint venture by professionals, parents, and students alike. Coupled with America Online's ease of use and graphical interface, it's not only one of the most comprehensive online resources available, it's really fun. Educators will tell you that learning is most effective when it's enjoy-able. The Learning & Culture Channel is that kind of experience— enlivening, satisfying, and encouraging to students of every age.

Those who know, however, will assure you that *research* is a signifi-cant portion of the education process. And research is rapidly becom-ing an electronic medium. There's good reason for that. Find out by turning the page.

CHAPTER 14

Reference

- Compton's NewMedia Forum
- Merriam-Webster
- American Business Information's Business Yellow Pages
- Pro CD's Phone Book on AOL (the White Pages)
- MEDLINE
- Nolo Press Self-Help Law Center
- Resources on the World Wide Web
- Online Databases

If ever there was a message in search of a medium, it's *reference*. The print medium—home to reference works for centuries—is losing its predominance. Large volumes containing thousands of pages are simply too inconvenient, too wasteful of natural resources, and too unwieldy to meet the push-button demands of the electronic information age.

A printed encyclopedia, for example, made sense 60 years ago, but to describe every aspect of today's society—especially today's technological society—a comprehensive encyclopedia would have to fill a room, not a shelf. Even if you had the room, you would hesitate to use the thing: searching—especially cross-referencing—would be too tedious; information would probably be out of date by the time it was printed (and certainly by the time you had it paid for); and the perpetual revisions would make indexing a nightmare.

Forget the printed encyclopedia. Forget the room to house it. Forget the payments and revisions. Turn on your computer, punch up AOL, and click the Reference Desk button on the Main Menu, or use the keyword: **Reference** (see Figure 14-1). It's all here, it's all topical, it's all affordable. And not a single tree fell to make it possible.

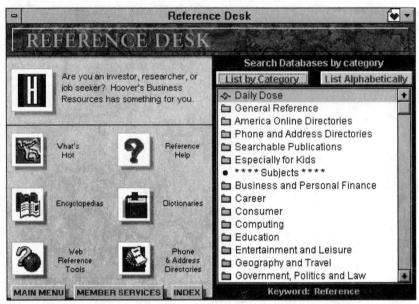

Figure 14-1:
AOL's Reference
Desk window.

Alternative Listings

Look carefully at Figure 14-1. Note the buttons immediately above the list box marked List by Category and List Alphabetically. Normally, this list appears with categories displayed, but if you know which reference work you're looking for, click the List Alphabetically button. *Zip!* The title of every reference work available on AOL will appear (an extraordinary number of them), ready for you to pursue.

Compton's NewMedia Forum

Four years ago, the keyword: **Comptons** brought you a rather plain presentation of Compton's Encyclopedia. It was an admirable resource—more than 9,000,000 words; 5,274 full-length articles; 29,322 capsule articles; 63,503 index entries—and won the Critics' Choice award for the best education program, as well as top honors at the 1991 Software Publisher's Association awards ceremony. But it remained primarily textual, a vestige of its print heritage; hardly a sterling example of the online medium.

That, of course, was in the days of 1200 baud modems and 16-color displays. Today, things have changed, including the Compton's NewMedia Forum (see Figure 14-2).

Figure 14-2: Compton's NewMedia Forum offers a newly enhanced multi-media encyclope-dia and a growing array of support services.

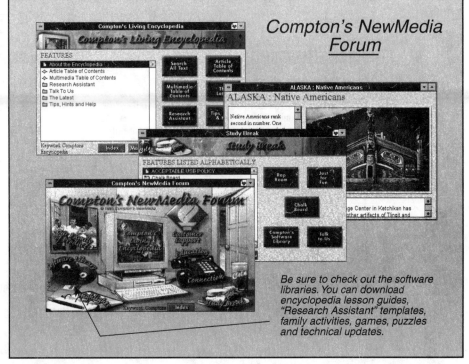

At the root of it all is *Compton's Living Encyclopedia*—an enhanced version of the printed work, and a multimedia extravaganza. The Encyclopedia offers not only text, but graphics, sounds, and videos as well. Oh it's a reference work all right, and as a reference work it's exhaustively comprehensive. But it's also a *multimedia* reference work, and that makes it fun as well.

I love trains. I love the sound and smell—and the romance—of trains. I ride a light rail system to town (Metropolitan Area Express [MAX] in Portland, Oregon), and Amtrak's most popular route—the Coast Starlight—passes within a few miles of my house. To test Compton's Living Encyclopedia as an effective resource, I searched for the word "railroad" and was more than gratified with the results (see Figure 14-3).

Figure 14-3:
Over a thousand
references to rail-
roads! Elysian
Fields for the
railnaut.

Compton's Living Encyclopedia

Search All Text

To Search on the full text of encyclopedia entries, type words that describe what you are looking for, then click "List Articles."

RAILROAD

Items 1-20 of 250 out of 1175 matches.

TRANSPORTATION : Growth of Railroads
TRANSPORTATION : Freight Transportation
RAILROAD : BIBLIOGRAPHY FOR RAILROAD
RAILROAD : Railroad Modernization
RAILROAD : Railroad Organization and Regulation
RAILROAD : Building a Railroad
RAILROAD : Development of Modern American Railroads
RAILROAD : Railroads Cross the Continent
RAILROAD

[List Articles] [More] [Help & Info]

Notable Passenger Trains

These are the trains I want to travel in someday. The text below is extracted from Compton's Living Encyclopedia, Online Edition, and downloaded from AOL.

Blue Train, South Africa

Said to be the most luxurious train in the world, the Blue Train makes a leisurely 1,000-mile, 26-hour trip once or twice a week between Pretoria and Cape Town.

Coast Starlight, United States

Though I've already mentioned this train as Amtrak's most popular, it warrants a second mention here. The Coast Starlight crosses the Cascade Mountains and follows the coastline of California in a 1,400-mile, 33-hour trip between Seattle and Los Angeles. Save your pennies and get a sleeper.

Indian Pacific, Australia

Another luxury train, the Indian Pacific crosses the Australian continent, from Sydney to Perth, in less than three days.

Orient Express, Europe
Europe's first transcontinental express, for years unmatched in luxury and comfort. From 1883 to 1977 (with interruptions during WWI and WWII), it ran from Paris to Constantinople (now Istanbul) in Turkey. Short runs are still made over portions of the original route.

Rheingold, West Germany
One of Europe's finest trains, the Rheingold runs between Amsterdam, the Netherlands and Basel, Switzerland, following the Rhine River and stopping at such cities as Cologne, Mainz and Munich.

Rossiya, Trans-Siberian Railway
The Rossiya runs daily between Moscow and Vladivostok. The trip takes a week. Call your travel agent (better yet, consult the Travel Forum, discussed in Chapter 11) before you pack: things are changing over there.

TGV, France
This is the fastest train in the world, cruising at 180 miles per hour and covering the 267 miles between Paris and Lyon in two hours.

Whoa! One hundred and eighty miles an hour! Few cars can reach that speed—in fact, few private aircraft can cruise at 180 miles an hour. But the TGV does it every day, with aplomb, replete with French cuisine and a most eclectic group of passengers.

Merriam-Webster

Forgive my rambling. I got sidetracked, so to speak, when the subject of trains came up. I was talking about antiquated media, and another has just come to our attention: the ubiquitous dictionary. Quickly now: name the first dictionary that comes to mind. Chances are, you said Webster's (actually, it's *Merriam*-Webster's now), and that's just what AOL has to offer (see Figure 14-4).

The dictionary is another message looking for an improved medium, and like the encyclopedia, the dictionary is perfectly served by the machinery of the online medium. So is the thesaurus, which Merriam-Webster also offers online. AOL's machines search Merriam-Webster's references with speed and accuracy, returning not only definitions, pronunciations, and synonyms, but fascinating information about the etymology of words—especially if you choose to consult *Word Histories*, Merriam-Webster's nutriment for the bibliophile appetite. You'll find all the Merriam-Webster offerings on the Reference Desk's main menu, or use the keywords: **Merriam-Webster**.

American Business Information's Business Yellow Pages

When you want to find a new restaurant, an electrician, the nearest theater, or an odd part for your bicycle, where's the first place you look? Virtually all of us would say the Yellow Pages, that ubiquitous corpus of commerce. Well now there is a worthy alternative to thumbing those familiar pages, and it's free on AOL!

You'll quickly find that AOL's American Yellow Pages offer some significant advantages over traditional printed Yellow Pages. Like AOL's other reference services, its American Yellow Pages are searchable. Whether your quest be common or exotic, you can quickly locate products or services by letting AOL's fingers, rather than yours, do the walking (see Figure 14-5).

Figure 14-5:
The American
Business Information Yellow Pages,
an AOL service
that's all business!

The Business Yellow Pages

Search the Business Yellow Pages

Search for directory information by category or company name. Limit a search by indicating city and state.

Search by: ○ Company Name ● Category

COMPUTERS

City: AUSTIN   State: TX

Search   About ABI   Help

Keyword: ABI; Yellow Pages

The Business Yellow Pages' Search feature helps you find the exact business you're looking for, locally or nationally.

Yellow Page Categories

Select a category for a search.

BAR CODE SCANNING EQUIPMENT & SUPPLIES
COMPUTER MANUFACTURERS
COMPUTER SERVICES
COMPUTER SOFTWARE
COMPUTER SOFTWARE MANUFACTURERS
COMPUTER SOFTWARE WHOLESALE
COMPUTER STORAGE DEVICES
COMPUTER SUPPLIES & PARTS MFRS
COMPUTERS

ABI Search Results

Double-click on an item to see the full record.

IONS INC AUSTIN	AUSTIN	TX 78741
JMC PRODUCTS	AUSTIN	TX 78758
NETSERV INC	AUSTIN	TX 78758
TECHNOLOGY WORKS	AUSTIN	TX 78758
VERBATIM CORP	AUSTIN	TX 78726

Open   More

Perhaps best of all, AOL's American Yellow Pages include nationwide listings; no longer will your curiosity be limited by the scope of your local telephone book. In just minutes you can locate business sources in the next town, or in Chicago, Bar Harbor, or San Diego. Just click the Yellow Pages entry on the main Reference Desk menu, or use the keywords: **Yellow Pages**.

Pro CD's Phone Book on AOL (the White Pages)

This morning I happened to think of an old friend, a musician from high school days. The last I heard he was in Iowa, but I haven't talked with him in years. I was wondering.

You're already ahead of me. Yes, if AOL offers the Yellow Pages, it must offer white pages too (see Figure 14-6). And like the Yellow Pages, AOL will do the looking for you, whether your goal be a business or residence. You can find the Online White Pages by using the keywords: **White Pages** and then clicking Pro CD. This is not only a viable alternative to long-distance Directory Assistance, it's much less expensive.

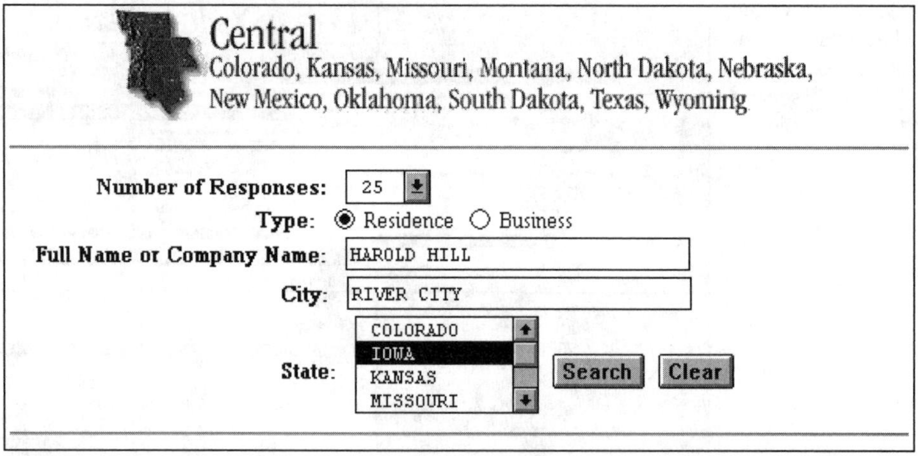

Figure 14-6:
Harold was always
a likable fellow; I
wonder what he's
up to.

Central
Colorado, Kansas, Missouri, Montana, North Dakota, Nebraska, New Mexico, Oklahoma, South Dakota, Texas, Wyoming

Number of Responses: 25

Type: ● Residence ○ Business

Full Name or Company Name: HAROLD HILL

City: RIVER CITY

State:
COLORADO
IOWA
KANSAS
MISSOURI

Search   Clear

MEDLINE

For at least the last hundred years, health care decisions have been solely the province of doctors, modern society's scientific experts on the machinery of the human body. In real life and in countless television and film productions, patients have traditionally played passive rather than active roles in the management of their personal health care and therapy. But as the end of the century approaches, deep and significant changes are afoot in the definition and delivery of complete health care, many of which offer patients greatly increased participation, understanding, and compassion—not to mention renewed status as human beings.

America Online's noteworthy contribution to this trend is found in MEDLINE, an online compendium of medical networks and resources that has been popular with doctors for years but now is available to everyone through AOL. If a single example were to be requested as to the benefits of the online medium, MEDLINE would be an excellent choice.

Access to MEDLINE is gained either via the main Reference Desk menu, or the keyword: **MEDLINE** (see Figure 14-7). The main MEDLINE window leads directly to several incredibly rich areas: MEDLINE's arsenal of search tools, the MEDLINE Message Board, the Better Health and Medical Forum and the Personal Empowerment Network.

Figure 14-7:
No longer the
exclusive province
of doctors,
MEDLINE is your
health information
gateway to medical
research, organiza-
tions, and health-
related groups.

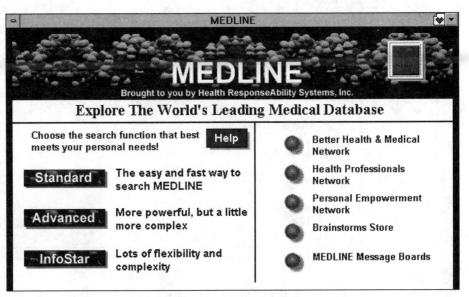

MEDLINE Search Tools

By now you are no doubt familiar with AOL's basic search mecha-nisms, all offering dialog boxes or menus that can help you find exactly what you are looking for. While MEDLINE Searches utilize this same structure, they differ in displaying not one but three different levels of search refinement.

MEDLINE's Standard Search is the one most like other AOL search dialog boxes—with a few enhancements. In addition to a standard search word dialog box, there are check boxes to focus the search (see Figure 14-8).

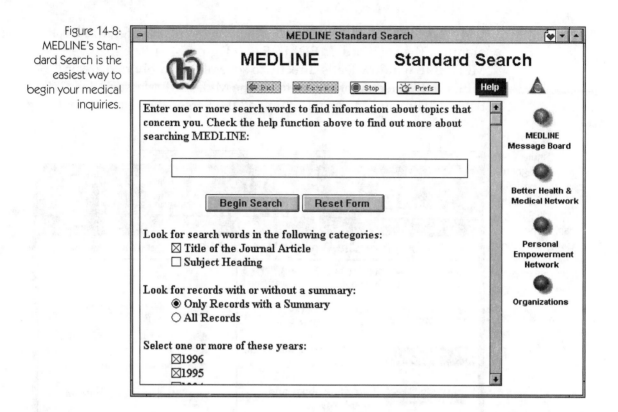

MEDLINE's Advanced Search adds another level of complexity, including the ability to specify title, summary, and years (see Figure 14-9).

Figure 14-9:
MEDLINE's
Advanced Search
is appropriate for
more experienced
users.

```
┌──────────────────────────────────────────────────────────────────────┐
│ ▢          MEDLINE Advanced Search                          ❤ ▾ ▲      │
│  ╭─╮                                                                    │
│  │ⓗ│   MEDLINE          Advanced Search                               │
│  ╰─╯     ◆ Back   ◆ Forward   ⬤ Stop   ☼ Prefs      Help    ▲         │
│ ─────────────────────────────────────────────────────────── ▲         │
│  Enter one or more search words to find information about topics that  │
│  concern you. Check the help function above to find out more about     │
│  searching MEDLINE.                                      MEDLINE       │
│                                                       Message Board    │
│      ┌──────────────┐  ┌──────────────┐                   ●           │
│      │ Begin Search │  │  Reset Form  │                                │
│      └──────────────┘  └──────────────┘               Better Health & │
│  Search in the following categories:                  Medical Network  │
│                                                           ●            │
│  Article Title:                                                        │
│  ┌──────────────────────────────────────────────┐    Personal         │
│  │                                              │    Empowerment       │
│  └──────────────────────────────────────────────┘    Network          │
│                                                           ●            │
│  Subject Headings:                                                     │
│  ┌──────────────────────────────────────────────┐    Organizations    │
│  │                                              │                       │
│  └──────────────────────────────────────────────┘                      │
│                                                                        │
│  Subject Headings, Central Concept(s):                                 │
│  ┌──────────────────────────────────────────────┐                      │
│  │                                              │                       │
│  └──────────────────────────────────────────────┘                      │
│                                                                        │
│  Summary:                                                   ▼          │
└──────────────────────────────────────────────────────────────────────┘
```

MEDLINE's InfoStar Search includes all the features of the Advanced Search, plus subject heading, central concepts, years, summary, language, author, and institution (see Figure 14-10).

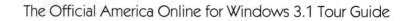

Figure 14-10:
InfoStar Search is
often used by
medical profes-
sionals.

```
─  http://search19.proxy.aol.com:8000/MedLine/MedLine04.html  ♥ ▼ ▲

       (h)   MEDLINE        InfoStar  Search
              ← Back  → Forward  ● Stop  ⚙ Prefs   Help   ▲

        ┌──────────────┐  ┌──────────────┐          ▲
        │ Begin Search │  │ Reset Form   │                ●
        └──────────────┘  └──────────────┘            MEDLINE
     Search in the following categories:            Message Board

        Article Title:                                   ●
        ┌────────────────────────────────────────┐   Better Health &
        └────────────────────────────────────────┘   Medical Network

        MeSH Headings:                                   ●
        ┌────────────────────────────────────────┐   Personal
        └────────────────────────────────────────┘   Empowerment
                                                      Network
        MeSH Headings, Central Concept(s):
        ┌────────────────────────────────────────┐      ●
        └────────────────────────────────────────┘   Organizations

        Abstract:
        ┌────────────────────────────────────────┐
        └────────────────────────────────────────┘

        Author:
        ┌────────────────────────────────────────┐
        └────────────────────────────────────────┘

        Institution:
        ┌────────────────────────────────────────┐  ▼
```

MEDLINE's Search array clearly offers search options appropriate to
a wide range of user backgrounds, and it's all available at the keyword:
MEDLINE.

MEDLINE Message Board

Message boards usually conjure a vision of hastily scribbled notes
tacked up where everyone can see. And that's a useful concept, both in
its simplicity and familiarity. But in regard to the MEDLINE Message
Board, such a concept doesn't quite seem to apply; the tone here is
more serious, more intent, and sometimes more urgent.

Here you'll find excellent tips on using MEDLINE's Standard,
Advanced, and InfoStar searches as well as other information useful to
first-time MEDLINE browsers. But most of all you'll find people who
are looking for knowledge, who possess knowledge, and who are
interested in helping. Look around. If you don't find what you're
looking for, choose the MEDLINE Suggestions folder and officially
enlist the help of some unseen friends.

Nolo Press Self-Help Law Center

Twenty-five years ago two former Legal Aid lawyers, dissatisfied with the lack of affordable legal information and advice available to the public, began writing understandable, easy-to-use self-help law books. Legal kits, software, and tapes all followed, but the purpose has never changed: to take the mystery out of law and make it accessible to Everyman.

Since they were already involved in print, audio, and video publications, it seemed only natural that Nolo Press would commit to the online medium as well, and they've done just that with their Nolo Press Self-Help Law Center at keyword: **Nolo** (see Figure 14-11).

Figure 14-11: Look to the Nolo Law Center for legal self-help.

Pay particular attention to Nolo's Pocket Guide to Family Law. You'll find chapters dedicated to adoption, alimony, child support, divorce, domestic violence, marriage, property & debt, reproductive rights, rights of unmarried people, and more.

Resources on the World Wide Web

AOL isn't your only source for online reference, and the first people to admit that are the people at America Online. Fortunately, you're not excluded from the remainder of the reference universe. That universe, you see, resides on the World Wide Web (the Web is discussed in Chapter 4, "Using the Internet"), and the Web is an integral feature of the Reference Desk.

Figure 14-12:
The World Wide Web is rife with reference resources, and they're all available via the Internet Link button on the main Reference screen.

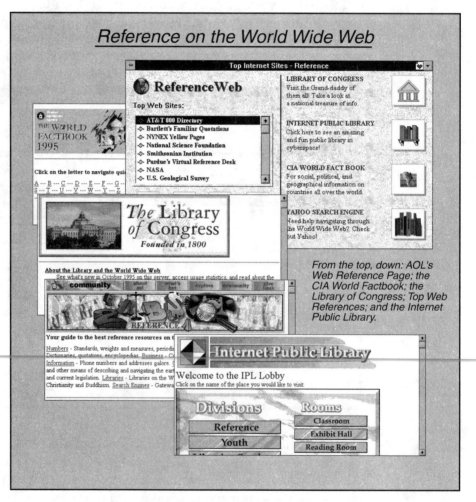

This is where reference comes into its own: the reference potential on the Web is worldwide, after all, and the world is a sea of information. Imagine having the Library of Congress, the Internet Public Library, the CIA Factbook, AT&T's 800-number directory, the National Science Foundation, the Smithsonian, NASA, the U.S. Geological Survey, the Rutgers University Law Library, and even a virtual hospital at your fingertips!

One of the best places to begin exploring the reference potential of the Web is with AOL's own Community Reference Home Page (see Figure 14-13, top). You'll find it on the Other Web Sites line in the Top Web Sites menu shown in Figure 14-12. The Community Reference Home Page is an encyclopedic inventory of nearly all of the reference sites on the Web, and probably the best jumping-off point for information exploration the Web has to offer.

Figure 14-13: AOL's own Community Reference page on the World Wide Web is an exhaustive listing of the Web's reference links. Only about a third of the page is pictured here.

Your guide to the best reference resources on the Web.

Numbers - Standards, weights and measures, periodic charts, even a currency converter! Words - Dictionaries, quotations, encyclopedias. Business - Company and consumer information. Directory Information - Phone numbers and addresses galore. Getting Around the Globe - Maps, Gazeteers and other means of describing and navigating the earth. Government and Law - Info on congress and current legislation. Libraries - Libraries on the Web. Religion - Visit home pages on Judaism, Christianity and Buddhism. Search Engines - Gateways and other ways to surf the Net.

Numbers

- Standards, weights and measures, periodic charts, even a currency converter!

- WebElements
- Periodic Table
- US Census Report - 1994 Statistical Abstract
- US Census Report - City and County Database
- Foreign Exchange Rates
- Local Times Around the World

Figure 14-13:
continued.

Words

- Dictionaries, quotations, encyclopedias.

- Dictionaries Ready Reference
- Dictionaries, Thesaurus, Acronyms
- Barlett's Familiar Quotations

Business

- Company and consumer information.

- Better Business Bureau
- GNN Business Pages
- Small Business Administration
- EDGAR Company Search
- PAWWS: Stock Quotes and Financial Game
- The Taxing Times: Tax Information

Directory information

- Phone numbers and addresses galore.

- AT&T 800 Directory
- NYNEX Interactive Yellow Pages
- Area Codes (US) via Stanford University
- US Postal Service ZIP+4 Lookup

Phone numbers and addresses galore.

Getting around the Globe

- Maps, Gazeteers and other means of describing and navigating the earth.

- CIA World Factbook - 1994
- Xerox PARC Map Viewer
- Geographic Nameserver
- The Perry-Castañeda Library Map Collection
- Geospatial Data and Information Resources, by Organization
- U.S. Gazetteer
- Virtual Tour of Israel
- Map of Asia

Online Databases

With the fall 1994 release of the Reference Desk, AOL effectively consolidated all its online databases into one place. Whether it's a telephone book or a dictionary of Wall Street terminology, if it's available online, it's available at keyword: **Reference**.

Print the List

If you conduct much online research, it helps to have a printed list of AOL's online databases, one that you can consult whether you're online or off. Just click the Index button on the bottom of the Reference Desk window and choose Print from the File menu.

We've explored many of AOL's databases in previous chapters, and others are highly specialized. But two warrant our attention here.

AOL Local Access Numbers

The list of telephone numbers you can use to contact AOL is a prodigious database in itself. America Online serves all of North America, after all, and that's a lot of territory (and a lot of access numbers). If you plan to travel with your computer, search this database for a list of access numbers for the localities you'll be visiting. Print the list, pack it with your modem and take it along. You can access the database from the Reference Desk, or by using the keyword: **Access**.

If you are a frequent traveler, you'll want to read Appendix D, "On the Road." There are lots of tips there for the AOL road warrior.

Software File Search

Speaking of searching, probably the places you'll search most frequently are AOL's own file libraries. Though the Reference Desk area lists Software File Search among the options in the main window's scroll box, you don't have to visit here to conduct a search. You can search AOL's file libraries at any time, from any location, by using the keywords: **File Search**, or by clicking the Find button on the toolbar.

File Search (you might hear it called "Quickfinder"—either term is accurate and the keyword: **Quickfinder**—or just **Quickfind**—works just as well) is AOL's mechanism for searching its list of online files. When you use the keyword, the Software Search dialog box will appear (see Figure 14-14).

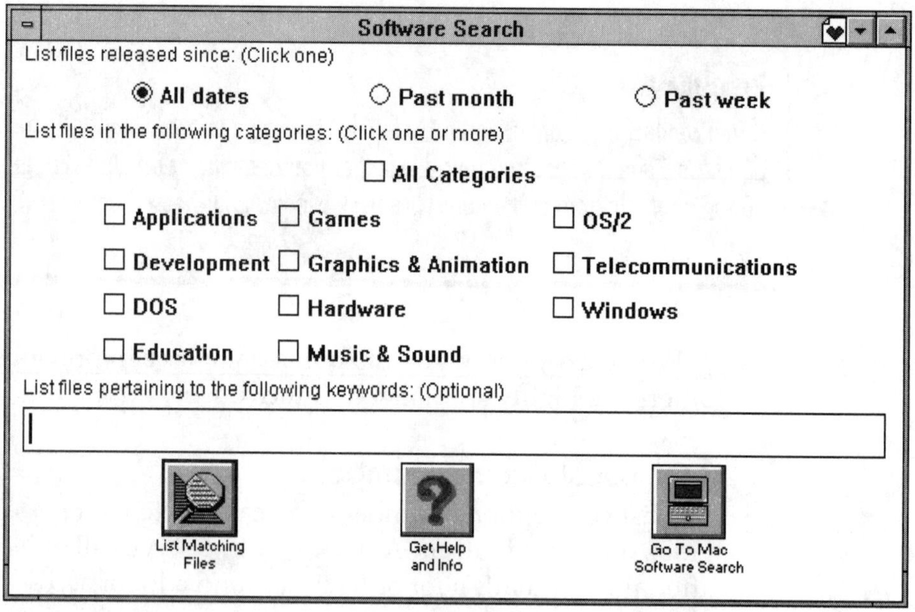

Figure 14-14:
The Software
Search dialog box.

Software Search

List files released since: (Click one)

◉ **All dates**   ○ **Past month**   ○ **Past week**

List files in the following categories: (Click one or more)

☐ **All Categories**

☐ **Applications**   ☐ **Games**   ☐ **OS/2**

☐ **Development**   ☐ **Graphics & Animation**   ☐ **Telecommunications**

☐ **DOS**   ☐ **Hardware**   ☐ **Windows**

☐ **Education**   ☐ **Music & Sound**

List files pertaining to the following keywords: (Optional)

List Matching
Files

Get Help
and Info

Go To Mac
Software Search

Most searches of AOL's online files are successful, but you might encounter situations in which the search fails (no files are found) even though you know there are files online that meet your criteria, or in which the search is too successful (wading through a hundred or more matches is just too much effort).

How Many Files Are Available?

One way of tracking AOL's growth is to periodically check the total number of files available online. When I first joined the service (I'm a "charter member," having first signed on in early 1990), there were fewer than 10,000 files. When I checked today, there were more than 80,000!

How did I determine the number of files available online? It's easy: just leave the Software Search dialog box empty (as it's pictured in Figure 14-14). Don't check any of the check boxes and don't put any criteria in the text box. Just leave the dialog as it appears when you first summon it, be sure the All Dates button is selected, then click the List Matching Files button.

America Online will respond by listing all the files available online and telling you how many there are. With this many files, you won't even want to browse the list, but the total number might be informative. Do this occasionally and watch AOL grow.

Let's say that you received a file from a friend who is using a Mac rather than a PC. It's common to compress files before sending them, and your friend used StuffIt to do so (indicated by the .sit filename extension). StuffIt is built into the Macintosh version of the AOL software, and most online files for Macs are "stuffed," as they say, so this isn't uncommon.

Unfortunately, you've got a PC, and PCs usually use the PKZIP compression software, not StuffIt. (StuffIt and PKZIP are discussed in Chapter 5, "Transferring Files.") Needing a PC utility that will decompress every imaginable Mac stuffed file, you sign on and use File Search to locate the utility.

Your first temptation is to simply type the category (or name) of the program you're looking for in the criteria text box, as shown at the top of Figure 14-15. You don't really want StuffIt itself; it only runs on Macs. You want something that will unstuff Mac stuffed files on the PC, so the generic term "Mac" is about the best criterion for your purpose.

Figure 14-15:
Homing in on an
unstuffing program
for the PC.

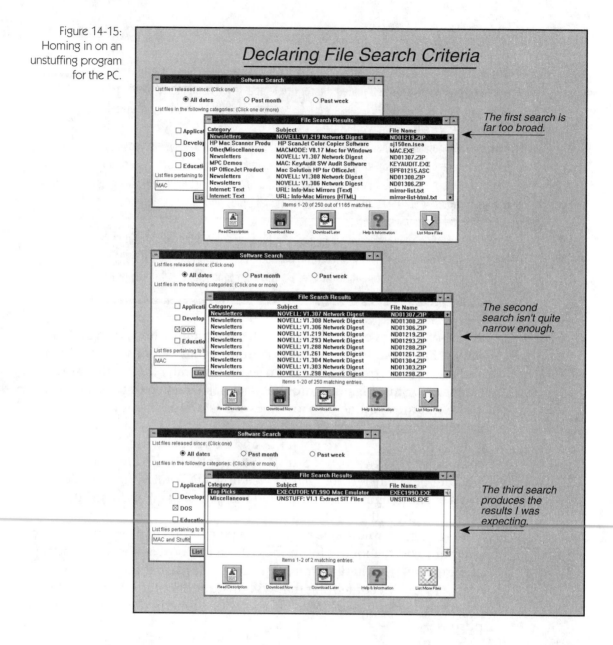

Notice the results of the first search: 1,165 files! Indeed, a few file-searching tips seem in order:

- Use check boxes to narrow your search. It's tempting to ignore the check boxes in the middle of the file search dialog box. If you do, All Categories is the default condition, even if it's not checked. By specifying a check box (I specified DOS in the second example in Figure 14-15), my search produced 250 files, hardly a manageable number.

- Narrow your search with *ands, ors,* and *nots.* I used an *and* function in the third example pictured in Figure 14-15 and eliminated all the other Mac-related files—whatever they were—that cluttered my results. (Be careful: mixing *ands* with *ors* or *nots* can sometimes produce misleading results.

- Don't specify version numbers. You might have heard that UnStuff 1.0.1 is the latest version. Searching with the criterion: UnStuff 1.0.1 would not produce the latest version, UnStuff 1.1.

- Criteria are not case-sensitive. Don't worry about uppercase and lowercase when you're typing criteria. America Online doesn't care. It also doesn't care if you make things plural or singular: "Mac" works no better or worse than "Macs."

- Use whole words. Abbreviations won't work, nor will wild cards. "UnS" (for UnStuff) or "UnS*" (using a wild card) won't find UnStuff.

- Search specific libraries if File Search fails. Using File Search to find "MajorTom," for example, will fail. Since the only MajorTom file posted online is a graphic, and because it's stored in the Gallery (discussed in Chapter 8, "The Community"), go to the Gallery and conduct your search there.

- To find the latest files, leave everything blank and specify "Past week." This finds all the files posted in just the past week.

Moving On

My overview of America Online's Reference Channel has lightly touched on topics representing the diversity of American culture. Yet, curiously, I've not written a single word about what may be the most popular of all American activities, an activity where time is information and information is literally money, an activity with a unique relationship to the online medium: the purchasing and selling of goods and services.

It's not as if America Online has not planned and prepared; indeed, AOL has been toiling in the background, constructing the virtual storefront and painting the virtual front door that you're about to enter. Get ready: "Buying & Selling" is up next.

Buying & Selling

CHAPTER 15

- The AOL Store
- 1-800-FLOWERS
- Hallmark Connections
- One Hanes Place
- OfficeMax Online
- Tower Records
- Health & Vitamin Express
- Shoppers' Advantage
- Classifieds Online
- atOnce Software
- KidSoft Super Store
- Omaha Steaks International
- Downtown AOL
- Caffè Starbucks

Ask ten people what a shopping excursion means to them and you'll probably get ten different answers. An elder might recall a time when shopping meant a once-a-month trip to "the store," where the selection was meager if not inadequate. Someone new to American shores might describe an open-air produce market, a Mediterranean bazaar, or the British post-shopping ritual of high tea. Another might recount stories of quests for unusual or arcane objects, spanning months or even years of browsing in dusty little shops. Globe trotters might speak excitedly of the streets of Paris, Sydney, Amsterdam, Hong Kong, or New York. And any one of these respondents might mention going to the Mall, alluding to the social scene as well as the plethora of goods to be found there.

Whether by car, carriage, ferry, or foot, all these shopping destinations have demanded transportation. Today, however, another shopping method is emerging and taking hold—one that offers exotica, style, selection, product information, speed—and above all, the ultimate convenience of home access. I speak, of course, of electronic commerce, and this chapter is your guide to a new generation of shopping, indeed a new definition of buying and selling, that is being written even as you read these words.

Electronic marketing is in its infancy. As you explore, remember that what you will find is important not only for the products and marketing models available now, but also as a prediction of product selection and store location of the future.

The AOL Store

The electronic communication medium is AOL's backyard, so what better place to begin than at the AOL Store (see Figure 15-1). Here you can find clothing, coffee mugs, and other products to let you proclaim your affiliation with AOL, as well as products such as modems, computer accessories, software, and books (like this one) to speed your online navigation and indulge your curiosity. Take a moment to check out the Multimedia Showcase, send an AOL gift certificate to a friend, or download one of AOL's hottest sound tracks. Just use the keywords: **AOL Store**.

Figure 15-1: Show your pride in America Online! Wear an AOL sweatshirt while you sip coffee from an AOL mug and read *America Online's Internet*.

1-800-FLOWERS

It's easy to forget that communication is much more than words. No matter the occasion, situation, or location, one of the most pleasant and touching messages you can send is the gift of flowers, a gift made simple by entering keyword: **Flowers**. (See Figure 15-2.)

You'll find seasonal and holiday suggestions for fresh cut flowers, as well as event and gift items including chocolates, cakes, centerpieces, gift baskets, wreaths, dried flower arrangements, and even a gift reminder service! You'll find it all at keyword: **Flowers**.

Figure 15-2:
1-800-FLOWERS:
the world's premier
florist and gift
shop.

> **Welcome to the World's Favorite Florist!**
>
> **1-800-FLOWERS**
>
> Submerge roses with bent necks under warm water for 30 minutes. This will help revive the roses.
>
> *Feature of the Day*
>
> *A Fresh Approach To Living And Giving*
>
> Shop Our Store
> Welcome & What's New
> Gift Concierge Service
> Customer Service
> Contests & Promotions
> Fresh Thoughts
> Flower Talk
> Featured Product
>
> Keyword: Flowers
> Shopping Cart Marketplace

Hallmark Connections

The Marketplace Channel has expanded quite a bit in recent months, and no doubt it will expand even more by the time this book reaches you. AOL has always been at the forefront of online technology, especially in the area of multimedia, so expect to see lots of new areas here. The Hallmark Connections area is a perfect example (see Figure 15-3).

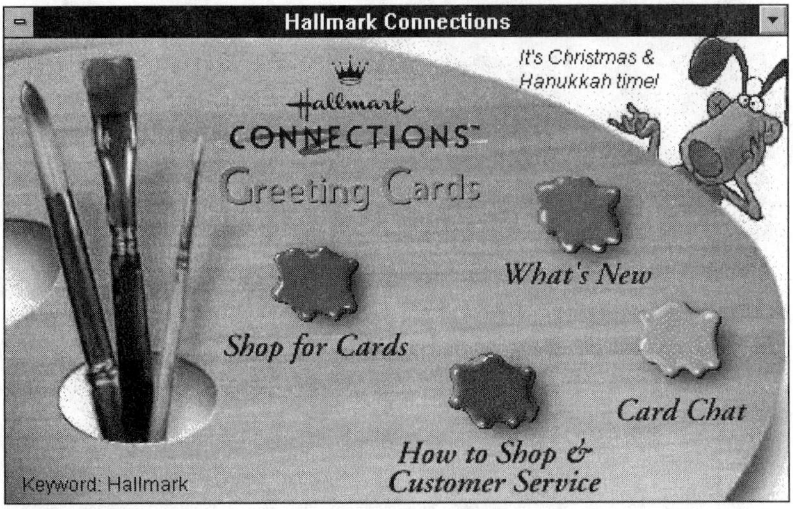

Figure 15-3:
Hallmark Connec-
tions—when you
care enough to
send the very
best (but don't
want to drive to
the store . . .).

> **Hallmark Connections**
>
> It's Christmas & Hanukkah time!
>
> *Hallmark* CONNECTIONS
> *Greeting Cards*
>
> *What's New*
>
> *Shop for Cards*
>
> *Card Chat*
>
> *How to Shop & Customer Service*
>
> Keyword: Hallmark

How many times has a birthday or anniversary slipped your mind until it was nearly upon you? What do you do? You could stop what you're doing, jump in your car, drive to a store, and get a card, but who has that kind of time these days? Well, Hallmark Connections is here to change all of that.

How would you like to be able to order high-quality, personalized greeting cards without ever leaving home (or work)? Better yet, how would you like to have someone mail those cards for you at the appropriate time? Talk about having a personal secretary!

The area is organized much like a real-world card department in any store you might visit. You can choose from seven departments, ranging from seasonal cards to business greeting cards. Once you've selected a card department, AOL will either ask you to narrow your search a bit further, or show you a list of available cards within your chosen department. Once you select a particular card, you'll be able to see what it actually looks like (see Figure 15-4).

Figure 15-4: Selecting a personalized card is as simple as clicking your mouse.

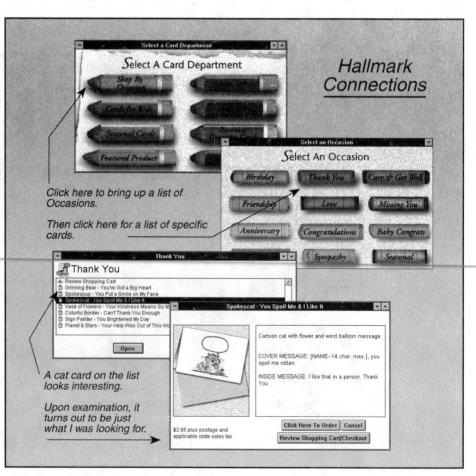

You'll also be able to personalize your card by supplying the recipient's name or other information as indicated, as well as your own closing message and name. The cards will be printed on recycled paper, and your closing message and name will be printed in a scripted font to simulate a signature. Your card will then be mailed to any address in the United States—either within 48 hours of your order or at any time you choose.

One Hanes Place

One Hanes Place (see Figure 15-5) is also a new addition to AOL. The Main Store at One Hanes Place is stocked with great everyday values on fashion legwear, intimate apparel, and activewear, as well as brand-name basics. You'll save up to 50 percent on Hanes, L'eggs, Bali, Playtex, Hanes Her Way, Champion, Just My Size, and Color Me Natural products.

Figure 15-5: The One Hanes Place Main Store and the Olympic Shop "store within a store."

The Olympic Shop at One Hanes Place is a "store within a store." Champion and Hanes are two of the sponsors of the 1996 Centennial Olympic Games in Atlanta. The Olympic Shop is where you can find authentic apparel from Champion and officially licensed apparel from Hanes. This shop was created with the whole family in mind—from Olympic printed apparel (collectible stuff!) to Looney Tunes goodies. Take a look around by typing the keyword: **Hanes**.

OfficeMax Online

So far we've seen interesting stores offering a wide selection of products at the Marketplace, but they've all been, for the most part, in the personal category. Don't worry. There are plenty of places where you can fulfill your practical needs—personal and business—as well.

OfficeMax OnLine is an exciting retail concept from one of the nation's largest and fastest-growing operators of high-volume, deep-discount office products superstores. OfficeMax opened its first store in suburban Cleveland, Ohio, on July 5, 1988, and in less than seven years grew to become one of America's largest specialty retailers, with more than 400 stores in 147 markets in 40 states from coast to coast, including Puerto Rico.

OfficeMax is able to buy in huge quantities and pass the savings on to you. They offer deep discounts on brand-name office products, business machines, electronics, furniture, computer hardware, software, and related products. Plus, everything they sell is backed by their low-price guarantee. And now with OfficeMax OnLine, you can buy their products from your keyboard and your order will be delivered directly to your door (see Figure 15-6).

Figure 15-6: OfficeMax Online—your one-stop office product shopping center.

Tower Records

When Tower Records went online, I went to heaven. I'm a music junkie—CDs are my habit—and without a weekly fix I'm petulant and sullen. Imagine my delight, then, when Tower offered me the ability to shop for music without having to leave my keyboard! (See Figure 15-7.)

Figure 15-7: Tower Records offers sustenance for the musically malnourished.

Perhaps most significantly, the online version of Tower Records provides a search mechanism for finding the music you're after. No more confusion and indecision, standing in front of incomprehensibly organized racks of tapes or CDs. At Tower Records Online you can bypass the stacks and quickly search by an artist's (or composer's) name, by an individual (not just album) song title, or by category. And if you're an inveterate browser, you'll find Tower Records's online listings diverse, extensive, easy to understand and follow, and pleasantly accessible.

Here's a fascinating tidbit: Tower Records's offerings aren't limited to music. Be sure to check out the Categories/Other Categories listing. You'll find comedy, TV and radio nostalgia; sound tracks; sound effects; nature sounds; and book, spoken word, self-help, and instructional recordings.

Health & Vitamin Express

Shopping for health care products can be as confusing as a foreign language. Claims and counterclaims, lists of ingredients as long as an IRS "clarification"—I've sometimes left health care stores as bewildered as a hound with hay fever. But with AOL's help, it doesn't have to be that way (see Figure 15-8).

Figure 15-8: Health & Vitamin Express offers health care products—and consultation too!

The people at Health & Vitamin Express (keywords: **Health EXP**) understand that health care can be complex and confusing, so they offer what any good store should offer: a comprehensive product array, low prices, and good information that's available for free. You can leave a message online and return later for a reply, or call their toll-free hotline for an immediate consultation about your individual needs and the products that can best meet those needs. And once you've determined what you're looking for, chances are very good you'll find it at Health & Vitamin Express at 10 to 15 percent off regular prices.

Shoppers' Advantage

Speaking of browsing, approximately 3.1 million members (more than 1 percent of the United States population!) browse Shoppers' Advantage on a regular basis. This is a little like the shopping "clubs" that

have sprouted up nationwide: you pay a small annual membership fee and you're rewarded with a warehouse full of products, attractively priced, in stock, and ready for shipment. Shoppers' Advantage not only adds the convenience of online shopping (no crowds, no parking lots, no waiting), it guarantees the lowest prices anywhere, or it will refund the difference. Now that's a powerful package!

You can browse the store whether or not you're a member of Shoppers' Advantage—a significant advantage over local shopping clubs—and you can enroll online at any time. Look at the benefits Shoppers' Advantage offers:

- Discounts from 10 to 50 percent on all manufacturers' list prices.

- More than 250,000 name-brand products, all in a searchable online database. If a product you're looking for is not on the database, you can contact the Product Research team, and they will try to get it for you.

- Automatic two-year free warranty extension. Even if there is only a three- or six-month manufacturer's warranty, the folks at Shoppers' Advantage will extend the warranty on any product purchased through them to two years, at no cost.

- Merchandise from name-brand manufacturers, including Panasonic, GE, JVC, Nikon, Sony, Pioneer, AT&T, Nintendo, Whirlpool, Quasar, Jordache, Hoover, Pentax, Timex, Memorex, Rayban, Radio Shack, Pierre Cardin, Singer, and Magnavox—an all-star roster of manufacturers.

- The Department Store (click the Shop Our Entire Store button), where browsing—rather than searching—is the order of the day, and the Best Buys section, where the staff posts their best bargains. If you want to compare prices and features for yourself, Shoppers' Advantage can compare as many as 50 similar items at the same time and display the results for your consideration.

- Guaranteed lowest price. If, within 30 days of buying something through Shoppers' Advantage, you find the same piece of merchandise being sold for a lower price by an authorized dealer, send the staff at Shoppers' Advantage a copy of the ad, and they will send you the difference.

A money-back membership guarantee. If you are not fully satisfied with Shoppers' Advantage, all you need to do is call its toll-free number to cancel your membership. Your current membership fee will be refunded in full.

New Toys

Searching the Shoppers' Advantage database the other day, I discovered the Sony compact disc player described in Figure 15-9.

Figure 15-9: The CD player I've been shopping for, at a $150 savings!

```
5-CD Carousel
SONY   CDPC745
  List Price:       $    480.00  Tax:          $       .00
  Your Price:       $    321.60  Shipping:     $     10.95
  Your Savings:     $    158.40
  Total Cost:       $    332.55

Product Description:
SONY 5 disc front loading carousel CD player. Features
play 1/exchange 4, 4 output hybrid pulse converter, 5
DSP soundfield modes, variable line output, digital
servo control, 5 key direct access disc selection  20
track music calendar, 6 repeat/6 play modes, optical
digital output, 170 disc music clip classification
system, headphone jack w/ volume control, time, program,
link edit, edit navigation, 170 disc custom file system
for memo, delete, level & DSP, 3 mode music scan,
variable manual fader and remote commander.

Shipping Options
   Type    Freight  Handling  Min / Max Del Days
   STD  $  10.95  $    .00        21/28
```

My old single-disc player is as ancient (and worn) as a crank telephone. With a five-disc changer, I could jockey the hits like Wolfman Jack or conduct an evening of symphony like George Szell. And if I buy it at Shopper's Advantage, I'll save 30 percent in the process!

Classifieds Online

This wouldn't be a fully operative communications medium without classified ads, and AOL has them—at no extra charge. AOL's Classifieds feature all the product categories you'd expect in any large newspaper, with no paper waste and an ease of accessibility that no newspaper could hope to match (see Figure 15-10). Just select Classifieds Online from the main Marketplace screen, or use the key-word: **Classifieds**.

Figure 15-10: Classifieds Online, where you can buy and sell computers and components, advertise your professional services, search the job postings, and take advantage of business opportunities—all without extra charges.

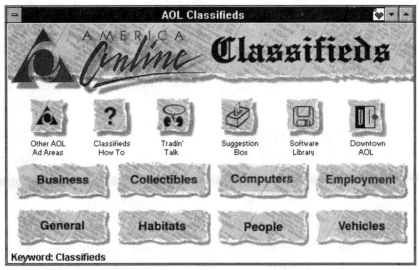

Classifieds Online offers, among other things, a library that adds unique value to the classifieds: ZIP Code and area code directories; UPS, FedEx, and U.S. Mail rate charts; a UPS manifest printing program; and the complete American Computer Exchange used-computer pricing guide.

The Hard Sell

Browsing the Classifieds Online library the other day, I came across the following excerpt from Direct-Marketing Firepower, an intriguing book by Jonathan Mizel. He's describing his friend Joe, who placed an ad on a local bulletin board system—a similar situation (though much more parochial) to AOL's Classifieds Online:

"So he decided this local BBS would be just the place to advertise it (an unneeded hard disk) since they allowed free classifieds for computer items. Joe placed the ad for this item on a Monday. I think he said he was selling it for $120.00. Guess how many responses Joe got by Wednesday. Go on, guess.

"Within 48 hours, Joe had received 220 responses to his little classified ad on a system that was only used by San Francisco technical computer people. The total number of people who are on the system is probably fewer than 5,000. He was freaked out, even mad, because people kept e-mailing him and calling him to get this damn piece of equipment (which, by the way, sold immediately)...

"Too bad old Joe didn't have 220 hard drives!"

Joe was advertising on a system with fewer than 5,000 members. America Online has more than 3 million. When I last checked, more than 211,000 classifieds were running, with more coming in every day. There's a portentious potential here.

And it's all free. All you pay is your regular AOL connect fee.

atOnce Software

Only a few years ago, an A-to-Z list of computer software would have been short and missing more than a few letters of the alphabet. Today that's all changed, and perusing software titles and capabilities is more like confronting the inventory of an entire library. Wouldn't it be nice if—like the library's catalogue system—there was a place where a comprehensive, detailed list of software information could be found?

Such a place does exist, and you need look no further than AOL's atOnce Software (see Figure 15-11). Here you'll find thousands of software titles nestled in a database that's much easier to explore and contains much more information than your local library's book catalogue. If you're looking for software, or information on software, this is a great place to start. Just use the keyword: **atOnce**.

Figure 15-11: Looking for software information? atOnce Software is the place to start.

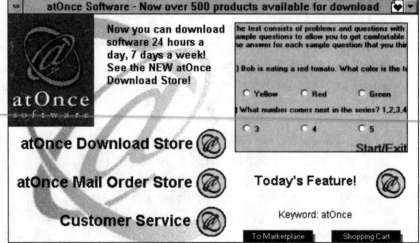

KidSoft Super Store

The KidSoft Super Store is the "kids" version of the atOnce Mail Order Store: a source for prescreened quality software just for children, with special emphasis on learning software (see Figure 15-12). You'll find software focusing on reading, math, spelling, music, creativity/art, geography, reference, and much more, featuring well-known names such as Mario, Putt-Putt, the Science Sleuths, Dr. Seuss, the Lion King, and Carmen Sandiego. And to make things easy as pie, you can search by age grouping, software title, or category to find descriptions and sample screens. You can get there with the keywords: **KidSoft Store**.

Figure 15-12: The KidSoft SuperStore: a software store just for kids.

Omaha Steaks International

Even though rampant change is a given in the online medium, some online discoveries tend to surprise more than others, such as food service businesses in general and Omaha Steaks in particular (see Figure 15-13). Omaha Steaks International's reputation as a premium purveyor of steaks, meats, and other gourmet foods spans 75 years, 8 states, and 28 locations, with its mail order branch claiming an astonishing 44-year history. So at second glance, Omaha Steaks's move to the online arena is a completely natural progression.

Figure 15-13:
From Omaha,
Nebraska, and the
heart of cattle
country direct to
your door, Omaha
Steaks's internation-
ally recognized
meats, seafood,
and desserts are
available now on
AOL!

Omaha Steaks's mission is the delivery of the very best beef, poultry, pork, veal, lamb, seafood, and desserts to your Omaha Steaks table, or to your front door. If your Epicurean interests are creative, you'll also find proven-delicious recipes from the nation's heartland. And don't forget to check out Omaha Steaks's Chocolate Ecstasy Cake and triple-trimmed filet mignons in the Specialties area. Are you hungry now? Just use the keyword: **Steaks**.

Downtown AOL

Are you shopping for something special or out of the ordinary, or maybe looking for a hard-to-find service? Or are you thinking about establishing an online presence for your business? Then be sure to explore Downtown AOL, AOL's fast-growing virtual community of shops and services (see Figure 15-14).

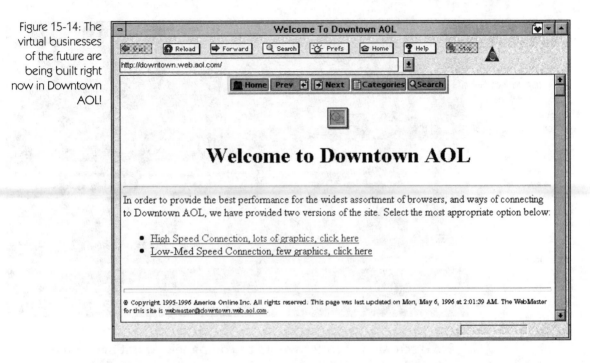

Downtown AOL is your gateway to the people, products, networks, businesses, and services that are rushing to establish an economic structure on one of the most vibrant of all online media, the World Wide Web. Customers can use AOL's easy-to-use Web software to quickly and efficiently search for that hard-to-find product or service. Businesses can take advantage of easily updated product descriptions and additions, full-color graphics, and focused links to consumer groups. And everyone benefits! Take an electronic stroll to city-center by typing the keywords: **Downtown AOL**.

Caffè Starbucks

After all this talk of shopping, you're probably ready for a good cup of coffee, right? Then you should not be surprised to find that Starbucks, one of the premier suppliers of gourmet coffees, is as close as AOL and the keyword: **Starbucks**. Being a top coffee contender is no mean feat in the northwest, where a request for a "double-skinny-mocha-decaf" is received with utter aplomb. And now you can join in the coffee revolution no matter where you live (see Figure 15-15).

Figure 15-15:
Coffee advice,
coffee philosophy,
coffee cups, even
regular coffee
deliveries—
Starbucks is your
one-stop coffee
resource!

No discussion of coffee would be complete without mention of the myriad delectables that can transform a superior coffee break into an extraordinary culinary experience. Just click the Sweets and Treats button and unleash your imagination.

Moving On

I've only scratched the surface of the Marketplace. You can select and purchase your groceries and pharmacy products here, and even have them delivered to your door. You can buy discounted books at the Online Bookstore. You can sell your old adding machine in the Classifieds, and you can buy a new one at OfficeMax. Of course, you don't really need an adding machine because you have a computer, but isn't it time for a new one? Computer Express has not only computers but components and software as well.

You've had a glimpse of Marketplace in the present and, young as it is, I'm sure you've also envisioned its future as well—bright and bristling with potential. But now it's time for some intangible rewards. This book's most popular chapter follows, and if you've read this far, you deserve the pot at the end of the rainbow. It's time for the Ten Best: the ten best tips, the ten best downloads, the ten best ways to meet people online—they're all available at the turn of the page.

Ten Best

When I was a boy, I believed that if I remained quiet and cooperative all day and all night Christmas Eve, Santa would be especially generous to me. For one 24-hour period every year, I was a model child. I did everything that was asked of me, exactly as requested. I must have been right: nowadays I receive paperweights and paisley ties on Christmas mornings rather than the electric trains and red wagons I received back in the days of deference.

Have you been naughty or nice? You haven't turned to this chapter first, have you? This chapter is a reward for faithful readers only. This is my Ten Best chapter, and I award it only to those who have read all of the preceding 15 chapters. If that's you, read on. . . .

Ten Best Tips

As long as we're discussing honor and privilege, let's begin with my list of the Ten Best Tips for using AOL. Most of these tips are intended to save you time online (so you save money); all of them will make your online activities more efficient and effective; and not a one of them is dishonorable.

1. *Read this book.*

   If you're reading this paragraph in spite of my admonition, at least plan to read the rest of the book eventually—the sooner the better. It's full of insights and techniques—not only mine but those of scores of other members as well. You don't have to be online to use this book. Take it on your next blue-water cruise: people will think you're very erudite, urbane, and jocose.

2. *Use keywords and keyboard shortcuts.*

This tip is so important that I've included a lengthy appendix—
Appendix B—listing all of AOL's keywords. Keywords can save
you tons of time. Don't worry about committing them all to
memory, just memorize those you use often. (Your most frequently
used keywords should be added to your Go To menu, which is
explained in Chapter 9, "Boards & Forums.") Keywords take you
to locations that normally require navigating menus within menus
within menus, and they do it in less than a second. To enter a
keyword, press Ctrl+K. To search AOL's list of keywords, press
Ctrl+K, provide an approximation of what you're looking for, then
click the Search button.

America Online's keyboard shortcuts are the same or so close to
the ones you use in Windows that only a few require additional
thought. A few are unique, and they're worth memorizing: Ctrl+K
to enter a keyword, Ctrl+M to compose new mail, Ctrl+F to find a
member, file, or place, Ctrl+I to send an Instant Message—that's
only four. It won't take long to learn them.

3. *Use Escape and hoodwink the hourglass.*

With all this talk about Control-key combinations, you may forget
the Escape key. Don't. Escape disconnects sluggish sign-ons;
cancels printing; and halts long articles and lists as you receive
them online. That's important: sometimes you'll double-click an
article icon only to find that you got yourself into a four-minute
feed that you don't want to read after all. No problem: press Esc.
The same goes for lists: Esc stops my list of Mail You Have Read,
for example, which contains hundreds of entries.

I don't want to give the wrong impression here: the Esc key does
not intervene in situations that produce the hourglass cursor. The
hourglass usually means that your computer is waiting for something from AOL's host computers, and if the system is sluggish or
for some reason you've become disconnected, the hourglass cursor
can become quite annoying. This leads us to our next topic of
discussion: how to circumvent the hourglass cursor. I'll describe
two methods below.

Whenever you see the hourglass cursor, try using it to manipulate various controls on the screen. This is especially convenient
when you want to manipulate scroll bars and menu bars. When

you're receiving a long list of items, you can start scrolling through that list without having to wait for the hourglass to go away. All you have to do is explore a bit: move that hourglass around, click your mouse, and watch what happens.

If manipulating screen controls isn't what you want to do, or if nothing happens when you try, it's time to get drastic. The solution? Press Ctrl+Esc. This will invoke the Windows Task Manager. When it appears, click once on the "America Online" listing, then click the End Task button. Unless things are terribly wrong, you'll soon see AOL's sign-off confirmation dialog box, the one that asks if you're sure you want to sign off. Click the No button.

If all goes well—it doesn't always—you will be rid of the hourglass, ready for more adventure. Be careful: Windows might intervene within a few seconds, claiming that AOL is "not responding." Be sure to click the Cancel button if you get this message, or you'll be signed off.

4. *Use FlashSessions, and read and compose mail offline.*
The Compose Mail command (Mail menu) works offline as well as on. You can compose all your mail offline while the clock's not running, perfecting every phrase. You can even attach files while you're composing mail offline. When you have finished composing a piece of mail, click the Send Later button at the left of the new mail (Untitled) window. America Online will store it (and any other mail you compose) on your disk for transmission either later when you're online (choose Read Outgoing FlashMail from the Mail menu, then click the Send All button) or more likely via a FlashSession(discussed in Chapter 6).

Likewise, resist the urge to read new mail online. Rather, wait until you've finished all your other online activity, then choose Activate FlashSession Now from the Mail menu. America Online will download all your incoming mail, then sign off. Once you're offline, choose Read Incoming FlashMail from the Mail menu and read your mail at your own pace.

5. *Use Help.*
Read the sidebar on page 24 and follow the tips there, in the order in which they appear.

6. *Keep track of your time and money.*
It's easy to lose track of time and money when you're online, but no one—neither you nor AOL—benefits from unexpected charges when the bill arrives. You can always check your current (and previous) month's bill by using the keyword: **Billing** (which is free), and the keyword: **Clock** tells you how long you've been online during any particular session. (It also tells you the current time, accurate to within a second or so.)

7. *Log your sessions and save to disk.*
Don't spend time reading material online that can just as easily be saved and read later while you're offline. Logging is a mechanism that allows you to capture all the text you encounter online without stopping to read it, whether it's text from the encyclopedia, messages on a board, or a discussion in a conference room. Any text that appears on your screen will be saved to a log if you open one before you start your online journey. (See Chapter 10, "Staying Informed," for a discussion of logging procedures.)

Logging is particularly valuable for new members. Start a log, sign on, and visit a few areas, then sign off. Once you're offline, review the log (use the Open command under the File menu to open logs). You'll learn a lot about AOL when you can review an online session at your leisure.

Of course, it's not easy to remember to open a log for each session, and sometimes you don't know you're going to run across something you want to save until you're there. Fortunately, all text received on AOL can be saved onto your hard drive for later review offline. Simply go to the File menu and select Save. This causes all the text in the article or message in the frontmost window on your screen to be transferred to any disk drive you specify, where it is saved as a plain text file that you can read using AOL or the word processor of your choice. Note that it isn't necessary for you to scroll through the entire article in order to save it. Even though you haven't seen the entire text of the article, your computer has, and everything is saved when you issue the Save command.

8. *Multitask and download when system activity is minimal.*
Your AOL software can download in the background while you're reading mail, working on a spreadsheet or using your word processor. If you start a long download—even if it's via a FlashSession—

and you have something else to do with your PC, do it. You can activate another application (use the Program Manager or the File Manager), or do most anything with the AOL software itself: visit a forum, read mail, or chat. Do not, however, engage in any activity that involves *another* download while one's already under way. Even if the AOL software lets you do it, it's uneconomical—it'll slow things down.

Here's another downloading tip: the AOL system—AOL's mainframes and the long-distance carrier in your local area—gets very busy in the evenings and on weekends. Your time on the system is allocated in slices, and these time slices get smaller as the system becomes more active. Your computer spends more of its time waiting in line for data when these time slices get small, yet the clock keeps running regardless.

Whenever you're planning a long download—say, anything over 10 minutes—plan it for the time of day when the system is least active. Typically, that's the morning: the earlier the better. Read about FlashSessions and the Download Manager in Chapter 6, and use both of them to reduce your download time.

9. *Look for More buttons.*
Lots of AOL windows include buttons or folders marked More. Don't overlook them. America Online doesn't tie up your system feeding you all 500 matching entries to a database search, for example. Rather, it offers the first 20, then waits to see if you want more. You might want to cancel at that moment, or you might want to see more. When the conditions are appropriate, AOL always offers the More option, but it's only useful if you choose to exercise it. America Online users who ignore the More buttons online never know what they're missing.

10. *Use the Find in Top Window command.*
The Find in Top Window command under the Edit menu allows you to specify text for the AOL client to find. While searching articles comes immediately to mind, this command is also handy for finding specific elements in long lists (in the File Search Results window, for example) and searching scrolling lists available in AOL's channels (for example, use the keyword: **Reference**, then find Dictionary in the List by Topic window). This command can save not only hours of reading but precious online time as well, by "reading" lists and scroll boxes for you.

Ten Best Downloads

This list is hardly objective and is most certainly in no particular order. These are just the shareware products I use, or readers use, most often. I've tested them all; they're all of the highest quality and well suited to their tasks.

To find any of the downloads mentioned, use the keywords: **File Search**, then specify the name of the file—excluding the version number (see the searching tips in Chapter 5, "Transferring Files")—as your search criteria. If you find more than one version of a particular program available, be sure to download the one with the highest version number, since it's the most recent release of that program.

1. *PKZIP and WinZip*

   PKZIP is offered as a commercial product, as shareware, and as an integral feature of your AOL software. PKZIP is a DOS-based product, however, so its commands are arcane and difficult to remember for the casual user. WinZip's interface is as easy to learn as they come. It's a Windows product and it's fully compatible with PKZIP files. One or both of these utilities should be on every Windows user's shelf, especially when you consider the minimal shareware fee. File compression is discussed in Chapter 5, "Transferring Files."

2. *WSCAN*

   This is the evaluation version of the popular virus-detection (and eradication) software from Chris McAfee and McAfee Associates. Virus-protection software is only as good as its most recent release—new viruses are hatched every day—and updates to WSCAN are posted on McAfee's own area on AOL.

   The latest release of WSCAN is fully integrated for Windows; it's not a Windows shell program. You can scan files on demand or set up configuration files for common uses. WSCAN detects, identifies, and disinfects known DOS computer viruses. It checks memory in both the system and data areas of disks for virus infections. If it finds a known virus, in most cases it will eliminate the virus and fully restore infected programs or system areas to normal operation. Use the keyword: **McAfee** for more information.

3. *PaintShop Pro*

Most of the really spectacular graphics available on AOL are in a format that your AOL software can open and display. Occasionally, however, you might run into one that chokes AOL's software or won't import into your word processing or desktop publishing program. For those occasions, you need a "Swiss Army knife" of a graphics program—one that opens anything (including .GIF, .JPG, .TIF, .BMP, and .PCX) and saves in formats that are useful to you. That program is PaintShop Pro, from JASC, Inc. PaintShop's new image-manipulation functions elevate it far above the average format conversion program. It's a great capture program for screen shots, but it's also one of the most expensive shareware packages available online. Use the keyword: **FileSearch**, then search with the criterion: Paint Shop.

4. *Makin' Waves*

Makin' Waves by Geoff Faulkner is a Windows sound conversion utility and .WAV file player. It converts the major sound formats: .VOCC, .SOU, and .SND to the .WAV format required by most sound-savvy Windows applications (including AOL). It also converts the sounds found on the Macintosh Music & Sound forum (keyword: **MMS**), and there are thousands of those. File search using the criterion: Faulkner.

You must have a sound card and speakers to make effective use of AOL's sounds.

5. *UUCODE*

UUCODE is Windows shareware that converts binary files (including graphics) to text files (and vice versa) through a process known as uuencoding. The conversion allows you to send and receive binary files via e-mail or Internet newsgroups (newsgroups make extensive use of uuencoded data).

Your AOL software will decode most uuencoded material found in newsgroups, but if you want to post uuencoded files yourself, you'll have to use a third-party program, and UUCODE is one of the best. Getting the hang of uuencoding takes a while (as a test, send some uuencoded mail to yourself first), but it's just about the only solution to a chronic Internet imperfection. File search: UUCODE.

6. *WAOL Express*

Bill Pytlovany is not only a skilled Windows programmer, he's also one of the most personable people you'll ever meet online. He has written Windows software for a number of clients, including AOL itself.

Thus, when I discovered Whale Express online (and saw that Bill was its programmer), I eagerly downloaded it.

Whale Express is a Windows-based scripting language designed specifically for America Online. Using Whale Express you can write "scripts" (macros) that run your WAOL (Windows AOL— pronounced "whale" by Everyone Who Matters) software automatically and unattended. Whale Express offers a "NewScreenName" command that allows you to change screen names automatically; scripts can call other scripts; and the help file serves as a complete reference to the utility. File search: Whale Express.

7. *Smileys*

There are lots of lists of smileys posted online. Use the keyword: **FileSearch**, then search with the criterion: Smileys. You'll find SMILEY.TXT, a venerable introduction to smiley etiquette; and you'll find SMILEYS.ZIP, a comprehensive (nearly 100k) smiley anthology with a frivolous little DOS application that displays a smiley and its meaning each time you enter SMILEY at the DOS prompt. The application is a little archaic in the Windows context, but it *is* something you can use the DOS prompt for. ;-)

8. *WinSpell*

This is a spell-checking addition that's ideal for WAOL users. It checks each word against its internal dictionary as you type, alerting you to spelling errors as they're made (a feature that can be turned off, if you can't stand the nagging). It works well with Windows AOL, checking your mail and message-board postings before you commit them to the scrutiny of the online proletariat.

9. *Dazzle*

I suppose you could call Dazzle a screen-saver, but who needs another screen-saver when Windows comes with one of its own?

I was skeptical. Dazzle isn't a Windows program—you have to stoop to DOS to use it—and it's not a screen-saver (actually, it is— if you send in your shareware fee, otherwise it's a stand-alone program), so why bother?

Because it's so good! Dazzle can calm fierce beasts, smooth turbulent waters, and lift tormented spirits. It's better than LSD (and perfectly legal). You've gotta see this thing. There are a lot of programs with Dazzle in their names. To be sure you get the one I'm talking about, file search with the criterion: Shiflett. J.R. Shiflett is the name of the person who wrote the program.

10. *GNNPress*

It used to be that to build a Web site, you had to learn what terms like HTML, URL, ISMAP, FTP, CGI, PERL, and C meant. No longer. You have your very own Web site already (see the discussion of My Place in Chapter 2), and GNNPress is a free Web page "authoring" tool that anyone can use.

Almost everything is done via menus. All you have to do is type the text and decide where your graphics (or sounds or videos) will appear. GNNPress creates the HyperText Markup Language code for you, which you can then upload to AOL and publish on the Web. GNNPress is so easy to use that you probably won't need a manual. (If you do, one's available—though it's not free.)

To find out about GNNPress, use the keyword: **NaviPress**. Note that this is a *keyword,* not a file search criterion.

Ten Most Frequently Asked Questions of Customer Relations

No one knows the nature of the questions asked of AOL's Customer Relations Department better than the Customer Relations Department staff itself, thus I went to them for this section of the book. I was aptly rewarded with the list below. Okay, it's more than ten, but who can fault a Customer Relations Department that offers more than it's asked for?

Huge thanks go to Steve Brannon, who prepared this material.

1. *I just installed AOL. Where do I begin? How do I get help?*
   Although not the question most often asked of member services, "How do I get help?" is likely the most often asked question by our members. When they run into a problem, who to call, how to get online information, etc. The write-up of "A methodical approach" to getting help in your book (see page 24) addresses this topic. One other important question on this topic, "What are the

minimum/recommended system requirements?" Minimum system requirements for AOL for Windows: Windows 3.1 or higher; 4MB of real memory (8MB is recommended if you intend to use the Web browser); 3MB of hard disk space; a 386 or better processor; Hayes or Hayes-compatible modem; and a standard phone line.

2. *How do I obtain the latest access number information for AOL?*
America Online is constantly adding new access numbers and new access methods. To discover the latest methods and phone numbers for accessing America Online, use the keyword: **Access**. You will discover information on the AOLNet 800 number, contacting AOL from foreign countries using AOLGlobalnet, how to request a local access phone number, and answers to the most often asked questions about access to AOL.

3. *Can I get information about my account while online?*
To obtain information on charges for using America Online, use the keyword: **Billing**. You can modify your address information, see a summary of your current bill, request a detailed bill, and access the list of frequently asked questions for the billing staff.

4. *I've just witnessed offensive behavior in a chat room; is there someone I can contact?*
We want the America Online community to be a friendly and safe place for our members to visit. Therefore, we enforce the AOL Terms of Service, and take appropriate action when violations are reported to us.

If you witness chat in a public chat room that violates AOL's Terms of Service, you may contact an AOL Service Guide by using the keyword: **GuidePager**. You may also contact AOL's Terms of Service Staff about any violation by using the "Write to the Community Action Team" icon located in the Terms of Service area (keyword: **TOS**).

Also, *never reveal your password to anyone!* No one from America Online will *ever* ask you for your password, as a means of identification, as a way to correct a "problem" with your account, or for *any* other purpose.

Anyone who knows your screen name and password can sign on with your account, and leave you to pay the bill! America Online is very much like a city with millions of residents (members). You wouldn't give your house keys to a stranger you met in a big city, and you shouldn't give your password, or any other account information, to people you meet online.

5. *Where can I find <my favorite subject> online?*
   Lots of questions are along the line of "Is AARP online?" and "I heard that *Consumer Reports* is on AOL—how do I find it?"
   One great way to find if an area you are interested in is on AOL is to use the "Where on AOL do I find. . ." message board in the Members Helping Members section of AOL. This message board can by found by entering the keyword: **MHM;** continue on any informative panels until you reach the Members Helping Members message boards. Double-click on the "Where on *AOL* do I find. . ." board. Browse for existing questions, or post your own.
   And don't forget the Find button on the toolbar!

6. *I use the menus and the screen panels to move from area to area. Is there a faster way?*
   Yes there is: use keywords. In addition, you can obtain a list of the latest keywords. Use the keyword: **Keywords**, of course.
   Use the keyword: **New** to discover the latest additions to America Online. By double-clicking one of the items in the NEW list, you'll be taken directly to that new service. If a keyword is available for the new area, it will be displayed on the lower portion of the panel. You can also access the NEW feature by clicking the What's Hot icon on the toolbar at the top of the screen.

7. *How can I determine if my friend has an AOL account? Is he logged on now?*
   For confidentiality reasons, America Online cannot give out personal account information about other members.
   However, many members create a Member Profile containing information such as their name, hobbies, and interests. To check a member's profile, select Get a Member's Profile from the Members menu. If you're not sure of the spelling of their screen name, or if you wish to search by last name or profile, go to the keywords: **Member Directory.**
   You can use AOL's Buddy List feature to receive notification whenever your friends log on. Buddy lists are discussed in Chapter 8.

8. *I know that AOL provides access to the Internet and the World Wide Web. How can I learn how to use them?*
Use the keyword: **AnswerMan** and explore what's offered there. If you still have a question after your review of AnswerMan, use the keyword: **Internet**, then post your question on one of the message boards there. The CyberJockeys who staff those boards are especially helpful.

9. *My Web browser has slowed considerably. What can I do to speed it up?*
AOL's browser comes with a "cache." This means that pages you use frequently are stored on your hard disk for fast reloading when you return to them during the same Web session. When the cache fills up, performance can slow down.

To purge your cache, go to the Members menu and select Preferences. Click WWW, then click Advanced, and finally press the Purge Cache button in the Advanced WWW Preferences window.

To increase the size of the cache so that more data can be saved, click on the up arrow by the "Maximum disk space to be used for cache" box in the Advanced WWW Preferences window, and increase the number of megabytes allocated to your cache. Your cache size (in megabytes) must be a whole number.

10. *What should I know about upgrading and maintaining my AOL software?*
Member *x* has AOL 2.5 and obtains the upgrades for 3.0. Now what? (Install it.) Will my preferences, favorite places, and Personal Filing Cabinet be retained? (Yes.) Will the old copy of AOL be deleted? (No.)

Many members don't understand that the upgrade files for AOL 3.0 are not automatically installed. The member must run the setup.exe program (the downloaded upgrade file). Once installed, the member must next start the new version of AOL and register their existing master screen name and password. Finally, the member should search their hard disk and consider erasing any old versions of AOL (we've heard from people who have many, many old copies of AOL on their machine).

11. *I love using e-mail, and I'd like to expand my use. How can I find out more?*

Questions that we get routinely are as follows:

- How can I determine if a friend has an e-mail address?

- How do I establish subaccounts?

- A friend of mine has an Internet address—how do I send mail to it?

- I have a friend on the Internet—what address should I give them so that they can send me mail?

- How do I attach a file to my mail?

- What is the least expensive way to send and receive e-mail?

- Can I send mail to several people at once?

- Can I send a copy of my mail without everyone else knowing I sent it?

- I just sent e-mail, can I get it back before the other person reads it?

- If I have to leave while writing a letter, can I save what I've typed and continue later?

- I sent mail yesterday, now I'd like to send the same mail to someone else. Do I have to type it all over again?

- Can I prevent my mail from being deleted after a few days?

- Someone sent me an "attached" file. What do I do with it?

Most of these questions are answered at keywords: **Mail Center** or keywords: **Mail Gateway**. If you don't see the answer you need at these two keywords, use the keyword: **Questions** and take it from there.

Ten Best Ways to Make Friends Online

Perhaps above all, AOL is a community. If you're not a part of it, you're missing a wealth of opportunity. Like any community, you're ahead of the game if you know how to break into it. Here's how:

1. *Visit the New Members Lounge.*
   If you're new to AOL, you'll find comfort in numbers in the New Members Lounge. From the Welcome Screen, click the People Connection button on the toolbar, then click the List Rooms button, then select New Members Lounge from the Public Rooms list. (Another tip: Remember that there can be as many as 200 rooms open—use the Find in Top Window option from the Edit menu, and search for "New" to find the New Members Lounge quickly.)

2. *Find a favorite room and hang out there.*
   Chapter 8 describes the different kinds of chat rooms that are available online. Look that chapter over, find a room that interests you, and visit it when it's available. You might also find a favorite room by visiting any of AOL's forums (forums are described in Chapter 9).

3. *Post your profile.*
   Don't neglect to post your profile. Use the keyword: **Profile**, or choose Edit Your Online Profile from the Members menu. Talk about yourself. Make your personality irresistible. People in chat rooms often peek at other occupants' profiles, and if you haven't posted a profile, you're a persona non grata.

4. *Use Personal Publisher to post a Web page.*
   Personal Publisher is the home of the AOL membership's home pages. Home pages incorporate text and graphics—and even sound and video. In less than a year they've become the electronic version of calling cards, and everyone has fun with them. Personal Publisher pages are searchable and available to any AOL member.
   There's lots of online help available, plus the Personal Publisher application itself at keywords: **Personal Publisher**.

5. *Use an effective screen name.*
   You can use the Edit Screen Names command under the Members menu to add a screen name to your account if the one you're using now isn't very effective in a social situation. People have a hard

time relating to a screen name like "Tlich6734," but many find "MajorTom" worthy of notice. If nothing else, include your first name or your nickname in your screen name so people can address you as the friend you want to be.

6. *Search the membership for others with similar interests.*
   Use the keyword: **Directory** to search the Member Directory for others with interests similar to yours. Read their profiles and send them e-mail. You'll be surprised at the number who reply.

7. *Read messages and reply.*
   Find a forum that interests you (see Chapter 9, "Boards & Forums"), go to its message boards, and start reading messages. Eventually, you'll see some that provoke a response. Go ahead: post your comment. It gives you a great sense of purpose the next time you sign on: you'll scramble to that message board to see if anyone responded to your posting.

8. *Post a message soliciting replies.*
   Members Helping Members (keyword: **MHM**; see Chapter 2, "The Abecedarium") is a great place for message posting, but any forum will do. Post a message asking for help or an opinion. People love to help, and everyone has an opinion.

9. *Read newsgroups and reply.*
   This is similar to item 7. Newsgroups (discussed in Chapter 4, "Using the Internet") are similar to forums, only they're not limited to the AOL membership. Anyone with Internet access to newsgroups—tens of millions of people in hundreds of countries— can participate, and most do. I've made friends as far away as Australia this way.

10. *Download a file posted by another member and reply.*
    This goes especially for fonts and graphics. Download a few files (downloading is discussed in Chapter 5, "Transferring Files") and reply to the originator via e-mail. In selecting the graphics for this book, I sent e-mail to dozens of online artists, and every one of them replied within a day or two—most with two or three pages of enthusiastic banter.

Ten Best Greenhouse Projects

I'm starting to feel like an online old-timer. A sea dog. Savant. Guru, even. This is my twelfth year online, my fifth year at AOL. I receive scores of tips from readers every day. For four months I was Forum Leader of one of AOL's largest departments—a job from which I had to resign in order to return to my Tour Guide activities.

Perhaps the most significant change I've witnessed has occurred in the past 18 months: commercialism in the online industry. My thesaurus lists mostly disreputable synonyms for the word "commercialism": barbarism, vulgarism, vandalism, philistinism, even artlessness. That's awfully judgmental and it's not what I'm talking about. I'm talking about a commercial online medium similar to the commercial broadcast medium: logos for Chevrolet and Coke, ads for pain relievers, even infomercials. Believe me, it's coming, and it's coming quickly.

As a commercial vehicle, this medium is in its infancy. No one knows exactly how to make effective commercial use of it. What the medium needs is a place where information-age entrepreneurs (infopreneurs?) can experiment with strategies, ideas, and technologies. A place to make mistakes and find solutions. A place to break the rules.

That place exists. It's at AOL, and it's called the *Greenhouse* (keyword: **Greenhouse**). If you want a peek at the future, this is the place to look. To see them all, use the keyword: **Greenhouse**. To see my favorite Greenhouse projects, read on.

1. *The Motley Fool* (keyword: **Motley Fool**) offers investment tips for novices and experts, with an irreverent spin.

2. *Follywood* (keyword: **Follywood**) offers movie ratings by AOL members, and an ongoing screenplay written by AOL members.

3. *iGOLF* (keyword: **iGOLF**) features timely coverage of golfing events worldwide, interactive gold games, and columns by golfing celebrities.

4. *Better Health and Medical Forum* (keyword: **Better Health**) is a trove of newsworthy health issues, health information updates, and support groups.

5. *NetNoir* (keyword: **NetNoir**) is the community room for the Afrocentric fellowship. Music, sports, and business information abounds.

6. *eGG* (keyword: **eGG**) is a haven for gastronomes, including cook-book reviews, meal planning guides and special appearances by cooking celebrities.

7. *Health Zone* (keyword: **HealthZone**) offers access to fitness and nutrition experts, diets and fitness support groups, and appearances by celebrity athletes.

8. *Hecklers Online* (keyword: **Hecklers**) offers absolutely nothing of socially redeeming value. It goes the extra mile to be politically incorrect. It's the Monty Python of the online community. If you refuse to be silenced by gatekeepers of monotonous information, heckle here.

9. *The Sixty-Second Novelist* (keyword: **Sixty**) is so cool, *WIRED* magazine finished preparing an article about it for their November 1995 issue before it had even gone online! I can't explain it in the space allotted here, you simply have to check it out for yourself.

10. *PicturePlace* (keywords: **Picture Place**) makes it fast, easy, and inexpensive to get your pictures scanned. You send the picture (or negative), it's scanned, put in a private area online for you to download, and the original is sent back to you. There are no floppy disks to wait for or additional software required to use your pictures.

Ten Best Tips From the Remote Staff

A visit to AOL's Vienna, Virginia, headquarters is impressive enough: two four-story buildings are packed with staff offices (there must be hundreds of them). And Vienna isn't AOL's only location any longer: there are many others, scattered all over the country.

As is often the case, however, it's what you *can't* see that's most impressive. Thousands of people are employed as *remote staff* at AOL: they work from their homes for the most part, managing forums and libraries, answering member mail, and more. I'm sure someone keeps track of all of these people—but I don't, thus my guess as to their number is a wild one at best. I'll bet there are over five thousand.

Working with members day in and day out, the remote staff is probably the most knowledgeable group of AOL users around, so it only makes sense that I would poll them for their ten best tips. In fact, I received hundreds of tips from the staff. The process of whittling them down to ten was painful. Someday I should write another book.

Below are their tips, along with their screen names. My thanks to each and every one of the remote staffers who participated.

1. *PCA Walt: Know the difference between keywords and search words.*
   I hear from members all of the time, and one of the most common areas of confusion is the difference between keywords and searching criteria.

   A *keyword* is a shortcut to a frequently visited area on AOL. To use a keyword, press Ctrl+K, then type in the keyword. There's a list of them in Appendix B of this book.

   Search criteria are words you use to find a specific file in AOL's download libraries. Let's say you're looking for WinZip. You wouldn't use WinZip as a keyword: it's not an area, it's a file. Instead, you would use the keyword: **File Search**—which puts you in the File Search area on AOL—then use the criterion: WinZip to find the file.

2. *CJ Daye: Use World Wide Web addresses as keywords.*
   Having a home page on the World Wide Web is tantamount to success in the marketplace, at least if television and print advertising are to be believed. World Wide Web addresses (*URLs*, or *Uniform Resource Locators*) appear on half the print and television ads published today, it seems, with more appearing every day.

   So what do you do if "http://www.hormel.com" appears in a Spam ad in *Bon Appetit*? It's easy: fire up AOL and sign on, then press Ctrl+K (for keyword) and enter the URL you saw *as a keyword*. That's all there is to it. It's even easier if someone sends you a URL via e-mail. While you're still online, copy the URL, press Ctrl+K, then paste the URL into the Keyword window. Click the Go button and you're there!

   You have to be signed on to use this tip, and the URL must begin with "http://" (which is often left out of advertising plugs) in order to work.

3. *CJ Jon: Search intelligently*

When searching for information on a particular topic, use the wide range of searching resources AOL has to offer. Start your search locally, then branch out to the Internet. Begin by using the Find button on the toolbar. For more detail, the keyword: **Services** allows you to conduct a topical search on areas available on AOL. You might also want to look at keyword: **Reference** for encyclopedias, dictionaries, and so forth. You can also do a keyword search at the keyword box by clicking on the Search button there.

If the resource you're after is on the Internet, use the keyword: **Webcrawler** and search there. You might also try using the keyword: **http://www.yahoo.com/** to use the Yahoo Web search engine.

4. *PC Tom: Want to search by filename? All I can recommend is* just don't do that*!!!*

Using a filename as a criterion for searching is the absolute worst way to conduct a search. Even though filenames are part of the search algorithm, unless you are absolutely sure of the filename for the last version of the program, this doesn't give you a reliable search. When version numbers change, so does the filename.

Instead, search less specifically. If you're searching for WinZip, try using "file compression" or "archive" as search criteria. The whole idea is to avoid version numbers (which change) and specific product names (which are often obtuse: is it "WinZip" or "Win Zip"?)

5. *CJ Sarah: To leave the free area, just pull down your Go To menu and select "Exit Free Area."*

Members are often caught behind AOL's "free curtain" where keywords don't work, mail can't be sent, and the Internet is off limits. Sure, the clock's not running, but what if you want to get back at it? I've had some people tell me that they turn off their modems to get out of free areas! Sarah's advice is the best there is.

6. *Host CWC: Turn off graphics in online documents.*

Online graphics can slow your AOL sessions to a crawl. Turning them off won't keep you from getting new artwork for a new *area* you try to access, but it will keep you from having to sit and wait if there is a picture connected to a particular *article* you are trying to access. In place of the picture, there's a "Get Graphic" button instead.

To turn off online graphics, pull down the Members menu, choose Personal Choices, then choose Multimedia Preferences.

This tip applies to the World Wide Web as well. Even with a fast modem, the Web is at best lethargic. To pump a little adrenaline into the Web's bloodstream, turn off its graphics. The Preferences button—which leads you to the graphics/no graphics option—is in plain view in the Web browser's window. If you encounter a page with graphics you want to see, turn the graphics preference back on, then click the Reload button.

7. *Teacher cc: Use the keyword:* **Shorthands** *to find out ways to help you communicate with more than just typed text.*
   Don't know what "ROTFLOL" means? Want to soften what might be interpreted as harsh criticism when it's not really meant that way? In speech, we use vocal intonations and facial expressions, but vocal intonations and facial expressions aren't available via the online medium, thus emotional "shorthands" (or *emoticons*) have been developed. To get a listing of them all, use the keyword: **Shorthands**.

8. *BillP: Use add-ons.*
   Many members aren't aware that their AOL software is explicitly designed to accept *add-on* applications. AOL programmers left numerous "hooks" for third-party programmers to utilize in designing software that becomes a part of—adds on to—the AOL client software. Add-ons expand your software, allowing it to perform tasks that serve a specific need.

   There are hundreds of add-ons available online. Many of them automate e-mail frequent operations for heavy e-mail users, but there are others that check your spelling, switch screen names, automate common chat responses, monitor your billing, download message board messages for offline reading and responding, and improve AOL's Address Book.

   You can see a listing of all of the available AOL add-on software by using the keyword: **File Search**, then searching with the criteria: AOL add-ons.

9. *Phylwriter: Learn about ASCII text!*

ACSII text (or just plain *text*) allows everyone on all platforms to read your work. If you write (and save) messages in AOL's text editor (that is, by choosing New from the File menu), they're guaranteed ASCII text. You can copy and paste from ASCII documents with impunity, and you can attach saved ASCII documents (use the filename extension ".txt" for best compatibility) to e-mail and rest assured that it will reach its destination with minimal hassle on the recipient's part, regardless of the recipient's choice of computers.

Remember this: Most of the nongraphical material you will encounter online is ASCII text. You can copy and paste it into e-mail documents or new text documents you create by choosing New from the File menu. When you're offline you can review saved text by choosing Open from the File menu, or you can open it with any word processor. ASCII text is as universal and useful as white flour, with no calories and zero grams of fat!

10. *FPC Mary: Use the Address Book to keep track of information about your online friends.*

Mary has no qualms about using the Address Book to her liking, rather than in the way we've been instructed to use it. She uses the Group Name field traditionally, but in the Screen Names field she might put the person's birth date, spouse's name, or primary interest *as well as* their screen name. Thus, whenever she looks up Tom Lichty in her Address Book, she might see "Author of Tour Guide, wife Victoria in medical school" in the Screen Names field, along with my screen name, "MajorTom." Then, when she writes to me, she can say, "How's Victoria doing in school?" and I'll feel all the more flattered.

Admittedly, she has lost some convenience: she can't click on the Address Book's To: or CC: buttons and watch a screen name pop into a mail form, but she's one who believes the inconvenience is worth it. She can always copy and paste the screen name, after all. I use this trick all of the time. Go ahead: break the rules. Nobody's watching.

Everybody Out of the Bus!

Our tour has concluded. Typical of tours everywhere, ours has been an abridgment, a synopsis of things I find most interesting about AOL. You will find your own favorites, and in so doing discover things that I not only didn't mention but didn't know myself. Moreover, AOL is a moving target: like most online services, AOL is almost fluid—flowing from opportunity to opportunity, conforming to trends and advances, relentlessly expanding to fill new voids. I'll try to keep up, and no doubt there will be another edition of this book someday to describe an even bigger and better AOL than the one we know today.

Meanwhile, this edition has reached its end. While you're waiting for the next one, sign on to AOL and send me some e-mail. Tell me what you want included (or excluded) in the next edition. Tell me what you liked or disliked about this book. Send me logs, files, articles—anything you think might complement *The Official America Online Tour Guide*. I look forward to hearing from you.

—MajorTom

APPENDIX A
Making the Connection

If you have never used America Online—if you have never even installed the software—this chapter is for you. It's written for novices—those who hold disks in their sweaty palms and wonder if they are stalwart enough to connect their PCs to the outside world.

If you *have* used America Online—if you already have an account and a password—read on. I'll tell you when it's appropriate to skip the new member material in this chapter, and what page to turn to.

Most of us think of computers as machines—functional, autonomous, and independent. We've come to accept computing as an isolated activity, and our dialogs with the computer as closed circuits. The only external device we've ever encountered is a printer. Oh, we might personify our PCs. We might give them names and even voices, and we might think of their error messages and dialog boxes as "communication." But we know better.

Computers don't think. Computers don't respond with imagination or indignation or intelligence. They react—to comply with our wishes—only as they have been preprogrammed to do. There are no threats to us here.

Connecting to America Online puts human intelligence at the other end of the line. That's because AOL isn't just a computer complex in Virginia. It's people, and people online expect a dialog. People respond, with innovation and humor.

This is not the familiar, predictable universe we're accustomed to. So why mess with it?

Because there's more to life, that's why. Think of your first car, your first love, your first job—experiences resplendent with reward but not without their share of anxiety. We're talking about discovery here, and while AOL and the Internet may not rank with finding love or starting a career, they do offer exceptionally rewarding opportunities.

Things You'll Need

Let's take inventory here. There are a few things you need before you can connect with America Online. You may already have them, but let's be sure.

The Computer

You need a PC, of course. It has to be capable of running Windows, which should already be installed and tested on your machine. A mouse is highly recommended, too. Though most Windows programs can be operated without a mouse, doing so is like eating with your fingers: it's much more difficult than using the proper tool, and in many circles it's socially unacceptable.

You will need at least 4 megabytes of RAM (random access memory): this is the minimum requirement for running Windows. You'll also need a hard disk with 3.5MB of free space. (If you plan to browse the World Wide Web, figure on another 2.5MB of free space—even more if you plan to use the cache. See the sidebar titled "The Fine Print.") You also will need a floppy disk drive capable of reading 3.5-inch floppy disks, or a CD-ROM drive if your AOL software is on a CD. If you need the software on a medium other than the one you have, call 800-827-6364.

The Fine Print

The minimum required disk space mentioned above is for the installation of the software only. America Online offers a disk-based cache feature for use with the World Wide Web that speeds the presentation of Web pages. The speed gain is so significant that anyone planning to use the Web should also plan to use the cache.

If you do plan to use the cache, assume you will need to allocate at least 10MB of disk space to it—more if it's available. The World Wide Web and other Internet features are discussed in Chapter 4, "Using the Internet."

Your AOL software also offers a Personal Filing Cabinet, where you can store your electronic mail, and Favorite Places (the Personal Filing Cabinet and e-mail are discussed in Chapter 3; Favorite Places are discussed in Chapter 4). If you intend to use the Personal Filing Cabinet, add another 5MB of hard disk space to the minimum requirement.

In other words, for a full installation, you will need 3.5MB for the essential software, 2.5MB for the Web browser, 10MB for the browser's cache, and 5MB for the Personal Filing Cabinet. That's a total of 21MB—ample room for AOL to roam.

Finally, a display system capable of displaying 256 colors is recommended. Your AOL software works with 16-color systems, but the presentation of the service is optimized for 256 colors. Refer to your Windows manual (or the manual for your video display adapter, if one is installed as an option) for information on how to change the number of colors your system displays.

I digressed. Essentially, any Windows-compatible machine will do. If yours isn't the latest model—if it doesn't have 435 horsepower and fuel injection and a five-speed transmission—don't worry.

The Telephone Line

You need access to a telephone line. Your standard residential phone line is fine. A multiline business telephone might be more of a challenge. What's really important is that your telephone plugs into a modular telephone jack (called an *RJ-11* jack, if you care about that sort of thing). It's the one with the square hole—measuring about a quarter-inch—on one side.

Whenever you're online, your telephone is out of commission for normal use. If you try to make a voice call using an extension phone on the same line, it's as if you picked up the phone and someone else was having a conversation—except that you'll *never* want to eavesdrop on an AOL session; the screeching sound that modems make when communicating with each other is about as pleasant as fingernails on a blackboard—and about as intelligible.

The Membership Kit

America Online membership kits come in a number of forms, but they all include three things: the software, a temporary registration number, and a temporary password. The software may come on a single floppy disk, two floppy disks, or a CD. Find the software, the registration number, and the password, and set them by your PC. Keep this chapter nearby as well.

If your kit came with floppy disks, make copies of them immediately. Consult the Windows help files for instructions on how to do this if you don't know already. Once you've copied the software, put the original AOL disk(s) somewhere safe. You never know when you might need them again.

The Modem

A modem (short for *mo*dulator/*dem*odulator) is a device that converts computer data into audible tones that the telephone system can transmit. Modems are required at both ends of the line: AOL has a number of them at their end as well.

Modems are rated according to their data-transmission speed. If you're shopping for a modem, get one rated at 28,800 bps if you can. Modems rated at 28,800 bps are fast and are capable of extracting every bit of performance AOL has to offer. (If AOL doesn't offer 28,800 bps capability in your area when you read this, be patient. It's probably in the works.) On the other hand, high-speed modems really only strut their stuff when you're browsing the World Wide Web or downloading files (discussed in Chapters 4 and 5, respectively). In other words, a 2400 baud modem might satisfy your needs if all you really want to do is exchange electronic mail. That's all I have on my laptop, for example. A 2400 baud modem, however, should be considered the minimum.

Baud Rates

The term *baud rate* refers to the signaling rate, or the number of times per second the signal changes. Don't confuse the baud rate with *bits per second* (bps)—they're not the same thing. By using modern electronic wizardry, today's modems can transmit two, three, or four bits with each change of signal, increasing the speed of data transfer considerably. Because it takes eight bits to make a byte, a modem rated at 28,800 bps can transfer anywhere between 3,600 and 14,400 bytes per second. A *byte* is the amount of data required to describe a single character of text. In other words, a modem with a baud rate of 28,800 should transmit at least 3,600 characters—about 45 lines of text—per second.

Alas, the world is an imperfect place—especially the world of phone lines. If there's static or interference of any kind on the line, data transmission is garbled. And even one misplaced bit can destroy the integrity of an entire file. To address the problem, AOL validates the integrity of received data. In plain English, this means that AOL sends a packet of information (a couple of seconds' worth) to your PC, then waits for the PC to say, "I got that, and it's okay," before it sends the next packet. Validation like this means things run a little slower than they would without validation, but it's necessary. We're probably down to a minimum of 3,000 characters per second once we factor in the time it takes to accommodate data validation.

Then there's noise. You've heard it: static on the line. If you think it interferes with voice communication, it's murder on data. Often your PC says, "That packet was no good—send it again," and AOL complies. The reliability of any particular telephone connection is capricious. Some are better than others. Noise, however, is a definite factor, and packets have to be re-sent once in a while. Now we're probably down to a minimum of 2,900 characters per second on a good telephone line on a good day—which is still over 40 lines of text per second at 28,800 bps.

In other words, a 28,800 bps modem isn't 16 times faster than a 2400 bps model, and a 9600 bps modem isn't four times faster than one rated at 2400 bps. On the other hand, a 28,800 bps modem doesn't cost 16 times as much as a 2400 bps model. What I'm trying to say is, in terms of baud per buck, 28,800 is your best buy.

I prefer modems with speakers and lights. Lights, of course, are only found on external modems, and external modems typically require an available serial port. If you have an internal modem, you won't need an available serial port (and you won't have any lights to watch). My modem has six or seven lights. I don't understand most of them, but they look important. The one marked RD (receiving data) is worth watching when you are transferring a file (I discuss file downloading in Chapter 5). It should stay on almost continuously. If, during a file transfer, your RD light is off more than it's on, you've either got a noisy phone line or the system is extremely busy. Whatever the cause, it's best to halt the file transfer (AOL always leaves a Finish Later button on the screen for that purpose) and resume it another time. That's why I advise buying a modem with lights: if you don't have them, how can you tell what's going on?

A number of PCs now offer internal modems: modems inside the PC itself. If you have an internal modem, you won't tie up a communications port on the back of your PC (leaving it available for some other purpose), but you won't have any lights to watch either. Life is full of compromises.

If your modem is the external variety, it will need power of some kind. Some external modems use batteries, but most use AC power and plug into the wall. Be sure an outlet is available.

Most important, be sure you have the proper cables. For an external modem, you need two: one to connect the modem to the PC and another to connect the modem to the phone jack. The modem-to-phone-jack cable bundled with many modems rarely exceeds six feet. If the distance between your modem and your phone jack exceeds that distance, you can buy an extension cable at a phone, electronics, or hardware store. Extension cables are standardized and are inexpensive.

Few external modems include a PC-to-modem cable. You probably will have to purchase one if you're buying an external modem. Check your modem's manual to see if your modem requires a hardware-handshaking (high-speed) cable. If it does, it's essential that you use one, as it will provide a more reliable connection at top speed.

You might also need to make some provision for using your phone on the same line when you're not online. It's less complicated if the modem has a jack for your phone. In that case, you can plug the modem into the phone jack, then plug the phone into the modem. The jacks on the back of the modem should be marked for this. **Note:** You will *not* be able to use your modem and your phone simultaneously: it's one or the other.

If your modem is internal, or if your external modem only has a single jack and you want to continue using your phone as well as your modem on the same line, you might also want to invest in a modular splitter, which plugs into the phone jack on your wall, making two jacks out of one. You plug your phone into one of the splitter's jacks and your modem into the other. Plugging both devices into the same jack won't interfere with everyday telephone communications; incoming calls will continue to go to your phone, just as they did before. You should be able to find a splitter at a phone, electronics, or hardware store for less than $3.

If all this sounds like a lot of wires to keep track of and you have trouble plugging in a toaster, don't worry. Most modems come with good instructions, and the components are such that you can't connect anything backward. Just follow the instructions and you'll be all right.

The Money

Before you sign on to AOL for the first time, there's something else you'll need: money. America Online wants to know how you plan to pay the balance on your account each month. Cash won't do. Instead, you can provide a credit card number: VISA, MasterCard, American Express, or Discover Card are all acceptable. So are certain bank debit cards. Or have your checkbook handy: AOL can have your bank automatically transfer the funds each month if you provide the necessary numbers.

The Screen Name

We're almost ready, but right now I want you to get all other thoughts out of your mind and decide what you want to call yourself. Every AOL member has a unique screen name. Screen names are how AOL tells us apart from each other. You must have one, and it has to be different from everybody else's.

A screen name must consist of from three to ten characters—letters, or letters and numbers. Punctuation and spaces are not acceptable. Millions of people use AOL, and they all have screen names of ten or fewer characters. Chances are, the screen name you want most is taken, so have a number of alternates ready ahead of time and prepare yourself for disappointment. Hardly anyone ever gets his or her first choice.

Though screen names aren't case-sensitive—you can address mail to majortom or MajorTom or MAJORTOM, and it will still get to me—they always appear onscreen the way they were first entered. I first entered my screen name, for example, as MajorTom. If you send mail to majortom, I will see MajorTom on the To: line of my incoming mail. I'm MajorTom in chat rooms and instant messages as well. Keep this in mind as you enter your screen name for the first time, and capitalize your screen name as you want others to see it.

There's no going back, by the way. Once AOL accepts your initial screen name, it's yours as long as you remain a member. Though your account can have as many as five screen names (to accommodate other people in your family or your alter egos), your initial screen name is the one AOL uses to establish and verify your identity. For this reason, your initial screen name can't be changed. Be prepared with a zinger (and a half-dozen alternates), otherwise, AOL will assign you something like TomLi5437, and you'll forever be known by that name. People have a hard time relating to a name like that.

MajorTom

I worked my way through college as a traffic reporter for an Oregon radio station. I was both reporter and pilot. It was a great job: perfect hours for a student, easy work and unlimited access to a flashy plane. It didn't pay much, but somehow that wasn't important—not in the halcyon days of bachelorhood.

I hate to date myself, but David Bowie was an ascending force on the music scene in those days. Impertinent, perhaps—a little too androgynous and scandalous for the conservative element of the Nixon era—but definitely a hit-maker. Our station played Bowie. On my first day, the morning show disk jockey switched on his microphone and hailed "Ground Control to Major Tom"—a line from Bowie's Space Oddity—to get my attention. The name stuck. I was known as Major Tom from then on.

When the time came for me to pick my screen name years ago, AOL suggested TomLi5437 and I balked. How about just plain Tom? I asked. It's in use, AOL replied. I tried four others, and AOL continued to remind me of my lack of imagination. In desperation I tried MajorTom, and AOL accepted it. Once an initial screen name is accepted, that's it. I'm MajorTom on AOL now, and I will be forever more.

The Password

Oh yes, you need a password. Without a password, anyone knowing your screen name can log on using your name and have a heyday on your nickel. Passwords must be from four to eight characters in length, and any combination of letters, or letters and numbers, is acceptable. (As is the case with screen names, punctuation and spaces aren't allowed in passwords.) You will enter your password every time you sign on, so choose something easy to remember—something that's not a finger-twister to type. It should be different from your screen name, phone number, Social Security number, address, or real name—something no one else would ever guess, even if they know you well.

A Case for Elaborate Passwords

In his book *The Cuckoo's Egg*, Cliff Stoll describes computer hackers' methods for breaking passwords. Since most computers already have a dictionary on disk—all spelling-checkers use dictionaries—the hackers simply program their computers to try every word in the dictionary as a password. It sounds laborious, but computers don't mind.

Read this carefully: *No one from AOL will ever ask you for your password.* This is another hacker's ruse: lurking in AOL's dark corners, hackers troll for new members. When they spot someone they think is new, they'll send e-mail or an Instant Message (a real-time message that pops onto your screen) masquerading as an AOL employee. They'll say they're verifying billing records, or something like that, and ask for your password—this is referred to as *phishing. Don't reply*! Instead, make a note of the perpetrator's screen name, then use the keyword: **TOS** (it's free) to access the Terms of Service and determine what you should do next.

In other words, I'm making a case for elaborate passwords here. Don't make it personal, don't use your Social Security number, don't write it down, select something that's not in a dictionary, and never ever give out your password to anyone. This is important.

Installing the Software

Finally, we're ready to get our hands dirty. Don't fret: installing the AOL software is a straightforward process. An installation program does all the work for you.

Again, be sure you have at least 3.5MB of space available on your hard disk, and be sure your PC has no trouble running Windows.

If your kit came with disks, insert the first (or single) copy of the AOL disk into your floppy disk drive. (The original AOL disk works just as well, but making—and using—a copy is just standard paranoid procedure.) If your kit came with a CD, insert the CD into your CD-ROM drive.

Connect your modem to your PC and turn it on. Refer to your modem's instruction manual if you're not sure how to connect it. The modem doesn't have to be connected in order to install the software, but the assumptions the installer program makes about your hardware will be more accurate.

Start Windows and, using the Program Manager, choose Run from the File menu. Enter **A:\SETUP.EXE** in the input box if you're installing from a floppy disk; if AOL came on a CD-ROM, change the "A" to the drive letter of the CD-ROM.

A few minutes might pass as SETUP determines the best way to install your software. It's looking at the amount of space on your hard disk, the communications port to which your modem is attached, and the modem itself. It's also looking for an earlier version of the AOL software on your disk. We'll discuss that potential later. The system examination process can take a while. Don't let it worry you: SETUP isn't making any changes to your machine during this time.

Eventually, Setup's Welcome screen will appear (see Figure A-1).

Figure A-1:
The Setup
program's Wel-
come screen is
displayed when
Setup is loaded
and ready to run.

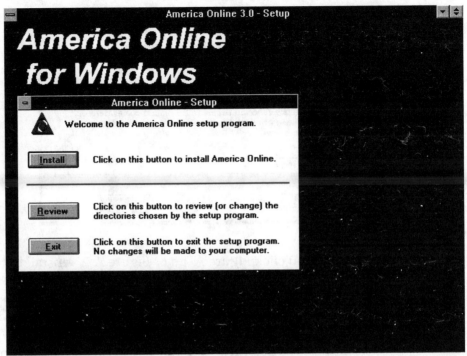

The Setup program assumes that you want to install the software in a C:\AOL30 directory on your hard disk. If you want to have the program installed in a different subdirectory, click the Review button (shown in Figure A-1), then click the Continue button to bypass the first review window, and type over the C:\AOL30 entry in the text box illustrated in Figure A-2. As the message says, if you change anything, be sure to include the drive letter and full path. **Note:** You need not create the directory—whatever it is—prior to installation. The Setup program creates the directory if it doesn't already exist.

Figure A-2:
By clicking the
Review button
shown in Figure
A-1 (and the Con-
tinue button on the
screen that fol-
lows), you'll arrive
at this screen.
Accept the
assumption or
change the path
(including the drive
letter if necessary)
as you see fit.

Once you click Figure A-1's or Figure A-2's Install button, the Setup
program does its work. This takes a couple of minutes. As it's working,
a progress indicator keeps you abreast of the program's progress (see
the center window in Figure A-3). If your membership kit contained
two disks, you will be asked to insert the second disk. When setup is
complete, AOL notifies you that you're "ready to use America Online"
(bottom window of Figure A-3).

Figure A-3:
Installation of the
America Online
software takes only
a few minutes.

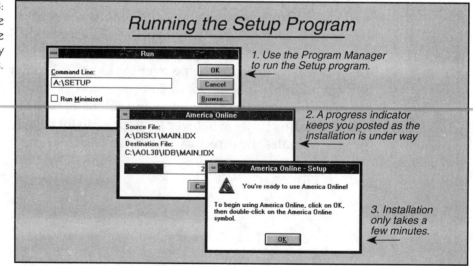

There. You've done it. You've installed the software, and you're ready to sign on. Eject the disk and put it in a safe place. Then let's get on with it.

Existing members, note: The upcoming pages discuss finding local phone numbers and declaring a billing method—matters that aren't your concern. Please turn to the Upgrading heading on page 544 to continue your upgrade.

The Initial Online Session

The initial online session takes about 15 minutes. Be sure you have the time and uninterrupted access to the phone before you begin. You needn't worry about money: though you'll be online for a while, the setup process is accomplished on AOL's dime, not yours. You needn't worry if you make a mistake either; plenty of Cancel buttons are offered during the initial session. If you get cold feet, you can always hang up and start over.

Configuring the Telephone Connection

Before it can successfully make the connection, AOL needs to know a number of things about your telephone. It needs to know whether you have touch-tone or rotary dialing, whether it needs to dial a 9 (or something else) to reach an outside line, and whether a 1 should be dialed before the 800 number. Canadian and international members will need to supply additional information.

Your modem should be connected to the phone line and to your PC before you begin the initial online session, and everything should be turned on.

SETUP has created an AOL program group and added it to your Program Manager. That group is probably showing on your screen at the moment. Double-click the WAOL icon to begin. The Confirmation screen will greet you as soon as the software loads (see the top window in Figure A-4).

If you click the No button in the top window pictured in Figure 2-4—something I recommend—you'll see Figure 2-4's second window. Make any necessary changes to the contents of this window, then click OK.

If you've followed the step above, a third screen will verify your modem and port settings (see the third screen in Figure A-4). Again, the assumptions displayed here are the result of the Setup program's investigation routines. Here's a tip: Even if your modem is Hayes-compatible, click the Select Modem button and select your modem brand and model from the list. Specificity pays under these circumstances.

A fourth screen tells you how to obtain a local access number if you are outside of the contiguous 48 states.

When you click on the Set up America Online window's OK button, the application dials an 800 number to find a local access number for you. You will be able to monitor the call's progress by watching the window pictured at the bottom of Figure A-4. Once you see the message that says "Connected at XXXX baud" (the baud rate is determined by the speed of your modem), you can be sure your PC and modem are communicating properly. You can be sure that your modem and the telephone system are connected as well. If the AOL software found anything amiss prior to this point, it would have notified you and suggested solutions.

Figure A-4:
Read these screens
carefully, make
changes if they're
necessary, and take
advantage of the
opportunity to
specify your mo-
dem. Once you OK
the Setup window,
AOL dials an 800
number for the
initial connection.

Welcome to America Online!

In just a minute you will sign on to America Online and can
begin exploring the service! But first, we need to make sure
we know how to call America Online from your computer.

America Online will automatically dial a special toll-free "800"
number and allow you to choose your access numbers.
These numbers will be used for all future connections.

You probably...
- live in the continental United Sta
- are using America Online at hor
- have a 9600 baud (or faster) mo
- need to dial a "1" to make a toll-
- have a touch-tone telephone

If this is all correct, or you're not sure, clic
Otherwise, click "No" to adjust America O
properly on your computer.

[Yes]   [No]

The Initial Phone Call

*1. First, the AOL application tells you what
it's going to do.*

*I recommend that you
answer No to the first
dialog in this illustration
so that you may specify
your modem's make
and model.*

Set up America Online

If you're trying to call America Online through a switchboard or
you need to dial "9" or another prefix to access an outside line,
enter that prefix in the box below. Please note that most phone
systems require a brief pause after the prefix. To indicate a
pause, enter a comma after the prefix you've entered in the box.

[   ] 1-800-xxx-yyyy

Select the type of phone line
◉ Tone ○ Pulse

☒ Require a "1" before "800"

Click on the

[OK]

*2. If you answer "No" to
the dialog box above,
AOL responds with the
form at right.* ———→

Set up America Online

We have determined that you have a modem on COM1 with a maximum
speed of 28800 baud.

If this is incorrect, please change the settings below. If you're not sure, just
click "OK".

Select the COM port to use:
◉ COM1 ○ COM2 ○ COM3 ○ COM4

Select your modem's fastest baud rate:
2400
4800
9600
14400
19200
28800

*3. When you click the OK button above,
this dialog appears. Even if you are
sure that your modem is Hayes compatible, click this button and see if you
can specify your make and model.*

If your modem is not Hayes compatible, click "Select Modem" to
customize America Online for use with your modem. Otherwise,
click "OK" to continue. If you're not sure, just click "OK."

[OK]   [Select Modem]   [Cancel]

AMERICA
Online

Step 1: Initializing modem

[CANCEL]

*4. When everything's squared away,
AOL dials its 800 number to consult
its access-number database.*

Isolating Connection Errors

Though they rarely do, things can go wrong during the connect process. The problem could be at your end (e.g., the modem or the phone
lines), or it could be at AOL's end. You'll know that the problem is at
your end if you don't hear a dial tone (assuming your modem has a
speaker) before your modem begins dialing. If you hear the dial tone,
the dialing sequence, and the screeching sound that modems make
when they connect, you'll know everything is okay all the way to the
common carrier (long-distance service) you're using. If your connection
fails during the initial connect process, don't panic. Wait a few minutes

and try again. If it fails a second time, call AOL Technical Support at 800-827-6364.

Selecting Your Local Access Numbers

Now you're connected, and AOL is anxious to say hello. Its initial greeting is friendly, if a bit prosaic (see the top window in Figure A-5). Its singular interest right now is to find some local access numbers for you. To do that, it needs to know where you are. It finds that out by requesting your local area code.

Figure A-5:
Using your area code, America Online attempts to select two local numbers for access to the service.

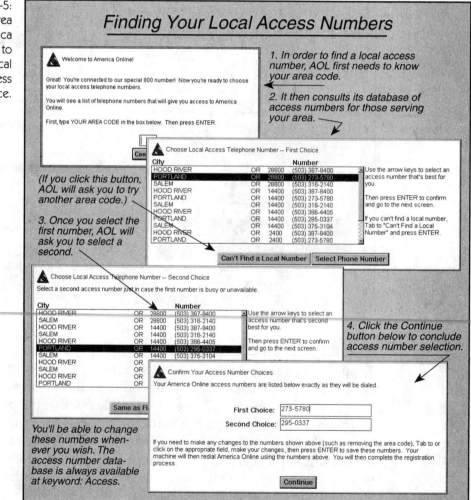

Using your area code, AOL consults its database of local access numbers and produces a list of those nearest you (see the second window in Figure A-5). Look over the list carefully. The phone number at the top of the list isn't necessarily the one closest to you. Also, note the baud rates listed in the third column. You can select any number with a baud rate that's as fast as your modem or faster.

If there isn't a local number listed for your area—that is, if you have to dial a 1 before your access number in order to complete the call—you might have to pay long-distance charges to your telephone company in order to connect to AOL. (There's an alternative: read "The Other 800 Number" sidebar.) Once the initial sign-on process concludes and you're online, use the keyword: **Access** and investigate AOL's database of access numbers on a regular basis. You may find a number there after all.

The Other 800 Number

AOL actually offers two 800 numbers. The first is the one the Setup program consults when it's searching for access numbers in your area. The second 800 number is there to save you money. In order to serve members who live in remote communities, AOL has established this 800 number for access from anywhere in the contiguous United States. While this number isn't exactly toll-free, the charge for its use is considerably less than most long-distance tariffs. If you must dial 1 to reach AOL, sign on and investigate the 800 number at keyword: **Access**.

It's a good idea to have a secondary number as well. A secondary number (if available) is just that: a second number for your modem to call if the first one is busy (which happens rarely) or bogged down with a lot of traffic (which happens more frequently). Interestingly, dozens of modems can use the same number at the same time by splitting their usage into tiny packets. This is all very perplexing to those of us who think of phone numbers as capable of handling one conversation at a time, but it's nonetheless true. There is a limit, however, and when it's reached, AOL tries the second number. The third window in Figure A-5 illustrates the screen used to select this alternate.

Finally, AOL presents the screen confirming your selections, pictured at the bottom of Figure A-5.

The Temporary Registration Number & Password

Assuming you've clicked on the Continue button shown in Figure A-5, your PC will disconnect from the 800 number and dial your primary local access number you've selected. Once the connection is reestablished, AOL presents the screen shown in Figure A-6. This is where you must enter the temporary registration number and password you received with your startup kit. These are the temporary equivalents of the permanent screen name and password you'll soon establish. Enter the words and numbers carefully; they're usually nonsensical and difficult to type without error.

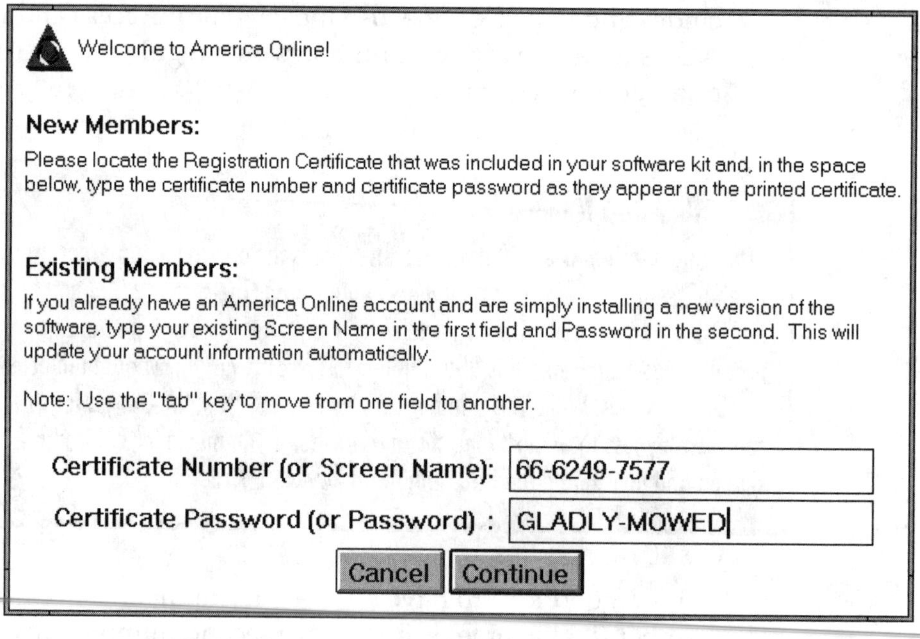

Figure A-6:
Enter your registration number and password here. Be sure to type them exactly as they appear on your certificate or label. (No sneaky trying to use the one in the picture—it won't work!)

Welcome to America Online!

New Members:

Please locate the Registration Certificate that was included in your software kit and, in the space below, type the certificate number and certificate password as they appear on the printed certificate.

Existing Members:

If you already have an America Online account and are simply installing a new version of the software, type your existing Screen Name in the first field and Password in the second. This will update your account information automatically.

Note: Use the "tab" key to move from one field to another.

Certificate Number (or Screen Name):   66-6249-7577

Certificate Password (or Password) :   GLADLY-MOWED

Cancel   Continue

Your Name & Address

When you click the Continue button shown in Figure A-6, AOL provides directions for using an online form like the one shown in Figure A-7. If you're not familiar with Windows, you'll want to read the directions carefully. If you've used Windows software before—even a little bit—you already know this stuff. It's traditional Windows protocol.

Once you've read the instructions, click the Continue button, and AOL will ask you for some personal information (see Figure A-7).

Figure A-7:
Provide your name,
phone number(s),
and address. Be
sure to use the
telephone number
format shown in
the illustration.

> ⚠ Please be sure to enter ALL of the following information accurately:
>
> First Name: _____   Last Name: _____
>
> Address: _____
>
> City: _____   State: ___
>
> Zip Code: _____   Daytime Phone: _____
>
> Country: [UNITED STATES ▼]   Evening Phone: _____
>
> Note: Please enter phone numbers area code first, for example, 703-555-1212, and enter state with no periods, for example, VA for Virginia.
>
> [Cancel] [Continue]

America Online uses this information to communicate with you offline. Although AOL never bills members directly (we'll discuss money in a moment), and though this information is not available online to other members, the AOL staff occasionally does need to contact you offline, and they use this information to do so. They might want to send you a disk containing an upgrade to the software, or perhaps you've ordered something from them (this book, for example) that needs to be mailed. That's what this information is for.

Your Phone Number

Your phone number becomes an important part of your record at America Online—not because anyone at AOL intends to call you but because AOL's Customer Service Department uses this number to identify you whenever you call. Should you ever need to call, the first question Customer Service will ask is, What's your phone number? It's unique, after all, so Customer Service uses it to look up your records. It's an efficient method, but only if you provide the number accurately during your initial sign-on.

Providing Your Billing Information

Let's be up-front about it: America Online is a business run for profit. In other words, AOL needs to be paid for the service it provides. It offers a number of ways to accomplish this. VISA and MasterCard are the preferred methods of payment. America Express and the Discover/ Novus card also are acceptable. Certain bank debit cards are acceptable as well, though you will have to confirm their acceptability with your financial institution. If none of these work for you, America Online also can arrange to debit your checking account automatically. (There's a fee for this—more than a credit card costs you—so you might want this option to be your last resort.)

When you click the Continue button shown in Figure A-7, another screen appears, identifying AOL's connect-time rates. Read it carefully—you need to know what you're buying and what it's costing you, after all—then move on (see Figure A-8).

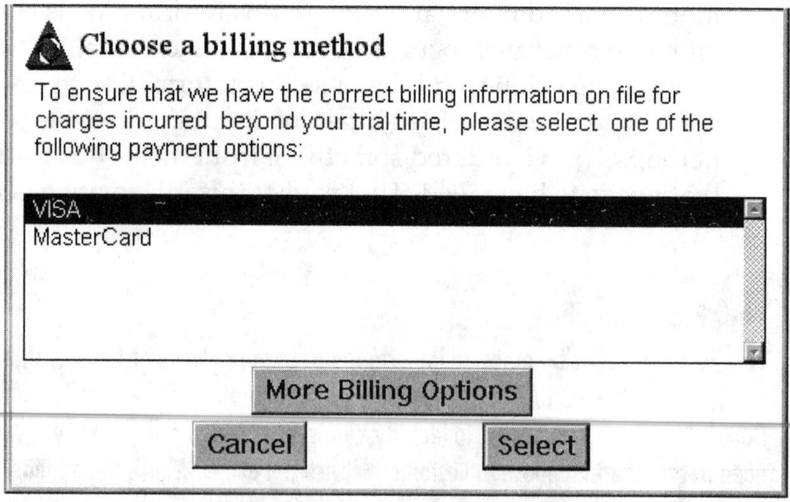

Figure A-8: VISA and MasterCard cards are welcome, and the More Billing Options button leads to information about using American Express or the Discover/ Novus card, or debiting your checking account.

Choose a billing method

To ensure that we have the correct billing information on file for charges incurred beyond your trial time, please select one of the following payment options:

VISA
MasterCard

More Billing Options

Cancel   Select

Figure A-9 shows an example of the billing information screen that lies under the options pictured in Figure A-8. This is the VISA form, but the forms for the other cards are about the same.

Figure A-9:
The VISA form is
about the same as
the one for
MasterCard,
American Express,
or the Discover/
Novus card. Use
the number formats
described.

By providing the following account information, I hereby authorize America Online to debit my
account for any charges I incur in excess of my 10 hour free trial period. Enter your
information for VISA

Card Number: [_____]   **Expiration Date:** [_____]

Bank Name : [_____]

Input as indicated here:
    Card Number: 0123-4567-8901-2345   Expiration Date: 09-91
    Bank Name   :   First Virginia Bank

Enter the name as it appears on the credit card:

First Name: [_____]   **Last Name:** [_____]

[Cancel] [Other Billing Method] [Continue]

Choosing a Screen Name & Password

When you click the Continue button shown in Figure A-9, AOL provides a series of screens informing you of the significance of screen
names, concluding with the screen name input form pictured at the top
of Figure A-10. AOL does not choose a screen name for you—an
incentive to have your own choices at hand.

Figure A-10:
Conclude the
registration process
by entering your
screen name and
password.

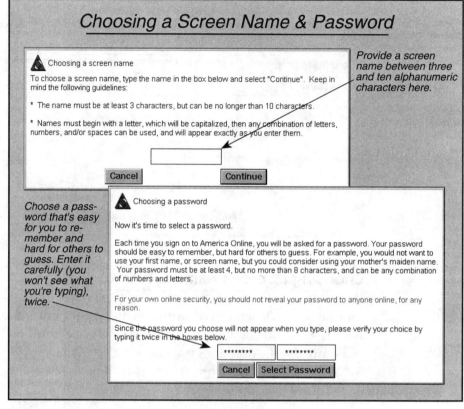

Note that the characters of your password don't appear on your screen as you type them. Substituting asterisks for the letters of your password is a standard security precaution—you never know who's looking over your shoulder. America Online asks you to enter your password twice to be sure you didn't mistype it the first time.

Upgrading

Like all good things, the America Online software is continually improving. You can always download the latest copy of the software online at keyword: **Upgrade**. In fact, you may want to stop in there to verify that you have the latest version of software. You can check to see what version you are currently running by selecting About America Online from the Help menu.

If you are already an AOL member and you're installing an updated version of the software, here are a couple of tricks that will expedite the process.

Use your Existing Account Information

Be sure you're signed off and you have quit your AOL software. Do *not* remove the outdated AOL software from your hard disk. The C:\AOL25 directory (or earlier) contains a bounty of account information that you probably want to retain: preferences, the Personal Filing Cabinet, your Web cache, newsgroups, Parental Controls, and Favorite Places. This information can all be transferred to your new software, *if* you leave the outdated software on your disk until the upgrading process has concluded.

Now follow the steps detailed in the Installing the Software section of this appendix, on pages 532 through 535. Be sure to click the Review button that appears in Figure A-1 to verify that the Setup program found the existing copy of your AOL software.

Unless you tell it otherwise, the Setup program will install the new software in a directory named C:\AOL30. Change the directory name if you wish, but *do not overwrite your existing AOL software.* This implies that you will temporarily have to have enough room on your hard disk for two AOL installations, until you're ready to delete the old one.

Follow the abbreviated instructions in Figures A-2 through A-5. Though there are ways to bypass the local-number lookup routine, let the Setup program jump though its hoops: you might find a new local access number in the process, and it might be better than the one(s) you've been using.

When you come to the Welcome screen pictured in Figure A-6, enter your existing screen name and password where indicated. When you do, the setup routine will conclude and you'll drop into AOL as if you'd signed on normally. When you do, check your preferences, Personal Filing Cabinet, and Favorite Places to verify that information has been retained from your old software.

Delete Your Old Software

Once you've signed off, use DOS or the File Manager to delete the old C:\AOL25 directory (or whatever your old directory was called). This will free up considerable space on your hard disk and prevent you from accidentally invoking your old software when you next sign on—a common error.

If you invoke AOL from Program Manager, the AOL icon there is probably linked to the software you just removed from your disk. To update the link, select the AOL icon and choose Properties from the Program Manager's File menu, then click the Browse button to point the icon to your new AOL software.

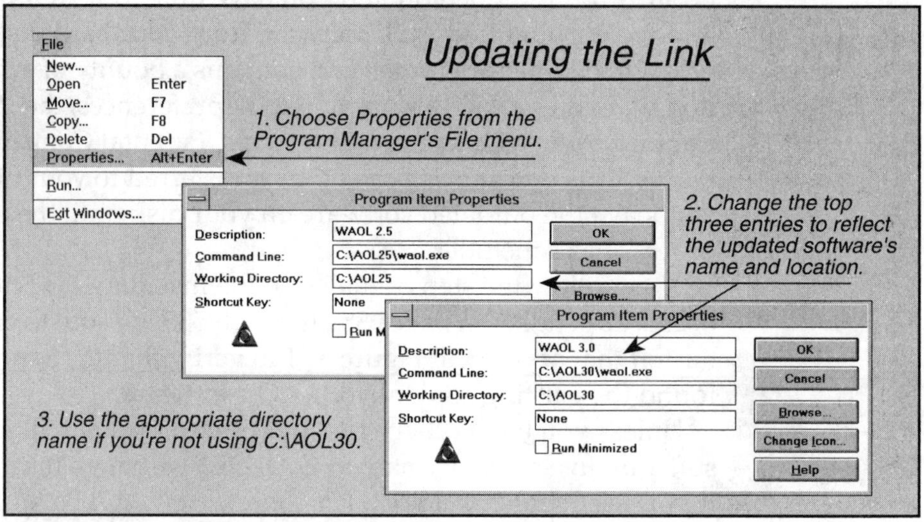

Figure A-11:
Be sure to update the Program Manager's link to your updated software.

Where To Go From Here

Once you're online, you have the entire AOL universe to explore. The thought is at once enticing and overwhelming. Here's what I suggest: if you're new, spend a half-hour wandering around aimlessly. You have quite a bit of free connect time coming, so you don't have to worry about money. Press Ctrl+K (for Keyword), then enter **Hot** to see what's hot online this month. Use the keyword: **Internet** to find an Internet feature that interests you; then, without any particular agenda, explore that feature and perhaps one other.

During this initial session, don't try to absorb the entire contents of AOL or the Internet. Rather, wander aimlessly, getting a feeling for the nature of the online universe. Note how much like Windows it is. Everything is predictable and familiar—at least to a Windows user.

After a half-hour or so, you might want to sign off. Choose Exit from the File menu, and click the Exit button on the Exit screen. Once the dust settles, turn to the chapter in this book that describes a feature you just visited. Read that chapter, then sign back on and explore that department again. See if you can find the things I described in the chapter. Spend another half-hour at this.

Now you're on your own. Explore another department if you wish, or turn to Chapter 3, "Electronic Mail & the Personal Filing Cabinet," and learn how to send mail to somebody. You'll probably get a response in a few days. People at AOL are very friendly. It really *is* a community.

APPENDIX B
Keywords

Keywords are the fastest way to get from one place to another on America Online. To go to a specific forum or area, you just click the Keyword button on the toolbar (or press Ctrl+K), and enter its keyword.

Of course, you need to know the keyword before you can enter it. The most current list of keywords is always available by using (what else?) a keyword: **Keywords**. It's a long list, and because of its length, you might have trouble finding the keyword you're after by consulting the list online. (Printing it is an option.)

Allow me to suggest two alternatives: (1) Click the Keyword button on the toolbar, enter a description of what you're after, then click the Search button in the Keyword window (instead of the Go button). This invokes the Directory of Services, a searchable database of services offered by America Online (and it's discussed in Chapter 2, "The Abecedarium"). Because it's searchable, the Directory is a faster method of locating an online area than reading through the list of keywords, and the Directory always lists keywords when they're available. (2) Use the lists of keywords appearing below. They're alphabetical by keyword. They may save you the trouble of printing a list of your own.

Keyword Tips
The three little keyword tips below may be of help to you.

⚠ Like screen names, keywords are neither case-sensitive nor space-sensitive. "directoryofservices" works just as well as "Directory of Services."

⚠ Many of AOL's areas identify their associated keywords in their primary window somewhere. Look for these.

If you find an area you think you'll visit again often, click the little heart icon on the title bar of that area's window. This will add the location to your list of Favorite Places, where you can organize and access it conveniently. The Favorite Places feature is discussed in Chapter 4: "Using the Internet."

The keyword lists below were compiled by Jennifer Watson (screen name: Jennifer) on 5/1/96. Please e-mail changes or additions to her, as she maintains the lists on a continuing basis. Thanks, Jennifer!

Entries with asterisks (*) are within free areas. Entries that are platform-dependent (those that are available only to members using specific types of computers) are indicated as such: "GAOL" is Gem AOL (DOS); "MAOL" is Mac AOL; "WAOL" is Windows AOL.

Alphabetical by Keyword

Keyword	Area
1-800-TREKER	800-TREKKER: 24 Hour Sci-Fi Collectibles Hotline
1-800-TREKKER	800-TREKKER: 24 Hour Sci-Fi Collectibles Hotline
1010	A Day in the Life of Cyberspace
17	Seventeen Magazine Online
1995	1995: The Year in Review
20	Twentieth Century Mutual Funds
20/20	ABC News-On-Demand
20TH	Twentieth Century Mutual Funds
21ST	Twentieth Century Mutual Funds
24 HOURS	24 Hours of Democracy
25 REASONS	Best of America Online showcase
2MARKET	Marketplace Gift Service
3-D	3D Resource Center
3-D RENDERING	3D Forum
3D	3D Forum
3D AUDIO	SRS Labs
3D REALMS	Apogee/3D Realms Support Center
3D RENDERING	3D Forum
3D SIG	3D Forum
3D SOUND	SRS Labs
3D-RENDERING	3D Forum
3DO	The 3DO Company
4DDA Entry	Mac Business Forum [MAOL only]
4RESOURCES	AT&T Home Business Resources
5	DOS Forum
5TH GENERATION	Symantec
60	60-Second Novelist
60 SECOND NOVELIST	60-Second Novelist
60 SECONDS	60-Second Novelist
7 WONDERS	Seven Wonders of the Web

Keyword	Area
777-FILM	MovieLink
777-FILM ONLINE	MovieLink
7TH	Seventh Level Software
800	AT&T 800 Directory Web Link
800 DIRECTORY	AT&T 800 Directory Web Link
800 FLOWERS	800-Flowers
800-FLOWERS	800-Flowers
800-TREKER	800-TREKKER: 24 Hour Sci-Fi Collectibles Hotline
800-TREKKER	800-TREKKER: 24 Hour Sci-Fi Collectibles Hotline
90210	90210 Wednesdays
90210 WEDNESDAYS	90210 Wednesdays
95 APPLY	AOL for Windows 95 Beta Test Application [WAOL only]
9600	High Speed Access Center*
9600 ACCESS	High Speed Access Center*
9600 CENTER	High Speed Access Center*
99.1	WHFS 99.1 FM
:)	Grateful Dead Forum
;)	Hecklers Online
;-)	Hecklers Online
;-D	Virtual Christian Humor
<><	Christianity Online
<Z>	The Health Zone
@ THE MOVIES	@ The Movies
@AOL DEAD	AOL Live Auditorium
@AOL LIVE	AOL Live auditorium
@BOWL	The Bowl auditorium
@COLISEUM	The Coliseum auditorium
@CYBER RAP	Cyber Rap auditorium
@CYBERPLEX	Cyberplex auditorium
@GLOBE	The Globe auditorium

@INC LIVE	Inc. Live Conference Room
@MAINSTAGE	Main Stage auditorium
@NEWS ROOM	The News Room Auditorium
@ODEON	The Odeon auditorium
@ROTUNDA	Rotunda Auditorium
@THE NEWS ROOM	The News Room Auditorium
@THE.MOVIES	@the.movies
@TIMES	@times/The New York Times Online
@TIMES CROSSWORD	The New York Times Crosswords
@TIMES STORE	@times Store
A&B	Simon & Schuster College Online
A'S	Major League Baseball Team: Oakland Athletics
AAC	Academic Assistance Center
AAFMAA	Army and Air Force Mutual Aid Association
AAII	American Association of Individual Investors
AAPMR	American Academy of Physical Medicine and Rehabilitation
AARP	American Association of Retired People
AARP ANNUIT	AARP Annuity Program
AARP ANNUITY	AARP Annuity Program
AARP BANK 1	AARP Credit Services
AARP FUND	AARP Investment Program
AARP HART	AARP Auto & Homeowners Program
AARP HARTFORD	AARP Auto & Homeowners Program
AARP LIFE	AARP Life Insurance Program
AARP NY LIFE	AARP Life Insurance Program
AARP PRU	AARP Group Health Insurance
AARP SCUDDER	AARP Investment Program
AATRIX	Aatrix Software, Inc.
ABBATE VIDEO	Abbate Video
ABC	ABC Online
ABC AUDITORIUM	ABC Online: Auditorium
ABC AUTO RACING	ABC Sports REV Speedway
ABC BASEBALL	ABC Sports Major League Baseball
ABC BETA	ABC Online: Beta area
ABC CLASS	The ABC Classroom
ABC CLASSROOM	The ABC Classroom
ABC COLLEGE FOOTBALL	ABC Sports College Football
ABC CROWN	ABC Sports Triple Crown
ABC DAYTIME	ABC Daytime/Soapline
ABC ENTERTAINMENT	ABC Prime Time
ABC EVENTS	ABC Online: Auditorium
ABC FIGURE SKATING	ABC Sports Figure Skating
ABC FOOTBALL	ABC Sports College Football
ABC GMA	ABC Good Morning America
ABC GUESTS	ABC Online: Auditorium
ABC HELP	ABC Online: Help
ABC HOCKEY	ABC Online: NHL Online
ABC KIDS	ABC KIDZINE
ABC KIDZINE	ABC KIDZINE
ABC LOVE	ABC Online: Love Online
ABC MNF	ABC Sports Monday Night Football
ABC NEWS	ABC News-On-Demand
ABC NEWS VIEWS	ABC Online: News Views
ABC NHL	ABC Online: NHL Online
ABC PRIMETIME	ABC Prime Time
ABC RADIO	ABC Radio
ABC SOAPS	ABC Daytime/Soapline
ABC SPORTS	ABC Sports
ABC SPORTS STORE	ABC SPORT STORE
ABC STATION	ABC Online: Stations
ABC STATIONS	ABC Stations
ABC TRACK	ABC Track
ABC TRANSCRIPTS	ABC Online: Auditorium
ABC TRIPLE	ABC Sports Triple Crown
ABC TRIPLE CROWN	ABC Triple Crown
ABC VIDEO	ABC Online: Video
ABC VIDEO	ABC Online: Video Store
ABC WOMEN	ABC Sports Women's Sports
ABC WOMEN'S	ABC Sports Women's Sports
ABF	Help Desk [Platform-dependent]
ABI	Business Yellow Pages
ABI YELLOW PAGES	Business Yellow Pages
ABM	Adventures by Mail
ABOTE THE RIM	NESN Basketball
ACADEMY	Starfleet Online
ACADEMY AWARDS	Academy Awards
ACCESS	Local access numbers*
ACCESS ERIC	AskERIC
ACCESS EXCELLENCE	Access Excellence
ACCESS NUMBERS	Local access numbers*
ACCESS SOFTWARE	Access Software
ACCESS.POINT	AccessPoint
ACCESSPOINT	AccessPoint
ACCOLADE	Accolade, Inc.
ACCORDING	Company Research Message Boards
ACCORDING TO BOB	Company Research Message Boards
ACE VENTURA	EXTRA Online
ACE VENTURE STORE	Extra Online
ACER	Acer America Corporation
ACLU	American Civil Liberties Union
ACS	American Cancer Society
ACSNATL	American Cancer Society
ACT	Kaplan Online/SAT, ACT
ACTING	The Casting Forum
ACTIVISION	Activision
ACTORS	The Casting Forum
ACTRESSES	The Casting Forum
ACUBED	America-3: The Women's Team
AD SIG	Advertising Special Interest Group
AD&D	AD&D Neverwinter Nights
ADD	AD&D Neverwinter Nights
ADDONS	BPS Software
ADOBE	Adobe Center menu
ADOBE PHOTOSHOP	Adobe Center menu
ADOPTION	Adoption Forum
ADVANCED	Advanced Software, Inc.
ADVANCED GRAVIS	Advanced Gravis

ADVANCED LOGIC	Advanced Logic Research
ADVENTURE	Outdoor Adventures Online
ADVENTURES BY MAIL	Adventures by Mail
ADVERTISING	Advertising Special Interest Group
ADVERTISING SIG	Advertising Special Interest Group
ADVICE	Advice & Tips
ADVISOR	Top Advisor's Corner
ADVISORS	Top Advisor's Corner
ADVSOFT	Advisor Software
AE	Awakened Eye SIG
AECSIG	Architects, Engineers and Construction SIG
AEN	American Entertainment Network
AF'S SECRET BARGAINS	Arthur Frommer's Secret Bargains
AFFINIFILE	Affinity Microsystems
AFFINITY	Affinity Microsystems
AFRICA	Afrocentric Culture
AFRICAN	Genealogy Forum
AFRICAN AMERICAN	The Exchange: Communities Center
AFRICAN-AMERICAN	Afrocentric Culture
AFROCENTRIC	Afrocentric Culture
AFT	American Federation of Teachers
AFTERWARDS	Afterwards Cafe
AGOL	Assemblies of God Online
AGRICULTURE	NAS Online
AHS	American Hiking Society
AIDS	AIDS and HIV Resource Center
AIDS DAILY	AIDS Daily Summary
AIDS QUILT	GLCF AIDS Quilt
AIR JORDAN	Michael Jordan area
AIRCRAFT	Flying Magazine
AIRCRAFTS	Flying Magazine
AIRPLANE	Aviation Forum
AIRPORTS	Flying Magazine
AIRSHOWS	Aviation Forum
AKIMBO	FullWrite
ALA	America Lung Association
ALADDIN	Aladdin Systems, Inc.
ALARM	Consumer Electronics
ALDUS	Adobe Systems Inc.
ALF	American Leadership Forum
ALL MY CHILDREN	ABC Daytime/Soapline
ALL STAR	MLB All-Star Ballot
ALLYN & BACON	Simon & Schuster College Online
ALOHA	Apple Aloha for eWorld Alumni
ALPHA TECH	Alpha Software Corporation
ALPT	The Grandstand's Simulation Golf
ALR	Advanced Logic Research
ALTERNATIVE MEDICINE	Alternative Medicine Forum
ALTSYS	Altsys Corporation
ALVIN	Hatrack River Town Meeting
ALYSIS	Alysis Software
AM GLOSSARY	AnswerMan Glossary
AMATEUR RADIO	Ham Radio Club
AMBROSIA	Ambrosia Software

AMC	ABC Daytime/Soapline
AMERICA ONLINE STORE	America Online Store
AMERICA OUT OF LINE	ABC Online: America Out Of Line
AMERICA'S CUP	America's Cup 1995 [May disappear without notice]
AMERICA3	America-3: The Women's Team
AMERICAN AGENDA	ABC News-On-Demand
AMERICAN AIRLINES	EAASY SABRE Travel Service
AMERICAN ART	National Museum of American Art
AMERICAN ASTROLOGY	Astronet
AMERICAN DIABETES	American Diabetes Association
AMERICAN DIALOGUE	American Dialogue
AMERICAN EXPRESS	ExpressNet (American Express)
AMERICAN HISTORY	National Museum of America History
AMERICAN INDIAN	The Exchange: Communities Center
AMERICAN LUNG	America Lung Association
AMERICAN LUNG ASSOC	America Lung Association
AMERICAN WOODWORKER	American Woodworker
AMERICAS CUP	America's Cup 1995 [May disappear without notice]
AMERICON	America Online Gaming Conference
AMEX	ExpressNet (American Express)
AMEX ART	ExpressNet Art Download*
AMPLIFIERS	Stereo Review Online
ANALOG	Science Fiction & Fantasy
ANDERTON	Craig Anderton's Sound Studio & Stage
ANDY PARGH	Andy Pargh/The Gadget Guru
ANGELS	Major League Baseball Team: California Angels
ANIMAL	Pet Care Forum
ANIMALS	Pet Care Forum
ANIMATED SOFTWARE	Animated Software
ANIMATION	Graphic Forum [platform-dependent]
ANOTHER CO	Another Company
ANSWERMAN	Answer Man
ANTAG	Antagonistic Trivia
ANTAGONIST	Antagonistic Trivia
ANTAGONIST TRIVIA	Antagonistic Trivia
ANTAGONISTIC TRIVIA	Antagonistic Trivia
ANTI-AGING	Longevity Magazine Online
ANTI-OXIDANTS	Longevity Magazine Online
ANTIAGING	Longevity Magazine Online
ANTIQUES	The Exchange: Collector's Corner
AOL BEGINNERS	Help Desk [Platform-dependent]
AOL CRUISE	AOL Member Cruise
AOL DEAD	AOL Live Auditorium
AOL DINER	Everything Edible!
AOL FAMILIES	AOL Families area
AOL GIFT	AOL Gift Certificates
AOL LIVE	AOL Live
AOL MEMBER CRUISE	AOL Member Cruise
AOL MOVIES	@the.movies
AOL PREVIEW	Upgrade to latest AOL software
AOL PRODUCTS	America Online Store
AOL SPORTS LIVE	AOL Sports Live

AOL STORE	America Online Store	ASK TODD ART	The Image Exchange: Ask Todd Art
AOL WORLD	AOL World	ASKAOL	Member Services*
AOLGLOBALNET	AOLGLOBALnet Test Center	ASKCS	Member Services*
AOLHA	Apple Aloha for eWorld Alumni	ASKERIC	AskERIC
AOLNET	AOLNET	ASNE	Newspaper Association of America
AOLSEWHERE	AOLsewhere	ASSEMBLY	Development Forum [platform-dependent]
AOOL	ABC Online: America Out Of Line	ASSN	Christianity Online: Associations & Interests
AOP	Association of Online Professionals	ASSN ONLINE PROF	Association of Online Professionals
APDA	Apple Professional Developer's Association [MAOL only]	AST	AST Support Forum
		ASTROGRAPH	Astrograph
APOGEE	Apogee/3D Realms Entertainment	ASTROLOGY	ASTRONET
APPLE	Mac Computing channel	ASTROMATES	Astronet
APPLE COMPUTER	Apple Computer	ASTRONAUTS	Challenger Remembered
APPLE UPDATE	Apple System 7.5 Update	ASTRONET	ASTRONET
APPLEBIZ	Apple Business Consortium	ASTRONOMY	Astronomy Club
APPLESCRIPT	AppleScript SIG	ASTROS	Major League Baseball Team: Houston Astros
APPLICATIONS	Business/Applications Forum [platform-dependent]	ASYMETRIX	Asymetrix Corporation
		AT	Antagonistic Trivia
APPLICATIONS FORUM	Business/Applications Forum [platform-dependent]	AT TIMES	@times/The New York Times Online
		AT&T	AT&T
APPMAKER	Bowers Development	ATAGONISTS	Antagonistic Trivia
APPMAKER	Bowers Development	ATHLETICS	Major League Baseball Team: Oakland Athletics
APPS	Applications/Business Forum [platform-dependent]	ATLANTA BRAVES	Major League Baseball Team: Atlanta Braves
		ATLANTIC	The Atlantic Monthly
ARCADE	Games Forum [platform-dependent]	ATLANTIC	The Atlantic Monthly Online
ARCHITECTURE	Home Magazine Online	ATLANTIC MONTHLY	The Atlantic Monthly Online
ARGOSY	Argosy	ATLANTIC ONLINE	The Atlantic Monthly Online
ARIEL	Ariel Publishing	ATLUS	Atlus Software
ARIZONA	Arizona Central	ATONCE	atOnce Software
ARIZONA CENTRAL	Arizona Central	ATT	AT&T
ARM	Real Estate Online	ATT WIRELESS	AT&T
ARSENAL	Arsenal Commmunications	ATTICUS	Atticus Software
ART	Graphics Forum [platform-dependent]	AUDIO	Stereo Review Online
ARTEMIS	Artemis Software	AUDITORIUM	Center Stage
ARTHUR FROMMER	Arthur Frommer's Secret Bargains	AUG	User Group Forum
ARTICULATE	Articulate Systems	AUSTRALIA	Australia
ARTIFICE	Artifice, Inc.	AUSTRIA	Austria
ARTIST	Artists on America Online	AUSTRIAN	Genealogy Forum
ARTIST GRAPHICS	Artist Graphics	AUTO	AutoVantage
ARTIST'S SPOTLIGHT	Artists' Spotlight	AUTO RACING	AOL Auto Racing
ARTISTS	Artists on America Online	AUTOCAD	CAD Resource Center
ARTISTS SPOTLIGHT	Artists' Spotlight	AUTODESK	Autodesk Resource Center
ARTS	Afterwards Cafe	AUTOEXEC	Tune Up Your PC
ARTSPEAK	The Hub: ArtSpeak	AUTOMATE	Affinity Microsystems
ASCD	Assoc. for Supervisor & Curriculum Development	AUTOMATION	Affinity Microsystems
ASCTECH	Alpha Software Corporation	AUTOMOBILE	Car/Cycle Selections
ASCTS	Alpha Software Corporation	AUTOMOTIVE	Car/Cycle Selections
ASFL	The Grandstand's Simulation Football	AUTOS	Road & Track Magazine
ASI	Articulate Systems	AUTOSOUND	Consumer Electronics
ASIAN	The Exchange: Communities Center	AUTOVANTAGE	AutoVantage
ASIMOV	Science Fiction & Fantasy	AV	AutoVantage
ASK AMERICA ONLINE	Member Services*	AV FORUM	Aviation Forum
ASK STAFF	Questions*	AVIATION	Aviation Forum
ASK TODD	The Image Exchange: Ask Todd Art	AVID	Avid Technology

AVID DTV	Avid Technology
AVOCAT	Avocat Systems
AVOCAT SYSTEMS	Avocat Systems
AWAKE EYE	Awakened Eye SIG
AWAKENED EYE	Awakened Eye SIG
AX GARDENING	Arizona Central: House/Home
AZ ALT	Arizona Central: ALT.
AZ ALT.	Arizona Central: ALT.
AZ ASU	Arizona Central: Sports
AZ AT EASE	Arizona Central: At Ease
AZ BIZ	Arizona Central: Small Business
AZ BUSINESS	Arizona Central: Your Money
AZ CACTUS	Arizona Central: Cactus League
AZ CALENDARS	Arizona Central: Plan On It
AZ CARDS	Arizona Central: Sports
AZ CAROUSING	Arizona Central: Carousing
AZ CENTRAL	Arizona Central
AZ COMMUNITY	Arizona Central: Your Community
AZ COMPUTERS	Arizona Central: Computers
AZ CONCERTS	Arizona Central: Carousing
AZ COUCHING	Arizona Central: Couching
AZ DESTINATIONS	Arizona Central: Destinations
AZ DIAMONDBACKS	Arizona Central: Sports
AZ ENTERTAINMENT	Arizona Central: At Ease
AZ FUN	Arizona Central: Plan On It
AZ GOLF	Arizona Central: Golf
AZ HIGH SCHOOLS	Arizona Central: Preps
AZ HOME	Arizona Central: House/Home
AZ HOUSE	Arizona Central: House/Home
AZ LIFE	Arizona Central: Your Life
AZ MONEY	Arizona Central: Your Money
AZ NEWSLINE	Arizona Central: Newsline
AZ PREPS	Arizona Central: Preps
AZ SCOREBOARD	Arizona Central: Scoreboard
AZ SCORES	Arizona Central: Scoreboard
AZ SMALL BUSINESS	Arizona Central: Small Business
AZ SPORTS	Arizona Central: Sports
AZ SPORTS CALENDARS	Arizona Central: Plan On It
AZ SPORTS SCHEDULE	Arizona Central: Plan On It
AZ STARDUST	Arizona Central: Stardust
AZ SUNS	Arizona Central: Sports
AZ THEATER	Arizona Central: Stardust
AZ THEATRE	Arizona Central: Stardust
AZ TRAVEL	Arizona Central: Destinations
AZ TRIPS	Arizona Central: Destinations
AZ TV	Arizona Central: Couching
AZ U OF A	Arizona Central: Sports
AZ VOLUNTEERS	Arizona Central: Volunteers
B&B	Bed & Breakfast U.S.A.
BA	Bank of America
BABY BOOMER	Baby Boomers area
BABY BOOMERS	Baby Boomers area
BABYLON	Babylon 5
BABYLON 5	Babylon 5

BACKCOUNTRY	Backpacker Magazine
BACKPACKER	Backpacker Magazine
BALANCE SHEET	Disclosure's Financial Statements
BALI	One Hanes Place
BALKAN	Balkan Operation Joint Endeavor
BALLOON	800-Flowers
BALLOONS	800-Flowers
BALTIMORE ORIOLES	Major League Baseball Team: Baltimore Orioles
BANK AMERICA	Bank of America
BANK OF AMERICA	Bank of America
BARGAINS	Checkbook Bargains
BARRONS	Barrons Booknotes
BARTLETT	Bartlett's Familiar Quotations [WAOL 2.5 only]
BARTLETTS	Bartlett's Familiar Quotations [WAOL 2.5 only]
BASEBALL	MLB Baseball area
BASELINE	Baseline Publishing
BASEVIEW	Baseview Products, Inc.
BASIC	Development Forum [platform-dependent]
BASKETBALL	NBA Basketball area
BASKETBALL TRIVIA	NTN Basketball Trivia
BATBOY	Weekly World News
BATMAN	DC Comics Online
BAUMRUCKER	Baumrucker Conference [May disappear without notice]
BBS	BBS Corner
BBS CORNER	BBS Corner
BC	Christian Books & Culture
BCS	Boston Computer Society
BEANIE	Pangea Toy Net
BEANIE BOY	Pangea Toy Net
BEATY	Company Research Message Boards
BEAUTY	Elle Magazine Online
BED & BREAKFAST	Bed & Breakfast U.S.A.
BED	Bed & Breakfast U.S.A.
BEE	BeeSoft
BEEPER	Consumer Electronics
BEER	Food & Drink Network
BEESOFT	BeeSoft
BEGINNER	Help Desk [Platform-dependent]
BEGINNERS	Help Desk [Platform-dependent]
BELCH	AOL Plays With Sounds [WAOL only]
BELGIUM	Belgium
BELIEFS	Religion & Beliefs
BERK SYS WIN	Berkeley Systems
BERKELEY	Berkeley Systems
BERKSYS	Berkeley Systems
BERNIE	Bernie Siegel Online
BEST OF AOL	Best of America Online showcase
BETA APPLY	Beta Test Application Area [May disappear without notice]
BETHEL	Bethel College and Seminary
BETHESDA	Bethesda Softworks, Inc.
BETHESDA SOFTWORKS	Bethesda Softworks, Inc.
BETHSEDA	Bethesda Softworks, Inc.

BETTER HEALTH	Better Health & Medical Forum
BETTER LIVING	Ideas for Better Living
BEVERAGES	Everything Edible!
BEVERLY HILLS	90210 Wednesdays
BEVERLY HILLS 90210	90210 Wednesdays
BEYOND	Beyond, Inc.
BI	Gay & Lesbian Community Forum
BIC MAG	Bicycling Magazine
BICYCLE	The Bicycle Network
BICYCLING	Bicycling Magazine
BICYCLING MAGAZINE	Bicycling Magazine
BIG TWIN	The All-Harley Magazine
BIKENET	The Bicycle Network
BILL GATES	The Hub: The Secret Files of Bill Gates
BILLING	Account and Billing*
BIOLOGY	Simon & Schuster Online: Biology Dept.
BIOSCAN	OPTIMAS Corporation
BIRDING	Birding Selections
BISEXUAL	Gay & Lesbian Community Forum
BIT JUGGLERS	Bit Jugglers
BIZINSIDER	Herb Greenberg's Business Insider
BK	Burger King College Football
BKG	American Dialogue
BLACK AMERICAN	Afrocentric Culture Selections
BLACK HERITAGE	Black History Month [May disappear without notice]
BLACK HISTORY	Black History Month [May disappear without notice]
BLACK VOICES	Orlando Sentinel Online: Black Voices
BLACK-AMERICAN	Afrocentric Culture Selections
BLACKBERRY	Blackberry Creek
BLACKBERRY CREEK	Blackberry Creek
BLACKS	Afrocentric Culture Selections
BLIND	DisABILITIES Forum
BLIZZARD	Blizzard Fun!
BLIZZARD ENT	Blizzard Entertainment
BLOC DEVELOPMENT	TIGERDirect, Inc.
BLOCKBUSTER	Blockbuster Music's Online Store
BLUE JAYS	Major League Baseball Team: Toronto Blue Jays
BLUE RIBBON	Blue Ribbon Soundworks
BLUEPRINT	Graphsoft, Inc.
BLUES	House of Blues Online
BMG	BMG Distribution Online
BMUG	Berkeley Macintosh Users Group
BOARDSAILING	Sailing Forum
BOAT	Boating Online
BOATING	Boating Selections
BOATS	The Exchange
BOB BEATY	Company Research Message Boards
BOBB	Company Research Message Boards
BOFA	Bank of America
BONK	60-Second Novelist: BOnKeRs Trivia
BONKERS	60-Second Novelist: BOnKeRs Trivia
BOOK	The Book Nook

BOOK BESTSELLERS	Books area
BOOKNOOK	The Book Nook
BOOKNOTES	Barrons Booknotes
BOOKS & CULTURE	Christian Books & Culture
BOOKS	Book areas
BOOKSTORE	Online Bookstore
BOSNIA	Balkan Operation Joint Endeavor
BOSOX	Major League Baseball Team: Boston Red Sox
BOSTON	Digital City Boston
BOSTON CELTICS	NESN Backsetball
BOSTON ONLINE	Digital City Boston
BOSTON RED SOX	Major League Baseball Team: Boston Red Sox
BOWL GAMES	NCAA Football Bowl Info
BOWLING	The Grandstand: Other Sports
BOWLS	NCAA Football Bowl Info
BOXER	Boxer*Jam Gameshows [WAOL only]
BOXER JAM	Boxer*Jam Gameshows [WAOL only]
BOXER*JAM	Boxer*Jam Gameshows [WAOL only]
BOXING	Sports channel
BP MARKETPLACE	Backpacker Online's Marketplace
BPS SOFTWARE	BPS Software
BRAINSTORM	Brainstorm Products
BRAINSTORMS	Brainstorms
BRAINSTORMS	Brainstorms Store
BRATS	Overseas Brats
BRAVES	Major League Baseball Team: Atlanta Braves
BRAVOS	Major League Baseball Team: Atlanta Braves
BREAKFAST	Bed & Breakfast U.S.A.
BREW	Food & Drink Network
BREWERS	Major League Baseball Team: Milwaukee Brewers
BREWING	Food & Drink Network
BRIDGES	The Hub: Even More Bridges of Madison County
BRINKLEY	ABC News-On-Demand
BRITISH	Genealogy Forum
BROADBAND	AOL's Cable Center
BROADWAY	Playbill Online
BRODERBUND	Broderbund
BROKEN ARROW	Broken Arrow
BROWSER FIX	AOL 2.6 for Macintosh* [MAOL 2.6 only]
BRYCE	MetaTools Inc.
BTS	Bethel Theological Seminary
BUCS	Major League Baseball Team: Pittsburgh Pirates
BUDDHISM	Religion & Ethics Forum
BUDDY	Buddy Lists
BUILDING	HouseNet
BULGARIA	Bulgaria
BULL	Merrill Lynch
BULL MOOSE	Bull Moose Tavern
BUNGIE	Bungie Software
BURGER KING	Burger King College Football
BURP	AOL Plays With Sounds [WAOL 2.5 only]
BUSINESS	Business News area
BUSINESS CENTER	Your Business

BUSINESS FORUM	Applications/Business Forum [platform-dependent]
BUSINESS INSIDER	The Business Insider
BUSINESS KNOW HOW	Business Strategies Forum
BUSINESS NEWS	Business News area
BUSINESS RESOURCES	Hoover's Business Resources
BUSINESS SCHOOL	Kaplan Online -or- The Princeton Review
BUSINESS SENSE	Business Sense
BUSINESS STRATEGIES	Business Strategies Forum
BUSINESS WEEK	Business Week Online
BUSINESSRANKINGS	Business Rankings
BW	Business Week Online
BW ONLINE	Business Week Online
BW SEARCH	Business Week: Search
BYTE	ByteWorks
BYTE BY BYTE	Byte By Byte Corporation
BYTEWORKS	ByteWorks
C	Development Forum [platform-dependent]
C&S	Computing channel [platform-dependent]
CA	Crossword America
CABLE	AOL's Cable Center
CABLE MODEM	AOL's Cable Center
CABLE NEWS	New England Cable News
CAD	CAD Resource Center
CADILLAC	Cadillac WWW Home Page
CAFFE STARBUCKS	Caffe Starbucks
CALENDAR	What's Hot in Mac/PC Computing [platform-dependent]
CALENDAR GIRLS	The Hub: Calendar Girls
CALIFORNIA ANGELS	Major League Baseball Team: California Angels
CALL	Accessing America Online*
CALLISTO	Callisto Corporation
CAMERA	Photography Selections
CAMERAS	Popular Photography Online
CAMEROON	Cameroon
CAMPAIGN 96	Today's News: The Campaign Trail
CAMPING	Backpacker Magazine
CAMPUS	Online Campus
CAMPUS LIFE	Campus Life Magazine
CANADA	Canada Launch Centre
CANADA CHAT	Canada Chat
CANCEL	Cancel Account*
CANCELLED TV SHOWS	Lost & Found TV Shows
CANCER	Cancer Forum
CANCER J SCIAM	Cancer Journal from Scientific American
CANCER JOURNAL	Cancer Journal from Scientific American
CANVAS	Deneba Software
CAPITAL	Politics Forum
CAPITAL CONNECTION	Politics Forum
CAPITAL MARKETS	Capital Markets Center [WAOL 2.5 only]
CAPITAL MARKETS CENTER	Capital Markets Center [WAOL 2.5 only]
CAPITALS	Washington Capitals
CAPMAR	Capital Markets Center [WAOL 2.5 only]
CAPS	Washington Capitals
CAPSTONE	Capstone Software
CAR	Car/Cycle Selections
CAR AND DRIVER	Car and Driver Magazine
CARDINAL	Cardinal Technologies, Inc.
CARDINALS	Major League Baseball Team: St. Louis Cardinals
CARDS	Hallmark Connections [WAOL and MAOL only]
CAREER	Career Selections
CAREER NEWS	USA Today Industry Watch section
CAREERS	Career Selections
CAROLE 2000	Astronet
CARPENTRY	HouseNet
CARS	Car/Cycle Selections
CARTOON NETWORK	Cartoon Network
CARTOONS	Cartoon collection
CASADY	Casady & Greene
CASINO	RabbitJack's Casino
CASTING	The Casting Forum
CASTING FORUM	The Casting Forum
CATHOLIC	Catholic Community
CATHOLIC NEWS	Catholic News Service
CATHOLIC NEWS SERVICE	Catholic News Service
CATHOLIC REPORTER	National Catholic Reporter
CB	College Board
CBD	Commerce Business Daily
CC	Computing Company Connection
CC MAG	Christian Computing Magazine
CCB	Chicago Online: Crain's Chicago Business
CCC	Computing Company Connection
CCDA	Christian Community Development Association
CCE	Columbia Encyclopedia
CCG	Christian College Guide
CCGF	Collectible Card Games Forum
CCI	Christian Camping International
CD	2Market
CDS	Stereo Review Online
CE	Consumer Electronics
CE SOFTWARE	CE Software
CEC	Christian Education Center
CELEBRITY CIRCLE	Oldsmobile/Celebrity Circle
CELEBRITY COOKBOOK	Celebrity Cookbook
CELLULAR	Consumer Electronics
CELLULAR PHONE	Consumer Electronics
CELTICS	NESN Basketball
CELTICS BASKETBALL	NESN Basketball
CENTER STAGE	Center Stage auditorium
CENTRAL	Symantec
CENTRAL POINT	Symantec
CENTURY	Twentieth Century Mutual Funds
CENTURY FUNDS	Twentieth Century Mutual Funds
CEP	Council on Economic Priorities
CEREBRAL PALSY	United Cerebral Palsy Association
CH	Christian History Magazine
CH PRODUCTS	CH Products
CHALLENGER	Challenger Remembered

CHAMPION	One Hanes Place
CHANGE PASSWORD	Change your password*
CHANGE PROFILE	Edit your member profile
CHANNEL C	CNN Newsroom Online [MAOL and GAOL only]
CHANNEL ZERO	The Hub: Channel Zero
CHARITY	Access.Point
CHARTER	Charter Schools Forum
CHARTER SCHOOL	Charter Schools Forum
CHARTER SCHOOLS	Charter Schools Forum
CHAT	People Connection
CHEESECAKE	Eli's Cheesecakes
CHEESECAKES	Eli's Cheesecakes
CHEF	Everything Edible!
CHEF'S CATALOG	Chef's Catalog
CHEFS	Everything Edible!
CHEFS CATALOG	Chef's Catalog
CHESS	Strategy & Wargaming Forum
CHICAGO	Chicago Online
CHICAGO CUBS	Major League Baseball Team: Chicago Cubs
CHICAGO ONLINE	Chicago Online
CHICAGO TRIBUNE	Chicago Tribune
CHICAGO WHITE SOX	Major League Baseball Team: Chicago White Sox
CHICO	California State University
CHILD SAFETY	Child Safety Brochure
CHILDREN'S HEALTH	Children's Health Forum
CHINESE ASTROLOGY	Astronet
CHIP	ChipNet Online
CHIPNET	ChipNet Online
CHISOX	Major League Baseball Team: Chicago White Sox
CHOCOLATE	The Health Zone
CHRIST	Christianity Online
CHRISTIAN	Religion & Ethics Forum
CHRISTIAN CAMPING	Christian Camping International
CHRISTIAN COLLEGES	Christian College Guide
CHRISTIAN COMPUTING	Christian Computing Magazine
CHRISTIAN CONNECTION	Christianity Online Chat & Live Events
CHRISTIAN EDUCATION	Christian Education Center
CHRISTIAN FAMILIES	Christianity Online: Marriage/Family Forum
CHRISTIAN FAMILY	Christianity Online: Marriage/Family Forum
CHRISTIAN HISTORY	Christian History Magazine
CHRISTIAN KID	Christianity Online: Kids
CHRISTIAN KIDS	Christianity Online: Kids
CHRISTIAN MAN	Christianity Online: Men
CHRISTIAN MEN	Christianity Online: Men
CHRISTIAN PRODUCTS	Christian Products Center
CHRISTIAN READER	Christian Reader
CHRISTIAN SINGLES	Christianity Online: Singles
CHRISTIAN STUDENT	Christianity Online: Student Hangout
CHRISTIAN STUDENTS	Christianity Online: Student Hangout
CHRISTIAN WOMAN	Christianity Online: Women
CHRISTIAN WOMEN	Christianity Online: Women
CHRISTIANITY	Christianity Online
CHRISTIANITY TODAY	Christianity Today
CHROL CHAT	Christianity Online Chat & Live Events

CHROL CLASSIFIEDS	Christianity Online Classifieds
CHROL RESOURCES	Christian Resource Center
CHURCH LEADERS	Christianity Online: Church Leaders Network
CHURCH LEADERS NETWORK	Christianity Online: Church Leaders Network
CIGAR	Food & Drink Network
CIGARS	Food & Drink Network
CINCINNATI REDS	Major League Baseball Team: Cincinnati Reds
CINEMA	@the.movies
CINEMAN	Movie Review Database
CINEMAN SYNDICATE	Movie Review Database
CINEMAPOV	CinemaPOV
CITIBANK	The Apple Citibank Visa Card
CITIZEN	Access.Point
CITY WEB	City Web
CIVIC	Access.Point
CIVIL LIBERTIES	American Civil Liberties Union
CIVIL WAR	The Civil War Forum
CJ CONTESTS	CyberJustice Contests
CL	Campus Life Magazine
CLARIS	Claris
CLASSES	Online Campus
CLASSIFIED	AOL Classifieds
CLASSIFIEDS	AOL Classifieds
CLASSIFIEDS ONLINE	AOL Classifieds
CLASSROOM	President's Day
CLEVELAND INDIANS	Major League Baseball Team: Cleveland Indians
CLICK HERE	The Hub: Click Here
CLIFE	Computer Life Magazine
CLINTON	White House Forum
CLN	Christianity Online: Church Leaders Network
CLOCK	Time of day and length of time online
CLOTHES	Elle Magazine Online
CLOTHING	Elle Magazine Online
CLS	Christianity Online Classifieds
CLUB KIDSOFT	Club KidSoft
CLUBCALL	ClubCall [WAOL 2.5 only]
CLUBS & INTERNET	Clubs & Interest's Top Internet Sites
CLUBS	Clubs & Interests Channel
CM	Christian Ministries Center
CMC	Creative Musician's Coalition
CMIL	University of California Extension
CMS	Christian Media Source
CMT	Coda Music Tech
CN	Christianity Online Newsstand
CNEWS	Christianity Online Newsstand
CNFA	The Grandstand's Simulation Football
CNN	CNN Newsroom Online
CNN GUIDES	CNN Newsroom Online
CNN NEWSROOM	CNN Newsroom Online
CNS	Catholic News Service
CO ASSOCIATIONS	Christianity Online: Associations & Interests
CO CLASSIFIEDS	Christianity Online Classifieds
CO CONTEST	Christianity Online: Contest
CO FAMILIES	Christianity Online: Marriage/Family Forum

CO FAMILY	Christianity Online: Marriage/Family Forum
CO INTERESTS	Christianity Online: Associations & Interests
CO KIDS	Christianity Online: Kids
CO LIVE	Christianity Online Chat & Live Events
CO MAN	Christianity Online: Men
CO MEN	Christianity Online: Men
CO NEWS	Christianity Online Newsstand
CO SINGLE	Christianity Online: Singles
CO SINGLES	Christianity Online: Singles
CO STUDENT	Christianity Online: Student Hangout
CO STUDENTS	Christianity Online: Student Hangout
CO TEEN	Christianity Online: Student Hangout
CO TEENS	Christianity Online: Student Hangout
CO WOMAN	Christianity Online: Women
CO WOMEN	Christianity Online: Women
CO YOUTH	Christianity Online: Student Hangout
COBB	The Cobb Group Online
COBB GROUP	The Cobb Group Online
CODA	Coda Music Tech
CODA MUSIC	Coda Music Tech
COINS	The Exchange
COL	Chicago Online
COL BUSINESS	Chicago Online Business Guide
COL CALENDAR	Chicago Online Calendar
COL CHAT	Chicago Online Chat
COL EDUCATE	Chicago Online Education Guide
COL EDUCATION	Chicago Online Education Guide
COL ENTERTAINMENT	Chicago Online Local Entertainment Guide
COL FILES	Chicago Online Libraries
COL GOVERNMENT	Chicago Online Election 96
COL GOVT	Chicago Online Election 96
COL LIFESTYLES	Chicago Online Local Entertainment Guide
COL MALL	Chicago Online Mall
COL MARKETPLACE	Chicago Online Marketplace
COL MEDIA	Chicago Online Media Guide
COL NEWS	Chicago Online Business Guide
COL PLANNER	Chicago Online Planner
COL SPORTS	Chicago Online Sports
COL TECH	Chicago Online Technology Guide
COL TICKET	Chicago Online Ticketmaster
COL VISITOR	Chicago Online Visitor Guide
COL WEATHER	Chicago Online Calendar & Almanac
COLISEUM	Center Stage
COLLECT	Collectibles Online
COLLECT CARDS	Collectible Card Games Forum
COLLECTIBLES	Collectibles Online
COLLECTIBLES ONLINE	Collectibles Online
COLLECTING	Wizard World
COLLECTOR	The Exchange
COLLEGE	College Selections
COLLEGE BOARD	College Board
COLLEGE FOOTBALL	AOL Football
COLLEGE ONLINE	Simon & Schuster College Online
COLOGNE	The Fragrance Counter

COLOR IMAGING	Advanced Color Imaging Forum
COLOR WEATHER MAPS	Weather area
COLORADO ROCKIES	Major League Baseball Team: Colorado Rockies
COLUMBIA	Columbia Encyclopedia
COLUMBIA.NET	Columbia's Health Today
COLUMBIA/HCA	Columbia's Health Today
COLUMBIANET	Columbia's Health Today
COLUMNISTS	Columnists & Features Online
COLUMNS	Columnists & Features Online
COMEDY	The Comedy Pub
COMEDY CENTRAL	Comedy Central
COMEDY PUB	The Comedy Pub
COMIC STRIP	Comic Strip Centennial
COMICS	Comics Selections
COMMANDO	Kim Komando's Komputer Clinic
COMMON GROUND	Common Ground Software
COMMONS	The Motley Fool
COMMUNICATIONS	Communications Forum [platform-dependent]
COMMUNITIES	The Exchange: Communities Center
COMMUNITY	Access.Point
COMMUNITY CENTER	Clubs & Interests Channel
COMP SITES	Computing Internet Sites [WAOL 2.5 and MAOL 2.6 only]
COMPANIES	Computing Company Connection
COMPANY	Company Research
COMPANY 3DO	The 3DO Company
COMPANY PROFILES	Hoover's Handbook of Company Profiles
COMPANY RESEARCH	Company Research
COMPANY UPDATES	Hoover's Company Updates
COMPAQ	Compaq
COMPOSER	Composer's Coffeehouse
COMPOSER'S	Composer's Coffeehouse
COMPOSERS	Composer's Coffeehouse
COMPTONS	Compton's NewMedia Forum
COMPTONS ENCYCLOPEDIA	Compton's Living Encyclopedia
COMPTONS SOFTWARE	Compton's Software Library
COMPUADD	CompuAdd
COMPUKIDS	CompuKids
COMPUMOMS	Mother's Day in Computing CyberSerials
COMPUSERVE	Prodigy Refugees Forum
COMPUSTORE	Shopper's Advantage Online
COMPUTE	I-Wire Online
COMPUTER	Computing channel [platform-dependent]
COMPUTER AMERICA	Craig Crossman's Computer America
COMPUTER BOWL	Computer Bowl
COMPUTER EXPRESS	Computer Express
COMPUTER FORUM	Computing channel [platform-dependent]
COMPUTER LAW	CyberLaw/Cyberlex
COMPUTER LIFE	Computer Life Magazine
COMPUTER PERIPHERALS	Computer Peripherals, Inc.
COMPUTER TERMS	Dictionary of Computer Terms
COMPUTING	Computing channel [platform-dependent]
COMPUTING AND SOFTWARE	Computing channel [platform-dependent]
COMPUTING DEPT	Computing & Software [MAOL only]

COMPUTING FORUMS	Computing channel [platform-dependent]
COMPUTING LIFESTYLES	Family Computing Forum: Lifestyles & Computing
COMPUTING NEWS	Computing News [MAOL and GAOL only]
COMPUTING SITES	Computing Internet Sites [WAOL 2.5 and MAOL 2.6 only]
COMPUTOON	CompuToon area
CON	Christianity Online: Contest
CONFIG	Tune Up Your PC
CONGRESS	Capital Connection
CONGRESSIONAL	Congressional Quarterly
CONNECT	Connect Magazine
CONNECTING	Accessing America Online*
CONNECTION	Intel Corporation
CONNECTIX	Connectix
CONSUMER	Consumer Reports
CONSUMER ELECTRONICS	Consumer Electronics
CONSUMER REPORTS	Consumer Reports
CONSUMERS	Consumer Reports
CONTACTS	Employer Contacts Database
CONTEST	AOL Contest area
CONTEST AREA	AOL Contest area
CONTEST CENTRAL	Family Computing Forum: Contest Central
CONTESTS	AOL Contest area
COOK	Everything Edible
COOKBOOK	Celebrity Cookbook
COOKIE	The Motley Fool
COOKING	Everything Edible
COOKING CLUB	Everything Edible
COOKS	Food & Drink Network
COOPER	JLCooper Electronics
CORBIS	Corbis media
CORBIS MEDIA	Corbis media
CORCORAN	Corcoran School of Art
COREL	Corel Special Interest Group
CORELDRAW	Corel Special Interest Group
CORKSCREWED	Corkscrewed Online
CORNER	Pro's Corner
CORPORATE PROFILES	Hoover's Handbook of Company Profiles
COSA	AfterEffects
COSTAR	CoStar
COSTARD	The Motley Fool
COUNTDOWN	NTN Trivia
COUNTRIES	AOL Around the World
COURSES	Online Campus
COURSEWARE	Electronic Courseware
COURT TV	Court TV's Law Center
COURTROOM TELEVISION	Court TV's Law Center
COURTS	CyberJustice's Courts of Karmic Justice
COW	Christianity Online: Women
COWLES	Cowles/SIMBA Media Information Network
COWLES SIMBA	Cowles/SIMBA Media Information Network
CP&B	Computing Print & Broadcast
CPB	Computing Print & Broadcast
CPC	Christian Products Center

CPI	Computer Peripherals, Inc.
CPOV	CinemaPOV
CPS	Symantec
CQ	Congressional Quarterly
CR	Christian Reader
CRAFTS	Crafts Selections
CRAIG CROSSMAN	Craig Crossman's Computer America
CRAIN'S	Chicago Online: Crain's Chicago Business
CRAIN'S SMALL BIZ	Chicago Online: Crain's Small Business
CRAINS	Chicago Online: Crain's Chicago Business
CRASH	Flight Sim Resource Center
CRAZY HORSE	Rockline Online
CREDIT	Credit Request Form for connect problems*
CREDIT REQUEST	Credit Request Form for connect problems*
CRIMINAL JUSTICE	Simon & Schuster Online: Criminal Justice Dept.
CRISPY	Pangea Toy Net
CRITIC	Critic's Choice
CRITICS	Critic's Choice
CRITICS CHOICE	Critic's Choice
CROATIA	Croatia
CROSSDRESSER	Transgender Community Forum
CROSSDRESSING	Transgender Community Forum
CROSSMAN	Craig Crossman's Computer America
CROSSWORD	The New York Times Crosswords
CROSSWORDS	The New York Times Crosswords
CRUISE	Cruise Critic
CRUISE CRITIC	Cruise Critic
CRUSADE	Avon's Breast Cancer Awareness Crusade
CRYSTAL	Crystal Dynamics
CRYSTAL BALL	The Crystal Ball Forum
CS	Center Stage
CS	Internet Connection Store
CSB	Chicago Online: Crain's Small Business
CSLIVE	Member Services*
CSMITH	CyberSmith
CSPAN	C-SPAN
CSPAN BUS	C-SPAN in the Classroom
CSPAN CLASS	C-SPAN in the Classroom
CSPAN CLASSROOM	C-SPAN in the Classroom
CSPAN ONLINE	C-SPAN
CSPAN SCHOOLS	C-SPAN Educational Services
CSUC	California State University
CT	Christianity Today
CUBBIES	Major League Baseball Team: Chicago Cubs
CUBS	Major League Baseball Team: Chicago Cubs
CURRICULUM	Assoc. for Supervisor & Curriculum Development
CUSTOMER SERVICE	Member Services*
CWUG	ClarisWorks User Group
CYBER 24	24 Hours in Cyberspace
CYBERCAFE	CyberSmith
CYBERJUSTICE	CyberJustice
CYBERLAW	CyberLaw/CyberLex
CYBERLEX	CyberLaw/CyberLex
CYBERSALON	Cybersalon

CYBERSERIALS	CyberSerials
CYBERSEX	NetGirl
CYBERSLEUTH	Murder Mysteries Online
CYBERSLIM	The Health Zone
CYBERSMITH	CyberSmith
CYBERSPORTS	The Grandstands' Cyber Sports Simulation Leagues
CYBERVIEW	This Week's Best Cyberviews
CYBERVIEWS	This Week's Best Cyberviews
CYBERZINES	Digizine Sites on the Web
CYCLE	Cycle World Online
CYCLEWORLD	Cycle World Online
CYCLING	Cycle World Online
CYRANO	The Hub: Cyrano
CZECH REPUBLIC	Czech Republic
DACEASY	DacEasy, Inc.
DAILY	Reference Daily Dose
DALAI LAMA	Dalai Lama Conference [May disappear without notice]
DAN HURLEY	60-Second Novelist
DANCE	@times: Music & Dance
DANISH	Genealogy Forum
DATABASE	Database Support SIG
DATABASES	Database Support SIG
DATAPACK	DataPak Software
DATAPAK	DataPak Software
DATAWATCH	Datawatch
DATING	Romance Connection
DAVIDSON	Davidson & Associates
DAYNA	Dayna Communications
DAYONE	ABC News-On-Demand
DAYSTAR	Daystar Digital
DAYTIMER	DayTimer Technologies
DC	Digital City -or- DC Comics
DC COMICS	DC Comics Online
DC COMICS ONLINE	DC Comics Online
DC EVENT	Digital City: The Event Source
DC FUN	Digital City: Entertainment)
DC MARKETPLACE	Digital City: Marketplace
DC NEWS	Digital City: News/Weather
DC PEOPLE	Digital City People
DC PEOPLE	Digital City: People
DC SPORTS	Digital City: Sports
DC WEB	City Web
DCL	Dictionary of Cultural Literacy
DD	Dial/Data
DEAD	Grateful Dead Forum
DEAD END	The Dead End of the Internet
DEADLY	Deadly Games
DEAF	Deaf & Hard of Hearing Forum
DEBATE	Politics Forum
DEC	Digital Equipment Corporation
DECISION	Decision Point Forum
DECISION 94	Decision '96

DECISION POINT	Decision Point Forum
DECORATING	Home Magazine Online
DEFENSE	Military City Online
DELL	Dell Computer Corporation
DELRINA	Symantec
DELTA	Delta Tao
DELTA POINT	Delta Point
DELTATAO	Delta Tao
DEMOCRACY	CNN Newsroom Online
DENEBA	Deneba Software
DENMARK	Denmark
DES	DeskMate
DESIGN	Elle Magazine Online
DESIGN SIG	Design SIG
DESIGNER	Design SIG
DESIGNERS	Elle Magazine Online
DESIGNS ONLINE	Designs Online
DESK REFERENCE	NY Public Library Desk Reference
DESKMATE	DeskMate
DESKTOP CINEMA	Desktop Cinema* [WAOL 2.5 and MAOL 2.6 only]
DESKTOP PUBLISHING	Desktop and Web Publishing area [platform-dependent]
DETROIT TIGERS	Major League Baseball Team: Detroit Tigers
DEV	Development Forum [platform-dependent]
DEVELOPER	Development Forum [platform-dependent]
DEVELOPMENT	Development Forum [platform-dependent]
DEVELOPMENT-FORUM	Development Forum [platform-dependent]
DF FOOD	Destination Florida: Restaurants and Nightlife
DF OUT	Destination Florida: Outdoors
DF PARKS	Destination Florida: Attractions
DF ROOMS	Destination Florida: Places to Stay
DF SHOP	Destination Florida: Shopping
DF SPACE	Destination Florida: Kennedy Space Center
DF SPORTS	Destination Florida: Sports
DF TICKET	Destination Florida: Ticketmaster
DG CHAT	Digital Glasgow City Chat
DI	Disney Interactive
DIABETES	American Diabetes Association
DIAL	Dial/Data
DIALOGUE	American Dialogue
DIAMOND	Diamond Computer Systems
DIAMOND COMPUTERS	Diamond Computer Systems
DICTIONARY	Dictionary Selections
DIGITAL	Digital menu
DIGITAL ECLIPSE	Digital Eclipse
DIGITAL IMAGING	Digital Imaging Resource Center
DIGITAL RESEARCH	Novell Desktop Systems
DIGITAL RESEARCHINC	Novell Desktop Systems
DIGITAL TECH	Digital Technologies
DIGIZINES	Digizine Sites on the Web
DILBERT	Dilbert Comics
DILBERT COMICS	Dilbert Comics
DILBOARD	Dilbert Comics
DINE	Everything Edible

DINE OUT	Dinner On Us Club
DINER	The Web Diner
DINER CREW	The Web Diner
DINING	Everything Edible
DIR OF SERVICES	Directory of Services
DIR OF SVCS	Directory of Services
DIRECTORY	Member Directory
DIRECTORY OF SERVICES	Directory of Services
DIS	DisABILITIES Forum
DISABILITIES	DisABILITIES Forum
DISABILITY	DisABILITIES Forum
DISCLOSURE	Disclosure Incorporated
DISCOVER	Discover AOL area
DISCOVER AOL	Discover AOL
DISCOVERY	The Discovery Channel
DISCOVERY ED	The Discovery Channel Education Area
DISNEY	Disney Services
DISNEY ADVENTURES	Disney Adventures Magazine
DISNEY INTERACTIVE	Disney Interactive
DISNEY JOBS	Disney Jobs
DISNEY MAGAZINE	Disney Adventures Magazine
DISNEY SOFT	Disney Interactive
DISNEY SOFTWARE	Disney Interactive
DISNEY.COM.LOW	Disney.com Sneak Preview
DIVA	Soap Opera Digest
DIVA LA DISH	Soap Opera Digest
DJ	Don Johnston, Inc.
DL	Dalai Lama [May disappear without notice]
DO SOMETHING	Do Something!
DOBSON	Focus on the Family
DOBSON	Focus on the Family
DOCL	Dictionary of Cultural Literacy
DOCTOR WHO	Doctor Who Online
DODGERS	Major League Baseball Team: Los Angeles Dodgers
DOGERS	Major League Baseball Team: Los Angeles Dodgers
DOMARK	Domark Software Inc.
DON JOHNSTON	Don Johnston, Inc.
DONATION	Access.Point
DONATIONS	Access.Point
DONT MISS	Directory of Services
DOROTHY	CyberJustice's Oasis of Xaiz
DOS	DOS Forum
DOS 5.0	DOS Forum
DOS 6	MS-DOS 6.0 Resource Center
DOS 60	MS-DOS 6.0 Resource Center
DOWNLOAD	Software Center [Platform-dependent]
DOWNLOAD 101	Download Help*
DOWNLOAD CREDIT	Credit Request Form for connect problems*
DOWNLOAD GAMES	Download Online Games* [WAOL and GAOL only]
DOWNLOADING	Software Center [Platform-dependent]
DOWNTOWN	Downtown AOL
DOWNTOWN AOL	Downtown AOL
DOWNTOWN MSG	Downtown AOL Message Boards
DP	Decision Point Forum
DPA	Decision Point Forum
DR DOS	DOS Forum
DR GAMEWIZ	Dr Gamewiz Online
DR WHO	Doctor Who Online
DRESSAGE	Horse Forum's Dressage MiniForum
DRI	Novell Desktop Systems
DRIVING	Car and Driver Magazine
DRUG REFERENCE	Consumer Reports Complete Drug Reference Search
DS	Do Something!
DSC	The Discovery Channel
DSC-ED	The Discovery Channel Education Area
DSCED	The Discovery Channel Education Area
DT	Downtown AOL
DT AOL	Downtown AOL
DTP	Desktop and Web Publishing area [platform-dependent]
DTV	Motley Fool: Desktop Video
DUBLCLICK	Dubl-Click Software
DUTCH	Genealogy Forum
DVORAK	Software Hardtalk with John C. Dvorak
DWP	Desktop & Web Publishing
DWP	Desktop and Web Publishing Forum
DYNAMIX	Sierra On-Line
DYNAWARE	Dynaware USA
DYNAWARE USA	Dynaware USA
E!	E! Entertainment Television
EAASY SABRE	EAASY SABRE Travel Service
EARL'S GARAGE	Pro's Corner
EARLS GARAGE	Pro's Corner
EARTH	Environmental Forum
EARTHLINK	TBS Network Earth/IBM Project [MAOL and GAOL only]
EASTERN EUROPEAN	Genealogy Forum
EASY	EAASY SABRE
EASY SABRE	EAASY SABRE Travel Service
EAT	Dinner On Us Club
EAT OUT	Dinner On Us Club
EATS	Good Morning America Recipes
ECOTOURISM	Backpacker Magazine
ECS	Electronic Courseware
ED ADVISORY	Education Advisory Council Online
EDA	Education Advisory Council Online
EDDIE BAUER	Eddie Bauer
EDELSTEIN	Fred Edelstein's Pro Football Insider
EDGAR	Disclosure's EdgarPlus
EDIT PROFILE	Edit your member profile
EDITOR'S CHOICE	Pictures of the Week
EDITORIALCARTOONS	InToon with the News
EDITORS CHOICE	Pictures of the Week
EDMARK	Edmark Technologies

EDTECH	Assoc. for Supervisor & Curriculum Development	EXCHANGE	The Exchange
EDUCATION	Education channel	EXERCISE	Longevity Magazine Online
EDUCATION CONNECTION	Compton's Education Connection	EXPERT	Expert Software, Inc.
EFORUM	Environmental Forum	EXPERT PAD	PDA/Palmtop Forum
EGG	Electronic Gourmet Guide	EXPERTSOFT	Expert Software, Inc.
EGG BASKET	Electronic Gourmet Guide	EXPOS	Major League Baseball Team: Montreal Expos
EGYPT	Egypt	EXPRESS NET	ExpressNet (American Express)
ELECTRIC	Electric Image	EXPRESSNET ART	ExpressNet Art Download*
ELECTRIC IMAGE	Electric Image	EXTRA	EXTRA Online
ELECTRONIC PUBLISHING	Desktop & Web Publishing Area	EXTREME FANS	Extreme Fans
ELECTRONICS	Andy Pargh/The Gadget Guru	EZ	The Entrepreneur Zone
ELI	Eli's Cheesecakes	EZINE	PDA/Palmtop Forum
ELI CONTEST	Elic's Cheesecakes Contest	EZINES	Digizine Sites on the Web
ELI'S	Eli's Cheesecakes	EZONE	Your Business
ELI'S CHEESECAKES	Eli's Cheesecakes	F2M	Transgender Community Forum
ELIS CHEESECAKES	Eli's Cheesecakes	FABFACTS	Fabulous Facts
ELLE	Elle Magazine Online	FABULOUS FACTS	Fabulous Facts
ELVIS	Weekly World News	FACE OFF	Face Off
EMAIL	Post Office [MAOL and WAOL Only]	FALL TV	Lost & Found TV Shows
EMERALD COAST	Emerald Coast	FALL TV SHOWS	Lost & Found TV Shows
EMERGENCY	Public Safety Center	FAMILY	Family Areas
EMERGENCY RESPONSE	Public Safety Center	FAMILY ALBUM	Family Computing Forum: The Family Room
EMIGRE	Emigre Fonts	FAMILY COMPUTING	Family Computing Resource Center
EMPOWERMENT	Personal Empowerment Network	FAMILY FINANCES	Real Life
ENCYCLOPEDIA	Enclopedias	FAMILY GAMES	Family Computing Forum: Family Games
ENDER	Hatrack River Town Meeting	FAMILY NEWS	Family Computing Forum: News & Reviews
ENDNOTE	Niles and Associates	FAMILY PC	FamilyPC Online
ENGINEERING	NAS Online	FAMILY ROOM	Family Computing Forum: Family Room
ENGLISH	Simon & Schuster Online: Education Dept.	FAMILY SHOWCASE	Family Product Showcase
ENTERTAINMENT	Entertainment Channel	FAMILY TRAVEL	Family Travel Network
ENTERTAINMENT NEWS	Entertainment News	FAMILY TRAVEL NETWORK	Family Travel Network
ENTERTAINMENT WEEKLY	Entertainment Weekly	FANS	Extreme Fans
ENTREPRENEUR ZONE	Your Business	FANTASY	Science Fiction & Fantasy
ENVIRONMENT	Environmental Forum	FANTASY BASEBALL	The Grandstand's Fantasy Baseball
ENVIRONMENTAL ED	Earth Day	FANTASY BASKETBALL	The Grandstand's Fantasy Basketball
ENVOY	Motorola	FANTASY FOOTBALL	The Grandstand's Fantasy Football
EPSCONVERTER	Art Age Software	FANTASY HOCKEY	The Grandstand's Fantasy Hockey
EPUB	Desktop & Web Publishing area	FANTASY LEAGUE	The Grandstand's Fantasy & Simulation Leagues
EPUBS	Desktop & Web Publishing area	FANTASY LEAGUES	The Grandstand's Fantasy & Simulation Leagues
EQUIBASE	Horse Racing	FAO	F.A.O. Schwarz
EQUIS	Equis International [MAOL and WAOL only]	FAO SCHWARZ	F.A.O. Schwarz
ERC	Public Safety Center	FARALLON	Farallon
ERIC	AskERIC	FASHION	Elle Magazine Online
ESH	Electronic Schoolhouse	FAVE FLICKS	Favorite Flicks!
ETEXT	PDA's Palmtop Paperbacks	FAVORITE FLICKS	Favorite Flicks!
ETHICS	Religion & Ethics Forum	FAX	Fax/Paper Mail
ETRADE	TradePlus	FC	Family Computing Forum
EUN	Electronic University Network	FCF	Family Computing Forum
EVENT	Today's Events in the Center Stage	FDN	Food & Drink Network
EVENTS	Today's Events in the Center Stage	FEATURES	Columnists & Features Online
EW	Entertainment Weekly	FED	Federation
EWORLD	Apple Aloha for eWorld Alumni	FEDERATION	Federation
EXAM PREP	Exam Prep Center	FEDEX	FedEx (Federal Express)
EXCELLENCE	Access Excellence	FEEDBACK	Member Services*

FELISSIMO	Felissimo
FELLOWSHIP	Fellowship of Online Gamers/RPGA Network
FELLOWSHIP HALL	Christianity Online Chat & Live Events
FERNDALE	Ferndale [WAOL 2.5 only]
FESTE	The Motley Fool
FFGF	Free-Form Gaming Forum
FICTION	The Atlantic Monthly Online
FID	Fidelity Online Investments Center [WAOL only]
FID AT WORK	Fidelity Online's Working Area
FID BROKER	Fidelity Online's Funds Area
FID FUNDS	Fidelity Online's Funds Area
FID GUIDE	Fidelity Online's Guide Area
FID NEWS	Fidelity Online's Newsworthy Area
FID PLAN	Fidelity Online's Planning Area
FIDELITY	Fidelity Online Investments Center [WAOL only]
FIFTH	Symantec
FIGURE SKATING	ABC Sports Figure Skating
FILE	Software Center [Platform-dependent]
FILE SEARCH	Search database of files
FILES	Software Center [Platform-dependent]
FILM REVIEW DATABASE	Movie Review Database
FILM REVIEW DB	Movie Review Database
FILM REVIEWS DATABASE	Movie Review Database
FILM STUDIOS	MovieVisions
FILMBALL	Follywood Games
FINANCE	Personal Finance channel
FINANCIAL ASTROLOGY	ASTRONET
FINANCIAL ASTROLOGY	ASTRONET
FINANCIAL STATEMENT	Disclosure's Financial Statements
FINANCIALS	Disclosure's Financial Statements
FINLAND	Finland
FIREBALL	Flight Sim Resource Center
FIRST	First Look at How New Products
FIRST BYTE	Baumrucker Conference [May disappear without notice]
FIRST CHICAGO ONLINE	First Chicago Online
FIRST LADY	Hillary Rodham Clinton
FIRST LOOK	First Look at How New Products
FISH	Boating Online
FISHING	Boating Online
FITNESS	Fitness Forum
FLIGHT	Flight Sim Resource Center
FLIGHT CENTER	Flight Sim Resource Center
FLIGHT SIM	Flight Sim Resource Center
FLIGHT SIMS	Flight Sim Resource Center
FLIGHT SIMULATIONS	Flight Sim Resource Center
FLORIDA	Destination Florida
FLORIDA KEYS	The Florida Keys
FLORIDA MARLINS	Major League Baseball Team: Florida Marlins
FLOWERS	800-Flowers
FLY	Aviation Forum
FLYING	Flying Magazine
FLYING MAG	Flying Magazine
FLYING MAGAZINE	Flying Magazine

FOCUS	Focus Enhancements
FOCUS ENHANCEMENTS	Focus Enhancements
FOF	Focus on the Family
FOG	Fellowship of Online Gamers/RPGA Network
FOLKWAYS	Folklife & Folkways
FOLLYWOOD	Follywood
FONTBANK	FontBank
FOOD & DRINK	Food & Drink Network
FOOD	Everything Edible!
FOOL	The Motley Fool
FOOL AIR	Motley Fool: Airlines
FOOL CHEM	Motley Fool: Chemicals
FOOL CHIPS	Motley Fool: Semiconductors
FOOL DOME	Fool Dome
FOOL DTV	Motley Fool: Desktop Video
FOOL HARD	Motley Fool: Hardware
FOOL SEM	Motley Fool: Semiconductors
FOOL VID	Motley Fool: Desktop Video
FOOLBALL	Fool Dome
FOOLISH	The Motley Fool
FOOTBALL	AOL Football
FORMZ	auto*des*sys, Inc.
FORTE	Forte Technologies
FORTNER	Fortner Research
FORTRAN	Fortner Research
FORUM	Computing channel [platform-dependent]
FORUM AUD	Rotunda Forum Auditorium
FORUM AUDITORIUM	Rotunda Forum Auditorium [MAOL and GAOL only]
FORUM ROT	Rotunda Forum Auditorium
FORUMS	Computing channel [platform-dependent]
FORUMS	Computing channel [platform-dependent]
FORUMS	PC Support Forums
FOSSIL	Fossil Watches and More
FOSSIL WATCHES	Fossil Watches and More
FOTF	Focus on the Family [WAOL and MAOL only]
FOTF	Focus on the Family
FOUND TV SHOWS	Lost & Found TV Shows
FOUR RESOURCES	AT&T Home Business Resources
FRACTAL	Fractal Design
FRACTAL DESIGN	Fractal Design
FRAGRANCE	The Fragrance Counter
FRANCE & ASSOCIATES	France & Associates
FRANCE	France
FRANKLIN	Franklin Quest
FRASIER	Fraiser Tuesdays
FRASIER TUESDAYS	Fraiser Tuesdays
FREE	Member Services*
FREELANCE	Freelance Artists SIG
FREEMAIL	FreeMail, Inc.
FREESHOP	The FreeShop Online
FREESHOP ONLINE	The FreeShop Online
FRENCH OPEN	French Open [May disappear without notice]
FRENCH TEST	France Beta Test*

FREQUENT FLYER	Inside Flyer	GATEWAY 2000	Gateway 2000, Inc.
FRIDAY	ABC Online: Friday @ 4ET	GAY	Gay & Lesbian Community Forum
FRIDAY @ 4ET	ABC Online: Friday @ 4ET	GAY BOARDS	Gay & Lesbian Community Forum Boards
FRIDAY AT 4	ABC Online Auditorium	GAY BOOKS	Lambda Rising Bookstore
FRIEND	Sign on a friend to AOL*	GAY CHAT	Gay & Lesbian Community Forum Events &
FRIEND IN FRANCE	France Beta Test*		Conferences
FROG	The WB Network	GAY MESSAGE	Gay & Lesbian Community Forum Boards
FROMMER	Frommer's City Guides	GAY NEWS	Gay & Lesbian Community Forum News
FROMMER'S	Frommer's City Guides	GAY ORG	Gay & Lesbian Community Forum Organizations
FROMMER'S CITY GUIDES	Frommer's City Guides	GAY ORGS	Gay & Lesbian Community Forum Organizations
FROMMERS	Frommer's City Guides	GAY POLITICS	Gay & Lesbian Community Forum News
FROMMERS CITY GUIDES	Frommer's City Guides	GAY SOFTWARE	Gay & Lesbian Community Forum Libraries
FRONTIERS	Scientific American Frontiers	GAY TRAVEL	Gay & Lesbian Community Forum Travel
FSRC	Flight Sim Resource Center	GAYME	Gay & Lesbian Community Forum Gaymeland
FTN	Family Travel Network	GAYMELAND	Gay & Lesbian Community Forum Gaymeland
FTP	Internet FTP	GAYMES	Gay & Lesbian Community Forum Gaymeland
FULL DISCLOSURE	AOL's Full Disclosure for investors	GAZETTE	CyberJustice's Gazette Online/Email
FULLWRITE	FullWrite	GBL	The Grandstand's Simulation Baseball
FUND	Morningstar Mutual Funds	GCACTION	Cames Channel Action
FUNDS	Morningstar Mutual Funds	GCACTION	Games Channel: Action Games
FURNISHINGS	Home Magazine Online	GCC	GCC Technologies
FURNITURE	Home Magazine Online	GCCLASSIC	Games Channel: Classic Games
FUTBOL	AOL Soccer	GCCONTESTS	Games Channel: Contests
FUTURE LABS	Future Labs, Inc.	GCFL	The Grandstand's Simulation Football
FUZZY	The Hub: Fuzzy Memories	GCINFO	Games Channel Information
FWM	Fighting Woman News	GCINFO	Games Channel: Gaming Information
GADGET	Andy Pargh/The Gadget Guru	GCKNOWLEDGE	Games Channel: Knowledge Games
GADGET GURU	Andy Pargh/The Gadget Guru	GCPERSONA	Games Channel: Persona Games
GALACTICOMM	Galacticomm	GCRPG	Games Channel: Role Playing Games
GALLERY	Portrait Gallery	GCS	Gaming Company Support
GAME	The Games Channel	GCSIMULATION	Games Channel: Simulation Games
GAME BASE	Game Base	GCSPORTS	Games Channel: Sports Games
GAME DESIGN	Game Designers Forum	GCSTRATEGY	Games Channel: Strategy Games
GAME DESIGNER	Game Designers Forum	GDT	GDT Softworks, Inc.
GAME DESIGNERS	Game Designers Forum	GDT SOFTWORKS	GDT Softworks, Inc.
GAME ROOMS	Games Parlor	GEMSTONE	GemStone III
GAME SITES	WWW Game Sites	GEMSTONE III	GemStone III
GAMEPRO	GamePro Online	GEN NEXT	Generation Next
GAMES & ENTERTAINMENT	The Games Channel	GENDER	Transgender Community Forum
GAMES	The Games Channel	GENEALOGY	Genealogy Forum
GAMES CHANNEL	The Games Channel	GENEALOGY CLUB	Genealogy Forum
GAMES DOWNLOAD	Download Online Games* [WAOL and GAOL	GENERAL AVIATION	Aviation Forum
	only]	GENERAL HOSPITAL	ABC Daytime/Soapline
GAMES FORUM	Games Forum [platform-dependent]	GENERAL MAGIC	General Magic
GAMES PARLOR	Games Parlor	GENERATION NEXT	Generation Next
GAMESTER	FamilyPC Online	GENERATIONS	Generations
GAMETEK	Gametek	GENESIS	Video Games area
GAMEWIZ	Dr. Gamewiz Online	GENIE EASY	Astronet
GAMEWIZ INC	Dr Gamewiz Online	GEO SDK	Geoworks Development [WAOL and GAOL only]
GAMING	Online Gaming Forums	GEOGRAPHIC	Odyssey Project
GARAGE	Pro's Corner	GEOGRAPHY	Simon & Schuster Online: Geography Dept.
GARDEN	Gardening Online Selections	GEOWORKS	Geoworks
GARDENING	Gardening Online Selections	GERALDO	The Geraldo Show
GATEWAY	Gateway 2000, Inc.	GERALDO SHOW	The Geraldo Show

GERMANY	International Channel
GERTIE	Mercury Center Trivia
GET A LIFE	The Hub: Get A Life
GETTING STARTED	Help Desk [Platform-dependent]
GETTING STARTED FORUM	Help Desk [Platform-dependent]
GGL	The Grandstand's Simulation Golf
GH	ABC Daytime/Soapline
GIANTS	Major League Baseball Team: San Francisco Giants
GIF CONVERTER	GIF Converter
GIFT CERTIFICATE	AOL Gift Certificates
GIFTED	Giftedness Forum
GIFTS	800-Flowers
GIGABRAIN	FamilyPC Online
GIGABYTES	The Hub: Gigabytes Island
GIX	Gaming Information Exchange
GLCF	Gay & Lesbian Community Forum
GLCF BOARDS	Gay & Lesbian Community Forum Boards
GLCF CHAT	Gay & Lesbian Community Events & Conferences
GLCF EVENT	Gay & Lesbian Community Forum Chat
GLCF EVENTS	Gay & Lesbian Community Forum Chat
GLCF H2H	Gay & Lesbian Community Forum Heart to Heart
GLCF HEART	Gay & Lesbian Community Forum Heart to Heart
GLCF HEART TO HEART	Gay & Lesbian Community Forum Heart to Heart
GLCF LIBRARY	Gay & Lesbian Community Forum Libraries
GLCF NEWS	Gay & Lesbian Community Forum News
GLCF ORG	Gay & Lesbian Community Forum Organizations
GLCF ORGANIZATIONS	Gay & Lesbian Community Forum Organizations
GLCF ORGS	Gay & Lesbian Community Forum Organizations
GLCF QUILT	GLCF AIDS Quilt
GLCF SOFTWARE	Gay & Lesbian Community Forum Libraries
GLCF TCF	Transgender Community Forum
GLCF TRAVEL	Gay & Lesbian Community Forum Travel
GLCF WOMAN	GLCF: Women's Space
GLCF WOMEN	GLCF: Women's Space
GLOBAL	Global Village Communication
GLOBAL VILLAGE	Global Village Communication
GLOBALNET	AOLGLOBALnet International Access*
GLOBE	Center Stage
GMA	ABC Good Morning America
GMAT	Kaplan Online -or- The Princeton Review
GMFL	The Grandstand's Simulation Football
GMME	Grolier's Encyclopeda
GNN	GNN Best of the Net
GNN BETA	GNN Best of the Net
GO SCUBA	Scuba Club
GODIVA	Godiva Chocolatiers
GOLF	AOL Golf area
GOLF AMERICA	Golfis Forum
GOLF COURSES	Golfis Forum
GOLF DATA	GolfCentral
GOLF INFORMATION	Golfis Forum
GOLF RESORTS	Golfis Forum
GOLFIS	Golfis Forum

GONER TV	Lost & Found TV Shows
GOOD MORNING AMERICA	ABC Good Morning America
GOPHER	Internet Gopher
GOSSIP	Entertainment Channel
GOURMET	Everything Edible!
GOVERNING	Governing Magazine
GOVERNMENT	Politics Forum
GPF	GPF Help*
GPFL	The Grandstand's Simulation Football
GPS	Trimble Navigation, Ltd.
GRADUATE SCHOOL	Kaplan Online -or- The Princeton Review
GRAFIK	Grafik/Animation (France) [WAOL 2.5 only]
GRANDSTAND	TheGrandstand
GRANDSTAND TRIVIA	The Grandstand's Sports Trivia
GRAPH SIM	Graphic Simulations
GRAPHIC	Graphic Simulations
GRAPHIC ARTS	Graphic Arts & CAD Forum [platform-dependent]
GRAPHIC DESIGN	Design SIG
GRAPHIC SIMULATIONS	Graphic Simulations
GRAPHICS	Graphic Arts & CAD Forum [platform-dependent]
GRAPHICS FORUM	Graphic Arts & CAD Forum [platform-dependent]
GRAPHISOFT	Graphisoft
GRAPHSOFT	Graphsoft, Inc.
GRATEFUL DEAD	Grateful Dead Forum
GRAVIS	Advanced Gravis
GRE	Kaplan Online -or- The Princeton Review
GREECE	Greece
GREEK	Genealogy Forum
GREENBERG	Kaplan Online
GREENHOUSE	AOL Greenhouse
GREET ST	Greet Street Greeting Cards
GREET STREET	Greet Street Greeting Cards
GROLIER	Grolier's Encyclopeda
GROLIER'S	Grolier's Encyclopeda
GROLIERS	Grolier's Encyclopeda
GROUP	McLaughlin Group
GROUPWARE	GroupWare SIG
GRYPHON	Gryphon Software
GRYPHON SOFTWARE	Gryphon Software
GS	WWW Game Sites
GS ARTS	The Grandstand's Martial Arts (The Dojo)
GS AUTO	The Grandstand's Motor Sports (In The Pits)
GS BASEBALL	The Grandstand's Baseball (Dugout)
GS BASKETBALL	The Grandstand's Basketball (Off the Glass)
GS BOXING	The Grandstand's Boxing (Squared Circle)
GS COLLECTING	The Grandstand's Collecting (Sports Cards)
GS FOOTBALL	The Grandstand's Football (50 Yard Line)
GS GOLF	The Grandstand's Golf (On The Green)
GS HOCKEY	The Grandstand's Hockey (Blue Line)
GS HORSE	The Grandstand's Horse Sports & Racing Forum
GS MAG	GS+ Magazine
GS OTHER	The Grandstand's Other Sports (Whole 9 Yards)
GS SIDELINE	The Grandstand's Sideline
GS SOCCER	The Grandstand's Soccer (The Kop)

GS SOFTWARE	The Grandstand's Sports Software Headquarters	HEALTH EXP	Health and Vitamin Express
GS SPORTS TRIVIA	The Grandstand's Sports Trivia	HEALTH EXPRESS	Health and Vitamin Express
GS SPORTSMART	The Grandstand's Sports Products (Sportsmart)	HEALTH FOCUS	Health Focus
GS TRIVIA	The Grandstand's Sports Trivia	HEALTH LIVE	Health Speakers and Support Groups
GS WINTER	The Grandstand's Winter Sports (The Chalet)	HEALTH MAGAZINE	Health Magazine
GS WRESTLING	The Grandstand's Wrestling (Squared Circle)	HEALTH MAGAZINES	Health Resources
GSC	Graphic Simulations	HEALTH REFERENCE	Health Resources
GSDL	The Grandstand's Simulation Basketball	HEALTH RESOURCES	Health Resources
GSFL	The Grandstand's Simulation Football	HEALTH TODAY	Columbia's Health Today
GSHL	The Grandstand's Simulation Hockey	HEALTH WEB	Health Web Sites
GSS	Global Software Suport	HEALTH ZONE	The Health Zone
GUAM	Guam	HEART TO HEART	Gay & Lesbian Community Forum Heart to Heart
GUFL	The Grandstand's Simulation Football	HEAVEN	The Hub: Heaven
GUIDE PAGE	Guide Pager	HECKLE	Hecklers Online
GUIDE PAGER	Guide Pager	HECKLER	Hecklers Online
GUITAR	Guitar Special Interest Group	HECKLERS	Hecklers Online
GUNS	The Exchange: Interests & Hobbies	HECKLERS ONLINE	Hecklers Online
GURU	Andy Pargh/The Gadget Guru	HELMETS	Cycle World Online
GVC	MaxTech Corporation	HELP	Member Services*
GWA	The Grandstand's Simulation Wrestling	HELP DESK	Help Desk [Platform-dependent]
GWA	The Grandstand's Simulation Wrestling	HELP WANTED	Search Help Wanted, USA
GWALTNEY	Gwaltney Hams & Turkeys	HEM	Home Education Magazine
GWF	The Grandstand's Simulation Wrestling	HERBS	Longevity Magazine Online
GWPI	The Hub: Global Worldwide Pictures Interqantional Ltd.	HERITAGE	Heritage Foundation
		HERITAGE FOUNDATION	Heritage Foundation area
GWU	George Washington University	HFM MAGNET WORK	Hachette Filipacchi Magazines
H2H	Gay & Lesbian Community Forum Heart to Heart	HFS	WHFS 99.1 FM
HACHETTE	Hachette Filipacchi Magazines	HH KIDS	Homework Help
HACK	MacHack	HIGH SPEED	High Speed Access area*
HACKER	MacHack	HIGHLIGHTS	Highlights Online for Children
HACKERS	Hackers movie area	HIKER	Backpacker Magazine
HALL OF FAME	Downloading Hall of Fame	HIKING	Backpacker Magazine
HALLMARK	Hallmark Connections [WAOL and MAOL only]	HILLARY	Hillary Rodham Clinton
HALLMARK CONNECTIONS	Hallmark Connections [WAOL and MAOL only]	HISPANIC	Hispanic Selections
HAM	Ham Radio Club	HISPANIC	The Exchange: Communities Center
HAM RADIO	Ham Radio Club	HITCHIKER	The Hub: John the Hitchhiker
HAMMACHER	Hammacher Schlemmer	HITS	Rockline Online
HAMMACHER SCHLEMMER	Hammacher Schlemmer	HIV	AIDS and HIV Resource Center
HAMS	Gwaltney Hams & Turkeys	HMCURRENT	Health Magazine's Current area
HANDLE	Add, change or delete screen names	HMFITNESS	Health Magazine's Fitness area
HANES	One Hanes Place	HMFOOD	Health Magazine's Food area
HARDBALL	Baseball Daily by Extreme Fans	HMRELATIONSHIPS	Health Magazine's Relationships area
HARDWARE	Hardware Forum [platform-dependent]	HMREMEDIES	Health Magazine's Remedies area
HARDWARE FORUM	Hardware Forum [platform-dependent]	HO	Hecklers Online
HARLEY	The All-Harley Magazine	HOB	House of Blues Online
HARLEY DAVIDSON	The All-Harley Magazine	HOBBIES	Clubs & Interests Channel
HASH	Hash, Inc.	HOBBY	Hobby Central
HATRACK	Hatrack River Town Meeting	HOBBY CENTRAL	Hobby Central
HATRACK RIVER TOWN	Hatrack River Town Meeting	HOC	Home Office Computing Magazine
HBS PUB	Harvard Business School Publishing	HOCKEY	NFL Hockey area
HDC	hDC Corporation	HOCKEY TRIVIA	NTN Hockey Trivia
HDC CORPORATION	hDC Corporation	HOF	Downloading Hall of Fame
HEADLINES	Today's News channel	HOL PRO	The Biz!
HEALTH	Health Channel		

HOLIDAY	AOL Holiday Central [May disappear without notice]
HOLIDAYS	AOL Holiday Central [May disappear without notice]
HOLLYWOOD	Hollywood Online
HOLLYWOOD ONLINE	Hollywood Online
HOLLYWOOD PRO	The Biz!
HOLMES	Mysteries from the Yard
HOME	House & Home area
HOME AUDIO	Consumer Electronics
HOME BANKING	Bank of America
HOME BREW	Food & Drink Network
HOME BREWING	Food & Drink Network
HOME DESIGN	Home Magazine Online
HOME EQUITY LOANS	Real Estate Online
HOME OFFICE	Home Office Computing Magazine
HOME OWNER	Homeowner's Forum
HOME OWNERS	Homeowner's Forum
HOME PAGE	Personal WWW Publishing area [WAOL 2.5 only]
HOME PC	HomePC Magazine
HOME REFINANCING	Real Estate Online
HOME SCHOOLING	Homeschooling Forum
HOME THEATER	Stereo Review Online
HOME VIDEO	Home Video
HOMEOPATHIC REMEDIES	Longevity Magazine Online
HOMER	Homer's Page at The Odyssey Project
HOMEWORK	Homework Help Selections
HONG KONG	Hong Kong
HOOPS	NCAA Hoops [May disappear without notice]
HOOPS BOARDS	Extreme Fans: Message Boards
HOOPS TRIVIA	NTN Basketball Trivia
HOOVER	Hoover's Business Resources
HOOVER'S	Hoover's Business Resources
HOOVERS	Hoover's Business Resources
HOOVERS UPDATES	Hoover's Company Masterlist
HOROSCOPE	Horoscopes
HOROSCOPES	Horoscopes
HORROR	Science Fiction & Fantasy
HORSE	The Horse Forum
HORSE RACING	The Grandstand: Horse Sports & Racing Forum
HORSE SPORTS	The Grandstand: Horse Sports & Racing Forum
HORSES	The Horse Forum
HOT	What's Hot This Month showcase
HOT BUTTON	The Hub: The Hot Button
HOT ENTERTAINMENT	What's Hot in Entertainment
HOT MAC	What's Hot in Mac Computing
HOT PC	What's Hot in PC Computing
HOT REFERENCE	Hot Reference
HOTLINE	Member Services*
HOUSE	Home Magazine Online
HOUSE OF BLUES	House of Blues Online
HOUSENET	HouseNet
HOUSTON ASTROS	Major League Baseball Team: Houston Astros
HP	Hewlett-Packard

HP FAX	Hewlett-Packard Fax Products
HP FILES	Hewlett-Packard: Support Information Files
HP HOME	Hewlett-Packard: Home Products Information
HP MULTI	Hewlett-Packard Multifunction Products
HP PLOT	Hewlett-Packard Plotter Products
HP SCAN	Hewlett-Packard Scanner Products
HP SCSI	Hewlett-Packard SCSI Products
HP SERVER	Hewlett-Packard Server Products
HP STORE	Hewlett-Packard Information Storage Products
HP VECTRA	Hewlett-Packard Vectra Products
HPPRN	HP Printer Products
HRS	Better Health & Medical Forum
HSC	MetaTools Inc.
HTML	Web Page Toolkit
HTML	Web Page Toolkit
HTML HELP	The Web Diner
HTS	Home Team Sports
HTTP	What is HTTP?
HUB	The Hub
HUM	Virtual Christian Humor
HUMAN SEXUALITY	Simon & Schuster Online: Human Sexuality Dept.
HUMOR	The Comedy Pub
HUNGARY	Hungary
HUNT	AOL Treasure Hunt
HURLEY	60-Second Novelist
HURRICANE	Tropical Storm and Hurricane Info
HYPERCARD	HyperCard Forum
HYPERSTUDIO	Roger Wagner Publishing
HZ	The Health Zone
I-WIRE	I-Wire Online
IA	Print Artist Resource Center
IBD	Investor's Business Daily
IBIZ	InBusiness
IBM	IBM Forum
IBM OS2	OS/2 Forum
IBVA	IBVA Technologies
IBVA TECH	IBVA Technologies
IC	Computing Company Connection
IC HILITES	IC Hilites
ICELAND	Iceland
ICF	Investors' Exchange
IDEAS	The Atlantic Monthly Online
IDEAS FOR BETTER LIVING	Ideas for Better Living
IDITAROD	Iditarod Trail Sled Dog Race
IE	Investors' Exchange
IES	Online Campus
IFORSOOTH	Murder Mysteries Online
IFR	Flying Magazine
IG	Intelligent Gamer Online
IG ONLINE	Intelligent Gamer Online
IGOLF	iGolf
IGOLF HISTORY	iGolf History
IHRSA	The Health Zone
IIN	New Product Showcase

ILLUSTRATOR	Mac Graphics Illustrator SIG
IMAGE	Image Exchange
IMAGE EXCHANGE	Image Exchange
IMAGING	Advanced Color Imaging Forum
IMH	Issues in Mental Health
IMMIGRATION	Genealogy Forum
IMPROV	The IMPROVisation Online
IMPROVISATION	The IMPROVisation Online
IN	Investors' Network
IN TOON	InToon with the News
INBIZ	InBusiness
INBOARD	Boating Online
INBUSINESS	InBusiness
INC	Inc. Magazine
INC MAGAZINE	Inc. Magazine
INC ONLINE	Inc. Magazine
INC.	Inc. Magazine
INC. MAGAZINE	Inc. Magazine
INC. ONLINE	Inc. Magazine
INCOME STATEMENT	Disclosure's Financial Statements
INDIANS	Major League Baseball Team: Cleveland Indians
INDUSTRY CONNECTION	Computing Company Connection
INDUSTRY PROFILES	Hoover's Industry Profiles
INDY	Indy 500
INDY 500	Indy 500
INFINITI	Infiniti Online
INFINITI ONLINE	Infiniti Online
INFORMATION	Member Services*
INFORMATION PROVIDER	Information Provider Resource Center
INFORMATION PROVIDERS	Information Provider Resource Center
INFORMATIQUE	AOL in France [WAOL 2.5 only]
INFORMED PARENT	Princeton Review Informed Parent
INLINE	Inline Design
INLINE SOFTWARE	Inline Design
INNOSYS	InnoSys Inc. [MAOL and GAOL only]
INSIDE	Industry Insider -or- The Cobb Group Online
INSIDE FLYER	Inside Flyer
INSIDE MEDIA	Cowles/SIMBA Media Information Network
INSIDER	Industry Insider
INSIGNIA	Insignia Solutions
INSIGNIA SOLUTION	Insignia Solutions
INSTANT ARTIST	Print Artist Resource Center
INSTANT ARTIST1	Print Artist Resource Center
INSURANCE	Real Life
INTEL	Intel Corporation
INTEL INSIDE	Intel Corporation
INTELLIGENT GAMER	Intelligent Gamer Online
INTERACTIVE ASTROLOGY	ASTRONET
INTERACTIVE ED	Online Campus
INTERACTIVE EDUCATION	Online Campus
INTERCON	InterCon Systems Corporation
INTEREST	Clubs & Interests Channel
INTERIOR DESIGN	Home Magazine Online
INTERNATIONAL	International Channel
INTERNATIONAL CAFE	International Cafe
INTERNET	Internet Connection channel
INTERNET BIZ	InBusiness
INTERNET CENTER	Internet Connection channel
INTERNET CHAT	Internet Connection Coming Attractions
INTERNET CONNECTION	Internet Connection channel
INTERNET GRAPHICS	Internet Graphic Sites [WAOL 2.5 and MAOL 2.6 only]
INTERNET MAGAZINES	Magazines on the Internet [WAOL 2.5 and MAOL 2.6 only]
INTERNET MAGS	Magazines on the Internet [WAOL 2.5 and MAOL 2.6 only]
INTERNET NEWS	Internet Newsstand
INTERPLAY	Interplay
INTREK	InTrek
INTUIT	Intuit, Inc.
INVEST	Investors' Network
INVESTING	Investors' Network
INVESTMENT	Investors' Network
INVESTMENT LINGO	Investment Lingo
INVESTMENTS	Investors' Network
INVESTOR	Investors' Network
INVESTOR RELATIONS	AOL's Full Disclosure for investors
INVESTOR'S BUSINESS	Investor's Business Daily
INVESTOR'S DAILY	Investor's Business Daily
INVESTOR'S NETWORK	Investors' Network
INVESTORS	Investors' Network
INVESTORS BUSINESS	Investor's Business Daily
INVESTORS DAILY	Investor's Business Daily
INVESTORS NETWORK	Investors' Network
IOMEGA	Iomega Corporation
IOTW	Editor's Choice News
IP	Information Provider Resource Center
IPA	Advanced Color Imaging Forum
IQ	Wizard World
IRELAND	Ireland
IRISH	Genealogy Forum
ISCNI	Institute for the Study of Contact with Non-human Intelligence
ISIS	ISIS International
ISIS INTERNATIONAL	ISIS International
ISKI	iSKI
ISLAM	Religion & Ethics Forum
ISLAND	Island Graphics Corporation
ISLAND GRAPHICS	Island Graphics Corporation
ISRAEL	Israel
ISREAL	Israel
ISS	Personal Finance Software Support
ISSUES	Politics Forum
ITALIAN	Genealogy Forum
ITALIAN FOOD	Mama's Cucina by Ragu
ITALY	Italy
IWIRE	I-Wire Online
JAPAN	International Channel

JAYS	Major League Baseball Team: Toronto Blue Jays
JAZZFEST	House of Blues Online
JCOL	Jewish.COMMunity
JCPENNEY	JCPenney
JET	Aviation Forum
JEWISH	Jewish.COMMunity
JEWISH COMMUNITY	Jewish.COMMunity
JL COOPER	JLCooper Electronics
JOB	Real Life
JOBS	Help Wanted Ads
JOEL SIEGEL	ABC Good Morning America
JOHN GRAY	Men Are From Mars
JOHN NABER	John Naber [May disappear without notice]
JOKES	Jokes! Etc.
JORDAN	Michael Jordan area
JPEGVIEW	JPEGView
JUDAISM	Religion & Beliefs Forum
JUDGMENT	CyberJustice's Record Your Judgment
KANSAS CITY ROYALS	Major League Baseball Team: Kansas City Royals
KAPLAN	Kaplan Online
KARATE	The Grandstand's Martial Arts (The Dojo)
KARROS	Eric Karros Kronikles
KASAN	Kasanjian Research
KASANJIAN	Kasanjian Research
KAUFMANN	The Kaufmann Fund
KAZAKHSTAN	Kazakhstan
KEEFE	InToon with the News
KEEPER	Internet Usenet Newsgroup area
KENNEDY SPACE	Challenger Remembered
KENNEDY SPACE CENTER	Challenger Remembered
KENNEHORA	CyberJustice's Kennehora Junction
KENNEHORA JUNCTION	CyberJustice's Kennehora Junction
KENS GUIDE	The Hub: Ken's Guide to the Bible
KENSINGTON	Kensington Microware, Ltd.
KENT MARSH	Kent*Marsh
KEYWORD	Keyword List Area
KEYWORD LIST	Keyword List Area
KEYWORDS	Keyword List Area
KID DESK	Edmark Technologies
KID TRAVEL	Family Travel Network
KIDS	Kids Only channel
KIDS DICTIONARY	Merriam-Webster's Kids
KIDS ONLY	Kids Only channel
KIDS WB	Kids' Warner Brothers Online
KIDS WEB	Kid's Top Internet Sites
KIDS' WB	Kids' WB Online
KIDSBIZ	KidsBiz
KIDSOFT	Club KidSoft
KIDSOFT STORE	KidSoft Superstore
KIDZINE	ABC KIDZINE
KING	Martin Luther King
KING OF THE BEACH	HVP Volleyball
KIP	Kiplinger TaxCut Software Support
KIPLINGER	Kiplinger TaxCut Software Support

KIRSHNER	Simon & Schuster College Online
KITCHEN	Everything Edible
KIVETCH	CyberJustice's Worry, Complain & Sob
KNITTING	Needlecrafts/Sewing Center
KNOWLEDGE BASE	Microsoft Knowledge Base
KO HELP	Kids' Guide Pager
KOB	HVP Volleyball
KODAK	Kodak Photography Forum
KODAK WEB	Kodak Web Site [WAOL 2.5 only]
KOMANDO	Kim Komando's Komputer Clinic
KOMPUTER CLINIC	Kim Komando's Komputer Clinic
KOMPUTER TUTOR	Kim Komando's Komputer Clinic
KONSPIRACY	The Hub: Konspiracy Korner
KOREA	Korea
KPT	MetaTools Inc.
KPTBRYCE	MetaTools Inc.
KR	Kasanjian Research
KRAMER	ASTRONET
KRANK	MTV Online: Krank
KURZWEIL	Kurzweil Music Systems
L & C	Lois & Clark
L AND C	Lois & Clark
L&C STORE	Learning & Culture Store
L'EGGS	One Hanes Place
LACROSSE	The Lacrosse Forum
LAMBDA	Lambda Rising Online
LAMBDA RISING	Lambda Rising Online
LAMDA	Gay & Lesbian Community Forum
LANDSCAPING	Home Magazine Online
LANGUAGE	International Cafe
LANGUAGE SYS	Fortner Research
LANGUAGES	International Cafe
LAPIS	Focus Enhancements
LAPTOP	PowerBook Resource Center
LAPUB	LaPub
LATINO	HISPANIC Online
LATINONET	LatinoNet Registration
LATVIA	Latvia
LAUNCE	The Motley Fool
LAVATCH	The Motley Fool
LAW	Court TV's Law Center
LAW CENTER	Court TV's Law Center
LAW SCHOOL	Kaplan Online -or- The Princeton Review
LAWRENCE	Lawrence Productions
LAX	The Lacrosse Forum
LEADER	Leader Technologies
LEADER TECH	Leader Technologies
LEADER TECHNOLOGIES	Leader Technologies
LEADERS NETWORK	Christianity Online: Church Leaders Network
LEADERSHIP	Leadership Journal
LEADERSHIP JOURNAL	Leadership Journal
LEADING EDGE	Leading Edge
LEARN	Education channel
LEARNING & REFERENCE	Education channel

LEARNING	Education channel
LEARNING AND REFERENCE	Education channel
LEARNING CENTER	Education channel
LEGAL	Online Legal Areas
LEGAL PAD	The Legal Pad
LEGAL SIG	Legal Information Network
LEISURE	@times: Leisure Guide
LENS	Lens Express
LENS EXPRESS	Lens Express
LESBIAN	Gay & Lesbian Community Forum
LESBIAN BOARDS	Gay & Lesbian Community Forum Boards
LESBIAN CHAT	Gay & Lesbian Community Forum Events & Conferences
LESBIAN LIBRARY	Gay & Lesbian Community Forum Libraries
LESBIAN MESSAGE	Gay & Lesbian Community Forum Boards
LESBIAN NEWS	Gay & Lesbian Community Forum News
LESBIAN ORG	Gay & Lesbian Community Forum Organizations
LESBIAN ORGS	Gay & Lesbian Community Forum Organizations
LESBIAN POLITICS	Gay & Lesbian Community Forum News
LESBIAN SOFTWARE	Gay & Lesbian Community Forum Libraries
LESBIAN TRAVEL	Gay & Lesbian Community Forum Travel
LETTER	Community Updates From Steve Case*
LETTER2	Community Updates From Steve Case*
LIA	Lost in America
LIBERTARIAN	Libertarian Party Forum
LIBERTARIAN PARTY	Libertarian Party Forum
LIBERTARIANS	Libertarian Party Forum
LIBRARIES	Software Center [Platform-dependent]
LIBRARY	Library of Congress Online
LIBS	Software Center [Platform-dependent]
LIFE	Computer Life Magazine
LIFESTYLES & HOBBIES	Clubs & Interests Channel
LIFESTYLES & INTEREST	Clubs & Interests Channel
LIFESTYLES & INTERESTS	Clubs & Interests Channel
LIFESTYLES	Clubs & Interests Channel
LIFETIME	Lifetime Television
LIFETIME TELEVISION	Lifetime Television
LIFETIME TV	Lifetime Television
LILLIAN	Lillian Vernon
LILLIAN VERNON	Lillian Vernon
LIN	Legal Information Network
LIND	Lind Portable Power
LINGO	Investment Lingo
LINKS	Access Software
LINKSWARE	LinksWare, Inc.
LINN SOFTWARE	LinnSoftware [MAOL and WAOL only]
LINNSOFT	LinnSoftware [MAOL and WAOL only]
LISTINGS	TMS TV Quest
LISTSERV	Internet Mailing Lists
LITERACY	Adult Literacy & Education Forum
LITERATURE	Saturday Review Online
LIVE	AOL Live
LIVE PICTURE	Live Picture Inc.
LIVE SPORTS	AOL Sports Live
LIVE!	AOL Live
LJ	Leadership Journal
LOC	Library of Congress Online
LOCAL NEWS	Newspaper Selections
LOCAL NEWSPAPERS	Newspaper Selections
LOCALS	CyberJustice's Meet The Locals
LOGICODE	Logicode Technology, Inc.
LOIS & CLARK	Lois & Clark
LOIS AND CLARK	Lois & Clark
LOL	The Comedy Pub
LONGEVITY	Longevity Magazine Online
LOS ANGELES DODGERS	Major League Baseball Team: Los Angeles Dodgers
LOST	Lost in America
LOST IN AMERICA	Lost in America
LOST TV	Lost & Found TV Shows
LOST TV SHOWS	Lost & Found TV Shows
LOTTERY	Lotteries
LOVE	Love@AOL
LOVE MOM	I Love My Mom Because...
LOVE ONLINE	ABC Online: Love Online
LOVE@AOL	Love@AOL
LSAT	Kaplan Online -or- The Princeton Review
LUCAS	LucasArts Games
LUCAS ARTS	LucasArts Games
LUV	ABC Online: Love Online
LUXEMBOURG	Luxembourg
LV426	Industrial Corps
LYNCH	Merrill Lynch
LYNX	Virtual Airlines
LYNX AIRWAYS	Virtual Airlines
M'S	Major League Baseball Team: Seattle Mariners
M2F	Transgender Community Forum
MAC	Mac Computing channel
MAC ALPT	The Grandstand's Simulation Golf
MAC ART	Graphic Art & CAD Forum
MAC BIBLE	The Macintosh Bible/Peachpit Forum
MAC BUSINESS	Business Forum
MAC COMMUNICATION	Mac Communications & Networking Forum
MAC COMMUNICATIONS	Mac Communications & Networking Forum
MAC COMPUTING	Mac Computing channel
MAC DESKTOP	Mac Desktop Publishing/WP Forum
MAC DEVELOPMENT	Mac Developers Forum
MAC DOWNLOADING	Mac Software Center
MAC DTP	Mac Desktop Publishing/WP Forum
MAC EDUCATION	Mac Education & Technology Forum
MAC ESSENTIALS	Macintosh Essential Utilities
MAC GAME	Mac Games Forum
MAC GAMES	Mac Games Forum
MAC GRAPHICS	Mac Graphic Art & CAD Forum
MAC HACK	MacHack
MAC HARDWARE	Mac Hardware Forum
MAC HELP	Help Desk [Platform-dependent]
MAC HOME	Mac Home Journal

MAC HOME JOURNAL	Mac Home Journal
MAC HOT	What's Hot in Mac Computing
MAC HYPERCARD	Mac HyperCard & Scripting Forum
MAC LIBRARIES	Mac Software Center
MAC MULTIMEDIA	Mac Desktop Video Forum
MAC MUSIC	Mac Music & Sound Forum
MAC O/S	Mac Operating Systems Forum
MAC OPERATING SYSTEMS	Mac Operating Systems Forum
MAC OS	Mac Operating Systems Forum
MAC PROGRAMMING	Mac Developers Forum
MAC SOFTWARE	Mac Software Center
MAC SOFTWARE CENTER	Mac Software Center
MAC SOUND	Mac Music & Sound Forum
MAC SPEAKERZ	True Image Audio [MAOL and GAOL only]
MAC TELECOM	Mac Communications & Networking Forum
MAC TELECOMM	Mac Communications & Networking Forum
MAC TODAY	Mac Today Magazine
MAC UTILITIES	Mac Utilities Forum
MAC WORLD PROCESSING	Mac Desktop Publishing/WP Forum
MACINTOSH	Mac Computing channel
MACINTOSH BIBLE	The Macintosh Bible/Peachpit Forum
MACMILLAN	MacMillan Information SuperLibrary
MACMILLAN	The Information SuperLibrary
MACRO	Affinity Microsystems
MACROMEDIA	MacroMedia, Inc.
MACROMIND	MacroMedia, Inc.
MACROS	Affinity Microsystems
MACSCITECH	MacSciTech SIG
MACTIVITY	Mactivity '95 Forum
MACWORLD	MacWorld Magazine [MAOL and GAOL only]
MAD	DC Comics Online
MAD MAGAZINE	DC Comics Online
MADA	MacApp Developers Association
MAGAZINES	The Newsstand
MAGIC LINK	Sony Magic Link
MAGICK	Pagan Religions & Occult Sciences
MAGICKAL	Pagan Religions & Occult Sciences
MAGNET	Hachette Filipacchi Magazines
MAGNETO	Hachette Filipacchi Magazines
MAIL	Post Office [MAOL and WAOL only]
MAIL GATEWAY	Mail Gateway
MAILING LIST	Business Yellow Pages
MAILING LISTS	Internet Mailing Lists
MAINSTAY	Mainstay
MALAWI	Malawi
MALL	Marketplace channel
MAMA	Mama's Cucina by Ragu
MAMA'S CUCINA	Mama's Cucina by Ragu
MANAGER	Manager's Network
MANAGER'S NETWORK	Manager's Network
MANAGERS	Manager's Network
MANAGING	Manager's Network
MANHATTAN GRAPHICS	Manhattan Graphics
MARCO	Motorola

MARINE	Boating Online
MARINERS	Major League Baseball Team: Seattle Mariners
MARKET	Market Master
MARKET NEWS	Market News area
MARKET PLACE	Marketplace channel
MARKETING PREFERENCES	Marketing Preferences*
MARKETING PREFS	Marketing Preferences*
MARKETS	Market News area
MARLINS	Major League Baseball Team: Florida Marlins
MARRIAGE	Marriage Partnership Magazine
MARRIAGE PARTNERSHIP	Marriage Partnership Magazine
MARS	Men Are From Mars
MARTIAL ARTS	The Grandstand's Martial Arts (The Dojo)
MARTIN	Martin Luther King
MARTIN LUTHER	Martin Luther King
MARTIN LUTHER KING	Martin Luther King
MARTINSEN	Martinsen's Software
MASS	Massachusetts Governor's Forum
MASS.	Massachusetts Governor's Forum
MASSACHUSETTS	Massachusetts Governor's Forum
MASSAGE	Longevity Magazine Online
MATH	NAS Online
MATHEMATICS	Simon & Schuster Online: Mathematics Dept.
MATT	Matt Williams' Hot Corner
MATT WILLIAMS	Matt Williams' Hot Corner
MAXIS	Maxis
MAXTECH	MaxTech Corporation
MBS	Mac Business & Home Office Forum
MC	Military City Online
MC BUSINESS	Mercury Center Business & Technology area
MC COMMUNICATION	Mercury Center Communication
MC ENTERTAINMENT	Mercury Center Entertainment area
MC LIBRARY	Mercury Center Newspaper Library
MC LIVING	Mercury Center Bay Area Living area
MC MARKET	Mercury Center Advertising
MC NEW	San Jose Mercury News [GAOL only]
MC NEWS	Mercury Center In the News area
MC PR	Mercury Center Newshound
MC SPORTS	Mercury Center Sports area
MC TALK	Mercury Center Communication
MC TRIVIA	Mercury Center Trivia
MCA	Last Call Talk Show
MCADS	Mercury Center Advertising
MCAFEE	McAfee Associates
MCAT	Kaplan Online -or- The Princeton Review
MCDONALD'S	McFamily Community
MCFAMILY	McFamily Community
MCINTIRE	University of Virginia Alumni/McIntire School of Commerce
MCINTIRE ALUMNI	University of Virginia Alumni/McIntire School of Commerce
MCL	McLaughlin Group
MCLAUGHLIN	The McLaughlin Group
MCLAUGHLIN GROUP	The McLaughlin Group

MCM	Communications & Networking Forum
MCO	Military City Online
MCO BASES	Military City Online Worldwide Military Installations Database
MCO COMM	Military City Online Communications
MCO HQ	Military City Online Headquarters
MCO SHOP	Military City Online Shop
MCO TOUR	Military City Online Tour
MDP	Mac Desktop Publishing/WP Forum
MDV	Mac Developers Forum
MEANWHILE	The Hub: Meanwhile
MECC	MECC
MED	Mac Education Forum
MEDIA	Cowles/SIMBA Media Information Network
MEDIA INFORMATION	Cowles/SIMBA Media Information Network
MEDICAL DICTIONARY	Merriam-Webster's Medical Dictionary
MEDICAL SCHOOL	Kaplan Online -or- The Princeton Review
MEDICINE	Health Channel
MEDLINE	Medline
MEGA NEWS	FamilyPC Online
MEGAZINE	FamilyPC Online
MEGAZONE	FamilyPC Online
MELROSE	Melrose Mondays
MELROSE MONDAYS	Melrose Mondays
MEMBER DIRECTORY	Member Directory
MEMBER PROFILE	Edit your member profile
MEMBER SURVEY	Member Survey
MEMBERS	Member Directory
MEN	The Exchange: Communities Center
MEN ARE FROM MARS	Men Are From Mars
MEN'S HEALTH	Men's Health Forum
MENTAL HEALTH	Mental Health Forum
MER	Merrill Lynch
MERCPR	Mercury Center Newshound
MERCURY	Mercury Center
MERCURY CENTER	Mercury Center
MERRIAM	Merriam-Webster Dictionary
MERRIAM-WEBSTER	Merriam-Webster Dictionary
MERRILL	Merrill Lynch
MERRILL LYNCH	Merrill Lynch
MES	Messiah College
MESSAGE PAD	Newton Resource Center
MESSIAH	Messiah College
MET HOME	Metropolitan Home
METRICOM	Metricom, Inc.
METROPOLITAN HOME	Metropolitan Home
METROWERKS	Metrowerks
METS	Major League Baseball Team: New York Mets
METZ	Metz
MEXICO	Mexico
MFOOL	The Motley Fool
MGM	Mac Games Forum
MGR	Mac Graphic Art & CAD Forum
MGX	Micrografx, Inc.

MHC	Mac HyperCard & Scripting Forum
MHJ	Mac Home Journal
MHM	Members Helping Members message board*
MHS	Mac HyperCard & Scripting Forum
MHW	Mac Hardware Forum
MICHAEL JORDAN	Michael Jordan area
MICHIGAN	Michigan Governor's Forum
MICHIGAN GOVERNOR	Michigan Governor's Forum
MICHIGAN J FROG	The WB Network
MICRO	AOL in France [WAOL 2.5 only]
MICRO J	Micro J Systems, Inc.
MICROFRONTIER	MicroFrontier, Ltd.
MICROGRAFX	Micrografx, Inc.
MICROMAT	MicroMat Computer Systems
MICROPROSE	MicroProse
MICROSEEDS	Microseeds Publishing, Inc.
MICROSOFT	Microsoft Resource Center
MIDI	Music & Sound Forum [platform-depedent]
MILESTONE	DC Comics Online
MILITARY	Military and Vets Club
MILITARY CITY	Military City Online
MILITARY CITY ONLINE	Military City Online
MILWAUKEE BREWERS	Major League Baseball Team: Milwaukee Brewers
MIN	Minirth Meier New Life Clinics
MIND & BODY	Your Mind & Body Online
MIND AND BODY	Your Mind & Body Online
MINDSCAPE	Mindscape
MINICAD	Graphsoft, Inc.
MINIRTH MEIER	Minirth Meier New Life Clinics
MINNESOTA TWINS	Major League Baseball Team: Minnesota Twins
MIRABELLA	Mirabella Magazine
MIRABELLA ONLINE	Mirabella Magazine
MIRROR	Mirror Technologies
MISST-U	CyberJustice: Misst-U & The 7 Pillars of Wisdom
MIX CITICORP	Citicorp Mortgage [WAOL 2.5 only]
MIX CMBA	California Mortgage Bankers Association [WAOL 2.5 only]
MIX DATA TRACK	Data Track Systems Inc. [WAOL 2.5 only]
MIX GENESIS	Genesis 2000 [WAOL 2.5 only]
MIXSTAR	Mixstar Mortgage Information Exchange
MJ	Michael Jordan area
ML	Merrill Lynch
MLB	ABC Sports Major League Baseball
MLK	Martin Luther King
MLPF&S	Merrill Lynch
MLS	Real Estate Online
MLS LIVE	The Grandstand's Major League Soccer Live
MM	PC Multimedia Forum
MM SHOWCASE	Multimedia Showcase* [WAOL 2.5 and MAOL 2.6 only]
MMC	Music Message Center
MME	Grolier's Encyclopeda
MMM	Mac Desktop Video Forum
MMNLC	Minirth Meier New Life Clinics

MMO	Murder Mysteries Online
MMS	Mac Music & Sound Forum
MMW	Multimedia World Online
MMW CLINIC	Multimedia World Online's Clinic
MMW LIBRARY	Multimedia World Online's Library
MMW NEWS	Multimedia World Online
MMW OFFICE	Multimedia World Online's Office
MMW PAVILION	Multimedia World Online's Pavilion
MMW TEST TRACK	Multimedia World Online's Test Track
MMW WELCOME	Multimedia World Online's Welcome area
MNF	ABC Sports Monday Night Football
MOBILE	Mobile Office Online
MOBILE MEDIA	Mobile Media
MODELS	Elle Magazine Online
MODEM	High Speed Access*
MODEM HELP	High Speed Access area*
MODERN LIVES	The Hub: Modern Lives
MODERN ROCK	WHFS 99.1 FM
MODUS	Modus Operandi
MODUS OPERANDI	Modus Operandi
MOM	AOL Families
MOMS	AOL Families
MOMS ONLINE	Moms Online
MONDAY NIGHT FOOTBALL	ABC Sports Monday Night Football
MONEY	Personal Finance channel
MONOLITH	The Hub: Monolith
MONSTER ISLAND	Adventures by Mail
MONTESSORI	Montessori Schools
MONTESSORI SCHOOLS	Montessori Schools
MONTREAL EXPOS	Major League Baseball Team: Montreal Expos
MOO	Gateway 2000, Inc.
MORGAN DAVIS	Morgan Davis Group
MORNINGSTAR	Morningstar Mutual Funds
MORPH	Gryphon Software
MORTGAGE	Real Estate Online
MORTGAGE RATES	Real Estate Online
MORTGAGES	Real Estate Online
MOS	Mac Operating Systems Forum
MOS UPDATE	Apple System 7.5 Update
MOSAIC	Spiritual Mosaic
MOTHER	AOL Families
MOTLEY	The Motley Fool
MOTLEY FOOL	The Motley Fool
MOTORCYCLE	Car/Cycle Selections
MOTORCYCLES	Car/Cycle Selections
MOTORCYCLING	Cycle World Online
MOTOROLA	Motorola
MOTORSPORT	Motorsport '95 Online
MOTORSPORTS	Motorsport '95 Online
MOTU	Mark of the Unicorn
MOUNTAIN BIKE	Bicycling Magazine
MOVIE	@the.movies
MOVIE FORUMS	Movie Forums area
MOVIE REVIEW DATABASE	Movie Review Database

MOVIE REVIEW DB	Movie Review Database
MOVIE REVIEWS	Movie Reviews
MOVIE REVIEWS DATABASE	Movie Review Database
MOVIELINK	MovieLink
MOVIES	@the.movies
MOVIEVISIONS	MovieVisions
MP	Multimedia Preferences [WAOL and MAOL only]
MPM	Marriage Partnership Magazine
MR SCIENCE	Kim Komando's Komputer Clinic
MRD	Movie Review Database
MS BIZ	Your Business
MS DOS 6	MS-DOS 6.0 Resource Center
MS DOS 60	MS-DOS 6.0 Resource Center
MS SUPPORT	Microsoft Resource Center
MS-DOS FORUM	DOS Forum
MSA	Management Science Associates
MSBC	Your Business
MSCOPE	Standard & Poor's Marketscope
MSKB	Microsoft Knowledge Base
MSTATION	Bentley Systems, Inc.
MTC	Mac Communications & Networking Forum
MTV	MTV Online
MTV NEWS	MTV News
MU	CyberJustice: Misst-U & The 7 Pillars of Wisdom
MUG	AOL Store
MULTIMEDIA	Multimedia menu
MULTIMEDIA PREFS	Multimedia Preferences [MAOL and WAOL only]
MULTIMEDIA WORLD	Multimedia World
MULTIPLE SCLEROSIS	Multiple Sclerosis Forum
MURDER	Murder Mysteries Online
MURDER MYSTERIES	Murder Mysteries Online
MURDER MYSTERY	Murder Mysteries Online
MUSEUM	Smithsonian Online
MUSEUMS	Smithsonian Online
MUSIC & SOUND	Music and Sound Forum [platform-dependent]
MUSIC	MusicSpace
MUSIC AND SOUND FORUM	Music and Sound Forum [platform-dependent]
MUSIC FORUM	Music and Sound Forum [platform-dependent]
MUSIC MEDIA	Music Media
MUSIC NEWS	MTV Online: News
MUSIC PROMO	MusicSpace Events
MUSIC TALK	MusicSpace Communications
MUSIC WEB	MusicSpace WEB TopStops
MUSICSPACE	MusicSpace
MUSTANG	Mustang Software
MUSTANG SOFTWARE	Mustang Software
MUT	Mac Utilities Forum
MUT AWARD	Mac Shareware Awards [MAOL only]
MUT AWARDS	Mac Shareware Awards [MAOL only]
MUTUAL FUND	Morningstar Mutual Funds
MUTUAL FUND CENTER	AOL Mutual Fund Center
MUTUAL FUNDS	Morningstar Mutual Funds
MVT	Mac Utilities Forum
MW	MasterWord

MW DICTIONARY	Merriam-Webster's Collegiate Dictionary
MY PLACE	My Place (for FTP sites)
MYOB	Best! Ware
MYSTERIES	Mysteries from the Yard
MYSTERIES FROM THE YARD	Mysteries from the Yard
MYSTERY	Science Fiction & Fantasy
N MARIANA ISLANDS	Northern Mariana Islands
NAA	Newspaper Association of America
NABER	John Naber [May disappear without notice]
NACHRICHTEN	German News [WAOL only]
NAEA	NAEA Tax Channel [May disappear without notice]
NAESP	NAESP Web Link
NAGF	Non-Affiliated Gamers Forum
NAME	Add, change or delete screen names
NAMES	Add, change or delete screen names
NAM!	National Alliance of Mentally Ill
NAN	Nick at Nite
NAPC	Employment Agency Database
NAQP	National Association of Quick Printers area
NAREE	Real Estate Online
NAS	NAS Online
NASCAR	AOL Auto Racing
NATIONAL DEBT	U.S. Treasury Securities
NATIONAL GEOGRAPHIC	Odyssey Project
NATIONAL PARENTING	The National Parenting Center
NATIVE AMERICAN	The Exchange: Communities Center
NATURE	The Nature Conservancy
NAVISOFT	Navisoft Home Page
NBA DRAFT	1995 NBA Draft
NBC	NBC... NOT!
NBR	The Nightly Business Report: Making Sense of It All
NBR REPORT	The Nightly Business Report: NBR Online Report
NC8	News Channel 8
NCAA	NCAA Hoops [May disappear without notice]
NCLEX	Kaplan Online
NCR	National Catholic Reporter
NCT	Next Century Technologies
NEA	Accessing the NEA Public Forum*
NEA ONLINE	Accessing the NEA Public Forum*
NEA PUBLIC	NEA Public Forum
NEC	NEC Technologies
NEC TECH	NEC Technologies
NECN	New England Cable News
NEIGHBORHOODS	Neighborhoods, USA
NEIGHBORHOODS, USA	Neighborhoods, USA
NEOLOGIC	NeoLogic
NESN BASKETBALL	NESN Backsetball
NET CHAT	Coming Attractions
NET EXPERT	Pro's Corner
NET HEAD JED	CyberSmith
NET HEAD RED	CyberSmith
NET NEWS	Internet Newsstand
NET SOFTWARE	Internet Connection Download Libraries
NET SUGGESTIONS	Internet Suggestions
NETGIRL	NetGirl
NETHERLANDS	Netherlands
NETNEWS	Internet News
NETNOIR	NetNoir
NETNOIRE	NetNoir
NETORGS	Net.Orgs
NETSCAPE	Netscape Web Link
NETWORKING	Communications/Telecom/Networking Forum [platform-dependent]
NETWORKING FORUM	Communications/Telecom/Networking Forum [platform-dependent]
NETWORKS EXPO	New Product Showcase
NET NOIR	NetNoir
NET NOIRE	NetNoir
NEVERWINTER	AD&D Neverwinter Nights
NEW	Features & Services Showcase
NEW AGE	Relgion & Ethics Forum
NEW AOL	Latest version of AOL software
NEW ENGLAND	Genealogy Forum
NEW ENGLAND CABLE	New England Cable News
NEW ENGLAND CABLE NEWS	New England Cable News
NEW ENGLAND NEWS	New England Cable News
NEW ERA	Tactic Software
NEW LIFE	Minirth Meier New Life Clinics
NEW MEMBER	Orientation Express (New Member Area)
NEW MOVIES	New Release/Movies area
NEW PRODUCT	New Product News
NEW PRODUCT SHOWCASE	New Product News
NEW PRODUCTS	New Product Information
NEW RELEASES	New Release/Movies area
NEW REPUBLIC	The New Republic Magazine
NEW TV SEASON	Lost & Found TV Shows
NEW WORLD	New World Computing
NEW YORK	@times/The New York Times Online
NEW YORK CITY	@times/The New York Times Online
NEW YORK METS	Major League Baseball Team: New York Mets
NEW YORK TIMES	@times/The New York Times Online
NEW ZEALAND	New Zealand
NEWBIE	Orientation Express (New Member Area)
NEWS & REVIEWS	Family Computing Forum: News & Reviews
NEWS	Today's News channel
NEWS 8	News Channel 8
NEWS AND FINANCE	Today's News channel
NEWS CHANNEL	News Channel 8
NEWS CHANNEL 8	News Channel 8
NEWS LIBRARY	Mercury Center Newspaper Library
NEWS ROOM	Today's News channel
NEWS SEARCH	Search News Articles
NEWS TEXT	Today's News channel
NEWS VIEWS	ABC Online: News Views
NEWS WATCH	Search News Articles
NEWS/SPORTS/MONEY	Today's News channel

NEWSBYTES	Newsbytes
NEWSGRIEF	NewsGrief
NEWSGROUP	Internet Usenet Newsgroup area
NEWSGROUPS	Internet Usenet Newsgroup area
NEWSHOUND	Mercury Center Newshound
NEWSLETTER	Games & Entertainment Newsletter
NEWSLETTERS	Genealogy Forum
NEWSLINK	Today's News channel
NEWSPAPER	Newspaper Selections
NEWSPAPER LIBRARY	Mercury Center Newspaper Library
NEWSPAPERS	Newspaper Selections
NEWSSTAND	The Newsstand
NEWTON	Newton Resource Center
NEWTON BOOK	PDA/Palmtop Forum
NEXT	Generation Next
NEY YORK YANKEES	Major League Baseball Team: New York Yankees
NFL DRAFT	NFL Draft
NGLTF	Nation Gay & Lesbian Task Force
NGS	Odyssey Project
NGUIDES	CNN Newsroom Online
NHL	NHL Online
NICK	Nickelodeon Online -or- Nick at Nite
NICK @ NITE	Nick at Nite
NICK AT NITE	Nick at Nite
NICKELODEON	Nickelodeon Online
NIGERIA	Nigeria
NIGHTLINE	ABC News-On-Demand
NIKON	Nikon Electronic Imaging
NILES	Niles and Associates
NINTENDO	Nintendo Power Source
NINTENDO POWER SOURCE	Nintendo Power Source
NISSAN	Nissan Online
NISUS	Nisus Software
NMAA	National Museum of American Art
NMAH	National Museum of American History
NMSS	National Multiple Sclerosis Society
NNFY	National Network for Youth
NNY	National Network for Youth
NO HANDS	Common Ground Software
NO HANDS SOFTWARE	Common Ground Software
NOA	Nintendo Power Source
NOIR-NET	NetNoir
NOIRENET	NetNoir
NOIRE NET	NetNoir
NOLO	Nolo Press' Self-Help Law Center
NOLO PRESS	Nolo Press' Self-Help Law Center
NOMADIC	Nomadic Computing Discussion SIG
NON PROFIT	Non-Profit Network
NON PROFIT NETWORK	Non-Profit Network
NONPROFIT	AccessPoint: Nonprofit Professionals Network
NORTON	Symantec
NORWAY	Norway
NORWEGIAN	Genealogy Forum
NOT NBC	NBC... NOT!

NOT-FOR-PROFIT	Access.Point
NOTEBOOK	PowerBook Resource Center
NOVEL	60-Second Novelist
NOVELIST	60-Second Novelist
NOVELL	Novell Desktop Systems
NOW	Now Software
NOW PLAYING	Directory of Services
NPC	The National Parenting Center
NPN	Non-Profit Network
NPR	National Public Radio Outreach
NPS	New Product Showcase
NSS	National Space Society
NTN	NTN Trivia
NTN BASKETBALL TRIVIA	NTN Basketball Trivia
NTN HOCKEY TRIVIA	ABC Hockey Trivia
NTN HOOPS TRIVIA	NTN Basketball Trivia
NTN PLAYBOOK	NTN Playbook
NTN TRIVIA	NTN Trivia
NUL	National Urban League
NUMBERS	Accessing America Online*
NURSING	Kaplan Online
NUTRITION	Nutrition Forum
NVN	Newspaper Association of America
NWFL	The Grandstand's Simulation Football
NWN	AD&D Neverwinter Nights
NY PUBLIC LIBRARY	NY Public Library Desk Reference
NY TIMES	@times/The New York Times Online
NYC	@times/The New York Times Online
NYNEX	@times/The New York Times Online
NYT	@times/The New York Times Online
NYT CROSSWORD	The New York Times Crosswords
NYT CROSSWORDS	The New York Times Crosswords
NYT STORE	@times Store
O'S	Major League Baseball Team: Baltimore Orioles
O.J.	O.J. Simpson Trial [May disappear without notice]
O.J. SIMPSON	O.J. Simpson Trial [May disappear without notice]
OADD	AD&D Neverwinter Nights
OAKLAND A'S	Major League Baseball Team: Oakland Athletics
OAKLAND ATHLETICS	Major League Baseball Team: Oakland Athletics
OAO	Outdoor Adventures Online
OBJECT FACTORY	Object Factory
OC	Owens Corning
ODEON	Center Stage
ODYSSEY	The Odyssey Project
ODYSSEY PROJECT	The Odyssey Project
OFFICE	OfficeMax Online
OFFICEMAX	OfficeMax Online
OFL	The Grandstand's Simulation Football
OGF	Online Gaming Forums
OJ	Court TV's Law Center
OLD DOMINION	Virginia Forum
OLD FAVES	Favorite Flicks
OLDS	Oldsmobile/Celebrity Circle
OLDSMOBILE	Oldsmobile/Celebrity Circle

OLDUVAI	Olduvai Software, Inc.	OSO SPORTS	Orlando Sentinel's Sports
OLTL	ABC Daytime/Soapline	OSO TO DO	Orlando Sentinel Online: Things To Do
OLYMPIC	Olympic Festival Online	OTHER NEWS	The Hub: The Other News
OLYMPIC FESTIVAL	Olympic Festival Online	OUR WORLD	Today's News channel
OLYMPIC SHOP	The Olympic Shop	OUTBOARD	Boating Online
OLYMPIC STORE	The Olympic Shop	OUTDOOR	Outdoor Adventures Online
OLYMPICS	Olympic Festival Online	OUTDOOR ADVENTURE	Outdoor Adventures Online
OMAHA	Omaha Steaks	OUTDOOR GEAR	Backpacker Magazine
OMAHA STEAKS	Omaha Steaks	OUTDOORS	The Exchange
OMEGA	Omega Research	P6	Intel Corporation
OMNI	OMNI Magazine Online	PACEMARK	PaceMark Technologies, Inc.
OMNI MAGAZINE	OMNI Magazine Online	PACKER	Packer Software
ON	ON Technology	PADRES	Major League Baseball Team: San Diego Padres
ONE LIFE TO LIVE	ABC Daytime/Soapline	PAGAN	Pagan Religions & Occult Sciences
ONE SOURCE	Columbia's Health Today	PAGE	Page Sender
ONLINE CLOCK	Time of day and length of time online	PAGER	Consumer Electronics
ONLINE GAMING	Online Gaming Forums	PALM	Palm Computing
ONLINE PSYCH	Psych Online	PALM COMPUTING	Palm Computing
ONYX	Onyx Technology	PALMTOP	PDA/Palmtop Forum
OPCODE	Opcode Systems, Inc.	PANASONIC	Andy Pargh/The Gadget Guru
OPCODE SYSTEMS	Opcode Systems, Inc.	PANGEA	Pangea Toy Net
OPERA	Afterwards Cafe	PANGEA TOY NET	Pangea Toy Net
OPRAH	Get Movin' With Oprah	PAP	Applications Forum
OPTIMAGE	Philips Media OptImage	PAPER MAIL	Fax/Paper Mail
OPTIMAS	OPTIMAS Corporation	PAPERPORT	Visioneer
ORANGE	Nickelodeon Online	PAPYRUS	Sierra Online
ORIENTATION	Orientation Express (New Member Area)	PARADOX	DC Comics Online
ORIENTATION EXPRESS	Orientation Express (New Member Area)	PARASCOPE	Parascope
ORIGIN	Origin Systems	PARENT	AOL Families
ORIGIN SYSTEMS	Origin Systems	PARENT ADVICE	Princeton Review Informed Parent
ORIOLES	Major League Baseball Team: Baltimore Orioles	PARENT SOUP	Parent Soup
ORLANDO	Orlando Sentinel Online	PARENT SOUP LOCAL INFO	Parent Soup: Local Information
ORLANDO SENTINEL	Orlando Sentinel Online	PARENTAL CONTROL	Parental Controls*
ORSON SCOTT CARD	Hatrack River Town Meeting	PARENTAL GUIDANCE	Princeton Review Informed Parent
OS TWO	OS/2 Forum	PARENTING	AOL Families area
OS2	OS/2 Forum	PARENTS	AOL Families area
OSCAR	Academy Awards	PARGH	Andy Pargh/The Gadget Guru
OSCARS	Academy Awards	PARKS, NPCA	America's National Parks
OSKAR'S	Oskar's Magazine	PARLOR	Games Parlor
OSKARS	Oskar's Magazine	PARSONS	Parsons Technology
OSO	Orlando Sentinel Online	PASSPORT	Passport Designs
OSO BUSINESS	Orlando Sentinel's Business	PASSWORD	Change your password*
OSO CLASSIFIED	Orlando Sentinel Online: Classified Ads	PASTA	Mama's Cucina by Ragu
OSO CLASSIFIEDS	Orlando Sentinel Online: Classified Ads	PAT O	The Pat O'Brien Report
OSO COLLEGE FB	Orlando Sentinel Online: College Football	PAT O'BRIEN	The Pat O'Brien Report
OSO COLLEGE FOOTBALL	Orlando Sentinel Online: College Football	PAT OBRIEN	The Pat O'Brien Report
OSO ENTERTAIN	Orlando Sentinel's Entertainment	PAUL HARVEY	ABC Radio
OSO LIVING	Orlando Sentinel's Living	PBM	Play-By-Mail Forum
OSO MAGIC	Orlando Sentinel's Magic	PBM CLUBS	Play-By-Mail Clubs & Messaging
OSO PHOTOS	Orlando Sentinel's Photos	PC	People Connection
OSO REAL ESTATE	Orlando Sentinel Online: Real Estate	PC ANIMATION	PC Graphics Forum
OSO RELIGION	Orlando Sentinel Online: Religion News	PC APPLICATIONS	PC Applications Forum
OSO SERVICES	Orlando Sentinel's Services	PC APPLICATIONSFORUM	PC Applications Forum
OSO SOUND OFF	Orlando Sentinel's Sound Off	PC APS	PC Applications Forum

PC AUD	Center Stage
PC BEGINNERS	PC Help Desk
PC BG	PC Help Desk
PC CATALOG	PC Today
PC DATA	PC Data
PC DESKMATE	DeskMate
PC DEV	Developers Forum [platform-dependent]
PC DEVELOPMENT	Developers Forum [platform-dependent]
PC DEVELOPMENT FORUM	Developers Forum [platform-dependent]
PC DM	DeskMate
PC FINANCIAL	PC Financial Network
PC FINANCIAL NETWORK	PC Financial Network
PC FORUMS	Computing channel [platform-dependent]
PC GAMES	PC Games Forum
PC GRAPHICS	PC Graphics Forum
PC GRAPHICS FORUM	PC Graphics Forum
PC HARDWARE	PC Hardware Forum
PC HARDWARE FORUM	PC Hardware Forum
PC HELP	PC Help Desk
PC HOT	What's Hot in PC Computing
PC MUSIC FORUM	PC Music and Sound Forum
PC PC	Personal Computer Peripherals
PC SECURITY	Computing channel [platform-dependent]
PC SOFTWARE	PC Software Center
PC SOUND	PC Music and Sound Forum
PC SOUND FORUM	PC Music and Sound Forum
PC STUDIO	PC Studio
PC TELECOM	PC Telecom/Networking Forum
PC TELECOM FORUM	PC Telecom/Networking Forum
PC TODAY	PC Today
PC UTILITIES	DOS Forum
PC WORLD	PCWorld Online
PC WORLD ONLINE	PCWorld Online
PC-LINK HOTLINE	Credit Reequest Form for connect problems*
PCFN	PC Financial Network
PCM	PC Telecom/Networking Forum
PCMU	PC Music and Sound Forum
PCMUSIC	PC Music and Sound Forum
PCS	MobileMedia
PCW ONLINE	PCWorld Online
PD	Dinner On Us Club
PDA	PDA/Palmtop Forum
PDA DEV	PDA Development SIG
PDA DEV SIG	PDA Development SIG
PDA FORUM	PDA/Palmtop Forum
PDV	Developers Forum [platform-dependent]
PEACHPIT	The Macintosh Bible/Peachpit Forum
PEACHTREE	Peachtree Software
PEAPOD	Peapod Online
PEN	Personal Empowerment Network
PEN PAL	Edmark Technologies
PENTIUM	Intel Corporation
PEOPLE	People Connection
PEOPLE CONNECTION	People Connection

PEREGRINE	Pictorius
PERFORMA	Performa Resource Center
PERFUME	The Fragrance Counter
PERSON OF THE WEEK	ABC News-On-Demand
PERSONAL CHOICES	Personal Choices area [MAOL and WAOL only]
PERSONAL FINANCE	Personal Finance channel
PERSONAL REPORTER	Mercury Center Newshound
PET	Pet Care Forum
PET CARE	Pet Care Forum
PETER JENNINGS	ABC News-On-Demand
PETER NORTON	Symantec
PETITIONS	Accessing America Online*
PETS	Pet Care Forum
PF	Personal Finance channel
PF SOFTWARE	Personal Finance Software Center
PFSS	Personal Finance Software Support
PGM	PC Games Forum
PGR	PC Graphics Forum
PH	Simon & Schuster College Online
PHILANTHROPY	Access.Point
PHILIPPINES	Philippines
PHILLIES	Major League Baseball Team: Philadelphia Phillies
PHOENIX	Arizona Central
PHONE BOOK	Phone Directories
PHONE DIRECTORY	Phone Directories
PHONE HELP	Accessing America Online*
PHONE NUMBER	Accessing America Online*
PHONE NUMBERS	Accessing America Online*
PHONES	Accessing America Online*
PHOTO	Photography area
PHOTO FOCUS	Graphics and Photo Focus area
PHOTODEX	Photodex
PHOTOGRAPHY	Photography area
PHOTOS	Popular Photography Online
PHOTOSHOP SIG	Photoshop SIG
PHS	Practical Homeschooling
PHW	PC Hardware Forum
PHYS ED	Simon & Schuster Online: Health, Pys. Ed. & Rec. Dept.
PHYSICALLY DISABLED	DisABILITIES Forum
PICTORIUS	Pictorius
PICTUREPLACE	PictureWb & PicturePlace
PICTURES	Pictures of the World
PIERIAN	P>ieiian Spring Software
PIERIAN SP	Piereian Spring Software
PILOTS	Flying Magazine
PIN	AOL Families
PINK TRIANGLE	Gay & Lesbian Community Forum
PIPE	Food & Drink Network
PIPES	Food & Drink Network
PIRATES	Major League Baseball Team: Pittsburgh Pirates
PITTSBURGH PIRATES	Major League Baseball Team: Pittsburgh Pirates
PIXEL	Pixel Resources
PIXEL RESOURCES	Pixel Resources

PKWARE	PKWare Inc.
PLACES	P.L.A.C.E.S. Interest Group
PLANETOUT	PlanetOut
PLANTS	800-Flowers
PLASTIC SURGERY	Longevity Magazine Online
PLAY	Entertainment Channel
PLAY KEYWORD	Preview Vacations' Travel Update
PLAY-BY-MAIL	Play-By-Mail Forum
PLAYBILL	Playbill Online
PLAYER	Viewer Resource Center
PLAYERS	Viewer Resource Center
PLAYTEX	One Hanes Place
PLAYWELL	U.S. Golf Society Online
PLF	The Positive Living Forum
PLF QUILT	GLCF AIDS Quilt
PLUS	Plus ATM Network
PMM	PC Multimedia Forum
PMU	PC Music and Sound Forum
PNO	PlanetOut
POETRY	Afterwards Cafe
POG	KidzBiz' POG Area
POGS	KidzBiz' POG Area
POLAND	Poland
POLICY REVIEW	Heritage Foundation area
POLITICAL SCIENCE	Simon & Schuster Online: Political Science Dept.
POLITICS	Politics Forum
POLLS	CyberJustice's Arch of Public Opinion Polls\
POP PHOTO	Popular Photography Online
POPE	Catholic Community
POPULAR PHOTOGRAPHY	Popular Photography Online
PORK	Pork Online
PORT FOLLY	The Motley Fool
PORTABLE	Mobile Office Online
PORTABLE COMPUTING	Mobile Office Online
PORTFOLIO	Your Stock Portfolio
PORTUGAL	Portugal
POSITIVE LIVING	The Positive Living Forum
POST OFFICE	Post Office [MAOL and WAOL only]
POSTAL STAMPS	Comic Strip Centennial
POSTCARD	Lost in America
POSTCARDS	Virtual Post Card Center
POV	3D Resource Center
POWER BOATS	Boating Online
POWERBOOK	PowerBook Resource Center
POWERMAC	PowerMac Resource Center
POWERPC	PowerMac Resource Center
POWERTOOLS	American Woodworker: Tool Reviews
PP	Personal WWW Publishing area [WAOL 2.5 only]
PPI	Practical Peripherals, Inc.
PR	Princeton Review/Student Access Online
PRACTICAL PERIPHERALS	Practical Peripherals, Inc.
PRAIRIE	Prarie Group
PRAIRIESOFT	Prairie Group
PRAYER NET	The Prayer Network

PREMIER	Dinner On Us Club
PREMIER DINING	Dinner On Us Club
PRENTICE HALL	Simon & Schuster College Online
PRESIDENT	President's Day
PRESIDENT 96	President '96
PRESIDENTIAL	President's Day
PRESS	AOL Press Release Library
PRESS RELEASE	AOL Press Release Library
PREVIEW VACATIONS	Preview Vacations
PRICE	Price Online
PRICE ONLINE	Price Online
PRIDE	Gay & Lesbian Community Forum
PRIMESTAR	Andy Pargh/The Gadget Guru
PRIN	Principians Online
PRINCETON REVIEW	Princeton Review/Student Access Online
PRINCIPALS	National Principals Center Web Link
PRINO	Principians Online
PRINT ARTIST	Print Artist Resource Center
PRO BOWL	1996 Pro Bowl
PRO'S	Pro's Corner
PRO'S CORNER	Pro's Corner
PROCD	ProCD National Telephone Directory Search
PRODIGY	Prodigy Refugees Forum
PRODIGY REFUGEES	Prodigy Refugees Forum
PRODUCTIVITY	Applications/Business/Productivity Forum [platform-dependent]
PRODUCTIVITY FORUM	Applications/Business/Productivity Forum [platform-dependent]
PROFILE	Edit your member profile
PROGRAMMER U	Programmer University
PROGRAMMING	Development Forum [platform-dependent]
PROGRAPH	Pictorius Inc.
PROS	Pro's Corner
PROS CORNER	Pro's Corner
PROUD	Gay & Lesbian Community Forum
PROVUE	ProVUE Development
PSC	Public Safety Center
PSION	Psion
PSYCH ONLINE	Psych Online
PSYCHOLOGY	Psychology Forum
PTC	PC Telecom/Networking Forum
PU	Programmer University
PUB	The Comedy Pub
PUBLIC DEBT	U.S. Treasury Securities
PUBLIC POLICY	Politics Forum
PUBLIC RADIO	National Public Radio Outreach
PUBLIC SAFETY	Public Safety Center
PUBLISHERS	Computing Company Connection
PUERTO RICO	Puerto Rico
QB1	NTN's QB1
QC	UK Chat Rooms
QMMS	Mac Music & Sound Forum
QMODEM	Mustang Software
QOTD	Grandstand's Sport Trivia Question of the Day

QUALITAS	Qualitas
QUALITY	The Health Zone
QUARK	Quark, Inc.
QUE	P.C. Studio
QUEER	Gay & Lesbian Community Forum
QUES DICTIONARY	Computer and Internet Dictionary
QUEST	Adventures by Mail
QUESTION	One Stop Infoshop*
QUESTIONS	One Stop Infoshop*
QUICK PRINTERS	National Association of Quick Printers area
QUICKCHAT	UK Chat Rooms
QUICKFIND	Search database of files [platform-dependent]
QUICKFINDER	Search database of files [platform-dependent]
QUICKTIME	Mac Desktop Video Forum
QUIKJUSTICE	CyberJustice's Reward & Punishment
QUILT	Quilting Forum
QUILTERS	Quilting Forum
QUILTING	Quilting Forum
QUOTE	StockLink: Quotes & Portfolios area
QUOTES	StockLink: Quotes & Portfolios area
QUOTES PLUS	Quotes Plus
R&R	ABC Online: Rock & Road
R&T	Road & Track Magazine
RABBITJACK'S CASINO	RabbitJack's Casino
RABBITJACKS CASINO	RabbitJack's Casino
RACING	Car/Cycle Selections
RADIO	Entertainment Radio Forum
RADIUS	Radius Inc.
RAGU	Mama's Cucina by Ragu
RAILROADING	The Exchange
RALPH Z	UniverseCentral.Com
RALPH ZERBONIA	UniverseCentral.Com
RAM DOUBLER	Connectix Corporation
RANGERS	Major League Baseball Team: Texas Rangers
RANKINGS	Business Rankings
RASTEROPS	Truevision
RAY	Ray Dream
RAY DREAM	Ray Dream
RAY TRACE	3D Resource Center
RBO	Ringling Online
RC	Christian Resource Center
RCA	Andy Pargh/The Gadget Guru
RDI	Free-Form Gaming Forum
REACTOR	Reactor
READ	Adult Literacy Forum
READ USA	Online Bookstore
READER'S DIGEST	Reader's Digest
READING	Saturday Review Online
READING ROOM	The Reading Room
REAL ESTATE	Real Estate Online
REAL LIFE	Real Life Financial Tips
REC CENTER	Entertainment Channel
RECIPES	Woman's Day Online
RECORD	Tower Records

RECORDS	Tower Records
RECREATION	Entertainment Channel
RECREATION CENTER	Entertainment Channel
REDGATE	New Product Showcase
REDS	Major League Baseball Team: Cincinnati Reds
REFERENCE	Reference Desk channel
REFERENCE DESK	Reference Desk channel
REFERENCE HELP	Reference Desk Help area
REFERENCE WEB	Reference Web Tools
REGISTER	Online Campus
RELIGION & BELIEFS	Religion & Beliefs
RELIGION	Religion & Beliefs
RELIGION NEWS	Religion News Update
RELIGIONS	Religion & Ethics Forum
REMODELING	Home Magazine Online
RENDERING	3D SIG
REPRISE	Warner/Reprise Records Online
RESEARCH	Academic Assistance Center
RESNOVA	ResNova Software
RESNOVA SOFTWARE	ResNova Software
RESOURCES	Your Business Resources
RESTAURANT	Everything Edible
RESTAURANTS	Everything Edible
RETIREMENT	Real Life
REV	ABC Sports' REV Speedway
REV SPEEDWAY	ABC Sports' REV Speedway
REVIEW	1995: The Year in Review
REVIEWS	Family Computing Forum: News & Reviews
RICKI LAKE	The Ricki Lake Show
RICOCHET	Metricom, Inc.
RINGLING	Ringling Online
RINGLING BROS	Ringling Online
RINGLING ONLINE	Ringling Online
RL	Real Life
RNU	Religion News Update
ROAD & TRACK	Road & Track Magazine
ROAD	Road & Track Magazine
ROAD TRIP	Road Trip Area [WAOL 2.5 only]
ROAD TRIPS	Road Trip Area [WAOL 2.5 only]
ROADSIDE	Roadside USA
ROCK & ROAD	ABC Online: Rock & Road
ROCK & ROLL	Rock and Roll Hall of Fame
ROCK AND ROLL	Rock and Roll Hall of Fame
ROCK N ROLL	Rock and Roll Hall of Fame
ROCKIES	Major League Baseball Team: Colorado Rockies
ROCKLINE	Rockline Online
ROCKLINK	RockNet Information Window & Web Link
ROCKNET	RockNet Information Window & Web Link
ROGER CLEMENS	Roger Clemens' Playoff Baseball Journal
ROGER WAGNER	Roger Wagner Publishing
ROGUE	Motley Fool's Rogue
ROLAND	Roland Corporation U.S.
ROLE PLAYING	Role-Playing Forum
ROLLERSKATING	The Grandstand: Other Sports

ROMANCE	Romance Connection
ROOTS	Genealogy Club
ROSES	800-Flowers
ROSH HASHANA	Jewish New Year area
ROTUNDA	Rotunda Forum Auditorium
ROYALS	Major League Baseball Team: Kansas City Royals
RPG	Role-Playing Forum
RPGA	Fellowship of Online Gamers/RPGA Network
RPGA NETWORK	Fellowship of Online Gamers/RPGA Network
RPM	RPM Worldwide Entertainment & Travel
RPM TRAVEL	RPM Worldwide Entertainment & Travel
RR	ABC Online: Rock & Road
RSFL	The Grandstand's Simulation Football
RSG	Manhattan Graphics
RSP	RSP Funding Focus
RT	Road Trip Area [WAOL 2.5 only]
RUBBERMAID	Andy Pargh/The Gadget Guru
RUSSIA	Russia
RX	Health and Vitamin Express
RYOBI	Ryobi
S&S	Simon & Schuster College Online
S.F. GIANTS	Major League Baseball Team: San Francisco Giants
SA	Shopper's Advantage Online
SA MED	Scientific American Medical Publications
SABRE	EAASY SABRE Travel Service
SAF	Scientific American Frontiers
SAFETY	Public Safety Center
SAILING	Sailing Forum
SALON	Saturday Review Online: Conference Room
SAN DIEGO PADRES	Major League Baseball Team: San Diego Padres
SAN FRAN GIANTS	Major League Baseball Team: San Francisco Giants
SAN JOSE	Mercury Center
SAT	Kaplan Online/SAT, ACT
SAT REVIEW	Saturday Review Online
SATELLITES	Ham Radio Club
SATIRE	Soundbites Online
SATURDAY REVIEW	Saturday Review Online
SAUCE	Mama's Cucina by Ragu
SAVINGS BONDS	U.S. Treasury Securities
SBC	The Entrepreneur Zone
SCANDINAVIAN	Genealogy Forum
SCANNERS	Digital Imaging Resource Center
SCHEDULE	Computing Calendar [Platform-dependent]
SCHOLAR'S HALL	Scholars' Hall
SCHOLARS	Scholars' Hall
SCHOLARS HALL	Scholars' Hall
SCHOLARS' HALL	Scholars' Hall
SCHOLASTIC	Scholastic Network/Scholastic Forum
SCHOOLHOUSE	Electronic Schoolhouse
SCI & MED	Scientific American Science & Medicine
SCI AM	Scientific American
SCI FI	Science Fiction & Fantasy
SCI-FI	Science Fiction & Fantasy
SCIENCE	Scientific American
SCIENCE FICTION	Science Fiction & Fantasy
SCIENTIFIC	Scientific American
SCIENTIFIC AMERICAN	Scientific American
SCIFI CHANNEL	The Sci-Fi Channel
SCOOP	Newsgroup Scoop
SCORPIA	Scorpia's Lair
SCORPIA'S LAIR	Scorpia's Lair
SCORPIAS LAIR	Scorpia's Lair
SCOT	Genealogy Forum
SCOTCH	Genealogy Forum
SCOUTING	Scouting Forum
SCOUTS	Scouting Forum
SCRAPBOOK	Member Scrapbook
SCREAM	MusicSpace Events
SCREEN NAME	Add, change or delete screen names
SCREEN NAMES	Add, change or delete screen names
SCRIPT	Affinity Microsystems
SCRIPTING	Affinity Microsystems
SCRIPTS	Affinity Microsystems
SCUBA	Scuba Club
SE	Shoppers Express
SEA-DOO	Sea-Doo Online
SEARCH	Software Center [Platform-dependent]
SEARCH NEWS	Search news articles
SEATTLE MARINERS	Major League Baseball Team: Seattle Mariners
SECRET BARGAINS	Arthur Frommer's Secret Bargains
SECURITY	Consumer Electronics
SEGA	Video Games area
SELF HELP	Self Help area
SELF-HELP	Self Help area
SEM	Motley Fool: Semiconductors
SEND PAGE	Page Sender
SENIOR	SeniorNet
SENIOR FRIENDS	Columbia/HCA Live Physician's Chat
SERIUS	Serius
SERVENET	SERVEnet
SERVICE	Member Services*
SERVICES	Directory of Services
SERVICES DIRECTORY	Directory of Services
SEVEN WONDERS	Seven Wonders of the Web
SEVENTEEN	Seventeen Magazine Online
SEVENTH	Seventh Level Software
SEW	Needlecrafts/Sewing Center
SEWING	Woman's Day Online
SEX	Entertainment (just try it)
SF	Science Fiction & Fantasy
SHADOW	Shadow Traffic
SHADOW BROADCASTING	Shadow Traffic
SHADOW TRAFFIC	Shadow Traffic
SHAREWARE SOLUTIONS	Shareware Solutions
SHARP	PDA/Palmtop Forum
SHARPER IMAGE	The Sharper Image

SHERLOCK	Mysteries from the Yard
SHERLOCK HOLMES	Mysteries from the Yard
SHOPPERS ADVANTAGE	Shopper's Advantage Online
SHOPPERS EXPRESS	Shoppers Express
SHOPPING & TRAVEL	Travel channel
SHOPPING	Marketplace channel
SHOPPING AND TRAVEL	Travel channel
SHORTHAND	Online Shorthands
SHORTHANDS	Online Shorthands
SHOW TIMES	MovieLink
SHOWBIZ INFO	Showbiz News & Info
SHOWBIZ NEWS	Showbiz News & Info
SHOWS	Center Stage
SHUTTLE	Challenger Remembered
SI	Smithsonian Online
SIERRA	Sierra On-Line
SIFS	Computing channel [platform-dependent]
SIGHTINGS	Sightings Online
SIGNUP	IES Registration Center
SIGS	Computing channel [platform-dependent]
SILICON	Hardware
SIM	Simming Forum
SIM	The Simming Forum
SIMBA	Cowles/SIMBA Media Information Network
SIMI WINERY	Simi Winery
SIMMING	Simming Forum
SIMON & SCHUSTER	Simon & Schuster College Online
SIMON	Simon & Schuster College Online
SIMS	Simming Forum
SIMULATION AUTO	The Grandstand's Simulation Auto Racing
SIMULATION BASEBALL	The Grandstand's Simulation Baseball
SIMULATION BASKETBALL	The Grandstand's Simulation Basketball
SIMULATION FOOTBALL	The Grandstand's Simulation Football
SIMULATION GOLF	The Grandstand's Simulation Golf
SIMULATION HOCKEY	The Grandstand's Simulation Hockey
SIMULATION LEAGUES	The Grandstand's Fantasy & Simulation Leagues
SIMULATION WRESTLING	The Grandstand's Simulation Wrestling
SIMULATIONS	Graphic Simulations
SIMULATOR	Games Forum [platform-dependent]
SINGAPORE	Singapore
SISTORE	Sharper Image
SIXTY	60-Second Novelist
SKI	Ski Reports
SKI CONDITIONS	Ski Reports
SKI REPORTS	Ski Reports
SKI WEATHER	Ski Reports
SKI ZONE	The Ski Zone
SKY DIVING	Aviation Forum
SKYLINE	Virtual Airlines
SKYLINE AIRWAYS	Virtual Airlines
SLIME	Nickelodeon Online
SM	Smithsonian Magazine
SMALL BUSINESS	Your Business
SMART WATCHING	The ABC Classroom
SMITHFIELD	Gwaltney Hams & Turkeys
SMITHSONIAN	Smithsonian Online
SMITHSONIAN MAGAZINE	Smithsonian Magazine
SML	Sony Magic Link
SN EXPERIMENTS	Exploring the Star System
SN LIBRARIES	Scholastic Libraries
SN SCIENCE	Exploring the Star System
SN SPACE	Exploring the Star System
SN WEATHER	Exploring the Star System
SNGUESTS	Special Guests
SNLITGAME	Bookwoman's Literature Game [K-6]
SOAP DIGEST	Soap Opera Digest
SOAP OPERA	Soap Opera Digest
SOAPLINE	ABC Daytime/Soapline
SOCCER	AOL Soccer
SOCIAL SCIENCE	NAS Online
SOCIAL WORK	Simon & Schuster Online: Social Work Dept.
SOCIETY	Saturday Review Online
SOCIOLOGY	Simon & Schuster Online: Sociology Dept.
SOD	Soap Opera Digest
SOFT	Software Center [Platform-dependent]
SOFTARC	SoftArc
SOFTDISK	Softdisk Superstore
SOFTSYNC	Expert Software, Inc.
SOFTWARE	Software Center [Platform-dependent]
SOFTWARE CENTER	Software Center [Platform-dependent]
SOFTWARE COMPANIES	Computing Company Connection
SOFTWARE DIRECTORY	Software Center [Platform-dependent]
SOFTWARE HARDTALK	Software Hardtalk with John C. Dvorak
SOFTWARE HELP	Software Center [Platform-dependent]
SOFTWARE LIBRARIES	Software Center [Platform-dependent]
SOFTWARE LIBRARY	Software Center [Platform-dependent]
SOFTWARE PUBLISHERS	Computing Company Connection
SOFTWARE SUPPORT	Personal Finance Software Support
SOFTWARE TOOLWORKS	Mindscape
SOHO	Home Office Computing Magazine
SOLIII	Sol III Play-by-Email Game
SONY	Sony Magic Link
SOPHCIR	Sophisticated Circuits
SOS	Wall Street SOS Forum
SOUND	Stereo Review Online
SOUND ROOM	Sound Room* [WAOL only]
SOUNDBITES	Soundbites Online
SOURCERER	The Hub: Sourcerer
SOUTH AFRICA	South Africa
SOVARC	Library of Congress Online
SOVIET	Library of Congress Online
SOVIET ARCHIVES	Library of Congress Online
SPA	Longevity Magazine Online
SPACE	National Space Society
SPACE A&B	Space: Above & Beyond
SPACE ABOVE & BEYOND	Space: Above & Beyond
SPACE SHUTTLE	Challenger Remembered
SPACEY	The Hub: Space

SPAIN	Spain
SPAS	Longevity Magazine Online
SPC	Software Publishing Corporation
SPEAKERS	Stereo Review Online
SPECIAL INTERESTS	Clubs & Interests Channel
SPECTRUM	Spectrum HoloByte
SPECULAR	Specular International
SPEEDBOATS	Boating Online
SPEEDWAY	ABC Sports' REV Speedway
SPEEDY	Designs Online
SPIDER	Spider Island Software
SPIDER ISLAND	Spider Island Software
SPIN	Spin Online
SPINNING	Needlecrafts/Sewing Center
SPINONLINE	Spin Online
SPIRIT	Spirit Technologies
SPIRITS	Food & Drink Network
SPIRITUAL	Spiritual Mosaic
SPOOFS	TV Spoofs
SPORTS	Sport News area
SPORTS ARCHIVE	AOL Sports Archive
SPORTS BOARDS	The Grandstand's Sports Boards
SPORTS CHAT	The Grandstand's Chat Rooms
SPORTS EVENTS	AOL Sports Live
SPORTS LIBRARIES	The Grandstand's Libraries
SPORTS LINK	Sports channel
SPORTS LIVE	AOL Sports Live
SPORTS NEWS	Sport News
SPORTS ROOMS	The Grandstand's Chat Rooms
SPOTLIGHT	Center Stage Spotlight
SPRINT	Sprint Annual Report (Old)
SRO	Saturday Review Online
SRO SALON	Saturday Review Online: Conference Room
SRS	SRS Labs -or- Transgender Community Forum
SRS LABS	SRS Labs
SSI	Strategic Simulations
SSS	Craig Anderton's Sound Studio & Stage
SSSI	SSSi
ST. LOUIS CARDINALS	Major League Baseball Team: St. Louis Cardinals
STAC	STAC Electronics
STAMPS	The Exchange
STAR WARS	Star Wars Sim Forum
STAR WARS SIM	Star Wars Sim Forum
STARBUCKS	Caffe Starbucks
STARFISH	Starfish Software
STARFLEET	Starfleet Online
STARPLAY	Starplay Productions
STARTER	Help Desk [Platform-dependent]
STARTREK	Star Trek Club
STATS	Pro Sports Center
STATS	STATS, Inc.
STATS BASKETBALL	Pro Basketball Center
STATS HOOPS	Pro Basketball Center
STATS INC	Pro Sports Center

STATS INC.	Pro Sports Center
STATS, INC	Pro Sports Center
STATS, INC.	Pro Sports Center
STD	Sexually Transmitted Diseases Forum
STEAKS	Omaha Steaks
STEREO	Stereo Review Online
STEREO EQUIPMENT	Stereo Review Online
STEREO REVIEW	Stereo Review Online
STEVE CASE	Community Updates from Steve Case*
STF	STF Technologies
STF TECHNOLOGIES	STF Technologies
STOCK	StockLink: Quotes & Portfolios area
STOCK CHARTS	Decision Point Forum
STOCK PORTFOLIO	Your Stock Portfolio
STOCK QUOTES	StockLink: Quotes & Portfolios area
STOCK TIMING	Decision Point Forum
STOCKLINK	StockLink: Quotes & Portfolios area
STOCKS	StockLink: Quotes & Portfolios area
STORE	Travel & Shopping Channel
STORES	Travel & Shopping Channel
STRATA	Strata, Inc.
STRATEGIC	Strategic Simulations
STRATEGIES	The Entrepreneur Zone
STRATEGY	Strategy & Wargaming Forum
STRIKE-A-MATCH	Boxer*Jam Gameshows [WAOL only]
STUDENT	Princeton Review/Student Access Online
STUDENT ACCESS	Princeton Review/Student Access Online
STUDIO	MusicSpace Studio
STUDIOWARE	Roger Wagner Publishing
STUDY	Study Skills Service
STUDY BREAK	Compton's Study Break
STUDYSKILLS	Study Skills Service
STUFFIT	Aladdin Systems, Inc.
STUMP	Rotunda Forum Auditorium
STW	Mindscape
STYLE	Elle Magazine Online
STYLE CHANNEL	Style Channel
SUGGEST	Suggestion boxes*
SUGGESTION	Suggestion boxes*
SUMMER SLAM	World Wrestling Federation
SUNAIR	Virtual Airlines
SUNAIR EXPRESS	Virtual Airlines
SUNBURST	Sunburst Communications
SUNSET	Sunset Magazine
SUNSET MAGAZINE	Sunset Magazine
SUPER BOWL	Super Bowl XXX Online
SUPERCARD	SuperCard SIG
SUPERDISK	Alysis Software
SUPERLIBRARY	The Information SuperLibrary
SUPERMAC	Radius-SuperMac
SUPERMAN	DC Comics Online
SUPERSTARS	World Wrestling Federation
SUPERSTORE	Softdisk Superstore
SUPPORT	Member Services*

SURF	SurfLink
SURF SHACK	The Surf Shack
SURFBOARD	SurfLink
SURFER	SurfLink
SURFERS	SurfLink
SURFING	SurfLink
SURFLINK	SurfLink
SURNAMES	Genealogy Forum
SURVIVOR	Survivor Software
SURVIVOR SOFTWARE	Survivor Software
SUSAN	The Hub: Susan
SWEDEN	Sweden
SWEDISH	Genealogy Forum
SWEETHEART	Omaha Steaks Offer
SWIMMING	The Grandstand: Other Sports
SWISS	Genealogy Forum
SWITZERLAND	Switzerland
SYMANTEC	Symantec
SYNEX	Synex
SYSOP	Member Services*
SYSTEM 7	Mac Operating Systems Forum
SYSTEM 7.0	Mac Operating Systems Forum
SYSTEM 7.1	Mac Operating Systems Forum
SYSTEM 71	Mac Operating Systems Forum
SYSTEM RESPONSE	System Response Report Area* [MAOL and WAOL only]
T SHIRT	AOL Products Center
T TALK	Teachers' Forum
TA	Traveler's Advantage
TA FOOTRACE	Trans-America Footrace
TAC	Top Advisor's Corner
TACTIC	Tactic Software
TAIWAN	Taiwan
TAKE 2	Take 2 Interactive Software
TAKE 2 INC	Take 2 Interactive Software
TAL	Turner Adventure Learning
TALENT	Talent Bank
TALK	People Connection
TALK SHOW	Future Labs, Inc.
TAROT	The Crystal Ball Forum
TARTIKOFF	Last Call Talk Show
TAX	Tax Forum [May disappear without notice]
TAX CHANNEL	NAEA Tax Channel [May disappear without notice]
TAX FORUM	Tax Forum [May disappear without notice]
TAX GUIDE	Ernst & Young Tax Guide
TAXCUT	Kiplinger TaxCut Software Support
TAXES	Tax Forum [May disappear without notice]
TAXI	TAXI Independent Artist & Repertoire Co.
TAY	Taylor University
TAYLOR	Taylor University

TBIBM	TBS Network Earth/IBM Project [MAOL and GAOL only]
TCF	Transgender Community Forum
TCW	Today's Christian Woman
TEACHER	Teachers' Information Network
TEACHER PAGER	Teacher Pager
TEACHER'S LOUNGE	Teachers' Lounge
TEACHERS	Teachers' Information Network
TEACHERS LOUNGE	Teachers' Lounge
TEACHERS' LOUNGE	The Teachers' Lounge
TEAM	Team Concepts
TEAM CONCEPTS	Team Concepts
TECH HELP LIVE	Tech Help Live*
TECH LIVE	Tech Help Live*
TECHNOLOGY	Computing channel [platform-dependent]
TECHNOLOGY WORKS	Technology Works
TECHNOTORIUM	@times/The New York Times Online
TECHWORKS	Technology Works
TEEN	Teen Scene message boards
TEEN SCENE	Teen Scene message boards
TEENS	Teen Scene message boards
TEKNOSYS	Teknosys Works
TEKTRONIX	Tektronix
TELECOM	Communications/Telecom/Networking Forum [platform-dependent]
TELECOM FORUM	Communications/Telecom/Networking Forum [platform-dependent]
TELECOMMUNICATIONS	Communications/Telecom/Networking Forum [platform-dependent]
TELEPHONE	Phone Directories
TELEPHONE NUMBERS	Phone Directories
TELEPORT	Global Village Communication
TELESCAN	Telescan Users Group Forum
TELEVISION	Soap Opera Summaries
TELNET	Telnet [WAOL 2.5 only]
TEMPO	Affinity Microsystems
TEMPO II	Affinity Microsystems
TEMPO II PLUS	Affinity Microsystems
TEN TEN	A Day in the Life of Cyberspace
TENNIS	AOL Tennis
TERMS	Terms of Service*
TERMS OF SERVICE	Terms of Service*
TEST PREP	Kaplan Online
TEXAS INSTRUMENTS	Texas Instrument
TEXAS RANGERS	Major League Baseball Team: Texas Rangers
TG	Transgender Community Forum
TGS	Pictorius
TGS	Prograph International, Inc.
THE DEAD	Grateful Dead Forum
THE EXCHANGE	The Exchange
THE FLORIDA KEYS	The Florida Keys
THE GRANDSTAND	The Grandstand
THE HUB	The Hub
THE KEYS	The Florida Keys

THE LAB	The Lab
THE MALL	Travel & Shopping Channel
THE MOVIES	@the.movies
THE NATURE CONSERVANCY	The Nature Conservancy
THE NEW REPUBLIC	The New Republic Magazine
THE POST OFFICE	Post Office [MAOL and WAOL Only]
THE TOY NET	Pangea Toy Net
THE WALL	Vietnam Veterans Memorial Wall
THE WB NETWORK	The WB Network
THE WHITE HOUSE	White House Forum
THE WORLD	The World
THEATER	Saturday Review Online
THEATRE	Saturday Review Online
THESAURUS	Merriam-Webster's Thesaurus
THREE SIXTY	Three-Sixty Software
THREEDO	The 3DO Company
THRUST MASTER	Thrustmaster
THUNDERWARE	Thunderware
TI	Texas Instruments
TIA	True Image Audio
TICF	International Corporate Forum
TICKET	Ticketmaster
TICKETMASTER	Chicago Online Ticketmaster
TIES	Woman's Day Online
TIGER	TIGERDirect, Inc.
TIGERDIRECT	TIGERDirect, Inc.
TIGERS	Major League Baseball Team: Detroit Tigers
TIME	Time Message Boards
TIME DAILY	TIME Daily News Summary
TIMECAPSULE	CyberJustice's Istorian's Time Capsule
TIMES	@times/The New York Times Online
TIMES ART	@times: Art & Photography
TIMES ARTS	@times: The Arts
TIMES BOOKS	@times: Books of The Times
TIMES DINING	@times: Dining Out & Nightlife
TIMES FILM	@times: Film
TIMES LEISURE	@times: Leisure Guide
TIMES MOVIES	@times: Movies & Video
TIMES MUSIC	@times: Music & Dance
TIMES NEWS	@times/The New York Times Online
TIMES REGION	@times: In The Region
TIMES SPORTS	@times: Sports & Fitness
TIMES STORE	@times Store
TIMES STORIES	@times: Top Stories
TIMES THEATER	@times: Theater
TIMESLIPS	Timeslips Corporation
TIMEWORKS	Timeworks
TIMEX	Andy Pargh/The Gadget Guru
TIN	Teachers' Information Network
TIPS	Advice & Tips
TITF	Tonight in the AOL Forums [Platform-dependent]
TL	Travel & Leisure Magazine
TLC	The Learning Channel
TMAKER	T/Maker

TMS	TMS TV Source
TNC	The Nature Conservancy
TNEWS	Teachers' Newsstand
TNPC	The National Parenting Center
TNR	The New Republic Magazine
TO MARKET	2Market Gifts & More
TO NETSCAPE	Netscape [WAOL 2.5 only]
TODAY PITCH	The Motley Fool
TODAYS NEWS	Today's News channel
TODAYS OTHER	The Hub: Today's Other News
TODAYS PITCH	The Motley Fool
TODD ART	The Image Exchange: Ask Todd Art
TOLL FREE	AT&T 800 Directory Web Link
TOM SNYDER	Tom Snyder Productions
TOOLKIT	Web Page Toolkit
TOOLWORKS	Software Toolworks
TOONS	Cartoon Network
TOP ADVISOR	Top Advisor's Corner
TOP ADVISORS	Top Advisor's Corner
TOP COMP SITES	Top Computing Internet Sites [WAOL 2.5 and MAOL 2.6 only]
TOP COMPANY SITES	Companies on the Internet [WAOL 2.5 and MAOL 2.6 only]
TOP COMPUTING SITES	Top Computing Internet Sites [WAOL 2.5 and MAOL 2.6 only]
TOP MODEL	TopModel Online
TOP NEWS	Today's News channel
TOP TIPS	Top Tips for AOL
TORONTO BLUE JAYS	Major League Baseball Team: Toronto Blue Jays
TOS	Terms of Service*
TOS ADVISOR	Terms of Service*
TOTN	National Public Radio Outreach
TOUR	AOL Highlights Tour
TOUR GUIDE	AOL Products Center
TOWER	Tower Records
TOWER RECORDS	Tower Records
TOY NET	Pangea Toy Net
TPN	The Prayer Network
TRACK	Road & Track Magazine
TRADEPLUS	TradePlus
TRAFFIC	Shadow Traffic
TRAIL GUIDES	Backpacker Magazine
TRAILS	Backpacker Magazine
TRAINING	Career Development Training
TRANSCRIPT	Center Stage Transcripts
TRANSCRIPTS	Center Stage Transcripts
TRANSGENDER	Transgender Community Forum
TRANSPORTATION	NAS Online
TRANSSEXUAL	Transgender Community Forum
TRANSVESTITE	Transgender Community Forum
TRAVEL & LEISURE	Travel & Leisure Magazine
TRAVEL	Travel & Shopping Channel
TRAVEL ADVISORIES	US State Department Travel Advisories
TRAVEL FORUM	Travel Forum

TRAVEL HOLIDAY	Travel Holiday Magazine	TWO MARKET	2Market Gifts & More
TRAVELER	Travel Forum	TYSON	Tyson vs. McNeely [May disappear without notice]
TRAVELERS ADVANTAGE	Traveler's Advantage	U.S. SAVINGS BONDS	U.S. Treasury Securities
TRAVELERS CORNER	Traveler's Corner	UA	Unlimited Adventures
TREASURE HUNT	AOL Treasure Hunt	UCAL	University of California Extension
TREASURES	Tell a Story	UCPA	United Cerebral Palsy Association, Inc.
TREASURY BILLS	U.S. Treasury Securities	UCX	University of California Extension
TREASURY BONDS	U.S. Treasury Securities	UFO	Institute for the Study of Contact with Non-human
TREASURY DIRECT	U.S. Treasury Securities		Intelligence
TREASURY NOTES	U.S. Treasury Securities	UFOS	Institute for the Study of Contact with Non-human
TREASURY SECURITIES	U.S. Treasury Securities		Intelligence
TREK	Star Trek Club	UGC	User Group Forum
TREKER	800-TREKKER: 24 Hour Sci-Fi Collectibles Hotline	UGF	User Group Forum
TREKKER	800-TREKKER: 24 Hour Sci-Fi Collectibles Hotline	UHA	Homeowner's Forum
TRENDS	Elle Magazine Online	UKRAINE	Ukraine
TRENDSETTER	Trendsetter Software	ULTRALIGHTS	Aviation Forum
TRIANGLE	Gay & Lesbian Community Forum	UNIQUE	Best of America Online showcase
TRIB	Chicago Tribuone	UNITED KINGDOM	United Kingdom
TRIB ADS	Chicago Online Classifieds	UNIVERSE	UniverseCentral.Com
TRIB CLASSIFIED	Chicago Online Classifieds	UNIVERSE CENTRAL	UniverseCentral.Com
TRIB COLUMNISTS	Chicago Online Columnists	UNIVERSITIES	Electronic University Network
TRIB SPORTS	Chicago Tribune: Sports Area	UNIVERSITY	Electronic University Network
TRIBE	Major League Baseball Team: Cleveland Indians	UNIX	Computing Resource Center
TRIBUNE	Chicago Tribune	UNLIMITED ADVENTURES	Unlimited Adventures
TRIMBLE	Trimble Navigation, Ltd.	UNPROFOR	Balkan Operation Joint Endeavor
TRINCULO	The Motley Fool	UPDATEADD	AD&D Neverwinter Nights
TRIPLE CROWN	ABC Triple Crown	UPDATES	Hoover's Company Updates
TRIVIA	Trivia Club	UPGRADE	Upgrade to the latest version of AOL*
TROPICAL STORM	Tropical Storm and Hurricane Info	URBAN LEAGUE	National Urban League
TRUE IMAGE AUDIO	True Image Audio	US MAIL	Fax/Paper Mail
TRUE TALES	True Tales of the Internet	US NEWS	U.S. & World News area
TS	Trendsetter Software	US SAVINGS BONDS	U.S. Treasury Securities
TSENG	Tseng	US TREASURY SECURITIES	U.S. Treasury Securities
TSP	Tom Snyder Productions	USA	USA Weekend
TSR	TSR Online	USA WEEKEND	USA Weekend
TSR ONLINE	TSR Online	USEFUL THINGS	The Hub: Useful Things
TUNE UP	Tune Up Your PC	USELESS THINGS	The Hub: Useless Things
TUNE UP YOUR PC	Tune Up Your PC	USENET	Internet Usenet Newsgroup area
TURKEY	Turkey	USER GROUP	User Group Forum
TURNER VISION	Andy Pargh/The Gadget Guru	USER GROUPS	User Group Forum
TUTORING	Academic Assistance Center	USER NAME	Add, change or delete screen names
TV	Key TV area	USERLAND	Userland
TV GOSSIP	TV Shows Gossip	USFSA	United States Figure Skating Association
TV GUIDE	TMS TV Source	USPS	United States Postal Service
TV LISTINGS	TMS TV Source	USROBOTICS	U.S. Robotics
TV NETWORKS	TV Networks area	UTAH	Utah Forum
TV SHOWS	TV Shows	UTAH FORUM	Utah Forum
TV SOURCE	TMS TV Source	UZBEKISTAN	Uzbekistan
TV VIEWERS	TV Viewers Forum	VA	Virginia Forum
TWENTEITH	Twentieth Century Mutual Funds	VA.	Virginia Forum
TWENTIETH	Twentieth Century Mutual Funds	VAA	Virtual Airlines
TWENTIETH CENTURY	Twentieth Century Mutual Funds	VACATION	Preview Vacations
TWENTIETH-CENTURY	Twentieth Century Mutual Funds	VACATIONS	Preview Vacations
TWI	Time Warner Interactive	VALLEY	Virgin's Virtual Valley

VANGUARD	Vanguard Online
VANGUARD ONLINE	Vanguard Online
VAS	Virtual Airlines
VATICAN	Library of Congress Online
VAX	Computing Resource Center
VB	Visual Basic Area
VCOMMS	Vanguard Online: Communications
VDISC	Videodiscovery
VEGAN	Cooking Club: Vegetarians Online
VEGETARIAN	Cooking Club
VENTANA	Ventana Communications
VERONICA	Internet Gopher & WAIS
VERTIGO	DC Comics Online
VERTISOFT	Vertisoft
VETERANS	Military and Vets Club
VETS	Military and Vets Club
VETSCLUB	Military and Vets Club
VFR	Flying Magazine
VFUNDS	Vanguard Online: Mutual Funds Campus
VG	Vanguard Online
VGA PLANETS	VGA Planets
VGAP	VGA Planets
VGS	Video Games area
VH	Virtual Christian Humor
VH1	VH1 Online
VIACOM	Viacom New Media
VIDEO	@times: Movies & Videos
VIDEO GAME	Video Games area
VIDEO GAMES	Video Games area
VIDEO SIG	Video SIG
VIDEO TOOLKIT	Abbate Video
VIDEO ZONE	Video Zone
VIDEODISC	Videodiscovery
VIDEODISCOVERY	Videodiscovery
VIDEOS	Home Video
VIDI	VIDI
VIETNAM	Vietnam Veterans Memorial Wall
VIEWER	Viewer Resource Center
VIEWERS	Viewer Resource Center
VIEWPOINT	Viewpoint DataLabs
VILLAGE	Village Software
VILLAGE SOFTWARE	Village Software
VIREX	Datawatch
VIRGIN	Virgin's Virtual Valley
VIRGINIA	Virginia Forum
VIRGINIA FORUM	Virginia Forum
VIRTUAL AIRLINES	Virtual Airlines
VIRTUAL HUMOR	Virtual Christian Humor
VIRTUAL REALITY	Virtual Reality Resource Center
VIRTUAL TOYS	Pangea Toy Net
VIRTUAL TRADESHOW	Virtual Tradeshow
VIRTUAL VALLEY	Virgin's Virtual Valley
VIRTUS	Virtus Walkthrough
VIRUS	Virus Information Center SIG

VIRUS2	Virus Letter*
VISION VIDEO	Vision Video
VISIONARY	Visionary Software [MAOL only]
VISIONEER	Visioneer
VISUAL BASIC	Visual Basic Area
VITAMIN EXP	Health and Vitamin Express
VITAMIN EXPRESS	Health and Vitamin Express
VITAMINS	Longevity Magazine Online
VMS	Computing Resource Center
VNEWS	Vanguard Online: Vanguard News
VOLLEYBALL	King of the Beach Invitational
VOLUNTEER	AccessPoint
VOLUNTEERS	Access.Point
VOTE AMERICA	Vote America
VOYAGER	The Voyager Company
VOYETRA	Voyetra Technologies
VR	Virtual Reality Resource Center
VRLI	Virtual Reality Labs, Inc.
VSTRATEGY	Vanguard Online: Planning & Strategy
VT	Virtual Tradeshow
VTOYS	Pangea Toy Net
VV	Vision Video
WAHL	Andy Pargh/The Gadget Guru
WAIS	Internet Gopher & WAIS
WALKTHROUGH	Virtus Walkthrough
WALL	Vietnam Veterans Memorial Wall
WALL STREET WORDS	Wall Street Words
WARNER	Warner/Reprise Records Online
WARNER BROS STORE	Warner Bros. Studio Store
WARNER BROS. STORE	Warner Bros. Studio Store
WARNER BROS. STUSTO	Warner Bros. Studio Store
WARNER MUSIC	Warner/Reprise Records Online
WARNER STORE	Warner Bros. Studio Store
WASHINGTON	Capital Connection
WASHINGTON WEB	City Web
WATER	Boating Online
WB	The WB Network
WB STORE	Warner Bros. Studio Store
WBNET	The WB Network
WC CHAT	Writer's Club Chat Rooms
WCN	World Crisis Network
WD	Woman's Day Online
WD KITCHEN	Woman's Day Kitchen
WDC	Western Digital
WDC	Western Digital Company
WEATHER	Weather
WEATHER MALL	WSC Weather Mall
WEATHER MAPS	Color Weather Maps
WEAVING	Needlecrafts/Sewing Center
WEB	World Wide Web [WAOL 2.5 and MAOL 2.6 only]
WEB ART	Web Page Clip Art Center
WEB BIZ	The Web Diner
WEB DINER	The Web Diner
WEB ENTERTAINMENT	WEBentertainment

WEB HELP	The Web Diner	WINDOWS 95	Windows Forum
WEB MAKEOVER	Web Makeover	WINDOWS FORUM	Windows Forum
WEB PAGE	Web Page Toolkit	WINDOWS MAG	Windows Magazine
WEB PAGE TOOLKIT	Web Page Toolkit	WINDOWS MAGAZINE	Windows Magazine
WEB PUB	Web Publishing SIG	WINDOWS NT	Windows NT Resource Center
WEB PUBLISH	Web Publishing SIG	WINDOWWARE	Wilson Windowware
WEB PUBLISHING	Web Publishing SIG	WINDSURFING	Sailing Forum
WEB RESEARCH	Reference: Web Research	WINE	Food & Drink Network
WEB REVIEW	Web Review [WAOL 2.5 only]	WINERIES	Food & Drink Network
WEB TOOLS	Reference Web Tools	WINERY	Food & Drink Network
WEB UNIVERSITY	Web University	WINNER	AOL Contest area
WEBCRAWLER	World Wide Web [WAOL 2.5 and MAOL 2.6 only]	WINNER'S CIRCLE	ABC Track
WEBD	The Web Diner	WINSOCK	Winsock Central [WAOL 2.5 only]
WEBSITE	The Web Diner	WIRED	Wired Magazine
WEBSOURCE	Websource	WIRELESS	Wireless Communication
WEBSTER	Merriam-Webster Dictionary	WISE GUYS	Hecklers Online
WEDDING	Food & Drink Network	WIZARD	Wizard World
WEDNESDAYS	90210 Wednesdays	WIZARD WORLD	Wizard World
WEEKLY READER	Weekly Reader News	WOMAN	Woman's Day Online
WEEKLY WORLD NEWS	Weekly World News	WOMAN'S DAY	Woman's Day Online
WEIGAND	Weigand Report	WOMANS DAY	Woman's Day Online
WEIRD SISTERS	The Hub: Weird Sisters	WOMEN	Women's Interests
WEISSMANN	Traveler's Corner	WOMEN'S HEALTH	Women's Health Forum
WELCOME TO PLANET EARTH	ASTRONET	WOMENS	Womens Interests
WELLNESS	Longevity Magazine Online	WOMENS SPACE	GLCF: Women's Space
WELSH	Genealogy Forum	WOMENS SPORTS	Women's Sports World
WESTERN DIGITAL	Western Digital	WOOD	American Woodworker
WESTERN EUROPEAN	Genealogy Forum	WOODSTOCK	Woodstock Online
WESTWOOD	Westwood Studios	WOODWORKER	American Woodworker
WESTWOOD STUDIOS	Westwood Studios	WOODWORKING	American Woodworker
WHATS HOT	What's Hot This Month showcase	WORD HISTORIES	Word Histories
WHEELS EXCHANGE	Wheels Exchange	WORD PERFECT	Word Perfect Support Center
WHFS	WHFS 99.1 FM	WORD PROCESSING	Mac Desktop Publishing/WP Forum
WHITE HOUSE	White House Forum	WORKING	Working Software
WHITE PAGES	ProCD National Telephone Directory Search	WORKOUTS	Longevity Magazine Online
WHITE SOX	Major League Baseball Team: Chicago White Sox	WORKSHOP	Family Computing Forum: Life's Workshop
WICCA	Pagan Religions & Magickal Groups	WORLD	The World
WIDE WORLD OF SPORTS	ABC Online: Wide World of Sports	WORLD BELIEFS	World Beliefs
WILDCAT	Mustang Software	WORLD CRISIS	World Crisis Network
WILDCAT BBS	Mustang Software	WORLD NEWS	U.S. & World News area
WILDERNESS	Backpacker Magazine	WORLD WIDE WEB	World Wide Web [WAOL 2.5 and MAOL 2.6 only]
WILSON	Wilson Windoware	WORRY	CyberJustice's Worry Free Zone
WIMBLEDON	Wimbledon [May disappear without notice]	WORTH	Worth Magazine Online
WIN	Windows Forum	WORTH MAGAZINE	Worth Magazine Online
WIN 500	Windows Shareware 500	WORTH ONLINE	Worth Magazine Online
WIN 95	Windows Forum	WORTH PORTFOLIO	Worth Magazine Online Portfolio
WIN FORUM	Windows Forum	WP MAG	WordPerfect Magazine
WIN MAG	Windows Magazine	WRD	Christianity Online: Word Publishing
WIN NEWS	Windows News area	WRESTLING	World Wrestling Federation
WIN NT	Windows NT Resource Center	WRITE	Writer's Club Chat Rooms
WINDHAM	Windham Hill	WRITE TO OUR STAFF	Questions*
WINDHAM HILL	Windham Hill	WRITE TO STAFF	Questions*
WINDOWS	Windows Services	WRITER'S	Writer's Club
WINDOWS 500	Windows Shareware 500	WRITERS	Writer's Club

WRITERS CLUB CHAT	Writer's Club Chat Rooms
WS	GLCF: Women's Space
WSF	Women's Sports World
WSW	Wall Street Words
WWF	World Wrestling Federation
WWIR	Washington Week in Review magazine
WWN	Weekly World News
WWOS	ABC Online: Wide World of Sports
WWW	World Wide Web [WAOL 2.5 and MAOL 2.6 only]
X	Multimedia World Online
X FILES	X Files Fan Club Forum
X FILES CLUB	X Files Fan Club Forum
X FILES SIM	X Files Simming Forum
XAOS	Xoas Tools
XAOS TOOLS	Xoas Tools
XCMD	XCMD SIG
XCMD SIG	XCMD SIG
XCON	Christianity Online: Contest
XOL	Christianity Online
XWORD	The New York Times Crosswords
XWORDS	Crossword America
YACHTING	Sailing Forum
YACHTS	Boating Online
YANKEES	Major League Baseball Team: New York Yankees
YANKS	Major League Baseball Team: New York Yankees
YAVIASA	The Hub: You Are Very Intelligent and Somewhat Artsy
YBERSMITH	CyberSmith
YC	Your Church Magazine
YEAR	1995: The Year in Review
YEAR IN REVIEW	1995: The Year in Review
YELLOW PAGES	Business Yellow Pages
YIR	1995: The Year in Review
YMB	Your Mind & Body Online
YOUNG CHEFS	Young Chefs
YOUNGNESS	Longevity Magazine Online
YOUR BUSINESS	Your Business
YOUR CHOICE	ABC News-On-Demand
YOUR CHURCH	Your Church Magazine
YOUR MIND & BODY	Your Mind & Body Online
YOUR MIND AND BODY	Your Mind & Body Online
YOUR MONEY	Your Money area
YOUR TOONS	Cartoon collection
YOUTH SERVICE AMERICA	SERVEnet
YOUTHFUL	Longevity Magazine Online
YOUTHNET	National Network for Youth
YOYO	Yoyodyne Entertainment
YOYODYNE	Yoyodyne Entertainment
YSA	SERVEnet
YUBBA	Today's Events in the Center Stage
YUGOSLAVIA	Balkan Operation Joint Endeavor
Z	The Health Zone
ZAGAT	Zagat Restaurant/Hotel/Resort/Spa Surveys
ZAGATS	Zagat Restaurant/Hotel/Resort/Spa Surveys

ZD	Computer Life Online
ZD NET	ZD Net
ZEDCOR	Zedcor, Inc.
ZELOS	Zelos
ZEOS	Zeos International Ltd.
ZIFF	ZD Net
ZIMA	Zima
ZIMA TALK	Zima Events
ZIP CODE	Zip Code Directory [WAOL 2.5 only]
ZIP CODE DIRECTORY	Zip Code Directory [WAOL 2.5 only]
ZIP CODES	Zip Code Directory [WAOL 2.5 only]
ZODIAC	ASTRONET
ZON	Zondervan Publishing House
ZONDERVAN	Zondervan Publishing House
ZONE	The Entrepreneur Zone
ZONED	The Health Zone
ZONIE	The Health Zone
ZOOM TELEPHONICS	Zoom Telephonics
ZP	Zondervan Publishing House

APPENDIX C
Locations, Modems & CCL Files

America Online's custom software is not only user-friendly, it's modem-friendly as well. The first time you sign on to America Online, the software asks you several questions as part of the initial installation process. Your answers supply such things as modem speed and type, and allow AOL to determine local access telephone numbers to use, and so on. This information automatically configures your America Online software to connect effortlessly. However, you may need to modify this information if, for example, you change your location, upgrade your modem, or discover that your nonstandard modem needs special configuration. This appendix will show you how to create and save multiple setups and how to modify your configuration. It also covers modem files and CCL scripts as they relate to successful America Online connection.

Locations

Your America Online software allows you to create and store multiple sets of network setup and connection information. These sets of information are known as "locations," and while they are handy for folks who move from location to location, they also are very useful for those who like to stay put. You can store configurations for different connection speeds as well as access numbers for various locations.

Think of locations as coats. If you live in a temperate region of the country, you may only own one light windbreaker. On the other hand, if you call a more diverse climate your home, you may collect an entire wardrobe of coats to meet a variety of weather conditions. Locations are no different: they allow you to successfully step out into the world of America Online, regardless of where you are, what time it is, or what you wish to accomplish. Best of all, creating and choosing your location before signing on is easier than purchasing a closet full of coats and deciding which one to wear.

New locations are simple to create. Launch the America Online software and, instead of signing on as you normally would, click the Setup button on the Welcome (sign-on) window, and click the Create Location button that appears to the right. In the new window that appears, enter your information (described below in "Changing Your Location"). When you're finished, save your new location by clicking the Save button in the lower left-hand corner of the window. When you're prompted to name the location, choose a title that reflects the function of the new information, such as "Ann Arbor" (for a different city or town) or "9600 Access" (for a different connection speed). To use the location you've just created, simply select it in the Network and Modem Setup window. The next time you sign on, your software will use the setup information in the selected location.

Changing Your Location

To create or modify locations, you need to change your network options. Creation is simple, as described above in this appendix. To modify a setup, click the Setup button in the Welcome (sign-on) window, then choose, from the Network & Modem Setup Location list, the location you want to change. In both creating and editing a setup, your software displays a window titled "Network Setup" with a number of options (see Figure C-1). Be sure to note your current settings in case you need to return to them. You can use this screen to change any number of options, all described below.

Figure C-1: Working offline, click the Setup button in the Welcome (sign-on) window and choose either Edit Location or Create Location to access your network setup information.

Network Setup	
Location:	Local 28.8 Access
Phone Type:	⦿ Touch Tone ○ Pulse
Phone Number: 273-5780	**Phone Number:** 224-0298
Modem Speed: 28800 bps	**Modem Speed:** 28800 bps
Network: AOLnet	**Network:** AOLnet
☐ Use the following prefix to reach an outside line:	9,
☐ Use the following command to disable call waiting:	*70,
Save	Swap Phone Numbers	Cancel

Below, we'll look at each one of the variables pictured in Figure C-1.

Location

The Location field gives you the option of editing or creating a name for the Network Setup. Choose a name you'll recognize immediately, as described earlier.

Phone Type

Touch-tone phones are standard equipment today in most homes and hotels. However, there are still a few local phone exchanges (or homes) that do not support tone dialing; they use pulse dialing instead. If your America Online software seems to be having trouble when first dialing the local access number, select the Pulse option.

Phone Number

This field contains the phone number your America Online software uses to connect with the host computer. You'll notice that this field, and the associated Modem Speed and Network fields, are shown twice in the window. AOL automatically uses the second set of information if the first try with the primary information is unsuccessful. This allows you to set up an alternate access number for your AOL software to dial if the primary number is busy or unavailable.

You will need to change these numbers if you've moved to a new area, if you're on the road, or if you just want to try a different local access number. You can find local access numbers online via the keyword: **Access**. If there is only one number for your area, use that as both primary and alternate number so the AOL software will redial it automatically if the number is busy on the first try. If you don't want AOL to dial a second number, leave the alternate number field empty.

Tip: In some areas you may need to dial an area code, even for a local call. If you normally need to do this when you place voice calls, you will need to do it when you call America Online access as well.

Note: Remember, any long-distance charges you incur reaching the America Online access number are your responsibility. They're not included as a part of your monthly America Online fee. If you have to dial the number 1 before you can reach AOL's nearest access number, you're no doubt incurring long-distance charges.

Modem Speed

You'll most likely only need to change this if you get a new modem with a speed different than your usual modem, or if you're currently using a local access node that doesn't take full advantage of your modem's speed. For instance, you may use a local access number that can only handle 2400 bps. But if you later switch to a different number that can serve 9600 bps modems and you have a 9600 bps modem (or faster), you need to change the Modem Speed setting your America Online software uses. Use the Modem Speed pop-up menu to change the speed to the highest setting your modem and node can handle.

Network

This pop-up menu is used to select which phone carrier handles your calls from the local access node to America Online's host computers. AOLNet is AOL's proprietary network of telephone lines across the country. Use AOLNet whenever you can. SprintNet is the most widely used carrier for America Online in the United States; DataPac is used in Canada. There might be a few others, depending on your location. You can use the Network pop-up menu to select the appropriate network as specified for your access number. (The keyword: **Access**—available only when you're online—lists all of AOL's access numbers.) TCP/IP connections are detailed later in this appendix.

Outside Line Prefix

Some telephone systems, particularly those in hotels, offices, and schools, require that you dial a 9 or some other prefix to get an outside line. Enter the number you want America Online to dial; then enter a comma. The comma tells the modem to wait two seconds before dialing the next number. If it takes longer than two seconds for your phone system to access an outside line and generate a dial tone, you might want to add a second comma just to be sure. Note that the America Online software already has entered a 9 for you in the appropriate field. To use this prefix whenever you dial America Online, all you have to do is click this check box.

Disable Call Waiting

When you're connected to America Online and someone tries to call you, he or she would normally get a busy signal. If you have Call Waiting, however, the caller hears a normal ring, and your modem hears the beep that ordinarily lets you know you have a call waiting. As you can imagine, this tends to confuse your PC (not to mention the host computers). Call Waiting, which is a convenience for voice communications, is an interference for telecommunications and will disconnect your modem from America Online. If you use Call Waiting, you can (and should) temporarily disable it (on most phone systems, by entering a code such as 1170, or *70,) before dialing America Online. Be sure to include the comma after the string of numbers: it tells the modem to wait two seconds before dialing the next number. Note that the America Online software has already entered 1170 for you in the appropriate field. To configure your software to turn off Call Waiting whenever you dial America Online (but not any other time), all you have to do is click this check box. When you're finished using AOL, however, you may need to enter the same code from your phone handset to turn Call Waiting back on (or you may start to wonder why everyone is getting busy signals). If you aren't sure what numbers you should enter to disable Call Waiting, check with your local telephone company or look in the front section of your local phone directory, under Call Waiting.

Swap Phone Numbers

This handy button allows you to easily swap the information you've set for your primary and alternate numbers. This is useful when the primary number is giving you difficulties and you'd rather use the alternate number initially.

TCP/IP Connections

America Online also provides access to the service through TCP/IP, which is a communications format for transferring data over the Internet. To sign on with a TCP/IP connection, you must first have a TCP/IP connection from an Internet service provider to your computer. You can download a listing of public access Internet providers by using keywords: **File Search**, then searching for PDIAL. To use TCP/IP with America Online, download and install Winsock (available at keyword: **Winsock**). Winsock is an America Online-supported add-on that allows you to use TCP/IP connections, as well as other Internet applications. Once installed, simply create a new Locality and choose TCP/IP for your network connection, leaving the phone numbers blank.

You can also connect to America Online through a SLIP or PPP connection (a modem-based TCP/IP connection). To connect through SLIP or PPP, you need a program such as Trumpet, which is available online by using keywords: **File Search**, then searching for Trumpet Winsock. If you have a local area network (LAN), ask your system administrator if you have TCP/IP capabilities.

AOLGLOBALnet Connections

AOLGLOBALnet is America Online's international access network. Access through AOLGLOBALnet carries an additional surcharge and offers high-speed local connections around the world. To use AOLGLOBALnet, download and install the special CCL file from keyword: **AOLGLOBALnet**. More information on using America Online outside of the United States is available at keyword: **AOLsewhere**.

Modem Files

For the majority of members, America Online has made it unnecessary to worry about such things as data bits, stop bits, or parity. All your connection information is collected when you initially run America Online. Should you need to change your modem setup for any reason, follow the steps below:

▲ Click the Setup button at the bottom of the Welcome (sign-on) window.

🔺 Click the Setup Modem button. It makes no difference which location you select from the Choose Location list box: it's assumed that your modem configuration is the same for each one.

The Modem Selection and Customization window will appear. Select your modem from the extensive list that appears there. If your modem doesn't appear there, read on.

America Online has taken the extra step of allowing you to customize your modem setup should you need to. If you use a modem that's not included in AOL's preconfigured modem settings, you may need to create a custom modem file. A modem file is simply information that allows your modem and the AOL software to work together smoothly. It tells the modem how to set itself up for dialing out, how to place a call, and how to behave once it is connected. Fortunately, you hardly ever need to alter your modem file, but the option is available on those rare occasions when it is necessary. In these cases, a number of simple solutions are available:

🔺 If you are able to sign on, drop by the free Tech Help Live area online (use the keyword: **TechLive** and click on the Tech Support Live icon), available weekdays and weekends. An America Online representative will guide you through the process of configuring the software for your modem.

🔺 If it is after hours for Tech Help Live (and you're able to sign on), you may be able to find a preconfigured file for your modem already available. Go to keyword: **Highspeed** and double-click the Modem Profile Library. The well-stocked library is very likely to contain what you need. If you find a file for your modem, download it to the MPM subdirectory located in your AOL directory. After you've downloaded the file, sign off and click Setup in the welcome window (actually, it'll be the goodbye window if you've just signed off). Then click Modem Setup, and your modem type will appear in the list for selecting. If something goes wrong and you don't see your modem listed, make sure the modem profile is in the right directory, and check the instructions you'll find in the Modem Profile Library to make sure you've followed the correct procedures.

- ▲ If you are unable to sign on, call America Online Technical Support at 1-800-827-6364. Like the Tech Help Live area, this service is available seven days a week, and the representatives can offer considerable guidance.

- ▲ If you are unable to sign on to America Online but you can sign on to other services, you can access the same Modem Drivers library described above through the America Online Technical Support BBS. Just dial 1-800-827-5808 with a standard telecommunications program (such as Terminal, which comes with Windows). Your settings should be: 8 data bits, no parity, 1 stop bit. You can access the BBS at modem speeds up to 14,400 bps. Complete instructions for dialing the BBS and using the Terminal program are available under AOL's Help menu.

- ▲ If you are an advanced user, you can create a custom modem file suited to your own needs. Please note that even if you are an expert telecommunicator, you are advised that before making changes you should consult your modem's manual or technical support line for the features you can enable or disable. If you'd like to give this option a go, read on.

Customizing Your Modem File

To customize your modem file, follow the steps below:

- ▲ Working offline, click the Setup button in the Welcome window.

- ▲ Click the Setup Modem button in the Network & Modem Setup window.

- ▲ Select the modem most closely resembles yours from the list in the Modem Selection and Customization window. If you can't find one, use the Generic (Hayes compatible) modem.

Figure C-2:
America Online
offers built-in
editors to custom-
ize a modem file.

Custom Modem Profile

Setup Modem String:	AT&FE1Q0V1X1^M
Restore Modem String:	AT&F^M
Dial Prefix:	ATD
Dial Suffix:	^M
Disconnect String:	ATH^M
Escape String:	~~~+++~~~
Reset String:	ATZ^M

OK   Cancel

Click the Edit Commands button. AOL will copy the modem you selected into the Custom Modem Profile (see Figure C-2), which you can then edit according to your modem manufacturer's instructions. If those instructions aren't available, use the table below. These are the most common modem setup strings.

Parameter	Setting	Usual Command
Data Compression	On	%C1
Error Correction	On	&Q5
Flow Control Hardware - Request to Send/Clear to Send	(RTS/CTS)	&K3
Local Echo	On	E1
Verbose Responses Word responses	V1	
Extended Result Codes Respond to dial tone and busy signal	X1 or X4 (preferably X4)	DCD
Track the state of data carrier from the remote modem	&C1	DTR
Monitor	DTR	&D2

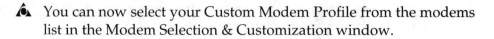

> You can now select your Custom Modem Profile from the modems list in the Modem Selection & Customization window.

Don't overlook the Modem Port option in the Modem Selection and Customization window. This tells the software where to look for the modem's physical connection to your computer, with the default being COM 1. If you want to use a modem connected to a port other than COM 1, select the appropriate port here. If you aren't sure which port your modem uses, check the ports on the back of the computer.

Solving Common Modem Problems

Here are some common modem problems and solutions:

Modem Won't Dial

America Online's software requires certain commands to connect properly to the host computer. To verify that these commands are included, click Edit Commands in the Modem Setup area and check the command strings. You may want to try adding "ATQ0V1E0" to your Setup Modem String, if something similar isn't already included. You should also check your dialing prefix field—for most modems this should read "ATV1 S11=55 Q0 E0 D" (those 0's are zeros).

Modem Dials but Won't Connect

If your connection fails at some point between the high-pitched carrier tone and the Welcome window, or if it fails after the first thing you try to do online, the culprits probably are flow control (XON/XOFF), data compression, or error-correction protocols. Make sure that these are disabled. Adding "AT&F" to the beginning of the Setup Modem String and adding "^M" to the very end should do the trick.

Modem Disconnects on Call Waiting

Sudden disconnections also can be caused by Call Waiting. The click that indicates a call is waiting on the line sounds like a "break" (disconnect immediately) signal to the modem, which obligingly hangs up. If this is a problem, you should disable Call Waiting when you connect to America Online. You can disable it offline by clicking the Setup button in the Welcome (sign-on) window, selecting your location in the list,

choosing Edit Location, and clicking in the check box marked "Use the following command to disable call waiting." The input field to the right of this line contains the pulse code to disable Call Waiting, which also works for touch-tone users in most areas. In some areas, you may need to change the default of 1170, to *70, for touch-tone use. Include a comma after the code: it tells the modem to wait two seconds before dialing the next number. If you aren't sure what numbers you should enter to disable Call Waiting, check with your local telephone company or look in the front section of your local phone book, under Call Waiting. Remember that once you're done on AOL, you may need to manually re-enable Call Waiting.

Modem Disconnects Frequently

If you have problems with line noise (static on your phone line while signed on to America Online), the result may be file-transfer errors, strange characters on the screen or occasional disconnections from America Online. One step you can take to cut down on line noise is to set your modem temporarily to a lower baud rate. Try the speed one step down from your current setting. You also can try another local access number (if available).

Another common cause of frequent disconnects is a phone cord with a bad connector (or jack) on one or both ends, or a faulty wall jack. If you hear lots of static when you're talking on the phone, odds are the same amount of static (line noise) is present when you use America Online. Check with your telephone company or an electrician to find out what can be done to improve your line quality.

Modem Speaker Stays On

To disable your modem speaker, click on Edit Commands in the Modem Setup area, and add M0 (the letter M and zero) to the Setup Modem String. If there are already characters present, add M0 immediately before the characters ^M, which fall at the end. For example, if you are using a Zyxel modem, your Setup Modem String would appear as AT&FM0^M.

Alternatively, M1 will enable the speaker until a connection is made, and M2 will keep the speaker turned on after a connection has been established.

CCL Files

The dysfunctionally curious will note the CCL subdirectory in the AOL directory. Normally, you won't need to worry about this, but to satisfy your curiosity, here is a brief description of CCLs and what they are all about.

A CCL file (Communication Control Language) is a modem "script" that allows your modem to talk to certain communication systems. Your America Online software comes with CCLs for networks like SprintNet, Tymnet, and DataPac, enabling them to work with America Online. CCL scripts are written in a programming language and can be modified with a simple text editor. The CCLs come preconfigured and already in place; you needn't do anything to take advantage of these, other than verify that the appropriate CCL for your access number is selected in the Network pop-up menu in the Network Setup screen. Additionally, it is unlikely you will need to alter a CCL script; modem files can handle virtually all your needs. There may be times, however, when the connection process is too complicated for a modem file. If you find that a modified or custom modem file does not solve your problems, contact America Online Technical Support for further details.

APPENDIX D
On the Road

Your access to America Online need not end where your wanderlust begins. Whether you travel across the country or use a notebook PC at work and at home, America Online is only a phone call away. This appendix gives you tips for calling America Online while traveling, finding local access numbers, and signing on using a computer other than your own.

Using America Online on the Road

Using America Online when you are traveling is easy with these few preparations and helpful hints:

- Inexpensive kits are available that help in setting up your modem when traveling. It's also a good idea to travel with an extra length of standard phone line with modular (RJ-11) jacks on each end, and a phone splitter. These items are available at many phone and electronics stores.

- If you're going to be staying in a hotel, ask for a "computer-ready" room: one with an extra phone jack for your modem (some hotels also use phones that have a special "data port" jack built into the side of the unit). If the hotel doesn't have phones set up for computer users, you can usually remove the phone cable from its phone jack and connect your modem cable. However, since many hotels use digital lines and private branch exchanges (PBXs), these jacks are often powered. Connecting your modem to one may toast your modem, and could damage your laptop as well. Line checkers are available from many electronics dealers.

If you need to dial a long-distance access number and do not want to pay the hotel's long-distance charges or accrue charges on a friend's phone bill, you can use your calling card. Edit your location's network setup (detailed in Appendix C) by inserting the following in the Phone Number field:

<Long-distance carrier number, if needed> + 0 + <area code> + <access number> + ,,,,, + <calling card number> + PIN (personal identification number, which may be optional)

For example: 10333-0-313-665-2900,,,,,12312312341234#

Those five commas cause AOL to wait 10 seconds while your long-distance carrier comes on the line and asks for your calling card number.

Note that your long-distance carrier number may be needed to override the default carrier for the phone you are calling from: AT&T is 10288, MCI is 10222, and Sprint is 10333. Call Waiting may cause problems here, so disable it if you are having difficulties. Also, be sure you've got the required prefix to access an outside line, entered in the "Use the following prefix..." box.

 Use America Online to back up your work while you're traveling. Send mail to yourself and attach the file you want to save. If you need to restore the file, you can read the mail and download the saved file. If you lose your work while you're on the road, or even after you return, you'll have a backup waiting online when you get home.

 In your travels, you may find yourself using America Online in places where sounds could be disruptive to others around you, such as a friend's guest room or a waiting room. In these situations, you can disable your America Online sounds (check your General Preferences under the Members menu) or turn your modem speaker off (refer to Appendix C: "Locations, Modems & CCL Files," or check your modem manual).

 Look up the local access numbers (by using the keyword: **Access**) for the area you'll be visiting. Do this before you leave: it's much easier. Create individual locations (discussed in Appendix C) for

your most frequent destinations, and name them appropriately. Now when you need to sign on you can simply select your location, say, Work, Branch Office, Home, or Cottage, through the Setup button on the Welcome (sign-on) window, and you're ready to go!

 If there is no local access number available in your area, you can access America Online anywhere in the United States, Puerto Rico, and the U.S. Virgin Islands by using a special 800 number. The number is 1-800-716-0023 and it does carry a surcharge for use. More information is available at keyword: **AOLnet**.

General help with signing on is available in the America Online Software under the Help menu.

Finding Local Access Numbers Offline

If you discover you need a new access number while you're on the road but you are unable to get online to search the number directory, you aren't alone. Many others have traveled down this path before, and a variety of options have opened up:

 Sign on with the NewLocal# option in the Screen Name pop-up menu on the welcome (sign-on) window. With this option enabled, America Online will call a toll-free number automatically and give you a list of access numbers to choose from.

 Call America Online's Customer Service Hotline at 1-800-827-6364 (within the United States) or 1-703-893-6288 (from Canada or overseas), between 6 a.m. and 4 a.m. Eastern time seven days a week.

 Phone the carrier network if you do not want to use AOLNet: Tymnet can be reached at 1-800-336-0149; SprintNet at 1-800-877-5045 ext. 5, and SprintNet's automatic access number listings at 1-800-473-7983.

 If you have a fax modem or access to a fax machine, call America Online's FAXLink service at 1-800-827-5551 and ask that a list of access numbers be faxed to you. An automated voice menu will guide you through the choices.

 Connect to America Online's Technical Support BBS at 1-800-827-5808 with a standard telecommunications program. Your settings

should be: 8 data bits, no parity, 1 stop bit. You can access the BBS at modem speeds up to 14,400 bps. Complete instructions for dialing the BBS and using the Terminal program are available under AOL's Help menu.

▲ If you're within the United States, you can connect to SprintNet's Local Access Numbers Directory with a standard telecommunications program. To access, simply dial any SprintNet node directly and, once connected, type **@D** and press the Return key twice. At the @ prompt, type **c mail** and press Return, then type **PHONES** for the username and **PHONES** again for the password. You can look up any local SprintNet number available.

Signing On as a Guest

In your travels you are likely to visit others who have America Online on their computers. While your screen names won't appear in their software, you can still use their machine to sign on with your account. Just select the "Guest" screen name from the pop-up menu on the welcome (sign-on) window and then click the Sign On button. (The "Guest" name option always appears in the list of screen names, no matter whose machine you're using or what kind of computer it is.) The software will dial the local access number and connect to America Online.

After you've made the connection, you'll see a dialog box that asks for a screen name and the password. Enter your screen name and password. America Online will connect using your account. Charges you accrue during the session (other than long-distance charges, if any) will be billed to your account rather than your friend's.

Note: Your password and your screen name will not be stored on the computer you're using to sign on as a guest. They will remain secure.

Note: Data such as your Address Book and FlashSession information is stored locally in your America Online software rather than on AOL's machines. As a result, you will not be able to see this information when signed on as a Guest on another computer. You are also unable to edit your screen names while signed on as a Guest.

To sign off from a Guest session, simply choose Sign Off from the Go To menu as you normally would.

AOL Abroad

If you travel out of the country and want to continue accessing America Online, don't leave home without visiting keyword: **AOLsewhere** first. The AOLsewhere area online provides access to AOLGLOBALnet international access numbers, technical support, international Web sites, the travel channel, and even a message board where you can network with other travelers. For information on connecting with AOLGLOBALnet access numbers, see Appendix C, and read the directions in the AOLGLOBALnet area carefully (you can get there quickly with keyword: **AOLGLOBALnet**).

APPENDIX E
Preferences

Like all good software, America Online offers the opportunity to configure the client to your liking via a group of user preferences. What if you work in a crowded office and don't want to hear sounds like "You have mail!" broadcast for all to hear? What if you get tired of typing in your password every time you sign on? Why does AOL close your Compose Mail window after you've sent mail?

All of these things—and a number of others—are covered by AOL's member preferences. Preferences can be set online or off, so you're best advised to set them offline when the meter isn't running.

Begin by choosing Preferences from the Members menu. Eight categories of preferences will appear in the form of the eight buttons pictured in Figure E-1.

Figure E-1:
The eight categories of preferences.
Click on any one of them to make changes.

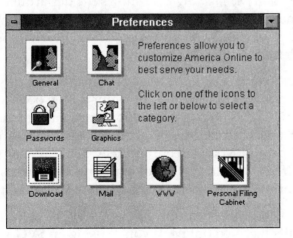

On the pages that follow, we will examine these preferences individually.

General Preferences

Here's where you have control over sounds, text, and Network News (see Figure E-2).

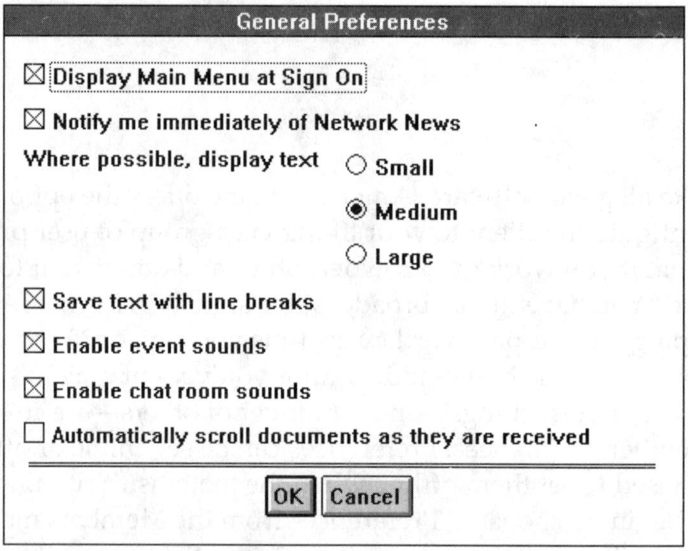

Figure E-2:
The General Prefer-
ences window
provides control
over the most
frequently changed
options in the
program.

General Preferences

☒ Display Main Menu at Sign On

☒ Notify me immediately of Network News

Where possible, display text   ○ Small

       ◉ Medium

       ○ Large

☒ Save text with line breaks

☒ Enable event sounds

☒ Enable chat room sounds

☐ Automatically scroll documents as they are received

[OK] [Cancel]

🔺 *Display Main Menu at Sign On* shows the departments window (the Main menu) when you first come online. If you don't use the Main Menu to navigate AOL, you may prefer to turn this option off. (On is the default setting.)

🔺 *Notify me immediately of Network News* turns on the Network News announcements that flash across your screen occasionally, such as when AOL is about to go down for regular maintenance. You don't need to do anything to get these messages—they automatically appear on your screen, and they don't interrupt what you're doing. If you would prefer not to receive these messages while you're online, turn off this option. (On is the default setting.)

🔺 *Where possible, display text* provides control over the size of most text that's received online. If you're using an SVGA monitor, incoming text may be too small for you to read. Some people have trouble with small text as well. No matter what causes the problem, this control offers the fix. (Default is Medium.)

🔺 *Save text with line breaks* gives you the option of curtailing the software's habit of adding a line break (also known as a *hard return*) at the end of each line. Though there are special conditions when you might need line breaks at the end of each line (some DOS word processors require it, for example), text shouldn't have breaks at the end of each line unless you insert one yourself with the Enter key on your keyboard. Disabling this function is useful if you want to type a reply to a message board posting offline and save it before signing on to post. (On is the default.)

🔺 *Enable event sounds* activates the sounds like "Welcome" when you sign on, and "You have mail!" when mail is waiting for you. If your machine can play these sounds (many machines can't—read Chapter 8, "The Community," for details on this subject) and you don't want to hear them, turn this control off. (On is the default.)

🔺 *Enable chat room sounds* activates member-sent sounds in chat rooms. Some chat rooms are especially sound-oriented. Try LaPub for an example. These people love to laugh out loud and slap one another on the back—quite aurally. To hear these sounds, you must have them installed on your machine, your machine must be sound-compatible, and you must leave this preference turned on. (For more about chat room sounds, read Chapter 8, "The Community.") (On is the default.)

🔺 *Automatically scroll documents as they are received* scrolls articles as they are received online. At 9600 baud, you can't read this fast, so scrolling incoming text is of no particular value at this speed or faster. It makes the screen a busy place to watch, and in some cases may actually slow down the transmission speed of text transfers. That's why the default is Off. It's always better to log incoming text (logging is discussed in Chapter 10, "Staying Informed"), and read text like this after you sign off. However, if you prefer to have articles scroll as they are received, for whatever reason, turn this preference on.

Chat Preferences

If you're fond of chat rooms, look these preferences over carefully. Chat rooms are discussed in Chapter 8, "The Community."

Chat Preferences

☐ Notify me when members arrive
☐ Notify me when members leave
☐ Double-space incoming messages
☐ Alphabetize the member list
☒ Enable chat room sounds

OK   Cancel

- *Notify me when members arrive* causes the "OnlineHost" to place a line in your chat room window announcing the entrance of every arriving member. Host and Guides love this feature, and it's helpful for all of us when we're in a room that doesn't have a lot of comings and goings. If the members in a room are transitory—as people in lobbies, for instance, tend to be—you will probably want to leave this preference off. (The default is Off.)

- *Notify me when members leave* is the same as the preference described earlier, except the notification is provided when the member leaves, rather than arrives in, the room. Again, it's helpful for Hosts and Guides. (The default is Off.)

- *Double-space incoming messages* just makes them easier to read. It also halves the amount of conversation that's displayed on your screen at any one time. It's a compromise, but the decision is yours. (The default is Off.)

- *Alphabetize the member list* offers you the choice of viewing the member list (the little scroll box of member names in the upper right corner of chat windows) in alphabetical order or in the order in which members arrive in the chat room. If you want to watch comings and goings (and the Notify preferences are turned off), leave this preference turned off. If you tend to refer to the list often—perhaps to look up the profiles of or send Instant Messages to other members in the room—alphabetizing it may help. (The default is Off.)

🔺 *Enable chat room sounds* is simply a second offering of the preference discussed earlier. It's listed under the General Preferences (see Figure E-2) as well. You may turn it on or off in either place— the change will be made for you in both places. (The default is On.)

Passwords Preferences

Passwords keep other people from using your account when you're not around. Once a password is stored, anyone using that machine can sign on and spend hours online, at your expense.

On the other hand, there are those of us for whom that potential simply doesn't exist. Perhaps you lock your computer when you're away, or the other people in your office or home are trustworthy beyond reproach. I sign on 5 or 10 times a day, and my computer is in my studio, which is sanctified ground. Typing my password 5 or 10 times a day is not only unnecessary, it's counterproductive. For this reason, I store my password (Figure E-4) and never have to type it in.

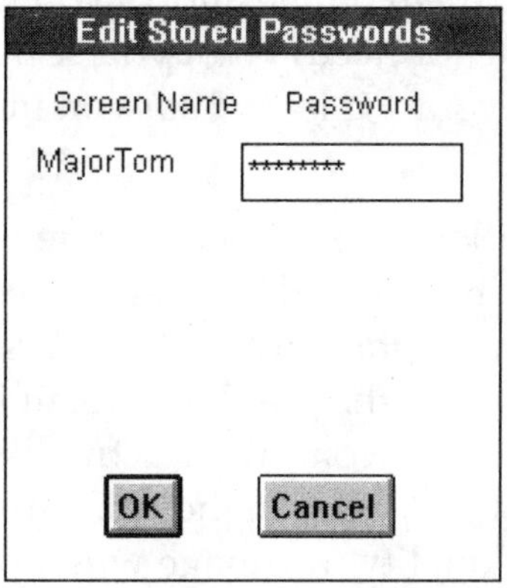

Figure E-4: You can't read my stored password. AOL displays only asterisks. The password, nonetheless, is there, and I don't have to type it in when I sign on.

Edit Stored Passwords

Screen Name   Password

MajorTom   ********

OK   Cancel

Use this option with care! AOL shows no pity when members call with unexpected bills run up by fellow office workers or members of the family. If there's a possibility that someone might access your account while you're away, don't utilize this feature. Finally, *never, ever, ever* use the stored password feature on a laptop installation. If someone is low enough to make off with your portable, they will undoubtedly be happy to run up a large AOL bill at your expense. (The default is Off.)

Graphics Preferences

These preferences pertain to the online viewing of graphics as they're received. Downloading graphics and the online graphics viewers are discussed in Chapter 5, "Transferring Files."

Figure E-5:
The Graphics
Preferences
provide control
over graphics that
are received
online.

Graphics Viewing Preferences

While you are online AOL will save online art to your PC's hard drive, this saves time when you enter the area again as you already have the necessary online art. You can control how much art is stored on your PC by changing the number below. If you increase the disk space AOL will run faster but take more space on your hard drive.

Maximum disk space to use for online art: 5   megabyte(s)

☑ **Display image files on download**

JPEG compression quality: 100

[Set Color Mode]   [OK]   [Cancel]

- *Display image files on download* allows you to view most graphics as they're received. Viewing them online allows you to abort the download if you don't like (or need) what you see. It's best to leave this preference on unless your PC is very low on memory, or very slow. (On is the default.)

- *JPEG compression quality* allows you to set the rate of compression for JPEG graphics as they're received. JPEG is actually a compression method rather than a graphic format. It's a *lossy* compression method, meaning that some of the graphic's detail is lost when it's saved in the JPEG format. The "compression quality" number in Figure E-5 ranges from 1 to 100. The higher this number, the less data is lost and the better quality the image when you save a graphic using the JPEG method. Smaller compression quality numbers cause more data to be lost and image quality to be diminished. On the other hand, small compression quality figures mean smaller files. What's best? I'd say leave this number set to 100 unless you are low on disk space or don't mind the quality loss. Always perform a test JPEG save before you commit a graphic to a lower number: once a graphic is saved, there's no going back. (The default is 100.)

⯅ *Set Color Mode*, available through the button on the bottom of the window, gives you the option of choosing the correct number of colors that your monitor can display (see Figure E-6). Normally AOL can determine this automatically, but not all monitors accurately report their capabilities. If you are noticing problems displaying images, you might try adjusting this control. (The default is Detect Automatically.)

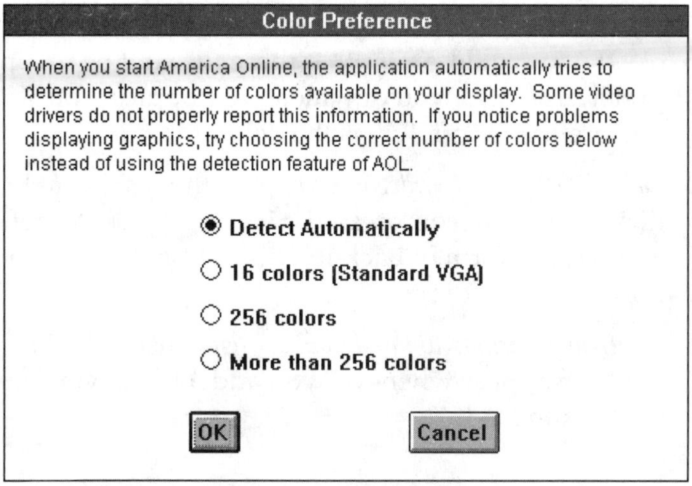

Figure E-6:
The Set Color
Mode preference
gives control over
the number of
colors AOL dis-
plays. Leave this at
Detect Automati-
cally unless you are
experiencing
problems.

Color Preference

When you start America Online, the application automatically tries to determine the number of colors available on your display. Some video drivers do not properly report this information. If you notice problems displaying graphics, try choosing the correct number of colors below instead of using the detection feature of AOL.

◉ **Detect Automatically**

◯ **16 colors (Standard VGA)**

◯ **256 colors**

◯ **More than 256 colors**

[OK]   [Cancel]

Download Preferences

If you do much downloading, you should (1) use the Download Manager, and (2) examine these preferences. (Downloading is discussed in Chapter 5; the Download Manager is discussed in Chapter 6.)

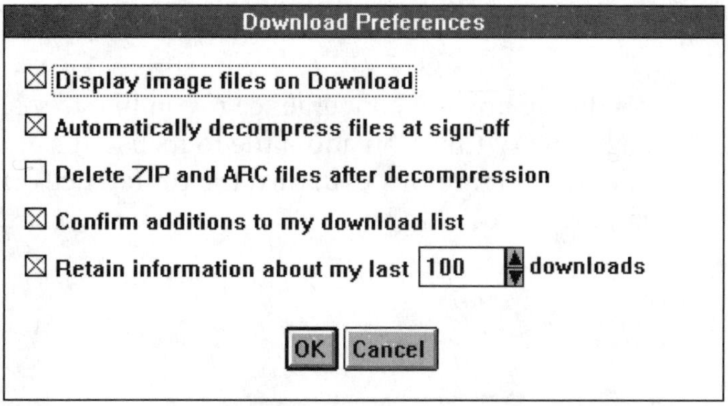

Figure E-7:
The Download
Preferences dialog
box provides
control over your
downloading
configuration.

Download Preferences

☒ **Display image files on Download**

☒ **Automatically decompress files at sign-off**

☐ **Delete ZIP and ARC files after decompression**

☒ **Confirm additions to my download list**

☒ **Retain information about my last** [100 ⭥] **downloads**

[OK] [Cancel]

🔺 *Display image files on Download* is a second offering of the preference discussed earlier under Graphic Preferences (see Figure E-5). Again, this preference allows you to view most graphics as they're downloaded. Again, changing the preference here will change it under the Graphics Preferences as well. (On is the default.)

🔺 *Automatically decompress files at sign-off* uses AOL's built-in version of PKUnZip (PKZip and PKUnZip are discussed in Chapter 5, "Transferring Files") to decompress any zipped files you have downloaded. AOL automatically unzips these files when you sign off. If you would prefer that these files not be unzipped, turn this preference off. If you download to floppies, you will want to turn this preference off. (On is the default.)

🔺 *Delete ZIP files after decompression* removes the archive from your disk after it's decompressed. Since many of us prefer to store the archive as a form of backup, this option defaults to the off condition.

🔺 *Confirm additions to my download list* causes the dialog box pictured in E-8 to appear whenever you add a file to your queue of files to be downloaded.

Figure E-8: AOL displays this dialog box whenever you add a file to your download queue. If you don't want to bother with it, turn the appropriate preference off.

The file has been added to your download list. To view your list or start the download, select 'Download Manager' below (or select from the File Menu or theToolbar later).

OK   **Download Manager**

This dialog box is a convenience if you like to visit the Download Manager every time you add a file to its list. It's an annoyance if you do not. If it annoys you, turn the preference off. (The default is On.)

▲ *Retain information about my last XX downloads* determines how many files are listed when you click on the Download Manager's Show Files Downloaded button. Each file that's retained consumes about 2K of your hard disk's storage space. You're the only one who knows how much of your hard disk you can afford to dedicate to this feature, so give this number some thought before changing it.

Mail Preferences

Electronic mail is an important part of America Online (e-mail is discussed in Chapter 3). Here are the preferences that apply to your e-mail.

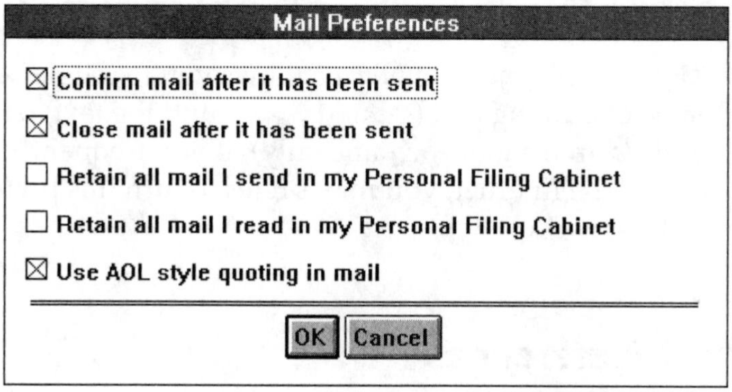

Figure E-9:
The Mail Preferences offer control over mail sent and received.

> **Mail Preferences**
>
> ☒ Confirm mail after it has been sent
> ☒ Close mail after it has been sent
> ☐ Retain all mail I send in my Personal Filing Cabinet
> ☐ Retain all mail I read in my Personal Filing Cabinet
> ☒ Use AOL style quoting in mail
>
> OK Cancel

▲ *Confirm mail after it has been sent* gives you a dialog box after your mail has been sent. If you send a lot of mail, you may prefer to turn this preference off. (The default is On.)

▲ *Close mail after it has been sent* will close an e-mail window after you've sent it to the recipient. If you would like to keep a document you've already sent open on your screen, turn this preference off. (The default is On.)

- *Retain all mail I send in my Personal Filing Cabinet* (the Personal Filing Cabinet is discussed in Chapter 3, "Electronic Mail & the Personal Filing Cabinet") keeps a copy on your hard disk of the mail you send. This is useful if you want to keep a permanent record of your mail. (**Note:** The Check Mail You've Sent command under the Mail menu accesses the mail that AOL holds for you on their hard disks in Vienna. This is a courtesy, and the amount of mail held there is subject to change. Only your Personal Filing Cabinet is capable of automatically storing your mail indefinitely.)

- *Retain all mail I read in my Personal Filing Cabinet* keeps a copy of the mail you have read on your hard disk. Be careful: under certain conditions this can balloon the size of your Personal Filing Cabinet on your hard disk. If you subscribe to Internet mailing lists for example, your Personal Filing Cabinet could grow in size very quickly. (The default setting is Off.)

- *Use AOL style quoting in mail* allows you to toggle between AOL's style of quoting text (<< and >> around the text) or the Internet's style (> in front of each line only). If you frequently send e-mail across the Internet, you may prefer to turn this preference off. (The default is On.)

WWW Preferences

America Online's Web browser may be fully integrated into the software, but it has enough features to be a stand-alone application. And like all good software, it can be configured to your liking (see Figure E-10). Keep in mind that these preferences should be set before you enter the Web.

Figure E-10:
The WWW Prefer-
ences provide a
number of configu-
ration options.

WWW Preferences

- ○ No Graphics
- ◉ Compressed Graphics
- ○ Uncompressed Graphics

Helper
Applications

- ☑ Don't show graphics at 2400 bps
- ☑ Show current location
- ☑ Show destination of hyperlinks
- ☐ Use a gray background in WWW docs

Security
Alerts

MajorTom's Home Page:

http://www.aol.com

OK | Advanced... | Cancel

- ▲ *No Graphics, Compressed Graphics* or *Uncompressed Graphics* gives you a choice in how you'd like to view (or not view) the graphics in Web pages. If you prefer speed over scenery, choose No Graphics and you will see a framed text placeholder (or an AOL logo, if there is no text associated with the graphic) wherever a graphic would have appeared. If you'd like to see the Web in its full glory (and you don't mind waiting a little longer), select Uncompressed Graphics. Compressed Graphics, the default, gives you the best of both worlds with quicker access and good-looking graphics. Keep in mind that the Compressed Graphics option will produced saved images (if you should elect to save them) in a special .ART format, which can be opened by your AOL client but not within other applications. To save a graphic in more traditional formats—.PCX or .BMP—make sure this option to set to Uncompressed Graphics.

- ▲ *Don't show graphics at 2400 bps* disables graphics in Web pages when you are connected at 2400 bps. The default for this option is on for your own protection—it could take hours for some graphic-intensive pages to download at 2400 bps. You can turn this option off it you prefer.

- *Show current location* gives you the URL address at the top of the window for the Web page you are on. This is useful if you want to double-check to see if you are where you meant to be, but it isn't necessary. You may disable this option if you'd prefer more room in your browser window. (The default setting is On.)

- *Show destination of hyperlinks* presents the URL address for a link when your cursor moves over the word/phrase (hypertext) or button (hypergraphic) that leads to it. The destination address appears in the lower left-hand corner of the browser window. This serves as an added clue that there is another link available from a Web page, as well as identifying the destination of the link. (The default setting is On.)

- *Use a gray background in WWW docs* changes the background from the default white to a light gray. You might want to change this to gray if the white is overly bright and difficult to read, or if you are used to the standard gray background used in other browsers. (The default setting is Off.)

- *[Your] Home Page* allows you to designate the page you'd like to start at when you first enter the Web. Change this to another URL address if you'd like to begin at that page instead. (The default setting is the address for AOL's own Web site.)

- *Advanced...* This button provides caching options in the event you'd like to adjust them. The cache keeps Web pages you've visited in memory so that when you return, you don't have to wait for the page to reload. The settings are already optimized for most users, but you have the option to configure them to your specific needs (see Figure E-11).

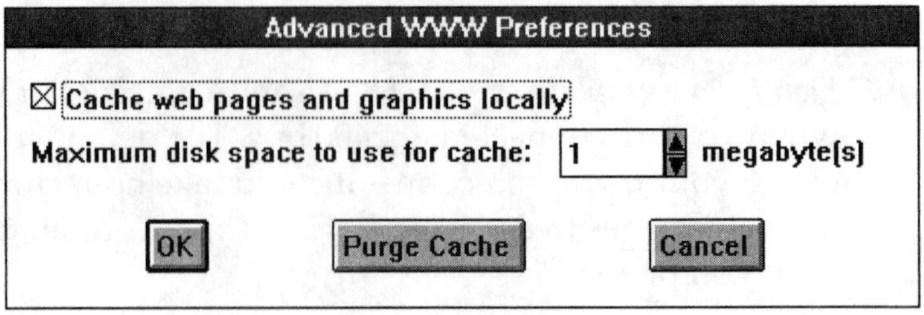

Figure E-11: Advanced WWW preferences offer the ability to change your cache settings.

Advanced WWW Preferences

☒ Cache web pages and graphics locally

Maximum disk space to use for cache: 1 megabyte(s)

[OK]   [Purge Cache]   [Cancel]

◮ *Cache web pages and graphics locally* is the toggle to cache pages or not. If you turn this off, you'll need to download pages you've already visited every time you visit them. If it's on, your browser will first look in your cache (which is on your hard disk) for the page, before going out on the Web to download it. Cached pages are much faster, but the cache consumes disk space. (The default setting is On.)

◮ *Maximum disk space to use for cache:* allows you to set the amount of hard disk space you want to allocate for the cache. You can click the arrows to increase or decrease the amount, or simply type the number (it must be a whole number) in the box. (The default setting is 1 megabyte.)

◮ The *Purge Cache* button will remove all pages that have been saved on your hard disk. You may wish to do this if you want to revisit those pages and have them update with new information, or if your browser has become extremely slow.

Personal Filing Cabinet Preferences

The Personal Filing Cabinet (PFC) organizes your Favorite Places, e-mail, and newsgroup messages, among other things. As it stores some important items, preferences are provided to protect against accidental deletion. Other preferences control its size and organization (see Figure E-12.)

Figure E-12:
The Personal Filing
Cabinet Prefer-
ences allow you to
control the behav-
ior and size of your
Personal Filing
Cabinet.

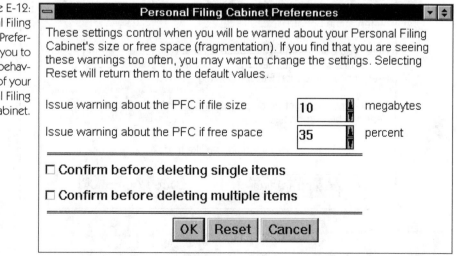

▲ *Issue warning about the PFC if file size (exceeds) XX megabytes* triggers the warning similar to that pictured in Figure E-13 whenever the size of your Personal Filing Cabinet reaches the specified value. Large PFC files slow down your software, especially when you start the AOL program or change screen names. The smaller you set this value, the more often you will receive warnings (assuming you're using your Personal Filing Cabinet in the first place). If your software seems to take an unusually long time to start, reduce this value.

▲ *Issue warning about the PFC if free space (exceeds) XX percent* triggers the messge shown in Figure E-13 whenever your PFC needs to be compacted. Free space will occur whenever you delete an entry or a number of entries from the PFC. Free space is cumulative, and if it exceeds the value shown in Figure E-12, you'll be notified. It's a simple matter to compact your Personal Filing Cabinet, and you can do it while you're offline (compacting the Personal Filing Cabinet is discussed in Chapter 3).

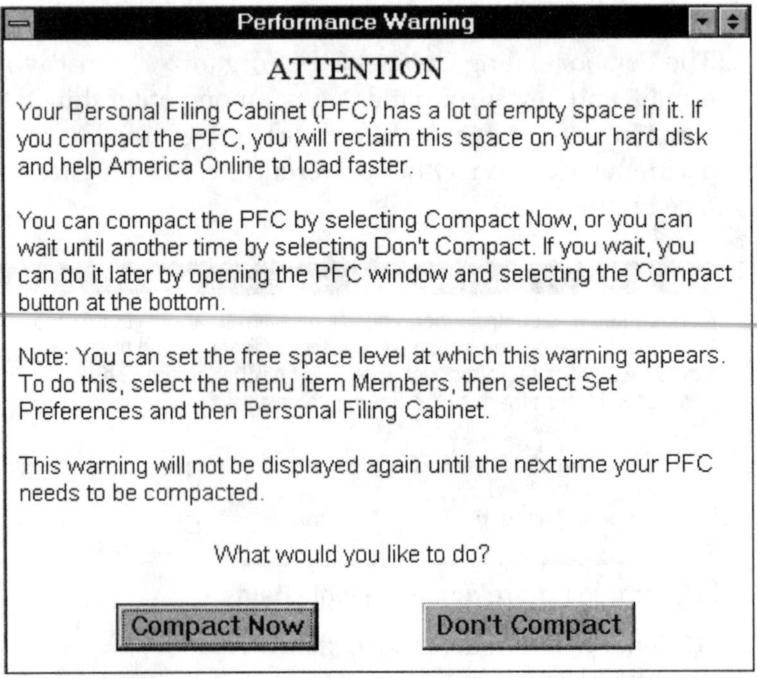

Figure E-13: If your Personal Filing Cabinet's free space exceeds the value set in the window pictured in Figure E-12, this warning appears.

Performance Warning

ATTENTION

Your Personal Filing Cabinet (PFC) has a lot of empty space in it. If you compact the PFC, you will reclaim this space on your hard disk and help America Online to load faster.

You can compact the PFC by selecting Compact Now, or you can wait until another time by selecting Don't Compact. If you wait, you can do it later by opening the PFC window and selecting the Compact button at the bottom.

Note: You can set the free space level at which this warning appears. To do this, select the menu item Members, then select Set Preferences and then Personal Filing Cabinet.

This warning will not be displayed again until the next time your PFC needs to be compacted.

What would you like to do?

[Compact Now]　　[Don't Compact]

🔺 (Referring again to Figure E-12) *Confirm before deleting single items* allows you to turn on or off the confirmation notice when deleting an item. You may wish to turn this off if you frequently delete items singly. (The default setting is On.)

🔺 *Confirm before deleting multiple items* gives you the option of enabling or disabling the confirmation notice when deleting two or more items. Unless you delete multiple items frequently, it is best to keep this on in case you accidentally select more than one item. (The default setting is Off.)

Buddy List Preferences

Buddy Lists are a convenient feature that allow you to keep a list of friends or colleagues and then find out if they are online at the click of a button (Buddy Lists are discussed in Chapter 8, "The Community"). Equally convenient are the controls AOL gives you to set up this feature to suit your needs. You cannot access Buddy List Preferences from the Preferences dialog. Instead, select Buddy Lists from the Members menu and click the Preferences button.

Figure E-14: Buddy List Preferences provide control over AOL's Buddy Lists feature.

Buddy List Preferences

Buddy List Preferences

☐ *Show me my Buddy List(s) immediately after I sign onto AOL*

Set My Buddy List Availability :
- ⦿ *Allow all members to add me to their list*
- ○ *Block all members from adding me to their list*
- ○ *Allow only the members below*
- ○ *Block only the members below*

[Save] [Cancel] [?]

▲ *Show me my Buddy List(s) immediately after I sign onto AOL* displays your Buddy Lists automatically, when you first connect to America Online. If this preference is off, you will have to issue the Buddy List command (from the Members menu) before AOL will monitor the comings and goings of your buddies for you. If you use Buddy Lists often, you may wish to turn this preference on. (The default setting is Off.)

▲ *Play sound when buddies sign on* gives you an aural alert any time someone in one of your buddy lists logs on to AOL. This keeps you from having to constantly check the Buddy List window.

▲ *Play sound when buddies sign off* is exactly the opposite, noisily notifying you that one of your buddies has taken off.

The next four Buddy List preferences determine who can add *your* screen name to *their* Buddy List. You may select only one of the four.

▲ *Allow all members to add me to their lists* lets any other AOL member put your name in their Buddy List.

▲ *Block all members from adding me to their lists* prevents anyone from listing your screen name.

▲ *Allow only the members below* allows you to enter into the text box a specific group of people who have your permission to list your name.

▲ *Block only the members below* prevents a specific group of people from listing your name.

These preferences are offered to protect the privacy of members who would rather not be Buddy Listed. Use them as you see fit.

Explore these preferences. Alter every one of them and live with the changes for a week. You may discover something you didn't know about yourself!

Glossary

This glossary was prepared by Jennifer Watson (screen name: Jennifer) and George Louie (screen name: NumbersMan) of the America Online staff (and to whom I express my heartfelt thanks for a job very well done). It's updated regularly and posted online. To find it, use the keyword: FileSearch, then search with the criterion: VirtualLingo.

800 number—AOL provides an 800 number, at a modest hourly rate, to members who are without local access numbers. To use this number, you must have WAOL 2.5 (or higher) or MAOL 2.5.1 (or higher) with the AOLnet CCL file available at keyword: AOLNet. Additional information on this number can be found at keyword: AOLNet. See also *access number* and *AOLnet*.

$im_off/$im_on—These are the commands for ignoring Instant Messages (IMs). Sending an IM to the screen name "$im_off" will block incoming IMs. Conversely, sending an IM to "$im_on" will allow you to receive IMs again. When using these commands to turn IMs off or on, do not include the quotation marks and type only in lowercase letters exactly as shown. To initiate the command, either type some text in the message box and send the IM (by clicking on the "Send" button) or simply click on the "Available?" button. You will receive confirmation in the form of an AOL dialog box when either turning IMs on or off. If members try to send you an IM or use the "Available?" button on the IM window, they will be told that "<your screen name> cannot currently receive Instant Messages." Note that IMs cannot be turned off for specific individuals—it is all or nothing. See also *IM*; contrast *ignore* and *parental chat controls*.

<< and >>—These symbols are used to quote text and often used in e-mail and posts. Members using WAOL 2.5 or higher can get automatic quoting simply by selecting and copying a block of text in an e-mail, and then clicking Reply. See also *e-mail* and *post*.

//roll—The command for rolling dice. When entered in a chat or conference room, AOL's host computer will return a random result for two six-sided dice to the room. For example:

```
OnlineHost : NumbersMan rolled 2 6-sided dice:   2 4
```

The command can also be used to roll other types and quantities of dice. The full syntax of the command is "//roll -diceXX -sidesYYY" (where XX is 0-15 and YYY is 0-999). Be sure to include the spaces. It is considered rude to roll dice in Lobbies or public chat areas (with the exception of the Red Dragon Inn, sims, and other special game rooms). This command is often used when role-playing or in lieu of "drawing straws." See also chat room, *OnlineHost*, and *sim*.

/ga—This is common shorthand for "go ahead," often used during conferences with protocol. See *protocol*.

abbreviations—These are acronyms for common online phrases used in chat, IMs, and e-mail. Examples include LOL (laughing out loud) and BRB (be right back). See also *chat* and *shorthand*; contrast with *body language*, and *emoticons*.

access number—A phone number (usually local) your modem uses to access America Online. To find an access number online, go to keyword: ACCESS or AOLNET. If you aren't signed on to AOL, there are a number of ways to get access numbers:

- Sign on with the "New Local#" (WAOL) or "Get Local#" (MAOL) option in the "Set Up & Sign On" window.

- Delete all your numbers in Setup; AOL will automatically call the 800 number and let you choose from the list of access numbers.

- Phone the network: Call SprintNet at 1-800-877-5045 ext. 5 or SprintNet's automatic access number listings at 1-800-473-7983; call Tymnet at 1-800-336-0149.

- Dial up SprintNet's Local Access Numbers Directory: Using a general telecommunications program, you can call in to a SprintNet node directly. Once connected, type **@D** and hit the <Enter> key twice. At the @ prompt given, type **c mail** and hit <Enter>, then type PHONES for the username and PHONES again for the password. You can look up any local SprintNet number available.

- Call America Online's Customer Service Hotline at 1-800-827-6364 (within U.S.A.) or 1-703-893-6288 (from Canada or overseas), open 24 hours a day, seven days a week.

🔺 Call AOL's FAXLink service at 1-800-827-5551 and request a list of access numbers be faxed to you. An automated voice menu will guide you through the choices.

🔺 Dial up AOL's Customer Service BBS with a standard telecommunications program at 1-800-827-5808 [settings: 8 data bits, no parity, 1 stop bit, up to 14.4K].

If you don't have a local access number, read the information in the Access Number area (keyword: AOLNET) on how to obtain one. See also *800 number, AOLnet, Datapac, SprintNet, Tymnet* and *node.*

Address Book—An AOL software feature that allows you to store screen names for easy access. Your Address Book may be created, edited, or used through the Address Book icon available when composing mail. You can also create or edit them with the "Edit Address Book" option under your "Mail" menu. You will need to specify an individual or group name in the first field and the screen name(s) of the account(s) in the second field. To use the names in your Address Book when composing mail, be sure your cursor is in either the "To:" box or the "CC:" box, and then click on the Address Book icon. You can then select the name(s) you'd like to have your e-mail addressed to. See also *e-mail* and *screen names.*

afk—Common shorthand for "away from keyboard." It's most often used in chat and IMs when it's necessary to leave the keyboard for an extended length of time. Upon return, "bak" is used, meaning "back at keyboard." See also *shorthands, abbreviations,* and *chat;* contrast with *body language* and *emoticons.*

Alt key—A special function key on the PC keyboard. Usually located near the space bar, you'll find the letters "Alt" printed on it. Holding down the Alt key while another key is pressed will often activate a special function. For example, <Alt> + <h> will bring up the Help section under WAOL and GAOL. (Note: Some Macintosh keyboards also have a key labeled "Alt," but this is primarily for use when operating a PC emulator on the Mac and is otherwise defined as the CommandKey.) See also *Control key, Command key,* and *Option Key.*

America Online, Incorporated (AOL)—The Vienna, Virginia-based online service. Formerly known as Quantum Computer Services and founded in 1985, AOL has grown rapidly in both size and scope. AOL has over four million members and hundreds of alliances with major companies. America Online's stock exchange symbol is AMER. To contact AOL headquarters call 1-703-448-8700, or use 1-800-827-6364 to speak to a representative. See also *AOL*; contrast *CompuServe, eWorld, Microsoft Network,* and *Prodigy.*

analog—Information composed of continuous and varying levels of intensity, such as sound and light. Much of the information in the natural world is analog while those man-made, such as from computers, are digital. For example, the sound of your significant other asking you politely and sensitively to get off AOL for the tenth time is analog. Yet if you were to convert that information to a computer sound file, it would become digital. Contrast with *digital.*

AOL—Abbreviation for America Online, Inc. Occasionally abbreviated as AO. See also *America Online Incorporated.*

AOLiversary—A date celebrated yearly on which a member first became an active on America Online. Considered an accurate yardstick by some to determine their state of addiction. See *AOLoholic.*

AOLnet—America Online's own packet-switching network that provides members with up to 28,800 bps local access numbers. To use this network, you must have WAOL 2.5 (or higher), or MAOL 2.5.1 (or higher) with the AOLnet CCL file available at keyword: AOLNet. AOLnet numbers are located across the country, mainly in large cities, and currently number over 275. For members who do not have a local access number, there is also an 800 number that is more affordable than most long-distance fees. To find AOLnet local access numbers, go to keyword: AOLNET. See also *800 number, packet-switching, and access number;* contrast with *SprintNet, Tymnet,* and *DataPac.*

AOLoholic—A member of AOL who begins to display any of the following behaviors: spending most of their free time online; thinking about AOL even when offline (evidenced by the addition of shorthands to non-AOL writings); attempting to bring all their friends and family online; and/or thinking AOL is the best invention since the wheel. A 12-step plan is in development. Many, but not all AOLoholics, go on to become remote staff. See also *member* and *remote staff.*

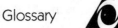

ARC—Short for archive, this is an older compression utility which was the PC standard prior to ZIP. This utility will compress one file, or multiple files, into a smaller file (called an archive), which will make for shorter transferring while uploading or downloading. Some older files online are still packaged in the ARC format. See also *archive, file, file compression, PKZip, ShrinkIt,* and *StuffIt.*

archive—1. A file that has been compressed smaller with file compression software. See also *file, file compression, ARC, PKZip,* and *StuffIt.* 2. A file that contains message board postings that may be of value, but have been removed from a message board due to their age, inactivity of topic, or lack of message board space. These messages are usually bundled into one document, and placed in a file library for retrieval later. See also *file* and *library.*

article—A text document intended to be read online, but may be printed or saved for later examination offline. Usually articles are less than 25k, as anything larger would probably scroll off the top of your window. Note that with GAOL only 8k of an article may be read at one time, with excess usually scrolling off the top; use your log feature to capture the entire article if this happens. See also *document*; contrast with *file.*

asbestos—A flame-retardant. Used as a modifier to anything intended to protect one from flames. For example, "donning asbestos underwear." This is usually used just before saying something that is expected to produce flames. Contrary to popular belief, hamsters are not flame-retardant, and system slowdowns can be attributed to the increased number of flames. See also *flame.*

ASCII—Acronym for American Standard for Computer Information Interchange (or American Standard Code for Information Interchange). ASCII is the numeric code used to represent computer characters on computers around the world. Because only seven bits are used in ASCII, there are no more than 128 (2^7) characters in the standard ASCII set. Variations of ASCII often extend the available characters by using an 8 bit means of identifying characters and thus may represent as many as 256 characters. The standard ASCII code set consists of 128 characters ranging from 0 to 127. America Online supports characters 28-127 in chat areas, IMs and message boards. Pronounced "ask-key." See also *ASCII text.*

ASCII art—Pictures created with no more than the 128 ASCII characters. ASCII art can be humorous, entertaining, or serious. It is popular in some chat rooms. Some members find it disruptive when large ASCII art is displayed in a chat room, so you are advised to ask before scrolling it. See also *ASCII* and *ASCII text*.

ASCII text—Characters represented as ASCII. Sometimes called "plain text," this is compatible with all platforms represented on AOL. See also *ASCII*.

"Ask the Staff" button—See *"Comment to Staff" button*.

asynchronous—Data communication via modem of the start-stop variety where characters do not need to be transmitted constantly. Each character is transmitted as a discrete unit with its own start bit and one or more stop bits. AOL is asynchronous. See also *synchronous*.

attached file—A file that hitches a ride with e-mail. Be the file text, sound, or pictures of your hamster "Bruno," it is said to be attached if it has been included with the e-mail for separate downloading by the recipient (whether addressed directly, carbon copied, or blind carbon copied). E-mail that is forwarded will retain any attached files as well. Files are usually attached because the information that they contain is either too long to be sent in the body of regular e-mail or is impossible to send via e-mail, such as with software programs. Multiple files may be attached by compressing the files into one archive and attaching the archive to the piece of e-mail with the "Attach File" icon. See also *archive, download, e-mail*, and *file*.

auditorium—Auditoriums are specially equipped online "rooms" that allow large groups of AOL members to meet in a structured setting. Currently, there are several auditoriums: AOL Live, The Bowl, The Coliseum, Cyberplex, CyberRap, The Globe, AOL Sports Dome, Main Stage, News Room, and The Odeon (for special and general events); Rotunda (for computing-related topics or computing company representatives); and Tech Live (for questions and help on AOL—this is in the free area). The auditoriums are divided into two parts: the stage, where the emcee and the guest speaker(s) are located, and the chat rows, where the audience is located. Upon entering an auditorium, a user is assigned to one of the chat rows, consisting of up to seven other audience members. Audience members in the same row may talk to each other without being heard by those on stage or by those in other rows. Nothing said in the audience can be normally heard by anyone on stage, although anything said on stage can be "broadcast" and heard by everyone in the audience. The OnlineHost will broadcast important information throughout the conference. The emcee moderates the conference and will broadcast more specific information. You can tell the difference between what is said on stage and what is said in your chat row because what is said in your chat row is preceded by a row number. More information on auditoriums can be found at keyword: SHOWS or ROTUNDA. See also *emcee, OnlineHost, The Coliseum, Odeon, Rotunda,* and *Tech Live*; contrast with *chat room* and *conference room*.

bandwidth—A measure of the amount of information that can flow through a given point at any given time. To use a popular analogy, low bandwidth is a two-lane road while high bandwidth is a six-lane superhighway.

bash—A get-together or party of AOL members in a particular area. Members who attend are often referred to as bashees, and popular bashes are the Big Apple Bash (in NYC) and the Texas Bash. Information on bashes can usually be found in "The Quantum Que," a community message board available at keyword: QUE.

basher—A particularly vile form of snert. A basher will usually target a certain group and harass them for the basher's pleasure. This usually takes place in a People Connection chat room dedicated to that group, but may also occur in conference rooms. See also *snert, People Connection, chat room,* and *conference room*.

baud rate—A unit for measuring the speed of data transmission. Technically baud rates refer to the number of times the communications line changes states each second. Strictly speaking, baud and bits per second (bps) are not identical measurements, but most non-technical people use the terms interchangeably. See also *bps*.

BBS (Bulletin Board System)—A system offering information that can be accessed via computer, modem, and phone lines. While that definition technically includes AOL, BBSs are typically much smaller in size and scope. Most BBSs maintain message boards and file libraries and some feature Internet access, newsfeeds, and online games. For more information online, go to keyword: BBS. BBSs are sometimes abbreviated as simply "board," and should not be confused with message boards on AOL. Contrast with *message board*.

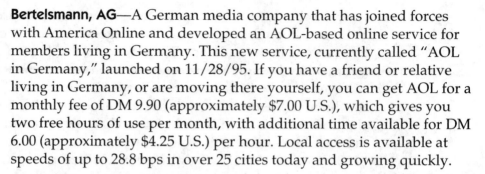

Bertelsmann, AG—A German media company that has joined forces with America Online and developed an AOL-based online service for members living in Germany. This new service, currently called "AOL in Germany," launched on 11/28/95. If you have a friend or relative living in Germany, or are moving there yourself, you can get AOL for a monthly fee of DM 9.90 (approximately $7.00 U.S.), which gives you two free hours of use per month, with additional time available for DM 6.00 (approximately $4.25 U.S.) per hour. Local access is available at speeds of up to 28.8 bps in over 25 cities today and growing quickly.

beta test—A period in a new product or service's development designed to discover problems (or "bugs") prior to its release to the general public. AOL often selects members to beta test its new software. If you are interested in beta testing AOL software, you may be able to apply at keyword: BETA APPLY. Hamsters are notoriously bad beta testers; the bugs distract their attention. See also *bug*.

blind carbon copy (bcc)—A feature of the AOL e-mail system that allows you to send e-mail to a member or members without anyone other than you being aware of it. To blind carbon copy, simply place parentheses around the screen name(s). For example, (JoeShmo) or (JoeShmo, HughHamstr). GAOL users will need to use two parentheses, as in ((JoeShmo)) or ((JoeShmo, HughHamstr)). When a blind carbon copy is made, it is said to be bcc'ed. See also *e-mail*; contrast with *carbon copy*.

board—An abbreviated reference to a message board or bulletin board service (BBS). See also *message board* and *BBS*.

body language—An online expression of physical movement and nonverbal emotions through text. Two popular methods have developed on AOL: colons (:::yawning:::) and brackets (<yawning and trying to stay awake for ten straight hours in front of a monitor>). See also *chat*; contrast with *abbreviations, emoticons*, and *shorthand*.

bounce—v. Something that is returned, such as e-mail. It isn't uncommon for e-mail sent to recipients outside of AOL to bounce and never make it to its intended destination. Sometimes users who are punted will refer to themselves as bounced. See also *e-mail* and *punt*.

bps (bits per second)—A method of measuring data transmission speed. Currently, 1200 through 28,800 bps are supported on AOL.

Speeds higher than 14,400 are generally only available in larger cities (see keyword: AOLNET for more information). See also *baud*.

brb—Common shorthand for "be right back." It is used by AOL members when participating in chat/conference rooms or talking in IMs (Instant Messages). See also *shorthands*, *abbreviations*, and *chat*; contrast with *body language* and *emoticons*.

browse—To casually explore rather than examine in detail. Typically used in reference to message boards and file libraries. Browsing information online without a specific target is one prominent trait of an budding AOLoholic. Contrast *search*.

browser—A way of accessing the World Wide Web. On WAOL 2.5 and higher, this is an integrated component of the software. On MAOL 2.6, it is a separate piece of software that may one day become integrated. See also *favorite place*, *Internet*, *hot list*, *page*, *Personal Filing Cabinet*, *site*, and *WWW*.

btw—Common shorthand for "by the way." It is used in IMs, chat/conference rooms, e-mail, and message postings. See also *shorthands*, *abbreviations*, and *chat*; contrast with *body language* and *emoticons*.

bug—A problem or glitch in a product, be it software or hardware. A bug may be referred to jokingly as a "feature." You can report a problem with AOL software or services by going to keyword: QUESTIONS and clicking on "Report a Problem." See also GPF.

bulletin board—See *message board* and *BBS*.

byte—Roughly (but practically) speaking, a byte is the amount of memory required to store one character typed from the keyboard. As this isn't much memory, bytes are often referred to in larger quantities: see *kilobyte* and *megabyte*.

carbon copy (cc)—A feature of the AOL e-mail system that allows you to address e-mail to a member for whom the e-mail is not directly intended or is of secondary interest. The primary addressee(s) are aware that the copy was made, similar to the carbon copy convention used in business correspondence. As such, the members carbon copied are not usually expected to reply. When a carbon copy is made, it is said to be cc'ed. Also known as a courtesy copy. See also *e-mail*, contrast with *blind carbon copy*.

CCL (Communication Control Language)—A script that allows you to control your modem. CCL scripts are most useful when the connection process is more complicated than can be handled by a modem file. For example, if your modem needs certain commands every time a connection is established, you can use or write a CCL script to automate this process. America Online uses standard CCLs and modem files to control your modem; in other words, you shouldn't need to worry about CCLs when connecting to AOL. See also *modem files*.

Center Stage—See *auditorium*.

channel—This is the broadest category of information into which America Online divides its material. Also known as department.

chat—To engage in real-time communications with other members. AOL members that are online at the same time may chat with each other in a number of ways: Instant Messages (IMs), chat/conference rooms, and auditoriums. "Chatting" provides immediate feedback from others; detailed discussions are better suited toward message boards; and lengthy personal issues are best dealt with in e-mail if a member isn't currently online. See also *Instant Message*, *chat room*, *conference room*, and *auditorium*, contrast with *message board* and *e-mail*.

chat rooms—Online areas where members may meet to communicate and interact with others. There are two kinds of chat areas—public and private. Public chat areas can be found in the People Connection area (keyword: PEOPLE) or in the many forums around AOL (see keyword: AOL LIVE for schedules). Public rooms may either be officially sanctioned rooms or member-created rooms (which are listed separately). All public rooms are governed by AOL's Terms of Service (TOS) and are open to anyone interested. Private chat rooms are available from most chat area and are open only to those who create them or know their names and meeting times. All chat rooms accommodate at least 23 members, while some of the chat areas in forums other than People Connection may hold up to 48 members. Those chat rooms that can be created by members (both public and private) must have names with no more than 20 characters, beginning with a letter, and containing no punctuation. Beware that Stratus hamsters have been known to escape and surprise unsuspecting members in chat rooms. See also *private room*, *chat*, *host*, *Guide*, *TOS*, and *People Connection*; contrast *auditorium* and *conference room*.

chat sounds—Sounds may be played and broadcast to others in chat areas by typing the following:

```
{S <sound>}
```

and sending it to the chat area. Be sure to type it exactly as shown and insert the exact name of the sound you wish to play where <sound> appears in the example. For example, {S Welcome} will play AOL's "Welcome" sound in a chat area. New sounds can be found online by searching the libraries. To install sounds into your AOL software for playing, you'll need a sound utility (also found in the libraries online). Keep in mind that other members will need to have the same sound installed in their AOL software to hear it when played. Sounds should be used sparingly so as not to disturb conversations or awaken slumbering hamsters. Please note also that GAOL users cannot hear chat sounds, nor can those without sound capabilities. See also *chat room* and *library*.

CIS—Short for CompuServe Information Service. May also be abbreviated as CI$. See also *Compuserve*; contrast with *AOL, eWorld, Microsoft Network*, and *Prodigy*

client—A computer that requests information from another. On AOL, your AOL software running on your computer is the client and the network of computers at America Online headquarters is the host. Contrast *host* (1).

close box—The small box in the upper-left corner of your window (and upper right in Windows 95). Clicking on this box closes the window. Not to be confused with a shoe box, boom box, or even clothes box. See also *window*; contrast *zoom box*.

club—See *forum*.

Coliseum, The—See *auditorium*.

Command key—A special function key on the Mac. Usually located near the space bar, you'll find printed on it either an open Apple symbol or a clover-leaf symbol (or both). Holding down the Command key while another key is pressed will often activate a special function. Also known as the Open-Apple key. See also *Control key, Option key*, and *Alt key*.

"Comment to Staff" button—A button available in file libraries that will allow you to send a note to the managers of the library. Note that it doesn't send a note to the uploader, only the library managers (often a forum leader or assistant). Note that this is labeled "Ask The Staff" on WAOL and GAOL. See also *download* and *library*.

compression—See *file compression*.

CompuServe (CIS)—A large, established commercial online service similar to America Online. While CompuServe Information Service (CIS) has more databases available, their service is priced higher and is less user-friendly than AOL. CIS is owned by H&R Block. May be referred to as "CIS" or "CI$" in shorthand during chat. Contrast with *America Online, eWorld, Microsoft Network*, and *Prodigy*.

conference room—A specific kind of chat area found in forums all around AOL where members can meet, hold conferences, and interact in real time. Conference rooms can hold up to 23 or 48 members at any one time (depending on location), and are located outside of the People Connection. Currently, there are over 250 public conference rooms with more being added all the time. Often special events are held in these rooms, and a protocol system may be used to make them proceed smoothly. Hosts or moderators often facilitate the discussions and conferences here. Hamster sightings are less frequent in these rooms. See also *host, moderator*, and *protocol*; contrast *chat room* and *auditorium*.

Control key—A special function key, usually located on the bottom row of keys, you'll find printed on it either "Ctrl" or "Control." Holding down the Control key while another key is pressed will often activate a special function. (Note: Some Macintosh keyboards also have a key labeled "Control," but this is primarily for use when operating a PC emulator on the Mac.) See also *Command key, Option key, Alt key*, and *Open-Apple key*.

corporate staff—Members who are usually company or IP (information provider) employees and work at the corporate offices of the company. In-house AOL, Inc. staff is often referred to in this manner as well. See also *in-house* and *IP*; contrast with *remote staff*.

cracker—One who violates security. Coined by hackers in the 1980s in defense against the growing assumption that all hackers are malevolent. A password scammer is a cracker. See also *password scammer*; contrast *hacker, phisher*, and *snert*.

cross-post—v. To place the same message in several folders, message boards, or newsgroups. Overuse of this is bad netiquette, and may result in having your posts hidden (if on AOL) or your mailbox barraged with flaming e-mail (if on the Internet). See also *flame, newsgroup, post,* and *spam.*

CS Live—See *Tech Live.*

Customer Relations—America Online's Customer Relations Hotline is open 24 hours a day, seven days a week. You can reach them at 1-800-827-6364. See also *Tech Live.*

cyberpunk—First used to designate a body of speculative fiction literature focusing on marginalized people in technologically enhanced cultural "systems." Within the last few years, the mass media has used this term to catergorize the denizens of cyberspace. Cyberpunks are known to cruise the information landscapes with alacrity, or lacking that, eagerness.

cyberspace—An infinite world created by our computer networks. Cyberspace is no less real than the real world—people are born, grow, learn, fall in love, and die in cyberspace. These effects may or may not be carried over into the physical world. America Online is an example of cyberspace created through interaction between the energies of the members, staff, and computers. See also *online community.*

daemon—An automatic program that performs a maintenance function on AOL. For example, a board daemon may run at 3 a.m. in the morning and clean up old posts on a message board. Rumored to stand for "Disk And Execution MONitor."

database—A collection of information, stored and organized for easy searching. A database can refer to something as simple as a well-sorted filing cabinet, but today most databases reside on computers because they offer better access. Databases are located all over AOL, with prominent examples being the Member Directory (keyword: DIRECTORY) and the Directory of Services (keyword: SERVICES). See AOL's Reference Desk (keyword: REFERENCE) for a large collection of databases. See also *Directory of Services, Member Directory,* and *searchable.*

DataPac—A packet-switching network operated by Bell Canada that provides local access numbers for Canadian members at an extra fee. See also *packet-switching network* and *access number;* contrast *AOLnet, SprintNet,* and *Tymnet.*

Delete—An AOL e-mail system feature that allows you to permanently remove a piece of mail from any and all of your mailboxes. To use, simply select and highlight the piece of mail you wish to delete (from either your "New Mail," "Check Mail You've Read," or "Check Mail You've Sent" windows, which can be found under your Mail menu) and click on the "Delete" button at the bottom of the window. The mail will be permanently deleted and cannot be retrieved. Mail you have deleted without reading first will appear as "(deleted)" in the Status box of the sender. The Delete feature is useful for removing unneeded mail from your Old Mail box. Do not confuse this feature with the "Unsend" option, which will remove mail you've sent from the recipient's mailbox. See also *e-mail* and *Status*; contrast *Unsend*.

demoware (demonstration software)—These are often full-featured versions of commercial software, with the exception being that the Save or Print features are often disabled. Some demos are only functional for certain periods of time. Like shareware, demonstration software is a great way to try before you buy. Contrast *freeware, public domain*, and *shareware*.

department—See *channel*.

digital—Information that is represented by two discrete states (either 1 or 0) and also referred to as binary information. Most information in the real world is not digital, but must be converted into this form to be used by computers. The converse is also true; digital information normally needs to be converted into analog information before people can use it. An example of this would be AOL chat sounds that are stored as digital information, but must be converted into their analog equivalents before they are actually heard by us. Contrast with *analog*.

Directory of Services—A searchable database that allows AOL members to quickly locate AOL's available services. This is available at keyword: SERVICES. See also *database* and *searchable*.

document—An information file, usually relating specific details on a topic. On AOL, these can be in the form of articles (which are read-only), or modifiable documents, usually created with the "New (Memo)" menu command within AOL. See also *article* and *file*.

DOD—Abbreviation for Download On Demand, a method of receiving artwork updates. AOL is rather unique in that as it grows and new areas are added, the custom artwork associated with new services and areas can be added on the fly. When you enter an area that includes new artwork, such as a logo or icon, it is automatically downloaded to your screen and stored on your computer. Once you've visited an area, you'll never need to wait for the artwork to download again. Similarly, if you never enter a new area with artwork updates, you will not need to wait for the DODs. At the time of this writing, DODs are only available on the MAOL and WAOL platforms. Contrast *UDO*.

DOS—Abbreviation for Disk Operating System. Different brands include PC DOS and MS-DOS (Microsoft). MS-DOS is the most widely used operating system for IBM PCs and compatibles. Pronounced "dahss." Contrast *OS/2, System*, and *Windows*.

download—The transfer of information stored on a remote computer to a storage device on your personal computer. This information can come from AOL via its file libraries, or from other AOL members via attached files in e-mail. Usually, downloads are files intended for review once you're offline. You download graphics and sounds, for instance. Download is used both as a noun and a verb. For example, you might download a graphic file to your hard drive, where you store your latest downloads. Hamsters have been known to defect via downloads. See also *archive, attached file, download count, download manager, FileGrabber*, and *library*.

download count—The download count (often abbreviated "Cnt" in a library window) refers to the number of times that file has been downloaded. This is often used as a gauge of the file's popularity. While this may not be too significant for a new upload, it is a good indication of the popularity of files that have been around for a while. For example, the file titled "Stuffit Expander 3.5.2 Installer" in the Macintosh Software Center's Helpful Utilities library has over 20,000 downloads. Often, however, the number of downloads is more reflective of the appeal of a file's name or description rather than of its content. Note that a newly uploaded file will always have a download count of 1, even though it hasn't been downloaded yet. So to divine the true number of downloads, always subtract one from the total. Also, if the system is slow, the download count visible at the top level of the library may not update immediately. See also *file, library*, and *download*.

download manager—An AOL software feature that allows you to keep a queue of files to download at a later time. You can even set up your software to automatically sign off when your download session is complete. You can schedule your software to sign on and grab files listed in the queue at times you specify. See also *download* and *file*. See also *Personal Filing Cabinet*.

drag-and-drop—The process of inserting data into a document by dragging it from a second window on the screen. Favorite Places, for example, can be hyperlinked in e-mail via drag-and-drop. See also *Favorite Places* and *hyperlink*.

e-mail—Short for electronic mail. One of the most popular features of online services, e-mail allows you to send private communications electronically from one person to another. No wasted paper, leaky pens, or terrible tasting envelope glue involved! E-mail is usually much faster and easier to send than ordinary mail; the shortcomings are that not everyone has an e-mail address to write to and your mail resides in electronic form on a computer system, although e-mail is considered as private and inviolable as regular U.S. Mail. With AOL's e-mail system, mail can be sent directly to scores of people, carbon copied, blind carbon copied, forwarded, and even include attached files. E-mail can also be sent (and forwarded) to any other service that has an Internet address. Your screen name's mailbox is limited to 550 pieces of mail at any one time, including both read and unread mail. Unread mail will remain in your New Mail box for four weeks after the date it was sent and mail you have read remains in your Old Mail box for three days. If the amount of mail in your mail box exceed 550 pieces, AOL will start to delete excess mail, starting with read mail—AOL will not delete any of your unread mail, however. These limits almost never present a problem for even frequent AOL users, however. See also *attached file, blind carbon copy, carbon copy, Delete, e-mail address, flashmail, gateway, Ignore, Keep As New, mailbomb, massmail, Personal Filing Cabinet, return receipt,* and *Status*; contrast *snail mail, message,* and *IM*.

e-mail address—A cyberspace mailbox. On AOL, your e-mail address is simply your screen name; for folks outside of AOL, you address is *yourscreenname*@aol.com. For example, if our friend Sharon wants to e-mail us from her Internet account, she can reach us as jennifer@aol.com or numbersman@aol.com. For mail outgoing from AOL, check out the E-Mail Gateway area (keyword: MAIL GATEWAY) for more information. See also *e-mail* and *screen name*.

Easter egg—A hidden surprise in software often left in at the whim of the programmers. Both Macintosh and Windows applications have Easter eggs, so does AOL.

echo—A rare AOL system bug that rapidly repeats a person's chat over and over in a chat or conference room. Also known as a system scroll. If this occurs, you should leave the room immediately and page a Guide using keyword: GUIDEPAGER.

emcee—A member who has been trained to moderate and host events held in auditoriums. See also *auditorium*; contrast with *host* and *moderator*.

emoticons—Symbols consisting of characters found on any keyboard that are used to give and gain insight on emotional states. For example, the symbol :) is a smile—just tilt your head to the left and you'll see the : (eyes) and the) (smile). The online community has invented countless variations to bring plain text to life and you'll see emoticons used everywhere from chat rooms to e-mail. Emoticons, like emotions, are more popular in "face-to-face" chat and some consider them unprofessional or overly cute. Regardless, they are one of the best methods of effective communication online. Emoticons may also be referred to as smileys, and collectively with other chat devices as shorthands. A brief list is available at keyword: SHORTHANDS. See also *shorthands* and *chat*; contrast with *abbreviations* and *body language*.

ET (EST or EDT)—Abbreviation for Eastern Time. Most times are given in this format as AOL is headquartered in this time zone. MAOL users can change this default time zone through their Preferences under the Members menu.

FAQ—Short for Frequently Asked Questions. FAQs may take the form of an informational file containing questions and answers to common concerns/issues. These are used to answer questions that are brought up often in message boards or discussions. These files may be stored online in an article or archived in a file library. See also *message board* and *library*.

favorite place—1. On WAOL 2.5 and higher, this refers to a feature that allows you to "mark" AOL and WWW places you'd like to return to later. These favorite places are stored in your Personal Filing Cabinet. Any WWW site can be made a favorite place, as well as any AOL window with a little heart in the upper right hand corner of the title bar. See also *Personal Filing Cabinet*.

2. On MAOL and GAOL, a favorite place is one of the user-definable locations at the bottom of the Go To menu. You can edit this with the "Edit Favorite Places..." option.

fax (facsimile)—A technique for sending graphical images (such as text or pictures) over phone lines. While faxes are usually sent and received with a stand-alone fax machine, faxes may also be sent to or from computers using fax software and a modem. You can also send a fax through AOL at keyword: FAX. Contrast with *e-mail* and *snail mail*.

file—Any amount of information that is grouped together as one unit. On AOL, a file can be anything from text to sounds and can be transferred to and from your computer via AOL. Collections of files are available in libraries for downloading, and files may be attached to e-mail. See also *download, library*, and *software file*, contrast with *article*.

file compression—A programming technique by which many files can be reduced in size. Files are usually compressed so that they take up less storage space, can be transferred quicker, and/or can be bundled with others. Files must be decompressed before they can be used, but the AOL software can be set to automatically decompress most files (check your Preferences). See also *file* and *download*.

file library—See *library*.

FileGrabber—A piece of software built into WAOL and MAOL that will automatically decode encoded data (also known as "binaries"), such as that found in some newsgroups. Besides making sure that your newsgroup preferences are set to allow you to decode files, you don't need to do anything to use—FileGrabber will automatically detect encoded data and ask you if you want to download the file. For more information, see the aol.newsgroups.help.binaries newsgroup. See also *download, file, Internet*, and *newsgroup*.

filename extensions—These are usually three character codes found suffixing a filename, and are primarily used for PC files. A comprehensive list would take several pages, but here are some common extensions:

Text/Word Processor formats:

DOC	Microsoft Word document
HLP	Help file
HTM	HyperText Markup Language (WWW) format

HTX	HyperText document
LF	Line Feeds added to text format
LET	Letter file, as to a friend (i.e., FRIEND.LET)
LOG	America Online log file, usually text
MW	MacWrite document
RTF	Rich Text Format
SAM	Ami Pro document
TXT	Unformatted ASCII Text
WS	WordStar document
WP (or WPD)	WordPerfect document

Graphic formats:

BMP	OS/2 or Windows Bitmap
EPS	Encapsulated PostScript
GIF	Graphic Interchange Format
JPG	Joint Photographic Experts Group (JPEG)
MAC	MacPaint (also PNT)
PIC	Macintosh PICT
PCX	Zsoft Paintbrush
TIF	Tagged-Image File Format (TIFF)
WMF	Windows MetaFile
WPG	WordPerfect Graphic

Compressed formats:

SIT	StuffIt (MacAOL v2.x can unstuff this automatically)
ZIP	PKZip (PC/GEOS, WAOL and Mac AOL v2.1 can unstuff this automatically)
ARC	Abbreviation for ARChive; similar to PKZip (PC/GEOS and WAOL can unstuff this automatically)
SEA	Self=Extracting Archive (usually a Mac file)

Other formats:

BAT	Batch file; executable file; DOS
BIN	Binary program file; often a subdirectory name
BMK	Windows Bookmark file; references Help segment
COM	Executable program file; DOS
DAT	Data file or subdirectory with data files
DBF	DBase file
DLL	Dynamic Link Library; program files recognized by Windows

EXE	PC executable file, can be a self-extracting archive
GRP	Windows Program Group
INI	Initilization file for Windows and other applications
MAC	Macro
MOV	QuickTime movie
MPG	MPEG animation
PM4	PageMaker version 4.x file
SLK	SYLK file
SYS	Device driver or System file
WAV	Windows sound file
XLC	Excel chart
XLS	Excel worksheet

flame—Made popular on the Internet, this means to chat, post messages, or send e-mail about something that is considered inflammatory by other members, and may cause fires among those who read and respond to it. "Flaming" may spark a lively debate when selectively and appropriately used. More often, it will cause misunderstandings and divided parties. Harassment and vulgarity are not allowed on America Online, and if you see this occurring, you may report the occurrence at keyword: TOS. See also *asbestos*, *chat*, *message board*, *e-mail*, and *TOS*.

flashmail—This is a feature of the AOL software that allows you to save your outgoing e-mail to your hard disk to send at a later time, or save your incoming e-mail so you can look at it later, online, or offline. These e-mails are stored in your Flashbox, and the outgoing files are sent with Flashsessions. See also *e-mail*.

folder—Groupings of messages by topic within message boards are termed "folders" on America Online. In most message boards, you may create a folder. Folder names are limited to 28 characters. See also *message* and *message boards*.

form—A window for an area online usually comprised of a text field, a list box (scrollable), and one or more icons. Often special artwork will be placed in the form as well, as in a logo. Examples of forms include OMNI Magazine Online (keyword: OMNI), MTV Online (keyword: MTV), and the Mac Games Forum (keyword: MGM). The Star Trek Club (keyword: TREK) is an example of a form without graphic elements. See also *icon* and *window*.

forum—A place online where members with similar interests may find valuable information, exchange ideas, share files, and get help on a particular area of interest. Forums (also known simply as areas or clubs) are found everywhere online, represent almost every interest under the sun, and usually offer message boards, articles, chat rooms, and libraries, all organized and accessible by a keyword. Forums are moderated by forum hosts or forum leaders. For example, in the Macintosh Computing department, each forum has a forum leader (denoted by AFL at the beginning of their screen name), and is assisted by Forum Assistants (denoted by AFA) and often assisted even further by Forum Consultants (denoted by AFC). See also *form* and *keyword*.

freeware—A file that is completely free and often made available in libraries of online services like AOL for downloading. Unlike public domain files, you are not able to modify it and the author retains the copyright. Since the author or programmer usually posts freeware and the user downloads it, distribution is direct and nearly without cost. Users are generally encouraged to make copies and give them to friends, even post them on other services. Check the file's documentation for limits on use and distribution. VirtuaLingo is freeware—you are encouraged to pass this along to anyone who may be interested, but please do not modify or incorporate it into another work without permission. See also *file*, *shareware*, and *public domain*.

FTP—Abbreviation for File Transfer Protocol. A method of transferring files to and from a computer that is connected to the Internet. AOL offers FTP access via the keyword: FTP, as well as personal FTP sites at keywords: MY PLACE. See also *Internet*, *WWW*, and *home page*; contrast *library*.

Fwd:—Short for "forward" as in forwarding e-mail to someone. See also *e-mail*.

gateway—A link to another service, such as the Internet, EAASY SABRE, or StockLink. Gateways allow members to access these independent services through AOL. Used as both a noun and a verb. See also *Internet*.

GAOL—The PC platform's DOS version of the AOL client software, based on the GeoWorks graphical operating system. The current version is 1.5a, although a special 2.0 version exists for GEOS users. May also be referred to as PC/GEOS, PCAO, or GEOS. Contrast with *MAOL* and *WAOL.*

GIF (Graphic Interchange Format)—A type of graphic file that can be read by most platforms; the electronic version of photographs. The GIF standard was developed by CompuServe as a standard for sharing graphical information across platforms (any with graphical display abilities). GIFs can be viewed with your AOL software or with a GIF viewer utility, which are located at keyword: VIEWERS. Member GIFs are also located in the Portrait Gallery (keyword: GALLERY). To view a Mac GIF on a PC you may need to strip off the Macintosh header with an application called "AOMAC2PC." This utility is located in the Viewer Resource Center. The g in "GIF" should not be pronounced like the brand of peanut butter, but rather like "gift." (Yes, we know others claim otherwise, but if it were to be pronounced like "JIF," it would have been spelled that way.)

Gopher—A feature of the Internet that allows you to browse huge amounts of information. The terms implies that it will "go-pher" you to retrieve information. It also refers to the way in which you "tunnel" through the various menus, much like a gopher would. See also *WAIS* and *Internet*; contrast *newsgroups* and *WWW.*

GPF—Abbreviation for General Protection Fault. If you get a GPF error, it means that Windows (or a Windows application) has attempted to access memory that has not been allocated for use. GPFs are the scourge of WAOL members everywhere. If you experience an GPF while using WAOL, write down the exact error message, then go to keyword: GPF HELP for assistance. (Note: As you may have guessed, GPFs occur only on PCs with Microsoft Windows installed.) See also *bug.*

GUI—Graphical User Interface. Some examples of GUIs include the Mac Operating System, OS/2, and Windows. See also *operating system, system, OS/2,* and *Windows.*

Guide—Experienced AOL members who have been specially chosen and trained to help other members enjoy their time online. All on-duty Guides wear their "uniforms"—the letters "Guide" followed by a space and a 2 or 3 letter suffix in all caps. If you would like to apply to become a Guide, send a request to the screen name "GuideApply" or ask a Guide for a copy of the application. Applicants must be at least 18 years of age, have an account that has been active six months or more, and be a member in good standing (no TOS or billing problems). To offer a compliment or lodge a complaint against a Guide, send mail to "Guide MGR." See also *Guide Pager, Lobby*, and *uniform*; contrast *host* and *moderator*.

Guide Pager—A feature of AOL that allows you to page a Guide when there is a problem in a chat or conference room, or when someone is requesting your password (a big no-no). Simply go to keyword: GUIDEPAGER, and you will be presented with a simple form to complete regarding the problem. If a Guide is unavailable, you may report the offending text at keyword: TOS or PC STUDIO. If you need to report a problem in the Kids Only area, you can use keyword: KIDS GUIDEPAGER. See also *Guide* and *TOS*.

gullible—Anyone who believes there are really hamsters on AOL. But seriously, the hamsters scattered throughout this glossary are just pranksters. The authors take no responsibility for their actions.

hacker—Not to be confused with hamsters, hackers are self-taught computer gurus who take an unholy delight in discovering the well-hidden secrets of computer systems. Blighted by a bad reputation of late, hackers do not necessarily denote those who intend harm or damage. There are those, however, who feed upon the pain inflicted by viruses. See also *password scammers*, *phishers*, and *virus*.

hamster—Unbeknownst to most users, AOL's host computers are actually powered by these small, efficient creatures with large cheek pouches. They are notorious for being temperamental workers. When things slow down or troubles mount online, it is a sure sign that an AOL employee forgot to feed the hamsters. See also *gullible*.

handle—An outdated term for your electronic nom de plume, or screen name. See also *e-mail address* and *screen name*.

help room—Online "rooms" where members can go to get live help with the AOL software/system as well as assistance in finding things online. There are two types of help rooms: Guide-staffed and Tech Live. The Guide-staffed rooms are located in the People Connection > Public Rooms area (keyword: PEOPLE). On weekdays, there is a generic help room, "AOL Help," open from 3 p.m. to 6 p.m. ET, with platform specific rooms open from 6 p.m. to 3 a.m. ET. On weekends, the generic help room opens at noon, with the platform specific rooms open from 3 p.m. to 3 a.m. For more information on the Tech Live help rooms, see Tech Live. See also *Guide*, *Help*, and *MHM*.

home page—1. The first "page" in a World Wide Web site.

2. Your own page on the WWW. Every member on AOL can now create their own home page—see keyword: MY HOME PAGE for more information.

3. The page you go to when you first enter the WWW.

See also *browser*, *favorite place*, *hot list*, *page*, *site*, *URL*, and *WWW*.

host—1. The AOL computer system, affectionately referred to as the Stratus. See also *Stratus*. The client/host computer paradigm as it relates to AOL is discussed in Chapter 1 of this book.

2. An AOL member who facilitates discussion in chat rooms. These are usually chat-fluent, personable individuals with particular expertise in a topic. You can find hosts all over the system, and they will often be wearing "uniforms"—letters in front of their names (usually in all caps) to designate the forum they host for. See also *Guide*, *chat room*, *conference room*, and *uniform*.

hot chat—A safe, euphemistic term which means to chat about (read "flirt") and engage in the popular online dance of human attraction and consummation. Virtually, of course. And usually in private rooms or IMs. Unfortunately, hamsters are prone to this activity but usually only on Mondays, Wednesdays, and Fridays in the early morning hours, for reasons man has yet to fathom.

hot list—On MAOL 2.6 (or higher) with the WWW browser, this is a place for storing your favorite WWW site addresses. See also *browser*, *page*, *site*, *URL*, and *WWW*.

hyperlink—As AOL uses the term, a hyperlink is a link to any item in your list of Favorite Places that has been inserted via drag and drop into e-mail. See also *drag-and-drop*, *Favorite Places*, *link*, and *URL*.

icon—A graphic image of a recognizable thing or action that leads to somewhere or initiates a process. For example, the icons in the "Compose Mail" window may lead you to the Address Book, allow you to attach a file, send the mail, or look up help. Icons are activated by clicking on them with a mouse; some may even be used with keyboard shortcuts. See also *keyboard shortcuts*.

Ignore—1. Chat blinders; a way of blocking a member's chat from your view in a chat/conference room window. Ignore is most useful when the chat of another member becomes disruptive in the chat room. Note that the Ignore feature does not block or ignore IMs from a member—it only blocks the text from your own view in a chat or conference room. To ignore a member's chat on MAOL or GAOL, click on the People icon, highlight the screen name of the person you wish to ignore, and click on the "Ignore" button. To ignore chat on WAOL, double click on the member's screen name from the list of member names in the upper right hand corner of the Chat room window. You will be presented with a dialog box which offers an option to ignore the selected member's text. Once ignored, a member's chat can be reinstated through the same process. See *$im_off/$im_on* for instructions on ignoring IMs.

   2. An AOL e-mail system feature that allows you to ignore mail in your New Mail box, causing it to be moved to your Old Mail box without having to read it first. To use, simply select and highlight the piece of mail you wish to ignore in your New Mail box and then click on the "Ignore" button at the bottom of the window. Mail you have ignored without reading first will appear as "(ignored)" in the Status box. See also *e-mail* and *Status*.

IM (Instant Message)—AOL's equivalent of passing notes to another person during a meeting, as opposed to speaking up in the room (chat) or writing out a letter or memo (e-mail). Instant Messages (IMs) may be exchanged between two AOL members signed on at the same time and are useful for conducting conversations when a chat room isn't appropriate, available, or practical. To initiate an IM conversation, select "Send Instant Message" from the "Member" menu or use the keyboard shortcuts listed below, enter the recipient's screen name and a message, and finally send the IM by clicking on "Send" or using the keyboard shortcuts. If your intended victim is currently online, they will receive the IM within seconds. IMs may be exchanged at any time and from any part of the service, although IMs may not be sent when you are in the free area or when you are uploading a file. On both the Mac and Windows versions of AOL, IMs are similar to a mini-chat room, but with a larger chat buffer. On GAOL, messages are displayed one at a time, with no continuous log kept onscreen. IMs can be logged with the Instant Message Log available in MAOL and WAOL, and with the System Log in GAOL. IMs may be ignored (see *$im_off/$im_on*). It is also possible to send an IM to yourself, and this is often used as a therapy exercise for recovering AOLoholics. IM is used as a noun ("I have too many IMs!") or a verb ("I'm IMing with him now"). See also *IMsect*.

Keyboard shortcuts for IMs:
MAOL:
    <Command> + <i>—to bring up a new IM window
    <Command> + <Return> -or- <Enter>—to send the IM
WAOL:
    <Control> + <i>—to bring up a new IM window
    <Control> + <Enter>—to send the IM
GAOL:
    <Control> + <i>—to bring up a new IM window
    <Tab> to "Send" button then <Enter>—to send the IM

IMsect—An annoying Instant Message (IM). These are usually from someone who insists on IMing you when you're busy, or when you've indicated you'd rather not talk in IMs. If this happens, you have the option of turning your IMs off completely (see *$im_off/$im_on* for directions). If someone persists in IMing you even though you've politely asked them to stop, this may be considered harassment and you should report it via keyword: TOS. See also *IM*.

in-house—Used to describe those employees that actually work at AOL in Vienna, Virginia, or one of the other satellite offices. May also be referred to as corporate staff. This is contrasted with remote staff, many of whom are actually volunteers and work from their homes. See also *corporate staff* and *remote staff*.

insertion point—The blinking vertical line in a document marking the place where text is being edited. The insertion point may be navigated through a document with either the mouse or the arrow keys. Also called *cursor*.

interactive—Having the ability to act on each another. AOL is interactive in the sense that you can send information and, based upon that, have information sent back (and vice versa). The chat rooms are an excellent example.

Internet—The mother of all networks is not an online service itself, but rather serves to interconnect computer systems and networks all over the world. AOL features the Internet Connection department, which includes access to e-mail service to and from Internet addresses, USENET Newsgroups, Gopher & WAIS Databases, FTP, Telnet, and the World Wide Web. AOL has even provided "CyberJockeys" who rove among the areas helping members out (they wear "CJ" in front of their screen names). To receive mail through the Internet gateway, you need to give others your Internet mailing address, which consists of your AOL screen name (without any blank spaces) followed by the "@" symbol and "aol.com" (i.e., jennifer@aol.com). To obtain more information about the Internet, use the keyword: INTERNET to go to the Internet Connection. For information about TCP/IP access to America Online, see *TCP/IP*. See also *browser, FTP, gateway, gopher, newsgroups, page, site,* and *WAIS*.

IP (Information Provider)—A person or party supplying material for use on AOL's services, and/or responsible for the content of an area on America Online's services. See also *corporate staff* and *remote staff*.

ISDN—Abbreviation for Integrated Services Digital Networks. ISDN is a relatively new type of access offered by local telephone companies. You can use an ISDN to connect to other networks at speeds as high as 64,000 bps (single-channel). AOL is expected to add support for ISDN in the future. See also *TCP/IP*; contrast *packet-switching network*.

Keep As New—An AOL e-mail system feature that allows you to keep mail in your New Mail box, even after you've read or ignored it. To use, simply select and highlight the piece of mail you wish to keep (in either your "New Mail" or "Old Mail" list [a.k.a. "Mail You Have Read" list]) and then click on the "Keep As New" button at the bottom of the window. Returning read mail to your New Mail box with the "Keep As New" button will not change the time and date which appears in the Status box of the sender. See also *e-mail*.

keyboard shortcuts—The AOL software provides us with keyboard command equivalents for menu selections. For example, rather than selecting "Send Instant Message" from the menu, you could type **<Control> + <i> on the PC (WAOL or GAOL), or <Command> + <i>** on the Mac.

keyword—1. A fast way to move around within America Online. For example, you can "beam" directly to OMNI Online by using the key-word: OMNI. To use a keyword, type either **<Command> + <k>** on the Mac or **<Control> + <k>** on the PC, and then the keyword, followed by the Return or Enter key. When online, keywords are communicated to others in a standard format: Keyword: NAME. The name of the key-word is shown in all caps to distinguish it from other words around it, but it does not need to be entered that way. Currently, there are almost 3000 public keywords. An updated list of all public keywords is avail-able in the AOL file libraries by searching for "keyword surf" (don't include the quotes) at keyword: FILESEARCH. See also Appendix B.

2. A single word you feel is likely to be included in any database on a particular subject. A keyword is usually a word that comes as close as possible to describing the topic or piece of information you are looking for. Several of AOL's software libraries, mainly those in the Computing department, can be searched for with keywords.

kilobyte—Roughly, a thousand bytes. Actually, a kilobyte is 1,024 bytes (two to the tenth power). See also *byte* and *megabyte*.

lamer—A colloquial term for someone who follows others blindly without really having a grasp on the situation. Used frequently within the hacker culture. See also *hacker*.

library—An area online in which files may be uploaded to and down-loaded from. The files may be of any type: text, graphics, software, sounds, etc. These files can be downloaded from AOL's host computer to your personal computer's hard disk or floppy disk. Some libraries are searchable, while others must be browsed. You may also upload a file that may interest others to a library. A library is the best way to share large files with other AOL members. To search libraries available for your platform, go to keyword: FILESEARCH. See also *file, download, upload, search,* and *browse*; contrast *FTP*.

line noise—Extraneous noise on telephone lines that is often heard as clicks or static. While line noise is usually only a nuisance to voice communications, it means trouble for data being transmitted through modems. If you are having problems remaining connected, it may be the result of line noise. Signing off, redialing, and getting a new connection will often help this problem.

link—A pointer to another place that takes you there when you activate it (usually by clicking on it). AOL has literally millions of links that criss-cross the service, but they can't compare to the links on the WWW (often called "hyperlinks") and can cross continents without you knowing it. See also *browser, favorite place, hot list, hyperlink, page, site, URL,* and *WWW.*

Lobby—Often seeming more like the Grand Central Station of AOL rather than a sedate hotel foyer, the Lobby is the default chat room of the People Connection. When you first enter the People Connection, you will most likely enter a Lobby where any other number of members are also gathered. Some prefer the bustling atmosphere of the Lobby, while others use it as a waystation for other rooms in the People Connection. There will usually be a Guide present in the main Lobby between the hours of 9 am and 6 am ET. If the main Lobby is full (with a maximum of 23 members at any one time), additional Lobbies will be created, and suffixed with 1, 2, 3 and so on. To get to the Lobby, go to keyword: LOBBY. Stop by on a chilly night for a warm mug of cocoa, but beware of pie fights and desk burnings. See also *chat, chat room,* and *Guide.*

LOL—Shorthand for "Laughing Out Loud," often used in chat areas and Instant Messages. Another variation is ROFL, for "Rolling On Floor Laughing." See also *shorthands, abbreviations,* and *chat;* contrast with *body language* and *emoticons.*

lurk—To sit in a chat room or read a message board, yet contribute little or nothing at all. Hamsters are known lurkers. See also *chat* or *conference room.*

MAOL—The Apple Macintosh version of the AOL client software. May also be referred to as Mac AOL. Contrast with *GAOL* and *WAOL.*

macro—A "recording" of keystrokes or mouse movements/clicks on a computer that allows you to automate a task. Macros are usually created with shareware and commercial software and can be initiated with a single key. They may contain something as simple as your signature for an e-mail note or a complex sequence that opens an application, converts the data, saves it in a special format, and shuts your computer down. Online, macros are most useful for sending large amounts of text to a chat area or for automating tasks such as archiving a message board or saving e-mail. Unfortunately, only Mac and Windows users can run macros; the GAOL environment doesn't allow macro use.

mailbomb—n. What you have when one person sends you an excessive amount of e-mail, usually done in retaliation for a perceived wrong. This is a serious offense, as it not only inconveniences you but occupies mail system resources. If you receive a mailbomb, you can report it at keyword: TOS. See also *e-mail, snert,* and *TOS.*

massmail—v. The act of sending a piece of e-mail to a large number of members. Also used a noun. See also *e-mail, cc,* and *bcc.*

megabyte—Roughly, a million bytes of data. Actually, a megabyte is 1,048,576 bytes (two to the twentieth power). See also *byte* and *kilobyte.*

member—An AOL subscriber. The term "member" is embraced because AOLers are members of the online community. See also *Online Community.*

Member Directory—The database of AOL member screen names that have profiles. To be included in this database, a member need only to create a Member Profile. Note that profiles for deleted members are purged periodically, therefore it's possible to have a Member Profile for a deleted screen name. You can search for any string in a profile. Wildcard characters and boolean expressions also may be utilized in search strings. The Member Directory is located at keyword: MEMBERS. See also *member, Member Profile, database,* and *searchable.*

Member Profile—A voluntary online information document that describes oneself. Name, address information, birthday, sex, marital status, hobbies, computers used, occupation, and a personal quote may be provided. This is located a keyword: MEMBERS or PROFILE. See also *member* and *Member Directory.*

message—A note posted on a message board for others members to read. Message titles are limited to 30 characters. Message texts are limited to 4038 bytes on MacAOL, 3978 bytes on WAOL, and 8990 bytes on GAOL. Note that GAOL users can only read 5095 bytes of text in a message (with any additional text scrolling off the top); MAOL and WAOL can read any message in its entirety. A maximum of 500 messages may be contained in a folder, with some containing considerably less. A message may also be referred to as a post. See also *message board*.

message board—An area where members can post messages to exchange information, ask a question or reply to another message. All AOL members are welcome and encouraged to post messages in message boards (or boards). Because messages are a popular means of communication online, message boards are organized with "folders," wherein a number of messages on a specific subject (threads) are contained in sequential order. A maximum of 50 folders may be created in one message board, with some boards having lower limits of 30 or 20 folders. While you can usually create a new folder your topic, you should try to find an existing topic folder for your related message before creating a new one. There are two kinds of message boards in use on AOL right now: regular and response-threaded. Message boards may be grouped together in a Message Center to provide organization and hierarchy. Message boards are occasionally called bulletin boards. See also *cross-post, folder, message, Message Center, spam*, and *thread*.

message board pointer—An automatic place-marker for message boards. AOL keeps track of the areas you have visited by date, allowing you to pick up where you left off upon your return. Once you've visited a message board, clicking on the "Find New" button will show you only the new messages that have been posted since your last visit. The pointers are updated each time you return. These pointers stay in effect for 60 days after your last visit.

Message Center—A collection of message boards in one convenient area. For example, the fifteen message boards in BikeNet (keyword: BIKENET) are organized into one Message Center. See also *message board*.

MHM (Members Helping Members)—A message board in the free area where America Online members can assist and get assistance from other members. Located at keyword: MHM.

Microsoft Network—A new online service that debuted the summer of 1995 and has over 500,000 users. Often abbreviated as MSN. See also *America Online, CompuServe, eWorld*, and *Prodigy*.

modem—An acronym for *mod*ulator/*dem*odulator. This is the device that translates the signals coming from your computer into a form that can be transmitted over standard telephone lines. A modem also translates incoming signals into a form that your computer can understand. Two modems, one for each computer, are needed for any data communications over telephone lines. Your modem speaks to a modem at AOL through a network of telephone lines provided by AOLNet, SprintNet, DataPac, or Tymnet, for example.

modem file—An information file that stores your modem settings for connecting to AOL. As modems differ, you often need to use a modem file configured specifically for your modem. Luckily, AOL offers over 90 standard modem files you can select from in the Setup window. If you cannot find a modem file for your modem, you can call AOL Customer Service, try the Modem Help area (keyword: MODEM HELP) or edit your modem file. See also *CCL*.

moderator—Typically a host who facilitates a discussion during a conference. The moderator usually manages protocol, if used. See also *host, conference room*, and *protocol*.

MorF—Acronym for Male or Female. To ask another member their sex. This happens frequently in Lobbies and chat rooms in the People Connection, but it is considered ill-mannered by most seasoned onliners. BorG (Boy or Girl?) is another manifestation of this virus that seems to infect some members. See also *Lobby, chat room*, and *People Connection*.

MSN—See *Microsoft Network*.

Net—Abbreviation for the Internet. See *Internet*.

netiquette—Net manners. Cyberspace is a subculture with norms and rules of conduct all its own. Understanding of these will often make your online life more enjoyable and allow you to move through more smoothly. Online etiquette includes such things as proper capitalization (don't use all caps unless you mean to shout). Basically, the most important rule to keep in mind is one we learned offline and in kindergarten of all places: Do unto others as you'd have them do unto you (a.k.a. The Golden Rule). See keyword: SHORTHANDS for a primer in AOL etiquette.

Network News—AOL maintenance broadcasts and feedback that are displayed in a small window. Network News can be enabled or disabled with the AOL software (select Preferences under the Members menu).

newbie—Affectionate term for a new member (under six months). The New Member Lounge in the People Connection is a popular haunt for the newly initiated. Contrast *wannabe*.

newsgroups—Internet's version of a public message board. Available on AOL at keyword: NEWSGROUPS. See also *FileGrabber* and *Internet*; contrast *ftp, gopher,* and *WWW*.

node—A single computer or device accessible via a phone number and used by one or more persons to connect to a telecommunications network, such as AOL. Everyone signs on to AOL via a node, which is usually local to them and doesn't involve long-distance charges. Sometimes a bad connection is the result of a busy node, and can be corrected by trying a new node. See also *packet-switching network, 800 number, access number, AOLnet, DataPac, SprintNet,* and *Tymnet*.

Odeon—An auditorium that focuses on conferences for media providers online, such as OMNI Magazine Online or NBC Online. The Odeon is accessible through individual forums or through the Center Stage at keyword: AUDITORIUM. See also *Auditorium*.

offline—The condition of a computer when it is disconnected from another machine—for example, disconnected from AOL's host. Note that you can be offline and still running the AOL software on your machine, as when you're composing mail offline. Contrast with *online*.

online—The condition of a computer when it is connected to another machine via modem. Contrast with *offline*.

online community—A group of people bound together by their shared interest or characteristic of interacting with other computer users through online services, BBSs, or networks. Because of the pioneer aspects of an online community, established onliners will welcome newcomers and educate them freely, in most cases. On AOL, elaborate conventions, legends, and etiquette systems have developed within the community. See also *cyberspace*.

OnlineHost—The screen name of AOL's host computer used to send information and usually seen in chat rooms, conference rooms and auditoriums. On WAOL and GAOL, the OnlineHost screen name may signal when a member enters or leaves the room. On all platforms, the OnlineHost screen name will give you the result of dice rolled. See also *chat room, conference room, auditorium*, and *//roll*.

Open-Apple Key—See *Command key*.

OS (operating system) —The software that is used to control the basic functions of a computer. Operating systems are generally responsible for allocation and control of a computer's resources. Some common operating systems are: MacOS, MS-DOS, UNIX, and OS/2. See also *DOS, System, UNIX*, and *Windows*.

Option key—A special modifier key commonly found on Mac keyboards. Usually located on the bottom row of keys and labelled "Option." Holding down the Option key while another key is pressed will often activate a special function.

OS/2—IBM's 32-bit operating system that offers a GUI interface for IBM PC and compatible machines. The current release of OS/2, version 2.1, runs Windows 3.1, DOS, and OS/2 specific applications. See also *operating system, DOS*, and *Windows*.

P*—Shorthand for Prodigy Service. See also *Prodigy*.

packet-switching network (PSN)—The electronic networks that enable you to access a remote online service by dialing a local phone number. Information going to and from your computer is segmented into "packets" and given an address. The packets are then sent through the network to their destination much as a letter travels through the postal system, only much faster. AOL uses a variety of PSNs to supply local nodes (local telephone numbers) for members' access. Also see *access number, node, AOLnet, DataPac, SprintNet*, and *Tymnet*; contrast *ISDN*.

page—A document on the World Wide Web, presented in the browser window. WWW pages can contain any combination of links, text, graphics, sounds or videos. A set of pages is often referred to as a site. See also *browser, favorite place, home page, hot list, link, site, URL,* and *WWW.*

palmtop—See *PDA.*

parental chat controls—Parental Control enables the master account holder to restrict access to certain areas and features on AOL (such as blocking IMs and rooms). It can be set for one or all screen names on the account; once Parental Control is set for a particular screen name, it is active each time that screen name signs on. Changes can be made by the master account holder at any time. To access controls, go to keyword: PARENTAL CONTROL. Contrast *$im_off/$im_on* and *ignore.*

parity—A method of error-correction at the character level, which is used in sending information via modems. Error correcton occurs less frequently now—every 1,024 characters isn't rare—so parity is almost a thing of the past.

partner—See *IP.*

password—Your secret 4–8 character code word that you use to secure your account. Because password security is so important, we've included a number of password-creation tips and reminders below. Please read these and pass these along to your friends (and enemies). See also *phish.*

—Your password should be as long as possible (use all 8 characters, if you can).

—Your password should not include any word found in your profile, any of your names (or your spouse's/kid's names), or anything commonly found in a dictionary.

—Your password should be a combination of letters and numbers.

—Try using the first letter of each word in an eight-word sentence.

—Or, use a word that is easy to remember and insert numbers into it such as SU8M3ER. (Important: Do *not* use any passwords you have ever seen used as examples.)

—Change your password often (use keyword: PASSWORD).

password scammer—See *phish.*

PC/GEOS—See *GAOL.*

PC-Link—A discontinued service for PC users which utilized a Deskmate-style interface with special support areas provided by the Tandy Corporation. PC-Link was phased out in late 1994. Abbreviated PCL. See also *AOL* and *Q-Link*.

PDA—Short for Personal Digital Assistant. A hand-held computer that performs a variety of tasks, including personal information management. PDAs are gaining in popularity and variety, although AOL is only officially supported on the Zoomer (Casio Z7000/Tandy Z-PDA/ AST Gridpad 2390), the Sharp PT9000, the Sony Magic Link, and the Motorola Envoy. The Zoomer, Magic Link, and Envoy versions of AOL only allows you to access a limited number of features. PT9000 allows almost complete access, and it can be run on the Zoomer. For those with an HP100LX, HP200LX, or other DOS-based palmtop with CGA capability, a work-around with GAOL v1.6 is possible. Wider PDA access to AOL is expected in the future, including the Apple Newton. If you can't wait for regular AOL access on the Newton, a shareware program called "Aloha" allows you to access your AOL e-mail. For more information, check out the PDA Forum at keyword: PDA. PDAs may also be referred to as palmtops.

People Connection (PC)—The AOL department dedicated to real-time chat. Many different rooms can be found here: Lobbies, officially sanctioned rooms, member-created rooms, private rooms, the Center Stage area, and PC Studio. You can access this area with keyword: PEOPLE. Feel free to surf PC, but please obey hamster crossing signs. See also *department, chat room*; contrast *conference room*.

Personal Filing Cabinet—On WAOL 2.5 and higher, this is a special feature of the AOL software that organizes your mail, files, newsgroup postings, and favorite places. Note that everything in your Personal Filing Cabinet is stored on your hard disk. You can set your Filing Cabinet preferences through by opening Preferences (<Ctrl> + <=>) and selecting Personal Filing Cabinet. This feature is not currently available for those on MAOL or GAOL. See also e-*mail, favorite place, file*, and *newsgroup*.

PKZip—A compression utility for PCs to compress one file, or multiple files, into a smaller file (called an archive), which will make for shorter up/downloading. WAOL 3.0 and MAOL 2.6 (and higher) can automatically decompress 2.04 ZIP archives. See also *archive, download, file, file compression, ARC*, and *StuffIt*.

phish—v. The act of tricking members into revealing their passwords, credit card numbers, or other personal information. Phishers will often disguise themselves as AOL staff, but remember that AOL staff will *never ever* ask you for your password or credit card information while you are online. They may also ask you to send certain files to them, or do something that seems odd to you. Phishers should always be reported to AOL so they don't continue to prey on other, less-knowledgeable members. If you get an IM from them, save the IM and then report them at keyword: GUIDEPAGER immediately. See also *hacker* and *password*.

phisher—One who phishes. See also *cracker*, *hacker*, and *snert*.

platform—As the word is used online, "platform" refers to the type of computer in use. Platforms include Macs, PCs (Windows or DOS), Unix workstations, and all of the others.

polling—v. The act of requesting information from everyone in a chat room. For example, a member may ask "Everyone here who is cool press 1" and the chat room will scroll with 1's for several minutes. This is considered disruptive and shouldn't be done in a public room. See also *chat room*.

post— 1. v. The act of putting something online, usually into a message board or newsgroup.

2. n. A message in a message board or newsgroup. See also *message board* and *message*; contrast *upload*.

private—adv. The state of being in a private room. It is considered taboo by some members to be "seen" in a private room because this is often the communication channel of choice for "hot chatters." In reality, however, private rooms are a convenient way to meet with someone when IMs would get in the way. If you are private and another member does a search for your screen name, they will be told that "<screen name> is online, but in a private room." See also *private room* and *hot chat*; contrast *chat room* and *conference room*.

private room—A chat room that is created by a member via an option in People Connection where the name is not public knowledge. Private room names have the same restrictions as chat room names: they may only contain up to 20 characters, must begin with a letter, and cannot contain punctuation. Some commonly named private rooms are rumored to be open 24 hours a day; AOLocholics have been known to

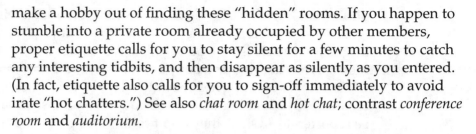

make a hobby out of finding these "hidden" rooms. If you happen to stumble into a private room already occupied by other members, proper etiquette calls for you to stay silent for a few minutes to catch any interesting tidbits, and then disappear as silently as you entered. (In fact, etiquette also calls for you to sign-off immediately to avoid irate "hot chatters.") See also *chat room* and *hot chat*; contrast *conference room* and *auditorium*.

Prodigy—An information service founded as a joint venture between IBM and Sears. It is currently one of the larger competitors that AOL faces. Prodigy is marred by continuous online advertising and other quirks. For all it's drawbacks, Prodigy still has a enormous subscriber base. For those members who defected from Prodigy to AOL, there is a Prodigy Refugees Forum online (keyword: PRODIGY). See also *P**; contrast *America Online*, *CompuServe*, *eWorld*, and *Microsoft Network*.

profile—AOL allows each screen name to have an informational file (a profile) attached to it. A profile tells a bit about who you are, where you live, what your interests are—anything you want others to know about you. A profile can be created or updated at keyword: PROFILE. You can only modify the profile of the screen name you are currently signed on under, and each screen name has a unique profile. To read another member's profile, press <Control> + <g> (<Command> + <g> on the Mac), enter their screen name and hit Enter. Not all members have profiles. You may search profiles through the Member Directory. A little-known AOL fact is that a Member Directory search reveals that over 250 "hamsters" are lurking among profiles. See also *member*, *Member Directory*, and *screen name*.

protocol—A system used in conference rooms to keep order and facilitate a discussion. When you have a question, you type **?**, when you have a comment, you type **!** and when you are finished, you type **/ga**. A queue of those waiting with questions and answers is displayed at regular points throughout the conference, and members will be invited to speak by the moderator or host. It is considered impolite and a breach of protocol to speak out of turn. See also *conference room*, *host*, and *moderator*.

public domain—A file that's completely free, uncopyrighted, and typically posted on services like AOL for distribution (via download-ing) directly to the user. Since the producer (or programmer) usually

posts this and the user downloads it, distribution is direct and nearly without cost. Users are generally encouraged to make copies and give them to friends—even post them on other services. Often little, or no, documentation is available for it, though. Contrast *freeware* and *shareware*.

punt—The act of being disconnected from AOL often as a result of difficulties at AOL or interference on your node (such as line noise). Used as a noun or verb. See also *bounce, node*, and *line noise*.

punt pillows—Virtual "pillows" given, via chat or IMs, to cushion the posterior of a member who was punted. Often depicted as () () () () or [] [] [] [] (the harder, concrete variety). See also *chat, IMs*, and *punt*.

'puter—An affectionate abbreviation for one's computer; often employed by enthusiasts and AOLoholics.

Q-Link—A discontinued service for Commodore 64 and 128 users. See also *America Online* and *PC-Link*.

quoting—To include parts of an original message in a reply. One or two greater-than characters (>) is the standard method for setting off a quote from the rest of the message. They are usually placed to the left of the sentence, followed by a space, but may also be placed on the right as well. For example:

```
 > Wow! That's great! How did you come by it?  (Internet-style)
 >> Wow! That's great! How did you come by it?
 >> Wow! That's great! How did you come by it? <<
 << Wow! That's great! How did you come by it? >>
```

WAOL 2.5 or higher users can quote text automatically in e-mail by first selecting it, then copying it (<Ctrl> + <c>), and then clicking on "Reply." See also >> and <<.

Re:—Short for "regarding" or "reply." See also *e-mail* and *message*.

release—v. To make something available to the general public, such as a file in a file library. See also *file* and *library*.

remote staff—AOL members who help in the various forums and areas. They usually work from their homes not AOL headquarters, hence "remote." Often these are Guides, Hosts, Forum leaders/assistants/consultants, etc. With Information Providers (IPs), the remote staff are usually those who do not work on the premises of the IP's offline physical location, whereas those IP employees who do are known as corporate staff. May also be called offsite staff or community leaders. See also *Guide, host, IP,* and *uniform*; contrast *corporate staff* and *in-house*.

return receipt—A feature available with the MAOL software that returns a piece of e-mail acknowledging that mail you sent to another AOL member (or members) has been received. To enable this function, you must check the "Return Receipt" box on the e-mail window before it is sent. Once the e-mail has been read by the member(s) it was addressed to (including those carbon copied and blind carbon copied), mail with the date and time it was read will be automatically generated and returned to the sender immediately. One note is sent for each member that reads the mail. If you check return receipt on a letter that is carbon copied to 100 people, 100 notes will trickle in as each addressee reads the mail. In general, return receipts are unnecessary as the Status feature can be used to determine when any piece of mail was read. Return receipts are most useful when you need to be immediately informed that the mail was read, usually so you can contact that person as soon as possible. Return receipts should be used sparingly as they can clutter up your mailbox. See also *e-mail, carbon copy, blind carbon copy,* and *status*.

revolving door—A chat or conference room has a "revolving door" when members are quickly moving in and out of the room. Lobbies and many popular chat rooms in the People Connection will often have "revolving doors." See also *chat room, conference room,* and *Lobby*.

Road Trip—An AOL feature, available for WAOL 2.5 (or higher) members, which allows you to create "tours" of the WWW and AOL, and then present these to others. For more information, see keyword: ROAD TRIP. See also *WWW*.

Rotunda—An auditorium that features conferences with companies or areas in the Computing & Software department. Accessible via keyword: ROTUNDA. See also *auditorium*.

savvy—To be knowledgeable or perceptive at something. Often seen as "computer-savvy" or "online savvy." Contrast *newbie* and *wannabe*.

screen name—The names, pseudonyms more often than not, that identify AOL members online. Screen names may contain no fewer than three and no more than ten characters, must be unique, and

cannot contain vulgarity or vulgar references. Also, some combinations of letters are reserved for online staff (such as "Guide" or "OMNI"). Screen names may not start with a number. Any one account may have up to five screen names, to accommodate family members or alter-egos, and each can have its own unique password. Either way, you cannot delete the original screen name you set up the account with, and the person that establishes the original screen name and account is responsible for all charges incurred by all five screen names. To add or delete your screen name, go to keyword: NAMES. Note that when you add a new screen name, it will be automatically blocked from entering Member Rooms in the People Connection. To disable this block, you will need to switch to the master screen name and use the Parental Control (keyword: PARENTAL CONTROL). See also *e-mail address, member,* and *uniform.*

scroll—1. Refers to the movement of incoming text and other informa-tion on your computer screen. See *scroll bar.*

2. The act of repeatedly typing similar words on screen, or spacing out the letters of a word. For example, if a member typed the word "hello" seven times in a row, with returns between each, this would be scrolling. So would hitting <Return> after each letter of a word. Polling also causes scrolling. Scrolling is prohibited in AOL's Terms of Service and you may be given a warning for this if observed by a Guide or Host. Go to keyword: TOS for more information. See also *polling.*

scroll bar—The bar on the right hand side of a window that allows you to move the contents up and down, or on the bottom of a window for moving things to the left or right. The area on the scroll bar between the up and down arrows is shaded if there is more information than fits in the window, or white if the entire content of the window is already visible. See also *scroll* (1).

search—Typically used in association with libraries and other search-able databases, the term *search* refers to a specific exploration of files or entries themselves, rather than a causal examination done line by line. See also *searchable, database, file,* and *library;* contrast *browse.*

searchable—A collection of logically related records or database files that serve as a single central reference; a searchable database accepts input and yields all matching entries containing that character string. The Members Directory is an example of a searchable database. See also *search, database, Directory of Services,* and *Members Directory.*

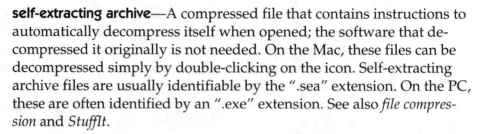

self-extracting archive—A compressed file that contains instructions to automatically decompress itself when opened; the software that decompressed it originally is not needed. On the Mac, these files can be decompressed simply by double-clicking on the icon. Self-extracting archive files are usually identifiable by the ".sea" extension. On the PC, these are often identified by an ".exe" extension. See also *file compression* and *StuffIt*.

shareware—A fully functional file that is distributed with the promise of "try before you buy." Made available with the downloader's good conscience in mind, the authors of shareware ask that if you continue to use their product, you pay the fee requested in their documentation. Shareware is often made available in libraries of online services like AOL for downloading or is distributed via CD-ROM collections. There are shareware programs of exceptional quality and many are often comparable to commercially distributed software. There are a great number of variations of the shareware theme such as demoware that is often fully functional except for printing or saving functions or is only functional for a short period of time; postcardware, which requests a postcard sent to the author; contributionware, and so on. See also file; contrast *demoware*, *freeware*, and *public domain*.

shorthands—The collective term for the many emoticons and abbreviations used during chat. These devices were developed by members over time to give information on the writer's emotional state when ASCII text only is available. A brief list of these is available at keyword: SHORTHANDS. See also *emoticons*, *abbreviations*, and *chat*; contrast with *body language*.

sig—Short for signature. A block of text that some folks include at their end of their newsgroup postings and/or e-mail. You can designate a sig for your own newsgroup postings through your newsgroup preferences. See also *newsgroup* and *post*.

sign-on kit—The free software, registration codes, and directions for creating a new AOL account. There are a number of ways to obtain sign-on kits. Online, go to keyword: FRIEND and follow the directions there to have kit sent via snail mail. Offline, you can always find a "free offer" card in a magazine, particularly those magazines that have online forums like *TIME* magazine. You may also find the sign-on kits

themselves bundled in one or more newsstand magazines, such as *MacWorld*, or with commercial software, modems, and computers. Sign-on kits can also be ordered via phone (1-800-827-6364, ext. 7776). Of course, you can always purchase *The Official America Online Membership Kit & Tour Guide* from your local bookstore; a sign-on kit is included in the back of the book. If you simply need new AOL software but not a entirely new account, you can download the latest software for your platform at keyword: UPGRADE or use the AOL Support BBS (see the access number entry for information regarding the AOL Support BBS).

sim—Short for simulation. A sim is a free-form game where participants role play in various scenarios. Sims are generally held in a chat or conference room, and may have rules associated with them. Check out the Simming Forum at keyword: SIM. See also *//roll*, *chat room*, and *conference room*.

simulchat—A chat held simultaneously with a radio call-in broadcast. Online chat participants listen to the broadcast and discuss the same topics being discussed on the air. The radio broadcast takes questions and comments from the online chat as well as from callers. Simulchats are organized through the Mercury Center (keyword: MC TALK), Chicago Online (keyword: COL), and OnLine Tonight (keyword: OLT). See also *chat*.

site—A specific place on the Internet, usually a set of pages on the World Wide Web. See also *link*, *page*, *URL*, and *WWW*.

smileys—See *shorthands* and *emoticons*.

snail mail—Mail that is sent via the U.S. Postal Service. Not meant as derogatory, but to point out the difference between nearly instantaneous e-mail versus the delivery of tangible packages. Despite its relative slowness, snail mail will be used until matter transfer becomes possible. See also *e-mail*.

snert—Acronym for Sexually Nerdishly Expressive Recidivistic Trolls. A member who is disruptive or annoying. Contrast *cracker*, *hacker*, *phisher*, and *troll*.

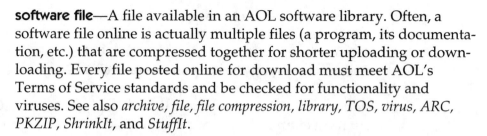

software file—A file available in an AOL software library. Often, a software file online is actually multiple files (a program, its documentation, etc.) that are compressed together for shorter uploading or downloading. Every file posted online for download must meet AOL's Terms of Service standards and be checked for functionality and viruses. See also *archive, file, file compression, library, TOS, virus, ARC, PKZIP, ShrinkIt*, and *StuffIt*.

sounds—see *chat sounds*.

Spam—1. n. A luncheon meat produced by the Hormel Foods Corporation. Spam is frequently the butt of many online jokes originally due to Monty Python's use of Spam as the topic of some of their skits. Lately, Spam jokes have taken on a life of their own online and you may see many references to it. There is even a newsgroup dedicated to Spam, as well as at least one WWW site.

2. v. To barrage a message board or newsgroup with inappropriate, irrelevant or simply numerous copies of the same post (as in cross-posting). Not only is this annoying, but it is exceedingly bad netiquette. Members who "spam" will often have their posts removed (if in an AOL message board) or find their mailbox full of e-mail from angry onliners (if in a newsgroup). See also *cross-posting, message board*, and *newsgroup*; contrast with *flame*.

SprintNet—Formerly known as Telenet, SprintNet is a packet-switching network that provides members with 1200, 2400, 9600, and 14,400 bps local access numbers to America Online. SprintNet networks are owned and operated by US Sprint. To find SprintNet local access numbers, go to keyword: ACCESS or call 1-800-877-5045 ext. 5. See also *packet-switching* and *access number*; contrast with *AOLnet, Tymnet*, and *DataPac*.

Status (of e-mail)—An AOL feature that allows you to check whether e-mail has been read yet and, if read, when. The status for an e-mail message will be either "(not yet read)," "(ignored)," "(deleted)," or will show the precise date and time when the mail was read. Status information includes recipients who were carbon-copied (and even those who were blind-carbon copied, if you were the sender). To check the current status of e-mail on the Mac platform, select and highlight the piece of mail you are interested in (either in the "New Mail," "Mail you have read," or "Mail you have sent" window) and then click on the "Status" button at the bottom of the window. On the PC platform, first

choose the "Check Mail You've Sent" option from the Mail menu, select and highlight the piece of mail, and then click on the "Show Status" button on the bottom of the window. See also *e-mail, carbon copy, blind carbon copy*, and *return receipt*.

Stratus—AOL's host computer is often referred to as "the Stratus." The term is a vestige from the days when Stratus was the only manufacturer AOL used. Today, AOL's host system is actually a collection of computers from a number of manufacturers including Cisco, Hewlett-Packard, IBM, and others. The system runs 365 days a year, 24 hours a day, and it's backed up by an impressive bank of batteries and a standby diesel generator in case the power fails. See also *host (1)* and *hamster*.

StuffIt—A popular compression program for the Apple Macintosh currently published by Aladdin Software and written by Raymond Lau. StuffIt is the standard method of compressing Mac files for uploading to AOL's file libraries. With StuffIt, it's possible to combine several files into one archive, which is convenient way of transferring several files at once. StuffIt files, also called archives, are often recognizable by the .sit extension to the filename. A file that has been compressed with StuffIt is said to be "stuffed." Files compressed with StuffIt can be automatically "unstuffed" when downloaded from Mac AOL or when opened using the Mac AOL software. StuffIt is currently distributed both as a shareware product, Stuffit Lite, and a commercial product, Stuffit Deluxe. Programs to extract stuffed files are free and exist both for the IBM and Mac. See also *archive, file compression, self-extracting archive, download*, and *shareware*; contrast *ARC* and *PKZip*.

surf—To cruise in search of information not readily evident in the hope of discovering something new. Usually paired with another word to describe the type of information being sought. Examples are room surfing and keyword surfing. The joy of surfing is only interrupted by the occasional "bump" when you forget to stop at the hamster crossing signs distributed randomly around AOL. See also *password scammer*.

synchronous—Data communication technique in which bits are transmitted and received at a fixed rate. Used to transmit large blocks of data over special communications lines. Much more complex than asynchronous communication, this technique has little application for most personal computer users. See also *asynchronous*.

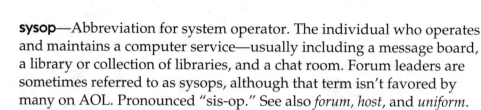

sysop—Abbreviation for system operator. The individual who operates and maintains a computer service—usually including a message board, a library or collection of libraries, and a chat room. Forum leaders are sometimes referred to as sysops, although that term isn't favored by many on AOL. Pronounced "sis-op." See also *forum, host*, and *uniform*.

system—Short for operating system, this refers to the software that controls the basic operations of a computer. System can also refer to the collection of components that have a functional existence when combined. Some examples of this include your computer system, the telephone system, or the AOL system. See also *operating system, OS/2*, and *Windows*.

TCP/IP—Acronym for Transmission Control Protocol/Internet Protocol. The protocol language that Internet machines use to communicate. WAOL 2.5 and MAOL 2.6 and higher allow you to sign-on via TCP/IP. AOL also uses TCP/IP to interconnect all of its host computers–a so-called "open architecture" system. See also *Internet*.

Tech Live—Previously known as CS Live, this is a free area where you can ask questions of AOL staff live. The Tech Live Auditorium is open from 6 a.m. to 4 a.m. Eastern time, seven days a week. Here you can get live help from experienced Customer Relations staff working in-house at AOL headquarters or remotely. This service is available in the Free Area through keyword: TECH LIVE. See also *Customer Relations*.

thread—In general terms, a discussion that travels along the same subject line. More specifically, a thread refers a group of posts in a message board under the same subject and (hopefully) topic. See also *message board*.

thwapp—v. To hit someone upside their screen name; a virtual slap. For example you may be ::thwapped:: for requesting an age/sex check in a chat room.

timeout—1. What happens when you've got two computers connected online and one gets tired of waiting for the other (i.e., when the hourglass [PC] or beachball [Mac] cursor comes up and the "host fails to respond"). You can report problems with frequent timeouts at keyword: SYSTEM RESPONSE.

2. The result of remaining idle for a certain amount of time while signed on to AOL. This timeout time is usually thirty minutes, but may

vary with different modems. In this case, AOL's computers are tired of waiting for you. It's also protection against staying signed on all night when an AOLoholic falls asleep at the keyboard.

title bar—The portion of a window where the name of the window is displayed. On the Mac the title bar also may include the close box and the zoom box. See also *close box, window,* and *zoom box.*

toast—Something totally ruined or unusable. For example, "Well, that file is toast." Also used as a verb.

TOS—Short for America Online's Terms of Service—the terms of agreement everyone agrees to when registering for and becoming a member of America Online. These terms apply to all accounts on the service(s). You can read these terms at keyword: TOS (in the free area), or by going to keyword: PC STUDIO and clicking on Terms of Service. Also included are avenues of reporting TOS violations to AOL. See *TOSAdvisor* and *TOS warning.*

TOSAdvisor—In days of olde, this was the screen name to which all TOS violations observed by members are sent to. These days, if you feel something violates TOS, you should go to keyword: TOS to report it. The Terms of Service Staff area can also be reached at keyword: PC STUDIO > Terms of Service/Parental Controls > Write to Terms of Service Staff. Note that there is no longer a screen name "TOSAdvisor." See *TOS, TOS warning,* and *OSW.*

TOSsable—The state of being likely to receive a TOS warning. For example, a TOSsable word is one which a TOS warning could be given to if typed online. See *TOS* and *TOS warning.*

TOS warning—An onscreen warning given by a trained Guide or Host for violating AOL's Terms of Service. These warnings are reported to AOL who takes action (or not, depending on the severity of the breach). See *TOS.*

Tour Guide—Short for *The Official America Online Membership Kit & Tour Guide*—i.e., this book.

Trojan horse—A destructive program that is disguised within a seemingly useful program. For example, a recent Trojan horse was a file called "AOLGOLD" which claimed to be a new version of AOL, but actually corrupted files if it was executed. A Trojan horse is only activated by running the program. If you receive a file attached to e-mail from a sender that you are not familiar with, you are advised not to download it. If you ever receive a file you believe could cause problems, forward it to screen name "TOSEmail1" and explain your concerns. Contrast *virus*.

troll—An online wanderer that often leaves a wake of disgruntled members before crawling back under their rock. It is unclear why trolls find AOL a popular watering hole, but it could be because they consider hamsters a delicacy. Contrast *cracker, hacker, password scammer*, and *snert*.

Tymnet—A packet-switching network that provides members with 1200 and 2400 bps local access numbers to America Online. Tymnet networks are owned and operated by BT Tymnet. To find Tymnet local access numbers, go to keyword: ACCESS or call 1-800-336-0149. See also *packet-switching* and *access number*; contrast with *AOLnet, DataPac*, and *SprintNet*.

typo—1. A typographical error.
　2. A dialect that many onliners have mastered with the advent of keyboards and late nights.

UDO—A method of receiving updates to the AOL software. Upon signing-on to AOL, the UDO sends all the necessary updates to your computer before you can do anything else. Rumor has it UDO stands for Unavoidable Delay Obstacle, but we haven't been able to verify it. Contrast *DOD*.

uniform—The screen name that's often "worn" by a staff member, either in-house or remote, when working online. The screen name usually consists of a identifiable prefix and a personal name or initials. Uniforms aren't usually worn when the member is off-duty. See also *Guide, Host*, and *screen name*. Some current uniforms include:

AFL	Apple/Mac Forum Leader
AFA	Apple/Mac Forum Assistant
AFC	Apple/Mac Forum Consultant
AOLive	AOL Live staff
CJ	CyberJockey

CNR	CNN News Room staff
CSS	Company Support Staff
FCL, FCA, or FCC	Family Computing staff
GLCF	Gay and Lesbian Community Forum staff
Guide	General system guide
GWRep	GeoWorks Representative
GWS	Game Wiz Staff
HOST	People Connection host
IC	Industry Connection
MCC	Manufacturers Corner staff (Consumer Electronics)
MW	MasterWord staff
NPR	National Public Radio Outreach staff
NWN	Neverwinter Night staff
OMNI	OMNI Magazine Online staff
PC	PC Forum Leader
PCA	PC Forum Assistant
PCC	PC Forum Consultant
PCW	PC World Online
REF	Reference Desk host
QRJ	RabbitJack's Casino staff
Teacher	IES Teacher
TECHLive	Tech Live representative (in-house)
TLA	Tech Live Advisor (remote)
VGS	Video Game Systems staff

UNIX—An easy-to-use operating system developed by Ken Thompson, Dennis Ritchie, and coworkers at Bell Laboratories. Since it also has superior capabilities as a program development system, UNIX should become even more widely used in the future. AOL does not currently have software for the UNIX platform. See also *operating system*; contrast *DOS, Windows*, and *system*.

Unsend—An AOL e-mail system feature that allows you to retrieve mail that has been sent but not yet read. To use, simply select and highlight the piece of mail you wish to unsend from the "Check Mail You've Sent" window and click on the "Unsend" button at the bottom of the window. The mail will be permanently deleted and cannot be retrieved. Note that only mail sent to other AOL members can be "unsent" or retrieved; Internet, Fax, and U.S. Mail cannot be retrieved. See also *e-mail*.

upload—1. v. The transfer of information from a storage device on your computer to a remote computer, such as AOL's host computer. This information may be uploaded to one of AOL's file libraries or it may be uploaded with a piece of e-mail as an attached file. Generally, any file over 16k (with the exception of text files) should be compressed before uploading to make the transfer faster and save money. Approved compression formats are ZIP, ARC, SIT, and SEAs. Important note: When uploading to AOL file libraries, be sure that the library you wish to upload to is the last one that you've opened after clicking on the "Upload" button; there is a bug that sends your file to the last opened library, regardless of whether it was the one you initially clicked on the "Upload" button in or not. See also *file, file compression,* and *library*; contrast with *download*.

2. n. The file or information that is sent or uploaded.

URL (Uniform Resource Locator)—An address for an Internet resource, such as a World Wide Web page or an ftp site. You can use a URL address to go to a WWW site by entering it directly into the WWW browser, or by typing it into the AOL keyword box (on WAOL 2.5 and MAOL 2.6 or higher). There is no list of URL addresses as they are constantly changing and growing. AOL's home page URL is http://www.aol.com. See also *browser, favorite place, hot list, page, site,* and *WWW*.

USENET—See *newsgroup*.

virus— Computer software that has the ability to attach itself to other software or files, does so without the permission or knowledge of the user, and is generally designed with one intent—to propagate themselves. They *may* also be intentionally destructive, however not all virus damage is intentional. Some benign viruses suffer from having been poorly written and have been known to cause damage as well. Virus prevention software and information may be found at keyword: Virus (on the Mac platform) or keyword: McAfee (on the PC platform). Contrast *Trojan horse*.

wannabe—Someone who aspires to something. Wannabes are often spotted by their obvious enthusiasm, or their frustration at not being able to acquire a skill. Most wannabes are self-proclaimed, and are considered a stage above newbies. For example, "He's a Guide wannabe." Contrast *newbie*.

WAOL—The PC platform's Windows version of the AOL client software. The current version is 3.0. (You can look up your revision number by selecting "About America Online" from the Help menu and then pressing <Control> + <r>.) Contrast with *MAOL* and *GAOL*.

Web— See *WWW*.

weeding—(Yes, that's "weeding" as in a garden of bliss.) An online wedding. Often held in the People Connection chat rooms like Romance Connection or in the LaPub. Nuptial announcements and well-wishes can often be found in The Que message board at keyword: QUE.

window—A portion of the computer screen in which related information is contained, usually with a graphical border to distinguish it from the rest of the screen. Especially important in graphic user interfaces, windows may generally be moved, resized, closed, or brought to the foreground or sent to the background. Some common AOL windows include the chat room window, e-mail windows, and IM windows.

Windows—A graphical extension to the DOS operating system used on IBM PCs and compatibles. Developed by Microsoft, the Windows environment offers drop-down menus, multi-tasking, and mouse-oriented operation. See also *DOS, system*, and *UNIX*.

WWW (Web)—Abbreviation for World Wide Web. One of the more popular aspects of the Internet, this is actually an overarching term for the many hypertext documents that a linked together via a special protocol called HyperText Transfer Protocol (or HTTP). WWW information is accessed through a WWW browser, which are available with WAOL 2.5 or MAOL 2.6 (or higher). You use "URL" addresses to get to various WWW sites, or pages, much like you use keywords on AOL. See also *browser, favorite place, home page, hot list, Internet, page, site*, and *URL*.

ZIP—see *PKZip*.

zoom box—The zoom box is the small box in the upper-right corner of the window. Clicking on the zoom box will cause a reduced window to zoom up to fill the entire screen; clicking on the zoom box of a maximized window will cause it to zoom down to its reduced size. Compare with *close box*.

Index

Explore the Internet

News Junkies Internet 500 🌐

$24.99, 500 pages, illustrated, part #: 461-8

Quench your thirst for news with this comprehensive
listing of the best news sites and sources on the Web.
Includes business, international, sports, weather, law,
entertainment, politics and more.

Walking the World Wide Web, Second Edition 🌐

$39.95, 784 pages, illustrated, part #: 298-4

More than 30% new, this book now features 500 listings
and an extensive index of servers, expanded and
arranged by subject. This groundbreaking bestseller
includes a CD-ROM enhanced with Ventana's WebWalker
technology; updated online components that make it the
richest resource available for Web travelers; along with a
full hyperlinked version of the text.

Internet Business 500 🌐

$29.95, 488 pages, illustrated, part #: 287-9

This authoritative list of the most useful, most valuable
online resources for business is also the most current list,
linked to a regularly updated *Online Companion* on the
Internet. The companion CD-ROM features a hyperlinked
version of the entire text of the book.

Stephen G. Kochan
Patrick Wood

Unix Shell
Programming
Third Edition

SAMS

800 East 96th Street, Indianapolis, Indiana 46240

Acquisitions Editor
Katie Purdum

Development Editor
Scott Meyers

Managing Editor
Charlotte Clapp

Copy Editor
Geneil Breeze

Indexer
Erika Millen

Proofreader
Jessica McCarty

Technical Editor
Michael Watson

Interior Designer
Gary Adair

Cover Designer
Gary Adair

Page Layout
Susan Geiselman

Contents at a Glance

Table of Contents